Stefan Th. Gries
Statistics for Linguistics with R

MW00397043

Stefan Th. Gries

Statistics for Linguistics with R

A Practical Introduction

3rd revised edition

DE GRUYTER
MOUTON

ISBN 978-3-11-071816-4
e-ISBN (PDF) 978-3-11-071825-6
e-ISBN (EPUB) 978-3-11-071829-4

Library of Congress Control Number: 2021930703

Bibliographic information published by the Deutsche Nationalbibliothek
The Deutsche Nationalbibliothek lists this publication in the Deutsche Nationalbibliografie;
detailed bibliographic data are available on the Internet at http://dnb.dnb.de.

© 2021 Walter de Gruyter GmbH, Berlin/Boston
Printing and Binding: LSC Communications, United States

www.degruyter.com

Für ergebnisoffene Forschung,
something that's getting lost ...

Statistics for Linguistics with R – Endorsements of the 3rd Edition

"This 3rd edition of *Statistics for Linguists with R* is a must-read for anybody who is interested in quantitative analyses of linguistic data – from absolute beginner to expert. The explanations are written in plain, down-to-earth but at the same time extremely precise language. In addition to introducing basic concepts of data analysis and working with R, the most common statistical procedures are described and exemplified in a very reader-friendly and didactically intelligent manner. I can highly recommend this new edition of *Statistics for Linguists with R* to teachers and students dealing with statistics in the language sciences."

Martin Schweinberger, Arctic University of Tromsø & Lab Director at the University of Queensland

"The 3rd edition of *Statistics for Linguistics with R* gives a boost to everything that was already great about its predecessors. Its major asset continues to be the accessible hands-on approach, which is supported by a wealth of well-tested data examples. In addition to that, the new edition gives us substantial updates that present and explain recent methodological developments. The book is thus not just excellent for teaching, but also as a highly usable resource for working linguists."

Martin Hilpert, University of Neuchâtel

"For many researchers and students of linguistics, Gries' *Statistics for Linguistics with R* is the water gear they wore when they first dipped their toes into the waters of quantitative data analysis – and many still use it when they find themselves lost at sea. With its clear (and sometimes refreshingly informal) explanations of basic concepts as well as more complex statistical models, and its abundance of demonstrations, exercises and 'think breaks' on linguistic case studies, this updated 3rd edition is an ideal textbook for taught courses and self-study alike. Beyond being a 'how to' for statistical analyses in R, the book also provides helpful tips on how to motivate (and critically evaluate) the use of quantitative methods in Linguistics, and how to structure and report quantitative studies."

Lauren Fonteyn, Leiden University Centre for Linguistics

https://doi.org/10.1515/9783110718256-202

Introduction

When I wrote the second edition, I never ever thought there was gonna be a third one. But then, over the last few years, so much has been happening with regard to quantitative methods in linguistics, I myself have learned so many things (many of which I should probably have known way earlier ...), I have reviewed so many papers from which I learned things, methods that in 2012 were still rarer and or being debated (in particular mixed-effects models but also a variety of tree-based approaches) have become somewhat better understood and, thus, a little more mainstream, and I've taught dozens of bootcamps and workshops where people wanted to go beyond the second edition. As a result, at some point I started thinking, ok, I guess there is interest, let's see what De Gruyter says – turns out they were happy to have a third edition so here we are.

While the first four chapters of course saw many changes and additions, it's actually again Chapter 5 that was revised quite a bit more: I'm still using two of the same data sets as in the 2nd edition and I still place great emphasis on the coefficients etc. that regression models return, but I got rid of the sum contrasts bits and added a ton of new stuff, all of which has been used in multiple courses and bootcamps over the years; these include more discussion of curvature, *a priori* orthogonal and other contrasts, interactions, collinearity, effects and now also emmeans, autocorrelation/runs, some more bits on programming, writing statistical functions, and simulations, exploring cut-off points in logistic regression etc.; also, there's now more discussion of issues of model selection, diagnostics, and (10-fold cross-)validation. And, 'by popular demand', there's now a whole new chapter on mixed-effects modeling, with detailed discussions of all sorts of aspects that are relevant there (and see Gries (to appear a in *Language Learning*) for a 'companion publication' to that new chapter of this book), plus there's a whole new chapter on trees and forests. I'm very grateful to (i) hundreds of bootcamp/workshop participants, who of course often requested that kind of content or invited me to teach just that, and to (ii) students who took (parts of) my 3-quarter statistics series at UC Santa Barbara or the regression block seminars at my other department at JLU Giessen for all the input/feedback I have received over the years, much of which allowed me to fine-tune things more and more. I'm certain that, if any of them read this book, they'll recognize some examples and sections of this book as having been 'test-driven' in 'their bootcamp' and I'm certain that readers of this book will benefit from the many iterations I've been able to teach this stuff till, I hope, it was structured in the best possible way – well, at least the best possible way I was able to come up with ...

https://doi.org/10.1515/9783110718256-203

I want to close with a plea to really engage with your data. Yes, *duh!*, obviously you were planning on doing that anyway, but what I mean is, treat your data analysis like detective work. Yes, that sounds like a trite cliché, but the more/longer I've been doing this myself, the more apt it seems: The data are a suspect trying to hide something from you and it's your job to unravel whatever it is the data are hiding. As I have seen over the years, it is (still!) soooo easy to fall into traps that your data are presenting and overlook small (or even big) red flags. Always be suspicious, always ask yourself "but didn't he (STG) or the author(s) of the paper you're reading just say ...?" And always be suspicious about what you just did yourself. Always ask yourself "if I wanted to shoot my paper down as a reviewer who had access to the data, how would I do it?" and then 'insure yourself' against 'that reviewer' by checking x, exploring alternative y, testing alternative method z ... Bottom line: to not be led astray, you need to interrogate your data in the most sceptical of ways, and with this book I'm trying to help you do this!

Table of Contents

1 Some fundamentals of empirical research

When you can measure what you are speaking about, and express it in numbers, you know something about it; but when you cannot measure it, when you cannot express it in numbers, your knowledge is of a meager and unsatisfactory kind. It may be the beginning of knowledge, but you have scarcely, in your thoughts, advanced to the stage of science. (William Thomson, Lord Kelvin, <http://hum.uchicago.edu/~jagoldsm/Webpage/index.html>)

1.1 Introduction

This book is an introduction to statistics. However, there are already very many introductions to statistics (and by now even a handful for linguists) – why do we need another (edition of this) one? Just like its previous two editions, this book is different from many other introductions to statistics in how it combines several characteristics, each of which is attested separately in other introductions, but not necessarily all combined:
- it has been written especially for linguists: there are many many introductions to statistics for psychologists, economists, biologists etc., but much fewer which, like this one, explain statistical concepts and methods on the basis of linguistic questions and for linguists, and it does so starting from scratch;
- it explains how to do many of the statistical methods both 'by hand' as well as with statistical functions (and sometimes simulations), but it requires neither mathematical expertise nor hours of trying to understand complex equations – many introductions devote much time to mathematical foundations (and while knowing some of the math doesn't hurt, it makes everything more difficult for the novice), others do not explain any foundations and immediately dive into some nicely designed software which often hides the logic of statistical tests behind a nice GUI;
- it not only explains statistical concepts, tests, and graphs, but also the design of tables to store and analyze data and some very basic aspects of experimental design;
- it only uses open source software: many introductions use in particular SPSS or MATLAB (although in linguistics, those days seem nearly over, thankfully), which come with many disadvantages such that (i) users must

https://doi.org/10.1515/9783110718256-001

buy expensive licenses that might be restricted in how many functions they offer, how many data points they can handle, how long they can be used, and/or how quickly bugs are fixed; (ii) students and professors may be able to use the software only on campus; (iii) they are at the mercy of the software company with regard to often really slow bugfixes and updates etc. – with R, I have written quite a few emails with bug reports and they were often fixed within a day!

– while it provides a great deal of information – much of it resulting from years of teaching this kind of material, reviewing, and fighting recalcitrant data and reviewers – it does that in an accessible and (occasionally pretty) informal way: I try to avoid jargon wherever possible and some of what you read below is probably too close to how I say things during a workshop – this book is not exactly an exercise in formal writing and may reflect more of my style than you care to know. But, as a certain political figure once said in 2020, "it is what it is ..." On the more unambiguously positive side of things, the use of software will be illustrated in *very* much detail (both in terms of amount of code you're getting and the amount of very detailed commentary it comes with) and the book has grown so much in part because the text is now answering many questions and anticipating many errors in thinking I've encountered in bootcamps/classes over the last 10 years; the RMarkdown document I wrote this book in returned a ≈560 page PDF. In addition and as before, there are 'think breaks' (and the occasional warning), exercises (with answer keys on the companion website; over time, I am planning on adding to the exercises), and of course recommendations for further reading to dive into more details than I can provide here.

Chapter 1 introduces the foundations of quantitative studies: what are variables and hypotheses, what is the structure of quantitative studies, and what kind of reasoning underlies it, how do you obtain good experimental data, and in what kind of format should you store your data? **Chapter 2** provides an overview of the programming language and environment R, which will be used in all other chapters for statistical graphs and analyses: how do you create, load, and manipulate different kinds of data for your analysis? **Chapter 3** explains fundamental methods of descriptive statistics: how do you describe your data, what patterns can be discerned in them, and how can you represent such findings graphically? In addition, that chapter also introduces some very basic programming aspect of R (though not in as much detail as my R corpus book, Gries 2016). **Chapter 4** explains fundamental methods of analytical statistics for monofactorial – one cause, one effect – kinds of situations: how do you test whether an obtained monofactorial result is likely to have just arisen by chance? **Chapter 5** introduces multifactorial regression modeling, in particular linear and generalized linear modeling using fixed effects.

While a lot of the above is revised and contains much new information, **Chapter 6**, then, is completely new and discusses the increasingly popular method of mixed-effects modeling. Finally, **Chapter 7** is also completely new and discusses tree-based approaches, specifically classification and regression as well as conditional inference trees and random forests.

Apart from the book itself, the companion website for this book at http:// www.stgries.info/research/sflwr/sflwr.html is an important resource. You can access exercise files, data files, answer keys, and errata there, and at http:// groups.google.com/group/statforling-with-r you will find a newsgroup "StatForLing with R". If you become a member of that (admittedly very low-traffic) newsgroup, you can

- ask questions about statistics relevant to this edition (and hopefully also get an answer from someone);
- send suggestions for extensions and/or improvements or data for additional exercises;
- inform me and other readers of the book about bugs you find (and of course receive such information from other readers). This also means that if R commands, or code, provided in the book differs from information provided on the website, then the latter is most likely going to be correct.

Lastly, just like in the last two editions, I have to mention one important truth right at the start: You cannot learn to do statistical analyses by reading a book about statistical analyses – you must *do* statistical analyses. There's no way that you read this book (or any other serious introduction to statistics) in 15-minutes-in-bed increments or 'on the side' before turning off the light and somehow, magically, by effortless and pleasant osmosis, learn to do statistical analyses, and book covers or titles that tell you otherwise are just plain wrong (if nothing worse). I strongly recommend that, as of the beginning of Chapter 2, you work with this book directly at your computer with R running (ideally in RStudio). This is really important because it will make parsing the code much much easier: For reasons of space, the R code in the book and especially its output is often presented in a much abbreviated format, with less commentary, and sometimes without the plots, but the code file(s) contain *much* more annotation and comments to help you understand everything, and then of course they also generate all requisite output. So, *do* statistical analysis, don't just read about it! Also, I think it's best to read this book in the order of the chapters because the statistical methods that are discussed and the computational and graphical tools used for them are becoming increasingly complex – unless you have really good prior knowledge, just starting with binary logistic regression modeling or mixed-effects modeling might be tricky because I explain a lot of things on the side in the earlier chapters.

1.2 On the relevance of quantitative methods in linguistics

> Linguistics has always had a numerical and mathematical side [...], but the use of quantitative methods, and, relatedly, formalizations and modeling, seems to be ever on the increase; rare is the paper that does not report on some statistical analysis of relevant data or offer some model of the problem at hand. (Joseph 2008:687)

Above I said this book introduces you to scientific quantitative research. But then, what are the goals of such research? Typically, one distinguishes three goals, which need to be described because (i) they are part of a body of knowledge that all researchers within an empirical discipline should be aware of and (ii) they are relevant for how this book is structured. The first goal is the **description** of our data on some phenomenon – i.e. answering the question "what's going on?" – which means that our data, our methodological choices, and our results must be reported as accurately and replicably as possible. This is already more important than it sounds and I regularly review papers whose methods sections do not even come close to that ideal – some don't even mention their sample sizes or the exact version of a statistical method they are using, rendering their studies non-replicable. All statistical methods described below will help us achieve this objective, but particularly those described in Chapter 3. The second goal is the **explanation** of what's going in our data – i.e. answering the question "why are things happening they way they are happening?" – usually on the basis of hypotheses about what kind(s) of relations you expected to find in the data. On many occasions, this will already be sufficient for your purposes. However, sometimes we may also be interested in a third goal, that of **prediction**, answering "what if?" question such as "what's going to happen in certain situations (in the future or when we look at different data)?". Chapter 4, but especially Chapters 5 to 7, will introduce you to methods to pursue these goals of explanation and prediction.

When we look at these goals, it may appear surprising that statistical methods were not in more widespread use in linguistics for decades. This is all the more surprising because such methods are very widespread in disciplines with similarly complex topics such as psychology, sociology, and ecology. To some degree, this situation is probably due to how linguistics has evolved over the past decades, but fortunately this has changed remarkably in the last 20 years or so. The number of studies utilizing quantitative methods has been increasing in nearly all linguistic sub-disciplines as the field is experiencing a seismic shift towards more quantitative methods (and of course the usual backlash from people who hate 'everything with numbers'). Even though such methods are commonplace in other disciplines, they – still! – often meet resistance in some linguistic circles: statements such as (i) "we've never needed something like that before", (ii) "the really interesting things are qualitative in nature anyway and are not in need of, or even obfuscated by, quantitative evaluation", or (iii) "I am a field linguist and don't need any of this", and there are even much more myopic statements I won't cite here.

Let me say this quite bluntly: quite often, such statements are just nonsense. As for (i), it's not obvious that such quantitative methods weren't needed so far – to prove that point, one would have to show that quantitative methods could impossibly have contributed something useful to previous research, which isn't very likely – and even then it wouldn't necessarily be clear that the field of linguistics is not *now* at a point where such methods are useful, which clearly more and more practitioners are thinking. As for (ii), in actual practice, quantitative and qualitative methods usually go hand in hand, sometimes to a point that makes contrasting the two approaches somewhat parochial, even if many people don't seem to get that. Quantitative analysis of the type discussed in this book is usually *preceded* by qualitative analysis (because it often is the qualitative annotation of data that is required for quantitative analysis) as well as *followed* by qualitative interpretation (because any study that doesn't just aim at predicting something, but also wants to explain/understand it, requires interpretation after the number-crunching). To put it maybe damagingly directly – the way I have often stated this in bootcamps/workshops, where I have more space to discuss this with examples – I've never understood why watching a video recording of, say, some conversation and noting down "at time index 01:46, speaker X uses expression Y with intonation Z; I think that 'constructs' S" and "at time index 01:48, speaker A performatively responds with word B and intonation type U; I think that 'indexes' Q" obviously leads to sharp, impactful/actionable, making-the-world-a-better-place insights, while doing the exact same thing but noting the results in a spreadsheet as in Table 1 for subsequent statistical analysis somehow, magically, turns the exact same thing into an oppressive, colonial, and overgeneralizing-to-the-point-of-being-meaningless exercise ...

Table 1: Schematic spreadsheet annotation of 'qualitative' data

CONVERSATION	SPEAKER	TIME	EXPRESSION	INTONATION	INTERPRETATION
1	X	01:46	Y	Z	S
1	A	01:48	B	U	Q

Any feature that a qualitative analysis wants to consider – *any* one feature! – can potentially be included in a quantitative analysis: One just adds a column for it to one's spreadsheet/data frame and enters what happened for subsequent analysis. How one can seriously consider a kind of qualitative analysis that takes pride in collecting data in a way that rules out proper subsequent quantitative analysis as 'superior' will forever elude me – but I do of course appreciate the fact that complex quantitative analysis of (qualitative) data increases the risk of not returning what one would like to find ...

As for (iii): Even, say, a descriptive (field) linguist who is working to document a near-extinct language can benefit from quantitative methods, as I've seen multiple times in my department at UCSB. If a chapter in a grammar on tense discusses whether the choice of some tense-marking morpheme is correlated with indirect speech or not, then quantitative methods can show whether there's such a correlation, in what kinds of circumstances (e.g., registers) this correlation is strongest, and when it doesn't arise (e.g. with specific verbs). Therefore, it will also forever elude me how such correlations can be argued to not be relevant to the description of a language and, for example, Berez & Gries (2010) show how quantitative methods were usefully applied in a study of how syntax and semantics are related to middle voice marking in a small corpus of narratives in the Athabaskan language Dena'ina.

Recommendation(s) for further study: Jenset & McGillivray (2017: Section 3.7) is a very well-argued must-read for anyone intransigent and narrow-minded enough to still reject the use of quantitative methods in linguistics. One excellent quote from there is this: "quantitative methods serve as necessary corrective steps for hypotheses formed based on qualitative methods. When generalizations are made based on qualitative methods alone, the results are at risk of missing important variation in the data, either due to cognitive bias, small samples (which means the samples may contain too few types or tokens to reveal the full variation), or by not detecting complex sets of connections between properties that are more readily disentangled by computers. Furthermore, relying exclusively on qualitative methods is potentially harmful to linguistics, since theorizing and development may be led astray by incorrect results".

This leads up to a more general argument already alluded to above: often only quantitative methods can separate the wheat from the chaff. Let's assume a linguist wanted to test the so-called aspect hypothesis, according to which imperfective and perfective aspect are preferred in present and past tense respectively (see Shirai & Andersen 1995). Strictly speaking, the linguist would have to test all verbs in all languages (covered by the hypothesis), the so-called population. This is of course not possible so the linguist studies a hopefully random and representative sample of sentences to investigate their verbal morphology. Let's further assume the linguist took and investigated a small sample of 38 sentences in one language and got the results in Table 2.

Table 2: A fictitious distribution of tenses and aspects in a small corpus

	Imperfective	Perfective	Sum
Present	12	6	18
Past	7	13	20
Sum	19	19	38

These data look like a very obvious confirmation of the aspect hypothesis: there are more present tenses with imperfectives and more past tenses with perfectives. However, a statistical analysis of such data – maybe using also information on the verbs used, the speakers, etc. – might show that this tense-aspect distribution can also arise just by chance with a probability p that exceeds the usual threshold of 5% adopted in quantitative studies (more on that below). Thus, the linguist wouldn't be allowed to reject the hypothesis that this distribution is due to random variation and wouldn't be allowed to accept the aspect hypothesis for the population on the basis of this sample no matter how much they would like to do so. The point is that an intuitive eye-balling of anecdotes or data, especially when accompanied by a strong desire to find a certain kind of result, is not only insufficient but also dangerous in how it can make one's work appear shoddy, arbitrary, or involving motivated reasoning to both colleagues in the field or outsiders – a proper statistical analysis is often needed to protect the linguist against producing invalid generalizations (more incisive examples for this await other contexts such as a workshop).

A more eye-opening example for when only proper statistical analysis shows what's going on is discussed by Crawley (2007:314f.). Let's assume a study showed that two variables XX and YY are correlated such that the larger the value of XX, the larger the value of YY (as indicated by the solid regression line summarizing the point cloud); see Figure 1:

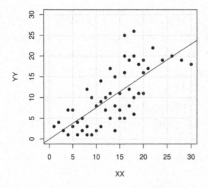

Figure 1: A correlation between two variables XX and YY

Note, however, that the spreadsheet actually also contains information about a third variable FF (with seven levels a to g). Interestingly, if you now inspect what the relation between XX and YY looks like for each of the seven levels of the third variable FF separately, you see that the relation suddenly becomes "the larger XX, the smaller YY"; see Figure 2 on the next page, where the seven levels are indicated with letters and dashed lines represent the regression lines summarizing the points for each level of FF. Such patterns in data are easy to overlook – they can only be identified through a careful quantitative study, which is why knowledge of statistical methods is indispensable.

For students of linguistics – as opposed to experienced practitioners – there's also a very practical issue to consider. Sometime soon you'll want to write a thesis or dissertation. Quantitative methods can be extremely useful and powerful if only to help you avoid pitfalls of this type (and others) posed by the data. Quantitative methods have a lot to offer, and I hope this book will provide you with some useful background knowledge.

This argument has an additional aspect to it. Much, though not all of, linguistics is an empirical science. Thus, it is necessary – in particular for students – to know about basic methods and assumptions of empirical research and statistics to be able to understand both scientific argumentation in general and how it pertains to linguistic argumentation in particular. This is especially relevant in the domains of, for example, contemporary quantitative corpus linguistics or psycholinguistics, where data are often evaluated with such a high degree of sophistication that quite some background knowledge of the relevant methods and terminology is required. Without training, what do you make of statements such as "The interaction between the size of the object and the size of the reference point does not reach standard levels of significance: $F_{1,12}=2.18$, $p=0.166$, partial $\eta^2=0.154$"?

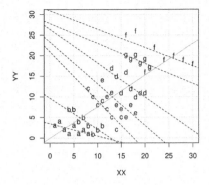

Figure 2: A correlation between two variables XX and YY, controlled for a 3rd variable FF

Or "Likelihood-ratio tests using ML-estimation indicated that both numeric predictors benefited significantly from permitting curvature with orthogonal polynomials to the second degree"? For that, you need some relatively solid training (of a type even this one book will already provide).

1.3 The design and the logic of quantitative studies

"The plural of anecdote is not data" -- or is it? (David Smith, <https://blog.revolutionana-lytics.com/2011/04/the-plural-of-anecdote-is-data-after-all.html>)

In this section, we will have a very detailed look at the design of, and the logic underlying, quantitative studies. I will distinguish several phases of quantitative studies and consider their structure and discuss the reasoning employed in them. The piece of writing in which we then describe our quantitative research will often have four parts: **introduction, methods, results,** and **discussion.** (If you discuss more than one case study in your writing, then typically each case study gets its own methods, results, and discussion sections, followed by a general discussion.) With few exceptions, the discussion of these matters in this section will be based on a linguistic example, namely the one and only phenomenon in linguistics that is really worthy of any study at all (why else would I have done my dissertation on it?), namely particle placement in English, i.e. the constituent order alternation of transitive phrasal verbs exemplified in (1).[1]

---

1 I print variables in the way that will be used in R, in caps SOMEVARIABLE, and I will print their levels in italics.

1. a.   He picked the book up. CONSTRUCTION: *vpo* (verb-obj-particle)
    b.   He picked up the book. CONSTRUCTION: *vpo* (verb-particle-obj)

An interesting aspect of this alternation is that, most of the time, both constructions appear to be functionally equivalent and native speakers of English usually
cannot explain well (if at all) why they produced (1a) on one occasion and (1b)
on some other occasion. In the past few decades, linguists have tried to describe,
explain, and predict the alternation (see Gries 2003), and in this section, we'll
use it to illustrate the structure of a quantitative study.

1.3.1 Scouting

At the beginning of a project/study, we want to get an overview of previous work
on the phenomenon you're interested in, which also gives us a sense of what still
can or needs to be done. In this phase, we try to learn of existing theories that
can be empirically tested or, much more infrequently, we enter uncharted territory in which we are the first to develop a new theory. This is a list of the activities that is typically performed in this scouting phase:
– a first (maybe informal) characterization of the phenomenon;
– studying the relevant literature;
– observations of the phenomenon in natural settings to aid first inductive generalizations;
– collecting additional information (e.g., from colleagues, students, etc.);
– deductive reasoning on your part.

If we take just a cursory look at particle placement, we will quickly notice that
there's a large number of variables that appear to influence the constructional
choice or, if we want to be careful, at least be correlated with it. A **variable** is "a
method for assigning to a set of observations a value from a set of possible outcomes" (Wilkinson & The Task Force 1999: 595), i.e., variables are characteristics
that – contrary to a constant – can exhibit at least two different states or levels
and can therefore be defined more intuitively, as "descriptive properties" (Johnson 2008:4). Variables that appear to influence particle placement include the
following:
– COMPLEXITY: is the direct object a simple direct object (e.g., *the book*), a let's
  call it phrasally-modified direct object (e.g., *the brown book* or *the book on the
  table*) or a clausally-modified direct object (e.g., *the book I had bought in Eu-
  rope*) (see, e.g., Fraser 1966);

- LENGTH: the length of the direct object (see, e.g., Chen 1986, Hawkins 1994), which could be measured in syllables, words, ...;
- DIRECTIONALPP: the presence of a directional prepositional phrase (PP) after the transitive phrasal verb (e.g. in *He picked the book up from the table*) or its absence (e.g. in *He picked the book up and left*) (see Chen 1986);
- ANIMACY: whether the referent of the direct object is inanimate (e.g. *He picked up the book*), or animate (e.g. *He picked his dad up*) (see Gries 2003a: Ch. 2);
- CONCRETENESS: whether the referent of the direct object is abstract (e.g. *He brought back peace to the region*), or concrete (e.g. *He brought his dad back to the station*) (see Gries 2003a: Ch. 2);
- TYPE: is the part of speech of the head of the direct object a pronoun (e.g. *He picked him up this morning*), a semipronoun (e.g. *He picked something up this morning*), a lexical noun (e.g. *He picked people up this morning*) or a proper name (e.g. *He picked Peter up this morning*) (see Van Dongen 1919).

During this early phase, it's often useful to summarize your findings in a tabular format. One possible table summarizes which studies (in the columns) discussed which variable (in the rows). On the basis of the above (hopelessly incomplete) list, this table could look like Table 3 and allows you to immediately recognize (i) which variables many studies have already looked at and (ii) the studies that looked at most variables.

Table 3: Summary of the literature on particle placement 1

	Fraser (1966)	Chen (1986)	Hawkins (1994)	Gries (2003a)	Van Dongen (1919)
COMPLEXITY	X				
LENGTH		X	X		
DIRECTIONALPP		X			
ANIMACY				X	
CONCRETENESS				X	
TYPE					X

Another kind of table summarizes the variable levels and their preferences for one of the two constructions. Again, on the basis of the above list, this table would look like Table 4, and you can immediately see that, for some variables, only one level has been associated with a particular constructional preference

Long complex NPs with lexical nouns referring to abstract things whereas CONSTRUCTION: *vop* is preferred with the opposite preferences. For an actual study, this first impression would of course have to be phrased more precisely. Much of this information would be explained and discussed in the first section of the empirical study, the introduction. In addition and in preparation for the next steps, you should also compile a list of other factors that might either influence particle placement directly or that might influence your sampling of verbs, particles, sentences, experimental subjects ...

Table 4: Summary of the literature on particle placement 2

CONSTRUCTION	*verb-object-particle*	verb-particle-object
COMPLEXITY		phrasally/clausally-modified
LENGTH		long
DIRECTIONALPP	presence	absence
ANIMACY	animate	inanimate
CONCRETENESS	concrete	abstract
TYPE	pronominal	

1.3.2 Hypotheses and operationalization

Once we have an overview of the phenomenon we're interested in and have decided to pursue an empirical study, we usually formulate hypotheses. To approach this issue, let's see what hypotheses are and what kinds of hypotheses there are.

1.3.2.1 Scientific hypotheses in text form

I will consider a scientific **hypothesis** to be a statement that describes a potentially falsifiable state of affairs in the world, where "potentially falsifiable" means it must be possible to think of events or situations that contradict the statement. Most of the time, this implies that the scenario described in the hypothesis must also be testable, but strictly speaking, these two characteristics are not identical. There are statements that are falsifiable but not testable such as "If children grow up without any linguistic input, then they will grow up to speak Latin." This statement is falsifiable, but you might find it hard to get human-subjects approval to test it (see Steinberg 1993: Section 3.1 on when some such hypothesis was in fact tested).

The following statement is a scientific hypothesis according to the above definition: "Reducing the minimum age to obtain a driver's license from 18 years to 17 years in Germany will double the number of traffic accidents in Germany within two years." This statement predicts that a certain state of affairs (a number of traffic accidents) will be observable after a certain action/treatment (reducing the minimum age ...), and it's falsifiable because it's conceivable – or shall we even say "quite likely"? – that, if one reduced the minimum age, the number of traffic accidents in Germany would not double within two years. Along the same lines, the following statement is not a scientific hypothesis: "Reducing the minimum age to obtain a driver's license from 18 years to 17 years in Germany could double the number of traffic accidents in Germany within two years." This statement is not a hypothesis according to the above definition because the word *could* basically means 'may or may not': The statement would be true if the number of traffic accidents were to double, but also if it didn't (after all, we only said could). In other words, whatever one observed two years after the reduction of the minimum age, it would be compatible with the statement; the statement has no predictive or discriminatory power.

We need to distinguish a variety of different kinds of hypotheses: independence/difference hypotheses and goodness-of-fit hypotheses on the one hand, and alternative and null hypotheses on the other. In the most general terms, alternative hypotheses stipulate the presence of differences/effects, whereas null hypotheses stipulate the absence of differences/effects, but let's break this down a bit. The prototypical hypothesis, i.e. what that term is colloquially understood to mean, is probably the combination of the first two kinds of each: An **alternative hypothesis** (often abbreviated as H_1) of the independence/difference kind is a statement that often consists of two parts, an *if*-part (the independent or predictor variable) and a *then*-part (the dependent or response variable). Most generally, the **dependent or response variable** is the variable whose values, variation, or distribution is to be explained (i.e. 'the effect'), and the **independent or predictor variable** is often assumed to be responsible for (changes in) the values of the dependent/response variable (i.e. a predictor is often seen as 'a/the cause'). This means, an alternative hypothesis of the **independence/difference kind** stipulates that the distribution of the response is not random because it can be explained, if only in part, by the values of the predictor(s), which result in some effect, or make a difference, in the response. That also means that, counter to what was implied in a recent overview article, there is really no difference between independence and difference hypotheses: Your H_1 that there is a *difference* in proficiency between native and non-native speakers is statistically equivalent to, and tested the same way as, the H_1 that proficiency is not *independent* of an L1-status variable/predictor with two levels *native* and *non-native*.

With regard to particle placement, the following statements are examples of scientific hypotheses:
- if a verb-particle construction is (going to be) followed by a directional PP, then native speakers will produce CONSTRUCTION: *vop* differently often than when no such directional PP is going to follow;
- if the direct object of a transitive phrasal verb is syntactically complex, then native speakers will produce CONSTRUCTION: *vpo* more often than when the direct object is syntactically simple;
- the longer the direct object of a transitive phrasal verb, the more likely it becomes native speakers will produce CONSTRUCTION: *vpo* (rather than CONSTRUCTION: *vop*).

(While the above examples are alternative hypotheses, they're not yet ready for statistical analysis – we haven't defined when a direct object of a transitive phrasal verb will be considered syntactically complex or long etc.; we'll deal with this in more detail in the next section.) If you pay attention to the formulations of the first two examples, you'll see that these also instantiate two different kinds of alternative hypotheses: The former is what is called **non-directional/two-tailed**: it stipulates a difference ("differently often") but it doesn't commit to the direction of the hypothesized difference: it doesn't say "more often" or "less often", which also means that either result would be compatible with the hypothesis as stated. The second example, however, is more committed: it doesn't just state "differently often", it also commits to the direction of the hypothesized difference ("more often") and is therefore called a **directional/one-tailed** hypothesis. Thus, in this second example, it is not the case that either result (more often or less often) would be compatible with the hypothesis as stated, it has to be "more often". This will be quite important later.

Second, an alternative hypothesis of the **goodness-of-fit** kind is a statement that stipulates that the distribution of a response variable differs from a random distribution or, often, from some well-known statistical distribution such as the normal (in the 'Gaussian, bell-shaped' sense) distribution or the uniform distribution. For example, in the particle placement example, one might hypothesize that the frequencies/frequency distribution of the two constructions *vop* and *vpo* differ/s from a random or uniform distribution (a fancy way of saying the two constructions are not equally frequent). For these hypotheses, we usually don't distinguish between one- and two-tailed hypotheses.

Now, what about null hypotheses? A **null hypothesis** (often abbreviated as H_0) defines which situations or states of affairs would falsify our alternative hypothesis H_1. They are, therefore, the logical opposite to our H_1 and we get such a H_0 by inserting the word not into our H_1. That means

- the H_0 counterpart to a H_1 of the non-directional/two-tailed independence/ difference kind would stipulate there's no difference/effect. For our above example, this would be: if a verb-particle construction is (going to be) followed by a directional PP, then native speakers will not produce CONSTRUCTION: *vop* differently often (i.e. they will produce *vop* equally often) than when no such directional PP is going to follow;
- the H_0 counterpart to a H_1 of the directional/one-tailed independence/difference kind would stipulate there's no difference/effect in the expected direction. For our above example, this would be: if the direct object of a transitive phrasal verb is syntactically complex, then native speakers will not produce CONSTRUCTION: *vpo* more often (i.e. as often or less often) than when the direct object is syntactically simple;
- the H_0 counterpart to a H_1 of the goodness-of-fit kind would stipulate that the frequencies/frequency distribution of the two constructions *vop* and *vpo* do/es not differ from a random or uniform distribution.

It is crucial to formulate the H_0 as mentioned above, i.e. by inserting *not*, because the idea is that both hypotheses – your H_1 and its opposite, H_0 – cover the whole result space, i.e. every result theoretically possible. Thus, if your H_1 was "if [...], then [...] more often" then your H_0 should not be "if [...], then [...] less often" because these two hypotheses do not cover all results possible – they don't cover the case where the two constructions are equally frequent.

It's useful for later to also mention confounding variables and moderator variables and represent all variables' interrelations in a simple plot like in Figure 3, in which unidirectional arrows mean something like 'affects' and bidirectional arrows mean something like 'is correlated with (but not necessarily causally)'.

Confounding variables are variables that are correlated with predictors and responses and they are important because, if overlooked/not included in an analysis, they can make it easier for a researcher to fall prey to spurious correlations, i.e. assuming cause-effect relations where none exist or exaggerating their importance (see Section 4.4.3 for more on correlation and causality). **Moderator variables**, on the other hand, can be defined as variables (often extraneous to at least the initial design of a study) that influence/moderate the relationship between the predictor(s) and the response(s), something we'll spend a huge amount of time on later.

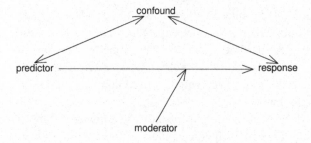

Figure 3: Variable types

With this terminology, we can state, for each of the above hypotheses, what the predictor and what the response is: In the first, the predictor is syntactic complexity of the direct object (COMPLEXITY); in the second, the predictor is the length of the direct object (LENGTH); in the third, the predictor is DIRECTIONALPP; the response in all three is the choice of construction (CONSTRUCTION with the two levels *vop* and vp*o)*.

Let's now turn to what might be the beginning of our methods section.

1.3.2.2 Operationalizing your variables

After having formulated our hypotheses in the above text form, there's still some more work left to do because it is as yet unclear how the variables invoked in our hypotheses will be investigated. For example and as mentioned above, we haven't defined (i) how exactly we will decide whether a PP following a transitive phrasal verb is "directional" or not, (ii) when exactly a direct object of a transitive phrasal verb will be considered syntactically complex, or (iii) how exactly the length of a direct object will be measured (letters (with or without spaces), phonemes, syllables, morphemes, words, syntactic nodes, miliseconds?). Therefore, we must find a way to **operationalize** the variables in our hypothesis, which means we decide what exactly we will observe, count, measure etc. when we investigate our variables and commit to a value we then enter into our spreadsheet. For example, if we want to operationalize a person's knowledge of a foreign language, we could do this as follows:

– we could develop a kind of 'ranking variable' reflecting the complexity of the sentences that a person can form in the language in a test (only main clauses? also compound sentences? also complex sentences? with sentence embeddings?);

– we could count the number of correctly/appropriately used morphemes between two errors in conversation;

– we could count the number of errors per 100 words in a text that the person writes in 90 minutes.

By contrast, what's wrong with proposing "amount of active vocabulary" or "amount of passive vocabulary"? These proposals are not (yet) particularly useful because, while knowing these amounts would certainly be very useful to assess somebody's knowledge of a foreign language, they're not directly observable: It is not (yet) clear what we would count or measure since it's not exactly practical to tell a learner to write down all the words he knows ... If we in turn operationalize the amount of, say, passive vocabulary on the basis of the number of words a person knows in a vocabulary test (involving, say, words from different frequency or dispersion bands) or in a synonym finding test, then we begin to know what to count – but the 'amount of' statement per se is too vague.

Sometimes, this process of operationalization can require developing something from scratch. For example, in several studies of constructional alternations in learner language, Wulff and I tried to find out whether, among other things, rhythmic alternation would be predictive of constructional choices. That is, the question was whether the preference for stressed-unstressed (S-U) syllable sequences over stress clashes (S-S) or stress lapses (more than two Us, as in S-U-U-U-S) would make people prefer the constituent order that allowed them to maintain, or at least stay closer to, an ideally alternating pattern. But that meant we needed to develop a metric that would allow us to compare S-U-U-S-S-U-U to U-U-S-U-U-S-U to S-S-U-S-S-U-U-S etc., something that quantified perfectly-alternating sequences (S-U), still-ok sequences (S-U-U) and dispreferred clashes and lapses, all the while also correcting for the length of the sequence ... Sometimes, this is the kind of challenge that operationalization poses.

From all of the above, it follows that operationalizing involves using levels or numbers to represent states of variables. A number may be a measurement (*402* ms reaction time, *12* words in a synonym finding test, the direct object is *4* syllables long), but it can also be presence-vs.-absence 'counts' (something happened *1* time, as opposed to *0* times) or a value on an ordinal scale, which allows us to encode discrete non-numerical states using numbers. Thus, variables are not only distinguished according to their role in the hypotheses – independent/predictor vs. dependent/response – but also according to their level of measurement:

– **categorical variables** are variables with the lowest information value. Different values of these variables only reveal that the objects with these different values exhibit different characteristics. (Another label for these variables is *nominal variables* or, when they can take on only two different levels, *binary variables*.) In our example of particle placement, the variable

DIRECTIONALPP could be coded with 1 for *absence* and 2 for *presence*, but note that the fact that the value for *presence* would then be twice as large as the one for *absence* doesn't mean anything (other than that the values are different) – theoretically, we could code *absence* with 34.2 and *presence* with 7 (although, if anything, it would be more practical and intuitive to code *absence* with 0 and *presence* with 1). Thankfully, however, R doesn't require that we use numbers for levels of categorical variables, we can just use words like absence or presence. Other typical examples of categorical variables are ANIMACY (e.g., *animate* vs. *inanimate*), CONCRETENESS (*abstract* vs. *concrete*), STRESS (*primary* vs. *secondary* vs. *none*), Vendlerian AKTIONSART (*accomplishment* vs. *achievement* vs. *activity* vs. *state*), etc.

– **ordinal variables** not only distinguish objects as members of different categories the way that categorical variables do, they also allow to rank-order the objects in a meaningful way but the exact differences between elements with different ranks cannot be meaningfully compared. Grades are a typical example: A student with an *A* (4 grade points) scored a better result than a student with a *C* (2 grade points), but just because 4 is two times 2, that doesn't necessarily mean that the A-student did exactly twice as well as the C-student – depending on the grading system, the A-student may have given three times as many correct answers as the C-student; in other words, ordinal variables indicate relative, but not absolute, magnitude. In the particle placement example, the variable COMPLEXITY is an ordinal variable if we operationalize it as above: *simple NP* < *phrasally-modified NP* < *clausally-modified NP*. It is useful to make the ranks compatible with the variable: If the variable is called COMPLEXITY, then higher rank numbers should represent greater degrees of complexity; if the variable is called ANIMACY, then higher rank numbers should represent greater degrees of animacy (e.g. *abstract* < *concrete inanimate* < *animate nonhuman* < *human*). Other typical examples are ranks of socio-economic status or degree of idiomaticity or perceived vocabulary difficulty (e.g., *low* vs. *intermediate* vs. *high*) or the levels of the Common European Framework of Reference (CEFR) for Languages broadly labeling language learners' language abilities (*A1* < *A2* < *B1* < *B2* < *C1* < *C2*).

– **numeric variables**, a term I will use to cover both interval and ratio variables. They do not only distinguish objects as members of different categories and with regard to some rank ordering, they also allow to meaningfully compare the differences and ratios between values. Consider a discrete numeric variable such as LENGTH (e.g. in syllables): when one object is six syllables long and another is three syllables long, then the first is of a different length than the second (the categorical information), the first is longer than the second (the ordinal information), but then it is also exactly twice as long as the second. Other examples are annual salaries, or reaction times in milliseconds.[2]

These differences can be illustrated in a table of a fictitious data set on lengths and degrees of complexity of subjects and objects – which column contains which kind of variable?

Table 5: A fictitious data set of subjects and objects

CASE	COMPLEXITY	SYLLENGTH	FILE	GRMRELATION
1	*high*	6	*D8Y*	*object*
2	*high*	8	*HHV*	*subject*
3	*low*	3	*KB0*	*subject*
4	*medium*	4	*KB2*	*object*

CASE is essentially a categorical variable: Every data point gets its own number so that we can uniquely identify it, but the number as such probably represents little more than the order in which the data points were entered, if that. COMPLEXITY is an ordinal variable with three levels. SYLLENGTH is a numeric variable since the third object can correctly be described as half as long as the first. FILE is another categorical variable: the levels of this variable are file names from the British National Corpus. GRMRELATION is a categorical variable with two levels *object* and *subject*. These distinctions help determine which statistical analyses/ tests can and cannot be applied to a particular question and data set, as we will see below. As a rule of thumb already, it's usually best to work with the highest level of measurement; I'll come back to this shortly.

This issue of operationalization is one of the most important of all. If we don't operationalize our variables properly, then all the rest might become useless since we may end up not measuring what we want to measure. In other words, without an appropriate operationalization, the validity of our study is at risk. If we investigated the question of whether subjects in English are longer than direct objects and looked through sentences in a corpus, we might come across the sentence in (2):

2. [SUBJECT The younger bachelors] ate [OBJECT the nice little parrot].

---

2 Numeric variables can be discrete as in the above LENGTH example, but also continuous (even if we may not be able to measure at an infinite degree of precision); see Baguley (2012: Section 1.3.2) for some critical discussion of this classification.

The result for this sentence depends on how length is operationalized. If length is operationalized as number of morphemes, then the subject is longer than the direct object: 5 (*The, young,* comparative *-er, bachelor,* plural *s*) vs. 4 (*the, nice, little, parrot*). However, if length is operationalized as number of words, the subject (3 words) is shorter than the direct object (4 words). And, if length is operationalized as number of characters without spaces, the subject and the direct object are equally long (19 characters). In this case, thus, the operationalization alone determines the result and, yes, this is obviously a contrived example, but should still make the point that different operationalizations can give rise to very different results (even just 20 examples like (2) could have a noticeable impact on the results of a regression of, say, 1000 sentences).

1.3.2.3 Scientific hypotheses in statistical/mathematical form

Once we have formulated both our own H_1 and the logically complementary H_0 in text form and have defined how the variables will be operationalized, we also formulate two statistical versions of these hypotheses. That is, we first formulate our H_1 (directional or non-directional) and the H_0 in text form, and in the statistical hypotheses we then express the numerical results we expect on the basis of the text hypotheses. Such numerical results usually involve one of five different mathematical forms: **frequencies, distributions,** means (or, more broadly, **central tendencies,** see Section 3.1 below for what that term means), **dispersions,** and **correlations.** (As you will see below in Section 3.3, correlation is in some sense actually the most general term of those five.) We begin by looking at a simple example of an H_1 regarding particle placement: If a verb-particle construction is (going to be) followed by a directional PP, then native speakers will use the constituent order *vop* more often than the constituent order *vpo*. If we assume we have found a way to define 'directional PP', then, in order to formulate the statistical-hypothesis counterpart to this text hypothesis, we have to answer this question: If we investigated, say, 200 sentences with verb-particle constructions in them, how would we know whether H_1 is (more likely) correct or not? (As a matter of fact, we actually have to proceed a little differently, but we will get to that later.) One possibility of course is to count how often CONSTRUCTION: *vop* and CONSTRUCTION: *vpo* occur in cases where the verb-particle construction is followed by a directional PP (i.e., co-occur with DIRECTIONALPP: *presence*). If the percentage of CONSTRUCTION: *vop* is higher than the percentage of CONSTRUCTION: *vpo* when there's a directional PP, then this looks like support for H_1. Thus, this possibility involves frequencies/proportions of a categorical dependent/response variable based on levels of a categorical independent/predictor variable:

- H_1 directional: if DIRECTIONALPP is *presence*, then the frequency/% of CONSTRUCTION: *vop* is greater than that of CONSTRUCTION: *vpo*;
- H_1 non-directional: if DIRECTIONALPP is *presence*, then the frequency/% of CONSTRUCTION: *vop* differs from that of CONSTRUCTION: *vpo*;
- H_0 (against the non-directional H_1): if DIRECTIONALPP is *presence*, then the frequency/% of CONSTRUCTION: *vop* is the same as that of CONSTRUCTION: *vpo*.

If we turn to the ordinal variable COMPLEXITY as operationalized on the basis of, for example, the three levels mentioned above, we could formulate hypotheses based on correlations:
- H_1 directional: the higher the value of COMPLEXITY, the higher the % of CONSTRUCTION: *vpo* out of both constructions with that value of COMPLEXITY;
- H_1 non-directional: the % of CONSTRUCTION: *vpo* out of both constructions varies across the values of COMPLEXITY;
- H_0 (against the non-directional H_1): the % of CONSTRUCTION: *vpo* out of both constructions doesn't vary across the values of COMPLEXITY.

Let's now turn to an example involving statistical hypotheses based on a numeric independent/predictor variable, and we will use it to make an important point. Consider the effect of LENGTH, whose effect we would hypothesize to be the following:
- H_1 directional: the higher the value of LENGTH, the higher the % of CONSTRUCTION: *vpo* out of both constructions with that length value;
- H_1 non-directional: the % of CONSTRUCTION: *vpo* out of both constructions varies across the values of LENGTH;
- H_0 (against the non-directional H_1): the % of CONSTRUCTION: *vpo* out of both constructions doesn't vary across the values of LENGTH.

Crucially, this text hypothesis – DO length affects constructional choice – can be checked in different ways. One of these ways, the above one, would correspond perfectly to the direction of causality we probably assume: LENGTH → CONSTRUCTION and we would accordingly check this by looking at each value of LENGTH (or groups of values of LENGTH) and determine the percentage distribution of CONSTRUCTION for each. Visually, this might be represented as in the left panel of Figure 4 by what you will later see as a stacked bar plot, where the x-axis lists values of LENGTH and the y-axis shows the percentage distribution of the two levels of CONSTRUCTION (dark grey: *vpo*, light grey: *vop*); we can clearly see that, indeed, on the whole the directional H_1 seems supported: for instance, once LENGTH is ≥10, CONSTRUCTION: *vop* doesn't occur at all anymore in these data.

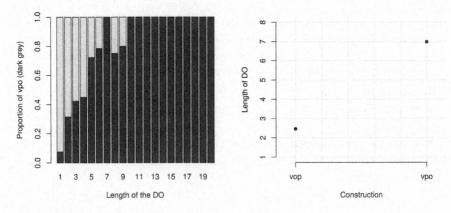

Figure 4: Ways to statistically check 'LENGTH affects CONSTRUCTION'

However, we could also take that same causal hypothesis LENGTH → CONSTRUC-TION and, merely for the statistical analysis, 'reverse its perspective': If LENGTH indeed affects CONSTRUCTION as hypothesized, then we should also be able to see the following:

- $H_{1\ directional}$: when CONSTRUCTION is *vop*, the average of LENGTH is less than when CONSTRUCTION is *vpo*;
- $H_{1\ non\text{-}directional}$: when CONSTRUCTION is *vop*, the average of LENGTH is different from when CONSTRUCTION is *vpo*;
- H_0 (against the non-directional H_1): when CONSTRUCTION is *vop*, the average of LENGTH is the same as when CONSTRUCTION is *vpo*.

In other words, a certain causal text hypothesis can, and probably ideally should, be operationalized and then tested with a statistical hypothesis that mirrors its direction of influence/argumentation, but doesn't always have to.

Above, I also told you that "it's usually best to work with the highest level of measurement" – what does that mean? To answer that question consider the following, different way to look at the same text hypotheses:

- $H_{1\ directional}$: when CONSTRUCTION is *vop*, the number of objects that are longer than the overall length average of all objects will be lower than when CON-STRUCTION is *vpo*;
- $H_{1\ non\text{-}directional}$: when CONSTRUCTION is *vop*, the number of objects that are longer than the overall length average of all objects will be different from when CON-STRUCTION is *vpo*;
- H_0 (against the non-directional H_1): when CONSTRUCTION is *vop*, the number of objects that are longer than the overall length average of all objects will not be different from when CONSTRUCTION is *vpo*.

Once you think about it, this makes sense: if a construction prefers longer objects, it will feature more of the above-average-length objects. So, in a table of observed frequencies as schematically represented in Table 6, the directional hypothesis would seem supported if $a<c$ and $b>d$, agreed?

Table 6: A schematic frequency distribution testing this H_1

	CONSTRUCTION: *vop*	CONSTRUCTION: *vpo*	**Sum**
DO > overall average	a	b	$a+b$
DO ≤ overall average	c	d	$c+d$
Sum	$a+c$	$b+d$	N

Yes, but the evaluation of this hypothesis could lose valuable information. In the first hypotheses involving LENGTH, each object contributed a numeric value to the computation of the averages, i.e. we used the highest level of measurement. But in this version of the hypotheses involving LENGTH, we're reducing the numeric length of each object to a binary *yes/no*, losing how much longer/shorter the object is – because now all we check is whether a certain object is longer than the average. If the overall average of all object lengths is 4.5, then that means we will code objects with lengths 5 and 15 the same, as *yes*. While that might occasionally (!) be justifiable, it should never be the starting point: always try to work on the highest information level that you have and only 'dumb things down' to lower levels if necessary.

Ok, now with similar operationalizations, the other text hypotheses from above can be transformed into analogous statistical hypotheses. Now, and only now, do we finally know what needs to be observed in order for us to reject H_0. (We will look at hypotheses involving distributions and dispersions later.) Also, all hypotheses discussed so far were concerned with the simple case where a sample of verb-particle constructions was investigated regarding whether the two constructions differ with regard to one predictor (e.g., DIRECTIONALPP). The statistical methods to handle such cases are the subject of Chapter 4. However, things are usually not that simple: most phenomena are multifactorial in nature, which means response variables are usually influenced by, or at least related to, more than one predictor variable. While the overall logic is the same as above, some complications arise and we'll postpone their discussion until Chapter 5.

1.4 Data collection and storage

Only after all variables have been operationalized and all hypotheses have been formulated do we actually collect our data. For example, we run an experiment or do a corpus study or ... However, we will hardly ever study the whole population of events but a sample so it is important that we choose our sample such that it is representative and balanced with respect to the population to which we wish to generalize. Here, I call a sample **representative** when the different parts of the population are reflected in the sample, and I call a sample **balanced** when the sizes of the parts in the population are reflected in the sample. Imagine, for example, we wanted to study the frequencies and the uses of the discourse marker like in the speech of Californian adolescents. To that end, we might want to compile a corpus of Californian adolescents' speech by asking some Californian adolescents to record their conversations. In order to obtain a sample that is representative and balanced for the population of all the conversations of Californian adolescents, all different kinds of conversations in which the subjects engage would be represented in the sample. A representative and balanced sample wouldn't just include the conversations of the subjects with members of their peer group(s), but also conversations with their parents, teachers, etc., and if possible, the proportions that all these different kinds of conversations make up in the sample would correspond to their proportions in real life, i.e. the population.

While it is important we try to stick to these rules as much as possible, why are they often more of a theoretical ideal?

THINK BREAK

This is often just a theoretical ideal because we don't know all parts and their proportions in the population. Who would dare say how much of an average Californian adolescent's discourse – and what is an average Californian adolescent anyway? – takes place within his peer group, with his parents, with his teachers etc.? And how would we measure the proportion – in words? sentences? minutes? Still, even though these considerations will often only result in estimates, we must think about the composition of your sample(s) just as much as we think about the exact operationalization of your variables. If we don't do that, then the whole study may well fail because we end up unable to generalize from whatever we find in our sample to the population we were trying to target. One important rule in this connection is to choose the elements that enter into our sample randomly, i.e. to randomize. For example, we could perhaps send a signal to our subjects' cell phone at random time intervals (as determined by a computer) whenever they are supposed to record the next five minutes of their conversation. This would make it more likely that we get a less biased sample of many different kinds of conversational interaction (than if we had the subjects record everyday from 15:05 to 15:15), which would then likely represent the population better.

Let's briefly look at a similar example from the domain of first language acquisition. It was found that the number of questions in recordings of caretaker-child interactions was surprisingly high. Some researchers suspected that the reason for that was parents' (conscious or unconscious) desire to present their child as very intelligent so that they asked the child "And what is that?" questions all the time so that the child could show how many different words he knew. Some researchers then changed their sampling method such that the recording device was always in the room, but the parents did not know exactly when it would record caretaker-child interaction. The results showed that the proportion of questions decreased considerably ...

In corpus-based studies, you will often find a different kind of randomization. For example, researchers sometimes first retrieved all instances of, say, a construction of interest and then sorted all instances according to random numbers. A researcher who then investigates the first 20% of the list, has a random sample. However, for corpus data, this is actually not a good way to proceed because it decontextualizes the uses that are studied and it makes it much harder to control for speaker-/file-specific idiosyncrasies, priming effects etc. It's better to randomly sample on the level of, say, the files and then study all instances of the construction (in their natural order) in the files that made it into the random sample. However one does it, though, randomization is one of the most important principles of data collection.

Once we have collected your data, we have to store them in a format that makes them easy to annotate, manipulate, and evaluate. There's a set of ground rules that defines the desired so-called case-by-variable format and that needs to be borne in mind.
– the first row contains the names of all variables;
– each of all other rows represents one and only one data point, where I'm using *data point* to refer to a single observation of the dependent/response variable (meaning, if one speaker contributes 10 reaction times to a study, these go into 10 rows, not 1);
– the first column just numbers all n cases from 1 to n so that every data point/ row can be uniquely identified and so that you can always restore one particular ordering (e.g., the original one or a chronological one);

- each of the remaining columns represents one and only one variable with respect to which every data point gets annotated. In a spreadsheet for a corpus study, for example, one additional column may contain the name of the corpus file in which the word in question is found; if we include data from multiple corpora, another column would contain the name of the corpus the current data point is from; yet another column may provide the line of the file in which the word was found. In a spreadsheet for an experimental study, one column should contain some unique identifier of each subject; other columns may contain the age, sex, ... of the subject, the exact stimulus or some index representing the stimulus the subject was presented with, the order index of a stimulus presented to a subject (so that we can test whether a subject's performance changes systematically over the course of the experiment), ...;
- especially for working with R, missing data are entered as NA and not just with empty cells (which also means no other variable level should be coded/ abbreviated as NA) in order to preserve the formal integrity of the data frame (i.e., have all rows and columns contain the same number of elements) and to be able to check up on the missing data to see whether, for example, there's a pattern in the missing data points which needs to be accounted for.

Some additional very helpful suggestions especially for working with R are to have the column names in the first row be in all caps, to never code the levels of categorical levels as numbers but as words/character strings in small letters, and to not use 'weird' characters such as spaces, periods, commas, tabs, #, single/double quotes or others in variable names or levels but stick to alphanumeric names (in whatever alphabet you wish).

To make sure these points are perfectly clear, let's look at two examples. Let's assume for our study of particle placement we had looked at a few sentences and counted the number of syllables of the direct objects. The predictor is the numeric variable LENGTH (in syllables), which can take on all sorts of positive integer values. The response is the categorical variable CONSTRUCTION, which can be either *vop* or *vpo*. When all hypotheses were formulated and, then, data were collected and coded, one possible format is the one represented in Table 7.

Table 7: A not-so-good table 1

	LENGTH: 2	LENGTH: 3	LENGTH: 4	LENGTH: 5
CONSTRUCTION: *vop*	//	//	///	//
CONSTRUCTION: *vpo*	////	///	//	

As a second example, let's look at the hypothesis that subjects and direct objects in transitive sentences are differently long (in words). Here, what is the dependent/response and what is the independent/predictor variable?

———
THINK BREAK
———

The predictor is a categorical variable we might call RELATION, which can be object or subject, the response is LENGTH, which can take on positive integer values. If we formulated all four hypotheses (H$_1$: text and statistical form; H$_0$: text and statistical form) and then looked at the small corpus in (3), then our spreadsheet should not look like Table 8.

3. a.   The younger bachelors ate the nice little cat.
    b.   He was locking the door.
    c.   The quick brown fox hit the lazy dog.

Table 8: A not-so-good table 2

SENTENCE	SUBJECT	OBJECT
The younger bachelors ate the nice little cat.	3	4
He was locking the door.	1	2
The quick brown fox hit the lazy dog.	4	3

Both Table 7 and Table 8 violate all of the above rules. In Table 8, for example, every row represents two data points, not just one, namely one data point representing some subject's length and one representing the length of the object from the same sentence; Table 7 is even worse: its second row represents 9 data points. Also, not every variable is represented by one and only column – rather, the four and two right columns of Table 7 and Table 8 respectively contain data points for one *level* of an independent variable, not one *variable*. How would you have to reorganize Table 8 to make it compatible with the above rules?

———
THINK BREAK
———

Every data point needs to have its own row and then be characterized with regard to all variables that are required or might be useful (if only for sorting or filtering the data), maybe like Table 9:

Table 9: A much better coding of the data in Table 8

CASE	SENTENCE	PHRASE	GRMREL	LENGTH
1	The younger bachelors ate the nice little cat.	The younger bachelors	subject	3
2	The younger bachelors ate the nice little cat.	the nice little cat.	object	4
3	He was locking the door.	He	subject	1
4	He was locking the door.	the door	object	2
5	The quick brown fox hit the lazy dog.	The quick brown fox	subject	4
6	The quick brown fox hit the lazy dog.	the lazy dog.	object	3

With very few exceptions (and I actually can hardly think of any), this is the format in which you should always save your data. Ideally, we enter the data in this format into a spreadsheet software and save the data (i) in the native file format of that application (to preserve colors and other formattings we may have added) and (ii) into a tab-delimited text file (ideally with a Unicode encoding such as UTF-8), which is easier to import into R. Here's the corresponding minimally required improvement of Table 7.

Table 10: A much better coding of the data in Table 7

CASE	CONSTRUCTION	LENGTH
1	vpo	2
2	vpo	2
3	vop	2
4	vop	2
5	vop	2
6	vop	2
7	vpo	3
8	vpo	3
9	...	...

1.5 The decision

When the data have been stored in a format that corresponds to that of Table 9/Table 10, we can finally do what we wanted to do all along: evaluate the data statistically. (For now I won't address how we decide which statistical test to choose but I'll return to this topic at the beginning of Chapter 4.)

As a result of that evaluation, we will obtain frequencies, distributions, averages/means, dispersions, or correlation coefficients. However, one central aspect of this evaluation is that we actually do not simply try to show that our H_1 is correct – contrary to what one might expect we try to show that the statistical version of H_0 is wrong, and since H_0 is the logical counterpart to H_1, this would support our H1. Specifically, we use the following four-step procedure, which is sometimes referred to as the **Null Hypothesis Significance Testing** (NHST) paradigm:

1. we define a so-called significance level $p_{critical}$, which is usually set to 0.05 (i.e., 5%) and which represents a threshold value for accepting/rejecting H_0;[3]
2. we analyze our data by computing some effect e using the statistic in your statistical hypotheses; that effect can be something like a difference in frequencies, distributions, a correlation, a difference in slopes, ...;
3. we compute the so-called probability of error p, which quantifies how probable it is to find e or something that deviates from H_0 even more in our sample when, in the population, it's actually H_0 that is true;
4. we compare $p_{critical}$ to p and decide
   a. if $p<p_{critical}$, then we consider the finding "significant": we can reject H_0 and accept H_1;
   b. if $p \geq p_{critical}$, then we consider the finding "not significant": we must stick with H_0 and cannot accept H_1.

In other words, *significant* has a technical meaning here: it doesn't mean 'important' or 'substantial', *significant* with regard to a result means 'the result is of a kind that is less likely to have arisen under the null hypothesis (which, typically, implies a random/chance distribution) than a previously-defined standard threshold (which, typically, is 0.05, or 5%).

For example, if in our sample the mean length difference between subjects and direct objects is 1.4 syllables, then we compute the probability of error p to find this difference of 1.4 syllables or an even larger difference in our sample when there's actually no such difference in the population we think our sample represents (because that is what H_0 predicts). Then, there are two possibilities:

– if this probability p (of finding a ≥1.4-syllable difference in our sample when there's none in the population that our sample represents) is smaller than $p_{critical}$ of 0.05, then we can reject the H_0 that there's no length difference between subjects and direct objects in the population. In the results section of our pa-

---

3 For a recent (renewed) suggestion to drastically lower the traditional threshold value of 0.05 to 0.005, see Benjamin et al. (2017).

per, we can then write that we found a significant difference between the means in our sample, and in the discussion section of our paper we would discuss what kinds of implications this has, etc.

– if that probability p is equal to or greater than $p_{critical}$ of 0.05, then we cannot reject the H_0 that there's no length difference between subjects and direct objects in the population. In the results section of our paper, we would then state that we haven't found a significant difference between the lengths in your sample. In the discussion part of our paper, we would then discuss the implications of this finding, plus we might speculate or reason about why there was no significant difference.

Note, however, that just because a significant result made us *accept* H_1, that doesn't mean that we have *proven* H_1. That's because there's still the probability of error p that the observed result has come about even though H_0 is correct – the probability of error p is small enough to accept H_1, but not to prove it.

This line of reasoning may appear a bit confusing at first especially since we suddenly talk about two different probabilities. One is the probability usually set to 5%, the other probability is the probability to obtain the observed result when H_0 is correct. The former, the significance level $p_{critical}$, is defined *before* data are collected whereas the latter, the probability of error or p-value, is computed *after* the data were collected, namely from the data. Why is this probability called *probability of error*? Because it is the probability to err when you accept H_1 given the observed data. Sometimes, we will find that people use different wordings and numbers of asterisks for different p-values:

– $p<0.001$ is sometimes referred to as *highly significant* and represented as ***;
– $0.001 \leq p < 0.01$ is sometimes referred to as *very significant* and represented as **;
– $0.01 \leq p < 0.05$ is sometimes referred to as *significant* and represented as *;
– $0.05 \leq p < 0.1$ is sometimes referred to as *marginally significant* and represented as *ms* or a period but since such p-values are larger than the usual standard of 5%, calling such results *marginally significant* amounts, polemically speaking at least, to saying "Look, I didn't really get the results to be significant as I was hoping, but c'mon, they are still pretty nice, don't you think?", which is why I typically discourage the use of this expression. Instead, if your p-value is greater than whatever your $p_{critical}$ was (typically 0.05), this is referred to as *not significant* (*ns*).

But while we have seen above how this comparison of the two probabilities contributes to the decision in favor of or against H_1, it is still unclear how this p-value is computed, which is what we will turn to now.

Warning/advice: You must never change your original H_1 after you have obtained your results and then sell your study as successful support of the 'new' H_1; I *have* seen people do this more than once. Also, you must never explore a data set – the nicer way to say 'fish for something usable' – and, when you then find something significant, sell this result as a successful test of a H_1 that you then pretend to have had in advance. You may of course explore a data set in search of patterns and hypotheses, but you have to say that that's what you did. In other words, don't sell the result of an exploratory approach as the result of a hypothesis-testing approach. (See Section 5.5 for more discussion of this in the thorny context of model selection.)

1.5.1 One-tailed *p*-values from discrete probability distributions

Let's assume you and I decided to toss a coin 100 times. If we get heads, I get one dollar from you, if we get tails, you get one from me. Before this game, you formulate the following hypotheses:
– text H_0: Stefan doesn't cheat;
– text H_1: Stefan is cheating.

This scenario can be easily operationalized using frequencies:
– statistical H_0: Stefan will win just as often as I will, namely 50 times (or both players will win equally often);
– statistical H_1: Stefan will win more often than I will, namely more than 50 times.

Now my question: if we play the game and toss the coin 100 times, what would the result need to be for you to suspect that I cheated?

THINK BREAK

Maybe without realizing it, you're currently thinking along the lines of significance tests. Let's make this more concrete by assuming you lost 60 times and also paraphrase it in terms of the above four steps of the null-hypothesis significance testing paradigm:
1. let's assume you set the significance level $p_{critical}$ to its usual value of 0.05;
2. you observe the effect *e*, namely that you lose 60 times, which is 10 times, or 20%, more often than a completely even distribution of 50:50 would have made you expect;
3. you're now in your mind 'trying to compute' the probability of error *p* how likely it is to lose 60 times or more often in our sample (the game of 100 tosses) when H_0 is true and you should have lost 50 times. Why "60 times or more often"? Because above we said you 'compute the so-called probability

of error p how likely it is to find e or something that deviates from H_0 even more' in your sample when, in the population, H_0 is true;

4. if you can compute p, you compare $p_{critical}$ and p and decide what to believe: if $p<p_{critical}$, then you can reject H_0, accept your H_1, and accuse me of cheating – otherwise, you must stick to H_0 and accept your losses.

Thus, you must ask yourself how and how much does the observed result deviate from the result expected from H_0. Obviously, your number of losses is larger: 60>50. Thus, the results that deviate from H_0 that much or even more in the predicted direction are those where you lose 60 times or more often: 60 times, 61 times, 62, times, ..., 99 times, and 100 times. That is, you set the significance level to 0.05 and ask yourself "is it less likely than 0.05 that Stefan did not cheat but still won 60+ times (although he should only have won 50 times)?" This is exactly the logic of significance testing.

It's possible to show that the probability p to lose 60 times or more often just by chance – i.e., without me cheating – is 0.028444, i.e., $\approx$2.8%. Since 0.028444<0.05 (or 5%), you can reject H_0 (that I played honestly) and accept H_1 (that I cheated). If we had been good friends, however, so that you wouldn't have wanted to risk our friendship by accusing me of cheating prematurely and had therefore set the significance level $p_{critical}$ to a more cautious 0.01 (or 1%), then you wouldn't be able to accuse me of cheating, since 0.028444>0.01.

This example has hopefully clarified the overall logic even further, but what's probably still unclear is how this p-value is computed. To illustrate that, let's reduce the example from 100 coin tosses to the more manageable amount of three coin tosses as in Table 11.

Table 11: All possible results of three coin tosses and their probabilities (when H_0 is correct)

TOSS1	TOSS2	TOSS3	HEADS	TAILS	PROBABILITY
heads	heads	heads	3	0	0.125
heads	heads	tails	2	1	0.125
heads	tails	heads	2	1	0.125
heads	tails	tails	1	2	0.125
tails	heads	heads	2	1	0.125
tails	heads	tails	1	2	0.125
tails	tails	heads	1	2	0.125
tails	tails	tails	0	3	0.125

in Table 11, you find all possible results of three coin tosses and their probabilities under the assumption that H_0 is correct and the chance for heads/tails on every toss is 50%. More specifically, the three left columns represent all possible results, column 4 and column 5 show how many heads and tails are obtained in each of the eight possible results, and the rightmost column lists the probability of each possible result. As you can see, these are all the same, 0.125. Why is that

Understanding this involves recognizing that, according to H_0, the probability of heads and tails is the same on every trial and that all trials are independent of each other. This notion of **independence** is important: trials are independent of each other when the outcome of one trial (here, one toss) doesn't influence the outcome of any other trial/toss. Similarly, samples (e.g., groups of trials) are independent of each other when there's no meaningful way in which we can match values from one sample onto values from another sample. For example, if we randomly sample 100 transitive clauses out of a corpus and count their subjects' lengths in syllables, and then we randomly sample 100 different transitive clauses from the same corpus and count their direct objects' lengths in syllables, then the two samples – the 100 subject lengths and the 100 object lengths – are pretty much independent. If, on the other hand, we randomly sample 100 transitive clauses out of a corpus and count the lengths of their subjects and their objects in syllables, then the two samples – the 100 subject lengths and the 100 object lengths – are dependent because we can match up the 100 subject lengths with the 100 object lengths perfectly by aligning each subject with the object from the very same clause. Similarly, if we perform an experiment twice with the same subjects, then the two samples made up by the first and the second experimental results are dependent, because we can match up each subject's data point in the first experiment with the same subject's data point in the second. This notion will become very important later on.

Returning to the three coin tosses: There are eight different outcomes of three tosses (each of which has two equiprobable outcomes) and they're all independent of each other. For each row/outcome, we obtain the probability to get that result by multiplying the individual events' probabilities: For the first row, that means computing 0.5 (p_{heads}) × 0.5 (p_{heads}) × 0.5 (p_{heads}) = 0.125 (the multiplication rule in probability theory). Analogous computations for every row show that the probability of each result is 0.125. Thus, we can show that H_0 predicts that each of us should win 1.5 times on average, e.g. if we played the three-toss game 100 times as the following code simulates (don't worry about understanding the code yet):

```
set.seed(sum(utf8ToInt("kassler"))) # replicable random number seed
collector <- rep(NA, 100) # collector for the 100 times 3 tosses
```

```
for (i in 1:100) { # do the following 100 times
   current.3.tosses <- sample(  # make current.3.tosses the result of
   x=c("H", "T"),               # 'tossing a coin'
   3,                           # 3 times
   replace=TRUE)                # where results can occur more >1 time
   # store in i-th slot of collector how many heads there were
   collector[i] <- sum(current.3.tosses=="H")
}
mean(collector) # how often should I win on average?
## [1] 1.5
```

Now imagine you lost two out of three times. If you had again set the level of significance to 5%, could you accuse me of cheating? Why (not)?

THINK BREAK

Of course not. Let me first ask again which events need to be considered. That would be (i) the observed result – that you lost two times – and (ii) the result(s) that deviate(s) even more from H_0 in the predicted direction – that's easy here: the only result deviating even more from H_0 is that you lose all three times. So let's compute the sum of the probabilities of these events. As you see in column 4 of Table 11, there are three results in which I win / you lose two times in three tosses: H H T (row 2), H T H (row 3), and T H H (row 5). Thus, the probability to lose exactly two times is 0.125+0.125+0.125=0.375, and that's already much much more than your level of significance 0.05 allows. However, to that you still have to add the probability of the event that deviates even more from H_0, which is H H H (row 1), which adds another 0.125. If you add all four probabilities up, the probability p to lose two or more times in three tosses when H_0 is true is 0.5 (obviously: losing 2 or 3 times covers half of all possible results). This is ten times as much as the level of significance so there's no way that you can accuse me of cheating. Note that even if you had lost all three tosses, you could still not accuse me of cheating, because the probability of that happening when H_0 is true is still 0.125, i.e. >0.05, which also means that 3 is simply too small a number of tosses to try and diagnose cheating (at least when your $p_{critical}$ is 0.05 or even 0.1).

We can also represent this logic graphically and at the same time go back to larger numbers of tosses. Figure 5 has four panels, one for 3 tosses, one for 6, one for 12, and then one for 24.

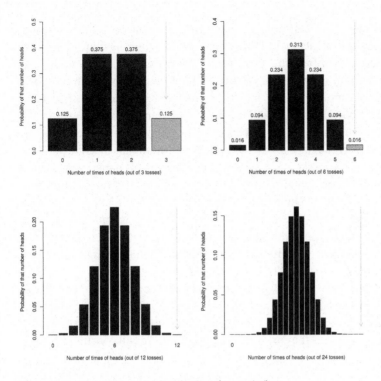

Figure 5: Bar plots of binomial distributions (one-tailed)

In each, the summed probabilities for all possible numbers of heads given the number of tosses made (i.e. column 4/HEADS of Table 11) are represented as bars, and the most extreme result (I always win) is always represented with a grey bar and an arrow pointing to it; in the cases of 3 and 6 tosses, I also plotted the summed probabilities of these outcomes (numbers of heads) on top of the bars.

Thus, if you lost more often than you should have according to H_0 and you want to determine the probability of losing as many times and even more often, then you move from the expectation of H_0, which is in the middle (along the x-axis) of the graph where the bars are highest, in the direction towards the observed result (say, at $x=3$) and then, once you hit the observed result (with $y=0.375$ in our example above), you start cumulatively adding the lengths of all bars as you continue to move in the same direction till you have added all remaining bars (in our simplest example, just the one more with $y=0.125$).

Figure 5 also illustrates another very important point. First, recall that the basic distribution underlying this data is a discrete and uniform (i.e. non-normal/bell-shaped) probability distribution, namely 0.5 (heads) vs. 0.5 (tails). But then, as the numbers of tosses in our games increase, the probability distribution of the possible results looks more and more like the bell-shaped curve we know from normal distributions. Thus, even i the underlying distribution is not normal but uniform, once we sample from it often enough, we still get a bell-shaped curve of times of heads, and the mathematical properties of that bell curve are well known and definable by just two parameters (its mean and its standard deviation).The more general implication of this is that, if data under investigation are distributed in a way that is sufficiently similar to some parametric distribution (i.e. a distribution defined by a fixed set of parameters such as the normal distribution, but also other widely used probability density functions such as the F-, t-, or chi-squared distribution), then one doesn't have to compute and sum up exact probabilities as we did above, but one can approximate the p-value from the parameters of the equations underlying the relevant distribution; this is often called using **parametric tests**, because the one assumes one's data are similar enough to probability functions defined by parameters – *not*, like a recent overview article suggested, because parametric tests test "hypotheses about population parameters"; that's something that non-parametric tests also do ... Crucially, however, the results from parametric tests are only as good as the data's distributional fit to the corresponding function. We will revisit this below.

1.5.2 Two-tailed p-values from discrete probability distributions

Now, we have to add another perspective to the mix. In the last section, we were concerned with directional H_1s. Your H_1 was "Stefan cheats", which means you were thinking I might do something to increase the probability of heads from 50% to some higher value. As discussed above, that means you had a directional/one-tailed hypothesis because you committed to the direction in which I'd change the probability of heads – because you knew you weren't going to cheat and you graciously enough didn't entertain the possibility I was stupid or self-sabotaging enough to cheat in a way that reduces the probability of heads. Thus, when you summed up the bar lengths in Figure 5 you only moved away from H_0's expectation in one direction, namely to the right tail where my potential cheating would make the number of heads go up.

However, often one only has a non-directional/two-tailed H_1. In such cases, one has to look at both ways in which results may deviate from the expected result. Let's return to the scenario where you and I toss a coin three times, but this time we also have an impartial observer watching us play who has no reason to suspect that only I would be cheating – that observer is open to the possibility that you are cheating as well and therefore formulates the following hypotheses (with a significance level of 0.05):

- text H_0: Both players will win equally often (or Stefan will win just as often as the other player);
- text H_1: One player will win more often than the other (or Stefan will win more or less often than the other player).

Imagine you lost three times. The observer now asks himself whether one of us should be accused of cheating. As before, he needs to determine which events to consider and he also uses a table of all possible results to help him figure things out. Consider, therefore, Table 12. To now compute the probability of error of accepting the non-directional H_1 after I won 3 times, the observer needs to compute the probability of *someone* winning three times – me *or* you (because both are covered by the H_1 "*One player* will win more often than the other"; both are highlighted in bold in Table 12). Thus, the observer first considers the result that you lost three times, which is what actually happened and which is listed in row 1 and arises with a probability of 0.125.

Table 12: All possible results of three coin tosses and their probabilities (when H_0 is correct)

TOSS1	TOSS2	TOSS3	HEADS	TAILS	PROBABILITY
heads	**heads**	**heads**	**3**	**0**	**0.125**
heads	heads	tails	2	1	0.125
heads	tails	heads	2	1	0.125
heads	tails	tails	1	2	0.125
tails	heads	heads	2	1	0.125
tails	heads	tails	1	2	0.125
tails	tails	heads	1	2	0.125
tails	**tails**	**tails**	**0**	**3**	**0.125**

But then, with his non-directional H_1, he also must consider the other way in which one player, this time you, can win as extremely as I did, so the observer also looks for deviations just as large or even larger in the other direction of H_0's expectation and finds it in row 8 of Table 12, where you win / I lose three times. The observer includes the probability of that event, too, and arrives at a cumulative probability of 0.25. This logic is graphically represented in Figure 6 on the next page in the same way as above.

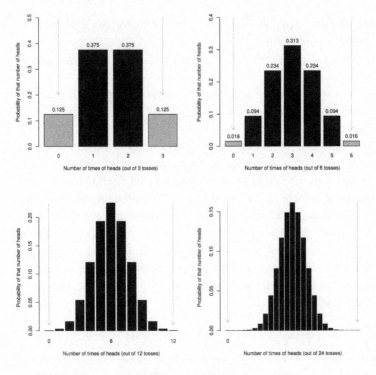

Figure 6: Bar plots of binomial distributions (two-tailed)

In other words, when *you* tested *your* directional H_1, *you* looked at the result 'you lost three times' (because you knew you didn't cheat and didn't have to consider that possibility in your H_1), but when *the observer* tested *his* non-directional H_1, *he* looked at the result '*somebody* lost three times.' This has one very important consequence: When you have prior knowledge about a phenomenon that allows you to formulate a directional, and not just a non-directional, H_1, then the result you need for a significant finding can deviate less extremely from the H_0 result and still be significant than if you only have a non-directional H_1. Usually, it will be like here: the *p*-value you get for a result with a directional H_1 is half of the *p*-value you get for a result with a non-directional H_1, meaning prior knowledge that allows you to commit to something more definitive is rewarded!

Let's now return to the example game involving 100 tosses. Again, we first look at the situation through your eyes (directional H_1), and then, second, through those of an impartial observer (non-directional H_1), but this time we change the point of time of analysis. Now, you and the observer try to determine *before the game* which results would be so extreme that you and the observer would be allowed to adopt the H_1. We begin with your perspective:

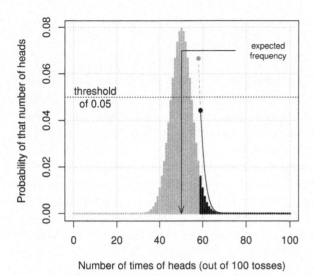

Figure 7: The probability distribution of 100 tosses of a fair coin (one-tailed)

In Figure 7, you find the by now familiar graph for 100 tosses with the null hypothesis expectation that the probability of heads is 0.5. (The meaning of the grey/black lines will be explained presently.)

Above, we had an empirical result whose p-value we were interested in, and in order to get that p-value, we moved from the expected H_0 results to the extreme values. Now we want to determine, but not exceed, a p-value before we have results and have to proceed the other way round: from an extreme point in the direction of the H_0 expectation. For example, to determine how many times you can lose without getting a cumulative probability exceeding 0.05, you begin at the most extreme result on the right – that you lose 100 times – and begin to add the lengths of the bars. (Obviously, you would compute that and not literally measure lengths.) R says the probability that you lose all 100 tosses is $7.8886091 \times 10^{-31}$. To that you add the probability that you lose 99 out of 100 times ($7.8886091 \times 10^{-29}$), the probability that you lose 98 out of 100 times ($3.9048615 \times 10^{-27}$), etc. In Figure 7, the cumulative sum of adding all those probabilities from $x=100$ on the right to further and further left is represented by the black line you can see in the right half rising as it goes towards the middle.

Once you have added all probabilities until and including 59 times heads (represented by the black bars), then cumulative the sum of all these probabilities reaches 0.044313 (represented by the black filled circle). Since the probability to get 58 heads out of 100 tosses is 0.0222923, you cannot add this event's probability to the cumulative sum of the others anymore without exceeding the level of significance value of 0.05: you can see how that addition would lead to the new cumulative sum of 0.0666053 (represented by the grey filled circle), which is above the threshold line of $y=0.05$. Put differently, if you don't want to cut off more than 5% of the summed bar lengths from the right (because you want to remain in 'significant' probability territory), then you must stop adding probabilities at $x=59$. You conclude: only if Stefan wins 59 times or more often can I accuse him of cheating, because the probability of that happening is the largest one that is still smaller than 0.05.

Now consider the perspective of the observer shown in Figure 8, which is very similar to Figure 7 (but simplified by leaving out the cumulative-summing bits). The observer also begins with the most extreme result, that I get heads every time, with the probability we know from above: $7.8886091 \times 10^{-31}$. But since the observer only has a non-directional H_1, he must also include the probability of the opposite, equally extreme result, that I get heads 0 times, i.e. that you win just as extremely, which is also $7.8886091 \times 10^{-31}$ (because the binomial distribution for $p_{success}=0.5$ is symmetric). For each additional number of heads – 99, 98, 97, etc. – the observer must now also add the corresponding opposite results – 1, 2, 3, etc. Once the observer has added the probabilities 61 times heads / 39 times tails and 39 times heads / 61 times tails, then the cumulative sum of the probabilities reaches 0.0352002 (see the black bars in Figure 8).

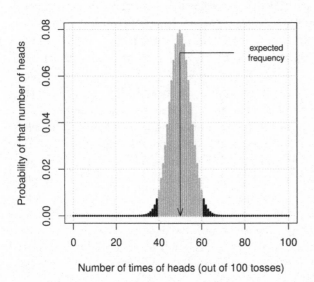

Figure 8: The probability distribution of 100 tosses of a fair coin (two-tailed)

Since the joint probability for the next two events – 60 heads / 40 tails and 40 heads / 60 tails – is 0.0216877, the observer cannot add any further results without exceeding the level of significance of 0.05. Put differently, if the observer doesn't want to cut off more than 5% of the summed bar lengths on both sides (because he wants to remain in 'significant' probability territory), then he must stop adding probabilities by going from the right to the left at x=61 and stop going from the left to the right at x=39. He concludes: only if someone – Stefan or his opponent – wins 61 times or more, can I accuse that someone of cheating.

Make sure you get what that entails: It entails that one and the same situation, e.g. me winning 60 times, can allow one person to accuse me of cheating (you, because your H_1 was directional), but not the other (the observer, because his H_1 was non-directional). You can already accuse me of cheating when you lose 59 times (only 9 times/18% more than the expected result), but the impartial observer needs to see you lose 61 times (11 times/22% more than the expected result) before he can start accusing me. This difference is very important and we will use it often below.

While reading the last few pages, you maybe sometimes wondered where the probabilities of events come from: How do I know that the probability to get heads 58 times in 100 tosses is 0.0222923? Essentially, those are computed in the same way as we handled Table 11 and Table 12, just that I did not write results up anymore because the sample space is too huge. These values were therefore computed with R on the basis of the so-called binomial distribution. You can easily compute the probability that one out of two possible events occurs x out of s times when the event's probability is p in R with the function dbinom; here's just one example (no need to understand the code yet):

```
dbinom(x=58, size=100, prob=0.5) # 58 heads/100 tosses of a fair coin
## [1] 0.02229227
# run this to get results like Table 11/12 for 3 tosses:
paste0(0:3, " times heads is this likely: ",
   sapply(0:3, function (af) sum(dbinom(af, 3, 0.5)))))
```

We'll do such computations again a few times, in particular in Chapter 4.

1.5.3 Significance and effect size

Finally, note one last important thing here: we said above that the *p*-value is '"how likely it is to find the effect *e* or something that deviates from H_0 even more in your sample'. From that you must not infer that the *p*-value is usually a good measure of the size of an effect. That's because the size of the *p*-value reflects multiple things at the same time: Yes, the effect size is one of them, but others are the sizes of the samples involved and the variability in the samples. Consider Figure 9 using made-up data: In each panel, female subjects on the left score a mean of approximately 105 whereas male subjects on the right score a mean of approximately 95 (the grey points are individual subjects' scores, the black points are the means.

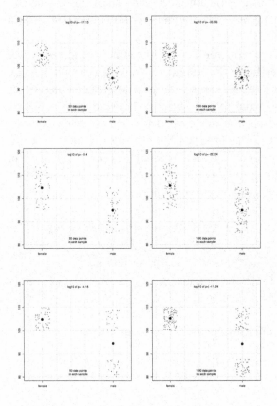

Figure 9: What contributes to effect sizes?

In other words, in each of the six plots the unstandardized effect size e, the raw observed difference between the female and the male average, is the same: 10. However,
- if you compare the three plots in each column, you see that with increasing variability (i.e. vertical spread of values for at least one sex), p increases by many orders of magnitude (i.e. becomes 'less significant', although the sample sizes stay the same);
- if you compare the two plots in each row, you see that with increasing sample size (i.e. more data points for, here, both sexes), p decreases by many orders of magnitude (i.e. becomes 'more significant', although the 'spread of the values' stays the same).

Thus, it is usually not a good idea to consider a p-value an effect size – it conflates more dimensions of information than just effect size – and it usually is a good idea to always clearly report (some form of) effect size as well.[4]

A similar logic applies to cross-tabulation. For instance, consider Table 13, which shows that two variables xs and ys are quite strongly associated to each other (the s in xs/ys stands for 'small').

Table 13: The correlation of two variables xs (rows) and ys (columns)

	ys: *n*	ys: *o*
xs: *a*	50	10
xs: *b*	10	30

When xs: b, the odds of ys: o are 15 times as high as when xs: a and that association is highly significant with a p-value of $<10^{-8}$:

```
## effect size (odds ratio)     log10 of p-value
##                  15.000              -8.265
```

But if we look at the same kind of cross-tabulation for a sample size 10 times as big (Table 14, the l in xl/yl stands for 'large')), but with the same effect size, you

---

4 Many people seem to think that standardized effect sizes are obviously and always superior to unstandardized effect sizes. While that might be so for meta-analytical purposes, it's not obviously true in other cases, see Baguley 2012: Section 7.3.2 or Pek & Flora 2018 for discussion).

can see that even just the increase in sample size has reduced the *p*-value by literally dozens of orders of magnitude:

Table 14: The correlation of two variables x1 (rows) and y1 (columns)

	y1: *n*	y1: *o*
x1: *a*	500	100
x1: *b*	100	300

```
## effect size (odds ratio)      log10 of p-value
##                     15.000              -75.256
```

Thus, again, do not equate *p*-values/significance tests with the sizes of effects: they are related if and when all other things are equal, but (i) even then not linearly and (ii) usually, all other things – sizes of samples, variabilities in samples – are not.

Recommendation(s) for further study: Gelman, Hill, & Vehtari (2020), in particular Chapter 4, for great discussion of problems with the NHST approach discussed here.

1.6 Data collection and storage

In this section, we will deal with a few fundamental rules for the design of experiments. The probably most central notion in this section is the token set (see Cowart 1997). I will distinguish two kinds of token sets, schematic token sets and concrete token sets. A **schematic token set** is typically a tabular representation of all experimental conditions. To explain this more clearly, let's return to the above example of particle placement.

Let's assume you want to investigate particle placement not only on the basis of corpus data, but also on the basis of experimental data. For instance, you might want to determine how native speakers of English rate the acceptability of sentences (the response ACCEPTABILITY) that differ with regard to the constructional choice (the first predictor CONSTRUCTION: *vop* vs. *vpo*) and the type of direct object (the second predictor OBJTYPE: lexical vs. pronominal). Since there are two levels for each of the two independent variables, there are 2×2=4 experimental conditions. This set of experimental conditions is the schematic token set, which is represented in two different forms in Table 15 and Table 16. The participants/subjects of course never get to see the schematic token set. For the actual experiment, you must develop concrete stimuli: **concrete token sets** that instantiate the variable level combinations (here indicated with the colon combining two variable names) of the schematic token set.

Table 15: Schematic token set for CONSTRUCTION:OBJTYPE, representation 1

	OBJTYPE: *lexical*	OBJTYPE: *pronominal*
CONSTRUCTION: *vop*	$vo_{lex}p$	$vo_{pron}p$
CONSTRUCTION: *vpo*	vpo_{lex}	vpo_{pron}

Table 16: Schematic token set for CONSTRUCTION:OBJTYPE, representation 2

CONDITION	CONSTRUCTION	OBJTYPE
1	*vop*	*lex*
2	*vop*	*pron*
3	*vpo*	*lex*
4	*vpo*	*pron*

However, both the construction of such concrete token sets and the actual presentations of the concrete stimuli are governed by a variety of rules that aim at minimizing undesirable effects. Three such sources of undesirable effects are particularly important:

– **knowledge of what the experiment is about**: we must make sure that the participants in the experiment do not know/figure out what's being investigated before or while they participate – after the experiment you can of course tell them. This is important because otherwise the participants might make their responses socially (or otherwise) more desirable or change the responses to 'help the experimenter';

– **undesirable experimental effects**: we must make sure that the responses of the subjects aren't influenced by, say, habituation to particular variable level combinations. This is important because in the domain of, say, acceptability judgments, Nagata (1987, 1989) showed that such judgments can change because of repeated exposure to stimuli and this may not be what we're interested in and, thus, something that should be controlled either by design (which is what we're talking about here) or in the statistical analysis (see, e.g., Section 5.2.8);

– **evaluation of the results**: we must make sure that the responses of the subjects can be interpreted unambiguously. Even a large number of willing and competent subjects is useless if your design doesn't allow for an appropriate evaluation of the data..

In order to address all these issues, we have to take the rules in (4) to (12) under consideration. Here's the first one in (4):

4.   The stimuli of each individual concrete token set differ with regard to the variable level combinations under investigation (and ideally only with regard to these and nothing else).

Consider Table 17 for an example, where the stimuli differ only with respect to the two predictors. If this was not the case (for example, because the right column contained the stimuli *John picked it up* and *John brought back it*) and we found a difference of acceptability between them, then we wouldn't know what to attribute this difference to – the different constructions (which would be what this experiment is all about), the different phrasal verb (that might be interesting, but is not what is studied here), an interaction of the two (i.e. a surprising effect when two things come together; this will be defined in more detail below) ... (4) is therefore concerned with the factor 'evaluation of the results'.

Table 17: Concrete token set for CONSTRUCTION : OBJTYPE 1

	OBJTYPE: *lexical*	OBJTYPE: *pronominal*
CONSTRUCTION: *vop*	John picked the key up	John picked it up
CONSTRUCTION: *vpo*	John picked up the key	John picked up it

When creating the concrete token sets, it's also important to consider variables which we're not interested in but which may make it difficult to interpret the results with regard to the variables that we are interested in (such as confounds and moderators). In the present case, for example, the choice of the verbs and the direct objects may be important. Or, it's well known that particle placement is also correlated with the concreteness of the referent of the direct object. There are different ways to take such variables, or sources of variation, into account. One is to make sure that 50% of the objects are abstract and 50% are concrete for each experimental condition in the schematic token set (i.e. we essentially introduce an additional variable, but it's 'only' a control variable, not a predictor). Another one is to use only abstract or only concrete objects, which would of course entail that whatever we find in our experiment, we could strictly speaking only generalize to that class of objects.

5. You must use more than one concrete token set, ideally as many concrete token sets as there are variable level combinations (or a multiple thereof).

One reason for (5) is that, if we only used the concrete token set in Table 17, then one point of critique would be that we could only generalize to other sentences with the transitive phrasal verb *pick up* and the objects *it* and *the key*, which might just not be the most interesting study ever (even though it is about particle placement). Thus, the first reason for (5) is again concerned with the factor 'evaluation of results', and the remedy is to create different concrete token sets with different verbs and different objects such as those shown in Table 18 and Table 19, which must of course also conform to (4).

Table 18: Concrete token set for CONSTRUCTION:OBJTYPE 2

	OBJTYPE: *lexical*	OBJTYPE: *pronominal*
CONSTRUCTION: *vop*	*Mary brought his dad back*	*Mary brought him back*
CONSTRUCTION: *vpo*	*Mary brought back his dad*	*Mary brought back him*

Table 19: Concrete token set for CONSTRUCTION:OBJTYPE 3

	OBJTYPE: *lexical*	OBJTYPE: *pronominal*
CONSTRUCTION: *vop*	*I eked my living out*	*I eked it out*
CONSTRUCTION: *vpo*	*I eked out my living*	*I eked out it*

A second reason for (5) is that if we only used the concrete token set in Table 17, then subjects would probably be able to guess the purpose of the experiment right away: Since our token set had to conform to (4), the subject would be able to identify the relevant variable level combinations quickly because those are the only things according to which the sentences differ, after all, we'd essentially be presenting minimal pairs; adhering to (5) begins to avoid that, as does adhering to (6):

6. Every subject sees maximally one stimulus from a concrete token set.

As I just mentioned, if we do not follow (5), the subjects might guess from the minimal-pair variations within one concrete token set what the whole experiment is about: The only difference between *John picked up it* and *John picked it up* is the choice of construction. Thus, when subject X gets to see the variable level combination (CONSTRUCTION: *vpo* and OBJTYPE: *pronominal*) in the form of *Mary brought back him*, then the other experimental stimuli in Table 18 must be given to other subjects. In that regard, both (5) and (6) are (also) concerned with the factor 'knowledge of what the experiment is about'. And the next:

7. Every subject is presented every variable level combination.

The motivation for (7) are the factors 'undesirable experimental effects' and 'evaluation of the results'. First, if several experimental stimuli we present to a subject only instantiate one variable level combination, then habituation effects may distort the results; this we could of course take into account by adding a variable to our analysis that mentions for each presentation of an experimental condition how often it has been presented already (see Sections 5.2.8, 5.6.3 below), but it would still complicate matters. Second, if we present one variable level combination to a subject very frequently and another one only rarely, then whatever difference you find between these variable level combinations may theoretically (also) be due to the different frequencies of exposure and not (just) due to the effects of the variable level combinations under investigation.

8. Every subject gets to see every variable level combination more than once and equally frequently.
9. Every experimental item is presented to more than one subject and to equally many subjects.

These rules are motivated by the factor 'evaluation of the results'. You can see what their purpose is if you think about what happens when we try to interpret a very unusual reaction by a subject to a stimulus. On the one hand, that reaction could mean that the stimulus itself is unusual in some respect in the sense that every subject would react unusually to it – but you can't test that if that stimulus isn't also given to other subjects, and this is the reason for the rule in (9). On the other hand, the unusual reaction could mean that only this particular subject reacts unusually to that variable level combination in the sense that the same subject would react more 'normally' to other stimuli instantiating the same variable level combination – but we can't test that if that subject doesn't see other stimuli with the same variable level combination, and this is the reason for (8). Next:

10. The experimental items are interspersed with distractors / filler items; there are minimally as many filler items as real experimental items per subject, but ideally two or three times as many.

The reason for (10) is obviously 'knowledge of what the experiment is about': We don't want the subjects to be able to guess the purpose of the experiment (or even just have them think they know the purpose of the experiment) so that they cannot distort the results.

An additional well-known factor that can distort results is the order in which items and distractors are presented. To minimize such effects, we must take into consideration the final two rules:

11. The order of experimental stimuli and filler items is pseudorandomized.
12. The order of experimental stimuli and filler items is pseudorandomized differently for every subject.

The rule in (11) requires that the order of experimental items and filler items is randomized using a random number generator, but it's not completely random – hence pseudorandomized because the ordering resulting from the randomization must usually be 'corrected' such that

- the first stimulus (e.g., the first question on a questionnaire) is not an experimental stimulus but a distractor;
- experimental stimuli do not follow each other directly;
- ideally, experimental stimuli exhibiting the same variable level combinations do not follow each other, which means that, after *John picked it up*, the next experimental item must not be *Mary brought him back* even if the two are interrupted by distractors.

The rule in (12) means that the order of stimuli must vary pseudorandomly across subjects so that whatever we find cannot be attributed to systematic order effects: Every subject is exposed to a different order of experimental items and distractors. Hence, both (11) and (12) are concerned with 'undesirable experimental effects' and 'evaluation of the results'. (This re-ordering of stimuli can be quite tedious, especially when your experiment involves many stimuli and subjects, which is why, once you are more proficient with R, it may be useful to write a function called, say, stimulus.randomizer to do this for you, which is how I do most of this.) Only after all these steps have been completed properly can we run our experiment. It probably goes without saying that we must carefully describe how the experimental design was set up in the methods section of your study.

One final remark about this: I know from experience (and long faces in classes) that the previous discussion can have a somewhat discouraging effect. Especially beginners hear/read this and think "how am I ever going to be able to set up an experiment for my project if I have to do all this? (I don't even know my spreadsheet software well enough yet ...)" And it's true: I myself might still need quite a bit of time before a spreadsheet for an experiment of mine looks exactly like it's supposed to. But if you don't go through what at first sight looks like a terrible ordeal, you're just postponing the ordeal, namely to the stage where your results might well be, what was the technical term again? oh yes, "useless"! Ask yourself what's more discouraging: spending maybe several days on getting the spreadsheet right, or spending maybe several weeks on doing a badly designed experiment and then having unusable results. In other words, be (nearly) as dedicated an experimenter as Michael L. Smith, who published Smith (2014), which says in the abstract: "This study rated the painfulness of honey bee stings over 25 body locations in one subject (the author)" – guess which location on his body was most painful (answer in the abstract) ...

Recommendation(s) for further study: Baayen (2010) for a great (but quite technical) discussion of a regression modeling perspective on factorial experiments.

Warning/advice: You must be prepared for the fact that usually not all subjects answer all questions, give all the acceptability judgments you ask for, show up for both the first and the second test, etc. Thus, you should plan conservatively and try to get more subjects than you thought you would need in the first place. As mentioned above, you should still include these data in your table and mark them with NA. Also, it's often very useful to carefully examine the missing data for whether their patterning reveals something of interest (it would be very important if, say, one variable level combination accounted for 90% of the missing data or if 90% of the missing data were contributed by only two out of, say, 60 subjects).

2 Fundamentals of R

> When we say that a historian or a linguist is 'innumerate' we mean that he cannot even be-
> gin to understand what scientists and mathematicians are talking about.
> (Oxford English Dictionary, 2nd ed., 1989, s.v. numeracy, from Keen 2010: 4)

2.1 Introduction and installation

In this chapter, you will learn about the foundations of R, which enable you to load and store data as well as perform some data processing operations preparing you for the applications in later chapters. Let's begin with the first step: the installation of R.

1. The main R website is <http://www.r-project.org>. From there, you can go to the CRAN website at <https://cran.r-project.org/mirrors.html>. Click on <https://cloud.r-project.org/> at the top and then the link for your operating system:
   a) for Windows, you will then click on "base", and then on the link to the setup program to download and then execute it;
   b) for Mac OS X, you immediately get to a page with a link to a .pkg file, which you can use to install R;
   c) for Linux, you choose your distribution and then either your distribution version or, if you use Ubuntu or a derivative such as Mint or Pop! OS, just go to the link <README.html>; more conveniently, you may be able to install R and many frequently-used packages using a package manager such as Synaptic or Muon;
2. then, after R is installed, I strongly recommend that you install RStudio, an excellent IDE for working with R, from <https://rstudio.com/products/rstudio/download/#download>.

You can now launch RStudio, which will in turn start R. If you're launching RStudio for the first time, I also recommend that you go through the following steps (these are a few of my own subjective preferences; as you become more experienced with RStudio, you may develop other preferences for your kind of work flow):
– configure RStudio: go to "Tools: Global Options..." and

https://doi.org/10.1515/9783110718256-002

- click "General" on the left and then, in the "Basic" tab, deactivate all options beginning with "Restore" and set "Save workspace to .RData on exit" to "Never" (so as to always start with a blank slate);
- click "Code" on the left and then,
  - in the "Editing" tab, activate the "Soft-wrap R source files" option (so long lines are wrapped at the end of the window);
  - in the "Display" tab, activate all options (so you have more visual input regarding aspects of the code);
- click "Pane Layout" on the left and then organize the quadrants such that
  - it says "Source" in the top left quadrant;
  - it says "Console" in the top right quadrant.
- install packages: If you're using R/RStudio for the first time, it might be simplest to install packages from within it: In RStudio, go to the quadrant whose pane contains a "Packages" tab, click on it, then click on Install, and then enter the names of the packages you want to install into the "Packages" field. For this book, I recommend you minimally install the following packages: car, doParallel, effects, faraway, lme4, lmerTest, magrittr, mlogit, MuMIn, nnet, nortest, partykit, pdp, randomForest, rgl, tree, and vioplot; I will occasionally refer to some other packages but these will cover just about all the code we will run. If you're more experienced, I recommend installing packages in an R terminal instance that you started with admin rights (on Linux, with "sudo R"). Finally, make sure you keep R, the packages you're using, and RStudio updated: I often see people not being able to replicate what they have been taught because R and/or a package are years old; this book was written with R 4.0.3 and RStudio 1.4.1103.

Then, download a zip archive with all materials for the book from the companion website of this edition of the book at <http://www.stgries.info/research/sflwr/sflwr.html> and unzip that archive (note: the companion website will also provide a file with errata as those get discovered). To unzip the zip file with the companion materials, you'll need to use a proper (!) unzipping software (e.g. 7-zip (Windoze or Linux) or StuffItExpander (Mac)) and the password **mockingbiRd**. This will return a folder called <sflwr3> that contains the code/R files for this book (<00_allcode.r> and <00_allcode.html>) plus exercise files, answer keys, and other things in several subdirectories: <_exercises>, <_inputfiles>, <_outputfiles>, and <_helpers>. (The book and the exercises were actually originally written in RMarkdown, I might make (some of) those files available at some point as well, *if* I can figure out how to do this without problems.) My recommendation is that, whenever you want to work on this book, you open a new instance of R/RStudio by double-clicking on the file

<sflwr3/00_allcode.r>; then, R/RStudio will already be in the right working directory and all file paths in the code file will work; if you're not in that directory, you can go there by going to the quadrant whose pane contains a "Files" tab, click on that tab, then click on the "..." button on the right, move to the folder, click "Open", and then click on "More" and then "Set As Working Directory".

R isn't just a statistics program – it's also a programming language (and environment) which has some superficial (!) similarity to Python or Julia. The range of applications is breathtakingly large as R offers the functionality of spreadsheet software, statistics programs, a general-purpose programming language, databases etc. This introduction to statistics, however, is largely concerned with functions to generate and process simple data structures in R and functions for probability distributions, statistical analysis, and graphical evaluation. We will therefore unfortunately not be able to deal with more complex data structures and many aspects of R as a programming language however interesting these may be – if you're interested in R as a corpus tool, I of course and shamelessly recommend Gries (2016). Also, I will not always use the simplest or most elegant way to perform a particular task but the way that I find most useful from a pedagogical and methodological perspective (e.g., to highlight commonalities between different functions and approaches). Thus, this book isn't a general introduction to R,[5] and I refer you to the recommendations for further study and the reference section for introductory books to R.

Now we have to address some typographical and other conventions. As already above, websites, folders, and files will be delimited by "<" and ">" as in, say, <_inputfiles/03_scmc.csv>. Package, function, or variables names as well as inline code snippets – anything you could enter into R – are formatted like variable names, i.e. like this mean(c(1, 2, 3)), but most code will usually be given in blocks like this, and if that code generates non-plot output, that will be shown like this, i.e. in a box with the same font as code but with "##" at the beginning of the line, like so:

```
a <- c(1, 2, 3)
mean(a)
## [1] 2
```

---

5 Note also that this book doesn't use what many people nowadays seem to equate with R, namely the tidyverse or ggplot2. In bootcamps, I usually spend a moment explaining why that is the case, but for here, let me simply refer you to the comprehensive discussion offered by Norman Matloff at <https://github.com/matloff/TidyverseSkeptic/blob/master/READMEFull.md>, who articulates my concerns and many more better than I would have been able to.

A lot of times, I will abbreviate the output shown in the book a bit, that will be indicated with a [...] in the output box, i.e. as ## [...].

As you enter things within R, usually you'll do so after a prompt like this ">", but you might occasionally also see lines that begin with "+". These plus signs R provides when it is still expecting further input from you before it begins to execute the function. For example, when you enter 2-, then this is what your R console will look like:

```
> 2 +
+
```

The plus sign means R is waiting for you to complete the subtraction. When you enter the number you wish to subtract and press ENTER, then this operation will be executed properly and you will get the result of -1:

```
3
```

Another example: If you wish to load the package effects into R to access some of the functions that it provides, you can load this package by entering library(effects). (Note: this only works if you already installed the package as explained above.) However, if you forget the closing parenthesis, R will wait for you to complete the input:

```
> 2 +
+
```

Once you enter just that missing) at the plus sign and press ENTER, the function will be executed. If, however, the code cannot be made to work by just providing the missing information, press ESC and start over.

2.2 Functions and arguments

As you may remember from school – please do! – one often doesn't use numbers, but rather letters to represent variables that 'contain' numbers. In algebra class, for example, you had to find out from two equations such as the following which values a and b represent (here $a={}^{23}/_7$ and $b={}^{20}/_7$):

$$a+2b=9$$
$$3a-b=7$$

In R, you can solve such problems, too, but R is much more powerful and variable names such as *a* and *b* can represent huge multidimensional elements so we'll refer to them here as **data structures** or **objects**. In this chapter, we'll deal with the data structures you need to know about for the statistical analyses I want to discuss. Such data structures can either be entered into R at the console or, more commonly, read into R from pre-existing files. I will present both means of data entry, but most of this book presupposes that the data are available in the form of tab-delimited text files that have the structure discussed in the previous chapter and were created in a text editor or a spreadsheet software such as LibreOffice Calc (but even a commercial spreadsheet software whose name rhymes a bit with "ick sell" might be ok in a pinch). In the following sections, I will explain how to create, load, and process data structures in R and how to save them from within R.

One of the most central things to understand about R is how you tell it to do something other than the simple calculations from above. We will always issue commands in R that consist of two elements: a function and, in parentheses, arguments; in that regard, R is similar to spreadsheet software, where you might use a function like AVERAGE and, as arguments, you give AVERAGE the cell coordinates of the numbers of which you want the average (e.g., "=AVERAGE(A1:B3)"). As in spreadsheet software, a **function** is an instruction to do something and **arguments** to a function represent (i) what the instruction is to be applied to and (ii) how the instruction is to be applied to it. (Arguments can be null, meaning, 'there might be no arguments', in which case the function name is just followed by opening and closing parentheses.) Let's look at a simple arithmetic function you know from school. If we want to compute the natural logarithm of 5 with R, we need to know the name of the function as well as how many and which arguments it takes. Well, the name of the function is log so let's now figure out what arguments it can take by using a function called args, whose argument is the name of another function:

```
args(log)
## function (x, base = exp(1))
## NULL
```

The output shows several important things about the arguments of functions in general and about log in particular. Apparently, log can take two arguments:
- the first argument is the number you want to log; internally to the function log, that argument is called x and since x is not defined in the function itself, it must be provided by the user (obviously, R cannot possibly guess let alone know which number(s) we want log);

– the second argument is the base of the logarithm we want to use; internally to the function log, that argument is called base and that one is defined in the function itself (namely as exp(1), which is 2.7182818), which means the user can either accept R's default log setting of base (because that might be what is needed) or the user can override R's default setting of base with their own desired one (e.g., if we want the logarithm to the base of 2 or 10).

```
# short form
log(x=5, base=exp(1))
## [1] 1.609438
# long form, broken down by arguments
log(             # compute the log
   x=5,          # of 5
   base=exp(1))  # to the base of e
## [1] 1.609438
```

However, since we're using the default setting of the base argument, R actually allows us to omit it: If we do not override R's default setting of an argument (because that's what we want), then R will use it:

```
log(5) # compute the log of 5 (to the base of e)
## [1] 1.609438
```

What R does here is 'think' this: 'Ok, the user wants a log and the user is giving me one argument but without telling me what the argument is: is the 5 supposed to be x or base? I guess I'll just map the argument(s) the user gave me to the arguments I expected in the order in which they occur. The first argument I wanted was x so I am going to make the first (unnamed) argument the user gave me x; and then, since the user didn't give me a second argument, I will use my default for base, which is exp(1)." Based on this logic, if we want the binary log of 5, we could get it in any of these ways (results not shown again):

```
log(x=5, base=2) # compute the
log(x=5, 2)      # log of 5
log(5, base=2)   # (to the
log(5, 2)        # base of 2)
```

And in fact, if we use the names of the arguments, we can change their order around simply because then R has the names to identify what's what (results not shown again):

```
log(x=5, base=2) # compute the log of 5
log(base=2, x=5) # (to the base of e)
```

In what follows, I will mostly use named arguments even when I give them in the default order so that you see what they are called and because I will often provide arguments in an order other than the default one (for didactic reasons).

Recommendation(s) for further study: Check the functions ? or help, which provide the help file/documentation for a function (try ?sample or help(sample) because we will need that function later).

2.3 Vectors

2.3.1 Generating vectors

Let's first make sure we have nothing lying around in our R workspace that might interfere with what's coming up now. For that, we can use the function rm (for "remove"). Its most frequent use in this book is exemplified in the following code chunk and shows you how can remove all objects from the current workspace. (If you wanted to remove only a single data structure, you just use the name of that data structure as the only argument to rm; thus, if there was an object aa in your workspace, you could remove it by typing rm(aa).)

```
rm(list=ls(all.names=TRUE)) # remove all ls finds in your workspace
```

The most basic data structure in R is a vector. **Vectors** are one-dimensional, sequentially ordered sequences of elements such as numbers or character strings (e.g., words). While it may not be completely obvious why vectors are important here, we must deal with them in some detail since many other data structures in R can ultimately be understood in terms of vectors. Vectors can be generated in R in a variety of ways. The simplest way is to take the name you want a vector to have (e.g. aa) and put into it <- (the 'assignment arrow') what you want the vector to contain (e.g. the number 5); the following creates a numeric vector aa:

```
aa <- 5
```

Now you can check whether this worked and 'print' the contents of aa:

```
aa
## [1] 5
```

Note: the [1] before the 5 means that the 5 is the first (and, here, only) element of the requested output. You can verify that aa is a vector using the function is.vector, which tests whether its argument is a vector or not and returns the result of its test in the form of another kind of vector, a **logical vector**, which can be either TRUE (R's version of *yes*) or FALSE (R's version of *no*):

```
is.vector(aa)
## [1] TRUE
```

You can also check what kind of vector aa is:

```
class(aa)
## [1] "numeric"
```

And you can check how long aa is, i.e. how many elements this vector contains:

```
length(aa)
## [1] 1
```

Of course you can also create logical vectors yourself; note how in this code snippet (and in many from now on), I will parenthesize an assignment to create a data structure and then also immediately display it:

```
(bb <- TRUE) # same as bb <- TRUE; bb # semicolons separate function
    calls in 1 line
## [1] TRUE
is.vector(bb)
## [1] TRUE
class(bb)
## [1] "logical"
length(bb)
## [1] 1
```

Also, we can create **character vectors**, i.e. vectors of character strings, which I will always provide between double quotes:

```
(cc <- "forklift")
```

```
## [1] "forklift"
is.vector(cc)
## [1] TRUE
class(cc)
## [1] "character"
length(cc)
## [1] 1
```

However, all of the above vectors are single-element vectors (what some might call a *scalar*), but typically we want to work with vectors that are (much) longer, that are multi-element vectors. We will discuss three ways to create such multi-element vectors: the functions c, rep, and seq. The function c (for "combine" or "concatenate") just puts one or more elements into a single vector:

```
# a multi-element numeric vector
(aa <- c(1, 3, 5))
## [1] 1 3 5
is.vector(aa)
## [1] TRUE
class(aa)
## [1] "numeric"
length(aa)
## [1] 3

# a multi-element character vector
(cc <- c("impetus", "klumpatsch", "facetiously"))
## [1] "impetus"     "klumpatsch"  "facetiously"
is.vector(cc)
## [1] TRUE
class(cc)
## [1] "character"
length(cc)
## [1] 3
```

In these examples, aa and cc were created by using c to combine three single-element vectors, e.g. the three words for cc. But c can also be used to combine one or more multi-element vectors:

```
numbers1 <- c(1, 2, 3) # generate ...
numbers2 <- c(4, 5, 6) # two vectors, then combine:
```

```
(numbers1.and.numbers2 <- c(numbers1, numbers2))
## [1] 1 2 3 4 5 6
length(numbers1.and.numbers2)
## [1] 6
```

Note that – unlike arrays in Perl – vectors can only store elements of one data type. For example, a vector can contain numbers or character strings, but not really both: If you try to force numbers and character strings into one vector, R will change the data type of one of the two vectors so as to make the resulting vector contain only one data type, and since you can interpret numbers as characters but not vice versa, R changes the numbers into character strings and then concatenates them into a vector of character strings:

```
numbers.num <- c(1, 2, 3) # generate ...
numbers.char <- c("four", "five", "six") # two vectors, then combine:
(nums.and.chars.become.chars <- c(numbers.num, numbers.char))
## [1] "1"    "2"    "3"    "four" "five" "six"
```

The double quotes around 1, 2, and 3 indicate that these are now understood as character strings, which means that you cannot use them for calculations anymore (unless you change their data type back).

The next function we look at is rep (for "repetition"). In the simplest scenario, the function takes two arguments:
– the first argument is internally called x and refers to the vector whose elements are to be repeated;
– the second argument is
    – either a numeric vector times, stating how often all of x is to be repeated;
    – or a numeric vector each, stating how often each element of x is to be repeated;
    – or a numeric vector length.out, stating how long the resulting vector should be.

Here are some straightforward examples:

```
rep(x="something", times=3)
## [1] "something" "something" "something"
rep(x="something", each=3)
## [1] "something" "something" "something"
rep(x=4, length.out=3)
## [1] 4 4 4
```

But remember: x is a vector, but nothing says it can only be a single-element vector as above and now we see the difference between times and each:

```
rep(x=c("anim", "inanim"), times=3)
## [1] "anim"   "inanim" "anim"   "inanim" "anim"   "inanim"
rep(x=c("anim", "inanim"), each=3)
## [1] "anim"   "anim"   "anim"   "inanim" "inanim" "inanim"
rep(x=c(1, 2, 3), length.out=10)
##  [1] 1 2 3 1 2 3 1 2 3 1
```

In the first case, R repeats all of x three times; in the second, R repeats each element of x three times before it goes on to the next; in the last one, R repeats the elements of x over and over again till it runs into the desired output length – then it stops right away, even if that means that not everything gets repeated equally often (we will use that for cross-validation much later).

Finally, can you guess what this will do, i.e. what happens if the times argument is a multi-element vector?

```
rep(x=c(4, 5, 6), times=c(3, 2, 1))
## [1] 4 4 4 5 5 6
```

This maps the elements of times onto the elements of x in a pairwise fashion and repeats them accordingly: The first element of x (4) is repeated as often as the first element of times states (3), etc. This pairwise mapping is something you need to bear in mind because of how useful and prevalent it is.

The final vector generation function we look at is seq (for "sequence"). Maybe a bit confusingly, it has four main uses; I will begin with the first two, which are similar to the uses of rep. These involve the following arguments:
– the first argument is called from and is a numeric single-element vector denoting the starting point of a numeric sequence;
– the second argument is called to and is a numeric single-element vector denoting the end point of a numeric sequence;
– the third argument is
  – either a numeric vector by in which case it states the increment which you add to from as often as needed to get from from to to;
  – or a numeric vector length.out, in which case it states how long the resulting vector should be (and R figures out for you what by needs to be for that).

The following examples should make this clear:

```
# using by
seq(from=2, to=6, by=0.4)
## [1] 2.0 2.4 2.8 3.2 3.6 4.0 4.4 4.8 5.2 5.6 6.0
seq(from=6, to=2, by=-0.4)
## [1] 6.0 5.6 5.2 4.8 4.4 4.0 3.6 3.2 2.8 2.4 2.0
# using length.out
seq(from=2, to=6, length.out=4)
## [1] 2.000000 3.333333 4.666667 6.000000
seq(from=6, to=2, length.out=4)
## [1] 6.000000 4.666667 3.333333 2.000000
```

The other two uses of seq I mention here involve what happens if you give it just a single argument and those are often used in programming applications involving so-called for-loops:
- if that argument is a positive integer, seq generates a sequence from 1 to that integer with by being 1;
- if that argument is a multi-element data structure, seq generates a sequence from 1 to however elements that data structure has with by being 1.

The following examples should make this clear again:

```
# using positive integers
seq(3) # same as seq(from=1, to=3, by=1)
## [1] 1 2 3
# using multi-element vectors
seq(c(2,5,8)) # same as seq(from=1, to=length(c(2, 5, 8)), by=1)
## [1] 1 2 3
```

Sometimes, you can do sequencing of integers with by=1 using a notation that involves the colon in its function as a range operator:

```
1:4
## [1] 1 2 3 4
6:4
## [1] 6 5 4
```

Another useful feature of vectors is that you can not only name the whole vectors, but also their individual elements:

```
numbers <- c(1, 2, 3); names(numbers) <- c("one", "two", "three")
```

```
numbers
##   one   two three
##     1     2     3
```

This is something that can be extremely useful in a variety of settings and I will use it multiple times below.

2.3.2 Loading and saving vectors

Since data for statistical analysis will usually not be entered into R manually, we now briefly discuss how to read vectors from, and save them into, files. (The discussion will only be brief because most of the time we will read in data frames, i.e. spreadsheet-like two-dimensional data structures and work with their columns.)

A very powerful function to load vector data into R is the function scan. This function can take many different arguments but here are some of its most important ones:
– the first argument is called file and is a single-element character vector specifying the location of the file you want to load;
– the second one is called what and is a single-element character vector defining what you are trying to load:
  – if you want to load a file that contains numbers, you need not specify that because that's scan's default expectation;
  – if you want to load a file that contains character strings, specify what= character() or what="";
– the last one mentioned here is called sep and is a single-element character vector providing the character that separates different entries (e.g., numbers or character strings) in the input file; often, this is set to
  – sep="\n", if every number/character string has its own line;
  – sep="\t", if the numbers/character strings are tab-delimited;
  – sep=",", if the numbers/character strings are comma-separated;
  – sep=" ", if the numbers/character strings are separated by spaces (the default).

There's a variety of other settings that can be useful and that I encourage you to explore once you have a bit more experience or feel you need them (especially quote, fileEncoding, and encoding). To load the file <_inputfiles/02_vector1.txt>, which contains what is shown in Figure 10, into a vector x, we would therefore enter this:

```
1
2
3
```

Figure 10: An example file

```
(x <- scan(file="_inputfiles/02_vector1.txt", sep="\n"))
## [1] 1 2 3
```

To load the file <_inputfiles/02_vector2.txt>, which is shown in Figure 11, into a vector x, ...

```
This is the first line
This is the second line
```

Figure 11: An example file

... we would probably want to enter this:

```
(x <- scan(file="_inputfiles/02_vector2.txt", what=character(),
    sep="\n"))
## [1] 1 2 3
```

Now, how do we save vectors into files. The required function – basically the reverse of scan – is cat and it takes very similar arguments:
– the first argument is the name of the vector to be saved;
– the second one is called file and is a single-element character vector specifying the location of the file into which you want to save the vector (if no file argument is provided, output is printed to the console);
– the third one is called sep and defines the character that separates the elements of the vector from each other just as in scan;
– the final argument I mention here is called append and is a single-element logical vector:
  – if append=FALSE (the default), then cat will save the vector in the specified file but if that target file already exists, then it'll be overwritten;
  – if append=TRUE, then cat will save the vector in the specified file but if that target file already exists, then the new output will be appended to what's already in that file.

Recommendation(s) for further study: Check the functions write, save, saveRDS, and dput to save vectors (or other structures) and save.image to save the whole workspace.

2.3.3 Working with vectors

Now that we can generate, load, and save vectors, we must deal with how you can edit them. The functions we'll be concerned with allow us to access particular parts of vectors to output them, to use them in other functions, or to change them. First, a few functions to edit numerical vectors. One such function is round. Its first argument is x, the vector with numbers to be rounded; its second is digits, the desired number of decimal places. (Note, R rounds according to an IEEE standard: The fact that 3.55 doesn't become 3.6, but 3.5, is not a bug; see the links in ?round.)

```
rm(list=ls(all.names=TRUE)) # clear memory
(aa <- seq(from=3.4, to=3.6, by=0.05))
## [1] 3.40 3.45 3.50 3.55 3.60
round(x=aa, digits=1)
## [1] 3.4 3.4 3.5 3.5 3.6
```

The function floor returns the largest integers not greater than the corresponding elements of the vector provided, ceiling returns the smallest integers not less than the corresponding elements of the vector provided, and trunc simply truncates the elements toward 0:

```
floor(x=c(-1.8, 1.8))    # compute the floor of those numbers
## [1] -2  1
ceiling(x=c(-1.8, 1.8)) # compute the ceiling of these numbers
## [1] -1  2
trunc(x=c(-1.8, 1.8))    # truncate these numbers
## [1] -1  1
```

The most important way to access parts of a vector (or other data structures) in R involves subsetting with square brackets. There are two main ways to do that:
– we can subset a vector with a logical vector of the same length, where that logical vector has TRUEs for the elements we do want and FALSEs for the elements we don't want;
– we can subset a vector with a numeric vector that lists the positions of elements we want.

In the simplest form, for example, this is how these two ways would allow us to access an individual vector element (here, the third):

```
cc <- c( "a"  , "b"  , "c" , "d"  , "e")   # spacing is just for
cc[   c(FALSE, FALSE, TRUE, FALSE, FALSE)] # ease of visual mapping
## [1] "c"
cc[3]          # show the 3rd element of cc
## [1] "c"
y <- 3; cc[y] # show the y-th (i.e., here, 3rd) element of cc
## [1] "c"
```

Since you already know how flexible R is with vectors, the following uses involving multi-element subsetting should not come as big surprises:

```
cc[c(TRUE, FALSE, TRUE, FALSE, FALSE)]
## [1] "a" "c"
cc[c(3, 1)]
## [1] "c" "a"

cc[c(TRUE, TRUE, TRUE, FALSE, FALSE)]
## [1] "a" "b" "c"
cc[c(1:3)]
## [1] "a" "b" "c"
```

With negative numbers, you can leave out elements:

```
cc[-2]
## [1] "a" "c" "d" "e"
```

However, there are many more powerful ways to access parts of vectors. For example, we can let R determine which elements of a vector fulfill a certain condition. Instead of typing a logical vector yourself like above, a usually better way is to present R with a logical expression so that it returns a logical vector for you. You should read this with a question intonation to realize how close to English R can be: cc is "d"?

```
cc=="d"
## [1] FALSE FALSE FALSE  TRUE FALSE
```

R checks for each element of cc whether it is "d" or not and returns its findings as a logical vector of FALSEs (*nos*) and TRUEs (*yess*). The only thing requiring a little attention here is that the logical expression uses two equal signs, which distinguishes logical expressions from assignments such as file="", which obviously use only one. Some other logical operators are:

– & means 'and' and | means 'or';
– >, >=, <, and <= mean what you think they mean;
– ! means 'not' and != means 'not equal to'/≠.

Here are some examples:

```
(bb <- 10:1)
## [1] 10  9  8  7  6  5  4  3  2  1
bb==4          # is bb 4?
## [1] FALSE FALSE FALSE FALSE FALSE FALSE  TRUE FALSE FALSE FALSE
bb<=7          # is bb <=7?
## [1] FALSE FALSE FALSE  TRUE  TRUE  TRUE  TRUE  TRUE  TRUE  TRUE
bb!=8          # is bb not 8?
## [1]  TRUE  TRUE FALSE  TRUE  TRUE  TRUE  TRUE  TRUE  TRUE  TRUE
(bb>8 | bb<3) # is bb >8 or <3?
## [1]  TRUE  TRUE FALSE FALSE FALSE FALSE FALSE FALSE  TRUE  TRUE
```

However, the above often don't scale well, meaning they become tedious very quickly as soon as the vectors involved become longer. This is because you get one TRUE/FALSE for every element of the tested vector, meaning if bb had 10,000 elements, your screen would be flooded with 10,000 responses even if you might only be interested in the few TRUE cases. There're two easy ways to deal with this. One involves the function any, which takes a logical vector as its argument and checks whether at least one of them is TRUE:

```
any(bb==4) # is there any 4 in bb at all? yes
## [1] TRUE
any(bb==0) # is there any 0 in bb at all? no
## [1] FALSE
```

The other involves the function which, which takes a logical vector as its first argument x and returns the positions of the TRUEs. Thus, which translates the first way of subsetting (with logical vectors) into the second (with numeric position indices of TRUEs).

```
bb # just to remind you what bb is
## [1] 10  9  8  7  6  5  4  3  2  1
# which position of bb (if any) contains ...
which(bb==4)        # ... a 4?
## [1] 7
which(bb<=7)        # ... values <=7?
## [1]  4  5  6  7  8  9 10
which(bb!=8)        # ... values that are not 8?
## [1]  1  2  4  5  6  7  8  9 10
which(bb>8 | bb<3) # ... values >8 or <3?
## [1]  1  2  9 10
```

Again and especially if you leave out the x= as I did here, you can read this nearly like a question in English: "which bb is 4?" or, a bit better, "which positions of bb are 4?" But note: don't confuse the position of an element in a vector with the element of the vector. The call which(bb==4) doesn't return the *element* 4, but the *position of the element* 4 in bb, which is the 7th, and the same is true for the other examples. And given what was said above, you can now subset bb not only with logical or numeric vectors you typed yourself (as above), but also with ones that you made R generate:

```
bb<=7 # a 1st log. expr.: which elements of bb are < 7?
## [1] FALSE FALSE FALSE  TRUE  TRUE  TRUE  TRUE  TRUE  TRUE  TRUE
bb[bb<=7]          # subsetting w/ a logical vector
## [1] 7 6 5 4 3 2 1
bb[which(bb<=7)] # subsetting w/ a numeric vector
## [1] 7 6 5 4 3 2 1

bb>8 | bb<3 # a 2nd log. expr.: which elements of bb are >8 or <3?
## [1]  TRUE  TRUE FALSE FALSE FALSE FALSE FALSE FALSE  TRUE  TRUE
bb[bb>8 | bb<3]          # subsetting w/ a logical vector
## [1] 10  9  2  1
bb[which(bb>8 | bb<3)] # subsetting w/ a numeric vector
## [1] 10  9  2  1
```

Since TRUE and FALSE in R correspond to 1 and 0, you can also easily determine how often a particular logical expression is true in/for a vector:

```
sum(bb==4)
## [1] 1
```

```
sum(bb>8 | bb<3) # how many elements of bb are >8 or <3?
## [1] 4
```

The above code involved examples where you tested whether each element of bb is one particular thing (4) and we did that with bb==4 or any(bb==4). What if we have several things to check bb for? For that, the operator %in% is useful and typically it gets used like this:

```
c(1, 6, 11) %in% bb # is 1 in bb? is 6? is 11?
## [1]  TRUE  TRUE FALSE
```

This checks for each element of the vector to the left of %in% whether it is attested in the vector to the right of %in%: 1 and 6 are in bb, 11 is not. (By the way, if you want to look up the help file for %in%, you can't say ?%in%, you have to use ? `%in%`.) If you would also like to know the exact position of the first (!) occurrence of each of the elements of the first vector (called x) in the second vector (called table), you can use match:

```
match(x=c(1, 6, 11), table=bb)
## [1] 10  5 NA
```

That is to say, the first element of the first vector (the 1) occurs the first time at the tenth position of bb; the second element of the first vector (the 6) occurs the first time at the fifth position of bb; the last element of the first vector (the 11) doesn't occur in bb. (The function match might remind you of VLOOKUP in spreadsheet software.)

Much of the above can of course not only be used to access parts of vectors, but also to change them. For example, one simple strategy to mitigate the effect that outliers might have is called winsorizing, which replaces outliers in a numeric vector by less extreme yet still attested values of that vector. Consider this vector aa:

```
(aa <- c(1, seq(from=30, to=70, by=4)))
## [1]  1 30 34 38 42 46 50 54 58 62 66 70
```

Obviously, the first value looks a bit like an outlier and one might decide, just for the sake of the current exemplification, to winsorize the vector by changing all of aa's values that are less than 30 to 30. Thus, we could do this:

```
aa.winsd <- aa                 # make aa.winsd a copy of aa
aa.winsd[aa.winsd<30] <- 30 # change values <30 to 30
aa.winsd                       # check result
##  [1] 30 30 34 38 42 46 50 54 58 62 66 70
```

R also offers several set-theoretical functions: setdiff, intersect, and union. Each of them takes two vectors x and y as their first and second arguments respectively and they all do what you probably expect them to do. The function setdiff returns the elements of x that are not in y:

```
aa <- c(10:1); bb <- c(2, 5, 9, 12)
setdiff(x=aa, y=bb) # what's in aa that's not in bb?
## [1] 10  8  7  6  4  3  1
setdiff(x=bb, y=aa) # what's in bb that's not in aa?
## [1] 12
```

The function intersect returns the elements of x that are also in y:

```
intersect(x=aa, y=bb) # what's the intersection of aa & bb?
## [1] 9 5 2
intersect(x=bb, y=aa) # what's the intersection of bb & aa?
## [1] 2 5 9
```

And union returns all elements that occur in at least one of the two vectors:

```
union(x=aa, y=bb) # what's the union of aa & bb?
##  [1] 10  9  8  7  6  5  4  3  2  1 12
union(x=bb, y=aa) # what's the union of bb & aa?
##  [1]  2  5  9 12 10  8  7  6  4  3  1
```

Another useful function is unique, which can be explained particularly easily to linguists: It goes through all the elements of a vector (the tokens) and returns all elements that occur at least once (the types) in their order of first occurrence:

```
(qwe <- letters[c(1, 3, 2, 2, 3, 4, 3, 4, 5)]) # (see ?letters)
## [1] "a" "c" "b" "b" "c" "d" "c" "d" "e"
unique(x=qwe) # what are the unique types in qwe?
## [1] "a" "c" "b" "d" "e"
```

But this doesn't tell us how often each of the types is attested, for which we can use the function table, which returns the frequencies of all types (in alphabetical order):

```
table(qwe) # how often does qwe contain which type?
## qwe
## a b c d e
## 1 2 3 2 1
```

In words, qwe contains a 1 time, b 2 times, etc.; this is an extremely useful function for corpus processing with R. (Note, extremely important: table by default ignores missing data – if you want to count those, too, one option to get those is using table(..., useNA="ifany").) Crucially, the values that table returns are the frequencies (1, 2, 3, 2, 1) and these frequencies have the names of the types they refer to ("a", "b", "c", "d", "e") This should remind you of what I told you earlier: one can name vector elements, which above we did with this bit of code:

```
numbers <- c(1, 2, 3); names(numbers) <- c("one", "two", "three");
    numbers
##   one   two three
##     1     2     3
```

One extremely useful thing is that one can then not only access parts of tables or vectors in the ways discussed above – with logical vectors and numeric position vectors – but now also with the names. Check this out:

```
qwe.t <- table(qwe)
qwe.t["b"] # & what's the frequency of "b" in the vector qwe?
## b
## 2
numbers["two"] # what is stored in the slot of numbers called "two"?
## two
##   2
```

This becomes interesting when you have a table called bnc.tab which contains the frequencies of 950,000 word types of, say, the British National Corpus, and you can just type bnc.tab["fish"] or bnc.tab[c("fish", "silk")] to look up the frequency of that word / those words in the corpus.

Let's now turn to some mathematical operations with vectors. There are two common scenarios and one special case, which I will discuss using simple multiplication as an example. Scenario 1 is that you want to multiply the elements of one numeric multi-element vector by the elements of another numeric multi-element vector and, crucially, the two vectors are equally long. In this case, R does what you saw above when I discussed rep, namely pairwise multiplication by position: aa[1]*bb[1], aa[2]*bb[2], aa[3]*bb[3], etc.:

```
(aa <- 1:5)
## [1] 1 2 3 4 5
(bb <- 5:9)
## [1] 5 6 7 8 9
aa*bb # 1*5, 2*6, 3*7, ...
## [1]  5 12 21 32 45
```

Scenario 2 is you want to multiply the elements of one numeric multi-element vector by the element of one numeric single-element vector. In that case, R starts as in scenario 1 – it does aa[1]*bb[1] but then there's no bb[2] to multiply aa[2] with. Therefore, R 'starts over' with the elements of bb and uses bb[1] again and does aa[2]*bb[1], then it runs into the same problem again for aa[3] and solves it the same way: aa[3]*bb[1], and so on:

```
(aa <- 1:5)
## [1] 1 2 3 4 5
(bb <- 5)
## [1] 5
aa*bb # 1*5, 2*5, 3*5, ...
## [1]  5 10 15 20 25
```

The special case, so to speak is, when the vectors aa and bb are not equally long *and* the length of the longer vector is not a multiple of the length of the shorter vector. In such cases, R will recycle the shorter vector as necessary and possible, but will also issue a warning:

```
(aa <- 1:5)
[1] 1 2 3 4 5
(bb <- 5:6)
[1] 5 6
aa*bb # 1*5, 2*6, 3*5, ...
[1]  5 12 15 24 25
Warning message: In aa * bb :
  longer object length is not a multiple of shorter object length
```

Finally, two functions to change the ordering of elements of vectors. The first of these functions is called sort, and its most important argument is of course the vector whose elements are to be sorted (and, as usual, it is called x); another important argument defines the sorting style: decreasing=FALSE is the default and for the opposite we can use decreasing=TRUE.

```
qwe <- c(1, 3, 5, 7, 9, 2, 4, 6, 8, 10)
(y <- sort(x=qwe))
## [1]  1  2  3  4  5  6  7  8  9 10
(z <- sort(x=qwe, decreasing=TRUE))
## [1] 10  9  8  7  6  5  4  3  2  1
```

The second such function is order. Its two most important arguments are one or more vectors according to which an ordering should be generated and then, like sort it can take a logical vector called decreasing as an additional argument (with decreasing=FALSE again being the default). However, what it returns is not usually immediately obvious. Can you see what order does?

```
z <- c("b", "c", "e", "d", "a")
order(z)
## [1] 5 1 2 4 3
```

THINK BREAK

The output of order when applied to a vector like z is a vector which tells you in which order you would need to put the elements of z to sort them as specified. To confuse you a bit more: z[order(z)] is the same as sort(z) ... Ok, let me now clarify: You look at order's output which tells you this: If you want to sort the values of z in increasing order,
– order's 1st output slot is a 5: you need to take the 5th value of z (the *a*);
– order's 2nd output slot is a 1: you need to take the 1st value of z (the *b*);
– order's 3rd output slot is a 2: you need to take the 2nd value of z (the *c*);
– order's 4th output slot is a 4: you need to take the 4th value of z (the *d*);
– order's 5th output slot is a 3: you need to take the 3rd value of z (the *e*);

This way, you get the alphabetical order of the elements in z and that's why z[order(z)] is the same as sort(z). If you provide order with more than one vector, these additional vectors are used to break ties in the previous vectors. As we will see below, order will turn out to be useful for data frames (where we cannot use sort).

Recommendation(s) for further study: Check out
- the function all (kind of a complement to any) to test whether all elements of a vector fulfill a particular logical condition;
- the function abs to obtain the absolute values of a numerical vector;
- the functions min and max to obtain the minimum and the maximum values of numeric vectors respectively.

2.4 Factors

The second data structure we will look at are factors. Factors are superficially similar to character vectors and we'll deal with them here only briefly.

2.4.1 Generating factors

The most straightforward way to generate a factor is by first generating a vector as introduced above and then turning it into a factor using the function factor with the vector to be factorized as the first and maybe only argument:

```
rm(list=ls(all.names=TRUE))
(f.vec <- c("open", "open", "open", "closed", "closed"))
## [1] "open"   "open"   "open"   "closed" "closed"
(f.fac <- factor(x=f.vec))
## [1] open   open   open   closed closed
## Levels: closed open
```

When we output a factor we created like that, we can see one difference between factors and vectors because the output includes a (by default alphabetically-sorted) list of all levels – the unique types the factor contains or, importantly, 'knows' it might contain – of that factor. When you create a factor, you can define the levels it's supposed to have and their order) with a second argument to factor, namely levels:

```
(f.fac.ll <- factor(x=f.vec, levels=c("closed", "open")))
## [1] open   open   open   closed closed
## Levels: closed open
```

```
(f.fac.12 <- factor(x=f.vec, levels=c("open", "closed")))
## [1] open    open    open    closed closed
## Levels: open closed
```

You'll see more of that in Section 2.4.3.

One other very useful way in which one sometimes generates factors is based on the function cut. In its simplest implementation, it takes a numeric vector as its first argument (x) and a number of intervals as its second (breaks), and then it divides x into breaks intervals:

```
num.vector <- 1:9
(cut.factor <- cut(x=num.vector, breaks=3))
##    [1]    (0.992,3.67]    (0.992,3.67]    (0.992,3.67]    (3.67,6.33]
##         (3.67,6.33]              (3.67,6.33]             (6.33,9.01]
##          [8]           (6.33,9.01]                       (6.33,9.01]
## Levels: (0.992,3.67] (3.67,6.33] (6.33,9.01]
```

As you can see, the vector with the numbers from 1 to 9 has now been changed into a factor with three levels whose names provide the intervals R used for cutting up the numeric vector; this is how you can check R created the right groups:

```
table(num.vector, cut.factor)
# [output not shown], henceforth abbreviated as [...]
```

You can see that num.vector's values 1, 2, and 3 are now conflated into the level "(0.992, 3.67]", etc. What do the three levels' names mean, though? The names define these levels:
– (0.992,3.67] means: 0.992 < interval/level 1 ≤ 3.67;
– (3.67,6.33] means: 3.67 < interval/level 2 ≤ 6.33;
– (6.33,9.01] means: 6.33 < interval/level 3 ≤ 9.01.

(See, for instance, the Wikipedia entry on Interval notation.) Also, cut has another way of using breaks and some other useful arguments so you should explore those in more detail: ?cut.

2.4.2 Loading and saving factors

We don't really need to discuss how you load factors because you'll usually get them as a by-product from loading the data structure of the next section, data frames – but if you really ever need to load a factor, you do it in the same way as you load vectors and then you convert the loaded vector into a factor as illustrated above. Saving a factor, however, is a little different. Imagine we have the following factor a.

```
(a <- factor(c("alpha", "charly", "bravo")))
## [1] alpha   charly bravo
## Levels: alpha bravo charly
```

If we now try to save this factor into a file as we would with a vector,

```
cat(a, sep="\n", file="_outputfiles/02_somefactor1.txt")
```

our output file will look like Figure 12:

```
1
3
2
```

Figure 12: Probably not quite successful factor output

This is because R represents factors internally in the form of integers from 1 to however many levels the factor has and since the default level order is alphabetical, *alpha* is internally 1, *bravo* is internally 2, and *charly* is internally 3. R then only outputs these numbers into a file. Since we want the words, however, we simply force R to treat the factor as a character vector, which will produce the desired result.

```
cat(as.character(a), # output a (as a character vector)
    sep="\n",        # w/ line breaks between elements
    file="_outputfiles/02_somefactor2.txt") # into this file
```

2.4.3 Working with factors

If you want to change an element of a factor into something else, you will face one of two scenarios. First, the simple one: you want to change a factor element into something for which the factor already has a level (most likely because it is already attested in the factor or was in the past). In that case, you can treat factors like vectors:

```
f.fac.11
## [1] open    open    open    closed closed
## Levels: closed open
f.fac.11[2] <- "closed"; f.fac.11
## [1] open    closed open    closed closed
## Levels: closed open
```

Second, the more complex one: We want to change a factor element into something that is not already an existing factor level. In that case, we first re-define the factor by adding the level that we want to change something into, and then we can treat that new factor like a vector again, as above:

```
f.fac.11 <- factor(f.fac.11, levels=c(levels(f.fac.11), "half-open"))
f.fac.11[3] <- "half-open"; f.fac.11
## [1] open        closed     half-open closed      closed
## Levels: closed open half-open
```

And again – because this can easily trip up analyses – a factor can have levels that are not attested among its elements. This can happen, for instance, when we change the third element of f back into what it was:

```
f.fac.11[3] <- "open"; f.fac.11
## [1] open    closed open    closed closed
## Levels: closed open half-open
```

The simplest way to get rid of those is to re-define the factor using `droplevels`, which, you're not gonna believe it!, drops unused levels from factors:

```
(f.fac.11 <- droplevels(f.fac.11))
## [1] open    closed open    closed closed
## Levels: closed open
```

2.5 Data frames

The data structure that's most relevant to nearly all statistical methods in this book is the data frame, if only in how data frames will just about always provide/contain the vectors and factors that constitute our variables. The data frame – basically what we would colloquially call a table (which I will not do because there's the function `table` that creates tables in R) – is actually only a specific type of another data structure, a list, but since data frames are the single most frequent input format for statistical analyses (within R, but also for other statistical programs and of course spreadsheet software), we will first concentrate only on data frames per se and then deal with lists separately below.

2.5.1 Generating data frames

Generating data frames from vectors (and factors) is very easy. Imagine we collected four different kinds of information for five parts of speech and wanted to generate the data frame in Table 20:
- the variable TOKENFREQ, i.e. the frequency of words of a particular part of speech in a corpus X;
- the variable TYPEFREQ, i.e. the number of different words of a particular part of speech in X;
- the variable POS, i.e. the parts of speech of those words;
- the variable POSCLASS, which represents whether the part of speech is from the group of open- or closed-class words.

Table 20: Concrete token set for CONSTRUCTION:OBJTYPE 3

TOKENFREQ	TYPEFREQ	POS	CLASS
421	271	adj	open
337	103	adv	open
1411	735	n	open
458	18	conj	closed
455	37	prep	closed

Step 1: We generate four vectors, one for each column:

```
rm(list=ls(all.names=TRUE))
TOKENFREQ <- c(421, 337, 1411, 458, 455)
TYPEFREQ <- c(271, 103, 735, 18, 37)
POS <- c("adj", "adv", "n", "conj", "prep")
CLASS <- rep(c("open", "closed"), c(3, 2))
```

Step 2: We can now just create our data frame with the function data.frame, which takes as arguments the relevant vectors and factors. In this case, we add the argument stringsAsFactors=TRUE so that the character vectors with our categorical variables become factors (because since R 4.0 character vectors are not automatically converted to factors anymore):

```
(x <- data.frame(TOKENFREQ, TYPEFREQ, POS, CLASS,
   stringsAsFactors=TRUE))
##   TOKENFREQ TYPEFREQ POS  CLASS
## 1       421      271 adj   open
## 2       337      103 adv   open
## 3      1411      735   n   open
## 4       458       18 conj closed
## 5       455       37 prep closed
```

As you can see, x contains the columns in the order in which we added the vectors into data.frame, the names of those vectors became column names of x, and since we didn't provide any row names, R just numbers them from 1 to 5. Let's look at the data frame using two very useful overview/summary functions: str and summary.

```
str(x)
## 'data.frame':    5 obs. of  4 variables:
##  $ TOKENFREQ: num  421 337 1411 458 455
##  $ TYPEFREQ : num  271 103 735 18 37
##  $ POS      : Factor w/ 5 levels "adj","adv","conj",..: 1 2 4 3 5
##  $ CLASS    : Factor w/ 2 levels "closed","open": 2 2 2 1 1
```

The output of str tells us the numbers of rows (5 obs.) and columns (4 variables) of x (which we could also get from nrow and ncol or dim for both, remember those for later), it tells us that columns 3 and 4 contain factors whereas columns 1 and 2 contain numeric vectors, and then we get a preview of the contents of each column; note again how the factors are internally represented with integer values that represent the (by default alphabetically-ordered) factor levels. Note also that there's a $ in front of each column name: that tells us that we can use the notation dataframe$columnname as a shortcut (as in x$TOKENFREQ or x$CLASS) to access a column from the data frame (if you have no-nonsense column names without spaces in them, as I would recommend):

```
summary(x)
##    TOKENFREQ         TYPEFREQ        POS       CLASS
##  Min.   : 337.0   Min.   : 18.0   adj :1   closed:2
##  1st Qu.: 421.0   1st Qu.: 37.0   adv :1   open  :3
```

```
##   Median : 455.0    Median :103.0    conj:1
##   Mean   : 616.4    Mean   :232.8    n   :1
##   3rd Qu.: 458.0    3rd Qu.:271.0    prep:1
##   Max.   :1411.0    Max.   :735.0
```

The output of summary summarizes each column depending on what it contains:
- if the column is a factor, we get (the beginning of) a frequency list of the factor (see esp. the column CLASS);
- if the column is a numeric vector, we get some numerical statistics including the vector's minimum, maximum, median, mean, etc.

(Note: the stringsAsFactors argument only changes character vectors to factors – it doesn't change numeric vectors into factors even if you as the analyst know that a certain numeric vector actually encodes something categorical. In other words and just to remind you of that, do not use a numeric vector to represent a categorical variable by, say, using 1 for *closed* and 2 for *open*, because R will 'think' such a vector is numeric. Instead, do what we did: define a character vector containing the properly human-readable strings closed and open and turn that into a factor.)

Two other useful functions are head and tail: They give you the first and last 6 elements of a vector or the first and last 6 rows of a data frame so you can quickly check whether everything looks as expected; if you want to see not 6, but a different number, make that number the second argument n of head/tail.

2.5.2 Loading and saving data frames

The more common way of getting R to recognize a data frame is to load a file that was generated with some spreadsheet software. Let's assume we generated a spreadsheet file </_inputfiles/02_dataframe1.ods> or a tab- or comma-delimited file <_inputfiles/02_dataframe1.csv> containing the above data frame x (using some spreadsheet software such as LibreOffice Calc or a text editor). Ideally, our spreadsheet would only contain alphanumeric characters and no whitespace characters (to facilitate later handling in R or other software). The first step is to save that file as a raw text file. In LibreOffice Calc, you would choose the Menu "File: Save As ...", choose "Text CSV (.csv)" from the menu on the bottom right, move to the directory where you want to save the file, enter a file name (ideally ending in ".csv"), and click "Save". Then you confirm that you want to save this in "Text CSV format". Then, you make sure you set the export options:
- Character set is probably best set to "Unicode (UTF-8)";

– Field delimiter should be {Tab};
– String delimiter should be empty;
– Save cell content as shown should be ticked, the other options shouldn't.

I myself am often more old-school, only use no-nonsense data frames, am on a UTF-8 operating system, and have many keyboard shortcuts so I just copy the whole spreadsheet into the clipboard, paste it into an empty text file, and save that text file with the file extension ".csv", and for me that's much faster than the above sequence of operations.

Recommendation(s) for further study: Check out the function expand.grid. (I mean that, we'll need it later.)

To import such a .csv file into R, the most comprehensive function for this is read.table. These are its most frequently-used arguments with frequently useful settings:
– file: defines the location of the file you want to import;
– header: whether the first row contains the labels for the columns (header=TRUE) – as it should be – or not (header=FALSE);
– sep: the character that separates columns; given the file we wish to import – and in fact always within this book – our setting should be sep="\t";
– dec: the character that is the decimal separator argument (by default the period, which means for some countries/locales this may need to be set to a comma);
– quote: the characters used for quoted strings; this should nearly always be set to an empty string, i.e. "".
– comment.char: the character that separates comments from the rest of the line; just like with quote, this should most likely be set to an empty string "";
– stringsAsFactors: whether columns with character vectors should be factors; the default has now become FALSE (unfortunately, from my backwards compatibility point of view) but for statistical data, I still prefer TRUE (for corpus data I would stick with the new default).

Thus, in order to import the table we may just have saved from LibreOffice Calc into a .csv file into a data frame called x, we enter the following (the first line is just to clear memory again and note how I immediately wrap summary() around the assignment x <- ... so that R reads in the data frame but also immediately shows the summary of what it imported):

```
rm(list=ls(all.names=TRUE))
summary(x <- read.table(file="_inputfiles/02_dataframe1.csv",
   header=TRUE, sep="\t", quote="", comment.char="",
   stringsAsFactors=TRUE))
##    TOKENFREQ         TYPEFREQ        POS        CLASS
## Min.    : 337.0  Min.    : 18.0  adj :1   closed:2
## 1st Qu.: 421.0  1st Qu.: 37.0  adv :1   open  :3
## Median : 455.0  Median :103.0  conj:1
## Mean    : 616.4  Mean    :232.8  n   :1
## 3rd Qu.: 458.0  3rd Qu.:271.0  prep:1
## Max.    :1411.0  Max.    :735.0
```

If our input file is a no-nonsense input file – no spaces or unusual characters anywhere and tabs between columns – we can usually just use the function read.delim with only the file argument, which is what I always do (unless I work with corpus data). Now, if we have a data frame in your R session and want to export it into a .csv file, we can do that with the counterpart to read.table, which is write.table. Here are the most frequently used arguments of write.table with frequently useful settings:
– x: the data frame to be saved;
– file: the file we want to save the data frame into;
– append, sep, and dec are used as introduced above;
– quote whether we want factor levels within double quotes, which is usually not particularly useful for editing data in a spreadsheet software so I always set this to FALSE;
– row.names and col.names specify whether we would like to include the names (or numbers) of the rows and the names of the columns in the file; the settings I usually use are the ones shown below:

```
write.table(x=x, file="_outputfiles/02_dataframe1.csv",
   sep="\t", quote=FALSE, row.names=FALSE, col.names=TRUE)
```

2.5.3 Working with data frames

If we have a data frame in memory/our workspace, there are several ways in which we can access the data in it. To access the columns of a data frame, i.e. the variables, we can not immediately just use the column names – that will most likely return an error. One alternative we can use instead is to use the function with like this:

```
with(x, TOKENFREQ)
## [1]  421  337 1411  458  455
```

A shorter alternative was shown above and uses the dollar sign (and this is what I will nearly always do in this book):

```
x$TOKENFREQ
## [1]  421  337 1411  458  455
```

Finally, we can use the function attach to make all columns of a data frame available without the name of the data frame:

```
TOKENFREQ # doesn't work
## Error in eval(expr, envir, enclos): object 'TOKENFREQ' not found
attach(x)
TOKENFREQ
## [1]  421  337 1411  458  455
detach(x) # see ?detach on detaching packages
```

Note that if a data frame that we attach has column names that are identical to names of variables in our environment – e.g. if we had a vector TOKENFREQ already defined in our workspace from whatever we did earlier – then after attaching the data frame, entering TOKENFREQ will return the variable from the attached data frame x, not the one defined before. This means one should be careful with attaching data frames to 'maintain order' in one's workspace so as to not confuse different data structures with the same name. If we want to 'undo' an attach, we can do that with detach and my recommendation is to only attach if you feel you really really need to, but if you did so, then, whenever you want to make any changes to a data frame you attached, detach it first (which forces you to explicate the data frame where this variable is from), then make your changes, and then (maybe) attach again – yes, super old-school and paranoid, but it works.

However, there's another way of accessing parts of data frames, one that applies not only to columns as above, but also rows, and that is again subsetting with square brackets. We saw above that we can use square brackets to select parts of vectors, which are one-dimensional data structures – since data frames are two-dimensional data structures, we now need two (sets of) figures, pretty much like (geographical) coordinates:

– one numeric vector restricting the output to the rows we want to see; that vector goes before a comma;

Recommendation(s) for further study: Check out the packages readODS, readr, readxl, or foreign and the functions read.delim2, read.csv/read.csv2, readRDS/saveRDS, and save.image
again.

– one numeric vector restricting the output to the columns we want to see; that
vector goes after the comma:

```
# I'm not showing output below; it's too long for the book
# since the columns are not restricted, all are returned
x[2,]      # returns row 2
x[2:3,]    # returns rows 2 & 3
x[c(4,2),] # returns rows 4 & 2
# since the rows are not restricted, all are returned
x[,2]      # returns column 2
x[,2:3]    # returns columns 2 & 3
x[,c(3,1)] # returns column 3 & 1
x[2,3]    # returns the cell area defined by row 2 & column 3
x[2,3:4] # returns the cell area defined by row 2 & columns 3 to 4
```

But if you can put numbers in there manually, you can also put code in there
that either returns TRUEs and FALSEs (and R will return the elements corresponding to TRUEs) or code that returns such numbers (by using which to return the
positions of TRUEs):

```
x$TOKENFREQ
which(x$TOKENFREQ>450) # same as: which(x[,2]>450)
x[x$TOKENFREQ>450,]     # same as: x[x[,2]>450,]
x$CLASS
which(x$CLASS=="open") # same as: which(x[,4]=="open")
x[x$CLASS=="open",]     # same as: x[x[,4]=="open",]
## [...]
```

You can also use the function subset for this and here I'm assigning the result to
an object qwe:

```
qwe <- subset(x, subset=TOKENFREQ>450)
qwe <- subset(x, subset=CLASS=="open")
```

But note that the factors in the reduced data frame qwe still have the levels in
them that are now not attested anymore:

```
summary(qwe)
   TOKENFREQ          TYPEFREQ        POS         CLASS
Min.    : 337    Min.    :103.0   adj :1    closed:0
1st Qu.: 379    1st Qu.:187.0   adv :1    open  :3
Median : 421    Median :271.0   conj:0
Mean    : 723    Mean    :369.7   n   :1
3rd Qu.: 916    3rd Qu.:503.0   prep:0
Max.    :1411    Max.    :735.0
```

Thus, when you create a data frame that's a part of a bigger data frame with sub-setting — [or subset — it's often a good idea to apply the above-mentioned function droplevels to the whole data frame: it reduces the levels of *all* factors in it to only those that are attested:

```
summary(qwe <- droplevels(subset(x, subset=CLASS=="open")))
   TOKENFREQ          TYPEFREQ        POS        CLASS
Min.    : 337    Min.    :103.0   adj:1    open:3
1st Qu.: 379    1st Qu.:187.0   adv:1
Median : 421    Median :271.0   n  :1
Mean    : 723    Mean    :369.7
3rd Qu.: 916    3rd Qu.:503.0
Max.    :1411    Max.    :735.0
```

Another useful function is split, whose first argument x can be a data frame and whose second argument amounts to a grouping variable using a vector/factor — either a vector/factor that is already part of x or one that is created on the fly (e.g. with a logical expression):

```
(x.split.1 <- split(x=x, f=x$CLASS))
(x.split.2 <- split(x=x, f=x$TOKENFREQ>450))
## [...]
```

We can also apply a split by more than one criterion; in that case, the f argument needs to be a list of vectors/factors:

```
(x.split.3 <- split(x=x, f=list(x$CLASS, x$TOKENFREQ>450)))
# add drop=TRUE to not return empty splits (like closed.FALSE)
## [...]
```

We will return to split in a moment in the section on lists.

Finally, let me mention a very practical way of reordering the rows of data frames by means of the function order introduced above. Recall that order returns a vector of positions of elements and recall that subsetting can be used to access parts of vectors, factors, and data frames (and later lists). As a matter of fact, you may already guess how you can reorder data frames from what you have read above (about order):

```
# the default ordering order is in ascending/increasing order
ordering.index <- order(x$TOKENFREQ)
x[ordering.index,]
## [...]
```

We can 'reverse' that ordering in two ways:

```
# using decreasing=TRUE
ordering.index <- order(x$TOKENFREQ, decreasing=TRUE)
# making the numbers to be sorted negative:
ordering.index <- order(-x$TOKENFREQ)
# and for the most part, this also works with factors:
# the default sort, which is decreasing=FALSE
ordering.index <- order(x$POS)
# reversing the sort w/ decreasing=TRUE:
ordering.index <- order(x$POS, decreasing=TRUE)
```

But with factors we cannot use the minus sign because what would -*open* be? For instance, imagine we want to sort the rows in the data frame x according to CLASS (ascending in alphabetical order) and, within CLASS, according to values of the column POS (in descending order). Now the problem is that we have two conflicting sorting preferences (ascending for CLASS and descending for POS) but we can't use the minus sign for either one. The solution to the problem is to use the function rank, which returns the ranks of vector values or, here, the integers that make up the levels of factors; see how the ranks correspond to the numbers reflecting an alphabetical sorting:

```
x$POS
## [1] adj  adv  n    conj prep
## Levels: adj adv conj n prep
rank(x$POS)
## [1] 1 2 4 3 5
```

Thus, we can do this now to get what we want (in a way that combines multiple sorting styles):

```
ordering.index <- order(x$CLASS, -rank(x$POS))
x[ordering.index,] # apply that ordering to x
```

2.6 Lists

While the data frame is probably the most central data structure for statistical evaluation in R and has thus received much attention here, you already know that data frames are actually just a special kind of another data structure, namely lists. More specifically, data frames are lists that contain vectors and factors which all have the same length. Lists are a much more versatile data structure, which can in turn contain various different data structures within them. For example, a list can contain different kinds of vectors, data frames, and other lists, as well as other data structures we will use implicitly, but not discuss explicitly, in this book (e.g., arrays or matrices):

```
some.vect <- c(1:10)
some.dafr <- x
some.fact <- factor(letters[1:10])
(a.list <- list(some.vect, some.dafr, some.fact)) # create a list
## [...]
```

As you can see, the three different elements – a vector of numbers, a data frame, and a factor – are now stored in a single data structure:

```
str(a.list)
## List of 3
##  $ : int [1:10] 1 2 3 4 5 6 7 8 9 10
##  $ :'data.frame':    5 obs. of  4 variables:
##   ..$ TOKENFREQ: int [1:5] 421 337 1411 458 455
##   ..$ TYPEFREQ : int [1:5] 271 103 735 18 37
##   ..$ POS      : Factor w/ 5 levels "adj","adv",..: 1 2 4 3 5
##   ..$ CLASS    : Factor w/ 2 levels "closed","open": 2 2 2 1 1
##  $ : Factor w/ 10 levels "a","b","c","d",..: 1 2 3 4 5 6 7 8 9 10
```

This kind of data structure is interesting because it can contain many different things and because we can access individual parts of it in ways similar to those we use for other data structures. As the above output indicates, the elements in lists are numbered and the numbers are put between double square brackets. Thus, we can access each element of the list like this:

```
a.list[[1]] # the 1st element of a list as a numeric vector
a.list[[2]] # the 2nd element of a list as a data frame
a.list[[3]] # the 3rd element of a list as a factor
## [...]
```

It is important to bear in mind that there are two ways of accessing a list's elements with subsetting. The one with double square brackets is the one suggested by how a list is shown in the console. This way, we get each element as the kind of data structure we entered it into the list, namely as a vector, a data frame, and a factor respectively. What, however, happens when we use the general subsetting approach, which you know uses single square brackets? Can you see the difference in the notation with double square brackets – what is happening here?

```
a.list[[1]] # the 1st element of a list as a ...?
## [1] 1 2 3 4 5 6 7 8 9 10
a.list[1]   # the 1st element of a list as a ...?
## [[1]]
## [1] 1 2 3 4 5 6 7 8 9 10
```

The difference is this: If we access a component of a list with *double* square brackets, we get that component as an instance of the kind of data structure as it was entered into the list (see the first output, which is a regular numeric vector). If we access a component of a list with *single* square brackets, we get that component as an instance of the data structure from which we're plucking it, i.e., here as a list. This may seem surprising or confusing, but it is actually consistent with what you already know: If we use single square-bracket subsetting on a vector, what do we get? A vector. If we use single square-bracket subsetting on a factor, what do we get? A factor, etc. Same thing here: If we use single square-bracket subsetting on a list, we get a list. So, once you think about it, no big surprise, but in all honesty, you will usually want a list component not as a list but as the (simpler) data structure in there, e.g. as a vector, so the more important and much more frequent way of subsetting lists is with double square brackets.

An alternative approach is to make sure the list components have names. We can do that just like we would with vectors when the list has already been created like above:

```
names(a.list) <- c("Part1", "Part2", "Part3") # give the parts names
## [...]
```

Or, you can actually do that already while you are creating the list:

```
a.list <- list("Part1"=some.vect, "Part2"=some.dafr,
   "Part3"=some.fact)
## [...]
```

Either way, once the list components have names, we can use by now familiar ways of subsetting as well:

```
a.list[[1]]        # all these three
a.list[["Part1"]] # return the same:
a.list$Part1       # a numeric vector
## [...]
```

And of course the same logic works for accessing parts of parts of lists:

```
a.list[[2]][2:3,3:4]
a.list[["Part2"]][2:3,3:4]
a.list$Part2[2:3,3:4]
## [...]
```

How do we delete a part of a list? Like this:

```
a.list[[2]] <- NULL # delete part 2 of the list, the data frame
```

Now, why am I discussing lists here? Here are two reasons: First, they're an extremely versatile/powerful data structure that can collect all sorts of information, a data frame with data, other vectors and factors that also pertain to the data, a regression modeling object that was generated from the data, etc. In other words, a list can be a structure that holds many completely different things together in one nicely accessible object, which can be useful when more comprehensive analyses are done.

Second, many functions return list objects. For example, very many statistical but also text processing functions such as strsplit, gregexpr, and others discussed in Gries (2016) return lists so you need to know how to handle them. But there are also other data wrangling functions that return lists. Above, we looked at split and did this:

```
(x.split.1 <- split(x=x, f=x$CLASS))
## [...]
```

The result of this, the object x.split.1, is actually a list as well, which contains two data frames, one with the rows of x when x$CLASS was *closed*, one for when it was *open*. If you now want to do a separate analysis of each data frame, you must know how you get those out of x.split.1 and you could do that as we've discussed above:

```
x.split.1$closed # or x.split.1[[1]]
x.split.1$open   # or x.split.1[[2]]
## [...]
```

Finally, a small function that is often very useful: Sometimes, a function returns a list object but you want the output to be an easier-to-process vector. It is sometimes then possible to use the function unlist to change the list object to a vector and often, though not always, that makes subsequent steps or displaying things much easier; you'll see that function in Section 4.2.2 below, for instance).

3 Descriptive statistics

> Any 21st century linguist will be required to read about and understand mathematical mod-
> els as well as understand statistical methods of analysis. Whether you are interested in
> Shakespearean meter, the sociolinguistic perception of identity, Hindi verb agreement vio-
> lations, or the perception of vowel duration, the use of math as a tool of analysis is already
> here and its prevalence will only grow over the next few decades. If you're not prepared to
> read articles involving the term Bayesian, or (p<.01), k-means clustering, confidence inter-
> val, latent semantic analysis, bimodal and unimodal distributions, N-grams, etc, then you
> will be but a shy guest at the feast of linguistics. (<http://thelousylinguist.blogspot.com/
> 2010/01/why-linguists-should-study-math.html>)

In this chapter, I'll explain how to obtain descriptive statistics for our data – no
p-values and/or significance testing yet: Section 3.1 discusses univariate statistics, i.e. statistics that characterize the distribution of one (response) variable, of
one vector, of one factor. Section 3.2 then is concerned with bivariate statistics,
statistics that characterize the relation of two variables, two vectors, two factors
to each other. Both these sections also introduce a variety of ways of representing such data and their relations graphically (with many additional graphs in
subsequent chapters). Section 3.3 is a brief, polemic, but important and hopefully also instructive excursus on the notion of 'correlation'; section 3.4 is similar
to that and provides my views on visualization. Finally section 3.5 is an excursus
on a few issues related to programming in R: conditional expressions, loops,
and writing your own functions (anonymous and otherwise). This section is useful, I think, because the more complex our data are, the more likely it becomes
that we will need/want to do more complex things or a lot of things for which we
know no existing functions – to my biased mind, a bit of programming knowledge is required for a linguist working with (a lot of) empirical data (and especially for a linguist who might decide to be open to or already pursue a career in
industry/data science rather than academia).

3.1 Univariate descriptive statistics

We'll begin with univariate statistics, i.e. statistics that describe (aspects of) the
behavior or distribution of a single (response) variable (i.e. one vector or one factor). We start out from the lower information value – categorical variables – and
work our way up via ordinal variables to numeric variables. Within each kind of

https://doi.org/10.1515/9783110718256-003

variable, we'll consider the overall distribution but also especially measures of central tendency and measures of dispersion. A **measure of central tendency** is the statistic that we would provide for a variable if we were given the following instruction: "Give me as much information about your variable as you can – but you're only allowed to give me one number!" A **measure of dispersion** is then the natural and pretty obligatory complement to that and answers the question: "That measure of central tendency you just gave me: how well does it actually summarize the variable it was computed from?" And then, finally, within each kind of variable, we'll also discuss simple ways of visualizing them.

To discuss all these things, we'll mostly work with a small data set that you will see again in Chapter 5 and that has a variety of things that are useful for didactic purposes. Let's load those data:

```
rm(list=ls(all.names=TRUE))
summary(x <- read.delim(file="_inputfiles/03_RT.csv",
    stringsAsFactors=TRUE)) ## [...]
```

It contains the following data:
- a categorical variable CASE, which contains 77 words for which the following variables were collected;
- a numeric variable RT: representing the reaction times to these words (in ms) in a lexical decision task (when we discuss linear modeling in later chapters, this will be the response variable);
- a numeric variable FREQ representing the frequency of the words in x$CASE in a small corpus;
- an ordinal variable FAM providing subjects' rated familiarity with the referent of the words in x$CASE;
- a categorical variable called IMA providing subjects' rated imageability with the referent of the words in x$CASE;
- a numeric variable MEAN with subjects' rated meaningfulness with the referent of the words in x$CASE.

Before we start, we want to prepare our data a bit with an eye to improve their immediate interpretability. If you look at the summary of the data frame x, you'll see that the factors in x are summarized with a frequency table in which the levels are listed in their default order, which is alphabetical. That's sometimes fine, and often not, especially for reasons having to do with plotting and modeling. For plotting, for instance, R will often generate plots plotting the levels in their order from left to right but that means that, in the case of x$FAM, it would give us a result for *hi* first, then a bit to the right of that the result for *lo*, and then further right the result for *med*, which means the alphabetical order of the levels is not reflecting the ordinal nature of the variable. Ideally, we would want the order of levels to be *lo*, *med*, and *hi* (and same ordering for x$IMA). (In fact, we would like x$FAM to be an ordered factor, but that is something we will, kind of, revisit again only later.) Thus, before we do anything else, we change the orders of the factors' levels around to make them more intuitive/useful:

```
x$FAM <- factor(x$FAM, levels=levels(x$FAM)[c(2, 3, 1)])
x$IMA <- factor(x$IMA, levels=levels(x$IMA)[c(2, 1)])
```

Also, note already that the data frame contains a variety of missing data indicated by NA; those are cases where, for some words, some measurements on the variables were not available. Being aware of this early on is incredibly important … To save some typing etc, just for now we're attaching the data frame:

```
attach(x)
```

3.1.1 Categorical variables

The simplest way of looking at a categorical variable is by determining how often each distinct outcome is attested by means of a simple frequency table and we have seen in Section 2.3.3 above how to do that:

```
table(IMA)
## IMA
## lo hi
## 23 30
```

Pay attention: We know from above that the data frame has 77 rows, but the two values do not sum up to that! Remember from above that the default setting of table excludes NAs in its counts; more precisely, table has an argument useNA, whose default setting is no. If we want missing data included as well, we have to say so with either of the following two options, which here of course return the same result:

```
table(IMA, useNA="ifany")   # shows an NA count only if there are any
## IMA
##   lo   hi <NA>
##   23   30   24
```

```
table(IMA, useNA="always") # always shows an NA count
[...]
```

If we want observed percentages, we can get those in two ways: We can compute them ourselves or we can use the function prop.table, which we apply to a table generated with table; but note, both functions only give us the percentages resulting from the frequencies shown (i.e., here, without the NAs):

```
table(IMA)/sum(table(IMA)) # same as
## IMA
##         lo        hi
## 0.4339623 0.5660377
prop.table(table(IMA))     # this
[...]
```

To involve the NAs in the computations, we have multiple options:

```
qwe <- table(IMA, useNA="ifany") # to shorten what follows
qwe/sum(qwe)      # same as
## IMA
##        lo        hi       <NA>
## 0.2987013 0.3896104 0.3116883
prop.table(qwe) # this, same as
[…]
qwe/length(IMA) # this (because length counts NAs)
[...]
```

3.1.1.1 Central tendency: the mode

The measure of central tendency of a categorical (or possibly of an ordinal variable with few levels) is the mode. Remember, a measure of central tendency is the one number that tells someone most about our data. If we're supposed to tell someone as much as possible about IMA but are allowed to state only one number, then our smartest choice is to tell them the frequency of the most frequent level, and that's what's called the **mode:**

```
table(IMA)
## IMA
## lo hi
## 23 30
```

```
max(table(IMA))
## [1] 30
```

Again, though: be ready for 'the unexpected': What does our approach do if two or more levels are equally maximally frequent?

```
some.factor <- factor(rep(letters[1:5], c(3, 5, 7, 7, 5)))
table(some.factor)
## some.factor
## a b c d e
## 3 5 7 7 5
max(table(some.factor))
## [1] 7
```

Sigh ... the function `max` doesn't tell us there are two levels of `some.factor` that occur 7 times. How can we do this better? Like this:

```
table(some.factor)[table(some.factor)==max(table(some.factor))]
## some.factor
## c d
## 7 7
```

That's better.

3.1.1.2 Dispersion: normalized entropy

As mentioned above, any measure of central tendency should always – as in always! – be accompanied by a measure of dispersion because otherwise we're not telling our readers how much information we have provided them with, or how good the information is we provided when we gave them our measure of central tendency. Thus, always – in case I didn't mention that before – provide a measure of dispersion. One measure we can use for categorical variables is a normalized entropy, written as H_{norm}. For a categorical variable with k different levels with observed percentages p_1 to p_k, H_{norm} is computed like this:

$$H_{norm} = -\frac{\sum_{i=1}^{k} p_i \times \log_2 p_i}{\log_2 k}$$

How do we do this in R?

```
percs <- prop.table(table(IMA))
-sum(percs * log2(percs)) / log2(length(levels(IMA)))
## [1] 0.98738
```

Note that if any of the *k* levels is not observed at all, then its value in percs will be 0, which will lead to an error message (because logs of 0 are not defined). We can avoid that by avoiding to log the percentages that are 0 in the first place:

```
percs <- percs[percs>0] # change percs to only non-0 elements
-sum(percs * log2(percs)) / log2(length(levels(IMA))) # same as above
## [1] 0.98738
```

H_{norm} falls into the interval [0, 1]: Values close to 0 mean that the distribution is very uneven such that most observations are concentrated in very few levels or even just one whereas values close to 1 mean that the distribution is very even/uniform. In other words, the higher H_{norm}, the less informative the mode is; see also Zar (2010: 43-44) for discussion of this measure, where it is referred to as *evenness* or *relative diversity*.

3.1.1.3 Visualization

Visualizing such data is fairly straightforward, there are very many ways in which such frequency information can be visualized. However, I will only show a small selection here. If one needs a plot at all (more on that below in Section 3.4), the probably best plot for such data according to criteria to be discussed there is a dot chart, which can be easily generated on the basis of a frequency table using the function dotchart, whose only obligatory argument is a numeric vector or a matrix x (or something that R can coerce into one such as a table; I am suppressing an irrelevant warning message here in the output, but you're of course seeing it anyway because you're reading this at your computer running the code as recommended, right?):

```
dotchart(x=table(IMA))
```

However, this is only the most basic version and a lot of times plots benefit in terms of interpretability, comprehensiveness of information, and self-sufficiency, if they're customized a bit. Below you find an example of dotchart with a few additional arguments that can actually be added to very many plotting functions (and that are commented in detail in the code):

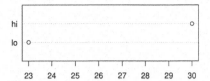

Figure 13: A basic dot chart of IMA

```
dotchart(main="The frequency distribution of IMA",
   xlab="Observed frequency", xlim=c(0, sum(table(IMA))),
   x=table(IMA), ylab="IMA", pch=16); grid()
```

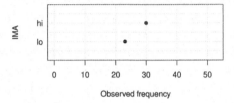

Figure 14: A nicer dot chart of IMA

Adding labels makes the plot more self-explanatory and setting the *x*-axis limits to include 0 (as the smallest possible frequency value) and the sum of all levels' frequencies helps with contextualizing the difference between the two observed values (contextualizing in the sense of 'making it appear less drastic than in the first untweaked plot').

Another frequently-used plot for such frequency data is a bar plot, whose most basic version can again be generated with just one simple function call:

```
barplot(height=table(IMA))
```

But again, we should customize that a bit:

```
qwe <- barplot(main="The frequency distribution of IMA",
   xlab="IMA", ylab="Observed frequency", ylim=c(0, sum(table(IMA))),
   height=table(IMA), col=c("lightgrey", "darkgrey"))
```

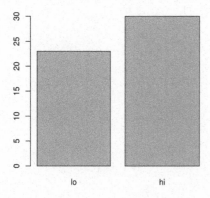

Figure 15: A basic bar plot of IMA

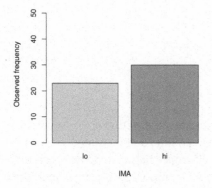

Figure 16: A nicer bar plot of IMA

You might wonder why I assigned the result of barplot to an object I just called qwe; after all, it doesn't seem like that did anything. But it did: Some plotting functions – barplot, boxplot, hist, to name a few basic ones – return some information as a 'by product'; this is why I recommend that, whenever you learn a new function, to read up on what exactly the value is that it returns (in the "Value" section of the function's documentation) and/or that you wrap str(...) around the function execution (to see whether R computes things it may not visibly return). Now, what does qwe contain? Two numbers ...

```
qwe # or str(qwe)
##        [,1]
```

```
## [1,]  0.7
## [2,]  1.9
```

What are those? These are the x-coordinates of the horizontal middles of the bars. That means, while the x-axis doesn't show a numeric axis with tickmarks like the y-axis, the plot still has an underlying two-dimensional coordinate system with x- and y-axis values and the two values in qwe can be used to add something to the plot that you want to be located at the mid-positions (in terms of the x-axis) of the bars. Thus, check out Figure 17:

```
# this is as before:
qwe <- barplot(main="The frequency distribution of IMA",
    xlab="IMA", ylab="Observed frequency", ylim=c(0, sum(table(IMA))),
    height=table(IMA), col=c("lightgrey", "darkgrey"))
# this is new:
text(x=qwe, y=table(IMA)/2, labels=table(IMA))
```

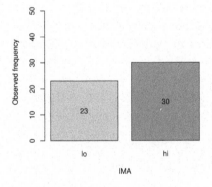

Figure 17: A even nicer bar plot of IMA

3.1.2 Ordinal variables

Ordinal variables, i.e. variables with categorical levels that also convey rank-order information, are sometimes in an awkward position because even though they provide more information than categorical variables, many studies treat them as categorical and the way they are handled best can depend on how many levels there are. In the present case, where our ordinal variable – FAM – has only three levels, most readers wouldn't blink if we treated it as we treated IMA in the last section (I am leaving out NAs here):

```
# distribution
table(FAM)
[...]
(percs <- prop.table(table(FAM)))
[…]
# mode
table(FAM)[table(FAM)==max(table(FAM))]
## med
##  31
# normalized entropy
percs <- percs[percs>0]
-sum(percs * log2(percs)) / log2(length(levels(FAM)))
## [1] 0.8988523
```

However, we can also treat **FAM** 'more properly' as an ordinal variable *if* we made sure, as we did, that its levels are in the right ordinal order (which, recall, is often not the alphabetical order); in that case as well as in cases of ordinal variables with more levels (e.g., Likert or other rating scales), one could describe that variable on the basis of the numbers representing the levels of such factors:

```
table(FAM)
[...]
table(as.numeric(FAM))
##
##  1  2  3
## 12 31 12
```

3.1.2.1 Central tendency: the median
The measure of central tendency for such ordinal variables is the **median**, which is the value we obtain when we sort all values of a distribution according to their size and then pick the middle one (e.g., the median of the numbers from 1 to 5 is 3); if we have an even number of values, the median is the mean of the two middle values (e.g., the median of the numbers from 1 to 4 is 2.5). We can compute the median with a function with the same name, but ...

```
median(x=as.numeric(FAM))
## [1] NA
```

Again, the missing data are rearing their ugly head. If the vector to which median is applied contains any NA, the default is to return NA. Thus, we need to override that default setting by telling median to remove NAs/any missing data it finds:

```
median(x=as.numeric(FAM), na.rm=TRUE)
## [1] 2
```

No surprises here: The mode of the three-level variable FAM is also the median.

3.1.2.2 Dispersion: quantiles etc.

As mentioned above, if our ordinal variable has just very few levels, we might treat it as categorical, which means we can use normalized entropy as our measure of dispersion. A useful measure of dispersion for ordinal data with many levels is the **interquartile range**; let's exemplify that here on the basis of a random vector some.ratings. Note, though, that the values in some.ratings will be random, but **replicably random**, meaning we will always get the same random numbers when we run the whole code chunk below. This is because the first line takes a word ("Kartoffelpuffer"), converts it into a series of integers (utf8ToInt), sums those up (sum, getting 1574), and then uses this number as a seed value for R's random number generator, which makes sure that the next random numbers generated will always be the same; whenever you do anything involving random numbers, you should do something like this to make sure you always can replicate your own results again later:

```
set.seed(sum(utf8ToInt("Kartoffelpuffer")))
some.ratings <- sample(1:7, 30, replace=TRUE)
table(some.ratings)
## some.ratings
## 1 2 3 4 5 6 7
## 1 6 5 4 3 5 6
median(some.ratings)
## [1] 4
```

The interquartile range is the difference of the values that cut off the lower 25% of the data and the upper 25% of the data (i.e., so to speak, the range of values that constitute the middle 50% of the data):

```
sort(some.ratings)
## [1] 1 2 2 2 2 2 2 3 3 3 3 3 4 4 4 4 5 5 5 6 6 6 6 6 7 7 7 7 7 7
```

The median here is the mean of sort(some.ratings)[15] (4) and
sort(some.ratings)[16] (4), the so-called 25% quartile is 3 and the so-called
75% quartile is 6, as you can count yourself above or have R tell you:

```
quantile(x=some.ratings)       # check out 25% & 75%
##   0%  25%  50%  75% 100%
##    1    3    4    6    7
summary(object=some.ratings) # check out 1st Qu. & 3rd Qu.
##    Min. 1st Qu.  Median    Mean 3rd Qu.    Max.
##   1.000   3.000   4.000   4.367   6.000   7.000
```

Thus, the interquartile range is 3, as we can confirm with IQR:

```
IQR(x=some.ratings)
## [1] 3
```

Recommendation(s) for further study: Check out the function mad for another robust measure of
dispersion.

3.1.2.3 Visualization
The visualization of ordinal data can typically done in the same way as for categorical variables, provided the factor levels are in the right ordinal order so that
the plotting functions return proper orderings on the relevant axes. Here's the
dot chart:

```
dotchart(main="The frequency distribution of FAM",
    xlab="Observed frequency", xlim=c(0, 55), x=table(FAM),
    ylab="FAM", pch=16); grid()
text(x=table(FAM), y=1:3, labels=table(FAM), pos=4)
```

And here's the bar plot:

```
qwe <- barplot(main="The frequency distribution of FAM",
    xlab="FAM", ylab="Observed frequency", ylim=c(0, 55),
    height=table(FAM), col=c("lightgrey", "grey", "darkgrey"))
text(x=qwe, y=table(FAM)/2, labels=table(FAM))
```

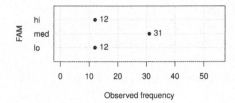

Figure 18: A dot chart of FAM

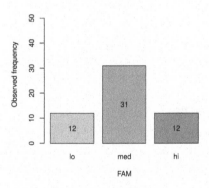

Figure 19: A bar plot of FAM

3.1.3 Numeric variables

You saw above that the treatment of ordinal variables can depend on their characteristics, specifically the number of levels they have. There's a bit of a similar situation with numeric variables, whose treatment also depends on their characteristics, in particular the distribution of the values. Simplifying a bit,

– if a numeric variable is roughly normally distributed (i.e. has a shape similar to that of a Gaussian bell-shaped distribution), we can use the arithmetic mean as a measure of central tendency and the standard deviation as a measure of dispersion;

– if a numeric variable is not normally distributed at all, it is often better to

- either apply the descriptive statistics usually reserved for ordinal variables, i.e. the median and the interquartile range;
- or, if possible, use statistics that were designed to be more robust to numeric variables deviating from normality much (see, e.g., Wilcox 2012, 2017).

Let's look at the two main options in turn for the three numeric variables in the data: RT, FREQ, and MEAN.

3.1.3.1 Central tendency: arithmetic mean

As you know, you compute the arithmetic mean by adding up all values of a numeric vector and dividing that sum by the number of values, but of course there's also a function for this:

```
mean(x=RT)
## [1] 631.86
mean(x=FREQ)
## [1] 9.25974
mean(x=MEAN)
## [1] NA
```

There we go ... missing data again:

```
mean(x=MEAN, na.rm=TRUE)
## [1] 435.9792
```

But how meaningful – no pun intended – are those means? Let's check the dispersion and the visualizations of the distributions (I'm following the order of exposition from the previous sections for the sake of consistency even if doing the plots now would be a good idea).

3.1.3.2 Dispersion: standard deviation etc.

The probably best known measure of dispersion for roughly normally-distributed numeric values is the standard deviation. There are two versions of it, one that is used for when your data are a sample of a larger population and one for when you have the data for the population; we will only discuss the former because in linguistics at large it's more likely that you only have sample data. That **standard deviation** of a vector with n elements x_1 to x_n and the mean m is computed as follows:

$$sd = \sqrt{\frac{\sum_{i=1}^{n}(x_i - m)^2}{n-1}}$$

In words: you subtract from each value the mean, square those differences, sum those squared values up, divide that sum by sample size minus 1 (which is a measure called **variance**), and take the square root of that. In R, we can compute it in, for instance, these two ways – I leave it up to you which one you find simpler:

```
(sum((RT-mean(RT))^2)/(length(RT)-1))^0.5    # way 1: manually
## [1] 60.16321
sd(x=RT); sd(x=FREQ); sd(x=MEAN, na.rm=TRUE) # way 2: using sd
## [1] 60.16321
## [1] 16.99334
## [1] 43.24374
```

However, note that it is difficult to compare standard deviations of distributions with very different means (even if they are normally distributed): All other things being equal, if the mean increases while the general variability of the distribution stays the same, the standard deviation increases as well:

```
sd(RT)
## [1] 60.16321
sd(RT*1000)
## [1] 60163.21
```

To make standard deviations from different distributions more comparable, a measure called the **variation coefficient** can be useful, which, so to speak, normalizes the standard deviation of a distribution by the distribution's mean:

```
sd(RT)/mean(RT)          # now both return ...
## [1] 0.09521604
sd(RT*1000)/mean(RT*1000) # ... the same result
## [1] 0.09521604
```

3.1.3.3 Visualization

Let's now turn to visualization of numeric variables, which will then actually also tell us whether it was a good idea to compute means and standard deviations in the first place. There are three main options I want to discuss here (although, as usual, the possibilities are endless): histograms, box plots, and empirical cumulative distribution plots. Histograms are probably the best known of these and we can plot them easily with the function hist. (Again, I am assigning that to qwe, which I then output, to show what hist returns on top of the plot.)

```
(qwe <- hist(x=RT))
[...]
```

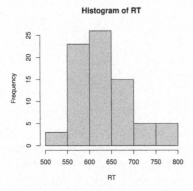

Figure 20: A histogram of RT

We get an already somewhat annotated histogram, which indicates quite a bit of similarity to a Gaussian bell-shaped normal curve. R 'looked at the data and decided' to bin the reaction times into 6 bins and the qwe object tells us where the breaks are between bins ($breaks) and how many reaction times are in each bin ($counts). If you do not use any plots other than histograms, my advice is to always generate at least one other histogram with a different number of bins to make sure that the visual appearance of the plot is not due to a particular binning choice. In the following line, I make R generate a histogram with approximately 12 bins – approximately, because R chooses a number for a pretty plot; see ?hist and ?pretty (no, the latter is not a joke). As you can see, this changes the visual appearance a bit: suddenly it looks like there are three bells next to each other (but bear in mind that the observed frequencies especially for the last six bins are really low, as we can see from the counts that labels=TRUE added on top of the bars).

```
hist(x=RT, breaks=12, labels=TRUE)
```

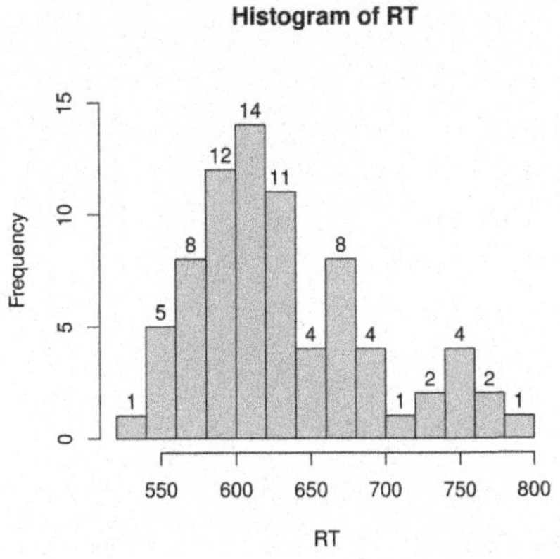

Figure 21: A more fine-grained histogram of RT

What about the histograms of the other two variables? Let's put them next to each other in one plotting window (see Figure 22 on the next page):

```
par(mfrow=c(2, 2)) # make the plotting window have 2 rows & 2 columns
hist(FREQ); hist(FREQ, breaks=12)
hist(MEAN); hist(MEAN, breaks=12)
par(mfrow=c(1, 1)) # reset to default
```

Clearly, reporting a mean and a standard deviation for FREQ is not useful: Either the variable should be transformed in some way (as we will do in Chapter 5) or we should report a median and an interquartile range (but even that will be of limited utility). For MEAN, the histograms are more in support of a mean/*sd* approach but we also see that there seems to be one value that looks a bit like an outlier. How do we we find out which word that is for?

```
CASE[which(MEAN>525)]
## [1] dog
## [...]
```

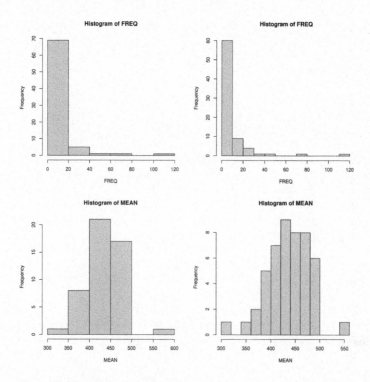

Figure 22: Histograms of FREQ and MEAN

Another frequent plot is the box plot, which can be generated as simply as this:

```
(qwe <- boxplot(x=RT))
[...]
```

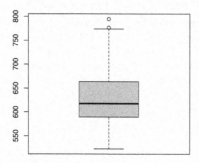

Figure 23: A box plot of RT

This plot contains a lot of valuable information (but see below ...):
- the heavy horizontal line represents the median (see qwe$stats[3,]);
- the regular horizontal lines that make up the upper and lower boundary of the boxes represent the hinges (corresponding to the 25%- and the 75% quartiles, see qwe$stats[2,] and qwe$stats[4,]);
- the whiskers – the dashed vertical lines extending from the box until the lower and the upper limit – represent the smallest and largest values that are not more than 1.5 IQRs away from the box (see qwe$stats[1,] and qwe$stats[5,]);
- the two unfilled circles at the top are two data points outside of the range of the whiskers (see qwe$out).

Let's make our box plots for FREQ and MEAN a bit nicer by adding some labeling and texting the mean into the plot as well:

```
par(mfrow=c(1, 2))
boxplot(x=FREQ, main="A boxplot of FREQ",
    ylab="Observed frequencies")
text(x=1, y=mean(FREQ), labels="x"); grid()
boxplot(x=MEAN, main="A boxplot of MEAN",
    ylab="Meaningfulness scores")
text(x=1, y=mean(MEAN, na.rm=TRUE), labels="x"); grid()
par(mfrow=c(1, 1))
```

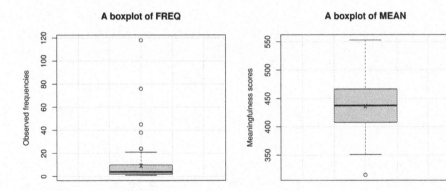

Figure 24: Box plots of FREQ and MEAN

Note in particular how

- the box plots of RT and MEAN represent the close-to-normal distributions: the medians are close to the means and kind of in the middle of the boxes and the (relatively symmetric) whiskers;
- the box plot of FREQ represents the skewness of the distribution: the box is at the very bottom of the distribution, the median is not in the middle of anything, not too close to the mean, and there are plenty of outliers but only on one side of the distribution. No one, ever, should look at this plot and try to summarize it only with a mean ...

One big downside of both histograms and box plots is that they bin – the histogram into the frequency bins and the boxplot bins at least the middle 50% into the box, and binning always loses information: You don't see what is happening within a bin/box and depending on the boundaries of the bin/box, neighboring data can also be distorted. One of the most revealing plots for numeric variables I know is the empirical cumulative distribution (function, abbreviated ecdf) plot. This plot doesn't bin, which means it loses no information, but it is admittedly not the easiest plot to understand – however, once one does understand it, it's very informative. For didactic reasons, let's begin with the ecdf plot for FREQ, which I am annotating here a bit:

```
# first a tabular summary that I will use to explain things
round(cumsum(prop.table(table(FREQ))), 2)
##    1    2    3    4    5    6    7    8    9   10   11
## 0.19 0.42 0.49 0.56 0.61 0.64 0.70 0.71 0.74 0.78 0.79
##   12   14   16   18   19   21   24   38   45   76  118
## 0.83 0.84 0.86 0.87 0.90 0.91 0.95 0.96 0.97 0.99 1.00
# then the ecdf plot:
plot(main="Ecdf plot for FREQ", verticals=TRUE, pch=4,
    xlab="Observed frequency values", x=ecdf(FREQ),
    ylab="Cumulative percentage"); grid()     # then some annotation:
arrows(x0=40, y0=0.2, x1= 2, y1=0.42, angle=20)
arrows(x0=40, y0=0.6, x1=12, y1=0.83, angle=20)
```

The table I provided first lists for every observed frequency value (1, 2, 3, ..., 76, 118) how much (in %) of the data in FREQ are maximally that high. For instance, it says 42% of all values of FREQ are ≤2, and this is where the lower arrow points. And, it says that 83% of all values of FREQ are ≤12, which is where the upper arrow points.

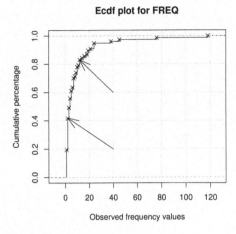

Figure 25: Defining an ecdf plot

That means,
- the more quickly this kind of curve rises (and this one does so pretty fast), the more the values of the plotted variable are (very) small (like here and we saw what kind of histogram/boxplot this corresponds to);
- the more slowly this kind of curve rises, the more of the values plotted are (very) large.

Now that (you think) you understood this, let me ask you this: What does an ecdf plot look like for (i) a normal distribution (i.e. like for RT/MEAN) and (ii) a uniform distribution?

THINK BREAK

Here are some answers (with the simplest versions of these plots):

```
par(mfrow=c(2, 2))
plot(ecdf(RT)); plot(ecdf(MEAN))
plot(ecdf(rnorm(5000))); plot(ecdf(runif(5000)))
par(mfrow=c(1, 1))
```

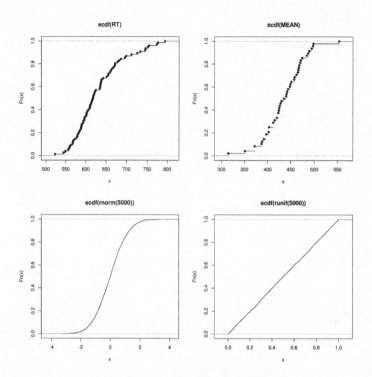

Figure 26: Ecdf curves for a normal and a uniform variable

A perfectly normal distribution results in an *S*-shaped curve, a perfectly uniform distribution results in pretty much a straight line. But again, the nice thing about the ecdf plot is that it doesn't bin. See in Figure 27 what happens if we have two normal distributions next to each other: The box plot doesn't tell you anything – it just gives us one big box of the type that we might also get if you had one normal distribution in your data or a fairly uniform distribution – but the ecdf plot shows us two *S*-shapes in the curve, a clear indication of two bells next to each other (which, here at least, hist would also see):

```
set.seed(sum(utf8ToInt("Räucherforelle"))) # two.normals.side.by.side
<- c(rnorm(200, 0, 2), rnorm(200, 8, 2))
par(mfrow=c(1, 2))
boxplot(two.normals.side.by.side)
plot(ecdf(two.normals.side.by.side), verticals=TRUE, main="")
par(mfrow=c(1, 1))
```

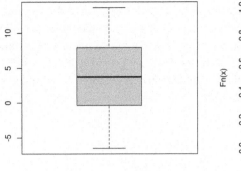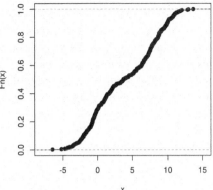

Figure 27: Two normal distributions side by side

Recommendation(s) for further study: Check out vioplot::vioplot. This notation means pack-agename::functionname, which here are identical, and thus stands for 'the function vioplot from the package vioplot. You can
- either load the whole package with library(vioplot) and then use the function like we use all functions, e.g. vioplot(RT);
- or not load the whole package but just access the function from it, e.g. vioplot::vioplot(RT).

3.1.3.4 Two frequent transformations

For reasons that will become particularly apparent later, numeric variables are sometimes transformed. As we will see, some transformations change the shape of a distribution: plot(ecdf(FREQ)) doesn't look the same as plot(ecdf(log(FREQ))), which often is in fact the reason why we transform a variable. Other transformations do not change the shape, but 'just' the values of a variable in ways that are useful. One of these transformations is called center-ing and consists of subtracting from every value of a numeric variable the mean of that variable:

```
MEAN.c <- MEAN-mean(MEAN, na.rm=TRUE) # manual
# shorter way to do this: MEAN.c <- scale(MEAN, scale=FALSE)
round(c(summary(MEAN),   "sd"=sd(MEAN,   na.rm=TRUE)), 2) # raw
##    Min. 1st Qu. Median    Mean 3rd Qu.    Max.    NA's       sd
##  315.00  409.75 437.50  435.98  466.25  553.00   29.00    43.24
round(c(summary(MEAN.c), "sd"=sd(MEAN.c, na.rm=TRUE)), 2) # transf.
##    Min. 1st Qu. Median    Mean 3rd Qu.    Max.    NA's       sd
## -120.98  -26.23   1.52    0.00   30.27  117.02   29.00    43.24
```

The point of this transformation is that the new, centered version of the variable has a mean of 0, which can be advantageous when it comes to regression modeling – other than that, the shape of the distribution and its *sd* haven't changed, as we can verify by comparing plot(ecdf(MEAN)) to plot(ecdf(MEAN.c)).

A related, frequent transformation is called *z*-standardization. This transformation begins with centering like above but then divides each centered value by the standard deviation of the whole variable:

```
MEAN.s <- MEAN.c/sd(MEAN, na.rm=TRUE) # manual
# shorter way to do this: MEAN.s <- scale(MEAN)
round(c(summary(MEAN.s), "sd"=sd(MEAN.s, na.rm=TRUE)), 2) # transf.
##    Min. 1st Qu.  Median    Mean 3rd Qu.    Max.    NA's      sd
##   -2.80   -0.61    0.04    0.00    0.70    2.71   29.00    1.00
```

This new variable also has a mean of 0, but now also an *sd* of exactly 1, which means you can more easily compare different values of variables with different means and *sd*s. For example, the word *asparagus* has an RT value of 696.21 (rounded to two decimals) in our data, while the mean of RT for all words is 631.86. That same word has a MEAN value of 442 while the overall mean of MEAN is 435.98. On which variable does *asparagus* differ more from the mean and how so? You do not want to look just at the numeric difference – 696.21-631.86 vs. 442-435.98 – because that neglects the scales and the distributions of the variables. Instead, we look at the *z*-standardized values (or *z*-scores) of each variable for *asparagus* and use the function scale to *z*-standardize now:

```
which.word.is.asparagus <- which(CASE=="asparagus")
scale(RT)[which.word.is.asparagus]
## [1] 1.069578
scale(MEAN)[which.word.is.asparagus]
## [1] 0.1392302
```

The RT value for *asparagus* is more than one *sd* greater than the mean reaction time of all words, but the MEAN value for *asparagus* is only 0.14 *sd*s greater than the mean meaningfulness of all words. You can see that also visually in Figure 28 below. The code plots the histogram for each variable (I am suppressing the big main headings) and then uses the function abline to draw vertical (v=) lines (and you would use abline(h=...) to draw horizontal lines): Each plot has one heavy line (lwd=3, which means 'make the line width 3 times the default') at the overall mean and one regular line at the value for *asparagus*.

```
par(mfrow=c(1, 2))
hist(RT, main=""); abline(v=mean(RT),lwd=3)
   abline(v=RT[which.word.is.asparagus])
hist(MEAN, main=""); abline(v=mean(MEAN, na.rm=TRUE), lwd=3)
   abline(v=MEAN[which.word.is.asparagus])
par(mfrow=c(1, 1))
```

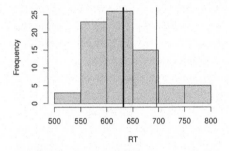 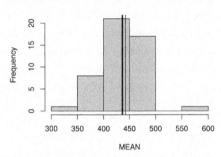

Figure 28: Histograms of RT and MEAN

Again, we will use this mostly in Chapters 5 and 6.

3.1.4 Standard errors and confidence intervals

Apart from the measures of dispersion discussed so far – normalized entropy, interquartile range, and the standard deviation/variance – there's another measure that quantifies, so to speak, the spread of a distribution, its dispersion, but it does so with a different motivation/emphasis. This measure is the **standard error** (often abbreviated as *se*), which can in turn be used to compute something maybe even more important and widespread, a so-called **confidence interval** (often abbreviated as *CI*).

The logic underlying these measures is the following. Consider first an example of the percentage of a certain outcome in multiple draws/trials from/of a binary categorical variable. If you take a (hopefully random) sample of observations from the population of interest, you can compute the percentage of the relevant variable level in your sample. Obviously, you hope that your sample percentage is close to the population percentage; just as obviously, your sample percentage is not likely to be exactly the population percentage – getting exactly 50 times heads in 100 fair coin tosses is not an extremely likely outcome, it's just the most likely outcome (p=0.0795892). That of course means, it would be nice to know how good an estimate of the population percentage your sample percentage is, and standard errors and confidence intervals quantify basically that (the computation of the latter is based on the former). One thing you do already know – if only instinctively: no matter how standard errors and confidence intervals work exactly, your sample percentage is probably going to be a better estimate of the population percentage if your sample is bigger. If you want to compute the percentage of vegetarians out of all people in the U.S. but you sample only two people, then there's a small chance that that sample will contain only vegetarians and that your sample percentage of 100% is pretty far away from the population mean – however, if you sample 500 people, your sample percentage is much more likely to be close to the actual population percentage.

The same is of course true for numeric variables and their means: If you were interested in the average height of people and decided to quantify that with a mean, you would take a (hopefully random) sample of observations from the population of interest and compute the mean of the variable in your sample. Again, you hope that your sample mean is close to the population mean and it would be nice to know how robust your sample mean is, which is again where standard errors and confidence intervals come in. But, as before, the bigger the sample, the more likely it is that your sample mean is close to the population mean – you don't want to end up having sampled only LeBron James and Hafþór Júlíus Björnsson …

Now, how do we compute standard errors? I will only discuss two of the most frequently-used standard errors, one for percentages or proportions, one for means, but there are many others (esp. standard errors for differences, etc.).

3.1.4.1 Standard errors for percentages

For percentages, the standard error of a percentage p is computed as follows:

$$se_{percentage} = \sqrt{\frac{p \times (1-p)}{n}}$$

Thus, if we suspect a coin is not fair and is biased in favor of heads, toss it 10 times and get heads 6 times, what is the standard error of the 60% heads percentage we found?

```
perc.heads <- 0.6; number.tosses <- 10
(se.perc <- sqrt((perc.heads*(1-perc.heads)) / number.tosses))
## [1] 0.1549193
```

What if we had achieved the same 60% percentage of heads in 50 times as many coin tosses? 50 times as many data points reduce the standard error massively:

```
number.tosses <- 500
(se.perc <- sqrt((perc.heads*(1-perc.heads)) / number.tosses))
## [1] 0.0219089
```

3.1.4.2 Standard errors for means

For means of a variable with n (non-missing) values, the standard error is computed as follows:

$$se_{means} = \frac{sd}{\sqrt{n}} = \sqrt{\frac{var}{n}}$$

In our data, the variable RT has the following descriptive characteristics:

```
c("mean"=mean(RT), "sd"=sd(RT), "n"=length(RT))
     mean        sd         n
631.85996  60.16321  77.00000
```

Thus, the standard error of the above mean of RT is this:

```
sd(RT)/sqrt(length(RT)) # sqrt(var(RT)/length(RT))
## [1] 6.856234
```

As an aside: the standard error of a mean is essentially the standard deviation of a large number of means (e.g. 50,000) computed from that many samples drawn with replacement from the variable in question. The following snippet of code draws 50,000 random samples with replacement from the reaction times and collects their means, and the *sd* of those 50,000 means is very close to the standard error we computed above: (As before, don't worry about understanding the for-loop yet, I will discuss those later in Section 3.5.2, just focus on the result you see in the console.)

```
set.seed(sum(utf8ToInt("Beutelteufel")))
sampled.means <- rep(NA, 50000); for (i in 1:50000) {
    sampled.means[i] <- mean(sample(RT, size=77, replace=TRUE))
}; sd(sampled.means) # see how close that is to 6.856234?
```

3.1.4.3 Confidence intervals

Confidence intervals (CI) 'bridge the gap' between descriptive statistics and analytical/hypothesis-testing statistics. Computing a standard 95%-CI for proportions or means is easy – understanding what they, or CIs in general, mean is less so. Let's begin with the CI for proportions, specifically for the example of 300 heads out of 500 tosses. For a 95%-CI, we can use part of the output of the function `binom.test` as follows (which I'm retrieving with the $ notation for lists from above):

```
round(binom.test(x=300, n=500, conf.level=0.95)$conf.int, 3)
## [1] 0.556 0.643
## attr(,"conf.level")
## [1] 0.95
```

The 95%-CI for our 60% heads percentage is [55.6%, 64.3%]. But what does such an interval mean both here in particular, but also more generally (e.g., for CIs of means, differences, slopes, etc.)? This is where it gets tricky and different sources will give you different interpretations. For example, you can find this:
– Sheskin (2011:75, 217): "a 95% confidence interval identifies a range of values a researcher can be 95% confident contains the true value of a population parameter (e.g., a population mean). Stated in probabilistic terms, the researcher can state there is a probability/likelihood of .95 that the confidence interval contains the true value of the population parameter."
– Fields, Miles, & Field (2012:45): "A different approach to assessing the accuracy of the sample [statistic] as an estimate of the [statistic] in the population is to calculate boundaries within which we believe the true value of the mean will fall. Such boundaries are called confidence intervals.", followed, two pages later, by "we calculate [confidence intervals] so that they have certain properties: in particular, they tell us the likelihood that they contain the true value of the thing we're trying to estimate".

This suggests that we could interpret the above as saying 'there's a 95% probability that the true/population heads percentage of this coin is between 55.56% and 64.32%'. But then other references will emphatically argue against this:
– Good & Hardin (2012:156): "A common error is to misinterpret the confidence interval as a statement about the unknown parameter [here, the percentage in the population, STG]. It is not true that the probability that a parameter is included in a 95% confidence interval is 95%. What is true is that if we derive a large number of 95% confidence intervals, we can expect the true value of the parameter to be included in the computed intervals 95% of the time";

– Zar (2010:86): "This means [...] (It doesn't mean that there's a 95% probability that the confidence interval computed from the one sample [...] includes [the statistic in the population])".

I actually recommend reading the Wikipedia article on this topic, in particular the section called "Meaning and interpretation", which is really interesting. That section (accessed 24 Sept 2020) discusses how CIs should and should not be interpreted (see also the recommendation for further study below) and also offers the maybe most, let's say, 'practical' interpretation of a CI for a non-statistician/practitioner: "A confidence interval is not a definitive range of plausible values for the sample parameter, though **it may be understood as an estimate of plausible values for the population parameter.**" (my emphasis). The two approaches towards understanding CIs that resonate most with me involve one based on significance-testing and one based on simulations so let's (briefly) talk about those.

As for the former, Cox & Hinkley (1974:214) say "we can regard confidence limits as specifying those parameter values consistent with the data at some level, as judged by a one-sided significance test", and from significance test and the CIs you've seen mentioned above, you've probably already inferred that a CI is typically defined for 1-p (the significance level, i.e., typically as 1-0.05=0.95). That means, in the above example of 500 tosses where we obtained 300 heads (i.e. 0.6 or 60%), we ask ourselves these two questions:

– what is the smallest number of heads you can get in 500 tosses that is not significantly different from the 300-out-of-500 result? It's 277, i.e. 0.554 or 55.4% (the result of `sum(dbinom(x=0:277, size=number.tosses, prob=perc.-heads))` is <0.025, the result of `sum(dbinom(x=0:278, size=number.tosses, prob=perc.heads))` is >0.025);

– what is the largest number of heads you can get in 500 tosses that is not significantly different from the 300-out-of-500 result? It's 322, i.e. 0.644 or 64.4% (the result of `sum(dbinom(x=322:number.tosses, size=number.tosses, prob=perc.heads))` is <0.025, the result of `sum(x=dbinom(0:321, size=number.tosses, prob=perc.heads))` is >0.025);

Thus, computing the 95%-CI for this example in this way returns [277, 322] or, in %, [0.554, 0.644], and you can see how similar they are to the result of `binom.test`, which was [0.556, 0.643]. Thus, the 95%-CI includes the values that do not differ significantly from the result you found and the interpretation of this approach would be to say "the 95%-CI boundaries are the numbers of heads that wouldn't be significantly different from the 0.6 result you got, i.e. between 277 and 322".

As for the latter, the simulation-based approach, we can approach CIs like this: We have a coin that, in one experiment of 500 tosses, yielded a proportion of heads of 0.6. What if we do that experiment 10,000 times and collect each proportion of heads in the 500 tosses? Some of those 10,000 repetitions/iterations of 500 tosses will lead to a heads proportion of 0.6 again, but – because there will be random variation – some will lead to a higher proportion of heads (e.g. 0.66), and some to a lower proportion of heads (e.g. 0.56). We just look at all 10,000 proportions and, using quantile, determine the boundaries of the middle 95% of those 10,000 proportions. In one such execution of 10,000 games of 500 tosses, the resulting 95%-CI I got was [278, 322] / [0.566, 0.644], i.e. again extremely close to the above values. So the interpretation of this approach would be to say "the 95%-CI boundaries are defined by the values of 278 and 322, which delimit the range of 95% likely results if you toss this coin with its heads probability of 0.6 500 times".

Crucially, and this is how CIs relate to significance testing, none of these extremely similar 95%-CIs (from binom.test, from the significance-testing approach, and from the simulation-based approach) includes 250, the value that would be most likely from the H_0 probability of heads from a fair coin of 0.5: All three results lead us to assume that the coin is in fact not fair, its heads percentage is just not compatible enough with H_0. In other words, in Section 1.5, we computed a *p*-value and would reject H_0 if that *p*-value was below the traditional 0.05% threshold; here, we computed a 95%-CI and would reject H_0 if that 95%-CI did not include the result expected from H_0 (250 heads in 500 tosses).

Now, how do we compute a 95%-CI of the mean of RT? Computing it with a function in R is easy, we can use part of the output of t.test like this:

```
round(t.test(x=RT, conf.level=0.95)$conf.int, 1)
## [1] 618.2 645.5
## attr(,"conf.level")
## [1] 0.95
```

The 95%-CI of the mean of RT is [618.2, 645.5]. Discussing in detail how one can apply the significance-testing approach and the simulation-based approach to the mean of RT here goes a bit further than I want to at this stage of the book so I will reserve this for classes/bootcamps and the exercises for this chapter. But all results for the 95%-CI of RT are again converging nicely: The significance-testing approach returns a 95%-CI of [618.2, 645.5] (i.e., exactly the same as t.test) and the simulation-based approach returns a 95%-CI of [618.6, 645.5] (i.e. very close to the other two results).

```
##      lower    upper
## 618.2127 645.4914
##       2.5%    97.5%
## 618.5992 645.4919
```

Recommendation(s) for further study: For much more comprehensive discussion and 23 misinterpretations of *p*-values and CIs, see Greenland et al. (2016).

3.2 Bivariate descriptive statistics

All descriptive statistics above pertained to only a single variable, but a lot of times – probably most of the time – one is interested in what two (or more) variables are 'doing together', especially what a response/dependent variable does given one or more predictor/independent variables. We will proceed again on the basis of variables' information values. As you'll see, a lot of the time what one does is a mere extension of the univariate case of the previous section.

3.2.1 Categorical/ordinal as a function of categorical/ordinal variables

If we have two categorical variables whose 'joint behavior' we want to explore, we can use the same function we have used above for just a single variable, namely `table`, to do cross-tabulation. (I used `table` like that once in Section 2.4.1 but didn't comment on it much.) For example, to see whether there's any relation between IMA and FAM, we give `table` not one vector/factor as an argument, but two. R then creates a two-dimensional table, which has the first-named variable's levels in its rows and the second-named variable's levels in the columns (don't forget about `table`'s default removal of the NAs):

```
(ima.fam <- table(IMA, FAM))
##      FAM
## IMA  lo med hi
##   lo  7  15  1
##   hi  3  16 11
```

It looks like these variables are related: it seems as if higher values of one variable make higher values of the other more likely. Note that we're not getting row and columns totals here, but adding those is easy:

```
addmargins(A=ima.fam)
## [...]
```

As above, we may want percentages, not frequencies, but, with two-dimensional tables, there are different ways to compute percentages and we can specify one with the argument `margin`. The default is `margin=NULL`, which computes the percentages on the basis of all elements in the table. In other words, all percentages in the table add up to 1:

```
prop.table(ima.fam)
##      FAM
## IMA          lo         med          hi
##    lo 0.13207547 0.28301887 0.01886792
##    hi 0.05660377 0.30188679 0.20754717
```

Another possibility is to compute row percentages, for which we set `margin=1` and we get percentages that add up to 1 in every row – a little mnemonic helper: 1 stands for 'by row' just like `table` puts the first-named variable into the rows.

```
prop.table(ima.fam, margin=1)
##      FAM
## IMA          lo         med          hi
##    lo 0.30434783 0.65217391 0.04347826
##    hi 0.10000000 0.53333333 0.36666667
```

Finally, we can choose column percentages by setting `margin=2`: now the percentages in each column add up to 1 – and we have the same mnemonic helper as above (because `table` puts the second-named variables into the columns).

```
prop.table(ima.fam, margin=2)
##      FAM
## IMA          lo         med          hi
##    lo 0.70000000 0.48387097 0.08333333
##    hi 0.30000000 0.51612903 0.91666667
```

A small recommendation if you have a clear separation of the two variables into a predictor and a response: make the percentages add up to 1 for the levels of the response per level of predictor. That is, the table just shown would be best if IMA was your response – for the sake of the argument, let's pretend that just for now

– because this table shows you for each level of the predictor FAM how the levels of IMA are distributed:

– when FAM is *lo*, 70% of the cases have IMA as *lo*;

– when FAM is *med*, 48.4% of the cases have IMA: *lo*;

– when FAM is *hi*, 8.3% of the cases have IMA: *lo*.

How can we visualize this kind of table? In this section, I will briefly mention two plots. The first plot is a mosaic plot for which we can use the function mosaicplot, which I already use here with some optional arguments (main and col). Note: the left plot shows the result of applying moscaicplot to the transposed version of ima.fam (i.e. a version where rows and columns were switched around, which I did so that the orientation of the plot is the same as that of the table ima.fam); the right plot uses the original, non-transposed version.

```
par(mfrow=c(1, 2))
mosaicplot(main="", x=t(ima.fam), col=c("grey35", "grey75"))
mosaicplot(main="", x=ima.fam, col=c("grey20", "grey50", "grey80"))
par(mfrow=c(1, 1))
```

In either plot, the widths of the bars represent the proportional distribution of the variable shown on the *x*-axis and, within each of the (stacked) bars, the heights indicate the proportional distribution of the levels of the variable on the *y*-axis. However, in spite of these commonalities, each plot highlights different things differently well: The left plot makes it super obvious that, as FAM increases, so does IMA:

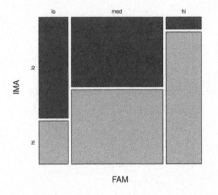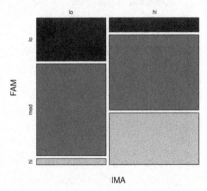

Figure 29: IMA as a function of FAM

- when FAM is *lo* (on the left), then the darker bar for IMA: *lo* is much higher than the lighter bar for IMA: *hi*;
- when FAM is *med* (in the middle), then the darker bar for IMA: *lo* is about as high as the lighter bar for IMA: hi;
- when FAM is *hi* (on the right), then the darker bar for IMA: *lo* is much smaller than the lighter bar for IMA: *hi*;

But try seeing this obvious pattern in the right plot – it's possible of course, but much harder, it doesn't show that in the same obvious way. This is a valuable lesson: Sometimes, the same data (ima.fam) can be plotted in the same kind of plot (moscaicplot), but a simple change in perspective – here, transposing – makes a huge difference in interpretability, and what are plots for if not that?

The second plotting option again uses barplot and in its most basic form we again just use barplot with just the table as its argument.

```
barplot(ima.fam)
```

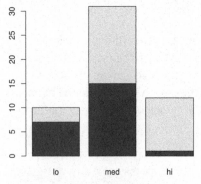

Figure 30: A stacked bar plot of ima.fam

Clearly, we should be able to do better than that: This kind of stacked bar plot is more useful for percentages, but if we want to plot the actual frequencies, then something like this might be nicer:

```
barplot(main="IMA per level of FAM", xlab="FAM", ylab="Frequency",
    ylim=c(0, 20), height=ima.fam, beside=TRUE,
    col=c("lightgrey", "darkgrey"))
legend(x="topright", title="IMA", legend=levels(IMA), ncol=2,
    fill=c("lightgrey", "darkgrey"), bty="n")
```

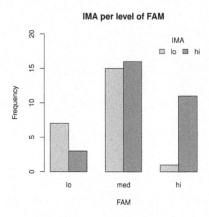

Figure 31: IMA as a function of FAM

But the most useful representation might be one where we use percentages as the input – how frequent is each level of IMA within each level of FAM? – and use a stacked bar plot where bar heights (summed percentages) always add up to 1 (i.e. 100%), which of course is extremely close to a mosaic plot, see Figure 32.

```
(ima.fam.perc <- prop.table(ima.fam, margin=2))
##      FAM
## IMA         lo        med         hi
##   lo 0.70000000 0.48387097 0.08333333
##   hi 0.30000000 0.51612903 0.91666667
barplot(axes=FALSE, main="IMA per level of FAM",
    xlab="Familiarity", ylab="Percentage", ylim=c(0, 1.3),
    height=ima.fam.perc, col=c("lightgrey", "darkgrey"))
axis(side=2, at=seq(0, 1, 0.25))
legend(x="top", title="Imageability", legend=levels(IMA),
    fill=c("lightgrey", "darkgrey"), ncol=2, bty="n")
```

This section discussed categorical/ordinal responses and predictors, but I have so far only talked about categorical variables and ordinal variables with very few levels (which, as mentioned before in Section 3.1.2) often get analyzed with the tools designed for categorical variables; Section 3.2.4 below will return to what to do if we have two ordinal variables each of which has many levels.

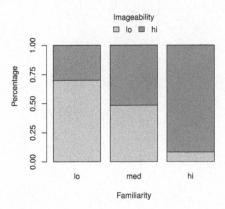

Figure 32: IMA as a function of FAM

3.2.2 Categorical/ordinal variables as a function of numeric variables

Now, what do we do if the dependent variable is categorical/ordinal, but the independent one is numeric? A linguistic example is whether the length of a direct object can help predict the choice of a verb-particle construction or whether the length difference between a recipient and a patient can help predict a binary constructional choice between the ditransitive or the prepositional dative. A non-linguistic example for this kind of question is whether annual income before taxes (a numeric predictor) helps predict voting for, say in the U.S., the Democratic or the Republican presidential candidate (the binary response variable). For expository simplicity and so we don't have to introduce new data, let's pretend here IMA is the response and MEAN is the predictor. Two very similar plots are available for this – one (cdplot) is essentially a smoothed version of the other (spineplot):

```
par(mfrow=c(1, 2))
qwe <- spineplot(IMA ~ MEAN) # this is the formula notation:
cdplot(IMA ~ MEAN)           # response ~ predictor(s)
par(mfrow=c(1, 1))
```

First, note the syntax of how the plots are generated, which involves something very important for the remainder of the book, namely a so-called **formula**. What we give to spineplot is not the usual kind of arguments (e.g., x=..., y=..., etc.), but a formula of the form 'response variable as a function of predictor(s)'.

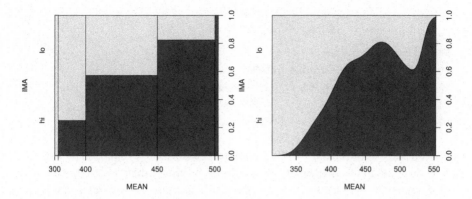

Figure 33: IMA as a function of MEAN

IMA is the response variable (which typically gets plotted on the *y*-axis; note, for spineplot, it needs to be a factor), the tilde ~ means 'as a function of' (and I will now usually use that to abbreviate things, esp. in code and (captions of) plots), and MEAN is the (only) predictor (which typically gets plotted on the *x*-axis).

What does this plot show exactly, however? To understand that, it is useful to quickly look at the additional results that spineplot creates.

```
qwe
##          IMA
## MEAN        lo hi
##    [300,350]  1  0
##    (350,400]  6  2
##    (400,450]  9 12
##    (450,500]  3 14
##    (500,550]  0  0
##    (550,600]  0  1
```

The function spineplot essentially changes the numeric predictor into a categorical predictor (by binning the numeric predictor like hist would, which we can check with hist(MEAN)$breaks) and then pretty much does what we did manually in the previous section, namely using a stacked bar plot to represent the percentages of the levels of the response variable. We can easily verify this by comparing the spine plot to a percentage version of qwe:

```
prop.table(qwe, 1)
##              IMA
```

```
## MEAN                  lo         hi
##   [300,350] 1.0000000 0.0000000
##   (350,400] 0.7500000 0.2500000
##   (400,450] 0.4285714 0.5714286
##   (450,500] 0.1764706 0.8235294
##   (500,550]
##   (550,600] 0.0000000 1.0000000
```

We can see a clear effect: as MEAN increases, so does the proportion of IMA: *hi*. Note also that in the spineplot, the widths of the bins correspond to the number of data points in each bin (i.e. to what, in a histogram, would be the bars' heights); because of that additional information, I usually prefer spine plots to the conditional density plots returned by cdplot.

3.2.3 Numeric variables as a function of categorical/ordinal variables

What if the situation is reversed, if the dependent variable is numeric and the predictor is categorical/ordinal? This is actually the case here: the real response variable in this data set is RT and variables such as IMA or FAM are the predictors. In this case, we can simply extend the box plot we used above for a single numeric variable by plotting a separate box plot of the response variable for each level of the predictor. We can use the formula notation again for this and I'm adding another argument to boxplot, which I will explain in a moment:

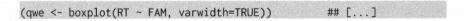

```
(qwe <- boxplot(RT ~ FAM, varwidth=TRUE))          ## [...]
```

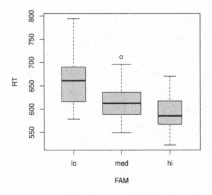

Figure 34: RT ~ FAM

We can see a clear trend that RT decreases as FAM increases (check out the development of the medians in qwe$stats[3,]) and you can probably already infer what varwidth=TRUE does: it makes the widths of the boxes proportional to the numbers of data points in each FAM category.

3.2.4 Numeric variables as a function of numeric variables

The final scenario to be discussed here is that of both the response and the predictor being numeric variables, e.g. when we consider the question of whether RT is related to MEAN. Such scenarios are usually referred to as **correlations** and measured with correlation coefficients. These correlation coefficients typically fall within the interval [-1, 1] and the following bullet list explains what the values mean (I am leaving aside the role that results of significance tests might play for one's choice of how to describe a correlation):

– the sign of a correlation coefficient reflects the **direction of the correlation:**
  – if the correlation coefficient is >0, we call this a *positive correlation*, which can be summarized with a sentence of the form "The more/higher ..., the more/higher ..." and/or "The less/lower ..., the less/lower ...";
  – if the correlation coefficient is (close to) 0, we say there is *no correlation*;
  – if the correlation coefficient is <0, we call this a *negative correlation*, which can be summarized with a sentence of the form "The more/higher ..., the less/lower ..." and/or "The less/lower ..., the more/higher ...";
– the absolute value of such a correlation coefficient reflects the **strength of the correlation**: the higher the absolute value of the correlation coefficient, or the more the correlation coefficient deviates from 0, the stronger the correlation between the two variables.

Computing a correlation coefficient couldn't be easier in R: We can use the function cor, which, if given no other arguments, computes the so-called Pearson product-moment correlation coefficient r:

```
cor(x=MEAN, y=RT, use="pairwise.complete.obs")
## [1] -0.3170991
```

That is, there's a negative correlation between the two variables – the higher MEAN becomes, the lower RT becomes – but it doesn't seem to be a strong one. To visualize it, we can use the very generic plot function, which, for this, minimally needs either the two variables x (typically for the predictor) and y (typically for the response) to be plotted or a formula:

```
plot(x=MEAN, y=RT) # same plot ...
plot(RT ~ MEAN)    # ... as this
```

But lets make it a bit nicer right away:

```
plot(main="RT ~ MEAN", xlab="Meaningfulness scores", xlim=c(300,
    600), x=MEAN, ylab="Reaction time (in ms)", ylim=c(500, 750),
    y=RT, pch=16); grid()
```

Note that correlations are bidirectional: the value of -0.3171 above means both 'the higher MEAN, the lower RT' and 'the higher RT, the lower MEAN'. The visual representation, however, was chosen such that what is conceptually the response (RT) is on the *y*-axis.

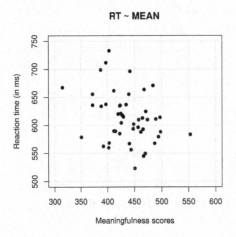

Figure 35: RT ~ MEAN

Now, if we look long and hard, we can discern a weak downward trend: It seems that if you go more to the right, the points are lower in the plot, but again, not a very strong trend at all. But we can actually do much more than this: We can try to 'predict' values of the response on the basis of the predictor using a method called **linear regression** by determining what the overall trend in the point cloud is. In its simplest form, it involves trying to draw a straight line through the point cloud in such a way that it represents/summarizes the point cloud best. But how does one define such a line (after all, there's an infinite number of lines one can draw through that point cloud) and how does one determine which of those fits "best"?

As for the former, any straight line through such a point cloud, here a so-called **regression line**, can be defined by an intercept and a slope, two absolutely essential concepts for later. The **intercept** is the y-axis value (i.e. the value of the response variable) that the line is at when the x-axis variable (i.e., the predictor variable) is 0; the intercept, therefore, kind of has to do with the latitude of the regression line, so to speak. The **slope**, on the other hand, is how much in y-axis units the line 'goes up' (if the slope is positive) or down (if the slope is negative) when you 'go one unit to the right' (i.e., the x-axis value increases by 1). Because of the importance of these notions, let me exemplify a few regression lines. First, their intercepts ...

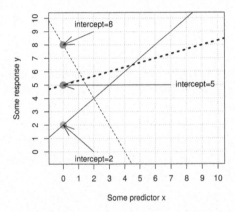

Some regression lines w/ intercepts

Figure 36: Regression lines and their intercepts

Then their slopes: For each slope, there's a first horizontal arrow starting from the regression line and going one x-axis unit to the right and a second vertical arrow that then, from that new x-axis position, 'catches up with' the line again (going up or down, as needed); next to that I state how much up or down one has to 'catch up', and that is the slope.

Any straight line in any such two-dimensional plot can be defined by a combination of an intercept and a slope (and plotted using the function abline, whose first argument a can be an intercept and whose second argument b can be a slope); even a completely horizontal line can be defined that way: its slope/b would be 0.

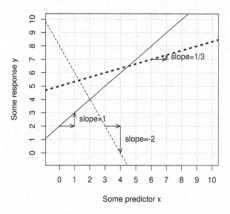

Figure 37: Regression lines and their slopes

But back to the above plot of MEAN and RT. The question now is, what is the 'best' line for that point cloud? In linear regression, best is operationalized as 'minimizing the sum of the squared residuals'. What does that mean? For instance, in Figure 38 below, the regression line through the three data points (the filled circles) has an intercept of 2 (again represented by the grey point) and a slope of 0.75 and the line embodies our y-axis value predictions for every x-axis value. In other words, the line summarizes our 'data' such that 'it says':
– when x is 2, we expect y to be 2 (the intercept) + 2 $(x) \times 0.75$ (the slope) = 3.5;
– when x is 4, we expect y to be 2 (the intercept) + 4 $(x) \times 0.75$ (the slope) = 5;
– when x is 6, we expect y to be 2 (the intercept) + 6 $(x) \times 0.75$ (the slope) = 6.5.

These predictions on the regression line are represented by the squares. Then, for every observed data point in our data, we compute the vertical distance from it to where the regression line is at the same x-axis value. These values, the lengths of these vertical lines in Figure 39, are called **residuals**: They are the differences between the observed y-values of our data (the filled circles) and the y-values predicted by (and, thus, on) our regression line (the squares). Then we just square these three residuals and add them up:

```
sum(c(-1.5, 3, -1.5)^2)
## [1] 13.5
```

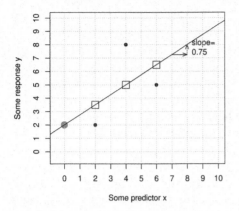

Figure 38: A regression line through 3 points

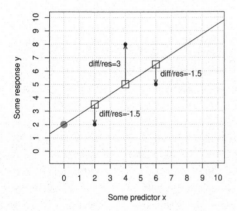

Figure 39: A regression line and its 3 residuals

"Best (regression) line" means there's no straight line that we can draw through these three points that would make this value smaller. As soon as we try to make the regression line fit better by
– moving it up/down a bit (i.e., changing its intercept from 2 to something else);
– tilting it up/down a bit (i.e., changing its slope from 0.75 to something else);
– doing both;

the corresponding sum of the squared residuals will become bigger. For instance, if you think 'why don't I increase the intercept by 0.5 to better catch the value at $x=4/y=9$'?, the residuals will change and this value will become worse:

```
sum(c(-2, 2.5, -2)^2)
## [1] 14.25
```

The same – some such increase – will happen if you try to tweak just the slope (e.g., to 1, when the above sum of squared residuals would become 17). Thus, according to this criterion at least, there's no better regression line. But now how do we get the intercept and the slope. I will not discuss the underlying math here but will just show how to do this in R. As a first step, let's quickly create a version of our original data that doesn't have any missing data (so we avoid having to deal with them now; I'll address this later). We detach the data frame x, determine where the missing data points are in the column MEAN (using the function is.na, which returns TRUE for NAs and FALSE for 'regular data points', check is.na(c(1, NA, 3))), subset the rows of x to avoid those (hence the minus), and store the result in a new data frame xx, which we attach:

```
detach(x)
where.is.meaningfulness.missing <- which(is.na(x$MEAN))
summary(xx <- x[-where.is.meaningfulness.missing,])
attach(xx)
## [...]
```

Computing the regression line is then fairly simple (treacherously simple, in fact, given everything we'll later see is involved): We define what is called a linear model, a certain kind of statistical model. What is a statistical model? A **statistical model** is a formal, mathematical characterization of the relationship between one or more predictors and one or more responses; often it is a schematic/idealized expression of the assumptions or hypotheses we have with regard to how data that we measured were generated (see Crawley 2013:389). A **linear model** is a statistical model of a certain kind that is typically expressed in the form of a (regression) equation whose purpose is to quantify the relationship between (a) predictor(s) and (a) response(s) and to generate predictions of the response(s). Let's do this here now and create a model called m using the function lm with a formula and immediately look at the object:

```
(m <- lm(RT ~ MEAN, data=xx)
## (Intercept)          MEAN
## 757.8901214   -0.3308923
```

That means the regression line for these data has a predicted *y*-axis value (i.e., a predicted reaction time) of 757.89, when MEAN is 0 and goes down (because the slope is negative) by -0.33 ms for every 1-unit increase of MEAN. Let's add the regression line to our previous plot:

```
plot(main="RT ~ MEAN", pch=16,
   xlab="Meaningfulness scores", xlim=c(300, 600), x=MEAN,
   ylab="Reaction time (in ms)", ylim=c(500, 750), y=RT); grid()
abline(a=757.89, b=-0.3309) # you could also just say abline(m)
```

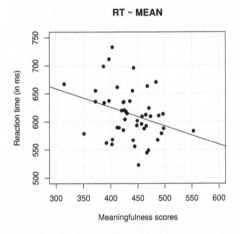

Figure 40: RT ~ MEAN (w/ regression line)

It's now also clear why the correlation isn't that high: Many of the predictions are quite bad, many observed points are quite far away from their predicted values. We can actually compute
- the predicted reaction time for each word (given its MEAN value) with the function predict, which only requires the model m as an argument (for this simple application at least, and you can also use the function fitted for that);
- the residual for each word with the function residuals, which also only requires the model m as an argument:

Let's add those values to the original data frame:

```
detach(xx)
xx$RTPREDICTIONS  <- predict(m) # or fitted(m)
xx$RTRESIDUALS  <- residuals(m) # or xx$RT - xx$RTPREDICTIONS
attach(xx); head(xx, 3)
##           CASE       RT FREQ FAM IMA MEAN RTPREDICTIONS RTRESIDUALS
## 2         ant 589.4347    7 med  hi  415      620.5698   -31.13514
## 3       apple 523.0493   10  hi  hi  451      608.6577   -85.60842
## 5 asparagus 696.2092      2 med  lo  442      611.6357    84.57345
```

In fact, we can even compute a reaction time prediction for a MEAN score that we don't see in our data like 355. We can do that in two ways: manually or using R's predict function again; the difference between the two results below is just due to rounding:

```
# manually:
757.89 + 355 * -0.3309
## [1] 640.4205
# using the function predict w/ the argument newdata
predict(m, newdata=list(MEAN=355))
##           1
## 640.4234
```

Let's see how this works: The vertical arrow in Figure 41 is at x=355 and you go up until you hit the regression line (where the square is), and then you turn left and read off the y-axis value when you hit the y-axis; you can see that it is indeed around 640 somewhere:

So that's what models are/do: They are a mathematical characterization of how parts of a system are related that is a generalization over, or an abstraction from, the individual data points that the model is derived from.

Can we visualize this better? I hope you haven't forgotten the function text, which I use for Figure 42.

```
plot(main="RT ~ MEAN", type="n",
    xlab="Meaningfulness scores", xlim=c(300, 600), x=0,
    ylab="Reaction time (in ms)", ylim=c(500, 750), y=0)
grid(); abline(m)
text(x=MEAN, y=RT, labels=CASE, cex=0.8, font=3)
```

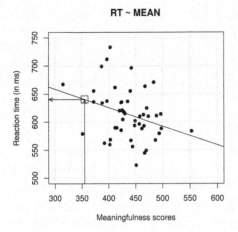

Figure 41: RT ~ MEAN (w/ prediction)

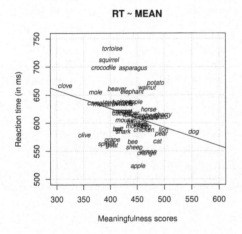

Figure 42: RT ~ MEAN (w/ words)

Note a few more important points: First, regression equations and lines are most useful for the range of values covered by the observed values. Here, the regression equation was computed on the basis of MEAN scores between 300 and about 550, which means that the regression line will probably be much less reliable for MEAN scores outside that range. Relatedly, note also that, if much much higher MEAN scores were theoretically possible (e.g. a value of 2291, check predict(m, newdata=list(MEAN=2289:2292))), our current model would actually predict a negative reaction time, which of course makes no sense; such considerations will become important later on.

Second, note that if you square the correlation coefficient – above, it was 0.3171 – you get an interesting statistic called the coefficient of determination:

```
(-0.3171)^2
## [1] 0.1005524
```

Given the range of the correlation coefficient r – which is [-1, 1] – the **coefficient of determination** (often also written as R^2 and no, the capital R is not a typo) – falls into the interval [0, 1], and it indicates how much of the variability of the response variable is explained by the predictor variable(s). What does that mean? Well, RT is variable: its values are not all the same, it has a standard deviation/variance greater than 0, and the coefficient of determination states how much of that variability is explained by the predictor. Note, however, that *explained* here has a technical meaning: it doesn't mean 'explain with regard to some theory or more fundamental mechanism' – that's what humans can hopefully do later based on the statistical results – it means something like 'account for'; just bear that statistical sense of *explain* in mind for the future. Obviously, in this case R^2 is relatively low (although what counts as low and what as high varies a lot within and between disciplines; blanket recommendations regarding such assessments are mostly somewhat arbitrary).

The Pearson product-moment correlation r is probably the most frequently used correlation. However, there are a few occasions on which it should not be used. First, if the relevant variables aren't numeric but ordinal (and have a decent number of different values), then one should use another correlation coefficient. One option is Spearman's ρ (read 'rho'), another is Kendall's τ (read 'tau'), Of the two, the former is intuitively easier to understand because it is essentially Pearson's r computed on ranks (at least when there are no ties, i.e. no values occurring multiple times):

```
cor(rank(RT), rank(MEAN))
## [1] -0.3096925
cor(RT, MEAN, method="spearman")
## [1] -0.3096925
```

Second, using Spearman's ρ or Kendall's τ is also advisable even if both variables are numeric but if the variables to be correlated differ quite a bit from a normal distribution and/or involve outliers.

Figure 43 shows you two variables x and y, which obviously contain one marked outlier at (5, 5). However, that one outlier makes a huge difference: It has a lot of influence on the product-moment correlation r and regression, but not so much on Spearman's ρ/Kendall's τ.

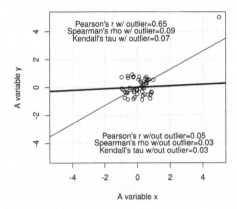

Figure 43: The effect of outliers on $r/\rho/\tau$

The Pearson product-moment correlation r with the outlier is quite high, but without it, it's pretty much non-existent; correspondingly, the outlier alone can change a data set of 50 completely uncorrelated value pairs and make its nearly horizontal regression line suddenly appear steep and noteworthy (something we'll revisit in Section 5.6.3 in more detail). However, the rank correlation Spearman's ρ doesn't 'fall into the same trap': yes, its value is higher with the outlier included, but not nearly as much as is the case with r; ρ/τ is the fallback for r much like the median sometimes is for the mean.

This example should also highlight the absolute indispensability of looking at your data and yes, I mean 'with your eyes'. Anyone who would have looked at the above scatterplot would hopefully immediately discarded their desire to simply compute Pearson's r on the data with the outlier. In fact, there's a very famous data set that shows how treacherous purely numerical analyses can be. The data sets in the four panels of Figure 44 all have
– identical means and variances of the x-variable;
– identical means and variances of the y-variable;
– identical correlations and regression lines;

although we can probably agree that only the top left one should be analyzed with a straight regression line / Pearson's r:

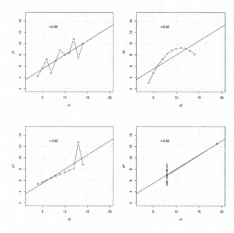

Figure 44: The Anscombe data

(And if you want to see much cooler example of this, the Datasaurus, look at this publication: https://www.autodeskresearch.com/publications/samestats.)

Finally, note that the linear modeling we did above (lm(RT ~ MEAN)) and, therefore, Pearson's product-moment correlation *r* assumes that the relation between the predictor and the response is one that is best captured with a straight line. Often that assumption might be ok, or ok enough, but one should still not simply take it for granted. I would recommend that one always also considers, if only briefly, the possibility that the regression line is curved. The last line of the following code chunk show you one simple way to do this by adding a so-called **smoother** to the data, in essence a regression line that is allowed to be curved:
– the function lines adds a line to the plot (remember, lwd determines the line width);
– the function lowess takes a formula argument just like lm.

In this case, it seems that the straight-line assumption/restriction is justifiable: the curved line is essentially hugging the straight one pretty well.

```
plot(main="RT ~ MEAN", pch=16, col="darkgrey",
    xlab="Meaningfulness scores", xlim=c(300, 600), x=MEAN,
    ylab="Reaction time (in ms)", ylim=c(500, 750), y=RT)
grid(); abline(m)
lines(lowess(xx$RT ~ xx$MEAN), lwd=2)
```

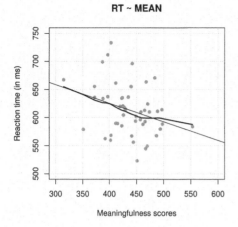

Figure 45: RT ~ MEAN (w/ smoother)

Some housekeeping, keeping the workspace clean:

```
detach(xx)
```

3.3 Polemic excursus 1: on 'correlation'

Before we move on with some comments on very basic R programming, I would like to clarify a few things. First, I want to make two comments with regard to the notion of correlation. From what I have heard people say or seen people write, it seems that some of them have an unhelpfully narrow understanding of what correlation actually means. It seems that, for quite a few people, correlation basically 'means' Pearson's *r* and straight-line linear regression of the type discussed above between RT and MEAN or the one shown here in Figure 46 for two arbitrary variables *x* and *y*.

In fact, I once heard someone say about data that looked like Figure 47 that the two variables were 'not correlated' ... I hope we can agree that not only do the data seem very clearly 'patterned': it is clearly possible to imagine a regression line through those points, just one that is curved. In fact, if one computes such a curved regression line of predicted values and its correlation with the observed values and adds it to the plot, as I obviously already did, then that *r*-value doesn't really look like there's "no correlation", because it's higher than most correlation coefficients reported for actual data: *r*=0.8462.)

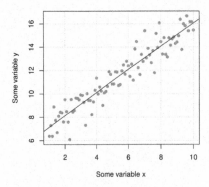

Figure 46: An arbitrary linear correlation

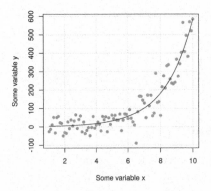

Figure 47: Points involved in a curvilinear correlation

Thus, correlation should not just be considered the type of correlation exemplified by the straight-line linear regression in Figure 46 – the most useful definition of correlation is that two variables are correlated if knowing the value of one variable helps you predict/narrow down the value range to expect for other variable. If you look at Figure 46 and I tell you "Oops, I found another data point behind the bathtub and its x-value is 9 – what do you think its y-value is gonna be?", I am hopeful you would guess a y-value of around 15 rather than around 7, because around 15 is where y-values are when x is around 9 in those data; put differently, given Figure 46, you have zero reason to believe 'if $x=9$, then $y=7$' and a lot of reason to believe 'if $x=9$, then $y=15$'. Obviously, the same is true of Figure 47 with its curved regression line: If there I tell you, "Oops, I found another data point in the hamper and its x-value is 9 – what do you think its y-value is gonna be?", please tell me you wouldn't guess -100, 0, or 5000, but something around 326. Why? For the same reason as above: The plot shows clearly what kind of *y*-values to expect when *x* is 9.

In fact, given the above definition, even the following, a relation between categorical variables as expressed in frequency tables, is a kind of correlation:

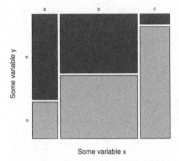

Figure 48: A correlation between two variables *x* and *y*

If I told you, "Oops, I found another data point in my trunk and its x-value is *c* – what do you think its y-value is gonna be?", you are hereby ordered to guess *o*, for reasons that should by now be more than obvious. A very fitting measure of correlation for categorical-variable situations like these, λ (read 'lambda', which falls into the interval [0, 1] and measures the **proportional reduction of error** in guessing the response once you know the predictor), returns a value of 0.174 here. That means knowing the level of x reduces your error in guessing the level of y by 17.4% – not huge, but I hope you agree that, given this plot, guessing anything but *o* when x is *c* makes no sense whatsoever.

Thus, don't fall into the trap of assuming an overly narrow view of what *correlation* actually means: The notion of correlation applies to all kinds of variables / variable combinations – why else would there be regression models for all all kinds of variables / variable combinations?

Before we go on to visualization, a second comment on 'correlation'. I can't remember how often I gave or heard a talk in which a correlation coefficient (or a coefficient of determination) was reported, e.g. an *r*-value of 0.3, 0.6, or perhaps even something as high as for the left panel of Figure 49 below, for which *r*≈0.95.

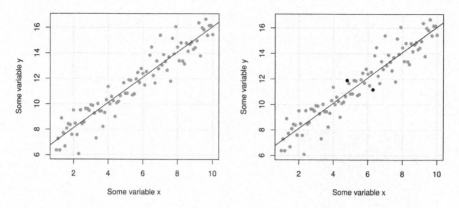

Figure 49: An arbitrary correlation, and then two new points

Or, you tell someone you read an online Econofact article by R. Akee from UCLA saying that, in the U.S., there's a strong correlation between family income and voter participation. What seems to be one of the most frequent kinds of reaction to such correlational statements? It's the pointing to 'an exception':
- "I don't think so: I just heard two sentences the subjects of which scored 4.8 and 6.3 on x, but 11.9 and 11.17 respectively on y, meaning their regression line would go down so I don't think there's a positive correlation like you report." (Those two data points have been added in the right panel of Figure 49.)
- "Nah, I don't think so, Uncle Irvin makes sooo much money and can never be bothered to vote."

What do those sentences show about the reported correlations? Not much in fact ... All they show is that the correlation isn't perfect, that r or ρ/τ or λ are not 1. But, duh!, we already knew that because the speaker probably didn't say the correlation was perfect in the first place and, more importantly, the graph shows that anyway. In spite of the high positive overall correlation, the left of the two scatterplots in Figure 49 has already literally hundreds of data-point pairs in it in which a data point more on the left can have a higher y-value than one a bit more on the right (so that a 'regression line' connecting them would go down just like the first of the two comments above). In fact in the left panel, there are exactly 376 pairs of points (like the two black ones) that would be connectable with lines going down! [cue sarcasm] Gee, I wonder whether that's why the correlation coefficient isn't 1 in the first place ... I already had 376 'counterexamples' to my trend, the fact that you added one more pair of values isn't really taking my breath away ...[end of sarcasm]. The point is the left plot still shows a strong positive correlation because there are ≈9.4 as many pairs of points (3540, to be precise) whose connecting lines would go up, which is why the correlation is as strong as it is (and in fact this comparison of how many lines between pairs of points would go up and how many would go down is what is used to compute the correlation coefficient Kendall's τ).

That means, such sentences don't really show much: think about whether the counterexamples you may come up with reflect something more fundamental about the data and whether your 377th counterexample is really going to make a crucial point – if not, don't be the correlation-'misunderstanding' exception presenter!

3.4 Polemic excursus 2: on visualization

The second slightly polemic (but actually slightly less subjective) excursus is on visualization. First, what is visualization good for? The way I see it is, we use visualization when the content of what we're visualizing would be (too) hard to comprehend if we put it there in prose. That means that several of the plots I showed above I would actually not want to see in a paper and I discussed and showed them here only because I was explaining how to generate plots with R in a didactic textbook setting. But out there in the research world, how often do I see something like the following in writing? "We found 126 examples of this construction in the 1m words native-speaker corpus and 135 examples of it in the 1m words learner corpus, see Figure 50", followed perhaps by some plot like this?

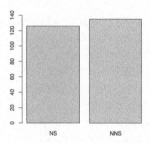

Figure 50: Some simple bar plot

Really?! The sentence "We found 126 [...] and 135 [...] didn't already say it all? I needed a visual aid to get it, to comprehend the mind-boggling complexity of ... those two (!) numbers? Call me elitist, but, sorry, no, I can handle two frequencies without visualization and so can every other reader of an academic (corpus-)linguistic paper in a peer-reviewed edited volume or journal – visualization here does nothing, nada, zip, nichts, ничего, so please, reserve it for when it's needed.

The second comment is actually even more important. Providing a graph when none is needed is just annoying, but doesn't really do much damage, but what happens a lot as well is that the graphs that are provided are, how do experts call it? Oh yes: "terrible". Let me first exemplify what I mean by showing the kind of plot that many people are still using and then I'll explain. Here is a case in point using the two frequencies above, a four-dimensional bar plot – it uses height, width, depth, and color – an even worse example would be a three- or four-dimensional pie chart.

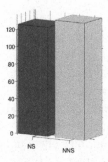

Figure 51: An unspeakable horror

What's so "terrible" about these? Simple: they are egregious violations of the idea to have a good ink-to-information ratio. How many values are we supposed to consider? Two frequencies which are close to each other and actually add up to 100% of the data. How many dimensions of information are we forced to process visually (if only to discard them as junk) to handle two (quite similar) frequencies/percentages? Like I said, four: three for each bar (length, width, and height) and the color of the bars. The lengths of the bars actually do not mean much: they are the same for both (even if the tilt does its best to hide that fact). Same with the width of the bars. The colors actually also don't add much because we already have the x-axis labels at the tickmarks to distinguish the bars. The only thing that actually means anything here is the bar height and there, too, the desire to have a 'fancy' 3-D plot resulted in the one dimension that actually matters getting displayed at an angle that makes recovering that information harder than it needs to be.

In sum, the plot was supposed to convey data on one dimension of information but offers three junk dimensions and one that is needlessly distorted, making it harder to process. (See Gries & Paquot, to appear for discussion of a similar (and authentic) example and Cleveland & McGill 1985 or Tufte 2001 for general discussion). Everyone knows that just because MS Word offers you 100 fonts to choose from, we don't want to see them all in your paper and you would probably never think of torturing your readers by using a font that is so ornamental that it's hard to read (such as Infiltrace or GuinevereCaps) – why would this be any different? Just because it's possible to use many dimensions, colors, etc. doesn't mean it's a good idea (unless they're needed for the dimensionality of the data).

But then how do we represent such data visually? Again, I don't think the 'complexity' of this frequency distribution calls for visualization in the first place, but if, *iff!*, your Ph.D. supervisor says you won't get your Ph.D. unless you provide a graph for it, then you go with a plot that uses a number of dimensions, an amount of information, that is commensurate with what you are trying to represent and this would be the first plot I showed you in this chapter:

```
frequencies <- c(126, 135); names(frequencies) <- c("NS", "NNS")
dotchart(pch=16, main="Frequencies of X in the NS & NNS corpora",
    xlab="Observed frequency", xlim=c(0, 260), x=frequencies,
    ylab="Corpus source"); grid()
    text(frequencies, 1:2, frequencies, pos=c(1, 3))
```

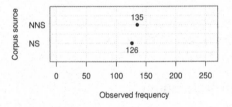

Figure 52: A merely unnecessary dot chart

Frequency is one-dimensional information, a point on a scale from, theoretically, 0 to ∞ so we can stay truest to the data if we locate each frequency on such a one-dimensional continuum. No extraneous dimensions, no extraneous colors, no other [insert a decent word here] – just two points, each one on a line starting at 0 and ending at an *x*-axis value that is large enough to accommodate even the most extreme distributions possible for 261 data points. The only other alternative we have discussed would be a bar plot, but only because people are so used to them (actually more than they are to dot charts), but, strictly speaking, that would again introduce at least one extraneous dimension: the likely meaningless bar width.

Again, I am aware of the fact that several plots above are not optimal from an ink-to-information ratio perspective, but then, this is a textbook trying to teach plotting functions and their settings so of course I sometimes tried to include more arguments than one might need, because that is the main focus of this book, not the actual data I am presenting – in a scientific article, however, the actual data is where the focus should be. Thus, for your own projects:

1. ask yourself "do I need a plot to convey what I want to convey?" – if the answer is *yes*,
2. ask yourself "really ...?!" – if the answer is still *yes*,
3. ask yourself "what is the critical 'dimensionality' of your data and what kind of plot represents it best?" – and when you think you're done,
4. critically check your plot: if you chose a plot but needed to write 1.5 pages to make a normal member of your target audience understand what it's about, you may need to reconsider and, for instance,
   a. change the perspective of the plot (recall the two mosaic plots for the same ima.fam table above);
   b. highlight dimensions differently (maybe use color/shading or font size instead of height in a plot), which might mean you actually
   c. choose an entirely different kind of plot;
   d. break your maybe big plot down into subplots ...

As you do more statistical work, your findings will often be complex – don't ruin a great analysis by presenting it in, let's say, ways that don't help.

3.5 (Non-polemic) Excursus on programming

In this section, I'll briefly introduce a few small aspects of R programming that are useful for statistical analyses; we'll deal with conditional expressions (Section 3.5.1), using loops (Section 3.5.2), not-using loops (Section 3.5.3), and how to write your own little functions (Section 3.5.4).

3.5.1 Conditional expressions

We will often be in the situation in which we want R to decide what to do next depending on something that happened before or that is happening elsewhere in our workspace. Several scenarios are conceivable:

1. if a condition *c* is met, do *x*, if not, do nothing;
2. if a condition *c* is met, do *x*, if not, do *y*;
3. if a condition *c* is met, do *x*, if not check whether condition *d* is met – if yes, do *y*, if not, do *z*, etc.

The most basic way of handling conditions in R involves a control-flow structure using the expression `if`. Scenario 1 can be expressed as follows:

```
if (some.logical.expression) {
    what to do if some.logical.expression evaluates to TRUE
}
```

For example, we might want to compute the percentage distribution of the frequencies of a vector x, but only if x has 3 or more different types:

```
x <- rep(2:4, 1:3) # x has 3 types: 2, 3, 4
```

We can use the following code to let R decide whether a percentage distribution will be returned or not:

```
if (length(unique(x))>=3) { # if x has 3 or more unique types
    prop.table(table(x))   } # then return a table of proportions
## x
##         2         3         4
## 0.1666667 0.3333333 0.5000000
```

If x had had fewer than 3 types, the above conditional returns nothing:

```
x <- rep(2:3, 3:4) # x has 2 types: 2, 3, now same as above:
if (length(unique(x))>=3) { # if x has 3 or more unique types
    prop.table(table(x))   } # then return a table of proportions
# no output
```

Scenario 2 can be expressed as follows:

```
if (some.logical.expression.1) {
    what to do if some.logical.expression.1 evaluates to TRUE
} else {
    what to do if that some.logical.expression.1 evaluates to FALSE
}
```

For example, we may want to compute a measure of central tendency of a numeric vector: the mean if the vector has 30 or more elements, the median otherwise (and let's make this work properly even with vectors containing NAs). Remember from above that x currently has 7 elements:

```
if (sum(!is.na(x))>=30) { # if x has 30+ non-NA elements
    c("mean"=mean(x, na.rm=TRUE))     # then return the mean of those
} else {                             # otherwise
    c("median"=median(x, na.rm=TRUE)) # return the median of those
}                                     # end of conditional
## median
##      3
```

But if x has enough elements that are not NA ...:

```
x <- rep(1:2, 15:16) # change x
if (sum(!is.na(x))>=30) { # if x has 30+ non-NA elements
    c("mean"=mean(x))     # then return the mean of those
} else {                  # otherwise
    c("median"=median(x)) # return the median of those
}                         # end of conditional
##     mean
## 1.516129
```

Note that I made the conditional return a named vector so that we know whether the number returned is a median or a mean, that's something we'll return to below.

Finally, scenario 3 can be expressed as follows:

```
if (some.logical.expression.1) {
    what to do if some.logical.expression.1 evaluates to TRUE
} else if (some.logical.expression.2) { # you can have more of these
    what to do if some.logical.expression.2 evaluates to TRUE
} else {
    what to do if some.logical.expression.2 evaluates to FALSE
}
```

For example, you want to log a number, but also be told explicitly if the logging 'ran into problems', i.e. when the number given to log was 0 or negative:

```
x <- 2 # change this value to see the other possible outputs
if (x>0) {                              # if x is greater than 0
   log(x)                               # log it
} else if (x<0) {                       # if x is less than 0
   c("The number you tried to log is negative.") # return this
} else {                                # otherwise
   c("The number you tried to log is 0.") # return this
}
## [1] 0.6931472
```

I get it, none of these examples is particularly exciting, but we have to start somewhere and the utility of the above will become clear(er) in the next two subsections (on loops and function writing). But before we get there, there's one final conditional expression that is very useful – especially for plotting: ifelse, which has the following structure:

```
ifelse(something.returning.TRUEs.and.FALSEs,
    what.to.return.for.each.TRUE,
    what.to.return.for.each.FALSE)
```

To see how useful this can be, let's generate some random normally-distributed numbers around 0:

```
set.seed(sum(utf8ToInt("facetiously")))
summary(y <- rnorm(30))
##      Min.  1st Qu.   Median     Mean  3rd Qu.     Max.
## -2.07884 -0.60728  0.01249 -0.01692  0.55302  2.24413
```

Now let's plot them such that every positive number is plotted with a blue filled circle and every negative number with a red filled circle; it's easy, see 53:

```
plot(y, pch=16, col=ifelse(y>0, "blue", "red"))
abline(h=0, lty=2)
```

Now let's plot them such that we use the same color decision as above, but then also such that every *y*-value whose absolute value is greater than 1 is plotted with a filled circle whereas all others are plotted with an unfilled circle (plot not shown here).

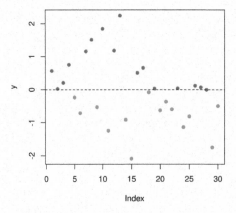

Figure 53: A plot exemplifying `ifelse` for colors

```
plot(y, pch=ifelse(abs(y)>1, 16, 1),
    col=ifelse(y>mean(y), "blue", "red"))
abline(h=c(1, 0, -1), lty=c(3, 1, 3))
```

Recommendation(s) for further study: Check out the function `switch`.

3.5.2 On looping

This section introduces loops, which are one useful way to execute one or more functions several times. While R offers several different ways to use loops, I will only introduce one of them here in a bit more detail, namely for-loops, I'm leaving `while` and `repeat`-loops for you to explore on your own. A for-loop has the following structure:

```
for (some.name in some.sequence) {
    what to do as often as some.sequence has elements
    this can be more than one line
}
```

This requires some explanation. The expression `some.name` stands for any name you choose to assign, and `some.sequence` stands for anything that can be interpreted as a sequence of values (where one value is actually enough to constitute a sequence); in this book, such a sequence will nearly always be a vector, namely a vector with integers from 1 to `length(some.sequence)` (either generated using the range operator : or seq). The values of that sequence are then usually used to access a part/subset of some data structure one at a time and do something with it. Let's first look at a very simple example, one that in fact one wouldn't use a loop for (and especially not like this), but that makes for a first straightforward example of the general logic of loops (and that we can build on afterwards). We first load a data frame (you need to look at the summary in R, it's too big for the book here):

```
rm(list=ls(all.names=TRUE))
summary(x <- read.delim(file="_inputfiles/03_scmc.csv",
   stringsAsFactors=TRUE)) ## [...]
```

Since we will deal with this data set a lot later, let me already introduce it a bit. This (corpus-based) data set contains
− a binary response ORDER: *mc-sc* vs. *sc-mc* indicating whether, in a complex sentence, the main clause precedes or follows the subordinate clause; i.e., the response is whether someone said/wrote *I was late because it rained* (*mc-sc*) or *Because it rained, I was late* (*sc-mc*);
− a categorical/binary predictor SCTYPE: *caus* vs. *temp* indicating whether the subordinate clause is a causal or a temporal one;
− a categorical predictor CONJ, which represents the conjunction used in the subordinate clause. Since these data are from a study involving parallel corpus data, the levels of CONJ are *als/when*, *bevor/before*, *nachdem/after*, and *weil/ because*;
− two numeric predictors LENMC and LENSC representing the numbers of words of the main and the subordinate clause respectively;
− a numeric predictor LENDIFF, which represents the result of main clause length minus subordinate clause length; that is, negative values indicate the main clause is shorter;
− a categorical predictor MORETHAN2CL: *no* vs. *yes* indicating whether or not there's more than just this main and subordinate clause in the sentence. This can be understood as a question of whether the sentence involves more com- plexity than just these two clauses.

One thing we might be interested in is getting an inventory of all unique values that each column contains. This could be useful to check for variables that are constant (because those would then not be useful) or to check for possible data entry errors (because if you see a variable having a level that you didn't expect to see, you need to check this). What does this task require? If we insist on doing this with a loop, it requires that we loop over the columns of the data frame and apply unique to each of it, maybe even sort(unique(...)). That means the sequence would involve 7 iterations (because we might not want to do this to the case numbers): one for each column of x (beginning with column 2) and that sequence could be easily generated with 2:8. Thus, this is how this could be done (in this didactic setting):

```
for (i in 2:8) {
   cat("The column called", colnames(x)[i],
      "has these unique values:\t",
      sort(unique(as.character(x[,i]))), "\n\n")
} ## [...]
```

This can be paraphrased as follows: Generate a variable called i as an index for looping. The value i should take on at the beginning is 2 (the first value in the sequence defined by 2:8), and then R executes the function(s) within the loop, i.e. those enclosed in curly brackets. Here, this means printing (with cat)
– "The column called", followed by
– the column names of x, the *i*-th one (i.e., the 2nd one), followed by
– "has these unique values:" (where "\t" is a tab stop), followed by
– the result of applying unique and then sort to the *i*-th column of x (i.e., the 2nd one), followed by
– two line breaks.

Then R gets to the } and 'checks' whether i has assumed all values of the sequence, and after the first iteration it of course hasn't. Thus, i gets to be the next/second value of the sequence – 3 – and R goes through the above body of the loop again, and again, and again, till i was 8. That means, i has assumed all values of the sequence and R exits the loop, done. (I am only showing abbreviated output here but you'll of course see all of it on your screen.)

```
## The column called ORDER has these unique values:  mc-sc sc-mc
## The column called SCTYPE has these unique values: caus temp
## [...]
```

Let's look at one other example, which is also only didactically motivated – one wouldn't really do this one with a loop either: Imagine you wanted to create a new vector/factor LENCOMP that contains for each case the information whether the main clause is longer or shorter than the subordinate clause or equally long. One important characteristic of this scenario is that we already know the length of the result of the loop: LENCOMP is going to have a length of 403, because it will contain one element for each row of x. In such cases, R's memory management and computation time benefits immensely from defining – before the loop! – an output 'collector' that already has the right length and whose slots we're filling or overwriting one-by-one as we iterate through the loop. I usually would create LENCOMP like this, with, here, 403 cases of NA, which means I can very easily see after the loop whether all NAs were overwritten as planned.

```
LENCOMP <- rep(NA, nrow(x))
```

Now we can use a loop with a conditional expression to fill LENCOMP's slots:

```
for (i in seq(nrow(x))) { # beginning of for-loop
   if (x$LENMC[i]>x$LENSC[i]) { # if mc is longer than sc
      LENCOMP[i] <- "m>s"        # fill LENCOMP[i] w/ "m>s"
   } else if (x$LENMC[i]<x$LENSC[i]) { # if mc is shorter than sc
      LENCOMP[i] <- "m<s"           # fill LENCOMP[i] w/ "m<s"
   } else {                       # if both are equally long
      LENCOMP[i] <- "m=s"        # fill LENCOMP[i] w/ "m=s"
   }}
```

This can be paraphrased as follows: Generate a variable called i as an index for looping. The value i should take on at the beginning is 1 (the first value in the sequence defined by seq(nrow(x))), and then R executes the function(s) within the loop, i.e. those enclosed in curly brackets. Here, this means
– checking if the *i*-th main clause length is greater than the *i*-th subordinate clause length: if yes, put *m>s* into the corresponding *i*-th slot of LENCOMP – if no,
– checking if the *i*-th main clause length is less than the *i*-th subordinate clause length: if yes, put *m<s* into the corresponding *i*-th slot of LENCOMP – if no,
– i.e. otherwise, put *m=s* into the corresponding *i*-th slot of LENCOMP.

When the loop is done, we check the results, add LENCOMP to the data frame x as a factor, and remove the vector on its own from working memory:

```
table(LENCOMP, useNA="ifany") # were all NAs overwritten?
## LENCOMP
## m<s m=s m>s
## 183  27 193
x$LENCOMP <- factor(LENCOMP); rm(LENCOMP)
```

While these were just two simple examples, I hope they've given you a feel for how loops can be useful, and you should now revisit the examples of loops in Sections 1.5.1 and 3.1.4.2 above. However, R is often much better at doing things in non-loop ways namely by relying on the fact that many operations can be done more efficiently in a vectorized way in particular with a family of functions that have the word `apply` in their name. You have already seen the vectorized way in general in action above: For instance, if you have two equally long vectors you can do pairwise addition of them just like this – you do not need to do that with a loop (like you might in other programming languages):

```
aa <- 1:5
bb <- 5:9
aa*bb # 1*5, 2*6, 3*7, ...
## [1]  5 12 21 32 45
```

Therefore, the second `for`-loop from above could be solved better like this:

```
LENCOMP.signf <- factor(sign(x$LENMC-x$LENSC))
levels(LENCOMP.signf) <- c("m<s", "m=s", "m>s")
table(x$LENCOMP, LENCOMP.signf)
## [...]
```

But the `apply` family of functions provides even more powerful options, which we'll discuss now.

3.5.3 On not looping: the `apply` family

The `apply` family of functions involves quite a few very useful functions but we will only look at two of them here: `apply` and `tapply`. The function `apply` usually takes three arguments:
- the first argument is called X and is usually a two-dimensional matrix (or an array), but it can also be a (part of a) data frame;
- the second argument is called MARGIN and is typically
  - *1* if you want to do something to each row of X; or
  - *2* (if you want to do something to each column of X);
- the third argument is called FUN and is a function that you want to apply to each row or column of X.

Above we used a loop to retrieve the unique values of each column of x but the first, but now we'll generate a frequency table of these columns of x and not with a loop, and this is actually all you need:

```
apply(X=x[,-1], MARGIN=2, FUN=table)
## [...]
```

You can see how much more efficient code can become with good uses of apply.

The other function is tapply. It usually takes three arguments as well:
– the first argument is called X and is a data structure (typically a vector/factor);
– the second argument is called INDEX and is
  – either another vector/factor that has as many elements as X;
  – or a list of other vectors/factors, each with as many elements as X;
– the third argument is called FUN and is a function that you want to apply to each subset of X as defined by INDEX.

This may sound complex but you probably know this already from Pivot tables in spreadsheets. For example, imagine you want to compute the average lengths of subordinate clauses for each conjunction. This is what you might do without knowing tapply:

```
mean(x$LENSC[x$CONJ=="als/when"])
mean(x$LENSC[x$CONJ=="bevor/before"])
mean(x$LENSC[x$CONJ=="nachdem/after"])
mean(x$LENSC[x$CONJ=="weil/because"])
```

But here's how to do this with tapply:

```
tapply(X=x$LENSC, INDEX=x$CONJ, FUN=mean)
##      als/when  bevor/before nachdem/after  weil/because
##      8.139785      7.217391     10.353846     10.105528
```

Not only is this much less work (and of course the savings would be even greater for arguments of INDEX with more levels), but this would also show you if there was a typo in your data: If there was an entry of "als/when " in your data, i.e. a conjunction with a space added erroneously, the tapply line would show you a mean for that so you'd be alerted to the error – the manual computation above wouldn't show you that because you'd never ask for a mean for "als/when ".

But then, the second argument can be a list, which means we can do groupings by more than one variable. Here's how to compute the average subordinate clause length for every combination of x$ORDER and x$CONJ (and round it to something decent):

```
round(tapply(X=x$LENSC, INDEX=list(x$CONJ, x$ORDER), FUN=mean), 1)
```

And tapply can also be useful in the context of plotting, for instance, when you want to add means to a boxplot: how are the lengths of subordinate clauses distributed for each of the four conjunctions?

```
boxplot(x$LENSC ~ x$CONJ, varwidth=TRUE) # as above, but now ...
text(x=1:4, y=tapply(x$LENSC, x$CONJ, mean), labels="x")
```

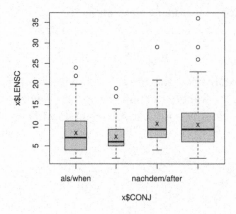

Figure 54: LENSC ~ CONJ (the CONJ labels don't all fit, that's why two seem to be missing)

Very useful ... While the above has hopefully already given you some impression or even ideas what is possible, things become really interesting when you realize that the argument FUN in these cases can be a function you define yourself, which is the topic of the next section.

Recommendation(s) for further study: Check out the functions sapply, lapply, and, much later, maybe rapply.

3.5.4 Function writing

The fact that R isn't just some statistics software but a full-fledged programming language means we're not limited by the functions that already exist in R or in any package that we may install – we can fairly easily write our own functions to facilitate and/or automate tedious and/or frequent tasks. In this section, I'll provide a few very small examples of the logic of how to write our own functions, which is something that will become extremely useful when we tackle larger and/or more complex data sets that might require functionality that isn't straightforwardly available. We begin with anonymous functions, which allow the user to quickly construct a new but unnamed function on the fly.

3.5.4.1 Anonymous functions

Let's return to one of the scenarios above: We have a data frame in our workspace and we want to check the columns for what they contain. Above, we used first a for-loop to just print them all to the screen and then we used apply with FUN=table to see the frequencies of all the different values, or types, each column contains. What if all we want to know is the number of different types per column? That is, we don't care what they are and how frequent they are – we just want to see the number of unique values. If there was a function called typecounter that returns the number of types of whatever it is given, the answer should by now be obvious; we would do this:

```
apply(X=x, MARGIN=2, FUN=typecounter)
```

But there is no such function in base R. But we do know what would probably be the core of that function: If we had a vector qwe of which we wanted the number of different types: typecounter(qwe) would essentially do length(unique(qwe)), However, we can just define this function anonymously in that slot (and I'm leaving out the column with the case numbers again):

```
apply(X=x[,-1], MARGIN=2, FUN=function(af) length(unique(af)))
## [...]
```

What happens here is that R 'gets handed' each column from apply and then it wants to apply a function to it, the argument of FUN. The function it is given in the FUN slot is one that is defined right there and then and it isn't given a name (hence it is an anonymous function). That anonymous function, when it is given a column from apply, function-internally labels that column/content af (for *anonymous function*, but you can call it whatever you want), and then it does to/with af what the function definition says: length(unique(af)) – done.

Here's another example: We can use an anonymous function to quickly compute the variation coefficient (from Section 3.1.3.2) for the two clause length variables in x:

```
apply(X=x[,5:6], MARGIN=2, FUN=function(af) sd(af)/mean(af))
##      LENMC     LENSC
## 0.5409923 0.5608361
```

How about computing for each column the percentage of tokens that are hapaxes, i.e. occur only a single time?

```
apply(X=x[,-1], MARGIN=2, function(af) sum(table(af)==1)/length(af))
## [...]
```

Again, I hope it becomes clear how elegantly you can do various different tasks in R – extremely fast and without loops – once you grasp this notion of anonymous functions. And once you've grasped that, why not write your own named, not anonymous, functions for things you need to do over and over again? That's the topic of the final section of this chapter.

3.5.4.2 Named functions

A lot of my work involved looking at 2x2 tables and computing an association measure that would quantify the degree of association between the two binary variables represented in the table, like here:

```
VAR1 <- rep(letters[1:2], each=500)
VAR2 <- rep(letters[c(13,14,13)], c(400, 300, 300))
(qwe <- table(VAR1, VAR2))
##      VAR2
## VAR1   m   n
##    a 400 100
##    b 300 200
```

One measure that can be computed for this is the so-called odds ratio, which is computed as follows:

```
(qwe[2,2]/qwe[2,1]) / (qwe[1,2]/qwe[1,1]) # (200/300)/(100/400)
## [1] 2.666667
```

What this means is that the odds of VAR2: n when VAR1: b (i.e. $^{200}/_{300}$) are 2.6667 times as high as when VAR1: a (i.e. $^{100}/_{400}$). But in base R, there is no function to compute this so it might be nice to have a function that can do this real quick. It would also be nice if that function could handle cases where the computation of the odds ratio would run into a division-by-0 error, which is sometimes solved by adding 0.5 to each cell before the above computation is done. Given everything we have discussed above, writing such a function (to be called odds.ratio) is not difficult. Step 1: we write the code that we would run if we didn't have a function:

```
(qwe <- qwe+0.5)
##      VAR2
## VAR1      m      n
##    a 400.5 100.5
##    b 300.5 200.5
(qwe[2,2]/qwe[2,1]) / (qwe[1,2]/qwe[1,1])
## [1] 2.658927
```

(The result is now slightly different because of our adding-0.5 strategy.) Step 2 is to look at that code and identify all the information R needs to run this. In this case, this is straightforward: all the above two lines of code need is the table in qwe. We, therefore, wrap a function definition around the above code that makes sure that we provide qwe to the function being defined:

```
odds.ratio <- function (qwe) { # function-definition introducing qwe
   qwe <- qwe+0.5                        # code from the
   (qwe[2,2]/qwe[2,1]) / (qwe[1,2]/qwe[1,1]) # previous code chunk
}                                # close the function definition
```

And step 3 is actually optional but advisable: We replace the (names of the) data structures the function needs by (more) generic and instructive ones and, we are fastidious, we make sure we explicitly tell the function what to return to the user when it's done (with return):

```
# qwe is replaced by a.2by2.table
odds.ratio <- function (a.2by2.table) {
   a.2by2.table <- a.2by2.table+0.5
   return((a.2by2.table[2,2]/a.2by2.table[2,1]) /
      (a.2by2.table[1,2]/a.2by2.table[1,1]))
}
```

Done:

```
qwe <- table(VAR1, VAR2) # recreate the original table qwe
odds.ratio(qwe)          # apply the new function to it
## [1] 2.658927
```

Now you might say, 'but I only want 0.5 to be added when there are 0s in the table, not otherwise ...' Fair enough, but if we change the function accordingly, the user also needs to be informed whether the odds ratio they are getting is based on unaltered cell frequencies or on ones that had 0.5 added to them. In other words, we now need two pieces of information in the output: the odds ratio and how it was computed. No problem: check out the code file for the code, but here's the result when applied to tables with and without 0s:

```
odds.ratio(qwe)
## $`with 0.5 added?`
## [1] FALSE
## $`odds ratio`
## [1] 2.666667

qwe[1,2] <- 0; qwe # now there's a zero in qwe[1,2]
odds.ratio(qwe)    # it does
## $`with 0.5 added?`
## [1] TRUE
## $`odds ratio`
## [1] 534.4443
```

Sure, again none of this will make you win the next big Kaggle competition, but it is a first step towards you writing your own functions (and theoretically, you could keep this function for when we use the odds ratio again in Section 4.1.2.1). And while we're at it, why don't we write a named function that computes a variation coefficient? Like so:

```
var.coef <- function (some.num.vector) {
   return(sd(some.num.vector) / mean(some.num.vector)) }
var.coef(1:10)
## [1] 0.5504819
```

Finally, do you remember how, in Section 3.1.1.1 above, we tried to compute the mode of a categorical variable and ran into the problem of variables where two or more levels of the variable may have the same maximal frequency? What we did up there is this:

```
some.factor <- factor(rep(letters[1:5], c(3, 5, 7, 7, 5)))
table(some.factor)
## some.factor
## a b c d e
## 3 5 7 7 5
max(table(some.factor)) # we don't see there are two 7s
## [1] 7
```

So why not turn our solution to that problem into a function mode?

```
mode <- function (some.vector.or.factor) {
    return(table(some.vector.or.factor)[table(some.vector.or.factor)
        ==max(table(some.vector.or.factor))]) }
mode(some.factor)
## some.vector.or.factor
## c d
## 7 7
```

As you become more proficient with R, you'll hopefully consider writing your own functions more often, which will make your analyses more efficient. Note that, depending on your R/RStudio settings, functions might not be available from one session to the next so put them in little files that you can source at the beginning of a new session (you will see examples of that in Chapter 5) or add them to your <Rprofile.site> file (on a Linux system, that file will likely be in </etc/R>; see also ?Startup and google around a bit) so that R loads them all whenever it starts up.

Recommendation(s) for further study: You should try and write some small functions for normalized entropies and standard errors of percentages and means.

---

4 Monofactorial tests

The most important questions of life are, for the most part, really only questions of probability. (Pierre-Simon Laplace, from <https://malouf.sdsu.edu>)

In my description of the phases of an empirical study in Chapter 1, I skipped over one essential step: how to decide which significance test to use. In this chapter, I will now discuss this step in some detail as well as then discuss how to conduct a variety of significance tests you may want to perform on your data. More specifically, in this chapter I'll explain how descriptive statistics from Chapter 3 are used in the domain of hypothesis-testing that either looks at a univariate scenario (there's only one response variable and you're testing for a H_1 of the goodness-of-fit kind) or at a bivariate scenario (you have a monofactorial situation with a predictor and a response variable and you're testing for a H_1 of the independence/difference kind). For example, in Section 3.1.3, I explained how you compute a measure of central tendency (such as a mean) or a measure of dispersion (such as a standard deviation) for a particular sample. In this chapter, you will see how you test whether such a mean or standard deviation differs significantly from a known mean or standard deviation (the univariate question) or the mean or standard deviation of a second sample (the bivariate/monofactorial question).

However, before we begin with actual tests: how do you decide which of the many tests out there is required for your hypotheses and data? One way to try to narrow down the truly bewildering array of tests is to ask yourself the six questions I will list in (13) to (18) and discuss presently, and the answers to these questions usually point you to only one or two tests that you would typically apply to your data. (A bit later, I will also provide a visual aid for this process.)

Ok, here goes. The first question is shown in (13).

13. What kind of study are you conducting?

Typically, there are three possible answers to that question, of which only one is relevant for this chapter and the following two: Studies, or case studies in studies, can be

– **descriptive**, in which case you likely use many of the things discussed in the previous chapter but probably no significance testing;

https://doi.org/10.1515/9783110718256-004

- **hypothesis-generating**: you're exploring a (typically/hopefully large) data set with the intentions of detecting structure(s) and developing hypotheses for future studies; your approach to the data is therefore data-driven, bottom-up, exploratory;
- **hypothesis-testing**, in which your approach to the data involves specific hypotheses you want to test and requires the types of approaches in the remainder of this book.

Thus, in this and the next few chapters, we'll assume the answer to this question is *hypothesis-testing*. Next question:

14. What kinds of variables are involved in your hypotheses, and how many?

There are essentially two types of answers. One pertains to the information value, or level of measurement, of the variables and we have discussed this in detail in Section 1.3.2.2 above so I won't repeat that here. The other allows for four different possible answers, of which we'll discuss the three relevant for this book. First and as already alluded to above, you may only have one response variable (i.e. a univariate scenario), in which case you normally want to compute a so-called **goodness-of-fit test** to test whether the statistic computed for this variable in your data corresponds to other results (from a previous study) or corresponds to a known distribution (e.g., a normal distribution). Examples include

- is the ratio of *no*-negations (e.g., *He is no stranger)* an*d not*-negations (e.g., *He is not a stranger*) in your data 1 (i.e., the two negation types are equally likely)?
- is the average acceptability judgment you receive for a sentence comparable to the average reported for the same (kind of) sentence in a previous study?

Second, you may have one predictor and one response (i.e. a monofactorial scenario). In both cases you typically want to compute a **monofactorial test for independence/differences** to determine whether the values of one/the predictor are correlated with those of the response. For example,

- does the animacy of the referent of the direct object (a categorical or ordinal predictor) correlate with the choice of one of two postverbal constituent orders (a categorical response)?
- does the average acceptability judgment (a mean of a numeric response or a median of an ordinal response) vary as a function of whether the subjects doing the rating are native speakers or not (a categorical predictor)?

Third, you may have one response and two or more predictors and you might be trying to determine whether the individual predictors (and maybe their interactions, see esp. Sections 5.2.4 and 5.2.8 below for that) correlate with, or predict, the response; this would be a **multifactorial analysis**. For example,

- does the choice of a negation type (a categorical response with the levels *no* vs. *not*; see above) depend on the mode of communication (a binary predictor with the levels *spoken* vs. *written*), the type of verb that is negated (a categorical predictor with the levels *copula*, *have*, or *lexical*), and/or the interaction of these predictors?
- does the reaction time to a word *w* in a lexical decision task (a numeric response) depend on *w*'s word class (a categorical predictor with possibly very many levels), *w*'s frequency in a reference corpus (a numeric predictor), whether the subject has seen a word semantically related to *w* on the previous trial or not (a binary predictor), whether the subject has seen a word phonologically similar to *w* on the previous trial or not (a binary predictor), and/or any interactions of these predictors?

Next question:
15. Are data points in your data related such that you can connect or group them meaningfully and in a principled way?

This question is concerned with whether you have what are called independent or dependent samples and this brings us back to the notion of independence discussed in Section 1.5.1. In the spirit of the discussion there, two samples – e.g., the numbers of mistakes made by ten male and ten female non-native speakers in a grammar test – are independent of each other if you cannot connect each male subject's value to that of one female subject on a meaningful and principled basis such that each male data point is connected to one and only one female data point and vice versa. You wouldn't be able to do so if you randomly sampled ten men and then randomly sampled ten women and let them take the same test.

We said above that samples can be dependent if, for instance, you test experimental subjects more than once, e.g., before and after a treatment. In that case, you could meaningfully connect each subject's value in the before-treatment sample to the same subject's value in the after-treatment sample because each subject's characteristics could affect both their data points.

The second way in which samples may be dependent was explained using subjects and direct objects sampled from the same sentences, in which case each subject could be connected to the object from the same sentence. But what about the above example of ten men and ten women taking a grammar test. We said that, if the ten men and ten women were sampled separately and randomly, these would be two independent samples – but can you imagine another scenario in which these two would be dependent samples?

THINK BREAK

If the ten men were the husbands of the ten women, then we would want to consider the samples dependent. Why? Because spouses are on average more similar to each other than randomly-chosen people: they often have similar worldviews, IQs, professions, diets, mannerisms, they spend more time and speak more with each other than with randomly-selected people, etc. Thus, they will be *probabilistically* correlated – which means, I don't want to hear of any counterexamples (see Section 3.3 and, for instance, Dolgalev et al. 2013 or Groyecka et al. 2018) – and one should associate each husband with his wife, making this two dependent samples.

Independence of data points is often a very important criterion: Many classical tests assume that data points are independent (most methods of Chapters 4 and 5) but there are many studies out there that applied tests that assume the independence of samples or data points to data that were not that, which can obviously lead to incorrect results (which is where some tests of Chapter 4 and all of Chapter 6 come in).

Next question:

16. What is the statistic of the response variable in the statistical hypotheses?

There are essentially five different answers to this question, which I already mentioned in Section 1.3.2.3 above. Your dependent variable may involve frequencies/counts, distributions, central tendencies, dispersions, or correlations.

The final two questions pertain mostly to this chapter – chapters 5 and 6 will deal with the underlying motivation of these questions in a different way:

17. What does the distribution of the data or your test statistic look like? For example, if your response is numeric, is it (roughly) normally distributed?
18. How big are the samples you collected? $n<30$ or $n\geq30$?

These questions relate back to Section 1.5, where I explained two things: First, if your data / test statistics follow a particular probability distribution, you can often use a (usually computationally simpler) parametric test, whereas if your data / test statistics don't, you often must use a (computationally more involved) non-parametric test. Second, given sufficient sample sizes, even means from a decidedly non-normal distribution can begin to look normal and, thus, allow you to apply parametric tests. It is safer, however, to be careful and, if in doubt, run both types of tests.

Let's now use a graph (<sflwr3_navigator.png>), which visualizes this process and which you should have downloaded as part of all the files from the companion website. Let's exemplify the use of this graph using the hypothesis that the average acceptability judgment (a median of an ordinal response) varies as a function of whether the subjects providing the ratings are native or non-native speakers (a categorical predictor). You start at the top left with the rounded red box with *approach* in it. Then, the above scenario is a hypothesis-testing scenario so you go down to *hypothesis-testing*. Then, the above scenario involves averages so you go down to the rounded blue box or bubble with *central tendency* in it. Then, the hypothesis involves both a response and a predictor so you go down to the right, via *1 R 1 P* (1 response, 1 predictor) to the transparent box with (tests for) *independence/difference* in it. You got to that box via the blue box with *central tendency* so you follow the color and continue to the next blue box containing *information value*. Now you make two decisions: first, the dependent variable is ordinal in nature, second, the samples are independent. Thus, you take the *ordinal* arrow down to the blue bubble which also is on the receiving end of the *indep* (samples) arrow. That blue bubble where the arrows arrive has *U*-test in it, which is the typical test for the above question, and the R function for that test is already provided there, too: `wilcox.test`.

Now, what does the dashed arrow mean that leads towards that box? It means that you might also end up doing a *U*-test if your response was numeric but the data were of a nature that did not permit the use of the normal default test for that scenario (a *t*-test for independent samples); that is, dashed arrows provide alternative tests for the first-choice test from which they originate.

Obviously, this graph is a simplification and doesn't establish every connection one could establish and doesn't contain everything one would want to know, but I think it can help beginners to make first choices for tests so I recommend that, as you continue with the book, you always determine for each section of Chapter 4 which test/method to use and how to identify this on the basis of the graph. One connection one could have made is that *correlation* (leading to *multifactorial modeling*) is actually a term broad enough to cover also frequencies and central tendencies, as you will recall from Section 3.3; Chapters 5 and 6 of this book deal with all such aspects of (regression) modeling.

Before we get started, let me remind you once again that in your own data your categorical variables should ideally always be coded with meaningful character strings so that R can recognize them as factors when reading in the data from a file.

4.1 Distributions and frequencies

In this section, I will illustrate how to test whether distributions and frequencies from one sample differ significantly from a known distribution (see Section 4.1.1) or from another sample (see Section 4.1.2). In both subsections, we begin with categorical variables and then proceed to numeric ones.

4.1.1 Goodness-of-fit

4.1.1.1 One categorical/ordinal response

Let's begin by returning to an example from Section 1.3, the constructional alternation of particle placement in English, which is again represented in (19).

19. a.   He picked the book up. (verb - direct object - particle)
    b.   He picked up the book. (verb – particle - direct object)

As we know, often both constructions are acceptable and native speakers can often not explain their preference for one of the two. Since there's a clear acquisitional difference between the two constructions – meaning, they are not acquired at the same time – one might hypothesize that the two constructions are not equally frequent, and this is what we're going to test. This scenario involves
– a categorical response variable CONSTRUCTION with the levels *verb-object-particle* vs. *verb-particle-object*;
– no predictor, because you do not investigate whether the distribution of CONSTRUCTION is dependent on anything else.

Such questions are generally investigated with tests from the family of **chi-squared tests,** which is one of the most important and widespread tests (in formulae, *chi-squared* is written as X^2). Since there's no predictor, we test the degree/goodness of fit between the observed distribution in our data and the distribution expected from H_0, which should remind you of Section 1.5 (where you/an observer decided whether certain frequencies resulting from tossing a coin repeatedly were compatible with the H_0 of 50:50). This **chi-squared test for goodness-of-fit** (check <sflwr3_navigator.png>) involves the following steps:

Procedure
1. Formulate the hypotheses;
2. describe the data statistically and visually;
3. compute the frequencies you would expect given H_0;
4. check/test the assumption(s) of the test:
     a. all observations are independent of each other;
     b. 80% of the expected frequencies are ≥ 5;
     c. all expected frequencies are >1;
5. compute the contributions to X^2 (chi-squared) for all observed frequencies;
6. compute the test statistic X^2, *df*, and *p*.

Step 1 is very easy here:[6] As you know, H_0 typically postulates that the data are distributed randomly/evenly, and that would mean that both constructions occur equally often, i.e., 50% of the time (just as tossing a fair coin many times will mostly result in a largely equal distribution). Thus:

- H_0: The frequencies of the two levels of CONSTRUCTION are identical – if you find a difference in your sample, this difference isn't due to a systematic frequency difference between the two constructions; $n_{\text{verb-object-particle}} = n_{\text{verb-particle-object}}$;
- H_1: The frequencies of the two levels of CONSTRUCTION are not identical; $n_{\text{verb-object-particle}} \neq n_{\text{verb-particle-object}}$.

Note that this is a two-tailed H_1: we're not committing to a specific direction of the difference, which is why we're not saying $n_{\text{verb-object-particle}} > n_{\text{verb-particle-object}}$ or $n_{\text{verb-object-particle}} < n_{\text{verb-particle-object}}$. Next, we would collect some data and count the occurrences of both constructions, but here we'll use frequencies from a picture description experiment reported in Peters (2001); we load a spreadsheet that contains this part of her data from the folder with the input files:

```
rm(list=ls(all.names=TRUE))
summary(x <- read.delim(file="_inputfiles/04_vpcs1.csv",
   stringsAsFactors=TRUE)) ## [...]
```

The summary of the data frame already shows us the observed frequencies but we'll just 'do it by the books' and compute the relevant tables as discussed in Section 3.1.1:

---

6 This threshold value of 5 (step 4b) is the one most commonly mentioned. There are a few studies that show that the chi-squared test is fairly robust even if this assumption is violated – especially when, as is the case here, H0 postulates that the expected frequencies are equally high (see Zar 2010:474). However, to keep things simple, I stick to the most commonly quoted threshold value of 5 and refer you the above pages in Zar (2010) for discussion. If one's data violate this assumption, then one can compute a binomial test (if, as here, one has two groups) or a multinomial test (for three or more groups); see the recommendations for further study.

```
(CX.obs <- table(x$CONSTRUCTION))
## verb-object-particle verb-particle-object
##                  150                    247
prop.table(CX.obs)
## verb-object-particle verb-particle-object
##            0.3778338            0.6221662
```

If we really feel the need to visualize information as simple as this – recall my discussion of this in Section 3.4 – we could do so with a dot chart or a bar plot:

```
dotchart(pch=16, xlab="Observed frequency", xlim=c(0, sum(CX.obs)),
    x=CX.obs); text(x=CX.obs, y=seq(CX.obs), labels=CX.obs, pos=1)
abline(v=mean(CX.obs), lty=3)
```

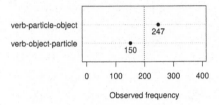

Figure 55: A dot chart of CONSTRUCTION

By the way, I want to highlight something important here. Note how in the call to dotchart I defined the x-axis limits: I wrote xlim=c(0, sum(CX.obs)), not xlim=c(0, 397) or xlim=c(0, 400), and in text I defined the y-values with a call to seq, instead of just saying 1:2 – can you imagine why?

THINK BREAK

Yes, typing 397/400 and/or 1:2 would have been shorter, but I nearly always try to write code in such a way that it is easily recyclable for the next analyses. If I had used xlim=c(0, 397) but my next analysis had involved 200 or 4000 data points, I'd need to adjust that number to make it fit the new data. If I had used y=1:2 but my next analysis had involved a table of 3 categories, I'd need to adjust that number to make it fit the new data; same for the call to abline. But if I do it like this, I let R do the work: As soon as I give R the object CX.obs, it can figure out the x-axis limits from there, the y-coordinates for text, the v for abline, etc. Thus, I can recycle all the code by either just making sure I call the table from the next analysis CX.obs or by doing a quick find-and-replace for the new name of the table, but then it's all done. In a way, I am writing the code as if I was already considering that, maybe, later this will be re-used or even turned into a function so I better make sure R can do as much as possible already from the data it needs to see anyway (as opposed to hard-coding all sorts of things into the code that then need to be replaced). This is why a lot of code below will be a bit longer than it would need to be: it's so you can quickly recycle it!

Step 3 is already half-way included in the plot (with the abline): If we have 397 instances and H₀ says the distribution is random/equal, then the expected frequency for each construction is of course straightforward:

```
(CX.exp <- rep(mean(CX.obs), length(CX.obs)))
## [1] 198.5 198.5
```

Step 4: checking whether we can actually do a chi-squared test here: We will assume (!, this is for didactic convenience, obviously this would have to be justified/explained for a real study) that the data points are independent (such that each construction has been provided by a different speaker and that all instances involve different transitive phrasal verbs, etc.). Both expected frequencies are greater than 5 and thus greater than 1, so we can proceed with steps 5 and 6 (in one go because of how closely connected they are). Each contribution to chi-squared (for each cell of our table) is computed as follows:

$$\text{Contribution to chi-squared} = \frac{(observed - expected)^2}{expected}$$

That is to say, for every value of our observed frequency table we (i) compute the difference between the observed and the expected frequency, (ii) square this difference, and (iii) divide it by the expected frequency again. In R:

```
(CX.cont2CS <- ((CX.obs-CX.exp)^2)/CX.exp)
## verb-object-particle verb-particle-object
##            11.85013             11.85013
```

The chi-squared test statistic is then just the sum of these:

```
(CX.chisq <- sum(CX.cont2CS))
## [1] 23.70025
```

Obviously, this value increases as the differences between observed and expected frequencies increase (because then the numerators of the contributions to chi-squared deviate more from 0 and the squaring makes all differences – positive or negatives ones – positive). That also means that chi-squared becomes 0 when all observed frequencies correspond to all expected frequencies because then the numerators become 0. Thus, we can actually simplify our statistical hypotheses to the following:

– H_0: $X^2=0$.
– H_1: $X^2>0$.

But the chi-squared value alone doesn't show you whether the differences are large enough to be statistically significant. So, what do we do with this value? Before computers became more widespread, a chi-squared value was used to look up in a chi-squared table whether the result is significant or not. We now can just compute the exact p-value directly. For that, we need the chi-squared value (which we already have) and a number called degrees of freedom (df), which indicates the number of frequencies that is free to vary while they all still sum up to our total. In our case, this number is 1 because, if we have a total of 397, then we can choose one frequency freely, but then the other is restricted because the sum total of both frequencies needs to be 397. We can then insert these values into the function pchisq, which computes areas under the curve of the chi-squared distribution like this:

```
pchisq(q=CX.chisq, df=1, lower.tail=FALSE)
## [1] 1.125678e-06
```

That value is obviously much smaller than the traditional significance level of 0.05 (the result means $p=0.000001125678$), which means we reject H_0 and, to the extent that her data were a representative sample of verb-particle constructions in the population, assume that the two constructions are indeed unequally frequent in the population in general. And now that I tortured you with the 'manual computation', let me show you how you can get this all much faster, namely with one short line of R code using the function chisq.test:

```
(CX.chisq <- chisq.test(x=CX.obs))
##  Chi-squared test for given probabilities
## data:  CX.obs
## X-squared = 23.7, df = 1, p-value = 1.126e-06
```

So why did I discuss all the manual stuff from above if it's that easy? Because it's important to understand at least a bit what actually goes into these statistics. As you can see, I assigned the result of chisq.test to an object CX.chisq. This is because that object contains more information than is shown in the console; remember the recommendation from Section 3.1.1.3 to usually look up the structure of an object with str whenever you learn a new function (you can often also use names). CX.chisq is a list with quite a few components:

```
names(CX.chisq)
## [1] "statistic" "parameter" "p.value"   "method"    "data.name"
## [9] "observed"  "expected"  "residuals" "stdres"
```

The first three components are what was shown above, but there's more. In particular, two components are often interesting:
— CX.chisq$expected: the expected frequencies we computed manually;
— CX.chisq$residuals: the residuals, which are computed like this: (CX.obs-CX.exp)/sqrt(CX.exp), which means, if you square these, you get the contributions to chi-squared. These are useful because, in a sense, for each cell of our table, they indicate whether an observed frequency is greater or less than its corresponding expected frequency (via their sign) and how much that particular cell contributes to the chi-squared value (via their absolute value); thus, it is the residuals of chi-squared tests that help you identify those numbers in your table that are most responsible for a significant result. In this case, the results aren't that interesting because we only have two cells and a H_0 of 50-50 so both residuals have the same absolute value. In more complex tables than this one, residuals can be very helpful in interpreting the results.

As an aside, the function chisq.test can take an additional argument p which specifies the expected probabilities. If this isn't specified, R just assumes an equal/random distribution, which was exactly what we needed: If we specify the expected/H_0 distribution of 50:50 explicitly, we get the same result.

```
chisq.test(x=CX.obs, p=c(0.5, 0.5))
##  Chi-squared test for given probabilities
## data:  CX.obs
## X-squared = 23.7, df = 1, p-value = 1.126e-06
```

However, if you ever need to test your observed data against another H_0 expectation, that is where you can enter a different percentage expectation. For instance, if you collect 300 more verb-particle constructions with a 1:2 distribution, you can test their distribution against Peters's data with this p argument:

```
chisq.test(x=c(100,200), p=CX.obs/sum(CX.obs))
```

Finally, this is how we might now summarize in our results section: "The construction where the particle follows the verb directly was observed 247 times and the construction where the particle follows the direct object was observed only 150 times; expected frequencies for both were 198.5. That difference between observed and expected frequencies is highly significant according to a chi-squared goodness-of-fit test (X^2=23.7, df=1, p<0.001)."

Warning/advice: Never, ever, compute a chi-squared test like the above on percentages or otherwise normalized frequencies – always on 'real' observed frequencies! I once saw a conference talk where someone reported the results of many chi-squared tests done on percentages – obviously, that ruined everything, the whole talk (although no one in the audience commented on it)
...

Recommendation(s) for further study: the function binom.test for an exact-test alternative to a chi-squared test on two frequencies (e.g. if your two expected frequencies are too low) or the function EMT::multinomial.test for an exact-test alternative to a chi-squared test on three or more frequencies (e.g. if your three expected frequencies are too low). Theoretically, you could also use a simulation for this (like in the section on confidence intervals, but I won't discuss that here.)

4.1.1.2 One numeric response

Let's now look at the equivalent goodness-of-fit question for a numeric response variable. The prototypical instance of this is probably the case where you want to know whether a certain numeric variable is normally distributed. Checking for normality like this is so often useful because many parametric tests require it. For this example, we're going to return to the reaction time data from the last chapter: We already saw the somewhat normal-looking variables RT and MEAN there and now we're going to 'formally' test this. This scenario involves
– a dependent numeric variable – one time RT, one time MEAN;
– no predictor because we're not testing whether the distribution of these variables is influenced by, or correlated with, something else.

There are many tests for normality, but we will use the **Lilliefors test for goodness-of-fit** (for normality), which in turn uses the same test statistic as the so-called Kolmogorov-Smirnov test (but then computes the *p*-value differently). The procedure here doesn't really involve much:

Procedure

1. Formulate the hypotheses (separately for each variable);
2. describe the data visually; (I am not discussing statistics like skewness and kurtosis in this book because I hardly ever see them used; see Sheskin 2011:16-30 if you want to learn about them);
3. compute the test statistic *D* and *p*.

Step 1 leads to these two hypotheses:
- H_0: the distribution of the variable (again, separately one at a time) does not differ from a normal distribution: $D=0$;
- H_1: the distribution of the variable differs from a normal distribution: $D>0$.

Let's load the data:

```
rm(list=ls(all.names=TRUE))
summary(x <- read.delim(file="_inputfiles/04_reactiontimes.csv",
   stringsAsFactors=TRUE)) ## [...]
```

Visualization is of course straightforward; we did that above so I am only showing the code again to remind you, but not the plots:

```
par(mfrow=c(2, 2))
hist(x$RT, main=""); plot(ecdf(x$RT), main="")
hist(x$MEAN, main=""); plot(ecdf(x$MEAN), main="")
par(mfrow=c(1, 1))
```

Like I said above, the Lilliefors test is based on the Kolmogorov-Smirnomv test statistic *D*, which involves the maximal vertical distance between the observed ecdf curve of the variable under consideration and the ecdf curve one would see if the data had the same mean and the same standard deviation as your data but were distributed exactly as postulated by H_0, i.e. here normally (compare the *D*-value of ks.test(x=x$RT, "pnorm", mean=mean(x$RT), sd=sd(x$RT)) with the one you will see in a moment). It is straightforward to compute this test in R:

```
nortest::lillie.test(x=x$RT)
##   Lilliefors (Kolmogorov-Smirnov) normality test
## data:  x$RT
## D = 0.1259, p-value = 0.004136
```

As you can see, p is much smaller than 0.05, which means we reject H_0 and assume that RT isn't normally distributed. We would report this by saying something like "According to a Lilliefors test for normality, the variable RT differs very significantly from a normal distribution ($D=0.1259$, $p=0.0041$)." Upon running the same for MEAN, we find that it does not differ significantly from normality ($D=0.055$, $p=0.9735$):

```
nortest::lillie.test(x=x$MEAN)
## Lilliefors (Kolmogorov-Smirnov) normality test
## data: x$MEAN
## D = 0.054922, p-value = 0.9735
```

Let me just show you what this test amounts to visually, so to speak. The plot in Figure 56 shows the observed ecdf plot for MEAN in black, which we have seen before. But then it also contains 100 grey ecdf curves, each of which is a random normal distribution with the same mean and the same *sd* as MEAN. In other words, if MEAN was perfectly normal, the black line would go through the middle of the grey curves and it pretty much does that and that's why the Lilliefors test returns a non-significant result for MEAN. The test (and the plot) are essentially saying (I am simplifying a bit here): 'if the meaningfulness values were normally distributed out there in the world at large, they'd be looking like the grey stuff and your distribution doesn't really differ that much from that." However, note that, as always, there are also people who reject the idea of a statistical significance test for normality using a p-value so be prepared to read/hear the recommendation one should only use visual diagnostics like the plot above or others; I won't engage in this tiresome debate here.

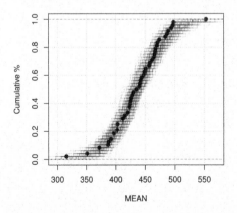

Figure 56: Normality-checking plots (w/ simulations)

4.1.2 Tests for differences/independence

Let's now move from the goodness-of-fit tests on to monofactorial tests (for frequencies/distributions); we'll proceed in the same order as before.

4.1.2.1 One categorical response and one categorical predictor (indep.samples)

We begin by revisiting the particle placement data of Peters (2001) because, when we discussed them above, I actually omitted a predictor that she was studying and that we're going to look at here, namely whether the discourse givenness of the referent of the direct object is correlated with CONSTRUCTION. In the picture-description experiment described above, she manipulated the givenness of the referent of the direct object and obtained the already familiar 397 verb-particle constructions. The expectation was that when the direct object's referent is given, subjects would prefer to describe the picture with CONSTRUCTION: *verb-object-particle* whereas when the direct object's referent is new, they would prefer CONSTRUCTION: *verb-particle-object*. This scenario involves
- a categorical response variable CONSTRUCTION: *verb-particle-object* vs. CONSTRUCTION: *verb-object-particle*;
- a categorical predictor GIVENNESS with the levels *given* and *new*.

Here, under certain conditions, we can also do a chi-squared kind of test, in particular a **chi-squared test for independence**, which involves the exact same steps as the chi-squared test above:

Procedure
1. Formulate the hypotheses;
2. describe the data statistically and visually;
3. compute the frequencies you would expect given H_0;
4. check/test the assumption(s) of the test:
   a. all observations are independent of each other;
   b. 80% of the expected frequencies are $\geq$ 5;
   c. all expected frequencies are >1;
5. compute the contributions to X^2 (chi-squared) for all observed frequencies;
6. compute the test statistic X^2, *df*, and *p*.

Step 1 is very similar to the above:
- H_0: The frequencies of the levels of CONSTRUCTION do not vary as a function of the levels of GIVENNESS; $X^2=0$.
- H_1: The frequencies of the levels of CONSTRUCTION vary as a function of the levels of GIVENNESS; $X^2>0$.

Next, we load the data:

```
rm(list=ls(all.names=TRUE))
summary(x <- read.delim(file="_inputfiles/04_vpcs2.csv",
    stringsAsFactors=TRUE)) ## [...]
```

Step 2 is computing the descriptive statistics and visualizing the data: As in Chapter 3, we cross-tabulate, compute percentages (note why we compute row, not column percentages), and we compute the odds ratio:

```
(CX.obs <- table(x$GIVENNESS, x$CONSTRUCTION))
##          verb-object-particle verb-particle-object
##  given                     85                  100
##  new                       65                  147
prop.table(CX.obs, 1)
##          verb-object-particle verb-particle-object
##  given             0.4594595            0.5405405
##  new               0.3066038            0.6933962
(CX.odds <- (CX.obs[2,2]/CX.obs[2,1]) / # odds
           (CX.obs[1,2]/CX.obs[1,1]))  # ratio
## [1] 1.922308
```

There seems to be an effect:
- the odds of CONSTRUCTION: *verb-particle-object* over *verb-object-particle* are 2.26 to 1 (147⁄65) when GIVENNESS: *new*;
- the odds of CONSTRUCTION: *verb-particle-object* over *verb-object-particle* are 1.18 to 1 (100/85) when GIVENNESS: *given*;
- the ratio of these two odds is the odds ratio of 2.26/1.18≈1.922, meaning CONSTRUCTION: *verb-particle-object* is more preferred when GIVENNESS is *new* than when GIVENNESS is *given* (as predicted).

Note that the way the odds ratio is computed means that it ranges from 0 to ∞ and is 'centered' around 1:
- if the odds ratio is 1, that means the two variables are not correlated;
- if the odds ratio is in the interval (1,+∞] and you computed it like we did – we started computing it from the lower right corner, i.e. we started with the odds of the second level of the response (in the columns) given the second level of the predictor (in the rows) – then that means the second level of the response is more preferred with the predictor's second level of the predictor than with the predictor's first level;

– if the odds ratio is in the interval [0,1) and you computed it the same way, then that means the second level of the response is less preferred with the predictor's second level of the predictor than with the predictor's first level.[7]

We can visualize this with a mosaic plot (maybe again of the transposed table, recall Section 3.2.1):

```
mosaicplot(x=t(CX.obs), xlab="CONSTRUCTION", ylab="GIVENNESS",
    col=c("grey35", "grey75"))
```

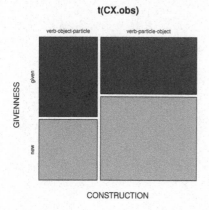

Figure 57: CONSTRUCTION ~ GIVENNESS

But how do we do step 3, in particular Steps 3a and 3b, for which we need the expected frequencies? The expected frequencies in the cells of the table follow from the so-called marginal frequencies/totals, i.e. the row and column totals:

```
addmargins(CX.obs)
##          verb-object-particle verb-particle-object Sum
## given                      85                  100 185
## new                        65                  147 212
## Sum                       150                  247 397
```

The two constructions are not equally frequent in the complete data set: CON-STRUCTION: *verb-object-particle* accounts for $^{150}/_{397}$ of the data (i.e. 0.3778) whereas CONSTRUCTION: *verb-particle-object* accounts for $^{247}/_{397}$ of the data (i.e.

---

7 You often also find the logarithm of the odds ratio (especially in the context of binary logistic regression, see Section 5.3.1.1 below).

0.6222). But if H_0 is true, namely that the distribution of the levels of CONSTRUC-
TION is independent of the levels of GIVENNESS, then we should always see this
0.3778 to 0.6222 distribution – not only in the totals (where we do see it) but also
within each level of GIVENNESS, because, again, H_0 says GIVENNESS doesn't matter for the distribution of CONSTRUCTION. Therefore, the expected frequencies
of both constructions when GIVENNESS is *given* should be this:

```
185 * prop.table(table(x$CONSTRUCTION))
## verb-object-particle verb-particle-object
##             69.89924            115.10076
```

And, analogously, the expected frequencies of both constructions when GIVEN-
NESS is *new* should be this:

```
212 * prop.table(table(x$CONSTRUCTION))
## verb-object-particle verb-particle-object
##             80.10076            131.89924
```

And we can actually put those together into one nice table using the function
rbind (rbind binds rows together into a two-dimensional data structure (e.g. a
table or a data frame), and there's a corresponding function cbind for binding
columns together):

```
addmargins(CX.exp <- rbind(
   "given"=185 * prop.table(table(x$CONSTRUCTION)), # row 1
   "new"=  212 * prop.table(table(x$CONSTRUCTION))  # row 2
)) # close rbind & addmargins
##         verb-object-particle verb-particle-object Sum
## given             69.89924            115.1008 185
## new               80.10076            131.8992 212
## Sum              150.00000            247.0000 397
```

The rest is now the same as before: Step 4 involves checking whether we can actually do a chi-squared test here. Again, just for didactic convenience (!), we will
assume that the data points are independent (such that each construction has
been provided by a different speaker, all instances involve different transitive
phrasal verbs, etc.). Also, all four expected frequencies are >5 and thus >1 – if
this assumption wasn't met, we could continue with the function fisher.test.
We can proceed with steps 5 and 6 and compute for each of the four cells the
contribution to chi-squared using the same formula as above, and we can sum

those up to get the overall chi-squared value; note how nicely you just need to give R the two tables, it will do the matching up of the cells for you:

```
(CX.cont2CS <- ((CX.obs-CX.exp)^2)/CX.exp)
##          verb-object-particle verb-particle-object
##   given              3.262307             1.981158
##   new                2.846825             1.728841
(CX.chisq <- sum(CX.cont2CS))             # chi-squared value
## [1] 9.819132
```

To compute a p-value from that, we again need to know the relevant degrees-of-freedom df-value, which is computed as follows:

```
(nrow(CX.obs)-1) * (ncol(CX.obs)-1)
## [1] 1
```

With this, we can proceed as before:

```
pchisq(q=CX.chisq, df=1, lower.tail=FALSE)
## [1] 0.001727059
```

Again, this value is obviously smaller than the traditional significance level of 0.05, which means we reject H_0 and, to the extent that her data were a representative sample of verb-particle constructions, do not assume anymore that there's no correlation between GIVENNESS and CONSTRUCTION in the population. But let's actually slow down a bit and discuss what this means 'graphically', so to speak.

Above, we discussed the decision-making process on the basis of the coin-tossing examples – 100 times, then 3 times. We approached computing the p-value there by (i) drawing up a distribution of all possible times heads might show up in 3 or more tosses and then (ii) going from the H_0 scenario – heads and tails are equally frequent, the peak of that histogram/bar plot – in the direction of the observed result and, once we got to the observed result, we started adding up all probabilities of that result and any results differing from the H_0 result even more extremely. In the example of the impartial observer, who had a non-directional/two-tailed hypothesis, you could go in either direction from the H_0 peak: left in the direction of 'fewer heads', right in the direction of 'more heads', or both (for a two-tailed hypothesis). With the chi-squared distribution, that's different because of how chi-squared is computed: We compute the differences between observed and expected values and then we *square them*! In other words, any *observed-expected* difference that was positive would be squared and stay positive, but any observed-expected difference that was negative would be squared and would also become positive. That's why

- H$_0$ was X^2=0 because if all observed frequencies are identical to all their expected counterparts, X^2 will be 0;
- H$_1$ was X^2>0 because, given how it is computed, it can only result in positive values no matter how the observed values differ from the expected ones.

That in turn means, there aren't two tails of that distribution: on the left, it begins at the H$_0$ expectation of 0 and then it can only go to the right, into the range of positive values, as is shown in the left panel below:

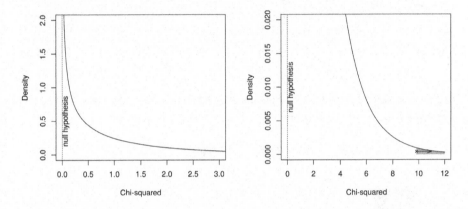

Figure 58: Chi-squared distribution for *df*=1

The right panel indicates with an × the chi-squared value we computed – 9.82 – and then, with grey shading and the arrow, all results more extremely away from H$_0$. The grey-shaded area under that curve, more precisely its share under the total area of the complete curve (which is set to 1), corresponds to the two-tailed *p*-value of the chi-squared test. This is sometimes confusing to people because we're actually only looking at one tail of that curve, but that's because whatever direction the observed frequencies differ from the expected ones, the squaring in the computation of chi-squared makes chi-squared positive; that also means that, in 2×2 tables at least, a directional/one-tailed hypothesis would allow us to halve the *p*-value we computed above.

While this was all a bit tedious, it is relevant both in general and for other tests and discussion following below, and the good news for now is that, again, we can get this all much faster:

```
(CX.chisq <- chisq.test(x=CX.obs, correct=FALSE))
## 	Pearson's Chi-squared test
## data: 	CX.obs
## X-squared = 9.8191, df = 1, p-value = 0.001727
```

As before, we can retrieve expected frequencies and residuals from this object:

```
CX.chisq$expected   # like what we computed manually
## 		verb-object-particle verb-particle-object
## 	given 		69.89924 		115.1008
## 	new 		80.10076 		131.8992
CX.chisq$residuals # the top left cell has the highest absolute value
## 		verb-object-particle verb-particle-object
## 	given 		1.806186 		-1.407536
## 	new 		-1.687254 		1.314854
```

A plot that summarizes these things nicely is the kind of association plot we can generate with assocplot (applied to the transposed table again):

```
assocplot(t(CX.obs), col=c("black", "lightgrey"))
```

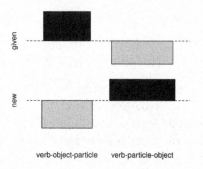

Figure 59: Association plot for CONSTRUCTION and GIVENNESS

In this plot, "the area of the box is proportional to the difference in observed and expected frequencies" (from ?assocplot). The black rectangles above the dashed lines indicate observed frequencies exceeding expected frequencies (i.e. positive residuals); grey rectangles below the dashed lines indicate observed frequencies smaller than expected frequencies (i.e. negative residuals). The heights of the boxes are proportional to the residuals and the widths are proportional to the (square roots of the) expected frequencies. Note, the absolute size of the boxes doesn't mean much: R tries to make the boxes as big as it can given the size of the plotting window. Thus, this plot is useful for interpretive purposes when you already know that the table differs significantly from H_0, but it's not useful to compare association strengths across tables.

One final comment before we write it all up: Above, we computed as an effect size the odds ratio. That's fine for 2×2 tables, but sometimes we have frequency tables that do not just have 2 rows and 2 columns and in that case an odds ratio is less straightforward. An effect size that can be applied to tables with more rows and/or columns is called Cramer's V; it theoretically falls into the interval [0, 1] and it is computed like this:

$$V = \sqrt{\frac{\chi^2}{n \times (min(nrow, ncol) - 1)}}$$

In R and using the function dim, which returns the row and column numbers (i.e., the same as c(nrow(...), nol(...))):

```
sqrt(CX.chisq$statistic / (sum(CX.obs) * (min(dim(CX.obs))-1)))
## X-squared
## 0.1572683
```

This is how you would summarize all the results: "[You'd obviously show the table with the observed frequencies, then:] New objects are preferred in the construction *verb-particle-object* and are dispreferred in *verb-object-particle*; the opposite kind of constructional preference is found for given objects. According to a chi-squared test for independence, this correlation is very significant (X^2=9.82, *df*=1, *p*<0.002), but the effect isn't particularly strong (V=0.157, odds ratio=1.9223 (or log odds ratio=0.6535)). [Maybe show a plot.]

4.1.2.2 One ordinal/numeric response and one categorical predictor (indep. samples)

Let's now look at an example in which two independent samples are compared with regard to their overall distributions. You will test whether men and women differ with regard to the frequencies of hedges they use in discourse (i.e., expressions such as *kind of* or *sort of*). Again, note that we're here only concerned with the overall distributions – not just means or just variances. We could of course do that, too, but it's of course possible that a test for different means or variances might not uncover, or react unambiguously to, the overall distributional difference(s).

Let's assume we recorded 60 two-minute conversations of a confederate, each with of 30 men and 30 women, and then counted the numbers of hedges that the male and female subjects produced. We now want to test whether the distributions of hedge frequencies differs between men and women. This question involves
– a numeric response variable HEDGES: the number of hedges produced;
– a categorical predictor SEX with two levels: *female* and *male.*

The question of whether the two sexes differ in terms of the distributions of hedge frequencies is investigated with the **Kolmogorov-Smirnov test for independence/differences** (again, don't forget to check <sflwr3_navigator.png>):

Procedure
1.   Formulate the hypotheses;
2.   describe the data visually;
3.   check/test the assumption(s) of the test: the data are continuous;
4.   compute the cumulative frequency distributions for both samples, the maximal absolute difference of both distributions' ecdf curves D and p.

Step 1 is straightforward because the situation is simple enough and we have dealt with ecdf curves before:
– H_0: The distribution of HEDGES does not differ depending on the levels of SEX; $D=0$
– H_1: The distribution of HEDGES differs as a function of the levels of SEX; $D>0$.

Step 2: we load the data:

```
rm(list=ls(all.names=TRUE))
summary(x <- read.delim(file="_inputfiles/04_hedges1.csv",
   stringsAsFactors=TRUE)) ## [...]
```

Given what is at issue is the overall distribution rather than any specific statistic describing the distribution, we immediately visualize (see the code file). This looks like a massive difference in distribution: The values of the women in black are on average higher (because that curve is rising further on the right where the high values are) and the values of the men (in grey) are distributed across a wider range of values (because their curve starts way earlier on the left, but ends nearly exactly with that of the women).

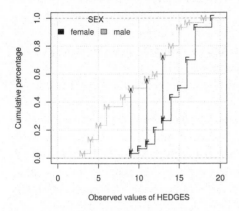

Figure 60: The ecdf of HEDGES by SEX

This looks like a massive difference in distribution: The values of the women in black are on average higher (because that curve is rising further on the right where the high values are) and the values of the men (in grey) are distributed across a wider range of values (because their curve starts way earlier on the left, but ends nearly exactly with that of the women).

Now, step 3, and here we're running into a small (but easily fixable) issue: our data are not actually continuous. They are numeric, but absolute frequencies, meaning they are discrete integers, and in fact multiple values of HEDGES are observed multiple times (the issue of ties again). We'll ignore this for a moment and proceed, but I will show you later a quick and dirty fix. So let's compute the Kolmogorov-Smirnov test with ks.test, which needs as input the two vectors to compare:

```
ks.test(x=x$HEDGES[x$SEX=="female"], y=x$HEDGES[x$SEX=="male"],
    exact=FALSE)
##  Two-sample Kolmogorov-Smirnov test
## data:  x$HEDGES[x$SEX == "female"] and x$HEDGES[x$SEX == "male"]
## D = 0.46667, p-value = 0.002908
## alternative hypothesis: two-sided
```

Obviously, we're getting the warning that at least one, but in fact quite a few, of the frequencies in HEDGES occur multiple times, which means the function doesn't compute an exact p-value. Instead, it produces an approximation – we'll see in a moment how good it likely is. The D-value is quite high and, correspondingly, the *p*-value is quite small, clearly under 0.05. We can therefore summarize as follows: "According to a two-sample Kolmogorov-Smirnov test, there is a significant difference between the distributions of hedge frequencies of women and men: women seem to use more hedges and behave more homogeneously than the men, who use fewer hedges (D=0.4667, p=0.0029)."

Ok, two small things: First, how do we deal with the ties? We can actually just jitter the values (with the eponymous function `jitter`), which means 'adding a bit of random noise to each value' so that, for instance, the four cases of male hedge frequencies of 13 are not the same values anymore. But now you might wonder, but won't that affect the results massively? Well, it will affect them a bit, but `jitter` is smart: it doesn't just add *any* random noise. It first checks for the smallest difference between the values (which here is 1), and then it generates random noise not bigger than 20% of that smallest difference, i.e. here 0.2. That means, as long as the noise is that small, two different values can never exchange ranks because of the jittering.

```
set.seed(sum(utf8ToInt("Schinkenwürfel"))); ks.test(x=jitter(
    x$HEDGES[x$SEX=="female"]), y=jitter(x$HEDGES[x$SEX=="male"]),
    exact=FALSE)
##   Two-sample Kolmogorov-Smirnov test
## D = 0.46667, p-value = 0.002908
## alternative hypothesis: two-sided
```

As you can see, with this random number seed, the result doesn't change at all. But I hope you're still suspicious of this and wonder "what if he had taken a random seed other than *Schinkenwürfel* and/or did more random tests? Maybe he wouldn't be that lucky then!" Glad you're asking; check out the code file for the script returning these results:

```
summary(D.values) # explore the distribution of the D-values
##    Min. 1st Qu. Median    Mean 3rd Qu.    Max.
##  0.4667  0.5000 0.5000  0.4999  0.5000  0.5333
summary(p.values) # explore the distribution of the p-values
##       Min.   1st Qu.    Median      Mean   3rd Qu.      Max.
## 0.0003936 0.0011062 0.0011062 0.0012332 0.0011062 0.0029083
```

Even if we jitter the values 1000 times, we get only get *D*-values that are at least as high as ours, which means we also only get *p*-values at least as significant as ours; our above results/conclusions seem pretty safe; the jittering with *Schinkenwürfel* did not affect the test decision anti-conservatively (that's a technical term: a test (decision) is **anti-conservative** if it is more likely to reject H_0 than it should be).

The final thing I still want to explain is how D is computed. Above I said that this test involves "the maximal absolute difference D of both distributions' ecdf curves". That means that the D-value corresponds to the biggest ever observed height difference between the curve of the women and the curve of the men; in fact, in the plot above, that's what the three arrows are showing; they have lengths of $D=0.4667$. And in a case like this, with discrete values, D is actually 'somewhat easy' to compute 'manually', as I do here. Check out the code (running bigger and bigger parts of it from the inside out so you see how it's working), but if you're new to programming and don't understand it yet, that's ok, too, it's just a little brain teaser but not essential for what follows.

```
max(apply(
   apply(
      prop.table(table(x$HEDGES, x$SEX), 2),
      2,
      cumsum),
   1, diff))
## [1] 0.4666667
```

4.2 Dispersion

Sometimes, it's necessary and/or interesting to not just look at the general characteristics of a distribution but also at more narrowly defined distributional characteristics. The two most obvious characteristics are the central tendency and the dispersion of a distribution. This section is concerned with the dispersion – more specifically, the variance or standard deviation – of a variable; Section 4.3 discusses measures of central tendency.

For some research questions, it's useful to know, for example, whether two distributions have the same or a similar dispersion. Put differently, do two distributions spread around their means in a similar or in a different way? To illustrate the point once more, consider Figure 61, which shows two distributions of each 10 values – 10 in grey, the other 10 in black. Obviously, the two distributions have pretty similar means (indicated by the horizontal lines in the respective colors, and a significance test shows that the means are not significantly different ($p>0.52$), but just as obviously the distributions have very different dispersions around their means, as indicated by the distances of the points from their mean lines (and by p of one test being <0.006).

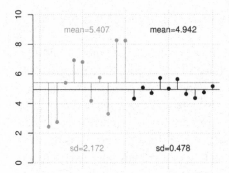

Figure 61: Similar mean, different dispersions

In Section 4.2.1, we discuss how to test whether the dispersion of a numeric response is significantly different from a known dispersion value; in Section 4.2.2, we discuss how to test whether the dispersions of numeric response differs significantly across two groups. (I won't discuss tests for normalized entropies or interquartile ranges, which are too rare to devote space to them.)

4.2.1 Goodness-of-fit test for one numeric response

As an example, let's again consider the already very familiar reaction time data set. Imagine you wanted to determine whether the meaningfulness scores we have are comparable with regard to their dispersion to those collected in other studies; let's assume some bigger norming studies found a variance of such meaningfulness scores of 1970. This question involves the following variable(s) and is investigated with a **one-sample chi-squared test for goodness of fit** (for variances) as described below. We have
– a numeric response MEAN;
– no predictor because you're not testing whether the MEAN is influenced by, or correlated with, something else.

As usual, here is the overall procedure:

Procedure
1. Formulate the hypotheses;
2. describe the data statistically and visually;
3. check/test the assumption(s) of the test: the population from which the sample whose variance is tested has been drawn, or at least the sample itself from which the variance is computed, is normally distributed;
4. compute the test statistic X^2, df, and p.

As usual, we begin with Steps 1 and 2 – hypotheses and descriptive statistics:
- H_0: The variance of MEAN is not different from the variance of the meaningfulness scores in the norming study; variance$_{MEAN}$=variance$_{MEANnormingdata}$=1970, χ^2=0.
- H_1: The variance of MEAN is different from the variance of the meaningfulness scores in the norming study; variance$_{MEAN}\neq$variance$_{MEANnormingdata}$, χ^2>0.

Next, we load the data:

```
rm(list=ls(all.names=TRUE))
summary(x <- read.delim(file="_inputfiles/04_reactiontimes.csv",
   stringsAsFactors=TRUE)) ## [...]
```

Then, we compute the variance of MEAN, and visualize the data (since we have done that already, I am only showing the code as a reminder):

```
(MEAN.var <- var(x$MEAN, na.rm=TRUE)) # the variance
## [1] 1870.021
plot(ecdf(x$MEAN), verticals=TRUE, main=""); grid()
```

Step 3 is testing the assumption of our test: are the values of MEAN normally-distributed? That, too, we have already tested in Section 4.2.1 above (so I'm showing only the *p*-value of the test):

```
nortest::lillie.test(x=x$MEAN)$p.value
## [1] 0.9734608
```

So, yes, we're allowed to proceed with this test. For this test, the chi-squared test statistic is computed as follows:

$$\chi^2 = \frac{(n-1)\times sample\ variance}{reference\ variance}$$

Which is of course very easy in R, but there's one trap you want to avoid: To compute *n*, do not use length because that would also count the NAs, which were not used for the computation of the variance – instead, do it like this, which essentially means 'the number of MEAN values that are not (!) NA':

```
(MEAN.chisq <- ((sum(!is.na(x$MEAN))-1)*MEAN.var) / 1970)
## [1] 44.61471
```

Since this chi-squared values has $df=n-1=47$ degrees of freedom, we can compute the p-value right away:

```
pchisq(q=MEAN.chisq, df=47, lower.tail=FALSE)
## [1] 0.5718904
```

Very clear result, and this is how we could summarize it: "According to a chi-squared test, the variance of the meaningfulness scores in the current sample (1870.021) doesn't differ significantly from the one found in the norming study (1970); $X^2=44.61$, $df=47$, $p=0.572$."

4.2.2 Test for independence for one numeric response and one categorical predictor

The probably more frequent scenario in the already rare domain of 'testing dispersions' is the case where we test whether two samples or two variables exhibit the same dispersion (or at least two dispersions that do not differ significantly). Since the difference or ratio of dispersions or variances is probably not a concept you spent much time thinking about so far, let's look at one more illustrative example, this time a linguistic one from sociophonetics. Gaudio (1994) studied the pitch range of heterosexual and homosexual men. At issue was therefore not the average pitch, but its variability, a good example for how variability as such can be interesting. In that study, four heterosexual and four homosexual men were asked to read aloud two text passages and the resulting recordings were played to 14 subjects who were asked to guess which speakers were heterosexual and which were homosexual. Interestingly, the subjects were able to distinguish the sexual orientation nearly perfectly. The only (insignificant) correlation which suggested itself as a possible explanation was that the homosexual men exhibited a wider pitch range in one of the text types, i.e., a result that has to do with variability/dispersion (of which range is the crudest measure).

We'll now look at an example from second language acquisition. Let's assume we want to study how native speakers of a language and very advanced learners of that language differed in a synonym-finding task in which both native speakers and learners were presented with words for which they were asked to name synonyms. We may now not be interested in the average numbers of synonyms that the learners and the native speakers come up with, but in whether these numbers of synonyms differ in their variability between learners and native speakers. This question involves

– a numeric response SYNONYMS, the numbers of synonyms subjects named;
– a categorical predictor SPEAKERTYPE: *learner* vs. *native*.

This kind of question would typically be investigated with the so-called F-test for homogeneity of variances, which involves the following steps:

Procedure
1. Formulate the hypotheses;
2. describe the data statistically and visually;
3. check/test the assumption(s) of the test:
   a. the population from which the sample whose variance is tested has been drawn or at least the sample itself from which the variance is computed is normally distributed;
   b. the samples are independent of each other;
4. compute the test statistic F, df_1 and df_2, and p.

First, let's formulate the hypotheses:
– H_0: The numbers of synonyms provided by the learners are not differently variable from the numbers of synonyms provided by the native speakers; the variances are the same ($var_{learner}=var_{native}$), i.e. the ratio of the two variances $F=1$.
– H_1: The numbers of synonyms provided by the learners are differently variable from the numbers of synonyms provided by the native speakers; the variances are not the same ($var_{learner}\neq var_{native}$), i.e. the ratio of the variances $F\neq1$.

We load the data from <_inputfiles/04_synonyms.csv>:

```
rm(list=ls(all.names=TRUE))
summary(x <- read.delim(file="_inputfiles/04_synonyms.csv",
   stringsAsFactors=TRUE)) ## [...]
```

Next, we compute the variances we want to compare. I show the 'clumsier' way first but then how one should really do this (based on Section 3.5.3 above):

```
var(x$SYNONYMS[x$SPEAKERTYPE=="learner"]) # or =="native"
tapply(X=x$SYNONYMS, INDEX=x$SPEAKERTYPE, FUN=var)
##   learner    native
## 10.31731 14.15385
```

For visualization, we'll use your new best friend, an ecdf plot (a box plot's resolution seems too crude); I'm only showing the plot here, not the code:

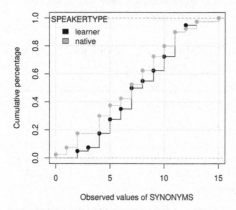

SYNONYMS ~ SPEAKERTYPE

Figure 62: SYNONYMS ~ SPEAKERTYPE

These look very similar ... But let's now test the normality assumption again for each group of SYNONYMS values: Again, I will show you the 'clumsier' way first, which consists of testing normality of the SYNONYMS values separately for each level of SPEAKERTPE:

```
nortest::lillie.test(x$SYNONYMS[x$SPEAKERTYPE=="learner"])
nortest::lillie.test(x$SYNONYMS[x$SPEAKERTYPE=="native"])
```

But here's the better way to do that, which uses tapply:

```
tapply(X=x$SYNONYMS, INDEX=x$SPEAKERTYPE, FUN=function (af)
    nortest::lillie.test(af)$p.value)
##    learner     native
## 0.1488194 0.6180459
```

Excellent: both groups of SYNONYMS values do not differ from normality, which means we can stick with the F-test. Thankfully, the first part of the test is easy: the F value is the ratio of the two variances (I usually recommend putting the smaller variance in the numerator and the larger in the denominator so that the value range of this fraction is (0, 1]):

```
(F.value <- var(x$SYNONYMS[x$SPEAKERTYPE=="learner"]) /
            var(x$SYNONYMS[x$SPEAKERTYPE=="native"]))
## [1] 0.7289402
```

The F-tests needs two degrees of freedom, which are also easy, because they are the two sample sizes each minus 1 (length again assumes no missing data):

```
tapply(X=x$SYNONYMS, INDEX=x$SPEAKERTYPE, FUN=length) - 1
## learner  native
##      39      39
```

But now the computation of the *p*-value is a bit more involved and while I will show you the shortcut in a moment, it's really necessary to understand this logic. Consider the left panel of Figure 63, which shows the *F*-distribution at df_1=39 and df_2=39 degrees of freedom; ignore the grey shading for now. Note that the H_0 expectation of the distribution is at *F*=1 because that's what you get as a ratio when both variances are the same, and the area under the curve on each side of *F*=1 is 0.5. But more importantly, note that the *F*-value can be <1 or >1, which depends on whether the variance in the numerator is smaller or greater than that in the denominator. In that regard, the *F*-distribution is unlike the X^2-distribution discussed in Section 4.1.2.1 but more like the bell-shaped coin-tossing probability bar plots in Section 1.5.1.

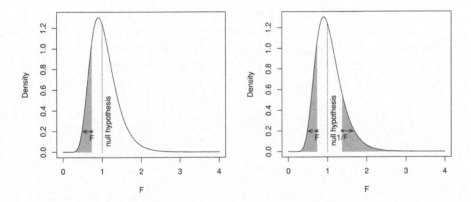

Figure 63: *F*-distribution for both *df*s=39

And I'm telling you this because …? Because the H_1 is non-directional/two-tailed. And recall our discussion of the coin-tossing example, where an observer watched you and me play and added up the heights of bars on both sides/tails of the, there, bell-shaped-distribution. Here, we do the same. The left panel also contains the *F*-value we found (with the ×) and, as discussed above, we go from the × away in the direction further away from H_0 expectation (i.e., following the arrow) and are essentially computing the grey-shaded area under the F-curve that deviates more extremely from the observed result. How big is that area?

```
pf(q=F.value, df1=39, df2=39, lower.tail=TRUE)
## [1] 0.163816
```

This at least allows us to decide already: Even this part of the p-value is already much greater than 0.05 so the variances of the learners and the native speakers do not differ significantly. But of course we continue to compute the full p-value in the right panel. Our hypothesis was two-tailed so, just like the impartial observer above, we now also have to consider the other side/tail of the distribution – what would have happened if the learner variance had been as much larger than the native-speaker variance than it is smaller, i.e. if the result had been the mirror image of the current one? The plot should make that clear and this is code that corresponds to that:

```
pf(q=1/F.value, df1=39, df2=39, lower.tail=FALSE)
## [1] 0.163816
```

The same value and our total p-value is the total of the two: 0.3276319.

Ok, this was long, I know, but a decent understanding of this two-tailed/one-tailed business is simply indispensable. The good news at last is that we now get to the easier part (easier in terms of coding). The function var.test can accept a formula notation and tells us all we now already know, but quicker:

```
var.test(x$SYNONYMS ~ x$SPEAKERTYPE)
## F = 0.72894, num df = 39, denom df = 39, p-value = 0.3276
## alternative hypothesis: true ratio of variances is not equal to 1
## 95 percent confidence interval:
##    0.385536 1.378221
## sample estimates:
## ratio of variances
##           0.7289402
```

(Don't be confused if ever the F-value you get from R isn't the same as the one you computed yourself. Barring mistakes, the value outputted by R is then $1/F$-value – R automatically puts the variance into the numerator whose level name comes first in the alphabet – here that works for us because we put *learner* in the numerator and *learner* precedes *native*.)

We can sum up as follows: "The native speakers' numbers of synonyms exhibit a variance that is approximately 40% larger than that of the learners (14.15 vs. 10.32), but according to an F-test, this difference is not significant: $F=0.73$, $df_{\text{learner}}=39$, $df_{\text{native}}=39$, $p=0.3276$." (Quick reminder: you can see that the difference between the variances is not significant not only from the p-value (0.3276) but also from the fact that the 95%-CI of our F-value includes the H_0-value of 1 ([0.386, 1.378]).)

Let me finally discuss something else here as well, namely how one would have proceeded if we had had a directional H_1, for instance that the learner variance would be less than the native speaker one. In terms of manual analysis, we would have computed F the same way as above, but then only checked the area under the curve for F being in the interval (0, 0.7289402] and would have arrived at the correct solution of 0.163816, fine, no surprises there. But if we want to use the function var.test for a one-tailed test, things can get 'confusing' (because I still can't always remember this, even after 15 or whatever many years of R-ing).

The thing is, there are three different ways in which we can compute the var.test and, for the two-tailed test, they all return the same p-value (though not the same F-values). I'm abbreviating the output here to just the F- and p-values (using [c("statistic", "p.value")]) and unlisting the list resulting from the single-square-bracket subsetting to get a shorter vector:

```
# the one from above: the formula
# F = alphabetically 1st level /2nd level: learner/native
unlist((var.test(x$SYNONYMS ~ x$SPEAKERTYPE)[c("statistic",
   "p.value")]))
## statistic.F     p.value
##   0.7289402   0.3276319
# the separate vectors approach, order 1
# F = 1st vector / 2nd vector: learner/native
unlist(var.test(
   x=x$SYNONYMS[x$SPEAKERTYPE=="learner"],
   y=x$SYNONYMS[x$SPEAKERTYPE=="native"])[c("statistic", "p.value")])
## statistic.F     p.value
##   0.7289402   0.3276319
# the separate vectors approach, order 2
# F = 1st vector / 2nd vector: now native/learner (!)
unlist(var.test(
   x=x$SYNONYMS[x$SPEAKERTYPE=="native"],
   y=x$SYNONYMS[x$SPEAKERTYPE=="learner"])[
c("statistic", "p.value")])
```

```
## statistic.F      p.value
##   1.3718546    0.3276319
```

But to do a one-tailed test, you need to define an argument called `alternative`, whose default setting is two-tailed (which is why we could omit it earlier). For a one-tailed test, you need to say `alternative="less"` or `alternative="greater"` and to make the right choice, you need to try and remember that the `alternative` setting for your H_1 applies,
- in the formula case, to the alphabetically first level of the predictor (i.e., SPEAKERTYPE: *learner*);
- in the two-vectors case, to the first-named/x argument vector.

In our hypothetical scenario, where we're hypothesizing the learner variance to be smaller than the native-speaker variance, that means this is what you'd have to write for each option:

```
unlist(var.test(x$SYNONYMS ~ x$SPEAKERTYPE,
   alternative="less")[c("statistic", "p.value")])
## statistic.F      p.value
##   0.7289402    0.1638160
unlist(var.test(
   x=x$SYNONYMS[x$SPEAKERTYPE=="learner"],
   y=x$SYNONYMS[x$SPEAKERTYPE=="native"],
   alternative="less")[c("statistic", "p.value")])
## statistic.F      p.value
##   0.7289402    0.1638160
unlist(var.test(
   x=x$SYNONYMS[x$SPEAKERTYPE=="native"],
   y=x$SYNONYMS[x$SPEAKERTYPE=="learner"],
   alternative="greater")[c("statistic", "p.value")])
## statistic.F      p.value
##   1.371855    0.163816
```

Just try to remember this (better than I apparently can ...).

Recommendation(s) for further study: Check out `car::leveneTest` for alternatives to the *F*-test (the Brown-Forsythe test and the Levene test) and the package the package `cvequality`, which has functions to test the difference between variation coefficients for significance.

4.2.2.1 A small excursus: simulation

What would we do if the samples had not been normally distributed, so we wouldn't have been able to do the *F*-test? For many years, I didn't know of any alternative test to fall back on (such as the Fligner-Killeen test, see ?fligner.test) so I would have had to do something else and I want to use this scenario to very briefly return to the notion of simulations in hypothesis testing, something we briefly touched upon in the section on confidence intervals. Remember what the *p*-value of a significance test means: it's the probability to find in our sample effect *e* or something that deviates from H_0 even more when, in the population, it is actually H_0 that is true. Well, if we know of no test that can give us a *p*-value, why don't we compute one by generating a H_0 distribution? We could 'just'

- generate a version of our data in which H_0 is true (or extremely likely to be true); in our present case, we could do that by randomly re-ordering either the predictor or the response, which would destroy any potential association of the two and, thus, create H_0 data;
- compute the relevant effect *e* in this H_0 version of the data and collect it somewhere;
- do that many times, say *s* times;
- and then simply count how often in our *s* results from H_0 data we obtained effects that were at least as big as *e* in our actual data: that count divided by *s* is then our *p*-value.

In R and using the logic on CIs (from Section 3.1.4.3) and on for-loops (from Section 3.5.2):

```
set.seed(sum(utf8ToInt("KinderMaxiKing")))
number.of.iterations <- 1397
F.value.collector <- rep(NA, number.of.iterations)
for (i in seq(number.of.iterations)) {
   SPEAKERTYPE.r <- sample(x$SPEAKERTYPE)
   F.value.collector[i] <- var(x$SYNONYMS[SPEAKERTYPE.r=="learner"])
   / var(x$SYNONYMS[SPEAKERTYPE.r=="native"])
}
(sum(F.value.collector<=F.value) + sum(F.value.collector>=1/F.value))
   / number.of.iterations
## [1] 0.241947
quantile(F.value.collector, probs=c(0.025, 0.975))
##      2.5%     97.5%
## 0.5876912 1.6409234
```

Our p-value is 0.241947: If one randomly jumbles the data, thereby destroying whatever relation there might be between the predictor and the response, we get F-values like the one in our actual data or others deviating from H_0 even more nearly 25% of the time. In other words, our F-value of 0.7289402 is pretty likely even with randomized versions of our data: we must stick with H_0.

In sum, sometimes, testing can be done by generating a H_0 distribution many times and then we just determine how many of those many times (in percent) were like or more extreme than the initial result on the actual data, and "generating a H_0 distribution" can be done by, for instance, re-shuffling the predictor. This kind of logic is something you should bear in mind in general, but also especially for variable importance values of random forests in Chapter 7.

4.3 Central tendencies

The probably most frequent use of simple significance tests apart from chi-squared tests are tests of differences between different measures of central tendency – medians and means. In Section 4.3.1, we'll be concerned with goodness-of-fit tests, i.e., scenarios where you test whether an observed measure of central tendency is significantly different from another already known one; in Section 4.3.2, we then turn to tests where measures of central tendencies from two samples are compared to each other (and comparisons of measures of central tendencies from more than two samples will be discussed in Chapter 5); last reminder: make sure you follow up with checking <sflwr3_navigator.png>.

4.3.1 Goodness-of-fit tests

4.3.1.1 One ordinal response

This section deals with a test that has two main applications: Either we have an ordinal variable and want to check its median against the known median of another ordinal variable, or we have a numeric variable and want to check its mean against the known mean of another numeric variable, but the test you want to do for that you're not permitted to do because your data violate the distributional assumptions of that test. We will explore the test of this section by looking at an interesting little morphological phenomenon, namely subtractive word-formation processes in which parts of usually two source words are merged into a new word. Two such processes are blends and complex clippings; some well-known examples of the former are shown in (20a), while (20b) provides a few examples of the latter.

20. a.   *brunch (breakfast × lunch), motel (motor × hotel), smog (smoke × fog), foolosopher (fool × philosopher)*
    b.   *scifi (science × fiction), fedex (federal × express), sysadmin (system × administrator)*

One question that may arise upon looking at these coinages is to what degree the formation of such words is supported by some degree of similarity of the source words. There are many different ways to measure the similarity of words, and the one we're going to use here is an extremely basic one, the so-called Dice coefficient (see Brew & McKelvie 1996 and Gries 2006 for using it on blends). You can compute a Dice coefficient for two words in two simple steps. First, you split the words up into letter (or phoneme or …) bigrams. For *motel*, you get:
– *motor*: *mo, ot, to, or*;
– *hotel*: *ho, ot, te, el.*

Then you count how many of the bigrams of each word occur in the other word, too. In this case, these are two (tokens): *ot* one time in *motor* and one time in *hotel*. This number, 2, is divided by the number of bigrams (8) to yield the Dice coefficient of $^2/_8$=0.25.[8] In other words, the Dice coefficient is the percentage of shared bigrams out of all bigrams (and hence numeric).

We will now investigate the question of whether source words that entered into subtractive word-formation processes are more similar to each other than words in general are similar to each other. Let's assume you know that the mean Dice coefficient of randomly chosen words is 0.225 (with a standard deviation of 0.0809) while the median is 0.151 (with an interquartile range of 0.125). These figures already suggest that the data may not be normally distributed.

This study involves
– a numeric response DICE, i.e. the Dice coefficients, which will be compared with the already known mean/median;
– no predictor since you do not test whether the Dice values are influenced by something else.

The hypotheses should be straightforward:
– H_0: The mean of DICE for the source words that entered into subtractive word-formation processes is not different from the known mean of randomly chosen word pairs; mean$_{DICE\ sourcewords}$=0.225, or mean$_{DICE\ sourcewords}$-0.225=0;

---

[8] Another shameless plug here (one has to make a living, you know?): If you want to learn how to do this kind of corpus/text processing with R, see Gries (2016).

– H_1: The mean of DICE for the source words that entered into subtractive word-formation processes is different from the known mean of randomly chosen word pairs; $mean_{DICE\ sourcewords} \neq 0.225$ or $mean_{DICE\ sourcewords}\text{-}0.225 \neq 0$.

Let's load the data:

```
rm(list=ls(all.names=TRUE))
summary(x <- read.delim(file="_inputfiles/04_dices1.csv",
   stringsAsFactors=TRUE)) ## [...]
```

The one-sample *t*-test that one would normally want to use here requires that the data are normally distributed so let's do some quick visualization:

```
par(mfrow=c(1, 2))
hist(x$DICE, main="")
plot(ecdf(x$DICE), verticals=TRUE, main="")
par(mfrow=c(1, 1))
```

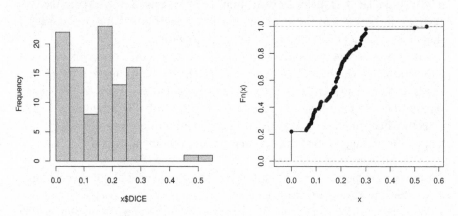

Figure 64: Descriptive plots for DICE

That doesn't look normal at all ... The Lilliefors test confirms that impression:

```
nortest::lillie.test(x=x$DICE)$p.value
## [1] 0.0003733424
```

Thus, we won't proceed with a test that assumes normality (even though DICE is numeric and we have more than 30 data points, we're being careful). Instead, we will use two other tests, which don't treat the data as having a numeric information value. The first of these tests is the **one-sample sign test**, which involves these steps:

Procedure
1. Formulate the hypotheses;
2. compute the frequencies of the signs of the differences between the observed values and the expected average;
3. compute the probability of error p.

We first rephrase the hypotheses to adjust them to the lower information value; I only provide new statistical ones:
- H_0: median$_{\text{DICE sourcewords}}$=0.151;
- H_1: median$_{\text{DICE sourcewords}}$≠0.151.

Then, we quickly re-compute the median (we had that in summary(x)) and its interquartile range. Obviously, the observed median Dice coefficient is a bit higher than 0.151, the median Dice-values of the random words, but it is impossible to guess whether the difference is going to be significant.

```
c("median"=median(x$DICE), "IQR"=IQR(x$DICE))
## median     IQR
## 0.16350 0.14425
```

For the one-sample sign test, we first determine how many of our observations are above and below the expected median. If the expected median of 0.151 was a good characterization of our own data, then 50% of our data should be above it and 50% should be below it. (Note that this means that the exact sizes of the deviations from the expected median are not considered here – we're only looking at whether the observed values are larger or smaller than the expected median, but not how much larger or smaller; we're incurring some of the kind of information loss that I warned you about at the end of Section 1.3) We do that by applying the function sign to the difference of each DICE value and 0.151:

```
table(sign(x$DICE-0.151))
## -1  1
## 46 54
```

46 of the 100 observed values are smaller than the expected median (the remaining 54 are greater than the expected median) – since you expected 50:50, it seems as if the Dice coefficients observed in our source words are larger than those of randomly-chosen words but maybe not enough for a significant result. (I hope by now this again reminds you of the coin-tossing example from Section 1.5.2; If you remembered that really well, you'd even know the outcome of this test here already ...) Thus, let's approach this graphically, using the logic from Section 1.5.2, Figure 8. Figure 65 shows the probabilities of all possible results you can get in 100 trials (because you look at the Dice coefficients of 100 subtractive formations). First, consider the left panel of Figure 65.

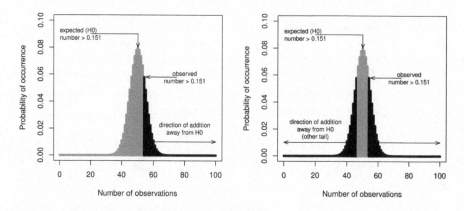

Figure 65: Binomial distribution for trials=100 and $p=0.5$

According to H_0, we expect 50 Dice coefficients to be larger than the expected median, but we found 54. Thus, we add the probability of the observed result (the black bar for 54 out of 100) to the probabilities of all those that deviate from H0 even more extremely, i.e., the chances to find 55, 56, ..., 99, 100 Dice coefficients out of 100 that are larger than the expected median; all those bars are also shown in black. These probabilities from the left panel sum up to ≈0.242:

```
sum(dbinom(x=54:100, size=100, prob=0.5))
## [1] 0.2420592
```

(This is how I computed the probabilities of coin tosses in Section 1.5, try it: sum(dbinom(2:3, 3, 0.5)) or sum(dbinom(c(0:39, 61:100), 100, 0.5)).)

While this already shows that you cannot possibly reach a significant result – this is already much greater than 0.05 – we're not finished yet ... As you can see in the left panel of Figure 65, so far we only included the deviations from H_0 in one direction – but our H_1 is non-directional, i.e., two-tailed. We must therefore also include the probabilities of the events that deviate just as much and more from H_0 in the other direction: 46, 45, ..., 1, 0 Dice coefficients out of 100 that are smaller than the expected median, as now also represented in the right panel of Figure 65. The probabilities sum up to the same value (because the distribution of binomial probabilities around $p=0.5$ is symmetric).

```
sum(dbinom(x=0:46, size=100, prob=0.5))
## [1] 0.2420592
```

The two-tailed p-value of 0.4841184 we arrive at isn't significant, because it's much greater than 0.05. We can sum up: "The investigation of 100 subtractive word formations resulted in an average source-word similarity of 0.1635 (median, IQR=0.144). According to a two-tailed one-sample sign test, that value isn't significantly different from the average similarity of random word pairs (median=0.151, IQR range=0.125): $p_{binomial}=0.484$."

Recall that this one-sample sign test only uses categorical information, i.e. whether each data point is larger or smaller than the expected reference median (but not how much). If the distribution of the data is rather symmetrical, then there's a better alternative test, one that also takes the sizes of the deviations into account, i.e. uses at least ordinal information. This so-called **one-sample signed-rank test** can be computed using the function wilcox.test like so:

```
wilcox.test(x=x$DICE, mu=0.151, correct=FALSE)
##   Wilcoxon signed rank test
## V = 2243, p-value = 0.3316
## alternative hypothesis: true location is not equal to 0.151
```

The test confirms the previous result: Both the one-sample sign test, which is only concerned with the directions of deviations, and the one-sample signed rank test, which also considers the sizes of these deviations, return a non-significant result; you would report this as above and just replace the $p_{binomial}$ with V and p.

4.3.1.2 One numeric response

Let's assume we're again interested in the use of hedges. Many studies suggest that men and women exhibit different communicative styles with regard to the frequency of hedges (and otherwise). In the data you explored in Section 4.1.2.2

with regard to distributions, you found an overall average hedge frequency of 12.35 hedges per person. You decided to add to the data and made 30 new two-minute recordings under the same conditions etc., but you couldn't use the same confederate as before. You now want to know whether the average number of hedges in your new recordings is significantly different from the value of 12.35 you found in your first round of data collection. This question involves
- a numeric response HEDGES, which will be compared to the value from the prior study;
- no predictor since you do not test whether HEDGES is influenced by something else.

For such cases, we might be able to use a one-sample t-test, which involves these steps:

Procedure
1. Formulate the hypotheses;
2. describe the data statistically and visually;
3. check/test the assumption(s) of the test: the population from which the sample whose mean is tested has been drawn or at least the sample itself from which the mean is computed is normally distributed;
4. compute the test statistic t, df, and p.

Step 1 is as always, the hypotheses:
- H_0: The average of HEDGES in the new recordings does not differ from the average of the previous recordings (12.35); $t=0$;
- H_1: The average of HEDGES in the new recordings differs from the average of the previous recordings; $t \neq 0$.

Step 2: we load the data:

```
rm(list=ls(all.names=TRUE))
summary(x <- read.delim(file="_inputfiles/04_hedges2.csv",
    stringsAsFactors=TRUE)); sd(x$HEDGES) ## [...]
```

The mean of this data is 14.33, i.e. higher than 12, but of course that doesn't yet mean it's significantly higher. Let's visualize to get an idea of the distribution:

```
par(mfrow=c(1, 2))
hist(x$HEDGES, main="")
plot(ecdf(x$HEDGES), verticals=TRUE, main=""); grid()
par(mfrow=c(1, 1))
```

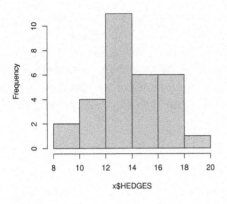 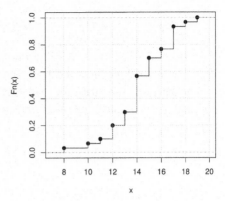

Figure 66: Descriptive plots for HEDGES

This looks really pretty normal, but of course we check for the record:

```
nortest::lillie.test(x$HEDGES)$p.value
## [1] 0.108652
```

Ok, we can proceed with the one-sample *t*-test. For this test, *t* is computed as follows, whose numerator also explains why the statistical H_0 is that *t*=0:

$$t = \frac{mean_{sample} - mean_{reference}}{se_{sample}}$$

```
(t.value ← (mean(x$HEDGES)-12.35)          / # numerator
   (sd(x$HEDGES)/sqrt(length(x$HEDGES))))   # denominator
## [1] 4.477968
```

To see what this value means, we need degrees of freedom again and, again, this is easy here: *df*=*n*-1=29. But let's now discuss the computation of the *p*-value again. We saw above in Section 4.1.2.1 that the X^2-distribution had only one tail (we could only have positive values), and we saw above in Section 4.2.2 that the F-distribution had two tails (from the H_0-value of 1, we could get *F*-values<1 and *F*-values>1). As you might guess from how the numerator of the *t*-value is computed, the *t*-distribution will be like the *F*-distribution with regard to the number of tails because, depending on the data, the numerator can be positive or negative. However, its peak is at 0 because that's the *t*-value corresponding to H_0: When both means are the same, their difference in the numerator of the *t*-value will be 0, as will be *t* itself. That, together with the fact that we again have a two-tailed H₁, means we proceed like with the *F*-test in terms of looking at two tails.

Figure 67 shows the *t*-distribution for *df*=29 with (i) the observed *t*-value of 4.477968 marked on the right, from which we would have to go to the more extreme right, and the other-tail *t*-value on the left, from which we would have to go to the more extreme left, each time adding up the, here obviously minuscule, area under the curve.

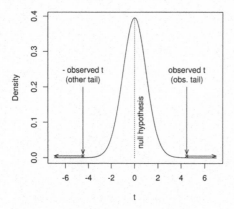

Figure 67: *t*-distribution for *df*=29

As you can kind of guess from the flatness of the curve when |*t*|>4.478, the sum of those two areas under the curve will be <0.05.

```
pt(q=-4.477968, df=29, lower.tail=TRUE) +
pt(q=+4.477968, df=29, lower.tail=FALSE)
## [1] 0.0001079073
```

And indeed, *p* is tiny, meaning we can reject H₀ and accept H₁. We sum up: "On average, the new recordings exhibit an average hedge frequency of 14.33 hedges (*sd*=2.43). According to a one-sample *t*-test, this average is highly significantly larger than the average from the first round of data collection value (which was 12.35): *t*=4.478, *df*=29, *p*≈0.0001."

With the right function, we can do this much quicker. We get the same results as before plus now also our mean's 95%-CI, which doesn't include 12.35 – hence the significant result.

```
t.test(x=x$HEDGES, mu=12.35)
```

```
##  One Sample t-test
## t = 4.478, df = 29, p-value = 0.0001079
## alternative hypothesis: true mean is not equal to 12.35
## 95 percent confidence interval:
##   13.42748 15.23918
## sample estimates:
## mean of x
##   14.33333
```

4.3.2 Tests for differences/independence

A particularly frequent scenario involves testing two groups of values with re-gard to whether they differ in their central tendency. As discussed above, there are several factors that determine which test to choose:
– the kind of samples: dependent or independent (see Section 1.5.1 and the be-ginning of Chapter 4);
– the information value of the response: ordinal vs. numeric;
– to some extent, the distribution of numeric responses: normal vs. non-normal;
– to some extent, the sample sizes.

If the response is numeric and normally-distributed or if both sample sizes are larger than 30 or if the differences between variables are normally distributed, then you can usually do a t-test (for independent or dependent samples, as re-quired) – otherwise, you should do a U-test (for independent samples) or a Wilcoxon test (for dependent samples) (or, maybe, computationally more de-manding exact or simulation-based tests). The reason for this decision proce-dure is that while the t-test for independent samples requires, among other things, normally distributed samples, we have seen that samples of 30+ ele-ments can be normally distributed even if the underlying distribution is not, but if you have doubts regarding the required distributional behavior of a variable, it's usually safer to not go with a parametric test. Strictly speaking, the t-test for independent samples also requires homogeneous variances, which we will also test for, but the version of the t-test we'll discuss (the t-test after Welch) can han-dle heterogeneous variances fairly well.

4.3.2.1 One ordinal response and one categorical predictor (indep. samples)
In this section, we discuss a non-parametric test for two independent samples of ordinal data, the U-test. Since I just mentioned that the U-test is not only used

when the samples to be compared consist of ordinal data, but also when they involve numeric data that violate the *t*-test's distributional assumptions, this section will involve such an example, a case where only a test of these distributional assumptions allows you to decide which test to use.

In Section 4.3.1.1 above, we looked at the similarities of source words entering into subtractive word formations and you tested whether these similarities were on average different from the known average similarity of random words to each other. However, in the above example no distinction was made between source words entering into different kinds of subtractive word formations. This is what we will do here by comparing similarities of source words entering into blends to similarities of source words entering into complex clippings. If both kinds of word-formation processes differed according to this parameter, this might be considered empirical motivation for distinguishing them in the first place. This example, thus, involves
- one numeric response DICE, the similarity of the source words whose averages you are interested in;
- one categorical predictor PROCESS: *blend* vs. *compclip*;
- independent samples since the Dice coefficient of any one pair of source words entering into a subtractive word formation has nothing to do with any one other pair of source words.

This kind of question would typically be investigated with the *t*-test for independent samples. However, that test requires normality of each of the two samples and given the non-normal shape of the Dice-values in the sample as a whole, we might be suspicious about them being normally distributed in each sample – but of course we'll check that. We load the data from a file that contains the Dice coefficients, but now also the word formation process for each Dice coefficient in an additional column.

```
rm(list=ls(all.names=TRUE))
summary(x <- read.delim(file="_inputfiles/04_dices2.csv",
    stringsAsFactors=TRUE)) ## [...]
```

Let's check for normality:

```
par(mfrow=c(1, 2))
tapply(X=x$DICE, INDEX=x$PROCESS, FUN=function (af)
    hist(af, main=nortest::lillie.test(af)$p.value))
## [...]
```

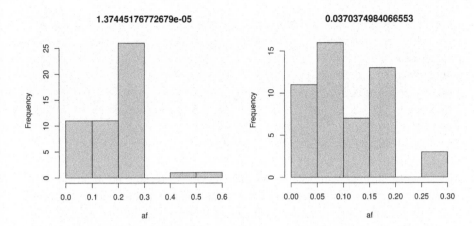

Figure 68: Descriptive plots for DICE by PROCESS

Both the plots and the tests make us decide to not go with a *t*-test and use a *U*-test instead. These are its steps:

Procedure
1.   Formulate the hypotheses;
2.   describe the data statistically and visually;
3.   check/test the assumption(s) of the test:
     a.   the samples are independent of each other;
     b.   the populations from which the samples whose central tendencies are tested have
          been drawn are identically distributed;
4.   compute the test statistic *W*, *z*, and *p*.

The hypotheses are straightforward:[9]
- H_0: The median of the Dice coefficients of the source words of blends is the same as the median of the Dice coefficients of the source words of complex clippings; their difference is 0, $W=0$.
- H_1: The median of the Dice coefficients of the source words of blends is not the same as the median of the Dice coefficients of the source words of complex clippings; their difference is $\neq 0$, $W>0$.

Step 2: we compute descriptive statistics. Instead of doing two separate applications of tapply, let's do this a bit more efficiently:

---

9 According to Bortz, Lienert, & Boehnke (2008:211-212), however, the *U*-test discovers differences of measures of central tendency fairly well even if the assumption in step 4b is violated.

```
tapply(X=x$DICE, INDEX=x$PROCESS, FUN=function (af) {
  c("median"=median(af), "IQR"=IQR(af)) })
## $blend
## median    IQR
##  0.204  0.096
## $complclip
## median    IQR
##  0.094  0.102
```

(We're not plotting again because we did that when checking normality.) Unfortunately, computing the U-test manually is annoyingly cumbersome (that's often the case for non-parametric tests, esp. when there are ties and no available approximations), which is why 'you're lucky' and we'll only discuss doing it with R's function wilcox.test. However, remember we have a directional hypothesis, which means, just like with the F-test above, you need to define an argument called alternative and you need to remember that the alternative setting for your H_1 applies (i) to the alphabetically first level of the predictor (blend) or the first-named/x argument: (I show only one result.)

```
# the formula approach
wilcox.test(x$DICE ~ x$PROCESS, alternative="greater", correct=FALSE)
##   Wilcoxon rank sum test
## W = 1855, p-value = 1.374e-05
## alternative hypothesis: true location shift is greater than 0
# the separate vectors approach, order 1 (x>y)
wilcox.test(alternative="greater", correct=FALSE,
  x=x$DICE[x$PROCESS=="blend"],
  y=x$DICE[x$PROCESS=="complclip"])
# the separate vectors approach, order 2 (x<y)
wilcox.test(alternative="less", correct=FALSE,
  x=x$DICE[x$PROCESS=="complclip"],
  y=x$DICE[x$PROCESS=="blend"])
```

We can now sum up: "According to a one-tailed U-test, the median Dice coefficient of the source words of blends (0.204, IQR=0.096) is highly significantly greater than the median of the Dice coefficients for complex clippings (0.094, IQR=0.102): W=1855 [or W=645, whichever you got], $p<0.0001$."

4.3.2.2 One ordinal response and one categorical predictor (dep. samples)

Just like the *U*-test, the test in this section has two major applications: You really may have two dependent samples of ordinal data (e.g. when you have a group of subjects perform two rating tasks to test whether each subject's first rating differs from the second), or, the probably more frequent application, you have two dependent samples of numeric data but cannot do the *t*-test for dependent samples because its distributional assumptions are not met. We'll discuss an example of the latter kind.

In a replication of Bencini & Goldberg's (2000) study of native speakers of English, Gries & Wulff (2005) studied the question whether German foreign language learners of English rely more on verbs or on sentence structures when they categorize sentences in terms of 'their overall similarity'. They crossed four syntactic constructions and four verbs to get 16 sentences, each verb in each construction. Each sentence was printed onto a card and 20 advanced German learners of English were given the cards and asked to sort them into four piles of four cards each. The question was whether the subjects' sortings would be (more) based on the verbs or on the constructions. To determine the sorting preferences, each subject's four stacks were inspected with regard to how many cards one would minimally have to move to create either four completely verb-based or four completely construction-based sortings. The investigation of this question involves

- one numeric response SHIFTS, the number of times a card had to be shifted from one stack to another to create the perfectly clean sortings, and we're interested in the averages of these numbers;
- one categorical response CRITERION: *construction* vs. *verb*;
- dependent samples, since each of the 20 subjects (called *S01*, to *S20*) comes with two numbers of shifts: one to create the verb-based sorting, one to create the construction-based sorting. Phrased the other way round: each of the numbers of card movements to get to a perfectly verb-based sorting has a corresponding number to get to a perfectly construction-based sorting.

To test such a result for significance, one should first consider a *t*-test for dependent samples since you have two samples of numeric values, Let's load the data that Gries & Wulff (2005) obtained in their experiment:

```
rm(list=ls(all.names=TRUE))
summary(x <- read.delim(file="_inputfiles/04_sortingstyles.csv",
    stringsAsFactors=TRUE)) ## [...]
```

The *t*-test for dependent samples that one would normally compute here requires that the pairwise differences between two SHIFT values per subject are normally distributed.

```
shift.diffs <- x$SHIFTS[x$CRITERION=="construction"] -
               x$SHIFTS[x$CRITERION=="verb"]
```

By the way ... Very important: note that the above only works like that because the input data are 'well-behaved': they are already sorted by x$CRITERION and then by x$SUBJECT – if this wasn't the case, you would of course compute the wrong pairwise differences! Can you figure out how to create that ordering (in R, obviously) if the data frame's rows weren't already ordered the right way?

```
x <- x[order(x$CRITERION, x$SUBJECT),]
```

Ok, back to checking shifts.diffs for normality:

```
hist(shift.diffs, main=nortest::lillie.test(x=shift.diffs)$p.value)
```

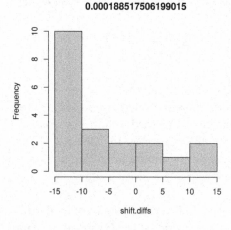

Figure 69: A histogram of shift.diffs

Maybe, just maybe, it's better to consider this ever so slightly non-normal, which means we don't do a *t*-test for dependent samples but a Wilcoxon-test, the equivalent to the *U*-test, but for dependent samples.

Procedure
1. Formulate the hypotheses;
2. describe the data statistically and visually;
3. check/test the assumption(s) of the test:
   a. the pairs of values are independent of each other;
   b. the differences of the pairwise values are symmetrically distributed (Bortz, Lienert, & Boehnke 2008:265, Zar 2011:184);
4. compute the test statistic T and p.

Step 1, the hypotheses: Given that Bencini & Goldberg found evidence for a construction-based sorting style, we might argue that, for the advanced learners of English we're looking at here, we might expect the same; thus, we formulate a directional/one-tailed hypothesis:
- H_0: median of the pairwise differences=0, $V=0$;
- H_1: median of the pairwise differences (computed as $\text{shifts}_{\text{towardsconstruction}}$ - $\text{shifts}_{\text{towardsverb}}$)<0, $V>0$.

Step 2, descriptive statistics:

```
tapply(X=x$SHIFTS, INDEX=x$CRITERION, FUN=function (af) {
    c("median"=median(af), "IQR"=IQR(af)) })
## $construction
## median    IQR
##   1.00   6.25
## $verb
## median    IQR
##  11.00   6.25
```

We see a big difference: On average, only 1 card needed be moved to get a perfect construction-based sorting, but 10 more, i.e. 11 altogether, cards had to be moved to get a verb-based sorting, which means the sorting styles exhibited by the subjects' stacks are much more similar to construction-based sorting. But the sample sizes are small – just 20 each – is that enough for significance?

The first assumption appears to be met because the pairs of values are independent of each other (since the sorting of any one subject, which gives rise to both SHIFTS-values, doesn't affect any other subject's sorting). The second assumption, not so much: The differences are highly asymmetric, as we saw in the histogram. That means, the Wilcoxon test is still a much better choice than the t-test for dependent samples, but still sub-optimal – I'll discuss the Wilcoxon test but, to be on the safe side, then also the paired version of the one-sample sign test (from Section 4.3.1.1) and a simulation-based test (as in Section 4.2.2.1).

As for the Wilcoxon test, just like with the *U*-test, we'll only discuss the direct R version:

```
wilcox.test(x$SHIFTS ~ x$CRITERION, alternative="less",
   paired=TRUE, exact=FALSE, correct=FALSE)
##  Wilcoxon signed rank test
## V = 36.5, p-value = 0.007634
## alternative hypothesis: true location shift is less than 0
```

To sum up: "On the whole, the 20 subjects exhibited a strong preference for a construction-based sorting style: The median number of card shifts to arrive at a perfectly construction-based sorting was 1 while the median number of card rearrangements to arrive at a perfectly verb-based sorting was 11 (both IQRs=6.25). According to a one-tailed Wilcoxon test, this difference is significant: V=36.5, p=0.0153." (As a side remark, that's actually really close to the p-value returned by the *t*-test for dependent samples, which is 0.0099306)

Now what about the paired version of the sign test? The H_0 expectation is that positive and negative values of shift.diffs would be symmetrical around 0. The histogram already showed that that's obviously not the case (which is why we didn't go with the *t*-test for dependent samples in the first place), and we can quantify this straightforwardly as well:

```
table(sign(shift.diffs))
## -1  0  1
## 14  1  5
```

Given that shift.diffs was computed as shifts$_{towardsconstruction}$ - shifts$_{towardsverb}$ and given our H_1 expectation of mostly negative values, this looks encouraging. But how likely is it to get 14 (or more) negative values of altogether 19 non-zero values? (You should again be thinking back to the coin tossing example.)

```
sum(dbinom(x=14:19, size=19, prob=0.5))
## [1] 0.03178406
```

The paired version of the sign test also says the difference is significant.

Finally, what about the simulation approach: We follow the same logic as in Section 4.2.2.1: We

– generate a version of our data in which H_0 is true (or extremely likely to be true); in our present case, we'll again do that by randomly re-ordering the predictor x$CRITERION, which would destroy its current association to x$SHIFTS;

- compute the relevant effect *e* the difference between the two medians (1 and 11) in this H_0 version of the data and collect it somewh*ere*;
- do that many times, say *s* times;
- and then simply count how often in our *s* results we obtained an effect that was at least as big as *e* in our actual data: that count divided by *s* is then *p*.

```
set.seed(sum(utf8ToInt("DönerKebap")))
number.of.iterations <- 1122
median.diff.collector <- rep(NA, number.of.iterations)
for (i in seq(number.of.iterations)) {
   CRITERION.r <- sample(x$CRITERION)
   median.diff.collector[i] <- diff(
      tapply(X=x$SHIFTS, INDEX=CRITERION.r, FUN=median))
} # end of for
(sum(median.diff.collector>= 10) + sum(median.diff.collector<=-10)) /
   number.of.iterations
## [1] 0.003565062
```

All results converge: the difference between the construction- and verb-based shift numbers is significant. I know all this testing seems excessive to some (and in bootcamps I am usually offering a very acerbic defense of this 'excess') but here in print it may suffice to say that it's better that you do all the tests that a reviewer might come up with or, even worse, that a reader comes up with after your paper was printed to demonstrate that you overlooked something, don't you agree? Some of the most blood-pressure-raising reviews I've received ultimately made the paper better because they forced me to do (more) things to make sure my/our results were not a fluke or due to mistakes in my/our analysis.

4.3.2.3 One numeric response and one categorical predictor (indep. samples)

This section deals with one of the most widely-used classical tests, the *t*-test for independent samples. To get to know it, we'll use an example from the domain of phonetics. Let's assume we wanted to study a pretty exciting directional H_1 that I developed the other day, that the first formants' frequencies of men are lower than those of women. We plan an experiment in which we record men's and women's pronunciation of a relevant set of stimuli, which we then analyze. This study involves

- one numeric response, namely F1FORMANT, whose averages we're interested in;
- one categorical predictor SEX: *female* vs. *male*;

– independent samples since, if every subject provides just one data point (and we pretend they do so for all different words), the data points are not related to each other.

The procedure for the *t*-test for independent samples involves these steps:

Procedure
1. Formulate the hypotheses;
2. describe the data statistically and visually;
3. check/test the assumption(s) of the test:
    a. the samples are independent of each other;
    b. the population from which the samples whose means are tested have been drawn or at least the samples itself from which the means are computed are normally distributed (esp. with samples of $n<30$);
    c. the variances of the populations from which the samples have been drawn or at least the variances of the samples are homogeneous;
4. compute the test statistic *t*, *df*, and *p*.

Step 1, we begin with the hypotheses and, given the precision and insightfulness of my observations from which I derived my exciting hypotheses, are bold enough to formulate a directional/one-tailed H_1:

– H_0: The average F1 frequency of women is the same as the average F1 frequency of men: $mean_{female}-mean_{male}=0$ or $t=0$;
– H_1: The average F1 frequency of women is higher than the average F1 frequency of men: $mean_{female}-mean_{male}>0$ or $t>0$.

The data we will investigate here are part of the data borrowed from a similar experiment on vowels in Apache; let's load them.

```
rm(list=ls(all.names=TRUE))
summary(x <- read.delim(file="_inputfiles/04_f1freqs.csv",
    stringsAsFactors=TRUE)) # […]
```

Step 2: some simple descriptive statistics, nothing new here:

```
tapply(X=x$F1FORMANT, INDEX=x$SEX, FUN=function (af) {
    c("mean"=mean(af), "var"=var(af), "sd"=sd(af)) })
## $female
##       mean        var         sd
##   528.8548 12276.8583   110.8010
## $male
##       mean        var         sd
```

```
##   484.27400 7726.60618    87.90112
```

It looks like we might find the expected difference, but the variances look quite different so assumption 3c might be violated. Let's now check all assumptions. With regard to step 3a, we will assume that each subject provided only one data point and each did so for a different word; with that, the data points can be considered independent. step 3b is next, for which I only show the plot:

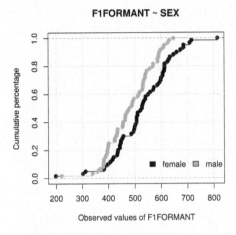

F1FORMANT ~ SEX

Figure 70: Ecdfs of F1FORMANT by SEX

Not the best S-shaped curves ever, but not too bad, and the two Lilliefors tests are fine: normality is ok. Not only is that good for our intention of doing the t-test for independent samples, it's also good because the test we might want to use to test for variance homogeneity before our planned t-test, the F-test, also requires normality. So, let's finally do Step 3c:

```
var.test(x$F1FORMANT ~ x$SEX)
## [...]
## F = 1.5889, num df = 59, denom df = 59, p-value = 0.07789
## ratio of variances
##              1.588907
```

This is more of a borderline case: Even though the variance for the female speakers is nearly 60% higher than that of the male speakers, the difference is just about not significant. Since we'll compute a version of the t-test that is known to be robust to differences in the variances (the t-test after Welch), we will accept the result of the *F*-test and go with our *t*-test, in which *t* is computed as follows (where subscripts 1 and 2 refer to the two levels of the predictor):

$$t = \frac{mean_1 - mean_2}{(\frac{var_1}{n_1} + \frac{var_2}{n_2})^{0.5}}$$

In R:

```
# preparation for computation of t & df
means <-      tapply(x$F1FORMANT, x$SEX, mean)
variances <- tapply(x$F1FORMANT, x$SEX, var)
lengths <-    tapply(x$F1FORMANT, x$SEX, length)

t.numerator <- means["female"]-means["male"]
t.denominator <- sum(variances["female"]/lengths["female"],
                    variances["male"]  /lengths["male"]  )^0.5
(t.value <- t.numerator / t.denominator)
##    female
## 2.441581
```

After that, Welch's *t*-test's *df*-value is computed in two steps like this: First, we compute a *c*-value like this:

$$c = \frac{var_1 \div n_1}{\frac{var_1}{n_1} + \frac{var_2}{n_2}}$$

```
c.numerator <- variances["female"]/lengths["female"]
c.denominator <- t.denominator^2 # !
(c.value <- c.numerator / c.denominator)
##      female
## 0.6137366
```

Then, sigh, that *c*-value is used to compute *df*:

$$df = (\frac{c^2}{n_1 - 1} + \frac{1 - c^2}{n_2 - 1})^{-1}$$

```
(df.value <- sum((c.value^2) / (lengths["female"]-1),
               ((1-c.value)^2) / (lengths["male"] -1))^-1)
## [1] 112.1946
```

Ok, after all this torture, we have t=2.4416 and df=112.1946 and can finally get a p-value from all this. Consider Figure 71, which shows the t-distribution at df=112.1946 with, as before, two tails and a peak at t=0 (the t-value corresponding to H_0). And, just like before, the t-value can be greater than 0 or less than 0; after all, that only depends on which value you subtract from which.

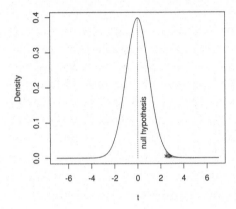

Figure 71: t-distribution for df=112.1946

In our case, we subtracted mean$_{male}$ from mean$_{female}$ and expected a positive result in our directional/one-tailed H_1. We did get that positive result, so we go from the H_0 middle to our positive t-value (again indicated with an "×") and then sum up the grey area under the curve from there to all the more extreme results on the right – but because it's a directional/one-tailed test, we this time do not also do that on the other/left tail as well.

```
pt(q=t.value, df=df.value, lower.tail=FALSE)
##       female
## 0.008092672
```

Ok, it's significant, as one might have imagined from the very small part under the curve that was grey. And now, finally, what you've all been waiting for, the short and sweet way to do it with one function:

```
t.test(x$F1FORMANT ~ x$SEX, alternative="greater")
##   Welch Two Sample t-test
## data:  x$F1FORMANT by x$SEX
## t = 2.4416, df = 112.19, p-value = 0.008093
```

```
## alternative hypothesis: true difference in means is greater than 0
## 95 percent confidence interval:
##   14.29739        Inf
## sample estimates:
## mean in group female   mean in group male
##             528.8548            484.2740
```

We can sum up our spectacular results as follows: "In the experiment, the average F1 frequency of the vowels produced by the female speakers was 528.9 Hz (sd=110.8), the average F1 frequency of the vowels produced by the male speakers was 484.3 Hz (sd=87.9). According to a one-tailed t-test for independent samples, the difference of 44.6 Hz between the means is statistically significant: t_{Welch}=2.4416, df=112.19, $p_{1\text{-tailed}}$=0.0081." (Again, do not be confused by the difference in signs between the t-value we computed and the one from t.test, this is again just due to the direction of subtraction in t's numerator.)

4.3.2.4 One numeric response and one categorical predictor (dep. samples)

For the test in this section, let's assume we want to compare if/how professional translators' performance differs when they translate into their dominant language (presumably their L1) from when they translate into their non-dominant language, because we might hypothesize that translation into the dominant language (so-called direct translation) is faster/more efficient than translation into the non-dominant language (so-called inverse translation). One possibility to measure 'efficiency' is the number of saccades translators exhibit in translating comparable texts in both directions: faster/more efficient translating could be associated with smaller numbers of saccades. This question involves
– one numeric response SACCADES, namely the number of saccades counted for each translation;
– one categorical predictor TASK, namely *direct* (when the translator translated into their dominant language) vs. *inverse* (when not);
– dependent samples since the each translator provides two values, which are therefore related.

The go-to test for such a scenario is the t-test for dependent samples, which requires the following steps:

Procedure
1. Formulate the hypotheses;
2. describe the data statistically and visually;
3. check/test the assumption(s) of the test: the differences of the paired values of the dependent samples are normally distributed;
4. compute the test statistic t, df, and p.

As usual, we formulate the hypotheses and our H_1 now is directional: We suspect that there will be a lower average of saccade values when TASK is *direct*:

- H_0: The average number of saccades does not differ depending on the direction of translation; $mean_{direct} - mean_{inverse}=0$, $t=0$;
- H_1: The average number of saccades differs depending on the direction of translation such that $mean_{direct} - mean_{inverse}<0$, $t<0$.

```
rm(list=ls(all.names=TRUE))
summary(x <- read.delim(file="_inputfiles/04_saccades.csv",
   stringsAsFactors=TRUE)) ## [...]
```

Step 2: We compute the pairwise differences between translation tasks for each translator and summarize them, plus we compute the descriptive statistics for all saccade values per level of TASK:

```
c(summary(sacc.diffs <- x$SACCADES[x$TASK=="direct"] -
   x$SACCADES[x$TASK=="inverse"]), "sd"=sd(sacc.diffs))
      Min.    1st Qu.     Median        Mean     3rd Qu.
-5988.0000 -1762.5000  -501.0000   -534.2188    374.7500
      Max.         sd
 6541.0000  2719.4438
tapply(X=x$SACCADES, INDEX=x$TASK, FUN=function (af) {
   c("mean"=mean(af), "var"=var(af), "sd"=sd(af))})
$direct
       mean         var          sd
   4037.125 8827287.145    2971.075
$inverse
       mean         var          sd
   4571.344 4947000.878    2224.185
```

Step 3: Can we do a t-test for dependent samples, are the pairwise differences normally distributed?

```
hist(sacc.diffs, main=nortest::lillie.test(x=sacc.diffs)$p.value)
```

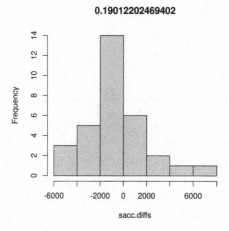

Figure 72: A histogram of sacc.diffs

"Yes we can." How can we visualize our data better? Here's what I *don't* want:

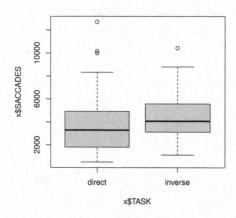

Figure 73: SACCADES ~ TASK

Why is this plot bad even if it seems to work so nicely in our direction (the median of the inverse translations is higher)?

THINK BREAK

It's bad because this plot doesn't represent the pairwise association of the measurements. For instance, you don't know from this plot whether the one outlier above the right box plot belongs to a very low value on the left or the one even higher outlier on the left. Thus, the simplest plot would actually be the histogram of the pairwise differences of Figure 72, because there every value represents the difference *within one person*. But a better plot might be something like Figure 74, though, in which every translator is represented by an arrow that connects that translator's direct-translation saccade value (on the left) to their inverse-translation saccade value (on the right), in which an incredibly subtle choice of colors reflects whether a translator's values behaved as we expected, and in which the black arrows represents the means.

```
plot(main="SACCADES ~ TASK (paired)", type="n", axes=FALSE,
    xlab="Task", xlim=c(0.9, 2.1), x=0,
    ylab="Saccades", ylim=c(0, 13000), y=0)
axis(1, at=1:2, labels=levels(x$TASK)); axis(2); grid()
arrows(angle=20, length=0.1, x0=1, y0=x$SACCADES[x$TASK=="direct"],
    x1=2, y1=x$SACCADES[x$TASK=="inverse"],
    col=ifelse(sacc.diffs>0, "red", "green"))
arrows(angle=20, length=0.1, lwd=3, x0=1,y0=mean(x$SACCADES[x$TASK==
"direct"]), x1=2, y1=mean(x$SACCADES[x$TASK=="inverse"]))
```

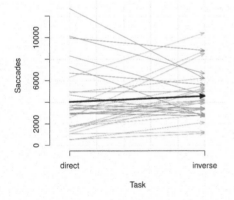

SACCADES ~ TASK (paired)

Figure 74: SACCADES ~ TASK (paired)

Much more useful, and it shows that many more arrows are green/going up than are red/going down and that some translators exhibit very big differences (steep arrows) whereas many exhibit much smaller ones (nearly horizontal arrows).

Now let's compute *t* and *df*, which is relatively straightforward here. We compute *t* like this and *df* is the number of value pairs *n*-1:

$$t = \frac{mean_{differences} \times \sqrt{n}}{sd_{differences}}$$

```
(t.value <- mean(sacc.diffs)*sqrt(length(sacc.diffs)) /
    sd(sacc.diffs))
## [1] -1.111256
(df.value <- length(sacc.diffs)-1)
## [1] 31
```

By now the next steps are hopefully somewhat familiar: In Figure 75, we have a *t*-distribution for *df*=31 with the usual two tails and a peak at the H_0 expectation of *t*=0. Again, *t* can be greater than 0 or less than 0, depending on what gets subtracted from what. In our case, we subtracted mean$_{inverse}$ from mean$_{direct}$ and expected a negative result in our directional/one-tailed H_1. We did get that negative result, so we go from the H_0 middle to our negative *t*-value (again indicated with an "×") and then sum up the grey area under the curve from there to all the more extreme results on the left.

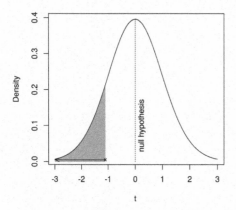

Figure 75: *t*-distribution for *df*=31

That grey area looks substantial – this can't be significant. Let's see:

```
pt(q=t.value, df=df.value, lower.tail=TRUE)
## [1] 0.1375015
```

Not significant. How would we have done all that with one function? Like this:

```
t.test(x$SACCADES ~ x$TASK, paired=TRUE, alternative="less")
## Paired t-test
## t = -1.1113, df = 31, p-value = 0.1375
## alternative hypothesis: true difference in means is less than 0
## 95 percent confidence interval:
##        -Inf 280.8753
## sample estimates:
## mean of the differences
##                 -534.2188
```

We sum up: "When the translators translated into their dominant language, they required on average 534.2 saccades fewer (sd=2719.4) than when they translated into their non-dominant language (mean$_{direct}$=4037.1, sd_{direct}=2971.1, mean$_{inverse}$=4571.3, $sd_{inverse}$=2224.2). [Maybe show Figure 74.] According to one-tailed t-test for dependent samples, this difference is not significant: t=-1.111, df=31, $p_{1\text{-tailed}}$=0.1375."

4.4 Correlation and simple linear regression

In this section, we discuss the significance tests for the coefficients of correlation discussed in Section 3.2.4. We begin with the correlations for ordinal data and then turn to numeric data.

4.4.1 Ordinal variables

By analogy to tests for central tendency and as discussed above in Section 3.2.4, ordinal correlation coefficients are used in two cases: (i) when at least of one of the two variables to be correlated is 'only' ordinal and (ii) when both are numeric but at least one of them isn't normally distributed (which is an assumption of the significance test of Pearson's r). Our example for ordinal correlations will involve a case of the latter: we'll revisit the reaction time data and check out the correlation between word frequency and the reaction time.

```
rm(list=ls(all.names=TRUE))
summary(x <- read.delim(file="_inputfiles/04_reactiontimes.csv",
    stringsAsFactors=TRUE)) ## [...]
```

The significance testing of any of the above correlation coefficients – r, ρ, or τ – involves the following steps:

Procedure
1. Formulate the hypotheses;
2. describe the data statistically and visually;
3. check/test the assumption(s) of the test:
   a. the data from both samples are at least ordinal;
   b. only for Pearson's r: the population from which the sample was drawn is bivariately normally distributed. Since this criterion can be hard to test (see Bortz 2005: 213f., but see the package MVN and I cannot remember seeing even a single study testing that), we simply require both samples to be distributed normally;
4. compute the test statistic t (for r) or S (for ρ) or z (for τ) and its p-value.

Step 1: We formulate the hypotheses. It seems reasonable to assume – not to mention obvious, given what must be thousands of studies – that there will be negative correlation between FREQ and RT: Glossing over any other predictors for now (like, maybe, word length?), the more frequent a word, the faster one will react to it in a lexical decision task; in other words, we have a directional/one-tailed hypothesis:

- H_0: There is no correlation between FREQ and RT, $r/\rho/\tau=0$;
- H_1: There is a negative correlation between FREQ and RT, $r/\rho/\tau<0$.

Step 2: which of the correlation coefficients will we compute? For plotting, I'm only showing the code, not the plots (see Section 3.1.3.3): RT looks normally distributed; FREQ looks very Zipfian-distributed:

```
par(mfrow=c(1, 2))
hist(x$RT, main="")
hist(x$FREQ, main="")
par(mfrow=c(1, 1))
```

What do corresponding tests say?

```
nortest::lillie.test(x$RT)$p.value
[1] 0.004136443
nortest::lillie.test(x$FREQ)$p.value
[1] 5.933414e-21
```

RT doesn't look all that bad, but the Lilliefors test says it's not normally distributed; FREQ, by contrast, is clearly non-normal. Thus, we won't compute Pearson's r, but Spearman's ρ, and its significance test, whose assumption – minimally ordinal information value of both variables – is met because both are in fact numeric. So let's plot the two variables and compute Spearman's ρ:

```
(qwe <- cor(x$FREQ, x$RT, method="spearman"))
## [1] -0.4851569
plot(main="RT ~ FREQ",  pch=16, xlab="Frequency", x=x$FREQ,
    ylab="Reaction time (in ms)", y=x$RT); grid()
text(x=90, y=725, paste0("Spearman's\nrho=", round(qwe, 3)))
```

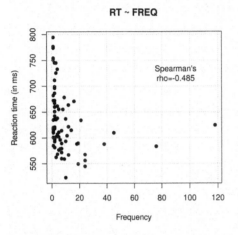

Figure 76: RT ~ FREQ

Note that the fact that we put RT on the y-axis reflects the notion that, while correlations are bidirectional, of the two variable RT is the response (and thus 'belongs' on the y-axis) whereas FREQ is the predictor (and thus goes on the x-axis).

Finally, we compute the significance test. You'll be delighted to see that I'm not walking you through the manual computation of ρ because, especially with ties, it is as tedious as many other non-parametric tests – we will only use an R function. Thankfully, this is then very easy: While we have used cor so far, there is in fact also a function called cor.test, which we use as follows (note the use of alternative: since no variable involved has levels, to which it could apply, alternative here pertains to how the correlation coefficient relates to 0):

```
cor.test(x$FREQ, x$RT, method="spearman", exact=FALSE,
    alternative="less")
##   Spearman's rank correlation rho
## S = 112985, p-value = 3.878e-06
```

```
## alternative hypothesis: true rho is less than 0
## sample estimates:
##        rho
## -0.4851569
```

We can sum up: "Since the variable FREQ is not normally distributed, we quantified its correlation with RT using Spearman's ρ. We found the predicted negative correlation (ρ=-0.485), which is highly significantly smaller than 0 (S=112985, $p_{\text{1-tailed}}$<0.0001): higher word frequencies are associated with shorter reaction times." Note that, in Chapter 5 below, we will revisit this correlation.

4.4.2 Numeric variables

To test the significance of Pearson's r, we look at an example from translation research again. 49 translators, who translated the same text from the dominant into their non-dominant language, did that at a computer where their numbers of key presses and mouse events were recorded. We want to see whether there's a correlation between those two variables, specifically, how well the (already logged) numbers of mouse events follow from the (already logged) numbers of key presses. The question involves
– a numeric response MOUSEEVENT;
– a numeric predictor KEYPRESS.

For such cases, we would try to use Pearson's product-moment correlation coefficient r and linear regression, the procedure is the same as in the previous section so we begin with step 1, the hypotheses:
  – H_0: There is no correlation between MOUSEEVENT and KEYPRESS, $r/\rho/\tau$=0;
  – H_1: There is a negative correlation between MOUSEEVENT and KEYPRESS, $r/\rho/\tau$<0.

We load the data:

```
rm(list=ls(all.names=TRUE))
summary(x <- read.delim(file="_inputfiles/04_keymouse.csv",
   stringsAsFactors=TRUE)) ## [...]
```

Is Pearson's r an option: are both variables normally distributed?

```
par(mfrow=c(1, 2))
hist(x$KEYPRESS, main=nortest::lillie.test(x$KEYPRESS)$p.value)
hist(x$MOUSEEVENT, main=nortest::lillie.test(x$MOUSEEVENT)$p.value)
par(mfrow=c(1, 1))
```

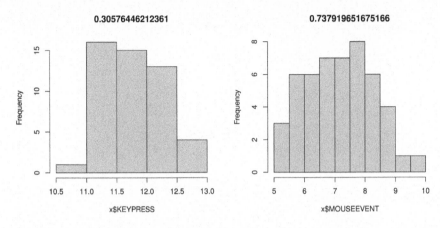

Figure 77: Histograms of KEYPRESS and MOUSEEVENT

Looking good so we compute Pearson's r and generate a scatterplot with the response on the y-axis, but for the color of the points, we're doing something new now with the argument col, namely use semi-transparent colors (to avoid overplotting and other 'visual effects') with a hexadecimal color code written like this: "#00000030", which you might look at as "RRGGBBOO":

- the first two 0s are the code for how much **red** you want, the second two 0s are how much **green** you want, the third two 0s are how much **blue** you want;
- the last two values (30) are the **opacity** of the point so 00 mean the point is actually completely transparent and FF means the point is fully opaque;
- that in turn might already tell you that these are values on the hexadecimal scale (where values from 0 to F correspond to values from 0 to 15), meaning they go from 00 (for 0) to FF (for 15×16+15=255). For example,
  - "#FF0000FF" is bright red, fully opaque whereas "#0000FFFF" is bright blue, fully opaque;
  - "#FFFF00FF" is red plus green, i.e. yellow, fully opaque;
  - "#FF00FF80" is red plus blue, i.e. purple, half opaque.

```
qwe <- cor(x$KEYPRESS, x$MOUSEEVENT, method="pearson")
plot(pch=16, col="#00000030", cex=2, xlab="Logged number of key
    presses", x=x$KEYPRESS, ylab="Logged number of mouse events",
```

```
    y=x$MOUSEEVENT); grid()
text(x=11, y=8.5, paste0("Pearson's\nr=", round(qwe, 3)))
```

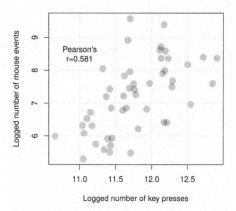

Figure 78: KEYPRESS ~ MOUSEEVENT

Finally, we compute the significance test, for which we can use cor.test again; pretty much everything stays the same:

```
cor.test(x$KEYPRESS, x$MOUSEEVENT, method="pearson",
    alternative="greater")
##  Pearson's product-moment correlation
## t = 4.8999, df = 47, p-value = 5.895e-06
## alternative hypothesis: true correlation is greater than 0
## 95 percent confidence interval:
##   0.3987573 1.0000000
## sample estimates:
##       cor
## 0.5814767
```

We sum up: "Since both variables KEYPRESS and MOUSEEVENT are normally distributed, we quantified their correlation with Pearson's r. We found the predicted positive correlation (r=0.581), which is significantly greater than 0 (t=4.9, df=47, $p_{\text{1-tailed}}$<0.0001): higher numbers of keypresses are associated with higher numbers of mouse events." But since we have a 'real' dependent variable, we can of course also look at a linear model for this correlation; let's do that in a way that will recur over and over again in the chapters to follow, namely with the summary function:

```
summary(m <- lm(MOUSEEVENT ~ KEYPRESS, data=x))
## [...] Coefficients:
##               Estimate Std. Error t value Pr(>|t|)
## (Intercept)   -7.5607      3.0185  -2.505   0.0158 *
## KEYPRESS       1.2555      0.2562   4.900 1.18e-05 ***
## [...]
## Multiple R-squared:  0.3381, Adjusted R-squared:  0.324
## F-statistic: 24.01 on 1 and 47 DF,  p-value: 1.179e-05
```

A lot of information (though abbreviated), but some of it we actually already know. We won't discuss everything here, but only what's relevant right now – much more will follow in Chapter 5. Let's begin at the bottom: The last line contains information we already know, kind of:
– the F-value is our t-value from cor.test squared;
– df_2 of the F-test at the bottom (47) is the df-value of our t-test from cor.test;
– the p-value is twice of what we computed (because lm reports two-tailed p-values whereas we computed a one-tailed one).

In the line above that, you find as "Multiple R-squared" the coefficient of determination R^2, which is Pearson's r squared; the second, adjusted, R^2, I will discuss later. And then, in the section called "Coefficients", you find the two values that the abbreviated model output we so far only considered already showed: the intercept of -7.5607 and the slope for KEYPRESS of 1.2555 (in the column labeled "Estimate"), followed by their standard errors, t-values – do you recognize the t-value from above in the row for KEYPRESS? – and then p-values. Importantly for later, each of the p-values tests the H_0 that the corresponding estimate is 0. Whether the intercept is 0 is usually not an interesting question but whether the slope for, here, KEYPRESS is 0 is of course more interesting. But again, we'll discuss regression modeling in so much more detail in the next two chapters that we'll leave it at this for now.

4.4.3 Correlation and causality

Especially in the area of correlations, but also more generally, you need to bear in mind the famous adage that, even if H_0 is rejected, correlation is a necessary (*only if*) condition for causation, but not a sufficient (*whenever*) one. Correlation doesn't imply causation, which is also the title of a Wikipedia article I recommend. As it says there (at least it did on 03 Oct 2020):

For any two correlated events, A and B, their possible relationships include:
- A causes B (direct causation);
- B causes A (reverse causation);
- A and B are both caused by C;
- A causes B and B causes A (bidirectional or cyclic causation);
- There is no connection between A and B; the correlation is a coincidence.

Wikipedia, s.v. "Correlation does not imply
causation", 03 Oct 2020

Thus, correlations can be spurious, in particular when they are of the third of the above quoted types; you can see this from many examples:

– A very pertinent example for me in California: There's a positive correlation between the number of firefighters trying to extinguish a fire and the amount of damage that is caused at the site where the fire was fought. This does of course not mean that the firefighters arrive at the site and trash/loot the place as much as they can – the correlation results from a third variable, the size of the fire: the larger the fire, the more firefighters are called to help extinguish it and the more damage the fire causes.

– There's a negative correlation between the amount of hair men have and their income, which, much to this author's chagrin, is unfortunately only due to the effect of a third variable: the men's age.

– There's a positive correlation such that the more likely a drug addict was to go to therapy to get off of his addiction, the more likely he was to die. This is not because the therapy leads to death – the confounding variable in the background correlated with both is the severity of the addiction: the more severely addicted addicts were, the more likely they were to go to therapy, but also the more likely they already were to die.

Note again that this is not a statistics problem: statistics provide you with numerical results and if there's a statistical correlation, the right statistics will tell you so. Making sense of such statistical results, interpreting them, and deciding which of the above five relationships holds is the job of the analyst, who, when facing such correlations, should be careful to not jump to conclusions ... And now you should do the exercise(s) for Chapter 4 ...

Recommendation(s) for further study: for unbelievably detailed overviews and great step-by-step discussions of monofactorial tests – those discussed here and many more – my go-to sources are Zar (2010) and Sheskin (2011); some chapters on some tests have more than 30 or even 50 pages, which may seem excessive, but both books explain things in extremely comprehensible ways. Also, for a quite different family of methods in the field of robust statistics, see the already mentioned references of Wilcox (2012, 2017) and the package WRS2.

5 Fixed-effects regression modeling

> The commonest mistake is to try to do the statistical modelling straight away. The best thing is to spend a substantial amount of time, right at the outset, getting to know your data and what they show. (Crawley 2013:389)

5.1 A bit on 'multifactoriality'

The monofactorial tests discussed above by definition all involved one response variable and one predictor and we investigated whether there's a correlation (as defined in Section 3.3) between them because such a correlation would be a necessary condition for a (hopefully) causal explanation. In many cases, proceeding like this might be the beginning of the empirical quantitative study of a phenomenon. Nevertheless, such a view on phenomena is usually a simplification: We live in a multifactorial world in which probably no phenomenon is really monofactorial – probably just about everything is correlated with several things at the same time. This is especially true for language, one of the most complex phenomena resulting from human evolution. For the sake of simplicity, let's explore this with a very mundane non-linguistic example, the efficiency of cars measured in mpg (miles per gallon); one mile is 1.609 km and one gallon is approximately 3.8 liters and note that miles per gallon has the opposite orientation of liters/100km: for mpg, high is good. (The following borrows from and extends discussion in Gries 2018; the example is maybe painfully obvious, but has its instructive advantages so bear with me.)

Imagine you think and read about the question of what determines cars' mpg efficiency and you find a study from the early 1990s that shows that cars with more cylinders need more gas (i.e. have a lower mpg-value). Imagine there's also another study from the late 1990s that shows that cars with more horsepower have lower mpgs, plus it kinda follows from basic physics that heavier cars would have lower mpgs. But then you get an idea: You develop the truly groundbreaking alternative hypothesis that cars with more displacement should have lower mpgs. That seems reasonable and you do a statistical test of your hypothesis on a sample of 32 different cars that comes with R:

https://doi.org/10.1515/9783110718256-005

```
rm(list=ls(all.names=TRUE));
summary(test.of.new.hyp <- lm(mpg ~ disp, data=mtcars))
## [...] Coefficients:
##                   Estimate Std. Error t value Pr(>|t|)
## (Intercept) 29.599855    1.229720   24.070  < 2e-16 ***
## disp        -0.041215    0.004712   -8.747 9.38e-10 ***
# [...]
## Multiple R-squared:  0.7183, Adjusted R-squared:  0.709
## F-statistic: 76.51 on 1 and 30 DF,  p-value: 9.38e-10
```

We haven't done that much linear modeling yet but, even from the bit we've done, this output should make you ecstatic: The penultimate line shows that the coefficient of determination R^2 of your model is awesome (around 0.72, meaning disp can 'explain' 72% of the variability of the mpg values in this (small) data set and r exceeds 0.8). Plus, the second line of the "Coefficients" part of the output shows that disp has a highly significant negative slope (just like expected). Even visually, this seems to look pretty good:

```
plot(main="The relation between displacement and mpg",
    xlab="Displacement (cubic inches; 61 ci = 1 ltr)", x=mtcars$disp,
    ylab="Miles per gallon", y=mtcars$mpg,
    pch=16, col="#00000030")
grid(); abline(test.of.new.hyp)
```

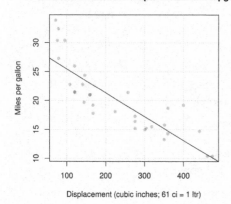

Figure 79: mpg ~ disp

You had a monofactorial hypothesis, you did a monofactorial test of it, it turns out highly significant and explains quite a large amount of the variability of the mpg values in your data – seems like it's time to write this up, send it to *Science* or *Combustion and Flame*, and await a congratulatory acceptance letter. But then, maybe not ... And not just because disp is not normally distributed or because diagnostics would reveal that this relationship should be curved, but, more importantly, because mpg values are a multifactorial phenomenon. But your test was a test of your monofactorial alternative hypothesis that disp is correlated with mpg against the H_0 that it isn't. That test is pretty anti-conservatively stacked in your favor because you didn't test your hypothesis against everything else you already knew to play a role. Put differently, you tested your hypothesis pretending you have no prior knowledge about mpg (leaving all of the variability of mpg, its variance, up for grabs by the one predictor you wanted to show is important, disp). But you *do* have some prior knowledge: You know that the number of cylinders, horsepower, and weight play a role, which statistically means they already account for a lot variability/variance. In fact, if you throw everything you already know about mpg values into a model, that model accounts for >84% of the variability of mpg, as you can see from the R^2-value here.

```
summary(prior.knowl <- lm(mpg ~ cyl+hp+wt, data=mtcars))$r.squared
## [1] 0.84315
```

That means what you should be interested in is not whether disp does anything (as opposed to nothing) regardless of everything else but whether your new pet variable disp (i) **adds to** what we already know or (ii) **replaces** what we already know.

With regard to 'adding to what we already know', you should determine the impact that disp has on the variability of mpg that we do not already account for with other things and whether that impact, when everything else is already controlled for, is significantly different from 0. With what you will learn below, one can show that disp has very little to contribute to what we already know: If you add disp to the statistical model of our prior knowledge, it makes no significant contribution: (p=0.3314).

Ok, but what about option 2, 'replacing what we already know'? Well, one can show that that's also not encouraging: The prior knowledge is many times more likely – in fact ≈766 more likely – to be the 'right model' than the displacement-only model. How is that possible, that you have such a strong and significant effect in your monofactorial model test.of.new.hyp but now nothing's left? In this trivial case, it's probably all too obvious: the predictors are all extremely correlated. All other things being equal (!), a car with more cylinders will usually have more displacement (because displacement 'is' the cylinder volume), which also means it will usually have more horsepower, and its engine will usually weigh more. In fact, these variables are all so highly interrelated that disp is >90% predictable from the other variables:

```
summary(what.accounts.4.disp <- lm(disp ~ cyl+hp+wt,
   data=mtcars))$r.squared
## [1] 0.9035985
```

Essentially and with only slight exaggeration, the idea of using disp as a great new predictor here is the equivalent of knowing that the favorite alternation of every linguist that has ever lived – *John picked up the book* vs. *John picked the book up* – can be explained well with the length of the direct object in morphemes but then having the 'new idea' that the length of the direct object in syllables might be a cool new predictor. Now you might say, 'ok, but these are extreme and unrealistic examples, no one in linguistics would do that', but that's not quite and obviously true. There are many studies on alternations such as the genitive alternation, the dative alternation, particle placement in native and non-native language and many of these studies proposed that predictors such as the length of the relevant constituents play a role for such ordering choices (e.g., short-before-long). But then others argued that the complexity of constituents plays an important role; yet others argued in favor of discourse-functional factors such as the givenness of the referents of the relevant constituents (e.g. given-before-new); yet others suggested that factors such as definiteness of NPs plays a role (definite-before-indefinite) ... However, clearly all these predictors are all in fact strongly interrelated: given referents tend to be encoded with short (and thus simple, not complex) definite or pronominal NPs and new referents tend to be encoded with longer (and thus potentially (more) complex), maybe indefinite and lexical NPs, ... so in linguistics, we often have to deal with predictors that are related like that.

Anyway, the main point of the current discussion is that even if you have a monofactorial hypothesis, you're still often likely to need a multifactorial exploration anyway – there's bound to be some prior knowledge, there's bound to be confounding and/or moderator variables you many need to consider – and that's what the rest of this book is all about, formulating and exploring (regression) models (using *model* as defined above in Section 3.2.4).

As discussed above, the logic of regression modeling is based on determining how much one can 'predict' what a response does depending on what one or more predictors do. These predictions are made by a regression model in the form of an equation and the (summary of the) model returns for each (coefficient of a) predictor:

- an (at least initially typically unstandardized) **effect size** stating how much it is correlated with the response; an effect typically is a difference in means (of the response between levels of a categorical predictor) or a slope (of the response for a 1-unit increase of a numeric predictor);
- an **effect direction** stating in what direction a predictor is correlated with the response; an effect can be positive (in the sense of 'increasing the predicted value of the response') or negative (in the sense of 'decreasing the predicted value of the response'); in the context of Pearson's r, this is r's sign;
- a **significance test**, stating the probability with which the obtained effect could arise when there's no effect in the population your data are a sample of; an effect can be significant (i.e., (too) unlikely to occur randomly to stick with H_0) or insignificant (i.e. (too) likely to occur randomly to accept H_1).

If a response is numeric, we typically do **linear regression modeling**; predictors can be

- numeric, and if you have just one such predictor, the regression model is actually intimately related to Pearson's r from Sections 3.2.4 and 4.4.2; if you have more than one such predictor, many textbooks would call this *multiple regression*;
- binary (i.e., categorical with 2 levels), and with just one such predictor, this kind of linear model amounts to a t-test for independent samples from Section 4.3.2.3;
- categorical with 3 or more levels, and with just one such predictor, this kind of linear model amounts to what is traditionally called a *one-way ANOVA*.

(Note: predictors can also be ordinal but we'll deal with that in a way that doesn't involve ordered factors.) These kinds of models – linear regression models – are the subject of Section 5.2. However, the linear model has been extended to what's called the **generalized linear model**, which are models that can have responses other than numeric values, but also all kinds of predictors:

- when the response is binary, we can do a **binary logistic regression** (the topic of Section 5.3); in monofactorial cases, such regressions are 'similar' to point bi-serial correlations or chi-squared tests for independence ;
- when the response is categorical, we can do a **multinomial regression** (the topic of Section 5.4.1); binary logistic regression is a special but very frequent subcase of multinomial regression;
- when the response is ordinal, we can do an **ordinal logistic regression** (the topic of Section 5.4.2).

(Check out the navigator plot again to orient yourself with regard to when different kinds of regression models are fit. And bear in mind, as you just read, this actually means that many of the test scenarios in Chapter 4 can actually be recast as the simplest cases of certain regressions.) In all cases, the quality of a regression model is determined by how well the model fits the data (given certain assumptions regarding the model). But how do we decide what kind of model to fit (first) and what to do with it? These seemingly innocuous questions open up an area of discussion involving notions such as **(initial) model formulation** and **model selection**, which we will later have to deal with in quite some detail. For now, we will postpone this part and begin with our discussion of (ultimately multifactorial) regression models with the three simplest kinds of models each testing one specific hypothesis; the fact that they are monofactorial and already known to us from Chapter 4 will help with understanding the more complex multifactorial ones later.

5.2 Linear regression

We are revisiting the lexical decision times from before but with a variety of different models using different variables as predictors. I will discuss them on the basis of separate data frames that contain only the variables of interest, i.e. subdata frames, so to speak, of the one with all variables we used before. I'm doing that only to make it unmistakably obvious that in a real analysis of those data you wouldn't fit a bunch of completely different unrelated models on them like I will now only for didactic reasons. We will discuss three models, each of them with RT as the response but each one with one different predictor – meaning, this chapter on multifactorial regression modeling will actually start with three monofactorial models. But there's a reason for that: you need to understand what the output of a regression means and that is best explained first using monofactorial models, plus the simplicity of these models also allows me to explain many additional important things; as you will see, in the three sections to follow, the excursus (pl.) are sometimes longer than the 'main section' on a certain kind of model.

The first thing to know, before you do any modeling at all, is that it is absolutely indispensable to do some thorough numeric and visual exploration before any statistical analysis, but especially regression modeling, is begun; that's why I spent so much time/space on Chapter 3 and probably irritated you to death with "describe the data statistically and visually" in Chapter 4. In a regression modeling context, the kinds of activity represented in Table 21 are very important and nearly all of these things will be discussed in different sections below:

Table 21: Exploration/preparation activities before the modeling starts

Major activity	Examples
descriptive stats & visualization	every variable on its own and with every other one
checking/correcting data	wrongly-entered/-converted/-imported data
discarding/trimming data	rare factor levels, certain kinds of influential data points
merging/conflating data	rare factor levels, collinear predictors
form-changing transformations	log, inverse, sqrt, (i)logit, power, etc.
form-preserving transformations	centering or z-standardizing
preparing factors	re-leveling, contrasts (successive diffs, ordinal, planned, …)

I also highly recommend Zuur et al. (2010) for a very nice discussion of these and other tasks, also see Fox & Weisberg (2019: Ch. 3), and the 'sister publication' to this book, Gries (to appear a), which discusses one mixed-effects modeling process and comes with an online supplement, the first >110 pages (when pdf-ed) of which are just this exploration and preparation process ... So, I am not just saying this is necessary – it actually is! I've been known to tell students that I don't want to see them in my office hours to, supposedly, discuss a regression model unless they have at least 100 lines of code first exploring the data on which the model is fit because that would likely amount to a waste of time ...

5.2.1 A linear model with a numeric predictor

As a point of entry, we begin with the kind of linear model that we actually already discussed in Section 4.4, but we now discuss it from the perspective of linear models proper and not so much as 'an addendum' to Pearson's r. Since this data set is so small and this kind of model already known to us, it is an ideal vehicle to develop many concepts we need. Let's imagine we had the following hypotheses with regard to the relation of FREQ and RT:
– H_0: There is no correlation between FREQ and RT; $R^2=0$;
– H_1: There is a correlation between FREQ and RT; $R^2>0$.

(Note that, for now, we're formulating H_1 as non-directional, although we would expect a negative correlation; this is only for didactic reasons, we'll revisit this below.) Let's load the data, which we actually already know well:

```
rm(list=ls(all.names=TRUE)); library(car); library(effects)
summary(x <- read.delim(file="_inputfiles/05_rt_freq.csv",
```

```
   stringsAsFactors=TRUE, row.names=1)) ## [...]
```

Using row names like that is only possible if the row names are all unique; check
head(x). Exploration for our present example is straightforward; since we already looked at the histograms above, I'm only showing the code for them, but
I'm showing Figure 76 again now with a smoother:

```
par(mfrow=c(1, 2))
hist(x$RT, labels=TRUE, main="")
hist(x$FREQ, labels=TRUE, main="")
par(mfrow=c(1, 1))
plot(x=x$FREQ, y=x$RT, pch=16); grid(); lines(lowess(x$RT ~ x$FREQ))
```

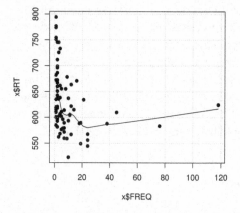

Figure 80: RT ~ FREQ (w/ smoother)

The histogram for RT looks 'fine'; it's kinda normal-ish (but actually, for regression, normality of the response is less important than normality of something
else, as you will see below in Section 5.6.2), but there's nothing 'exciting' about
it: no super-systematic skew, no gaps, no outliers – just 'fine'. The one for FREQ is
more problematic and was the reason why, above, we computed Spearman's ρ
for this correlation: The histograms has six bins but approximately 90% of all
the values ($^{69}/_{77}$) are squeezed into the leftmost bin; in other words, a regression
line for FREQ would cover a numeric range of values $^5/_6$ths of which it hardly has
any data for. We see that same thing in the our current plot, where our curved
smoother basically tells us that fitting a straight line through this point cloud
might not be the smartest idea ever.

What to do? There are multiple options. One solution is what we did above: 'downgrade' the values to an ordinal information level, and compute Spearman's ρ. Another one is to transform the offending variable into something that is more 'well-behaved'. Recall that in Section 3.1.3.4 above we talked about two kinds of transformations: one that did not change a distribution's shape (like centering and z-standardization) and one that did, and it is the latter kind that might help here, given how unhappy we are with FREQ's shape. And FREQ is in fact a particularly good candidate for this because one might know from previous work that frequency effects in language are often logarithmic in nature. So let's see whether logging helps, and since we know from the summary that FREQ contains no 0s, for which a log would not be defined, we can just do this:

```
par(mfrow=c(1, 2))
hist(log2(x$FREQ), main="")
plot(x=jitter(log2(x)$FREQ), y=x$RT, pch=16); grid()
    lines(lowess(x$RT ~ log2(x$FREQ)))
par(mfrow=c(1, 1))
```

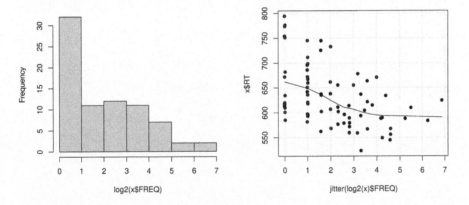

Figure 81: Exploratory plots when FREQ is logged …

Ok, still not great, but much better than before: There is clearly still some skew in the left plot and there is clearly still some curvature in the smoother, but especially looking at the right plot now, it is possible now to envisage a straight line through the points such that the curved one would hug it much of the (x-axis) 'time'. We therefore adopt the log transformation and, since that transformation is easily to un-do, we just overwrite the original values (as opposed to adding a new column FREQLOG to x):

```
x$FREQ <- log2(x$FREQ)
```

Other transformations that are regularly applied to numeric variables are the ilogit transformation, taking the inverse, or the square root of a variable.

Recommendation(s) for further study: Zar (2010: Ch. 13) for discussion of transformations and, e.g., Fox & Weisberg (2019: Section 3.4) for the Box-Cox and Yeo-Johnson transformations, which are implemented in car::powerTransform and are very useful to make variables whose distributions are skewed more amenable to various statistical approaches.

5.2.1.1 Numerical exploration

Let's now fit (and immediately summarize) the regression model, which for reasons that will become clear later will be called m.01 (for 'model 1') and is essentially the same as cor.test(xRT, xFREQ):

```
summary(m.01 <- lm(RT ~ 1 + FREQ, data=x, na.action=na.exclude))
## [...]
## Residuals:
##      Min      1Q  Median      3Q     Max
## -88.108 -45.072  -5.911  35.165 127.420
## Coefficients:
##              Estimate Std. Error t value Pr(>|t|)
## (Intercept)   667.033      9.801  68.060  < 2e-16 ***
## FREQ          -16.820      3.668  -4.585 1.78e-05 ***
## ---
## Signif. codes:  0 '***' 0.001 '**' 0.01 '*' 0.05 '.' 0.1 ' ' 1
##
## Residual standard error: 53.52 on 75 degrees of freedom
## Multiple R-squared:  0.2189, Adjusted R-squared:  0.2085
## F-statistic: 21.02 on 1 and 75 DF,  p-value: 1.78e-05
```

(Note that specifying the intercept explicitly with the 1 is optional, I am doing this to familiarize you with something we need in Chapter 6; also, I added na.action=na.exclude to the lm call to handle missing data but won't always list that argument in the book – it'll be in the code though) We already know some of this from above: the overall model (a simple correlation) is significant (see p in the last line) and the predictor explains 21.89% of the variance of the response (see multiple R-squared). Also note again the equivalence to cor.test: The model's F-value is cor.test's t squared, the model's df_2 is cor.test's df, the p-value is the same, etc. But now what is the adjusted R^2? This R^2-value is adjusted such that you 'incur a slight penalty' for every parameter estimated in your model. This is because regressions are so good at finding patterns in data that if you added completely random noise as another predictor, the regression would be able to find some little trend in there that might help explain an additional 1% or 0.5% of RT's variability. Like here: I make 77 random numbers (rnorm(77)) a new predictor and R^2 increases by 0.002 – but the adjustment is like adding a negative penalty to your multiple R^2 so if your additional predictor doesn't explain at least enough to overcome the penalty, which random numbers are not likely to do, then your adjusted R^2 will actually go down, like in this case:

```
set.seed(sum(utf8ToInt("Blagl")))
summary(lm(RT ~ 1 + FREQ + rnorm(77), data=x))[
    c("r.squared", "adj.r.squared")]
## $r.squared
## [1] 0.2212475
## $adj.r.squared
## [1] 0.2002001
```

That is to say, this adjustment/penalty 'disincentivizes' you to add junk predictors to your model in a desperate search for nice R^2-values. Adjusted R^2 is computed like this (with n being the sample size and p being the number of parameters that is estimated (without the intercept):

$$adj. R^2 = 1 - (1 - mult. R^2) \times \frac{n-1}{n-p-1}$$

Another way to compute this from some linear model m would be this (but of course we don't have to, given that it's already provided in the summary, and so I won't explain this bit of code further):

```
numer <- (deviance(m.01)/m.01$df.residual)
denom <- deviance(update(m.01, ~ 1)) / (nrow(model.frame(m.01))-1)
1-(numer/denom) # same as 1-((1-0.2189334) * ((77-1)/(77-1-1)))
## [1] 0.2085192
```

Thus, this adjustment is one way in which Occam's razor enters into regression modeling and it's probably best to always report both R^2-values. Now, what's Occam's razor? Write down what you think it is before you read on!

THINK BREAK

Occam's razor is usually cited as "entia non sunt multiplicanda praeter necessitatem", a regression-based paraphrase of which would be something like 'do not make your model more complex than is justified by your data', where
- a model m2 can be "more complex" than a model m1 because m2 involves more coefficients, and you might have more coefficients because m2
  - has more predictor variables than m1;
  - has predictor variables with more levels than m1;
  - has interactions between predictors that m1 doesn't have;
  - involves curved numeric predictors when m1 only has straight-line numeric predictors; etc.
- m2's higher degree of complexity can be "justified" if the way in which m2 is more complex makes a significant contribution (in terms of a p-value) or makes a substantial contribution (in terms of some criterion other than p such as information criteria, see Section 5.5 below).

It's important you understand that well: Counter to what I often hear in bootcamps or classes, Occam's razor does not mean "the simplest model is the best" (in fact, in terms of unadjusted R^2, the simplest model is *never* the best) – it means 'if two models trying to account for the same data do not 'differ enough' (as defined by your 'justification' criterion above, which could be a p-value), then prefer the simpler one'.

Now, maybe the most important part of the output again, the coefficients table, which we will discuss in excruciating detail by building on what we said earlier. With regard to the intercept, I told you above that the intercept is "the y-axis value that the [regression] line is at when the x-axis variable is 0". If we rephrase that a bit and make it more general at the same time (to cover later kinds of models already), we can define the intercept as follows (and you should tattoo this on the inside of your left eyelid so you never forget that!): The intercept is the value the regression model predicts when
- all categorical predictors in the model are set to their first level; and/or (!)
- all numeric predictors in the model are set to 0.

That means here, the intercept of our model m.01 is the predicted RT when
- (there are no categorical predictors so this part of the rule doesn't apply;)
- the predictor FREQ is 0. (Though recall that the predictor FREQ is the logged version of the original variable, which means that the intercept is the prediction for when the original, unlogged FREQ value is 1.)

Now what about the coefficient for FREQ? Above I said that this value, the slope of FREQ, is "how much in y-axis units the line goes up (if the slope is positive) or

down (if the slope is negative) when the *x*-axis value increases by 1". But again to look ahead, we rephrase that a bit and make it more general at the same time by defining the coefficient as follows (and this is for your right eyelid!): Each coefficient/estimate for any predictor X (main effect, interaction, or factor level – anything but the intercept) is the value you must add to the intercept to,
- in the case of (levels of) categorical predictors, predict the response value for the level of X whose coefficient/estimate you're looking at;
- in the case of numeric predictors, predict the response value that results from a 1-unit increase of X (and of course more often for more 1-unit changes);

while, and this is crucial!,
- all categorical predictors not mentioned/involved in X are still set to their first level (i.e. what they were at for the intercept),
- all numeric predictors not mentioned/involved in X are still set to 0 (i.e. what they were at for the intercept).

That means here, where we don't have any categorical predictors,
- the intercept is the predicted RT when FREQ is 0; put differently (and redundantly, but for consistency with what will follow), the intercept plus 0 times the slope of FREQ (of -16.82) is the predicted RT when FREQ is 0;
- the intercept plus 1 times the slope of FREQ is the predicted RT when FREQ is 1;
- the intercept plus 2 times the slope of FREQ is the predicted RT when FREQ is 2; you get the idea ...

Now, let's return to the other columns of the coefficients table. To remind you, we get the standard errors of each estimate (the intercept and the slope), the *t*-value is the estimate divided by its standard error, and the *p*-value always tests whether the estimate is significantly different from 0. Usually, we don't care about whether the intercept is different from 0, but we do care about the slope. Note that the *p*-value of the slope in the coefficients table is the same as the one for the whole model in the last line: that's of course because our model has only that one predictor.

For reasons that will become apparent later, whenever I compute and summarize a model like above, I follow that up with the following (although, here, this is redundant):

```
drop1(m.01, test="F")
## Single term deletions
## Model: RT ~ 1 + FREQ
##             Df Sum of Sq   RSS    AIC F value   Pr(>F)
```

```
## <none>                    214864 614.91
## FREQ      1       60226 275090 631.94   21.023 1.78e-05 ***
```

This is an extremely useful function. To anthropomorphize a bit, the function
- looks at the model and identifies all predictors in there that can be dropped from the model (more on that below);
- then drops each one of them at a time to create one of possibly several sub-models, here one that differs from m.01 only by missing that one dropped predictor;
- returns a significance test for, and this is the key point, whether the sub-model from which the predictor was dropped is significantly worse than the original model from which the predictor was not dropped.

In drop1's output, the first line contains two statistics about what happens when <none> of the predictors is dropped (we will talk about *AIC* later). The second line contains what happens when FREQ is dropped; it's R's version of saying this: "if you drop FREQ from m.01, then the resulting model – one that has no predictor at all anymore, which could be written as lm(RT ~ 1) – is significantly worse (p=1.78e-05)." And, again, this is redundant here, because, in a model with only one predictor, that is the same p-value as the one in the last line of the summary output; I only do this here already to build up a routine I recommend you follow all the time.

Another thing one will often want to do is compute the 95%-CIs of all estimates; thankfully, this part is easy. Base R actually has a function confint for that, but we will use car::Confint because it works the same for all models I'll discuss whereas confint does not. Thus:

```
Confint(m.01) # return estimates w/ their 95%-CI
##              Estimate     2.5 %      97.5 %
## (Intercept) 667.03260 647.50869 686.556518
## FREQ        -16.82015 -24.12815  -9.512145
```

Finally, in terms of numeric exploration, we usually want to see what the model's predictions are. For that, we can use one of my absolute favorite R packages, effects. I usually do the following, which you need to parse carefully because it involves two assignments before it outputs a result:

```
(ph <- data.frame(fre <- effect("FREQ", m.01)))
##   FREQ      fit       se    lower    upper
## 1    0 667.0326 9.800660 647.5087 686.5565
```

```
## 2    2 633.3923  6.108811 621.2229 645.5617
## 3    3 616.5722  6.951498 602.7241 630.4202
## 4    5 582.9319 12.291530 558.4459 607.4178
## 5    7 549.2916 19.013221 511.4153 587.1678
```

What effect does is, it looks at the numeric predictor FREQ, determines its range of values, and then picks a few somewhat equally-spaced values from that range. For these values, it then computes the predictions of the regression model, their standard errors, and their CI boundaries. The code above then puts that into the object fre, and then a data frame version of that gets stored in ph. This way I keep the code short, but retain both the effects object fre (for automated plotting later) and a data frame ph (for my own plotting later). The columns of ph are:

- FREQ: the values of the predictor for which effect decided to give you predictions based on m.01;
- fit: the predictions (of RT for the values in ph$FREQ) based on m.01;
- se: the standard errors of the predictions;
- lower: the lower bound of the 95%-CI of the predictions;
- upper: the upper bound of the 95%-CI of the predictions.

If you want predictions for a slightly better set of values of FREQ, you can get those with xlevels:

```
(ph <- data.frame(fre <- effect("FREQ", m.01,
   xlevels=list(FREQ=0:7))))
## [...]
```

Note how this output confirms my explanation of the intercept and slope above; the function all.equal, which tests whether target and current are the same, returns TRUE in both cases:

```
all.equal(target=ph$fit[1], current=coef(m.01)[1],
   check.names=FALSE)
## [1] TRUE
all.equal(target=ph$fit[2], current=coef(m.01)[1]+1*coef(m.01)[2],
   check.names=FALSE)
## [1] TRUE
```

In a simple model like this, plots might not really be needed, but for consistency's sake, we will quickly plot things anyway.

5.2.1.2 Graphical model exploration

The easiest way to get an already very decent plot is to just plot the effects object `fre`, here with a few additional arguments; note, that for this class of object/ plot, we say `grid=TRUE` as part of the call to plot, we don't add `grid()` later:

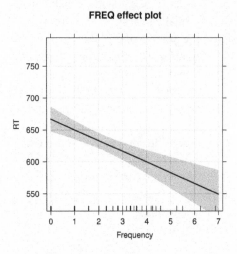

Figure 82: The effect of FREQ

Already very informative – I would normally at least probably add the observed values and jitter them a bit to reduce overplotting of points (see Figure 83):

```
plot(xlab="Frequency (logged, base of 2)", x=jitter(x$FREQ),
    ylab="Reaction time in ms", y=jitter(x$RT), pch=16,
    col="#00000060"); grid()
lines(x=ph$FREQ, y=ph$fit)
polygon(x=c(ph$FREQ, rev(ph$FREQ)), y=c(ph$lower, rev(ph$upper)),
    col="#00000020", border=NA)
abline(h=mean(x$RT), lty=3); abline(v=mean(x$FREQ), lty=3)
```

You might now summarize all of this: A linear regression model was fit with RT as the response and FREQ as the only predictor (logged to the base of 2 after initial graphical exploration). The model indicated a highly significant fit (F=21.02, df_1=1, df_2=75, p<0.0001). The model fit was decent (mult. R^2=0.2189, adj. R^2=0.2085).

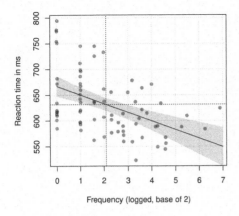

Figure 83: The effect of FREQ

Then you would show the "Coefficients" table of the summary output (ideally with the confidence intervals as well and one of the plots with the regression line and summarize: For every 1-unit increase in the logged FREQ predictor RT decreases by 16.8 ms."

5.2.1.3 Excursus: curvature and anova

The above model looked pretty good in terms of our three main kinds of regression results: the effect size (R^2) was decent, the effect direction was in the right direction (negative), and the model was significant in spite of the small number of data points. However, there are two things with regard to which the above can be improved a bit.

First, recall that we formulated or hypothesis in a non-directional/two-tailed way and the summary output actually tells us explicitly that the reported p-values for the intercept/slope are two-tailed: it says "Pr(>|t|)", that means the p-value is based on the (minuscule) areas (plural!) under the curve between $[-\infty, -2.12]$ and $[2.12, +\infty]$ in Figure 84. And that area is the two-tailed p-value we see in the model output:

```
pt(q=-4.585, df=75, lower.tail=TRUE)   +
pt(q=+4.585, df=75, lower.tail=FALSE)
## [1] 1.780013e-05
```

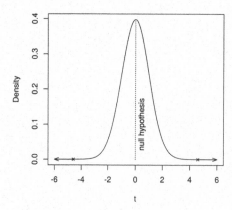

Figure 84: *t*-distribution for *df*=75

But given previous knowledge of the effects of word frequency, we would have had good reason to formulate a directional hypothesis, namely that the slope of FREQ would be negative. Since it is, it would then have been legit to use a one-tailed test and report half of this *p*-value for the slope, i.e. $8.9000671*10^{-6}$ (with some sensible rounding).

Believe me, I reviewed quite a few papers in the past where authors formulated a directional hypothesis and then (I guess unknowingly) did a non-directional/two-tailed test and reported that their result of, say, *p*=0.07 was not significant! (And, I have to admit, I once made this mistake myself.) Maybe you don't want to make that mistake (I certainly don't want to do it again): Rewriting a discussion section because (i) the effect one wanted is actually there and (ii) one's two pages of hand-wringing speculation why (one thought) it didn't show up is no one's idea of a good time ...

The second thing I want to draw your attention to is something I see even more often in submissions and papers. The result above looked pretty good, right? But who says that the straight line we chose to model RT with is the best we can do? Just because that's the simplest regression model doesn't mean it's the one we should stick with – maybe another model that permits the effect of FREQ to be curved (while still returning a result where, on the whole, FREQ speeds up RT) would be significantly/substantially better and, thus, permitted by Occam's razor. In fact, many things we're looking at in linguistics involve curved relations: learning, forgetting, priming, language change, and many more; as Harrell (2014:64) says, "[i]n the vast majority of studies, however, there is every reason to suppose that all relationships involving nonbinary predictors are nonlinear". In the present case, there are two reasons we might consider curvature, one *a priori*, the other not so much. As for the former, it is more than just reasonable to assume that word frequency isn't going to speed up subjects *ad infinitum*: at one point, you do not get faster anymore, if only for physiological reasons. Thus, there has to be some leveling off somewhere, and maybe that somewhere is included in our data – right now, we're not even checking that. As for the latter, recall that in our initial descriptive exploration, the curved smoother leveled off on the right (once FREQ exceeded 4).

How can one do this? One simple possibility is this: we do not enter FREQ as a predictor but poly(FREQ, 2). This essentially means adding FREQ, but also FREQ^2 (i.e. squared), as predictors into the model (and the squaring is what is responsible for the possibility of curving now). Let's see what happens:

```
summary(m.02 <- lm(RT ~ 1 + poly(FREQ, 2), data=x))
## [...] Coefficients:
##                    Estimate Std. Error t value Pr(>|t|)
## (Intercept)         631.860      6.031 104.761  < 2e-16 ***
## poly(FREQ, 2)1     -245.411     52.926  -4.637 1.49e-05 ***
## poly(FREQ, 2)2       87.060     52.926   1.645    0.104
## [...]
## Multiple R-squared:  0.2465, Adjusted R-squared:  0.2261
## F-statistic:  12.1 on 2 and 74 DF,   p-value: 2.834e-05
```

Well, both R^2-values of m.02 are higher than those of m.01, but really not by much. There's a straightforward way in the summary output of m.02 to see whether m.02 is significantly better – do you see it? – but the more generally useful way is by the absolutely key notion of model comparison: If you have two models that were fit to the same data set *and* if one model (here, m.01) is a submodel of the other model (here, m.02), typically such that they differ only by one predictor/term, then you can use the function anova to compare the two models to see whether the more complex model (here, m.02) can justify its higher degree of complexity by being significantly better than the less complex model (here, m.01). This is how it's done:

```
anova(m.01, m.02, test="F")
## Analysis of Variance Table
## Model 1: RT ~ 1 + FREQ
## Model 2: RT ~ 1 + poly(FREQ, 2)
##   Res.Df    RSS Df Sum of Sq      F Pr(>F)
## 1     75 214864
## 2     74 207285  1    7579.4 2.7058 0.1042
```

This output amounts to R saying the following: "I took a first model (m.01) and a second model (m.02); the two differ by df=1 but are not significantly different from each other (F=2.7058, df_1=1, df_2=74, p=0.1042)." (You can verify this by running pf(q=2.7058, df1=1, df2=74, lower.tail=FALSE). In other words, the added complexity of m.02 isn't accompanied by a correspondingly significantly better amount of variance explanation, which is why Occam's razor now says you have to go with the simpler one, i.e. m.01 without curvature.[10] Note how, in this case, the F-value and the p-value of this anova comparison are already in the summary output of m.02: If you check the coefficients row for poly(FREQ, 2)2, you find the p-value at the end and the t-value there is the square root of the anova F-value. The two plots, which compare the regression lines and their confidence bands side by side, also do not seem to differ a lot (at least not for the vast majority of the data):

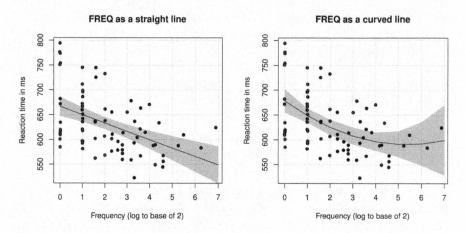

Figure 85: Straight vs. curved effect of FREQ

So, it might be nice to add to the previous write-up a sentence such as "A test for whether a curved effect of FREQ (an orthogonal polynomial to the second degree) would improve the model fit returned a non-significant result (F=2.7058, df_1=1, df_2=74, p=0.1042)."

---

10 This is a really tricky case because other model selection criteria (*AIC*) give a very weak recommendation to keep the curvature in the model; we will discuss those criteria later.

Recommendation(s) for further study: There are other ways to test for curvature, some of them much more powerful than polynomials, but I leave those up for you to explore at your 'leisure': check out the packages `splines` and especially `mgcv` for the extremely powerful (and complex) method of **generalized additive models**. Regarding the latter, see Pedersen et al. (2019) for a nice overview from an ecology point of view, Wieling (2018) or Baayen & Linke (to appear) for great yet still demanding overviews from a linguistics point of view and Wieling et al. (2014) for an application.

5.2.1.4 Excursus: model frames and model matrices

There are two notions I want to introduce now because the current model is so easy and straightforward and we'll need them later: The first one is the so-called **model frame**. The model frame is essentially just all the rows and columns used in the regression model. If our data frame had additional columns that are not used in the formula of m.01, they wouldn't be included in the model frame; if our data frame had rows with missing data in the relevant variables, those would also not be included. (From a model frame, you can also extract just the response with model.response(mf).)

```
head(mf <- model.frame(m.01), 3)
##                  RT      FREQ
## almond     650.9947 1.000000
## ant        589.4347 2.807355
## apple      523.0493 3.321928
```

The second, more important notion is the **model matrix**, which you get like so:

```
head(mm <- model.matrix(m.01), 3)
##           (Intercept)     FREQ
## almond              1 1.000000
## ant                 1 2.807355
## apple               1 3.321928
```

These are the values that you need to multiply the regression coefficients with – the intercept and the slope – and when you then sum up those products you get the predictions for each data point. (The intercept is always 1 because it's always included in the summation for every prediction and now you see why it's labeled "1" in the regression formula.). Look, these are the regression coefficients again:

```
coef(m.01)
## (Intercept)        FREQ
##   667.03260   -16.82015
```

So to get the prediction for *ant* you multiply and sum:

```
sum(coef(m.01) * mm["ant",]) # same as
## [1] 619.8125
1 *           # coef(m.01)[1]    , the intercept
667.03260 + # mm["ant",1]        , 1 for the intercept
2.807355 *  # coef(m.01)[2]      , the slope for FREQ
-16.82015   # mm["ant",2]        , FREQ for "ant"
## [1] 619.8125
```

We will see below why understanding this is useful, specifically when we talk about contrasts or something called *VIFs*.

5.2.1.5 Excursus: the 95%-CI of the slope

Very very brief final excursus, just as a 'proof of concept'. The slope and the intercept of m.01 came with 95%-CIs of [647.5, 686.6] and [-24.1, -9.5] respectively and we saw the resulting confidence band in the effects plots. One can apply a simulation-based approach to confidence intervals using a method called bootstrapping. **Bootstrapping** is another simulation-based approach where you
- take your data with its *n* data points and draw *n* values from it but with replacement (so that some data points will end up being chosen more than once and some data points will end up not chosen at all), then
- apply some statistical computation to that sample yielding a result *r*, and then
- do that again, and again, etc., always collecting *r*.

If you do that, say, 1000 times, you collect 1000 *r*-values, which give you an idea of the volatility of the *r*-value you got for your overall data set. That is because you just simulated 1000 times what *r* might have been if your data had been slightly different from what they actually are.

The 95%-CIs I obtained (from 1000 random-sampling-with-replacement draws) are [645.2, 689] and [-25.6, -9.5] so again quite similar to what Confint returned above, and if we plot the 1000 regression lines (in blue) on top of the confidence band (in red), we see the pretty good match of the two in Figure 86.

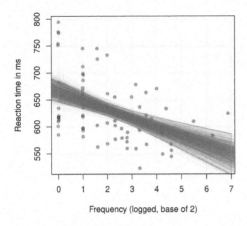

Figure 86: Parametric (red) vs. simulation-based (blue) 95%-CI

5.2.2 A linear model with a binary predictor

Let's now turn to a different kind of model, one where the predictor is categorical, specifically binary: We'll test the hypothesis that RT varies as a function of IMA (a scenario similar to that of Section 4.3.2.3 on the t-test for independent samples):
– H_0: There is no correlation between IMA and RT; $R^2=0$;
– H_1: There is a correlation between IMA and RT; $R^2>0$.

We load the data:

```
rm(list=ls(all.names=TRUE)); library(car); library(effects)
summary(x <- read.delim(file="_inputfiles/05_rt_ima.csv",
    stringsAsFactors=TRUE, row.names=1)) ## [...]
```

First, we do what we did above already, namely fix the ordering of the levels of IMA so that they are in a nice ascending order:

```
x$IMA <- factor(x$IMA, levels=levels(x$IMA)[c(2, 1)])
```

Next we would do some exploration of the data. Since we have already done some univariate exploration of every variable in previous sections, we just quickly do a box plot of RT ~ IMA:

```
boxplot(x$RT ~ x$IMA, varwidth=TRUE)
points(x=1:2, y=tapply(X=x$RT, INDEX=x$IMA, FUN=mean), pch=4)
```

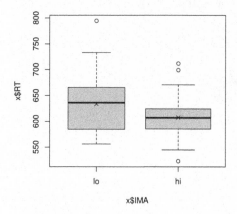

Figure 87: RT ~ IMA

It seems like there might be an effect, but the variability is big and the data set is small ... Let's fit our model.

5.2.2.1 Numerical exploration

The syntax doesn't change just because the predictor is categorical/binary now:

```
summary(m.01 <- lm(RT ~ 1 + IMA, data=x))
## [...] Coefficients:
##               Estimate Std. Error t value Pr(>|t|)
## (Intercept)    633.65      10.53   60.177   <2e-16 ***
## IMAhi          -25.97      14.00   -1.856   0.0693 .
## [...]
## Multiple R-squared:  0.06326,    Adjusted R-squared:  0.0449
## F-statistic: 3.444 on 1 and 51 DF,  p-value: 0.06925
```

Ok, the model isn't significant (F=3.444, df_1=1, df_2=51, p=0.06925) and the R^2-values are quite small (mult. R^2=0.063 and adj. R^2=0.045); this is the same as the t-test: The model's F-value is the t-test's t squared, the model's df_2 is the t-test's df, the p-value is the same, etc. But the real question is, what do the intercept (633.65) and the value for IMAhi (-25.97) mean? Remember me talking about something with your eyelids? This is that again, because the explanation is the same as before: The intercept is the value the regression model predicts when all categorical predictors in the model are set to their first level and/or all numeric predictors are set to 0. We don't have any numeric predictors so this part of the rule doesn't apply, which leaves us with the intercept being the predicted RT when IMA is its first level, which is *lo* (we fixed it that way). That is, the intercept of the output is the model saying, 'when IMA is *lo*, I predict an RT value of 633.65' (and that of course also mirrors the first mean reported by the *t*-test).

Now, what's the IMAhi value? That value is both a difference in means and a slope. This is because under the hood, so to speak, R conceptualizes the binary variable IMA such that it says, 'its first level (the user made that *lo*) is 0 and the second level (the user made that *hi*) is 1'. That way, the categorical difference between IMA *lo* and *hi* is like a slope of a discrete numeric variable which indicates how much the predicted value changes when you go from 0 (*lo*) to 1 (*hi*). Thus, that IMAhi value in the coefficients table (-25.97) is what you add to the intercept value (633.65) to get the prediction for IMA: *hi*:

```
coef(m.01)[2] + coef(m.01)[1]
##     IMAhi
## 607.6787
```

The way of how the difference in means (*lo* vs. *hi*) corresponds to a slope (0 to 1) is also visualized here; the arrow 'is' the regression line, its angle (relative to the *x*-axis) 'is' the slope:

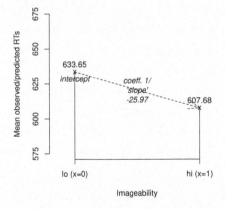

Figure 88: The regression coefficients/estimates of m.01

Another way of looking at this neat little conceptual trick is the following. Check out what happens if you create a version of IMA that to R is numeric, like IMA.num:

```
x$IMA.num <- as.numeric(x$IMA)-1; table(x$IMA, x$IMA.num)
##        0  1
##   lo  23  0
##   hi   0 30
```

If you now fit a linear model (or a correlation) with IMA.num as the predictor, you get the same results as we did with the categorical/binary factor IMA because that's what R does anyway:

```
summary(m.02 <- lm(RT ~ 1 + IMA.num, data=x)) ## [...]
```

And you can see that that's what's happening when you check out m.02's model frame and matrix (the matrix that R uses for the computations):

```
head(mf <- model.frame(m.01), 3)
##                RT IMA
## ant      589.4347  hi
## apple    523.0493  hi
## apricot  642.3342  lo
head(mm1 <- model.matrix(m.01), 3)
##          (Intercept) IMAhi
## ant                1     1
## apple              1     1
## apricot            1     0
head(mm2 <- model.matrix(m.02), 3)
##          (Intercept) IMA.num
## ant                1       1
## apple              1       1
## apricot            1       0
```

See? The *hi* in m.01's model frame column IMA is a 1 (like a logical TRUE) in m.01's model matrix column IMAhi just as it is a 1 in m.02's model frame column IMA.num, and the opposite for *lo* in m.01's model frame column IMA. In other words, a binary predictor to R is just something that can be made a 0 (*no*/FALSE) vs. 1 (*yes*/TRUE) numeric predictor (often called an **indicator variable**) so it can run the same linear model as if it has numeric data like in the previous section.

Now what does the *p*-value of summary output of `m.01` tell us? It says that the difference in the predicted RT-values isn't significant with a two-tailed hypothesis – it would have been significant, if we had formulated a one-tailed hypothesis because then you'd have been allowed to take half of that *p*-value: `pt(q=-1.856, df=51, lower.tail=TRUE)`.

As above, I follow that up with the following although it is just as redundant here as it was in the previous section – it will be different next time, I promise.

```
drop1(m.01, test="F")
## Single term deletions
## Model: RT ~ 1 + IMA
##          Df Sum of Sq    RSS     AIC F value  Pr(>F)
## <none>                130059  417.69
## IMA       1    8783.6 138843  419.15  3.4443 0.06925 .
```

It says, if you drop `IMA` from `m.01`, that makes no significant difference (*p*=0.06925). Let's get the 95%-CIs:

```
Confint(m.01) # return estimates w/ their 95%-CI
##              Estimate      2.5 %      97.5 %
## (Intercept) 633.65337 612.51383  654.792918
## IMAhi        -25.97463 -54.07247    2.123205
```

The CI for the difference in means/'slope' includes 0, which is R's way of saying, 'there being a difference of 0 between the two levels, i.e. none at all, that's plausible given the data.' Finally, the predictions, which in a monofactorial model like this are actually just the observed means (that `t.test` would return, see above); no surprises here, we already did much of that manually:

```
(ph <- data.frame(ima <- effect("IMA", m.01)))
##   IMA     fit       se    lower    upper
## 1  lo 633.6534 10.529844 612.5138 654.7929
## 2  hi 607.6787  9.219879 589.1691 626.1884
```

5.2.2.2 Graphical model exploration
Now, let's visualize. The simple plot is as before, a direct plotting of the `ima` effects object we just created:

```
plot(ima, xlab="Imageability", ylim=range(x$RT), grid=TRUE)
# [plot not shown, see code file ...]
```

But again, one might want to create a more detailed version that includes the observed data. Here I am showing a strip chart that uses the function arrows with 90-degree angles at the tips to draw error bars and/or confidence intervals; see the file for the code, I'm only showing the plot here:

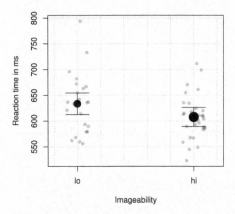

Figure 89: The effect of IMA

You can now write it all up: A linear regression model was fit with RT as the response and IMA as the only predictor. Observed/predicted RT means for IMA being *lo* and *hi* were 633.65 and 607.68 respectively [you could add CI information here]. However, given our non-directional H_1, the model indicated a non-significant fit (F=3.444, df_1=1, df_2=51, p=0.0693). The model fit was weak (mult. R^2=0.063, adj. R^2=0.045). [Then you would probably show the "Coefficients" table of the summary output and one of the plots.]

5.2.2.3 Excursus: coefficients as instructions

Because I have seen in many workshops how people struggle with the coefficients etc., here's yet another way to wrap your head around this is this: You gave lm a predictor IMA with two levels. Obviously that means you are interested in two means of RT, one for each of IMA's levels. But in the summary output, R doesn't give you two means – it gives you one mean (the one for IMA: *lo* as the intercept) and the other number it gives you is an instruction for you how to figure out the other one yourself: "Here's one mean for IMA: *lo* (I'm calling that an intercept), if you want the other one, just add the coefficient for IMAhi to the one I gave you, then you have it." And why does it do that? Because it tests each result for whether it could be 0 and gives you a *p*-value for that, which means if it gives you the *p*-value for the difference between IMA: *lo* and *hi*, then you can see whether that difference is significantly different from 0 and here it is not. As we will see, this logic extends to categorical variables with more levels.

The fact that regression coefficients are instructions on how to get from one mean to the next also reinforces something I said before: A traditional analysis of variance (ANOVA) is *the same* as a linear regression model! I read an overview article the other day that discussed ANOVA in a section on methods testing whether 'A is different from B' but put regression into a separate section on methods testing 'which predictors are associated with A'? That is misleading at best, as you know from (i) me pointing out in Section 1.3.2.1 that tests for independence and differences are not different (no pun intended) and now from (ii) the last few sections on linear regression modeling: The two are the same; see Gelman, Hill, & Vehtari (2020: Section 7.3) for more discussion.

5.2.3 A linear model with a categorical predictor

Let's now turn to a different kind of model, one where the predictor is categorical: we'll test the hypothesis that RT varies as a function of FAM:
- H_0: There is no correlation between FAM and RT; $R^2=0$;
- H_1: There is a correlation between FAM and RT; $R^2>0$.

We load the data and immediately fix the ordering of the levels of FAM to a nice ascending order:

```
rm(list=ls(all.names=TRUE)); library(car); library(effects)
summary(x <- read.delim(file="_inputfiles/05_rt_fam.csv",
    stringsAsFactors=TRUE, row.names=1)) ## [...]
x$FAM <- factor(x$FAM, levels=levels(x$FAM)[c(2, 3, 1)])
```

Next we would do the usual exploration of the data but again we already did a univariate explorations of every variable (response, predictor(s), ...) earlier so we just quickly do a box plot of RT ~ FAM:

```
boxplot(x$RT ~ x$FAM, varwidth=TRUE)
text(x=1:3, y=tapply(X=x$RT, INDEX=x$FAM, FUN=mean), labels="x")
```

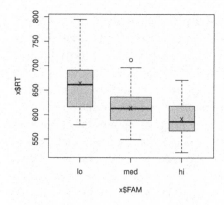

Figure 90: RT ~ FAM

It seems like there might be an effect, but the variability is big and the data set is small ... Let's fit our model.

5.2.3.1 Numerical exploration

As before, fitting/formulating the model doesn't change just because the predictor is categorical now. And, good, the model is significant ($F=7.982$, $df_1=2$, $df_2=52$, $p=0.0009481$) and the R^2-values are not all that bad (mult. $R^2=0.2349$ and adj. $R^2=0.2055$):

```
summary(m.01 <- lm(RT ~ 1 + FAM, data=x))
## [...] Coefficients:
##                 Estimate Std. Error t value Pr(>|t|)
## (Intercept)       663.29      13.23  50.118  < 2e-16 ***
## FAMmed            -49.64      15.59  -3.185 0.002449 **
## FAMhi             -71.90      18.72  -3.842 0.000334 ***
## [...]
## Multiple R-squared:  0.2349, Adjusted R-squared:  0.2055
## F-statistic: 7.982 on 2 and 52 DF,  p-value: 0.0009481
```

But the coefficients are what will be interesting now. From the above, I hope it is by now clear what the intercept is, namely the regression model's prediction when all categorical predictors in the model equation are set to their first level and/or all numeric predictors are set to 0. We again don't have any numeric predictors, which leaves us with the intercept of 663.29 being the predicted RT-value when FAM is its first level, which we set to *lo*. The other two coefficients follow the same logic as with IMA: Both are a difference in means as well as a slope because R extends the logic we saw for IMA by conceptualizing the ternary variable FAM in term of two contrasts:

– for the first contrast, R says, the first level of FAM is *lo* and I already mapped that onto the intercept (as 0) so let me contrast this intercept with all *cases* where FAM is *med* (which I make 1 in the column FAMmed in the model matrix) and then give the user the RT difference between those two levels of FAM as a difference in means/a slope;

– for the second contrast, R says, the first level of FAM is still *lo* and I already mapped that onto the intercept (as 0) so let me contrast this intercept now with all the cases where FAM is *hi* (which I make 1 in the model matrix) and then give the user the RT difference between those two levels of FAM as a difference in means/a slope.

Thus, that FAMmed value in the coefficients table (-49.64) is what you add to the intercept value (663.29) to get the prediction for FAM: *med*, and that FAMhi value in the coefficients table (-71.9) is what you add to the intercept value (663.29) to get the prediction for FAM: *hi*. That way, this is like a slope of a numeric variable which indicates how much the predicted value changes when you go, one time, from 0 (*lo*) to 1 (*med*), and the other time, from 0 (*lo*) to 1 (*hi*):

```
coef(m.01)[2] + coef(m.01)[1]
##    FAMmed
## 613.6471
coef(m.01)[3] + coef(m.01)[1]
##    FAMhi
## 591.3879
```

You can confirm that again by looking at the model frame and the model matrix:

```
head(mf <- model.frame(m.01), 3)
##               RT FAM
## ant      589.4347 med
## apple    523.0493 hi
## apricot  642.3342 lo
head(mm <- model.matrix(m.01),3)
##          (Intercept) FAMmed FAMhi
## ant                1      1     0
## apple              1      0     1
## apricot            1      0     0
```

This making the differences in means (*lo* vs. *med*, then *lo* vs. *hi*) slopes (0 to 1) is also visualized here. With this graph in particular, you should recognize that this kind of testing, which uses what are called **treatment contrasts**, is often great for situations where one of the levels of the predictor is a control group: Barring other considerations, make that one the first level of your factor so that all other groups are compared to the control and you get significance tests for how the control group/condition differs from everything else.

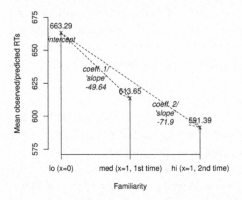

Figure 91: The regression coefficients/estimates of m.01

In other words, we have the same logic as before, but with an important twist: You gave lm a predictor with three levels. Obviously that means you are interested in three means of RT, one for each level of FAM. But in the summary output, R doesn't give you three means – it gives you one mean (the one for FAM: *lo*) and tells you to figure out the other two yourself: To get the predicted mean for FAM: *med*, take the intercept and add to it the coefficient for FAMmed, and to get the predicted mean for FAM: *hi*, take the intercept and add to it the coefficient for FAMhi. That way you can see whether the differences between the RT means (*lo* vs. *med* and *lo* vs. *hi*) are significant." But ...

1. that means we're neither explicitly given the difference between *med* and *hi* nor whether it is significant. From what we are given, we can infer what the difference is (-49.64 - -71.90), but not whether it's significant.
2. that also means that the coefficients output doesn't tell you one 'overall *p*-value' for FAM. In fact, it can happen with categorical predictors that the summary output for a 3-level predictor X shows you only 2 non-significant results, but X is still highly significant. This can happen in scenarios like the one in Figure 92, where the

a. the intercept is the prediction for X's level *a* (here, ≈11.5);
b. the first coefficient will be written as Xb and tells you how much you have to add to the intercept to predict the response when X is *b* (here, ≈1.9 and not significant here: *p*=0.089);
c. the second coefficient will be written as Xc and tells you how much you have to add to the intercept to predict the response when X is *c* (here, ≈-2.1 and not significant here: *p*=0.0575).
d. but it's the third possible comparison Xb vs Xc – i.e. exactly the one comparison difference (of ≈4) that we don't see in the summary output – that is actually significant here (*p*=0.0004) and that makes the predictor 'as a whole' significant (with a *p*-value of 0.06514).

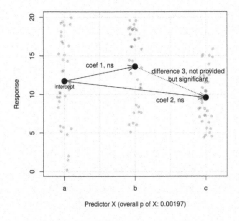

Figure 92: Differences between levels of predictor X

If you want one *p*-value for 'all of FAM', you can get that with anova again: You have a model with FAM, but you can also create one without it, i.e. a so-called **null model** without any predictors and just an intercept and then do a model comparison again:

```
m.00 <- lm(RT ~ 1, data=x); anova(m.00, m.01, test="F")
## Analysis of Variance Table
## Model 1: RT ~ 1
## Model 2: RT ~ 1 + FAM
##   Res.Df    RSS Df Sum of Sq      F     Pr(>F)
## 1     54 142847
## 2     52 109294  2     33553  7.982  0.0009481 ***
```

But you already know the nicer shortcut which we have used above for this: drop1, and you can see the results of both processes are identical:

```
drop1(m.01, test="F")
## Single term deletions
## Model: RT ~ 1 + FAM
##          Df Sum of Sq     RSS    AIC F value    Pr(>F)
## <none>               109294 423.70
## FAM      2    33553 142847 434.42   7.982 0.0009481 ***
```

It says, if you drop FAM from m.01, that makes a highly significant difference (p=0.0009481). (In this case, that's of course also the p-value of the full model, but in a multifactorial setting you can of course not use the p-value of the complete model to make inferences about a single predictor.) Here's how drop1 is essentially a shortcut for multiple manual anovas (I am leaving out all arguments other than the models and variables):

```
model.1 <- lm(Y ~ 1 + X1 + X2 + X3)
# this use of drop1 ...
drop1(model.1)
# ... does the same as the following 3 anova lines:
model.2a <- lm(Y ~ 1 +      X2 + X3); anova(model.1, model.2a)
model.2b <- lm(Y ~ 1 + X1      + X3); anova(model.1, model.2b)
model.2c <- lm(Y ~ 1 + X1 + X2     ); anova(model.1, model.2c)
```

Warning/advice: Given the above
- don't get into the habit of inferring the significance of predictor variables from the summary output if the predictor has more than 1 *df*, i.e. is not binary or numeric – use drop1; and
- don't summarize a coefficient with a sentence like "PREDICTOR's level x is significant (its coefficient is -49.6 [or whatever value it is])." That sentence doesn't mean much: That coefficient is a *difference* between two things, namely (i) the response's mean for when PREDICTOR is *x* and (ii) the response's mean when PREDICTOR is the intercept level – that's what you need to say. So, don't say 'FAM being *med* is significant', say 'the difference in predicted RT between when FAM is *med* and when FAM is *lo* is significant'.

But now how do you get the one missing contrast: *med* vs. *hi*? One way is with the very useful emmeans package, which has a function with the same name:

```
pairs(emmeans::emmeans(object=m.01, ~ FAM), adjust="none")
##  contrast estimate   SE df t.ratio p.value
##  lo - med     49.6 15.6 52   3.185  0.0024
```

```
##  lo - hi      71.9 18.7 52 3.842    0.0003
##  med - hi     22.3 15.6 52 1.428    0.1593
```

The first two contrasts we already knew from summary(lm(...)) but the third one is the new one and, here, the difference between *med* and *hi* isn't significant (p=0.1593).

The rest is all as before: 95%-CIs, ...

```
Confint(m.01) # return estimates w/ their 95%-CI
##              Estimate      2.5 %      97.5 %
## (Intercept) 663.28798  636.73111  689.84484
## FAMmed       -49.64091  -80.91828 -18.36354
## FAMhi        -71.90007 -109.45716 -34.34299
```

... and predictions:

```
(ph <- data.frame(fam <- effect("FAM", m.01)))
##    FAM      fit        se    lower     upper
## 1   lo 663.2880 13.234451 636.7311 689.8448
## 2  med 613.6471  8.234092 597.1242 630.1700
## 3   hi 591.3879 13.234451 564.8310 617.9448
```

5.2.3.2 Graphical model exploration

With regard to visualization of FAM's effect, there are no changes to our treatment of IMA: we can do the default effects plot ...

```
plot(fam, xlab="Familiarity", ylim=range(x$RT), grid=TRUE)
# [plot not shown, see code file ...]
```

... or we can customize another plot (the code would literally just be pasted from above – the only changes are the variable names (and this is possible because, as mentioned above in Section 4.1.1.1, I usually try to write the code such that R gets all the information from the data rather hard-coding in some numbers, that's why I don't say points(x=1:3, ...) etc.):

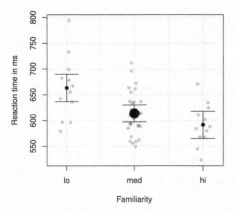

Figure 93: The effect of FAM

To sum up: "A linear regression model was fit with RT as the response and FAM as the only predictor. Observed/predicted RT means for FAM being *lo*, *med*, and *hi* were 663.29, 613.65, and 613.65 respectively [you could add CI information here]. The model indicated a significant fit (F=7.982, df_1=2, df_2=52, p<0.0001). The model fit was decent (mult. R^2=0.235, adj. R^2=0.206). [Then you would probably show the "Coefficients" table of the summary output and/or the output of pairs(emmeans...) and one of the plots.] All reaction times contrasts but *med* vs hi were significantly different from each other."

5.2.3.3 Excursus: conflation, model comparison, and contrasts

There are at least three things with the previous model that require additional explanation – this excursus is long! The first has to do with the last sentence of our write-up: 'all but *med* vs *hi* were significantly different from each other'. Depending on how entrenched Occam's razor is in your mind and depending on how much you took my "don't trust anyone's analysis, least of all your own!" to heart, this should make you perk up. Does the following characterization of our current situation remind you of something? We have a model whose coefficients table contains an intercept and two more terms (both related to one predictor), but the results (here from emmeans) indicate that not all terms (beyond the intercept) are significant.

What that should remind you is the situation when we checked for lm(RT~FREQ) whether FREQ needed to be curved. There, with FREQ, we had a more complex model (with curvature) and when we compared it to a less complex model (without curvature), we found Occam's razor preferred the simpler one. Here, by analogy, we have a model that involves three contrasts within FAM

– *lo* vs. *med*, *lo* vs. *hi*, *med* vs. *hi* – but maybe it's the same here and we don't need all the info currently in the model. So, let's compare ...

For this, we first create a version of FAM that conflates the two (adjacent ordinal) levels that exhibit the smallest difference (and that, just here, we actually already know are not significantly different (from pairs(emmeans(...))); this is didactically motivated) and then we create a second model that is simpler than m.01 because it now uses this conflated/reduced predictor:

```
x$FAM.confl <- x$FAM
levels(x$FAM.confl) <- c("lo", "med/hi", "med/hi")
table(x$FAM, x$FAM.confl)
##        lo med/hi
##    lo  12      0
##   med   0     31
##    hi   0     12
summary(m.02 <- lm(RT ~ 1 + FAM.confl, data=x))
## [...] Coefficients:
##                    Estimate Std. Error t value Pr(>|t|)
## (Intercept)          663.29      13.36  49.634  < 2e-16 ***
## FAM.conflmed/hi      -55.85      15.11  -3.696 0.000521 ***
## [...]
## Multiple R-squared:  0.2049, Adjusted R-squared:  0.1899
## F-statistic: 13.66 on 1 and 53 DF,  p-value: 0.0005209
```

The R^2-values are going down, but the *p*-value is smaller. You can see that the intercept is the same – of course, it's still the prediction for FAM: *lo* – but the slope for *med/hi* has of course changed. Now, which model to prefer? Same answer as above: If you have two models that were fit to the same data set *and* if one model (here m.02) is a sub-model of the other model (m.01), typically such that they differ only by one predictor/term, then you can use anova to compare the two models to see whether the more complex model can justify its higher degree of complexity by being significantly better than the less complex model. Thus:

```
anova(m.01, m.02, test="F")
## Analysis of Variance Table
## Model 1: RT ~ 1 + FAM
## Model 2: RT ~ 1 + FAM.confl
##   Res.Df    RSS Df Sum of Sq      F Pr(>F)
## 1     52 109294
## 2     53 113580 -1   -4286.4 2.0394 0.1593
```

The models are not significantly different from each other (F=2.04, df_1=1, df_2=52, p=0.1593), and this is the p-value that emmeans reported for *med* vs. *hi*. (You can check this by running pf(q=2.039385, df1=1, df2=52, lower.tail=FALSE). In other words, the higher degree of complexity of m.01 as opposed to m.02 (distinguishing three levels of FAM as opposed to two) isn't justified by a significantly better amount of variance explanation, which is why Occam's razor now says you have to go with the simpler one, i.e. m.02 with only two levels. That of course means that now you'd have to do everything again: drop1 (for consistency's sake), but definitely the CIs, the plot(s), and the write-up. Final comment on this first bit though: You might wonder, ok, I see how this works (i) in the case of truly categorical predictors where I conflate levels that behave alike and (ii) here where the predictor is actually ordinal (!) and the levels that behave alike are adjacent – but what do I do if a predictor is ordinal and, for whatever reason, the highest and the lowest rank behave alike (e.g., here, *lo* and *hi*)? Answer: then, most likely (!), you shouldn't conflate. We do conflation where indicated to follow Occam's razor and get a good (final) model, but most of the time we do so to then interpret the model and unless you come up with an ingenious explanation for why *lo* and *hi* should in fact behave the same (e.g., some hypothesis predicting a *U*-shaped trend), we shouldn't make a model 'statistically nicer' if that amounts to it being linguistically/conceptually less interpretable or not at all.

Ok, the second thing we need to briefly consider is this: Recall that, when we looked at m.01, we only had two of the three possible contrasts in there with p-values. We then used pairs(emmeans...) to get the third contrast. In the above case, I think that is fairly uncontroversial, but what if you have a predictor PARTOFSPEECH with 7 levels. The summary output of the model for that predictor would give you 6 contrasts: the intercept/first level of PARTOFSPEECH against the 2nd, against the 3rd, ..., against the 7th. But the number of those 6 contrasts pales in comparison to all the others you are not shown: 2nd vs. 3rd, 2nd vs. 4th,, ... 5th vs. 6th, 6th vs. 7th. With 7 levels, there are t(combn(7, 2))=$^{7 \times 6}/_2$=21 possible pairwise contrasts, meaning the summary table showed you only less than a third of the pairwise comparisons that one could theoretically do. Now, you can of course do some version of pairs(emmeans...) again to get them all, but then you are testing the living ... out of this single predictor, which can be dangerous. Why/how?

Remember we're normally assuming a significance level of 0.05, meaning 1 in 20 tests likely returns a significant result even if it shouldn't. But in this example, you'd be squeezing 21 tests out of PARTOFSPEECH so chances are at least one significant test will come out of that even if PARTOFSPEECH does absolutely nothing. In fact, if you do 13 tests at a significance level of 0.05, the chance that you are right in accepting the H_1 all the time is already close to that of a coin toss:

```
significance.level <- 0.05; number.of.tests <- 13
(1-significance.level)^number.of.tests
## [1] 0.5133421
```

Thus, the more tests you perform on one and the same data set/predictor, the more you should adjust your significance level from $p=0.05$ to something less lenient so that you reduce the risk of accepting H$_1$s you shouldn't be accepting. This can be done with the function p.adjust and here's an example using the above scenario. I first create a vector p.values.of.21.tests that contains 6 significant results and 15 non-significant ones, which could be the result of your testing every single contrast there is:

```
set.seed(sum(utf8ToInt("Erdbeerschnitte")))
p.values.of.21.tests <- c(runif(6, 0, 0.049), runif(15, 0.05, 1))
```

And now we adjust for the fact that we do such a high number of tests:

```
p.values.adjusted.for.doing.21.tests <- p.adjust(
    p=p.values.of.21.tests, method="holm")
sum(p.values.adjusted.for.doing.21.tests<0.05) # no * ones remain!
## [1] 0
```

The spirit of this adjustment is somewhat similar to how R^2-values get adjusted: Those get adjusted to penalize you for including too many maybe not so great predictors; here, the p-values get adjusted to penalize you for testing the hell out of your predictor. The above is the general approach using the function p.adjust from R base, but as you saw above, pairs, when applied to an emmeans object, can already take the same kind of adjust argument – I only always set that to *none* above because I wanted to show you how, with no adjustments, emmeans replicates the values from summary(lm(...)). Now, in the – I think – highly unlikely event that every single one of your 21 pairwise contrasts is in fact grounded in carefully-developed *a priori* theory (how likely is that ...?), forget I said anything and don't adjust, but down here on Earth, where I live, it is quite likely that at least some of these contrasts are not really motivatable well and then you have to be careful.

The third and final "additional consideration" has two parts, both of which are related to the previous one in terms of how they both speak to the contrasts you see quantified in the summary output. In keeping with my telling you to always be 'on the lookout', I hope it hasn't escaped your notice that we've actually been treating FAM as if it was categorical, when in fact it is ordinal! And R does in fact allow us to declare a factor to not just have categorical, but in fact ordinal levels; look at the difference in how the levels are reported:

```
head(x$FAM)
## [1] med hi  lo  med hi  med
## Levels: lo med hi
head(factor(x$FAM, ordered=TRUE))
## [1] med hi  lo  med hi  med
## Levels: lo < med < hi
```

However, summary outputs of models with such ordered factors are not straight-forward to interpret at all (because of the numerical contrasts resulting from R making a factor ordered) so we will use a different option that will make the summary output be very instructive. Instead of the treatment contrast coding we have been using so far, we can use a different one that I have found useful for ordinal factors. If you already made sure the factor levels are in the nice ascending order, as we did, it is very simple to apply to a factor the so-called **successive differences contrast coding** (using a function from the package MASS):

```
library(MASS)
x$FAM.sdif <- x$FAM; contrasts(x$FAM.sdif) <- contr.sdif
```

Nothing seems to have happened but let's compare the coefficients table of m.01, repeated here for convenience, ...

```
summary(m.01)$coefficients
##               Estimate Std. Error   t value      Pr(>|t|)
## (Intercept) 663.28798   13.23445 50.118286 1.074102e-45
## FAMmed      -49.64091   15.58688 -3.184787 2.448529e-03
## FAMhi       -71.90007   18.71634 -3.841567 3.340358e-04
```

... to this one based on the new version of the factor:

```
summary(m.03 <- lm(RT ~ 1 + FAM.sdif, data=x))$coefficients
##               Estimate Std. Error   t value      Pr(>|t|)
## (Intercept) 622.77431   6.815844 91.371556 4.235953e-59
## FAM.sdif2-1 -49.64091  15.586884 -3.184787 2.448529e-03
## FAM.sdif3-2 -22.25916  15.586884 -1.428070 1.592504e-01
```

Everything that would be at the bottom of the model output (not shown here) is the same (R^2, F, p, etc.), but the intercept is now the (unweighted!) mean of all three means of RT for the levels of FAM:

```
mean(tapply(x$RT, x$FAM, mean))
## [1] 622.7743
```

But what we care about is what's below that: The first coefficient is called FAM.sdif2-1, which means it's the difference between FAM's second and first level and that one we also got in the previous output. However, the second coefficient is called FAM.sdif3-2, which means it's the difference between FAM's third and second level. Thus, the p-values are now for the successive differences between the levels of the predictor in the right order and for the difference 3-2, i.e. what we before called *med* vs. *hi* we get the same p-value as with pairs(emmeans...) but without doing all sorts of tests – we're just testing each step in the sequence. Thus, this is a very nice (and for once really simple) alternative to take the ordinal nature of the factor more seriously while still getting an easily interpretable summary output.

The final discussion of contrasts here in this section is, in a sense, the most powerful and general one (and therefore long ...). Most of the studies I see use R's default treatment contrasts – only occasionally do I see other contrasts such as sum coding (see ?contr.sum) or Helmert (see ?contr.helmert) and very rarely do I see what follows now. Often, R's default contrasts do the job well enough (especially if one's interpretation is mostly based on effects plots), but we can also define our own set of contrasts that can not only test a very specific set of *a priori* hypotheses, but that are also nicely statistically independent of each other; these contrasts are called **planned orthogonal contrasts** and I will explain them here with two examples (and we will then use them occasionally in what follows). Since these are *a priori*/planned contrasts, we will just for now pretend that we actually had two *a priori* alternative hypotheses: that (i) that *lo* would definitely slow people down compared to 'not *lo*' (i.e. *med* and *hi* combined) and that (ii) the means of RT for *med* and *hi* wouldn't differ significantly. That is a set of hypotheses we can 'code into the factor FAM directly' so as to make the summary output of the regression model 'answer all our questions' right away. (Just like with the default treatment contrasts, we can formulate *l*-1 contrasts for a predictor, where *l* is the number of levels of our predictor.)

The optimal formulation of such planned orthogonal contrasts is governed by a set of rules we need to discuss:
1. levels that are ignored in a comparison are set to 0;
2. each level can only participate in one comparison in isolation.

3. the sum of all value tokens of a contrast vector is 0;
4. (groups of) levels that are contrasted with each other differ in their sign;
5. the sum of all absolute values of types is 1;
6. the products of weights sum to 0.

Without an example, this is probably close to incomprehensible, so let's look at what this means for our two FAM hypotheses/contrasts; since we will have to define this within R as a matrix, we will do so here as well. Check out Table 22:

Table 22: Orthogonal contrast settings for our hypotheses (i) and (ii)

FAM	contrast 1: *lo* vs. *med/hi*	contrast 2: *med* vs. *hi*
lo	+0.66667	0
med	-0.33333	+0.5
hi	-0.33333	-0.5

So, let walk through those rules separately for each of the hypotheses/contrasts;
1. with regard to rule 1,
   a. contrast 1: no level is ignored in this contrast, all three levels of FAM are involved, so none of them gets a 0, ✓;
   b. contrast 2: as per rule 2, the level *lo* was already compared on its own against something else so it cannot be compared again, which means it must now be ignored, and it does have a 0, ✓;
2. each level does only participate in one comparison in isolation:
   a. *lo* is used in isolation only once, in contrast 1, ✓;
   b. *med* and *hi* are each used in isolation only once, in contrast 2, ✓;
3. if we add up the three values in the each column of the contrast table, we do get 0 for each column, ✓;
4. with regard to rule 4,
   a. contrast 1: the two groups of values that are contrasted do differ in their sign: *lo* has a positive contrast weight (+2/3) whereas the other two have a negative weight (-1/3), ✓;
   b. contrast 2: the two values that are contrasted do differ in their sign: *med* has a positive contrast weight (+0.5) whereas *hi* has a negative weight (-0.5), ✓;
5. with regard to rule 5,
   a. contrast 1: if we take the two value types (+$^2/_3$ and -$^1/_3$), make them both positive, and add them up, we do get 1, ✓;
   b. contrast 2: if we take the two value types (+0.5 and -0.5), make them both positive, and add them up, we do get 1, ✓;

6. this sum is indeed 0: $^2/_3 \times 0 + -^1/_3 \times 0.5 + -^1/_3 \times -0.5$, ✓.

Believe it or not but I can see your face, even from within this book, ... because I have seen hundreds of bootcamp participants' faces before ... You're thinking, how the hell would I get from rules 1 to 6 to those numbers in the table?! This is one of these good-news-bad-news kind of situations and you don't get to choose, you get to hear the bad one first. So how do you arrive at those numbers? By traveling back in time to when you sat in, I dunno, 8th grade and maybe thought, "it doesn't get more useless than this!" You have to solve a small system of equations: For hypothesis/contrast 1, you need three weights that will have to be composed of two distinct values (because of rule 4), let's call those x for *lo* and y (for each *med* and *hi*) and you do know from rule 3 that $x+2y=0$, plus you know from rules 4 and 5 that $x+-y=1$. To do this in the slowest, most fine-grained way possible (of course there's a shortcut): From the former, it follows that $x=-2y$. If we insert that into the latter, we get $-2y+-y=1$, thus $-3y=1$, thus $y=-^1/_3$. That, we insert into $x=-2y$ and we get $x=-2\times-^1/_3=^2/_3$, done, there's our values for *lo* (x) and *med* and *hi* (y). For contrast 2, it's even simpler because *lo* is already restricted to 0.

If that was the bad news, what's the good one? It's that once you've done this a few times, you 'just know'. For instance, the first contrast involves all 3 levels of FAM, so the denominator in the fractions involved will be 3, etc.; trust me, I can't even remember when I composed my contrasts like this the last time.

Now, how do we do this in R? It's actually pretty easy (no, I'm not kidding):

```
x$FAM.contr <- x$FAM
lo_vs_med.hi <- c(2/3, -1/3, -1/3)
med_vs_hi <-    c(0  , 1/2, -1/2)
(contrasts(x$FAM.contr) <-    cbind(lo_vs_med.hi, med_vs_hi))
##        lo_vs_med.hi med_vs_hi
## [1,]     0.6666667       0.0
## [2,]    -0.3333333       0.5
## [3,]    -0.3333333      -0.5
```

Now we can fit our model with that predictor:

```
summary(m.04 <- lm(RT ~ 1 + FAM.contr, data=x))$coefficients
##                          Estimate Std. Error   t value      Pr(>|t|)
## (Intercept)             622.77431   6.815844 91.371556 4.235953e-59
## FAM.contrlo_vs_med.hi    60.77049  15.358659  3.956758 2.313189e-04
## FAM.contrmed_vs_hi       22.25916  15.586884  1.428070 1.592504e-01
```

All overall statistics (F, R^2s, p, again not shown) are the same, only the coefficients table changes. The intercept is again the (unweighted!) mean of all three FAM means, but check out the rest of the coefficients table now. It exactly answers our questions in the hypothesized scenario: the first row says the difference between *lo* and *med/hi* is highly significant (with a 60.77 ms difference) and the second row says the difference between *med* and *hi* isn't significant (with the by now familiar 22.26 ms difference, which comes with the by now familiar p-value of 0.1593).

I know this seems like a lot of work for something that you can get much more easily from elsewhere, but (i) it's only a lot of work while it's still new to you, after that it's effortless, and (ii) there are cases where it's not obvious at all how else you would get the kind of information planned contrasts can provide easily, which is where our second example comes in, a learner corpus study that included native speakers of English and learners of four different L1s, namely *French*, *German*, *Norwegian*, and *Spanish*. While that study did not do a regression, it still involved what in a regression modeling context would have been a 5-level predictor L1. My question to you: how would you set up the contrasts of this vector? Yes, treatment contrasts with L1: *English* as the first level would already be not bad – then each learner L1 gets compared to the native speaker results – but I want something that's probably even better so how do you do it?

THINK BREAK

Assuming the levels of the factor L1 are in alphabetical order – *en*, *fren*, *germ*, *norw*, *span* – I hope you agree with me on this:

```
contrasts(x$L1) <- cbind(
#                          en     fren    germ   norw   span
   native_vs_nonnative= c(0.8,  -0.2,   -0.2,  -0.2,  -0.2),  # contrast 1
   romance_vs_germanic= c(0  ,   0.5,   -0.5,  -0.5,   0.5),  # contrast 2
   spanish_vs_french=   c(0  ,  -0.5,    0  ,   0  ,   0.5),  # contrast 3
   norwergian_vs_german=c(0  ,   0  ,   -0.5,   0.5,   0  ))) # contrast 4
```

I won't bore you with how we get to those numbers, that torture, I mean "privilege"!, is reserved for bootcamp participants, but they are of course constructed according to the same rules as above. Such orthogonal contrasts can often be usefully conceptualized as forming a tree structure of comparisons:

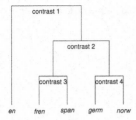

Figure 94: Orthogonal contrasts as a tree

This kind of stuff isn't that easily done with conflation etc. – knowing how to formulate such contrasts can make your regression modeling much more efficient.

Recommendation(s) for further study: For more on contrasts (especially in a mixed-effects modeling context), check out Schad et al. (2020), but it's quite technical (so maybe wait till after you've read the mixed-effects modeling chapter as well).

5.2.4 Towards multifactorial modeling

5.2.4.1 Simpson's paradox

Ok, now we're getting serious ... no more monofactorial stuff. Above, I spent some time on the mpg/displacement example to motivate multifactorial studies (likely even when your hypothesis is monofactorial). I will now discuss another very important motivation to consider your data multifactorially. Go back to Figure 1 for a moment (Section 1.2), which shows a reasonably strong and highly significant correlation between a predictor XX and a response YY. However, as you hopefully recall, both the plot and the correlation/linear regression are missing a second (categorical) predictor FF that was also part of the data; in fact, that factor FF denoted the field location where the XX and YY-values were sampled and that factor's correlation with YY is shown in the left panel of Figure 95 here (where the plotted letters represent the means). As you can see, FF's correlation with YY is quite strong (in fact, it's even stronger than that of XX, whose R^2 is a mere 0.5212). But now the 'magic' is what happens in the right panel (a version of Figure 2 with R^2 added), namely when one fits a multifactorial model in which XX, FF, and their interaction are used to model/predict YY: within each level of FF (i.e., within each field site), the correlation between XX and YY is actually negative, the opposite of what the left panel showed (reasonably strongly and highly significantly).

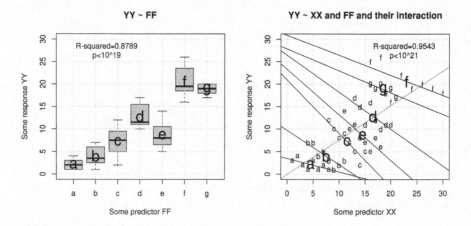

Figure 95: Simpson's paradox

This phenomenon is called **Simpson's paradox**: the fact that an effect in aggregate data (the positive slope in Figure 1) disappears or even gets reversed when the data are data are disaggregated (the right panel). Thus, whether a predictor (e.g., FF) is absent or present from a model can change what another predictor (e.g. XX) does (e.g., changing XX's positive slope to a negative one); thus, what one predictor does can depend on what one or more others are doing. This phenomenon is called an interaction, which is a concept everyone knows really well in real life, but that often gets omitted or misunderstood in research.

5.2.4.2 Interactions
Let me exemplify this notion with a non-linguistic example from my teaching: Imagine a well-being scale from 0 to 10: 0 means you're dead, 10 means you feel perfectly healthy and great. Let's imagine one evening you feel kinda crappy (WELLBEING=3). From past experience, you know that there are things that might make you feel better. Maybe, whenever in the past you felt like you feel now and you took medication *x*, it always made you feel better by 3 well-being points so you think 'if I change a variable TAKENMED from *no* to *yes*, that'll boost my score from 3 to 6'. Maybe, depending on your lifestyle, you also always feel 3 points better if you drink a bottle of vodka (changing the variable VODKAINTAKE from 0 to 1 (bottles)). So you conclude, 'cool, why don't I do both, then I'll be at 9!', and that embodies the null hypothesis of **additive behavior,** the assumption that what each predictor does as an effect is independent of what the other(s) do(es) so their individual effects just add up. But unless you're having a bottle of vodka

just now as you're reading this, I'm pretty sure you see where this is headed: some medications don't go all that well with alcohol. Thus,

- taking only the medication would boost WELLBEING from 3 to 6, i.e. the coefficient/difference in means for TAKENMED *no* → *yes* would be 3;
- drinking only the vodka would boost WELLBEING from 3 to 6, i.e. the coefficient/slope of VODKAINTAKE 0 → 1 would be 3;
- doing both would reduce your WELLBEING to 0, i.e. something would change the predicted value from 3 (where you were) + 3 (TAKENMED *no* → *yes*) + 3 (VODKAINTAKE 0 → 1), which should be 9, down to 0.

That something with a -9 effect would be an interaction (term). In fact, the highly technical definition I always use in teaching is: **an interaction is if something doesn't do the same everywhere/always.** That medication doesn't *always* make you feel better (by 3 points) – not if you down it with a bottle of vodka. Vodka doesn't *always* make you feel better (by 3 points) – not if you take the medication with it. More formally, two or more predictors are not just additive but interacting if the outcome of their joint behavior isn't the one you would predict from knowing their individual effects. Straightforward, right? Well, we'll see how in linguistics it often doesn't seem to be. But let's first discuss this in a bit more detail using a (made-up) linguistic example.

Let's return to an example from the beginning of the book: We again assume you wished to study whether the lengths of grammatical-relation constituents – captured in the response LENGTH – are correlated with two predictors: GRAMREL: *object* vs. *subject* and CLAUSE: *main* vs. *subordinate*; let's further assume you had equally many data points for all four combinations. Let's finally assume you determined the syllabic lengths of all constituents to compute the means for the four variable level combinations – objects in main clauses, objects in subordinate clauses, objects in main clauses, subjects in subordinate clauses – and obtained the following results:

- the average length of all subjects (i.e., across main and subordinate clauses) is less than that of all direct objects;
- the average length of all constituents (i.e., across subjects and objects) in main clauses is less than that of constituents in subordinate clauses.

Given these results, which of the four types of constituents would you expect to be longest and which to be shortest? I'm hoping that you think you'd expect main-clause subjects to be shortest and subordinate-clause objects to be longest, because, in the absence of indications to the contrary (which you were not given), that kind of additive behavior is H_0:

If two things each of which promote shortness come together, the effect should be something really short. In the most extremely homogeneous of cases, the result might be something like that visualized in Figure 96: The x-axis represents the predictor CLAUSE, the y-axis the response LENGTH, and the second predictor GRAMREL is represented by the two differently-colored lines. Also, the m and s represent the means for all main and subordinate clauses respectively (across levels of GRAMREL), and the two points in the middle are, as indicated on the x-axis, the means for objects and subjects (across levels of CLAUSE).

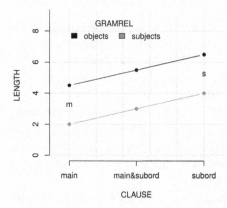

Figure 96: Additive behavior of two binary predictors

We can also represent these results in pivot-table like form: The four central cells are the observed means from the plot, the diff row and column indicate the differences of the two values in each row and column:

Table 23: Additive behavior of two binary predictors

	main	subord	$\text{diff}_{\text{main}\to\text{subord}}$
objects	4.5	6.5	2
subjects	2	4	2
$\text{diff}_{\text{subj}\to\text{obj}}$	2.5	2.5	

(The discussion of this is better with dynamic slides, but ok, here goes:) This graph and this table represent perfect additivity. Visually, because the two lines for objects and subjects are perfectly parallel (and it was the desire to show that which made me use a line plot connecting results for levels of categorical vari-

ables, which is usually frowned upon). Numerically, we can explain the additivity as follows: If I
- told you that main clause subjects have an average length of 2, and that
  - main-clause objects are on average 2.5 syllables longer than those (the left column difference);
  - subordinate-clause subjects are on average 2 syllables longer than those (the lower row difference);
- then asked you how long you think subordinate-clause objects will be,

you'd guess 2 (the starting value) + 2.5 (the first difference) + 2 (the second difference) = 6.5, and you'd be right on target, as shown in the plot and the table, because these 'data' are indeed perfectly additive. In fact, if you look at the diff row and column, you can even already see the perfect additivity there, because, remember how we defined *interaction*? "something doesn't do the same everywhere/always". Well, but here 'it' does:
- switching from subjects to objects leads to an increase of 2.5 *no matter which clause type you're looking at* (see the row for diff);
- switching from main to subordinate clauses leads to an increase of 2 *no matter which grammatical relation you're looking at* (see the column for diff).

How would we fit a linear model for this? Like this and, to understand the output, you have to know that I made *subject* the first level of GRAMREL:

```
round(summary(m.1 <- lm(LENGTH ~ 1 + GRAMREL + CLAUSE,
    data=s1))$coefficients, 3)
##              Estimate Std. Error t value Pr(>|t|)
## (Intercept)     2.010      0.014 143.001        0
## GRAMRELobj      2.500      0.016 154.019        0
## CLAUSEsubord    2.003      0.016 123.400        0
```

As you will remember (right?!):
- what is the intercept? "the value the regression model predicts when all categorical predictors in the model equation are set to their first level and/or all numeric predictors are set to 0. We have no numeric predictors; thus the intercept, ≈ 2, is the prediction when GRAMREL is *subject* and when CLAUSE is *main*;
- what are the coefficients? 'the value you must add to the intercept to, in the case of (levels of) categorical predictors, predict the value for the level of X you are looking at [...] while, and this is the crucial point, all categorical predictors not mentioned [...] are set to their first level'; thus,

- the value for GRAMRELobj is ≈2.5, meaning it's what you need to add to the intercept of 2 (for main clause subjects) to predict main-clause objects;
- the value for CLAUSEsubord is ≈2, meaning it's what you need to add to the intercept of 2 (for main clause subjects) to predict subordinate-clause subjects.

And then R/the model expects you to know that if you want to predict the length of subordinate-clause objects, you have to add both 2.5 and 2 to the intercept.

This is a model that has two so-called **main effects**, effects of predictors on their own that apply everywhere/always. As we see in the table/plot, it does pretty well; in these simulated data, R^2 is 0.997. But what if you forced an interaction into this model. In R, you'd do that like this:

```
round(summary(m.1b <- lm(LENGTH ~ 1 + GRAMREL + CLAUSE +
    GRAMREL:CLAUSE, data=s1))$coefficients, 3)
##                             Estimate Std. Error t value Pr(>|t|)
## (Intercept)                    2.011      0.016 123.396    0.000
## GRAMRELobj                     2.497      0.023 108.349    0.000
## CLAUSEsubord                   2.000      0.023  86.789    0.000
## GRAMRELobj:CLAUSEsubord        0.005      0.033   0.145    0.885
```

The interaction term GRAMREL:CLAUSE (the order doesn't matter, CLAUSE:GRAMREL would be just as fine) means you're permitting the effect GRAMREL to vary across the levels of CLAUSE (and the other way round). As you can see, the estimates in the first three rows are nearly exactly the same as before, but the fourth row is new. With m.1, to predict the length of subordinate-clause objects, you added to the intercept the two coefficients from before, then you were done. Now with m.1b, if you want to predict the length of subordinate-clause objects, you proceed like this: You start from the intercept (always), which is the mean for main-clause subjects; but you want to predict subordinate-clause objects, so to the intercept of ≈2 you need to add three things, namely
- as before and to change GRAMREL to *object*, you add the coefficient of GRAMRELobj, ≈2.5; according to the coefficients table, that makes a significant difference so your interim sum is ≈4.5;
- as before and to also change CLAUSE to *subord*, you add the coefficient of CLAUSEsubord, ≈2; so your interim sum is ≈6.5;
- but now the coefficient table also says 'oh, and when these two changes happen at the same time (GRAMRELobj:CLAUSEsubord), *then* you also add ≈0.005 – but actually, you don't need to because that makes no significant difference (*p*=0.885), you're already nearly perfectly at 6.5 already anyway.

This is confirmed by the by now familiar anova-based model comparison of the simpler model m.1 and the more complex model (by one term) m.1b:

```
anova(m.1, m.1b, test="F")
## Model 1: LENGTH ~ 1 + GRAMREL + CLAUSE
## Model 2: LENGTH ~ 1 + GRAMREL + CLAUSE + GRAMREL:CLAUSE
##    Res.Df    RSS Df   Sum of Sq      F Pr(>F)
## 1     117 0.92447
## 2     116 0.92430  1 0.00016752  0.021  0.885
```

So this is additive behavior: Both predictors do the same no matter what so R says you can make good (enough) predictions just by looking at the two predictors and don't need to also let the effect of one predictor be modified by the other; your prediction doesn't benefit significantly from an interaction. But then what would be an interaction? Consider Figure 97 (ignore the dashed line and the unfilled circle for now).

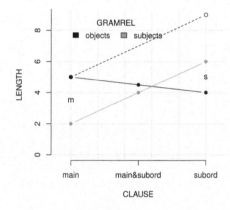

Figure 97: Interactive behavior of two binary predictors (1)

And here's the table:

Table 24: Interactive behavior of two binary predictors 1

	main	subord	diff$_{main \to subord}$
objects	5	4	-1
subjects	2	6	4
diff$_{subj \to obj}$	3	-2	

This is an interaction: visually, because the solid lines are far from parallel and, numerically, because the diff row and column show that each level of each predictor does something different depending on the other: When CLAUSE is *main*, changing from *subject* to *object* is a difference of 3, but when CLAUSE is *subord*, changing from *subject* to *object* is a difference of -2. If I
- told you that main clause subjects have an average length of 2, and that
  - main-clause objects are on average 3 syllables longer than those;
  - subordinate-clause subjects are on average 4 syllables longer than those;
- then asked you how long think subordinate-clause objects will be,

you'd guess 2 (the starting value) + 3 (the first difference) + 4 (the second difference) = 9, and you'd be totally off: You'd be where the dashed line leads, the unfilled circle, but you'd be totally overshooting the mark. You'd be predicting 9 when, according to the data, you should be predicting 4; you need a correction of -5 – an interaction term – to get from the additive assumption to what's actually happening in the data.

Here's the model with the interaction term:

```
round(summary(m.2b <- lm(LENGTH ~ 1 + GRAMREL + CLAUSE +
    GRAMREL:CLAUSE, data=s2))$coefficients, 3)
##                             Estimate Std. Error  t value Pr(>|t|)
## (Intercept)                    2.011      0.016  123.396        0
## GRAMRELobj                     2.997      0.023  130.043        0
## CLAUSEsubord                   4.000      0.023  173.565        0
## GRAMRELobj:CLAUSEsubord       -4.995      0.033 -153.254        0
```

See how this says, 'oh, if you want to start from the intercept and predict the length of subordinate-clause objects, then take the intercept (2), add the two main effects (3 and 4), but then you also need to 'correct' downwards by adding -5, and that -5 correction, you need that, it's highly significant ($p{\approx}0$, it's in fact $<10^{-135}$).

A final example of an interaction in the plot and the table is shown on the next page. By now, I hope it's clear what's going on. Without the interaction term, here you'd now be *under*shooting the mark: You'd predict subordinate-clause objects to be 2+2+2=6 syllables long when in fact they are 8 syllables long.

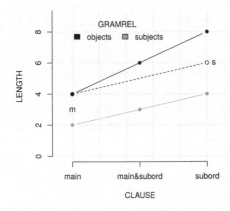

Figure 98: Interactive behavior of two binary predictors (2)

Table 25: Interactive behavior of two binary predictors 2

	main	**subord**	diff$_{main \to subord}$
objects	4	8	4
subjects	2	4	2
diff$_{subj \to obj}$	2	4	

Thus, an interaction term will be required and it is ≈2:

```
round(summary(m.3b <- lm(LENGTH ~ 1 + GRAMREL + CLAUSE +
   GRAMREL:CLAUSE, data=s3))$coefficients, 3)
##                           Estimate Std. Error t value Pr(>|t|)
## (Intercept)                  2.011      0.016 123.396        0
## GRAMRELobj                   1.997      0.023  86.655        0
## CLAUSEsubord                 2.000      0.023  86.789        0
## GRAMRELobj:CLAUSEsubord      2.005      0.033  61.505        0
```

Hoping that the above was clear, let's have you take a little 'test' to see whether you've understood this: Going back to the example discussed in the section on Simpson's paradox: if you return the right panel of Figure 95 above, what would it mean if the interaction between XX and FF was not significant?

THINK BREAK

If the interaction between XX and FF was not significant, that would mean that the seven negative slopes for factor levels *a* to *g* wouldn't be significantly different from each other, that the differences in the slopes of the lines, or angles between them, can be explained as random variation too well to assume otherwise, and that in turn would mean that we should have only one slope value that applies to each level of FF rather than permit the slope of XX to be different for each level of FF. Let's check this: We fit a model without the interaction, then we fit one with it, and then we do a model comparison:

```
m.withoutintact <- lm(YY ~ XX + FF)
m.withtheintact <- lm(YY ~ XX + FF + XX:FF)
anova(m.withoutintact, m.withtheintact, test="F")
## Analysis of Variance Table
## Model 1: YY ~ XX + FF
## Model 2: YY ~ XX + FF + XX:FF
##   Res.Df    RSS Df Sum of Sq      F Pr(>F)
## 1     46 151.42
## 2     40 119.25  6    32.169 1.7984 0.1241
```

The interaction isn't significant (p=0.1214), meaning the variability of the slopes has to be considered non-systematic at this point, which means Occam's razor would recommend to go with the simpler of the two models, m.withoutintact, which, visually, would look like Figure 99 (compare that to the right panel of Figure 95).

YY ~ XX and FF but no interaction

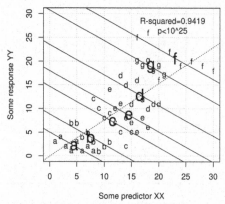

Figure 99: Simpson's paradox (w/out interaction term)

Ok, we will now use what we just discussed to cover interactions in our reaction time data. Specifically, we will discuss three models that give rise to three different kinds of interactions:
- when the interacting predictors are both categorical, we're concerned with how the differences between means for one predictor change across levels of the other (that's like the GRAMREL/CLAUSE example);
- when one interacting predictor is categorical and one is numeric, we're usually concerned with how the slopes for the numeric predictor differ across levels of the categorical predictor (that's like the Simpson's paradox example);
- when the interacting predictors are both numeric, we're concerned with how slopes for one predictor change across numeric values of the other (in essence, we're concerned with surfaces/planes in 3-or higher-dimensional space).

Note that I will leave interactions in models even if they are not significant. This is only for didactic purposes – so that I can discuss their numeric results and visualization – whereas in a real research study, one might delete them (depending on the study design). Given how much we've already covered and given our discussion of the object/subject lengths example, we can now go a little faster.

5.2.5 A linear model with two categorical predictors

Imagine you hypothesized that RT varies as a function of FAM and IMA, but also that the effect of FAM would vary by IMA. This means, you're not just expecting two main effects, but also that they interact:
- H_0: There is no correlation between FAM, IMA, and their interaction and RT; $R^2=0$;
- H_1: There is a correlation between FAM, IMA, and their interaction and RT; $R^2>0$.

Let's load the data:

```
rm(list=ls(all.names=TRUE)); library(car); library(effects)
summary(x <- read.delim(file="_inputfiles/05_rt_famima.csv",
   stringsAsFactors=TRUE, row.names=1)) ## [...]
```

As usual, we first fix the ordering of the levels of FAM and IMA so that they are in a nice ascending order:

```
x$FAM <- factor(x$FAM, levels=levels(x$FAM)[c(2, 3, 1)])
x$IMA <- factor(x$IMA, levels=levels(x$IMA)[c(2, 1)])
```

By now, we have done all the required exploration of each predictor and their correlations with the response often enough so we won't do this again here – obviously, with new data you'd have to. The one thing worth repeating here real quick (recall Table Table 21) is cross-tabulating the two predictors. Doing that is a good idea for two reasons: (i) to get an idea whether there are very infrequent combinations of factor levels, which is often a problem for regression modeling (how do you estimate a reliable coefficient if you only have very very few data points for a certain combination of things?) and (ii) to get an initial but incomplete heuristic idea of how much the predictors might be related to each other. In this case, we see two red flags:

```
table(x$IMA, x$FAM)
     lo med hi
  lo  7  15  1
  hi  3  16 11
```

Three of the six table cells are really very much underpopulated – if this was a real research context and we didn't use such a small data set for ease of didactic discussion only etc., we'd need to get more data or even give up the idea of modeling this with regression (see Section 5.6.1 on sample size requirements). The other reason for cross-tabulating also raises cause for concern: Clearly, the two predictors are related: the more FAM goes up, the more does IMA. This can be worrisome because if two (or more) predictors are (quite) correlated (a phenomenon called **(multi)collinearity**), the parts of variability of the response they explain will overlap so it becomes hard to decide what to attribute to which predictor. We will ignore this for now because we're still at the beginning of multifactorial regression modeling and can't do everything at the same time, but we will get back to collinearity in a moment.

5.2.5.1 Numerical exploration
The model is significant (F=3.352, df_1=5, df_2=47, p=0.0114). However, from this output, we cannot see whether the interaction is significant: the two contrasts we're shown don't exhaust all possible contrasts. Thus, we also run drop1:

```
summary(m.01 <- lm( RT ~ 1 + IMA + FAM + IMA:FAM, data=x))
## [...] Coefficients:
##              Estimate Std. Error t value Pr(>|t|)
## (Intercept)    676.30      17.64  38.344  < 2e-16 ***
## IMAhi          -26.11      32.20  -0.811  0.42161
```

```
## FAMmed          -58.94       21.36  -2.759  0.00823 **
## FAMhi           -96.80       49.89  -1.940  0.05834 .
## IMAhi:FAMmed     18.91       36.31   0.521  0.60495
## IMAhi:FAMhi      39.08       58.42   0.669  0.50681
## [...]
## Multiple R-squared:  0.2628, Adjusted R-squared:  0.1844
## F-statistic: 3.352 on 5 and 47 DF,  p-value: 0.01138
drop1(m.01, test="F")
## Single term deletions
## Model: RT ~ 1 + IMA + FAM + IMA:FAM
##          Df Sum of Sq    RSS    AIC F value Pr(>F)
## <none>                102349 412.99
## IMA:FAM   2    1081.9 103431 409.55  0.2484 0.7811
```

Dropping the interaction FAM:IMA from m.01 makes no significant difference (p=0.7811). But why aren't we getting p-values for the main effects? The answer is the **principle of marginality** (Fox 2016: Section 7.3.2). As its name implies, drop1 drops one predictor at a time. So it drops the interaction and gives us the p-value above, fine. But then it starts again from the full model in m.01 and wants to drop, say, only FAM. But, and I am simplifying a bit here, 'it can't' because FAM is still needed for the interaction term, and the same happens when drop1 'looks into the possibility' of dropping only IMA, which again 'it can't' do because that one, too, is still needed for the interaction term, and then it's done because there are no other predictors to consider for dropping. That's why we only get one p-value, but that's actually also kind of cool, because what that amounts to is that, typically, drop1 will return p-values for all predictors you 'should still be concerned with'. Look at it this way: If for whatever reason, the interaction FAM:IMA is still in your model then that's usually because it's significant and that in turn means that you can't place much trust in the main effects of FAM or IMA anyway, because if they interact, that means that FAM's effect isn't constant across IMA anyway (and vice versa). So, as long as an interaction of two or more predictors is still justifiably in your model, any lower-order effects would have to be interpreted with extreme caution anyway. If you revisit for a moment the second of the three object/subject length plots we discussed for interactions above (Figure 97), you'll recall that we saw a clear interaction between CLAUSE and GRAMREL, right? Would you really want to look at Figure 97 and tell someone something about CLAUSE's and/or GRAMREL's main effects? I hope not because what ever you'd tell them about a main effect would actually only be true of half of that data.

In a lot of cases, one would now actually delete the interaction term, or create a new model without it – say, m.02 – because after all drop1 showed the interaction didn't do anything significant. As mentioned above, we will omit this step here (and talk about model selection in detail later) only because I want to discuss the meanings of the coefficients and the visualization of the interaction. So, the coefficients, what do they mean? We talked about that above in the CLAUSE/GRAMREL example, but I want to revisit it here again from a slightly different angle (because I've had too many people in bootcamps who wanted to do mixed-effects modeling but couldn't pass what should be the entrance exam before one embarks on mixed-effects modeling, namely the ability to explain what any coefficient in a model like m.01 means ...).

You have two predictors, one with 2 levels, one with 3, which means you ultimately want 6 means. As we saw above, R doesn't give you 6 means, it gives you 1 (the intercept) and then 'instructions' how to get the others in the form of the coefficients (which are differences, here with their CIs):

```
Confint(m.01) # return estimates w/ their 95%-CI
##                Estimate      2.5 %      97.5 %
## (Intercept)   676.29971   640.81714  711.782290
## IMAhi         -26.10705   -90.88907   38.674976
## FAMmed        -58.93762  -101.90915  -15.966088
## FAMhi         -96.80151  -197.16139    3.558365
## IMAhi:FAMmed   18.90918   -54.13237   91.950731
## IMAhi:FAMhi    39.07763   -78.44255  156.597811
```

One way I see work well in bootcamps is this: We draw up a table that has cells for all means we expect predictions for and then we put in each cell which coefficients you have to sum up to get the right prediction:

Table 26: How to compute predicted reaction times in m.01

	FAM: *lo*	FAM: *med*	FAM: *hi*
IMA: *lo*	coef1 (intercept)	coef1+coef3	coef1+coef4
IMA: *hi*	coef1+coef2	coef1 + coef3 + coef2 + coef 5	coef1 + coef4 + coef2 + coef6

And you can easily verify this by (i) doing the math so you explain what happens there and why and (ii) checking the output from the effects package:

```
ph <- data.frame(ia <- effect("IMA:FAM", m.01))
ia # either you now look at ia
```

```
## IMA*FAM effect
##      FAM
## IMA         lo        med        hi
##   lo 676.2997 617.3621 579.4982
##   hi 650.1927 610.1642 592.4688
ph # or at the usual data frame ph
##   IMA FAM      fit       se    lower    upper
## 1  lo  lo 676.2997 17.63775 640.8171 711.7823
## 2  hi  lo 650.1927 26.94211 595.9921 704.3932
## 3  lo med 617.3621 12.04888 593.1229 641.6013
## 4  hi med 610.1642 11.66627 586.6947 633.6337
## 5  lo  hi 579.4982 46.66510 485.6201 673.3763
## 6  hi  hi 592.4688 14.07006 564.1635 620.7741
```

But from this you can also see that you're again missing all possible contrasts: You are getting 5 in the coefficients table, but there are $^{6\times5}/_2$=15 possible ones (if you really want to go desperately hunting for anything significant ...). You can get those with pairs(emmeans...) again; I am showing you three options, two more restricted and, thus, more justifiable ones and one that screams "please, please, can there please be something?". The first one compares means of FAM within each level of IMA; within the above table, these are comparisons within rows between columns, which amount to 6 means:

```
pairs(emmeans::emmeans(object=m.01, ~ FAM | IMA), adjust="none")
## IMA = lo:
##  contrast estimate   SE df t.ratio p.value
##  lo - med     58.9 21.4 47   2.759  0.0082
##  lo - hi      96.8 49.9 47   1.940  0.0583
##  med - hi     37.9 48.2 47   0.786  0.4360
##
## IMA = hi:
##  contrast estimate   SE df t.ratio p.value
##  lo - med     40.0 29.4 47   1.363  0.1793
##  lo - hi      57.7 30.4 47   1.899  0.0637
##  med - hi     17.7 18.3 47   0.968  0.3379
```

The second one compares means of IMA within each level of FAM; within the above table, these are 3 comparisons within columns between rows:

```
pairs(emmeans::emmeans(object=m.01, ~ IMA | FAM), adjust="none")
## FAM = lo:
##  contrast estimate   SE df t.ratio p.value
##  lo - hi      26.1 32.2 47   0.811  0.4216
## FAM = med:
##  contrast estimate   SE df t.ratio p.value
##  lo - hi       7.2 16.8 47   0.429  0.6698
## FAM = hi:
##  contrast estimate   SE df t.ratio p.value
##  lo - hi     -13.0 48.7 47  -0.266  0.7913
```

The third one compares all means with all others, which is all 15 comparisons:

```
pairs(emmeans::emmeans(object=m.01, ~ IMA:FAM), adjust="none")
## [...]
```

Recommendation(s) for further study:
- Note again that I am only showing *p*-values not adjusted for multiple comparisons here so that you can compare the *p*-values from emmeans easily with those of the summary output; in a real study, especially the third exploration above would most likely require some such correction. For this and related issues, the package multcomp may also be interesting for targeted *post-hoc* comparisons;
- also, don't forget that we're again treating FAM as categorical here but there's nothing that rules out the option discussed above, namely at least assign it the successive-differences contrast coding and use that version in this model (with m.02 <- lm(RT ~ 1 + IMA + FAM.sdif + IMA:FAM.sdif, data=x)). You should run that as well to make sure you understand the results;
- see Gelman, Hill, & Vehtari (2020: Section 6.3) for a nice explanation of regression coefficients as comparisons.

Now, how do we visualize this?

5.2.5.2 Graphical model exploration

We essentially do the kinds of plots we did for FAM or IMA in the previous two sections again, just this time for each level of the other predictor separately. We can use the effects package again for a good first shot:

```
plot(ia, ylim=range(x$RT), grid=TRUE) ## [...]
```

No wonder the interaction isn't significant: that's pretty parallel.

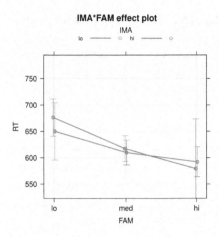

Figure 100: The effect of IMA:FAM

One recommendation when it comes to visualizing interactions, though: Note that, here, the effects package put FAM on the *x*-axis (and created separate panels for the levels of IMA). However, as already mentioned in Section 3.2.1, I recommend to always, *always!*, also generate the reverse perspective plot. Yes, I know it's the same numbers, but I've seen a lot of pairs of plots like that where each plot highlights different aspects of the results differently well. For example, with the above plot, you can not look at this and not *immediately* see in both panels that the blue line goes down, i.e. the nice ordinal effect of FAM. It's impossible not to notice. Here's the other perspective:

```
plot(ia, ylim=range(x$RT), grid=TRUE, x.var="IMA") ## [...]
```

Yes, one kind of sees that here as well, from left to right, the three short blue lines are lower in the coordinate system, but (i) the other plot shows that better (at least to me) and (ii) this plot, on the other hand, made me see much more easily how the ratio of IMA *lo* to *hi* differs across the levels of FAM (e.g., that the line connecting the IMA values goes down when FAM is *lo*, but up when FAM is *hi*). So, don't be lazy – do both plots!

You can also force all lines into one panel or of course create your own plot.

```
plot(ia, ylim=range(x$RT), grid=TRUE, multiline=TRUE, confint=list(
    style="auto"))
```

Remember: we glossed over some things for didactic reasons / expository convenience, in particular the data sparsity in 3 of the cells of the design and the fact that, if the interaction isn't significant, we wouldn't usually study it at this level of detail but rather drop it. But what about the collinearity? Time for another excursus ...

5.2.5.3 Excursus: collinearity and *VIFs*

As I said before, correlated – collinear – predictors are tricky because they make models unstable and uninterpretable. If your model contains several highly collinear predictors, what can happen is that, for instance, a seemingly small change in a model – e.g. dropping one of many (like, e.g., 12, 15, 20, ...) predictors – suddenly changes many other predictors' effect' size, direction, and *p*-value: You drop predictor A and suddenly

– predictors B to F, which were not significant with A in the model, suddenly become significant, and
– predictors G to I, which had a positive slope with A in the model, suddenly get a negative slope.

This makes multicollinearity a problem when it comes to interpreting regression results: if effect directions vary 'erratically' up and down depending on what else is in the model, how does one interpret such results? Maybe somewhat counterintuitively, it is important to realize, however, that multicollinearity is not a problem for prediction so if you build a model just for prediction, high multicollinearity isn't an issue – it's only an issue if you then want to interpret what is happening and why. (I recently skimmed a study where someone decided to not pursue a certain mode of analysis because of collinearity in a regression when in fact the point of that regression really was just prediction; that unnecessary decision cut off a potentially much better way of analysis than the one the author then fell back on.)

How does one detect multicollinearity? A first step can be looking at pairwise correlations of predictors, but that's not even close to enough, as I have written in many a review: High pairwise correlations between predictors are a sufficient condition for multicollinearity, but not a necessary one. Thus, it is not . ever . enough, period. One better diagnostic is a statistic called **variance inflation factors** (*VIFs*). It is useful to briefly discuss what those react to, for which we have to go back to the notion of a model matrix discussed above:

```
(mm <- model.matrix(m.01))[1:2,]
##         (Intercept) IMAhi FAMmed FAMhi IMAhi:FAMmed IMAhi:FAMhi
## ant              1     1      1     0            1           0
## apple            1     1      0     1            0           1
```

Remember that the model matrix consists of numeric predictor columns:
– for numeric variables (e.g. for FREQ, if we had that predictor in our current model), those would just be the numeric values of the predictor, but
– for categorical variables, those are *l*-1 (*l* being the number of levels of the categorical predictor) columns with 0s (essentially FALSEs) and 1s (essentially TRUEs) that encode which level a certain exhibits.

Here, we can infer from the model matrix that the first case – *ant* – has IMA: hi (see the 1 there?) and FAM: med (see the 1 there and the corresponding 0 for FAMhi); and that of course also means that ant has a 1 in IMAhi:FAMmed and a 0 in IMAhi:FAMhi. Now, what *VIF*s measure is how much each of the columns (but the intercept) in a model matrix is predictable from all others – that's **multicollinearity**. And this should explain to you why doing *only* pairwise correlations as a multicollinearity diagnostic is futile. Briefly and polemically: where's the *multi* in *pairwise* correlations (which are by definition *mono*factorial)? More usefully: Imagine you have a model with 10 numeric predictors. Then, the pairwise correlation tester checks whether predictor 1 is collinear by checking it against the 9 other predictors: 1 & 2, 1 & 3, ..., 1 & 10. But maybe predictor 1 isn't predictable by one other predictor, but by the combination of predictors 2, 4, 5, 8, and 9? Or maybe one level of a categorical predictor is highly predictive of something, which might be underestimated by checking the correlation of that categorical predictor with all its levels at the same time. The pairwise approach alone really doesn't do much: if you're worried about collinearity, great!, but if you then only check for it with pairwise correlations, consider your study an automatic *revise and resubmit* because then, by definition, the reader won't know how reliable your model is (and might also begin to think you haven't really understood the notion of collinearity in the first place), it's as simple as that.

Let's see how we can compute *VIF*s here. For the current kind of fixed-effects models of this chapter, there are two functions for this that I've used a lot, one in the package car, one in the package rms. For didactic reasons, we will use rms::vif, and it's easy:

```
sort(rms::vif(m.01))
##      FAMmed       IMAhi IMAhi:FAMmed       FAMhi IMAhi:FAMhi
##    2.696137    6.199461     6.761725   10.609164    13.660377
```

Let's look at the highest value. What that value means is that, in the model matrix, the column IMAhi:FAMhi is extremely predictable from the others. How does it say that? Remember that this column was the 6th and last in the model matrix? See how well it is predictable from all others?

```
summary(lm(mm[,6] ~ mm[,1]+mm[,2]+mm[,3]+mm[,4]+mm[,5]))$r.squared
## [1] 0.9267956
```

That column is nearly 93% predictable from all others, i.e. it's highly collinear. Now how do we get a *VIF* from that? I'll answer that question with a function:

```
R2.to.VIF <- function (some.modelmatrix.r2) {
   return(1/(1-some.modelmatrix.r2))
}
R2.to.VIF(0.9267956) # there's the VIF
## [1] 13.66038
```

So, *VIF*s quantify how much a column in a model matrix is predictable from all others with a value derived from an R^2. Which of course raises two questions: (i) What's the threshold value for *VIF*s, when are they 'too high'? (ii) And what to do if that happens? I am not discussing (ii) here in the book – it would lead too far (but see Fox & Weisberg 2019: section 8.8 on collinearity) – but as for the first: It's not like there's great agreement on that, but it seems (!) as if *VIF*s of 10 and above are definitely considered problematic (but of course some people suggest even smaller values); if *VIF*=10, then that column in the model matrix is explainable from the others with an R^2 of 0.9, and if *VIF*=5, then that column in the model matrix is explainable from the others with an R^2 of 0.8.

Recommendation(s) for further study:
- Check out the package performance, which has functions such as check_collinearity (to compute *VIF*s), but also other functions that are great for model diagnostics (e.g., performance or check_overdispersion);
- for a very thorough (but maybe a bit daunting) overview of methods to address collinearity, see Tomaschek, Hendrix, & Baayen (2018); you can find a maybe easier yet still thorough discussion in Ch. 13 of Fox (2016);
- you should also write a function VIF.to.R2 that takes as input a *VIF* and returns the R^2-value for that column.

5.2.6 A linear model with a categorical and a numeric predictor

Imagine now we hypothesized that RT varies as a function of FAM and FREQ, but also that the effect of FREQ would vary by FAM. This means, we're not just expecting two main effects, but also that they interact:
- H_0: There is no correlation between FAM, FREQ, and their interaction and RT; $R^2=0$;
- H_1: There is a correlation between FAM, FREQ, and their interaction and RT; $R^2>0$.

Let's load the data, log FREQ and fix the order of FAM's levels:

```
rm(list=ls(all.names=TRUE)); library(car); library(effects)
x <- read.delim(file="_inputfiles/05_rt_famfreq.csv",
   stringsAsFactors=TRUE, row.names=1)
x$FREQ <- log2(x$FREQ)
x$FAM <- factor(x$FAM, levels=levels(x$FAM)[c(2, 3, 1)])
summary(x) ## [...]
```

Again, we have done all the required exploration of each predictor and their correlations with the response so we only check for a possible relation between the two predictors:

```
par(mfrow=c(1, 2))
spineplot(x$FAM ~ x$FREQ)
boxplot(x$FREQ ~ x$FAM)
par(mfrow=c(1, 1))
```

Unsurprisingly, Figure 101 on the next page suggests there is a correlation already so we'd have to tread carefully ...

5.2.6.1 Numerical exploration
We fit our model with the interaction and summarize the results. The model is significant ($F=4.554$, $df_1=5$, $df_2=49$, $p=0.0017$) with actually a kind of decent R^2. However, we can again not see whether the interaction is significant so we immediately run drop1 on this model. The interaction FREQ:IMA from m.01 makes no significant difference ($p=0.3891$) so one would usually drop it, but we'll leave it in for now.

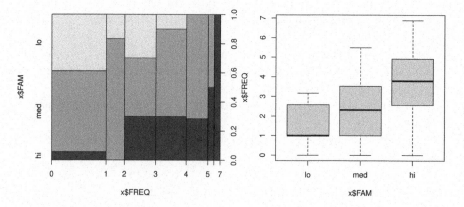

Figure 101: The relation of FAM and FREQ

```
summary(m.01 <- lm(RT ~ 1 + FREQ + FAM + FREQ:FAM, data=x))
## [...] Coefficients:
##              Estimate Std. Error t value Pr(>|t|)
## (Intercept)  697.96      22.65   30.809   <2e-16 ***
## FREQ         -22.69      12.20   -1.860   0.0688 .
## FAMmed       -66.40      26.82   -2.476   0.0168 *
## FAMhi        -94.76      37.78   -2.508   0.0155 *
## FREQ:FAMmed   15.01      13.22    1.135   0.2619
## FREQ:FAMhi    19.60      14.14    1.386   0.1719
## [...]
## Multiple R-squared:  0.3173,  Adjusted R-squared:  0.2476
## F-statistic: 4.554 on 5 and 49 DF,  p-value: 0.001728
drop1(m.01, test="F")
## Single term deletions
## Model: RT ~ 1 + FREQ + FAM + FREQ:FAM
##            Df Sum of Sq    RSS    AIC F value Pr(>F)
## <none>                  97528 423.43
## FREQ:FAM    2    3830.9 101359 421.55  0.9624 0.3891
```

Again, we want to understand the coefficients (here with their CIs):

```
Confint(m.01) # return estimates w/ their 95%-CI
##              Estimate        2.5 %      97.5 %
## (Intercept) 697.96237   652.435964  743.488779
## FREQ        -22.68790   -47.194802    1.818994
## FAMmed      -66.39724  -120.292054  -12.502427
```

```
## FAMhi          -94.75672 -170.680732 -18.832702
## FREQ:FAMmed    15.00512  -11.563262  41.573503
## FREQ:FAMhi     19.59873   -8.810438  48.007906
```

We draw up a table that has cells for means we want to consider predictions for and then we put in each cell which coefficients you have to sum up (how often) to get the right prediction:

Table 27: How to compute predicted reaction times in m.01

	FAM: *lo*	FAM: *med*	FAM: *hi*
FREQ: 0	coef1 (intercept)	coef1+coef3	coef1+coef4
FREQ: 1	coef1+coef2	coef1+coef3+coef2+coef5	coef1+coef4+coef2+coef6
FREQ: 2	coef1+2×coef2	coef1+coef3+2×coef2+2×coef5	coef1+coef4+2×coef2+2×coef6

And we check it against effects:

```
ph <- data.frame(ia <- effect("FREQ:FAM", m.01, xlevels=list(
   FREQ=0:7)))
ph[sort(sample(nrow(ph), 3)),] # here's a random sample of 3 rows
##    FREQ FAM      fit       se    lower    upper
## 9     0 med 631.5651 14.353462 602.7208 660.4095
## 10    1 med 623.8823 10.510947 602.7598 645.0049
## 21    4  hi 590.8490 12.939072 564.8469 616.8510
```

And we can use the package emmeans again – this time with the function emtrends – to make all 3 comparisons of FREQ slopes across the 3 levels of FAM; the first 2 we already knew from the summary output, the last one is new:

```
pairs(emmeans::emtrends(object=m.01, ~ FAM, var="FREQ"),
   adjust="none")
##   contrast estimate    SE df t.ratio p.value
##   lo - med   -15.01 13.22 49  -1.135  0.2619
##   lo - hi    -19.60 14.14 49  -1.386  0.1719
##   med - hi    -4.59  8.79 49  -0.523  0.6035
```

I hope you're getting to know the sequence pretty well by now.

5.2.6.2 Graphical model exploration

We essentially do the kinds of plots we did for FREQ in Section 5.2.1 above again, just this time for each level of the FAM separately. We can use the effects package again for a good first shot (using the exact same code):

```
plot(ia, ylim=range(x$RT), grid=TRUE) ## [...]
```

Here we won't generate the reverse-perspective interaction plot: numeric predictors 'belong' on the *x*-axis. But you can of course develop your own plot to include the observed data as well. Note how I am using a loop to plot the regression lines and confidence bands separately for each level of FAM and how I use the function rainbow with the argument n=3 to have R give me 3 maximally distinctive colors (so, for once!, I hard-coded the number 3 in there to keep complexity lower; look up ?rainbow). (I'm only showing the plot.)

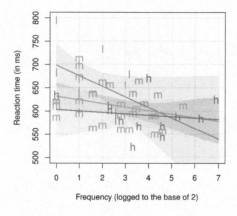

Figure 102: The effect of FREQ:FAM

You didn't really think there wasn't gonna be an excursus, right?

5.2.6.3 Excursus: *post-hoc* comparisons and predictions from effects

We used emtrends above to determine whether the slopes of FREQ differed significantly between pairs of levels of FAM. But can we actually also do something similar to what we did earlier, namely compare differences between RT means of different levels of FAM? Yes, we can, but we must of course not forget that there's another variable in the model, FREQ, which we need to control for at the same time. Above, we did stuff like this: emmeans(m.01, ~ IMA | FAM ...) to make IMA comparisons given a certain level of FAM and vice versa and then we saw the differences from the summary output and the additional ones we wanted to see. What happens if we do this here?

```
pairs(emmeans::emmeans(object=m.01, ~ FAM | FREQ), adjust="none")
## FREQ = 2.48:
##  contrast estimate   SE df t.ratio p.value
##  lo - med     29.1 19.1 49   1.523  0.1341
##  lo - hi      46.1 23.7 49   1.949  0.0570
##  med - hi     17.0 18.0 49   0.944  0.3500
```

It does something but none of the estimate values in this little table looks at all like the coefficients for FAM in the summary output – so is this right? It is, it is just a bit different: in lm's summary output of the regression table, the value for FAMmed (-66.40) is the change from FAM: *lo* to FAM: *med* when, "all numeric predictors not mentioned in X [i.e., here FREQ] are set to 0" but emmeans does something different: Here, the *lo* vs. *med* difference (29.1) is for, see what it says at the top?, when FREQ=2.48. Why is that? Because that's the mean of FREQ! So emmeans holds FREQ constant just like lm's summary output does, just at a different value: 2.48 (the mean), not 0 (the intercept). Which I hope reminds you of something ... Wouldn't it be great if one could get both of these things together? And yes, you can, namely if you had centered FREQ as discussed in Section 3.1.3.4, because that transformation – FREQ – mean(FREQ) – makes sure that the mean of this transformed version is 0. You should check that: Create a centered version of FREQ, use it to create m.02, and then run pairs(emmeans...) on that and you will see that, then, the both the summary and emmeans will have the same estimates for FAMmed and *lo - med* / FAMhi and *lo - hi*.

Recommendation(s) for further study: Check out Schielzeth (2010) for a nice discussion of the benefits of this kind of centering (potentially even of categorical predictors).

This brings me to another related and very important aspect. Remember that we always even discuss the non-significant interactions here so that see how interactions of such a type would be discussed and visualized if they were significant. But let's for a moment see what happens if we followed a kind of model selection procedure (see Section 5.5 below). To remind you, this was the coefficients table of m.01 and these were the effects we saw (note the practical overview function effects::allEffects):

```
round(summary(m.01)$coefficients, 4)
##             Estimate Std. Error t value Pr(>|t|)
```

```
## (Intercept) 697.9624    22.6547 30.8087   0.0000
## FREQ        -22.6879    12.1951 -1.8604   0.0688
## FAMmed      -66.3972    26.8190 -2.4758   0.0168
## FAMhi       -94.7567    37.7811 -2.5080   0.0155
## FREQ:FAMmed  15.0051    13.2209  1.1350   0.2619
## FREQ:FAMhi   19.5987    14.1369  1.3864   0.1719
allEffects(m.01, xlevels=list(FREQ=0:2))
##   model: RT ~ 1 + FREQ + FAM + FREQ:FAM
##   FREQ*FAM effect
##       FAM
## FREQ       lo       med       hi
##    0 697.9624 631.5651 603.2057
##    1 675.2745 623.8823 600.1165
##    2 652.5866 616.1996 597.0273
```

Now let's see what happens when we delete the interaction FREQ:FAM from m.01:

```
round(summary(m.02 <- lm(RT ~ 1 + FREQ+FAM, data=x))$coefficients, 4)
##             Estimate Std. Error t value Pr(>|t|)
## (Intercept) 675.2912    14.2022 47.5483   0.0000
## FREQ         -7.8539     3.9305 -1.9982   0.0510
## FAMmed      -43.3271    15.4827 -2.7984   0.0072
## FAMhi       -53.8580    20.3166 -2.6509   0.0107
allEffects(m.02, xlevels=list(FREQ=0:2))
##   model: RT ~ 1 + FREQ + FAM
##   FREQ effect
##          0        1        2
## 639.1197 631.2658 623.4119
##   FAM effect
##        lo      med       hi
## 655.7928 612.4657 601.9348
```

This should be a little disconcerting for a second: If you look at the summary output of m.01 and the effects of m.01, they match perfectly:
- the intercept in the summary output is the value in row 1, column 1 of the effects object;
- the coefficient for FREQ added to the intercept is the value in row 2, column 1 of the effects object;
- the coefficient for FAMmed added to the intercept is the value in row 1, column 2 of the effects object; etc.

just like I've been saying the whole time. But you can also see that this doesn't seem to work anymore for m.02. Yes, the slope for FREQ in the summary output (-7.8539) is in fact the difference between the effects for FREQ in the allEffects output and, yes, the differences for FAM in the summary output correspond to the differences in the allEffects output but it seems impossible to get from the summary output of m.02 to the predictions allEffects returns. For example, how do you look at the summary output of m.02 with its intercept value of 675.2912 and infer from it that the prediction for FAM being lo is 655.7928? What's going on?

THINK BREAK

The answer is that effects does something really nice here. Like emmeans, it makes the predictions for one predictor while holding the other predictors constant, controlling for them. But how exactly? Well, for the effect of FAM, it does the same as emmeans: it gives its predictions for FAM while FREQ is held constant at its typical value, the mean (which can be changed with the argument fixed.predictors). If we want to check that manually, we first generate a small data set which contains exactly those combinations of things for which we want predictions and then we feed that to predict's argument newdata:

```
(temp.new.data <- data.frame(
   FAM=levels(x$FAM), FREQ=rep(mean(x$FREQ), 3)))
##   FAM     FREQ
## 1  lo 2.482649
## 2 med 2.482649
## 3  hi 2.482649
predict(m.02, newdata=temp.new.data)
##        1        2        3
## 655.7928 612.4657 601.9348
```

See, those are the predictions for FAM from allEffects for m.02 so, ok. But what about the predictions for FREQ? What is 'the typical value' for FAM? You might think that's the mode, so FAM will be held constant by setting it to the max of table(x$FAM), which would be *med*. But that's not what effects does, as you can easily verify with the code shown in the code file. Those are not the predictions of allEffects. But *this* is how we get them (for when FREQ is 0):

```
# for FREQ = 0
(temp.new.data <- data.frame(FAM=levels(x$FAM), FREQ=0))
```

```
##    FAM FREQ
## 1  lo    0
## 2 med    0
## 3  hi    0
(temp.preds <- predict(m.02, newdata=temp.new.data))
##         1        2        3
## 675.2912 631.9641 621.4332
weighted.mean(x=temp.preds, w=table(x$FAM))
## [1] 639.1197
```

Replace the FREQ=0 by FREQ=1 and you get the corresponding predictions. (This can be done more compactly in one step with tapply but I wanted to break things down maximally.) So, instead of giving you predictions for FREQ that hold FAM constant at its mode, which would utilize just one of the three levels of FAM for the prediction, the effects package uses the proportional distribution of all levels of FAM, which arguably provides a more reliably interpretable estimate. (Imagine a case where the mode is a level that accounts only for 30% of the cases of a, say, 4-level predictor and one that is behaving somewhat more extremely than others; I know from my own experience that, in such cases, it is easier to misinterpret the results or overlook things than with the nice proportionally-weighted effects predictions.) This is one of the many reasons this package is so useful. (Note: emmeans::emmeans can do this kind of weighted computations as well; check out the argument weights of emmeans later.)

There's another important consequence of this: Remember what I said above about what effects does: "it makes the predictions for one predictor while holding the other predictors constant". That means, even if you look at the effect of one predictor, the other predictors are also relevant to the computations of the predicted values. The upshot of that, however, is that it is usually not a great practice to summarize the effect of a predictor on the response in a *multi*factorial model on the basis of its observed *mono*factorial effect in the data because, unless the predictors in your data are perfectly orthogonal/uncorrelated with each other – which is possible with experimental data, but much less likely in observational data – it is likely that plotting the observed effect will overestimate the effect's representation because it doesn't control for anything else in the model.

Think back to our mpg example in Section 5.1; you will remember that we had 'the idea' that, on top of everything else we know about mpg-values, they might (also) be explicable in terms of displacement. But then, in our regression model that contained 'everything else we know about mpg-values', disp had no significant effect anymore and the reason for that was that disp is so highly correlated with all the other predictors:

```
round(summary(real.test.of.new.hyp <- lm(mpg ~
    cyl+hp+wt+disp, data=mtcars))$coefficients, 3)
##              Estimate Std. Error t value Pr(>|t|)
## (Intercept)   40.829      2.757  14.807    0.000
## cyl           -1.293      0.656  -1.972    0.059
## hp            -0.021      0.012  -1.691    0.102
## wt            -3.854      1.015  -3.795    0.001
## disp           0.012      0.012   0.989    0.331
```

But from that it should be obvious that you must not summarize the effect of disp in this model just by showing the observed correlation between mpg and disp. Check out Figure 103 below: The points show the observed values for disp (*x*-axis) and mpg (*y*-axis) and these observed data points and their dashed monofactorial regression line suggest a nice strong negative correlation.

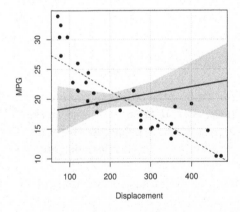

Figure 103: The effect of disp on mpg (monofact vs. in multifact)

But this is useless because these points just capture the monofactorial effect of disp. In other words, that dashed regression line is the effect of disp in the *mono*factorial model lm(mpg~disp) – you cannot use it to try and summarize the effect of disp in the *multi*factorial model real.test.of.new.hyp, because the dashed line summarizes a model that doesn't know whatever other contributions all other predictors are making in real.test.of.new.hyp. To summarize what disp does in real.test.of.new.hyp, we need to control for all the contributions of the other predictors and compute the relevant predicted values for disp with everything else in the model, as we've always done with effects. The solid regression line you see in the plot, *that* represents the effects predictions for disp when you control for everything else in the model. Obviously, it isn't significant, in fact it goes up a bit (when we 'hypothesized' a negative correlation) – the solid line and grey confidence band from effects of real.test.of.new.hyp show what disp is doing in the context of everything else in the model, namely not much (because of its high collinearity with the other predictors) – just the observed data and its regression line, which I have seen people use, are completely misleading.

Thus, as a general guideline: if you summarize a regression model, do so on the basis of the model's (effects) predictions (which guarantees you control for everything else in the model), not on the basis of (descriptive/monofactorial) plots of the observed data points. In monofactorial regression models and/or in perfectly orthogonal models or traditional ANOVAs, the two kinds of values will be identical, but elsewhere they will most likely not (in mixed-effects models, see Singmann & Kellen 2019) and then the predicted values are probably more useful/realistic. Thus, if you just always plot predictions, you'll just avoid this kind of problem.

5.2.7 A linear model with two numeric predictors

Nearly done with this part: Imagine now we hypothesized that RT varies as a function of MEAN and FREQ, but also that the effect of MEAN would vary by FREQ. This means, we're not just expecting main effects, but also that they interact.
- H_0: There is no correlation between MEAN, FREQ, and their interaction and RT; $R^2=0$;
- H_1: There is a correlation between MEAN, FREQ, and their interaction and RT; $R^2>0$.

Let's load the data and log FREQ:

```
rm(list=ls(all.names=TRUE)); library(car); library(effects)
x <- read.delim(file="_inputfiles/05_rt_freqmean.csv",
   stringsAsFactors=TRUE, row.names=1)
x$FREQ <- log2(x$FREQ)
summary(x) ## [...]
```

Again, we have done all the required exploration of each predictor and their correlations with the response so we only check for a possible relation between the two predictors:

```
par(mfrow=c(1, 2))
plot(x=x$MEAN, y=x$FREQ, pch=16, col="#00000030"); grid()
   lines(lowess(x$FREQ ~ x$MEAN)) # add a smoother
plot(x=x$FREQ, y=x$MEAN, pch=16, col="#00000030"); grid()
   lines(lowess(x$MEAN ~ x$FREQ)) # add a smoother
par(mfrow=c(1, 1))
```

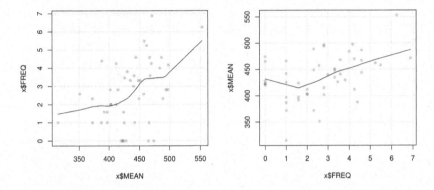

Figure 104: The relation of MEAN and FREQ

There seems to be a bit of a (collinear) trend.

5.2.7.1 Numerical exploration
We fit our model with the interaction:

```
summary(m.01 <- lm(RT ~ 1 + FREQ + MEAN + FREQ:MEAN, data=x))
## [...] Coefficients:
##                Estimate Std. Error t value Pr(>|t|)
## (Intercept) 841.07328  119.64545    7.030 1.03e-08 ***
## FREQ         -49.97544   38.38823   -1.302   0.1997
## MEAN          -0.48152    0.27759   -1.735   0.0898 .
## FREQ:MEAN      0.09678    0.08453    1.145   0.2584
## [...]
## Multiple R-squared:  0.1718, Adjusted R-squared:  0.1153
## F-statistic: 3.042 on 3 and 44 DF,  p-value: 0.03871
```

The model is just about significant (F=3.042, df_1=3, df_2=44, p=0.039) with an actually not terrible R^2 (although the adjusted one is really kinda low). In this case, we can see that the interaction isn't significant – we run drop1 on this model only for consistency's sake:

```
drop1(m.01, test="F")
## Single term deletions
## Model: RT ~ 1 + FREQ + MEAN + FREQ:MEAN
##            Df Sum of Sq   RSS    AIC F value Pr(>F)
## <none>                  79265 363.65
## FREQ:MEAN  1   2361.7 81627 363.06   1.311 0.2584
```

Dropping the interaction FREQ:MEAN from m.01 makes no significant difference (p=0.2584). So again one would usually drop the interaction, but we'll discuss it to explore this kind of interaction (between two numeric predictors, because that's gonna be fun). Again, we want to understand the coefficients (here with their CIs):

```
Confint(m.01) # return estimates w/ their 95%-CI
##                Estimate        2.5 %        97.5 %
## (Intercept) 841.07327624  599.94371228 1.082203e+03
## FREQ        -49.97544323 -127.34184509 2.739096e+01
## MEAN         -0.48151550   -1.04095688 7.792588e-02
## FREQ:MEAN     0.09678081   -0.07356989 2.671315e-01
```

Just so everyone's on the same page: What does the fact that the coefficient for FREQ is 100 times greater than the one for MEAN mean in terms of effect size?

THINK BREAK

Not much, really. The coefficients are answers to the question "what happens if this predictor increases by 1?", but since the range of the values of FREQ is less than 7 units whereas the range of the values of MEAN is 240 (plus they come with completely different dispersions) – you should compare their variation coefficients!) – you really can't compare those well with regard to effect size. However, you *could* compare them to learn more about their effect sizes *iff* you had z-standardized all variables in the model (as per Section 3.1.3.4). We would then obtain a standardized effect size for each predictor and see that the effect of FREQ is 1.383 times as strong as that of MEAN.

To see how the coefficients lead to the predictions, we use the usual table:

Table 28: How to compute predicted reaction times in m.01

	MEAN: 0	MEAN: 1
FREQ: 0	coef1 (intercept)	coef1 +coef3
FREQ: 1	coef1 +coef2	coef1 +coef2+coef3 +coef4
FREQ: 2	coef1 +2×coef2	coef1 +2×coef2+coef3 +2×coef4

And we check it against effects; to make sure we can do that, I am including MEAN values 0 and 1 in there:

```
ph <- data.frame(ia <- effect("FREQ:MEAN", m.01,
    xlevels=list(FREQ=0:7,MEAN=c(0:1, seq(300, 550, 50)))))
ph[c(1:2,9:10),]
##    FREQ MEAN    fit       se      lower     upper
## 1   0    0  841.0733 119.64545 599.9437 1082.2028
## 2   1    0  791.0978  91.19017 607.3161  974.8796
## 9   0    1  840.5918 119.36928 600.0188 1081.1647
## 10  1    1  790.7131  90.97721 607.3606  974.0656
```

5.2.7.2 Graphical model exploration

Visual exploration is now interesting because we suddenly have 3 numeric dimensions: FREQ, MEAN, and predicted RT. The effects package visualizes this by essentially making one of the predictors categorical (or, strictly speaking ordinal) and then giving you the kind of plot we saw in the previous section) but that doesn't always work very well. I want to therefore suggest two different kinds of 3-D approaches. For both, we first recreate ph but give it a more fine-grained resolution covering now only the observed range of values:

```
ph <- data.frame(ia <- effect("FREQ:MEAN", m.01, xlevels=list(
    FREQ=seq(0, 7, 0.5), MEAN=seq(300, 550, 10)))))
```

One possibility now is to do an actual rotatable 3-D plot using the package rgl (which on Mac seems to be cumbersome to install):

```
rgl::plot3d(                         # generate a 3-D plot
    xlab="Meaningfulness", x=ph$MEAN, # MEAN on the x-axis
    ylab="Freq. (logged)", y=ph$FREQ, # FREQ on the y-axis
    zlab="Predicted RT",   z=ph$fit)  # pred. RT on the z-axis
```

You can click onto the plot and move the mouse to turn the coordinate system. Usually, you have a bit of turning of the plot to do before you can see what's happening in the data – I do recommend, however, to let the predicted values be on the vertical axis most of the time. I explain how to work with such plots in workshops, but won't do so here because I cannot rotate the plot here to highlight things and you can't usually publish something like this anyway. Instead, I present a different kind of approach. The key to it is to recognize that we have three dimensions of information to present but no one is holding a gun to our head saying "and they – the three dimensions – all need to be represented spatially!" And usually it's easier to represent the third dimension, the size of the predicted values, not in a third spatial dimension but, for instance, with colors or symbols. Here is one approach that I use most of the time:

```
ph$fitcat <- as.numeric(cut(ph$fit, breaks=9))
```

What does `ph$fitcat` contain now? Values from 1 to 9, whose size reflects, at a lower level of resolution, the size of the numeric predicted RT values: 9 means slowest/highest RT, 1 means fastest/shortest RT, which is then plotted like this:

```
plot(type="n", x=ph$FREQ, y=ph$MEAN, xlab="Frequency",
    ylab="Meaningfulness"); grid()
text(x=ph$FREQ, y=ph$MEAN, labels=ph$fitcat, cex=0.5+ph$fitcat/6,
    col=grey(level=ph$fitcat/10))
```

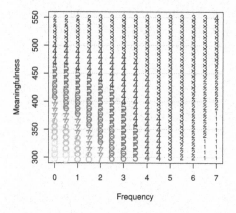

Figure 105: A 'numeric heatmap' of predictions for `m.01`

Other people prefer a heatmap of this kind (plot not shown, see the code file):

```
lattice::contourplot(ph$fit ~ ph$FREQ * ph$MEAN,
    xlab="Frequency", ylab="Meaningfulness", zlab="Predicted RT",
    cuts=20, region=TRUE, pretty=TRUE)
```

Or a greyscale-kind-of plot like this:

```
plot(x=ph$FREQ, y=ph$MEAN, pch=16, cex=4,
    col=grey(1-(as.numeric(ph$fitcat)/10), alpha=0.5)); grid()
```

Pretending we need to interpret the interaction because it's significant, both plots of course suggest the same (I will use mine because I am more used to it):
- for nearly every kind of MEAN value (300 to 500), as FREQ increases (i.e., you go from the left to the right), the numbers decrease, i.e. the predicted RT values get smaller – only for very high MEAN does this trend stop or ever so slightly gets reversed (see esp. the 4 in the top right corner);
- for most of the FREQ values (0 to 4.5), as MEAN increases (i.e. you go from the bottom to the top), the predicted reaction times decrease – only for very high FREQ does this trend stop or gets reversed a bit.

5.2.7.3 Excursus: where are most of the values?

I just couldn't end this part without adding something, it just didn't feel right, like I'd let you down ... but this actually is important/useful. One thing that many of the plots above did not communicate (well or at all) is the frequency distribution of the predictors, which is especially important in this 6th model, but also in the other cases. I had cases in my own work where I didn't pay attention to this at first and stared for what seems like hours at some plot(s) to understand certain trends in it only to later think, "wait, but where are actually most of the data points?" This applies here, too, though not as extremely as the cases I sometimes discuss in workshops. Consider this version of the numeric heatmap again, which has been augmented by the observed points plotted into the background as well as a data ellipse to nicely show for which combinations of predictor values we actually had data:

```
plot(type="n", x=ph$FREQ, y=ph$MEAN,
    xlab="Frequency", ylab="Meaningfulness"); grid()
text(x=ph$FREQ, y=ph$MEAN, labels=ph$fitcat,
    cex=0.5+as.numeric(ph$fitcat)/6)
points(x=x$FREQ, y=x$MEAN, pch=16, col="#00000020", cex=4)
```

```
car::dataEllipse(x=jitter(x$FREQ), y=x$MEAN, levels=0.9, add=TRUE,
    pch="", col="darkgrey")
```

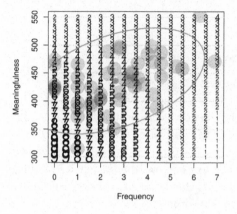

Figure 106: A 'numeric heatmap' of predictions for m.01 (w/ a data ellipse)

How does this help? (For those of you who have used mgcv::vis.gam, doing this is not unlike the logic motivating vis.gam's argument too.far.) In this particular case, the effect isn't really mind-blowing, but it shows clearly, for example, that the speeding-up effect of FAM is observed for more than 75% of the observed MEAN values or that the speeding-up effect of MEAN is observed for more than 75% of the observed FAM values. Also, it shows that there are in fact no words in your data with really high frequencies and really low meaningfulness scores (or vice versa). That might seem trivial to you here, but trust me, there will be situations where it isn't. Adding some quantile/decile information to a plot or adding rugs (?rug) etc. has sometimes made a huge difference in my (ease of) understanding of complex data – suddenly it was clear that certain kinds of predictions were 'less relevant' in the sense that they were for combinations of predictor values that were theoretically possible, but really rare or completely unattested.

5.2.8 Interactions (yes, again)

Now why have I been emphasizing this interaction stuff sooo much? Because interactions are often neglected, which means main effects can be overstated, theoretically interesting things can be missed, and/or whole studies can go down the toilet. For example, I once saw a conference presentation where someone wanted to discuss how some response was affected by some predictor differently over, let's say, three time periods (each represented by a different corpus representative of one time period). Let's also say for the sake/ease of exposition here the response variable was numeric and there was one numeric predictor. What the person presented was equivalent to this:

```
##              Estimate Std. Error t value Pr(>|t|)
## (Intercept)    4.134       0.636   6.505        0
## PREDICTOR      2.706       0.102  26.423        0
##              Estimate Std. Error t value Pr(>|t|)
## (Intercept)    4.625       0.642   7.202        0
## PREDICTOR      2.280       0.103  22.025        0
##              Estimate Std. Error t value Pr(>|t|)
## (Intercept)    3.592       0.478   7.508        0
## PREDICTOR      1.905       0.077  24.701        0
```

In other words, the presenter fit a separate linear model for each time period/ corpus and then compared the slopes of PREDICTOR across models by pointing out how the slopes became lower over time, maybe even, I don't remember, using plots like this. (The left plot shows the slope for CORPUS1, the middle one the slope for CORPUS2 in black and the one for CORPUS1 in grey, the right one the slope for CORPUS3 in black and the one for CORPUS2 in grey):

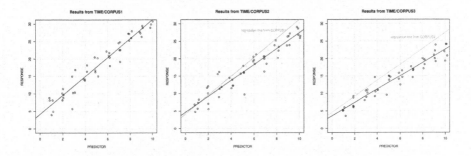

Figure 107: The effects of PREDICTOR per CORPUS

Why, in the context of this presentation's stated goal, is this 'really not useful', to put it mildly?

THINK BREAK

This isn't useful because you see that the slopes are different across the three time periods/corpora: 2.7 (corpus 1) > 2.3 (corpus 2) > 1.9 (corpus 3) and you see in the *p*-value that each one of them is significantly different *from 0*. But, what you don't see is whether they are *significantly different from each other*! Why did the presenter think they could say much about the diachronic change of the effect of PREDICTOR as long as they didn't show that the slopes are so different that it's likely not just random variability? Maybe the effect of PREDICTOR doesn't differ significantly / is constant across time/corpora – the statistical analysis presented certainly didn't say ... so what to do instead?

First, we merge the three data frames. Second, we add another column that says where the data are from. Third, we could give CORPUS an 'ordinal-like' successive differences contrast coding (see Section 5.2.3.3 above).

```
ALLCORPORA <- rbind(CORPUS1, CORPUS2, CORPUS3)
ALLCORPORA$CORPUS <- factor(paste0("C", rep(1:3, each=10)))
summary(ALLCORPORA)
##      RESPONSE          PREDICTOR       CORPUS
##  Min.    : 3.558   Min.    : 1.0    C1:50
##  1st Qu.:10.572    1st Qu.: 3.0    C2:50
##  Median :16.479    Median : 5.5    C3:50
##  Mean    :16.750   Mean    : 5.5
##  3rd Qu.:22.133    3rd Qu.: 8.0
##  Max.    :33.939   Max.    :10.0
contrasts(ALLCORPORA$CORPUS) <- MASS::contr.sdif
```

Finally, we do one model, not three!, followed up by a use of emtrends; crucially, the one model contains as predictors
- PREDICTOR: a significant effect here would show that there is a correlation between PREDICTOR and RESPONSE everywhere/always (i.e. in the combined data of all three time periods/corpora; I hope these two words are tipping you off already where I'm going with this);
- CORPUS: a significant effect here would show that there is a correlation between CORPUS and RESPONSE, which, since CORPUS is essentially something like TIMEPERIOD means that over time, the use of RESPONSE changes (regardless of what PREDICTOR does);
- PREDICTOR:CORPUS because a significant effect here would show – remember my technical definition of *interaction* – that PREDICTOR doesn't do the same everywhere/always, that there are significant differences between the different time periods/corpora in terms of how much PREDICTOR is related to CORPUS. *This* is the evidence of diachronic change that that study would have needed.

You can imagine the result we'll find in my carefully made-up data:

```
summary(m <- lm(RESPONSE ~ 1 + PREDICTOR + CORPUS +
    PREDICTOR:CORPUS, data=ALLCORPORA))
## [...] Coefficients:
##                       Estimate Std. Error t value Pr(>|t|)
## (Intercept)            4.11718    0.51125   8.053 2.77e-13 ***
## PREDICTOR              2.29685    0.08240  27.876  < 2e-16 ***
## CORPUS2-1              1.28299    1.25231   1.025   0.3073
## CORPUS3-2             -0.51894    1.25231  -0.414   0.6792
## PREDICTOR:CORPUS2-1   -0.37181    0.20183  -1.842   0.0675 .
## PREDICTOR:CORPUS3-2   -0.01497    0.20183  -0.074   0.9410
## [...]

## Multiple R-squared:  0.8454, Adjusted R-squared:   0.84
## F-statistic: 157.5 on 5 and 144 DF,  p-value: < 2.2e-16
drop1(m,test="F")
## [...]
##                   Df Sum of Sq    RSS    AIC F value  Pr(>F)
## <none>                         1209.8 325.14
## PREDICTOR:CORPUS   2    39.608 1249.4 325.97  2.3572 0.09833 .
```

Of course, there's not much: the successive differences are not significant (in two-tailed tests!, $p=0.0675$ and $p=0.941$), the whole interaction PREDICTOR:CORPUS isn't significant ($p=0.09833$), which means, it would probably be dropped because the slope of PREDICTOR is 'the same' across time periods. Given the lack of significance of the interaction, one would usually not even look at emtrends – just to demonstrate that there's not even a significant difference between the two time periods/corpora furthest apart, I am showing the results here anyway:

```
pairs(emmeans::emtrends(m, ~ CORPUS, var="PREDICTOR"), adjust="none")
##   contrast estimate    SE  df t.ratio p.value
## C1 - C2       0.372 0.202 144   1.842  0.0675
## C1 - C3       0.387 0.202 144   1.916  0.0573
## C2 - C3       0.015 0.202 144   0.074  0.9410
```

That means the actual finding would be this (only showing the plot):

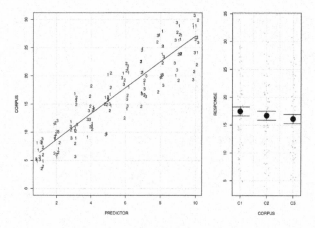

Figure 108: The effects of PREDICTOR and CORPUS

Don't get me wrong: I'm not saying the author didn't have *data* demonstrating the hypothesized change, which was 'how some response was affected by some predictor differently over three time periods' – I am saying, the author didn't have an *analysis* demonstrating the hypothesized change. Without having the interaction results, talk about diachronic change regarding the effect of PREDICTOR on the basis of just comparing slopes from *separate* analyses *visually* runs the risk of not saying anything at all – we need to check the interaction term. Now of course, if the effect of CORPUS is significant, there is a diachronic effect: RESPONSE is decreasing over time/CORPUS, but that wasn't what the author wanted: they wanted the effect of PREDICTOR to change over time/CORPUS. And before you think that this is a rare mistake: this happens so often that it's mistake #2 in a great overview paper called "Ten common statistical mistakes to watch out for when writing or reviewing a manuscript" (Makin & Orban de Xivry 2019) – so no, this isn't rare, I see it all . the . time and in submissions to the best journals! Just one week before I finalized this section, I reviewed a paper that eviscerated several earlier studies on the same topic for their statistical short-comings (which were indeed problematic) with a tone that surpassed even my sometimes acerbic comments, but then the author(s) of that ms did the above kind of slope comparisons by impressionistically comparing the visual similarity of their slopes ... So, repeat after me: interactions can be really really important. Chances are that, whenever you want to say 'the effect of X is not the same everywhere', you need an interaction term, and this is even true for experimental controls, as you will see in Section 5.6.4 when I return this one last time.

Recommendation(s) for further study: the package rms and its functions ols and anova: ols is similar to lm and returns most of the statistics that summary(lm(...)) would return, but anova applied to the output of ols returns something very interesting for later, namely for every predictor in the model, it returns the result of a significance test for that predictor and all its higher order factors (i.e. the predictor and the higher-order interactions the predictor is involved in).

5.3 Binary logistic regression

We're revisiting the clause-order data from Section 3.5.2 above so you might quickly want to read up on the question and variables involved there. Thus, our focus now becomes what to do when our response variable is a categorical/binary factor, not a numeric variable anymore. We will again discuss a few models on the basis of data frames that contain only the variables of interest in a certain subsection, i.e. sub-data frames, so to speak, of the one with all variables we used before. For didactic reasons, we will change the order of discussion and begin with a binary predictor for now.

5.3.1 A binary logistic regression with a binary predictor

Let's assume we hypothesize that subordinate clause placement – relative to the main clause, that is – is correlated with whether the subordinate clause is a causal or a temporal one.
- H_0: There is no correlation between SCTYPE and ORDER; $R^2=0$;
- H_1: There is a correlation between SCTYPE and ORDER; $R^2>0$.

You load the data:

```
rm(list=ls(all.names=TRUE)); library(car); library(effects)
source("helpers/R2.r"); source("helpers/C.score.r")
summary(x <- read.delim(file="_inputfiles/05_scmc_sctype.csv",
    stringsAsFactors=TRUE)) ## [...]
```

5.3.1.1 Numerical exploration
How would you have dealt with that before this section? Hopefully you're saying "with a chi-squared test for independence (from Section 4.1.2.1)". What did we do there? We
- generated a frequency table of observed frequencies;
- computed the table of expected frequencies;
- computed a chi-squared test and an odds ratio.

Let's do that here real quick because it'll help us understand the simplest kind of binary logistic regression:

```
(CLAUSES.obs <- table(x$SCTYPE, x$ORDER))
##         mc-sc sc-mc
##   caus    184    15
##   temp     91   113
(CLAUSES.exp <- chisq.test(table(x$SCTYPE, x$ORDER),
  correct=FALSE)$expected)
##          mc-sc     sc-mc
##   caus 135.794  63.20596
##   temp 139.206  64.79404
(CLAUSES.chisq <- sum(((CLAUSES.obs-CLAUSES.exp)^2)/CLAUSES.exp))
## [1] 106.4365
(CLAUSES.odds <- (CLAUSES.obs[2,2]/CLAUSES.obs[2,1]) /
                 (CLAUSES.obs[1,2]/CLAUSES.obs[1,1]))
## [1] 15.23223
```

There seems to be an effect:
- when SCTYPE is *temp*, the odds of ORDER being *sc-mc* over *mc-sc* are $^{113}/_{91} \approx 1.2418$ to 1;
- when SCTYPE is *caus*, the odds of ORDER being *sc-mc* over *mc-sc* are $^{15}/_{184} \approx 0.0815$ to 1;
- the ratio of these two odds is the odds ratio of $^{1.242}/_{0.081} \approx 15.23$.

We again started computing the odds ratio from the lower right corner – i.e. we computed the odds of the second level of the response – so we see that *sc-mc* is much more prevalent when SCTYPE is *temp* than when it is *caus*. Now, one thing I don't like about the odds ratio is its 'asymmetry': The preference of the second level of the response is in the vast numeric space from 1 to $+\infty$ whereas equally strong dispreferences of the second level of the response are 'squeezed into' the tiny numeric space from 1 to 0. (Yes, I get the math of it, but it doesn't feel intuitive to me, I'm too 'linear'.) What can we do about that? As mentioned in a note before, we can log the odds ratio and that helps:
- if the odds ratio is >1 because the second level of the response is more preferred with the predictor's second level, then its log becomes a positive value in the interval $(0,+\infty]$;
- if the odds ratio is 1 because the two variables are not correlated at all, then its log becomes 0;

– if the odds ratio is <1 because the second level of the response is less preferred
with the predictor's second level, then its log becomes a negative value in the
interval [-∞,0).

Suddenly, everything is symmetric around the 'no correlation' 0-point on the
scale – nice! So, let's log the odds ratio:

```
(CLAUSES.logodds <- log(CLAUSES.odds))
## [1] 2.723414
```

Log odds values can sometimes be a little easier to interpret when it comes to
comparing different ones. For example, if you have two odds ratios such as odds
ratio$_1$=0.5 and odds ratio$_2$=1.5, then you cannot completely intuitively (!) see
which effect is larger. The logs of the odds ratios – log odds ratio$_1$=-0.693 and log
odds ratio$_2$=0.405 – tell you immediately the former is larger because its logged
odds are further away from 0.

   What does any of this have to do with binary logistic regression modeling?
Let's fit our model and you'll see. Defining the model is really similar to the linear model cases, just a few small changes: (i) the function changes from lm to
glm and (ii) we add an argument family=binomial to tell glm that the response is
binary; we again also immediately apply drop1, which needs its test argument
changed from "F" (for linear models) to "Chisq" (for a so-called **likelihood ratio test** (LRT) for generalized linear and other models):

```
summary(m.01 <- glm(ORDER ~ 1 + SCTYPE, data=x, family=binomial))
## [...] Coefficients:
##             Estimate Std. Error z value Pr(>|z|)
## (Intercept)  -2.5069     0.2685  -9.336   <2e-16 ***
## SCTYPEtemp    2.7234     0.3032   8.982   <2e-16 ***
## [...]
## (Dispersion parameter for binomial family taken to be 1)
##     Null deviance: 503.80  on 402  degrees of freedom
## Residual deviance: 386.82  on 401  degrees of freedom
## AIC: 390.82
## [...]
drop1(m.01, test="Chisq")
## [...]
##         Df Deviance    AIC    LRT  Pr(>Chi)
## <none>      386.82 390.82
## SCTYPE   1  503.80 505.80 116.97 < 2.2e-16 ***
```

Similar to lm's output, but also different. For example, in the summary output, you get no R^2-values and also no overall p-value at the bottom. (You can of course infer that the model is significant from the fact that its only predictor is.) However, the bottom of the output also gives you 'a clue' about the overall model significance: If you subtract from the null deviance (503.8, indicating how well the null model with no predictors fits the data) the residual deviance (386.82, indicating how well our model with, here, one predictor fits the data), you get a value of 116.98, which is a value called G^2, which is a bit like X^2. Remember how X^2 was computed? We just used it again, it's the sum of the contributions to X^2, which quantify the discrepancy between observed and expected values in the c cells of the frequency table. G^2 is similar, it just computes the discrepancy between observed and expected values in a slightly different way: Rather than subtracting expected values from observed values (like for X^2), you divide observed values by expected values:

$$G^2 = 2 \sum_{i=1}^{c} observed \times \log \frac{observed}{expected}$$

```
2*sum(CLAUSES.obs*log(CLAUSES.obs/CLAUSES.exp))
## [1] 116.9747
```

In fact, X^2 and G^2 are quite highly correlated and the significance test for G^2 indeed uses the X^2 distribution:[11]

```
pchisq(q=116.9747, df=1, lower.tail=FALSE)
## [1] 2.90753e-27
```

As always, when our model has just one predictor, its drop1 p-value is also the p-value for the whole model. Now, to the coefficients. The good news is that the intercept and the coefficients have the same general meaning as above in the linear model; they are used to compute predictions in the same way as above, but this time they are not predictions of the actual value of the dependent variable (like the lm examples generated RT predictions), they are predicted log(ged) odds of **the second level of the response variable:**
– the intercept is the log odds value of the second level of the response that the regression model predicts when all categorical predictors in the model equation are set to their first level and all numeric predictors are 0. Thus, if -2.5069 is a logged odds value, we can exponentiate/antilog it with exp(-2.5069),

---

11 While this seems to be the most widely-used approach, it is not uncontroversial, see Harrell (2015:36f.)

which returns 0.0815206, which you should recognize from above as the odds of ORDER being *sc-mc* when SCTYPE is its 1st level, *caus*;
- the coefficient is what you add to the intercept to predict the log odds of the second level of the response for when SCTYPE changes to the other level, *temp*: -2.5069+2.7234=0.2165, which, when exponentiated/anti-logged is 1.2417231, which you should recognize from above as the odds of ORDER being *sc-mc* when SCTYPE is its 2nd level, *temp*;
- and those two things together mean that, if you exponentiate/antilog the coefficient of 2.7234, you get the odds ratio: exp(2.7234) returns 15.2320232.

As before, we can compute confidence intervals of these coefficients:

```
Confint(m.01) # return estimates w/ their 95%-CI
##              Estimate     2.5 %     97.5 %
## (Intercept) -2.506886 -3.076455  -2.016328
## SCTYPEtemp   2.723414  2.156967   3.352559
```

And as before, we can use the effects package to get predictions:

```
(ph <- data.frame(sub <- effect("SCTYPE", m.01)))
##   SCTYPE       fit         se      lower      upper
## 1   caus 0.07537688 0.01871434 0.0459497 0.1212547
## 2   temp 0.55392157 0.03480284 0.4851215 0.6207159
```

Wait, what? What are those predictions in the fit column? Those are not the predicted odds of 0.0815206 or 1.2417231, nor are they the predicted logged odds of -2.5069 and -2.5069+2.7234=0.2165! Turns out there's a third way to talk about the predictions of these kinds of models, namely in terms of **predicted probabilities of the second level of the response** variable, *sc-mc*, which are 15/(15+184)=0.07537688 when SCTYPE is *caus* and 113/(113+91)=0.55392157 when SCTYPE is *temp*, and the effects package returns this third option. And for me at least, that's great, because my preferred way of talking about predictions for these models is indeed also the predicted probabilities of the second level of the response. You need to realize, however, that these three options are of course equivalent: each scale – odds, log odds, and probabilities – can easily be converted into each other, as is indicated here in Figure 109, where preference and dispreference pertain to what binary logistic regression models predict: the second level of the response (and the fact that that is what such models predict, that would go on the inside of your third eyelid, people always forget that!):

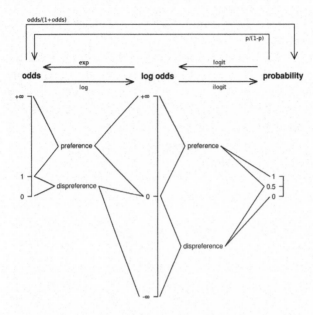

Figure 109: Three ways to look at results from a binary logistic regression

The logit and ilogit (or inverse logit) transformations are fairly straightforward:

$$logit\ x = \log \frac{x}{1-x} \qquad\qquad ilogit\ x = \frac{1}{1+\exp(-x)} = \frac{\exp(x)}{1+\exp(x)}$$

You can quickly write such functions yourself or use the functions `faraway::logit` (or `qlogis`) and `faraway::ilogit` (or `plogis`). And this actually also clarifies how we get from the numeric results to the binary/categorical predictions we're also interested in. You predict the second level of the response, *sc-mc*, when whichever numeric result you're considering – odds, log odds, predicted probabilities – is in its 'preference space' in Figure 109, i.e. when
– its predicted odds are ≥1;
– its predicted log odds are ≥0;
– its predicted probability is ≥0.5.

Otherwise, you predict *mc-sc*. Let's do that now for our data:

```
x$PREDS.NUM <- predict(m.01, type="response")
x$PREDS.CAT <- factor(ifelse(x$PREDS.NUM>=0.5,
  levels(x$ORDER)[2], levels(x$ORDER)[1]))
```

Then we can check how well our model is doing by generating what is some-times called a **confusion matrix**:

```
(qwe <- table(x$ORDER, x$PREDS.CAT))
##           mc-sc sc-mc
##   mc-sc    184    91
##   sc-mc     15   113
```

A first piece of good news is that the highest values are in the main diagonal, so maybe our model isn't that bad. We can now compute a variety of statistics, in particular accuracy, precision, and recall. To understand those, we need two easy distinctions:
- positives vs. negatives: **positives** are the cases where the model predicts the level it was tasked to predict, i.e. here *sc-mc*, **negatives** are when it predicts the other level. (This terminology comes from applications where the two levels of the response are massively different qualitatively and in terms of impact and often also in terms of frequency. For example, when you do cancer screening, the test is tasked with finding cancer so that would be the 'positive' prediction; when credit card companies monitor transactions for being likely fraudulent, then the algorithm saying 'this use of your credit card is fraudulent' is the 'positive' prediction – those are the predictions that are important and require (a re)action.)
- **true** vs. **false** is just whether the prediction/classification of the model is correct or not.

That means, we can define the four possible outcomes like this:

Table 29: The confusion matrix (for when one predicts the 2nd level of ORDER)

	predicted: ORDER: *mc-sc*	predicted: ORDER: *sc-mc*
observed: ORDER: *mc-sc*	184 (true negatives, *tn*)	91 (false positives, *fp*)
observed: ORDER: *sc-mc*	15 (false negatives, *fn*)	113 (true positives, *tp*)

And from that, we can compute statistics called precision and recall. **Precision** is computed as $(tp/(tp+fp))$ and answers the question 'how often (in %) was the model right when it predicted what it was tasked to predict?'; **recall** is computed as $(tp/(tp+fn))$ and answers the question 'how many of the things the model was tasked to find did it find (in %)?'. While current events might actually have resulted in everyone knowing these statistics now, let me nevertheless give a cancer screening example: Precision is 'how often is the test right when it says someone has cancer?', recall is how many of the n people that have cancer and were tested did the test find?'. In cases like ours, where there isn't a huge qualitative difference between the two levels of the response, it might be nice to report precision and recall for both levels, not just for the second one that the model technically predicted (only showing the results):

```
##      Class. acc. Prec. for sc-mc  Rec. for sc-mc
##        0.7369727       0.5539216       0.8828125
## Prec. for mc-sc  Rec. for mc-sc
##        0.9246231       0.6690909
```

Now, are those values good, e.g. the accuracy of 0.7369727? Unlike what you might think, you should not just automatically compare it to a chance accuracy of 0.5 (because you have two orderings) – why? Because the two orderings are not equally frequent. The more frequent ordering, *mc-sc*, accounts for 0.6824 of all the data, so even the dumbest of models could already get that much right by always 'guessing' the mode of the response variable. Accuracies should be compared to one of two baselines, and since one of them is by definition easier to beat, you actually always want to beat the harder one.

– baseline$_1$ is the accuracy a model would achieve if it always guesses the most frequent of the two orderings; that's the one I just mentioned, the harder one;
– baseline$_2$ is the accuracy a model would achieve if it guesses, for each case separately, a level of ORDER randomly but with the random guessing weighted by the frequencies of the two levels.

This is how we compute both:

```
(baseline.1 <- max(prop.table(table(x$ORDER))))
## [1] 0.6823821
(baseline.2 <- sum(prop.table(table(x$ORDER))^2))
## [1] 0.5665265
```

That means you can now use the same method we used for tossing a coin etc. to compute whether the accuracy you achieved is significantly better than either baseline: if you run the code in the code file, we're significantly better than either baseline although one really has to admit that an improvement to 0.7369 from 0.6824 hardly seems great. However, classification accuracy is widely-used, but not really an ideal evaluation metric.[12] More useful, though of course also not uncontroversial, are a version of an R^2 designed to work with generalized linear models and the so-called C-score, a score in the interval [0.5, 1], which is widely used to evaluate model fit. To get those, we use the two functions that we sourced from the helpers folder, which require only the model object as their only argument:

```
c("R2"=R2(m.01), "C"=C.score(m.01))
##        R2         C
## 0.3530766 0.7759517
```

This R^2-value, Nagelkerke's R^2, ranges from 0 to 1 like the one for linear models (even if its mathematical interpretation is actually different from that of a linear model, this is a so-called pseudo-R^2); its size here isn't great, but also not terrible (what an expert way of putting this ... this is *exactly* how you should put it in your results section) (See Tjur 2009 for an interesting alternative R^2). As for the C-score, following Baayen (2008:204) and Hosmer, Lemeshow, & Sturdivant (2013:177), C-scores of 0.8 and above are considered good or "excellent" so we're not really making the cut, arriving only at what Hosmer et al. call "acceptable".

5.3.1.2 Graphical model exploration

In terms of visualization, there's not much to add to what we talked about in the linear-modeling part: We visualize as before, just that now the y-axis features predicted probabilities rather than direct predictions of the response variable – everything else stays the same. Thus, you can use `effects` objects or you create your own plot; here's one example:

```
plot(sub, type="response", ylim=c(0, 1), grid=TRUE) ## [...] or
dotchart(xlab="Predicted probability of sc-mc", xlim=c(0, 1),
   x=ph$fit, ylab="SCTYPE", labels=levels(x$SCTYPE), pch=16,
   pt.cex=4*prop.table(table(x$SCTYPE))); abline(v=0.5, lty=3)
for (i in seq(nrow(ph))) {  # for each row in ph
   arrows(x0=ph$lower[i], y0=i, x1=ph$upper[i], y1=i,
      angle=90, code=3)
}
```

---

12 See Hosmer, Lemeshow, & Sturdivant (2013:170-173) or Harrell (2015:258) for discussion why this kind of accuracy, while usually provided in papers, is ultimately not a really good measure of predictive ability and also see Section 5.7.

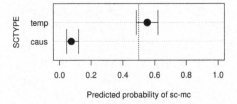

Figure 110: The effect of SCTYPE

You might now summarize all of this: "A binary logistic regression model was fit with ORDER as the response (predicting *sc-mc*) and SCTYPE as the only predictor. The model indicated a highly significant fit (*LR*-statistic=116.97, *df*=1, *p*<0.0001). The model fit was decent in terms of R^2 (0.3531); however, its accuracy was less good: While the accuracy (0.737) was very significantly better than baseline ($p_{binomial}$<0.01), precision was relatively low (0.554), recall was good at 0.883, but the *C*-score (of 0.776) did not reach the standard level of 0.8 [maybe provide the other precision/recall scores, too]. [Then you would probably show the "Coefficients" table of the summary output, ideally with the CIs, and one of the plots and summarize:] causal subordinate clauses are strongly associated with *mc-sc*, temporal subordinate clauses are weakly associated with *sc-mc*."

5.3.2 A binary logistic regression with a categorical predictor

We'll pick up the pace now and study the hypothesis that subordinate clause placement – relative to the main clause, that is – is correlated with the conjunction of the subordinate clause. Note that this variable – CONJ – is a finer resolution version, so to speak, of SCTYPE: One conjunction is causal, the other three are temporal. We formulate the hypotheses and load the data:
– H₀: There is no correlation between CONJ and ORDER; R^2=0;
– H₁: There is a correlation between CONJ and ORDER; R^2>0.

```
rm(list=ls(all.names=TRUE)); library(car); library(effects)
source("helpers/R2.r"); source("helpers/C.score.r")
summary(x <- read.delim(file="_inputfiles/05_scmc_conj.csv",
    stringsAsFactors=TRUE)) ## [...]
```

If you look at the four conjunctions that we're dealing with, do you have any thoughts on what one might want to do before modeling?

I hope you had at least one of two thoughts:

1. making the one causal conjunction the reference level so that it gets compared to each temporal one;[13]
2. defining *a priori* orthogonal contrasts. For instance you might say you want to compare
   a. the causal one vs. all three temporal ones combined;
   b. the temporal ones used for non-contemporaneous events (*bevor/before* and *nachdem/after*) vs. the contemporaneous one (*als/when*);
   c. *bevor/before* vs. *nachdem/after*.

In real research-life, you'd decide in favor of one, but for exposition's sake we will prepare the data for both:

```
x$CONJ <- factor(x$CONJ, levels=levels(x$CONJ)[c(4, 2, 1, 3)])
x$CONJ.ORTH <- x$CONJ
#                    w/b    b/b    a/w    n/a
caus_vs_temp <-    c(3/4, -1/4, -1/4, -1/4) # contrast 1
samet_vs_difft <- c(0  ,  1/3, -2/3,  1/3) # contrast 2
earl_vs_lat <-    c(0  ,  1/2,    0, -1/2) # contrast 3
contrasts(x$CONJ.ORTH) <- cbind(caus_vs_temp, samet_vs_difft,
    earl_vs_lat)
```

Let's also do a very quick cross-tabulation to check for data sparsity etc.

```
table(x$ORDER, x$CONJ)
        weil/because bevor/before als/when nachdem/after
  mc-sc          184           28       37            26
  sc-mc           15           18       56            39
```

Two combinations of levels are a bit rare again, but nothing too bad.

---

13 This has the positive side-effect that the reference level is the most frequent one, something that can help deal with collinearity.

5.3.2.1 Numerical exploration

Let's (re-)compute (only) the (harder) baseline, but then also follow it up with our model; let's use CONJ.ORTH here and let's do a whole bunch of things together at the same time:

```
(baseline <- max(prop.table(table(x$ORDER))))
## [1] 0.6823821
summary(m.01 <- glm(ORDER ~ 1 + CONJ.ORTH, data=x, family=binomial))
## [...] Coefficients:
##                          Estimate Std. Error z value Pr(>|z|)
## (Intercept)               -0.5322     0.1305  -4.079 4.52e-05 ***
## CONJ.ORTHcaus_vs_temp     -2.6329     0.3072  -8.572  < 2e-16 ***
## CONJ.ORTHsamet_vs_difft   -0.4326     0.2894  -1.495   0.1349
## CONJ.ORTHearl_vs_lat      -0.8473     0.3942  -2.150   0.0316 *
## [...]
##     Null deviance: 503.80  on 402  degrees of freedom
## Residual deviance: 380.48  on 399  degrees of freedom
drop1(m.01, test="Chisq")
## [...]
## ORDER ~ 1 + CONJ.ORTH
##             Df Deviance    AIC    LRT Pr(>Chi)
## <none>          380.48 388.48
## CONJ.ORTH    3   503.80 505.80 123.32 < 2.2e-16 ***
pchisq(q=123.23, df=3, lower.tail=FALSE)
## [1] 1.554985e-26
c("R2"=R2(m.01), "C"=C.score(m.01))
##        R2         C
## 0.3694436 0.7978125
```

The overall model is significant (LR-statistic=123.32, df=3, p<0.0001). The model fit is about decent-ish in terms of R^2 (0.369), but the C-score only reaches the standard level of 0.8 if you round to the most marketable number of digits ... Let's look at the coefficients and their confidence intervals:

```
Confint(m.01) # return estimates w/ their 95%-CI
##                          Estimate      2.5 %      97.5 %
## (Intercept)             -0.5322049 -0.7914933 -0.27883358
## CONJ.ORTHcaus_vs_temp   -2.6329076 -3.2686321 -2.05740569
## CONJ.ORTHsamet_vs_difft -0.4326176 -1.0049404  0.13146984
## CONJ.ORTHearl_vs_lat    -0.8472979 -1.6334824 -0.08296622
```

We see that
- the one causal conjunction (*weil/because*) is significantly different from all temporal ones (significant contrast in the summary output and a CI not including 0);
- the same-time conjunction (*als/when*) is not significantly different from the different-time ones (non-significant contrast in the summary output and a CI including 0);
- *nachdem/after* is significantly different from *bevor/before* (significant contrast in the summary output and a CI not including 0).

What about the predicted probabilities?

```
(ph <- data.frame(conj <- effect("CONJ.ORTH", m.01)))
##       CONJ.ORTH        fit         se     lower      upper
## 1   weil/because 0.07537688 0.01871434 0.0459497 0.1212547
## 2   bevor/before 0.39130435 0.07195791 0.2623180 0.5375019
## 3        als/when 0.60215054 0.05075402 0.4997995 0.6962850
## 4 nachdem/after 0.60000000 0.06076436 0.4773236 0.7112984
```

When CONJ/CONJ.ORTH is *weil/because*, there's a strong preference for ORDER being *mc-sc*; when it is *bevor/before*, there's a weak preference for *mc-sc*, otherwise there's a weak preference for *sc-mc*. How well does the model do in terms of its predictions? Better than the previous model, and therefore of course again better than both baselines: (I'm only showing the confusion matrix and its statistics.)

```
##            mc-sc sc-mc
##    mc-sc    212    63
##    sc-mc     33    95
##      Class. acc. Prec. for sc-mc  Rec. for sc-mc
##        0.7617866       0.6012658       0.7421875
## Prec. for mc-sc  Rec. for mc-sc
##        0.8653061       0.7709091
# better than baseline: 0.0002796997
```

5.3.2.2 Graphical model exploration
Nothing new here: You make a plot based on the plotting functions of the effects package ...

```
plot(conj, type="response", ylim=c(0, 1), grid=TRUE) ## [...]
```

... or you don't:

```
qwe <- barplot(height=ph$fit, width=prop.table(table(x$CONJ.ORTH)),
   xlab="Conjunction", ylab="Predicted probability of sc-mc",
   names.arg=levels(x$CONJ.ORTH), ylim=c(0, 1)); abline(h=0.5, lty=3)
arrows(x0=qwe, y0=ph$lower, x1=qwe, y1=ph$upper, angle=90, code=3)
```

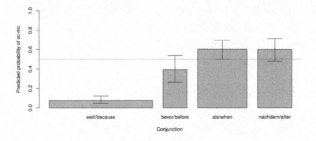

Figure 111: The effect of CONJ

That was quick and painless ...

5.3.3 A binary logistic regression with a numeric predictor

Now, imagine we hypothesized that the clause ordering should exhibit the widely-attested short-before-long effect: we're correlating ORDER with LENDIFF; remember that the predictor was computed as LENMC-LENSC, negative values mean the main clause is shorter. We formulate the hypotheses and load the data:
– H_0: There is no correlation between LENDIFF and ORDER; $R^2=0$;
– H_1: There is a correlation between LENDIFF and ORDER; $R^2>0$.

```
rm(list=ls(all.names=TRUE)); library(car); library(effects)
source("helpers/R2.r"); source("helpers/C.score.r")
summary(x <- read.delim(file="_inputfiles/05_scmc_lendiff.csv",
   stringsAsFactors=TRUE)) ## [...]
```

Wow, the mean of LENDIFF is really close to 0 (where both clauses are equally long), as if we had centered the variable and if you create a histogram with hist(x$LENDIFF), you'll see a nice bell-like distribution. Let's model ...

5.3.3.1 Numerical exploration

As before, we do a lot of things in one go: (I will only show the main results.)

```
## baseline: 0.6823821
## glm(formula = ORDER ~ 1 + LENDIFF, family = binomial, data = x)
## [...]
## glm's coefficients:
##              Estimate Std. Error z value Pr(>|z|)
## (Intercept) -0.77673    0.10849  -7.160 8.08e-13 ***
## LENDIFF      0.04418    0.01639   2.695  0.00704 **
## [...]
## drop1:  Df Deviance    AIC    LRT Pr(>Chi)
## <none>         496.22 500.22
## LENDIFF  1   503.80 505.80 7.5822 0.005895 **
##          R2          C
## 0.02612148 0.60339489
```

Ok, that might seem a bit weird: The overall model is significant (*LR*-statistic=7.58, *df*=1, *p*<0.006), but the model fit is terrible: R^2=0.026 and *C*=0.603. Let's compute CIs and focus on the coefficients – do you see what's happening?

```
Confint(m.01) # return estimates w/ their 95%-CI
##              Estimate        2.5 %      97.5 %
## (Intercept) -0.77673305 -0.99253183 -0.5668164
## LENDIFF      0.04418255  0.01257435  0.0770071
```

THINK BREAK

What is the intercept? The predicted log odds when the numeric predictor LENDIFF is 0. What is the predicted probability for *sc-mc* then?

```
1/(1 + exp(--0.77673))
## [1] 0.3150251
```

In other words, fairly low. What is the predicted probability for *sc-mc* when LENDIFF increases by/to 1?

```
1/(1 + exp(-(-0.77673+0.04418)))
## [1] 0.3246354
```

Not much higher ... In fact, you can already infer that the predicted log odds will only be greater than 0 and that therefore the predicted probability of *sc-mc* will only be greater than 0.5, when you have added +0.04418 often enough to 'over-come' the intercept of -0.77673, i.e. about 18 times. In other words, this model only predicts *sc-mc* when the main clause is 18+ words longer than the subordinate clause. But how many such data points do we even have?!

```
sum(x$LENDIFF>=18)
## [1] 5
```

Aha ... So we have 403 data points altogether, but the model we currently have only predicts *sc-mc* for 5 of those (a.k.a. a measly 1.2%) – not exactly the greatest degree of discriminatory power. You can see that really well in the predictions from the effects package:

```
(ph <- data.frame(lend <- effect("LENDIFF", m.01, xlevels=list(
   LENDIFF=seq(-32, 32, 8)))))
##   LENDIFF       fit          se      lower      upper
## 1     -32 0.1006001 0.04936021 0.03697592 0.2457632
## [...]
## 7      16 0.4825540 0.06850256 0.35262579 0.6148849
## 8      24 0.5704404 0.09759072 0.37825966 0.7434996
## 9      32 0.6540996 0.11894387 0.40293131 0.8412400
```

That of course suggests accuracy, precision, recall, those will all be more than terrible, too:

```
##              mc-sc sc-mc
##   mc-sc       272     3
##   sc-mc       126     2
##     Class. acc. Prec. for sc-mc Rec. for sc-mc
##       0.6799007       0.4000000      0.0156250
## Prec. for mc-sc Rec. for mc-sc
##       0.6834171       0.9890909
```

It doesn't get much worse than that: the accuracy is worse than the baseline: 0.6799007<0.6823821! Of course, recall for *mc*-sc is great – because the model nearly always predicts it ... We will also recognize our problem clearly when we visualize it now.

5.3.3.2 Graphical model exploration

First, the effects plot would be the usual one and you would already see that the predicted probabilities of *sc-mc* hardly ever go above 0.5 – only a bit on the very right where 5 points are located. But here's a plot that combines the predicted regression line and its confidence band with a representation of the observed data; check out the code for how this is done.

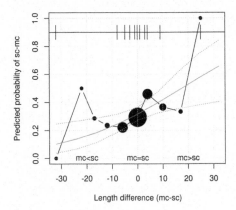

Figure 112: The effect of LENDIFF

By the way: The model fit is really bad and all, but is there at least a tendency of evidence of short-before-long or not?

THINK BREAK

There is: on the left, the length differences are negative, which means main clauses are shorter than subordinate clauses, and the predicted probabilities of *sc-mc* are low, which means with short(er) main clauses *mc-sc* is more likely, and the opposite for the right side. Still, this is obviously not great. So, either you give up at this point, just summarize and present it all, and then launch into a discussion section that speculates on why the results are such a bummer, or ... what else might you do?

THINK BREAK

You check whether LENDIFF's effect requires a curved regression line.

```
summary(m.02 <- glm(ORDER ~ 1 + poly(LENDIFF, 2), data=x,
    family=binomial)) ## [...]
```

```
## Coefficients:
##                    Estimate Std. Error z value Pr(>|z|)
## (Intercept)         -0.7806     0.1087  -7.179 7.01e-13 ***
## poly(LENDIFF, 2)1    6.0323     2.2999   2.623  0.00872 **
## poly(LENDIFF, 2)2    0.1788     2.4153   0.074  0.94100
anova(m.01, m.02, test="Chisq")
## Model 1: ORDER ~ 1 + LENDIFF
## Model 2: ORDER ~ 1 + poly(LENDIFF, 2)
##   Resid. Df Resid. Dev Df Deviance Pr(>Chi)
## 1       401     496.22
## 2       400     496.21  1 0.005445   0.9412
```

Well, it was worth a shot, but a *p*-value of 0.9412 isn't the best of justifications to add curvature to a model ... This seems to be the end of the road for this hypothesis. (I leave it up to you to check that a third-degree polynomial also doesn't help (even a generalized additive model allowing much more flexible curvature (not shown here) doesn't); also, you should re-run the model with the other version of CONJ (treatment contrasts) so you know you understand the output.)

5.3.3.3 Excursus: on cut-off points

There's one other way one could try to make the model perform better because there's one other parameter one could easily tweak: the cut-off point where we flip from one prediction (*sc-mc*) to the other (*mc-sc*). We've always used 0.5, i.e. the middle of the probability continuum and that *is* the default/unmarked choice (in the sense of 'if you use that, you don't have to justify it, but if you use something else, you better motivate that'). However, it's at least conceivable to use another one (although I'm not sure I can remember seeing a study in linguistics that did that). I want to briefly mention two approaches to this.

The first one is very easy: Instead of using 0.5 as the cut-off point, we could use the mean or the median of all predicted probabilities. That means, we're not saying 'predict *sc-mc* when it's more likely than *mc-sc*' (that would be the 0.5 threshold) – we're saying 'predict *sc-mc* when it's more likely than the average of all predictions'. This is how to do this and what happens as a result:

```
x$PREDS.CAT <- factor(ifelse(x$PREDS.NUM>=mean(x$PREDS.NUM),
   levels(x$ORDER)[2], levels(x$ORDER)[1]))
(qwe <- table(x$ORDER, x$PREDS.CAT))
##         mc-sc sc-mc
##   mc-sc   160   115
```

```
##    sc-mc    50    78
## evaluate the confusion matrix
##      Class. acc. Prec. for sc-mc  Rec. for sc-mc
##        0.5905707        0.4041451       0.6093750
## Prec. for mc-sc  Rec. for mc-sc
##        0.7619048       0.5818182
```

Now that the model is more discriminatory and predicts *sc-mc* much more often,
– accuracy goes actually way down (from 0.6799007 to 0.5905707);
– precision is nearly unchanged (from 0.4 to 0.4041451);
– recall is way up (from 0.015625 to 0.609375)!

So, if for whatever reason recall was super-important to you, this procedure could be better for your goals. For instance, high recall is needed when you screen patients for cancer or when you screen airplane luggage for explosives. In such scenarios, recall is very important, but accuracy and precision are much less so: If you get a (false) positive, you just check again, little harm done. In the second scenario, 'paying for 5 minutes of a TSA rep/luggage screener's time' to re-check a bag to make sure an alarm was a false positive is a small price to pay compared to the false negative of letting a bomb on a plane.

The second approach is a bit more involved and would make for a great assignment, but I'll discuss it here anyway. It's letting the data decide what the best cut-off point is by looking at all possible ones and picking the one that leads to the highest accuracy (or precision or recall). This code file shows how that can be done and visualized, but you will see that this, too, doesn't help. Even the best cut-off point, which turns out to be the predicted probability of 0.5484551 doesn't boost our accuracy much: (The code file shows how to get these results.)
– accuracy is the highest possible now (increasing from 0.6799007 to 0.6848635) but still bad because it's still pretty much the baseline;
– precision is perfect now (from 0.4 to 1) but that's of course just a single case!
– recall is even worse than the already terrible result before (decreasing from 0.015625 to 0.0078125).

Anyway, you can see how different cut-off points have different consequences and you need to decide what's most relevant for your current study (because, of course, we could use an analogous approach to find the cut-off point for the best precision or recall). For this model on these data, however, it's clear there's no magic bullet: LENDIFF is just not a great discriminatory predictor.

Recommendation(s) for further study: check out Kuhn & Johnson (2013: Section 16.4) on this notion of "alternate cut-offs" and ways to compute them with the caret package as well as Hosmer, Lemeshow, & Sturdivant (2013: Section 5.2.4).

5.3.4 A binary logistic regression with two categorical predictors

One might hypothesize that the ordering of the two clauses is affected by processing-ease considerations (esp. since we already saw a (bit of a) short-before-long effect). But we also know that the conjunctions have a huge effect – especially *weil/because* – so that might be able to override, or moderate/modify any effect that MORETHAN2CL, the predictor indicating the presence of more material in the sentence, might have. That's what we'll look at here (quickly).
– H_0: There is no correlation between MORETHAN2CL, CONJ, and ORDER; $R^2=0$;
– H_1: There is a correlation between MORETHAN2CL, CONJ, and ORDER; $R^2>0$.

```
rm(list=ls(all.names=TRUE)); library(car); library(effects)
source("helpers/R2.r"); source("helpers/C.score.r")
x <- read.delim(file="_inputfiles/05_scmc_conjmorethan2.csv",
   stringsAsFactors=TRUE)
x$CONJ <- factor(x$CONJ, levels=levels(x$CONJ)[c(4, 2, 1, 3)])
summary(x) ## [...]
```

Let's quickly check whether we will run into data sparsity issues in some of the 8 cells for which we will want predictions: (Results not shown here, see code file.)

```
table(x$MORETHAN2CL, x$CONJ)
ftable(x$CONJ, x$MORETHAN2CL, x$ORDER)
```

The upper table isn't too bad: We have 22 cases or more per cell, we can work with that. The lower table is also not that bad, but the first row has a quite extreme distribution of 87 to 5 (i.e. if CONJ is *weil/because* and MORETHAN2CL is *no*, we have very few cases of *sc-mc*), which I will use it to at least mention the important topic of **complete separation**, which refers to the situation where a predictor or combination of predictors perfectly predicts the response variable, e.g. if the first row of the ftable output above had been, say, 92 to 0. This is something that will throw the estimation of the model off because, if you think of the binary predictor case, the computation of the odds might involve division by 0 etc. Proper exploration at the beginning of an analysis should help you detect this, but if you ever don't find it during that stage, but R throws you a message saying fitted probabilities numerically 0 or 1 occurred and/or extremely high standard errors in a model output, then complete separation is one possible culprit. So, better do your exploration right at the beginning ...

5.3.4.1 Numerical exploration

Since everything else is as before, let me use this otherwise straightforward application to introduce some other things. First, two syntactic shortcuts: So far, when we had two predictors, say A and B, and their interaction in our regression formulae, we wrote that very explicitly as A + B + A:B, but there's a shortcut for that: A*B. Combining predictors with an asterisk means 'all main effects and all their interactions'. That means, A*B*C means A + B + C + A:B + A:C + B:C + A:B:C. And if you want to restrict the degree of 'interactivity' to a certain number, you can do that as well. For example, you may have four predictors A, B, C, and D, but if you only want to consider all main effects and all two-way interactions, you can do that like this: (A+B+C+D)^2, which is the same as A + B + C + D + A:B + A:C + A:D + B:C + B:D + C:D. But let's go with our simple-asterisk case in our small example now:

```
## baseline: 0.6823821
summary(m.01 <- glm(ORDER ~ 1 + CONJ*MORETHAN2CL, data=x,
    family=binomial)) ## [...]
Confint(m.01) # return estimates w/ their 95%-CI
##                                  Estimate       2.5 %      97.5 %
## (Intercept)                    -2.85647020  -3.9002522  -2.058707
## CONJbevor/before                1.75785792   0.4618588   3.099479
## CONJals/when                    3.00307368   1.9815496   4.197561
## CONJnachdem/after               2.85647020   1.7463550   4.114818
## MORETHAN2CLyes                  0.58434432  -0.4906360   1.782886
## CONJbevor/before:MORETHAN2CLyes 0.69658953  -0.9938187   2.381287
## CONJals/when:MORETHAN2CLyes    -0.09495903  -1.5407933   1.274635
## CONJnachdem/after:MORETHAN2CLyes 0.14962486 -1.3957095   1.637886
pchisq(q=132.06, df=7, lower.tail=FALSE)
## [1] 2.33246e-25
drop1(m.01, test="Chisq")
## [...]
##                    Df Deviance    AIC    LRT Pr(>Chi)
## <none>                371.74 387.74
## CONJ:MORETHAN2CL    3  372.88 382.88 1.1425   0.7668
c("R2"=R2(m.01), "C"=C.score(m.01))
##        R2         C
## 0.3915948 0.8198437
```

The overall model is significant (*LR*-statistic=132.06, *df*=7, *p*<0.0001). The model fit is decent in terms of R^2 (0.392) and the *C*-score is good (0.82). Note, however, that the interaction isn't significant (see the drop1 output). Here, I will leave it in nonetheless and even plot it for the usual didactic reasons. Specifically, I want to go over one more time how the coefficients lead to the predictions here. The following table lists the additions you have to do with the coefficients' log odds values, if you want to get the predicted probabilities; to check my steps (and compare with effects in a minute), you need to ilogit the sums of the coefficients.

Table 30: How to compute predicted log odds in m.01

	MORETHAN2CL: *no*	MORETHAN2CL: *yes*
CONJ: *weil/because*	coef1 (intercept)	coef1+coef5
CONJ: *bevor/before*	coef1+coef2	coef1+coef5+coef2+coef6
CONJ: *wenn/when*	coef1+coef3	coef1+coef5+coef3+coef7
CONJ: *nachdem/after*	coef1+coef4	coef1+coef5+coef4+coef8

This looks right when compared to our effects-based data frame:

```
ph <- data.frame(ia <- effect("CONJ:MORETHAN2CL", m.01)); ia ## [...]
##                  MORETHAN2CL
## CONJ                     no        yes
##    weil/because   0.05434783 0.09345794
##    bevor/before   0.25000000 0.54545455
##    als/when       0.53658537 0.65384615
##    nachdem/after  0.50000000 0.67567568
```

As usual, you have the option of using pairs(emmeans...): Given our interests/ expectations stated above, let's assume we want to see whether there are MORETHAN2CL differences within each conjunction:

```
pairs(emmeans::emmeans(object=m.01, ~ MORETHAN2CL | CONJ),
   adjust="none")
## CONJ = weil/because:
##  contrast estimate    SE  df z.ratio p.value
##  no - yes    -0.584 0.567 Inf -1.030  0.3030
## CONJ = bevor/before:
##  contrast estimate    SE  df z.ratio p.value
##  no - yes    -1.281 0.637 Inf -2.011  0.0443
## CONJ = als/when:
```

```
##  contrast estimate    SE  df z.ratio p.value
##  no - yes   -0.489 0.428 Inf -1.144  0.2527
## CONJ = nachdem/after:
##  contrast estimate    SE  df z.ratio p.value
##  no - yes   -0.734 0.516 Inf -1.423  0.1549
## Results are given on the log odds ratio (not the response) scale.
```

Note the comment at the end: these differences are on the log odds scale, not on the scale of odds or predicted probabilities. However, the *p*-values suggest that MORETHAN2CL only makes a difference for *bevor/before*. How well does the model do in terms of predictions? (I'm only showing the results here.)

```
##      Class. acc. Prec. for sc-mc  Rec. for sc-mc
##        0.7667494       0.5944444       0.8359375
## Prec. for mc-sc  Rec. for mc-sc
##        0.9058296       0.7345455
```

Is this better than baseline? Of course it is because we saw in previous sections that even worse accuracies are already good enough so this one will be, too, and I will save space by not going over this again.

5.3.4.2 Graphical model exploration
Here, too, there's little news – just a reminder of my recommendation to always plot both perspectives of an interaction: the one suggested by plot.effect by default and the one that reverses what's on the *x*-axis and what's in the panels. To me, the first plot you get from the code file highlights the overall similarity of the conjunctions' behavior for both levels of MORETHAN2CL in how both 'curves' go up similarly, whereas the latter highlights (i) how low both values for *weil/ because* are and (ii) how *bevor/before* exhibits the largest difference between MORETHAN2CL: *no* and MORETHAN2CL: *yes*. (Again, though, don't forget the interaction was not significant to begin with.)

5.3.5 Two more effects plots for you to recreate

Unlike in the previous edition of this book, I won't discuss the last two kinds of model one might expect from the section on linear models, so, no detailed sections of binary logistic regressions with (i) a categorical and a numeric predictor or (ii) two numeric predictors. However, before you get too sad about this on social media and to get you motivated to still practice them, I present two plots here – one for each model and each with the (non-significant) interaction in there – and encourage you to try and generate them, as practice for understanding the coefficients and how they translated in predictions and for plotting.

Here's the plot for a model with the predictors CONJ and LENDIFF and their interaction, and this one should be pretty straightforward:

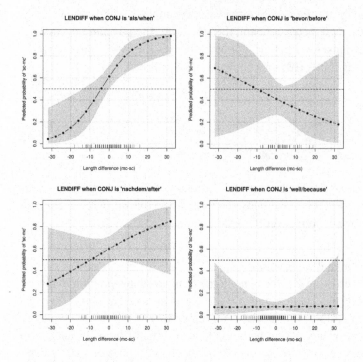

Figure 113: The effect of CONJ:LENDIFF

And here's the plot for the model with two numeric predictors, namely LENMC and LENSC, and their interaction: *m* and *s* mean what is predicted is *mc-sc* and *sc-mc* respectively and the size and darkness of the letters represent the certainty of the predictions (I used a function called mtext, which you haven't seen yet for the top *x*-axis label and the right *y*-axis label):

Recommendation(s) for further study: the package rms and its functions lrm and anova: lrm returns output similar to summary(glm(..., family=binomial)) (incl. R^2 and C, and, again, anova applied to the output of lrm returns, for every predictor in the model, the result of a significance test for that predictor and all higher-order predictors it's involved in.

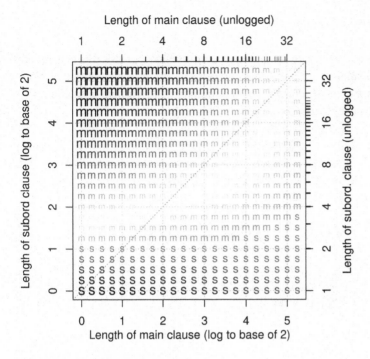

Figure 114: The effect of LENMC:LENSC

5.4 Other regression models

The two kinds of regression models discussed so far – for numeric and binary responses – are probably the by far most widely used ones in linguistics, There are two others, however, that I want to mention as well because they are probably underutilized. One is **multinomial regression**, a kind of modeling where the response is categorical with more than two levels; the other is **ordinal logistic regression**, where the response is ordinal (we will discuss the so-called proportional-odds cumulative logit model). In fact, binary logistic regression can be shown to be just the limiting sub-case, so to speak, of multinomial regression, which is why we will begin with this one now. The discussion will only deal with a smaller subset of models rather than all six kinds of predictor combinations from above and, for the most part at least, I will go over things more quickly.

5.4.1 Multinomial regression

The example we will explore to approach multinomial regression is concerned with which of a small set of predictors allows us to predict which of three different end-of-term exams or assignments foreign-language learners of English will choose. It involves these variables:
– a categorical response ASSIGNMENT: *lab_report* vs. *oral_exam* vs. *thesis*;
– a categorical predictor REGION, the geographic region the student is from: *centr_eur* vs. *hispanic* vs. *mid_east*;
– a numeric predictor MISTAKES, the number of mistakes the students made in their last assignment for this class.

```
rm(list=ls(all.names=TRUE)); library(car); library(effects);
    library(nnet)
source("helpers/R2.r"); source("helpers/summarize.multinom.r")
summary(x <- read.delim(file="_inputfiles/05_assign.csv",
    stringsAsFactors=TRUE)) ## {...]
```

Specifically, we will look at only two different hypotheses (in the same artificially-separated way as before):
– that MISTAKES predicts ASSIGNMENT, i.e.,
  – H_0: There is no correlation between MISTAKES and ASSIGNMENT; $R^2=0$;
  – H_1: There is a correlation between MISTAKES and ASSIGNMENT; $R^2>0$;
– that REGION predicts ASSIGNMENT, i.e.,
  – H_0: There is no correlation between REGION and ASSIGNMENT; $R^2=0$;
  – H_1: There is a correlation between REGION and ASSIGNMENT; $R^2>0$.

Before we do any modeling at all, this means we're in for some descriptive exploration. I'm referring you to the code file to save space but again, you should, minimally, look at each variable in isolation and each variable with each other one to identify distributional peculiarities, potential data sparsity issues, complete separation, potential collinearity issues, etc. (I am not repeating the monofactorial frequency tables here since we have those in the above summary of x.) The tables and plots do not seem to indicate many/severe problems and do suggest there may be some very predictive correlations with ASSIGNMENT to be found; there's a potential for complete separation for the relation between MISTAKES and ASSIGNMENT, but since that only arises when the numeric predictor MISTAKES is binned we'll need to wait and see whether it has an impact on the regression model later.

5.4.1.1 A multinomial regression with a numeric predictor

Fitting a model is actually fairly straightforward and doesn't differ much from what we've done so far – main change: we use nnet::multinom, not glm – but ...

```
summary(m.01 <- multinom(ASSIGNMENT ~ 1 + MISTAKES, data=x,
   model=TRUE, na.action=na.exclude)) ## [...]
## Coefficients:
##            (Intercept)    MISTAKES
## oral_exam     3.715382  -0.2343503
## thesis       -5.435598   0.2970226
## Std. Errors:
##            (Intercept)    MISTAKES
## oral_exam    0.8235303  0.05119224
## thesis       1.0018750  0.05395567
```

... interpreting a multinomial model on the basis of the coefficients, on the other hand, is awful. Even the intercepts are already a pain – they are logged ratios of predicted probabilities:
– exponentiating the intercept value for *oral_exam* (3.715382) is 41.074268, which is how much higher the predicted probability of *oral_exam* is than that of *lab_report* (the first level of the response) when MISTAKES is 0;
– exponentiating the intercept value for *thesis* (-5.4355976) is 0.004359, which is how much 'higher' the predicted probability of *oral_exam* is than that of *lab_report* (the first level of the response) when MISTAKES is 0.

How do you get predicted probabilities from that? Well, you know that the three predicted probabilities for when MISTAKES is 0 sum up to 1, so you essentially have this 'equation to solve' (and again this is the slowest pace to do so):

$$pred. \; prob_{labreport} + 41.07427 \times pred. \; prob_{labreport}$$
$$+ 0.004359 \times pred. \; prob_{labreport} = 1$$

Thus:

$$42.07863 \times pred. \; prob_{labreport} = 1$$

Thus:

$$pred. \; prob_{labreport} = 1 \div 42.07863 = 0.02376503$$
$$pred. \; prob_{oralexam} = 41.07427 \times 0.02376503 = 0.9761313$$
$$pred. \; prob_{thesis} = 0.00435863 \times 0.02376503 = 0.000103583$$

Or, shorter, but looking quite convoluted:

```
c(1,    exp(coef(m.01)[1,1]),  exp(coef(m.01)[2,1])) /
sum(c(1+exp(coef(m.01)[1,1]) + exp(coef(m.01)[2,1])))
## [1] 0.023765034 0.976131383 0.000103583
```

While that's already not my idea of fun, wait till we add the slopes – then it becomes positively dreadful:
– exponentiating the sum of the intercept for *oral_exam* and one time the slope of MISTAKES for *oral_exam* (3.481032) is 32.493222, which is how much higher the predicted probability of *oral_exam* is than that of *lab_report* when MISTAKES is 1;
– exponentiating the sum of the intercept for *thesis* and one time the slope of MISTAKES for *thesis* (-5.138575) is 0.005866, which is how much 'higher' the predicted probability of *thesis* is than that of *lab_report* when MISTAKES is 1.

Unbearable – can you imagine doing this for a multifactorial model? Let's agree to never do that again so we will from now on look at the predicted values from effects. Since multinomial models predict more than two levels of the response, here's another complication, however: With binary responses, it was enough to get one predicted probability – that of the second level of the response – because the other predicted probability would then just be 1 minus that one. But here, this doesn't work, which means we need as many predicted probabilities as there are levels, just as many standard errors, and as many lower and upper confidence bounds. The following code generates our familiar ph object, in which the columns beginning
– with *prob* are predicted probabilities of the then listed level of the response;
– with *L.prob* are those predicted probabilities' lower bounds of the CIs;
– with *U.prob* are those predicted probabilities' upper bounds of the CIs;

but then it trims it down to only those columns we might use for plotting:

```
ph <- data.frame(mist <- effect("MISTAKES", m.01, xlevels=list(
   MISTAKES=0:26)))
ph <- ph[,c(1, grep("prob", names(ph)))]
(ph <- ph[,c(grep("se.prob", names(ph), invert=TRUE))])[1:3,1:4]
##   MISTAKES prob.lab_report prob.oral_exam  prob.thesis
## 1        0      0.02376503      0.9761314 0.0001035830
## 2        1      0.02985156      0.9699733 0.0001751105
## 3        2      0.03743526      0.9622692 0.0002955435
```

Ok, this is better. However, as you will have noticed, there's really very little else we have right now: We don't even have *t*- or *z*-values for our coefficients, we have no *p*-values for them either; also missing is an overall significance test for this model and an R^2-value. So let's get all this. As you probably remember, the *t*-values in linear models and the *z*-scores in the binary logistic regression models were computed by dividing the estimates by the standard errors, which is easy:

```
(m.01.zscores <- summary(m.01)$coefficients /
    summary(m.01)$standard.errors)
##            (Intercept) MISTAKES
## oral_exam    4.511530 -4.577849
## thesis      -5.425425  5.504939
```

And then it's also easy to compute the *p*-values, which are by default the two areas under the standard normal curve, one time the lower tail on the left, one time the upper tail on the right, but since the normal distribution is symmetric, we just take twice the area to the right of the positive *z*-score:

```
(m.01.pvalues <- 2*pnorm(abs(m.01.zscores), lower.tail=FALSE))
##            (Intercept)     MISTAKES
## oral_exam 6.436168e-06 4.697824e-06
## thesis    5.781677e-08 3.692971e-08
```

Ok, now what about the *p*-value for the predictor and, therefore, here for the model as a whole? Above we typically used drop1 for this, but drop1 doesn't take multinom objects (not sure why not ...) so we just do what drop1 does 'automatically' manually: we make use of anova again and compare the null model – a model with no predictors and just an intercept – against the model we have (recall this from Section 5.2.3.1). The null model in turn we now create with the super useful function update, whose first argument is a model object that you want to change and whose second argument is typically one of the following two:
– it might just be ~ 1, which means that you update the model by deleting all predictors on the right hand side (of the ~) and fitting the model with only the overall intercept (1), which is exactly our null model application here;
– it might be .~. (which means, the complete model formula, both the response before the tilde and the predictors after it) followed by
  – -X, meaning your update consists of deleting the predictor(s) X from the model formula;
  – +P, meaning your update consists of adding the predictor(s) P to the model formula;

— -X+P, meaning your update consists of both deleting the predictor(s) X from
the model formula and inserting the predictor(s) P into it.

Here, we just have the very simple null model case, but you'll see the other use
of update in Chapter 6.

```
m.00 <- update(m.01, ~ 1); anova(m.00, m.01, test="Chisq") ## [...]
## Likelihood ratio tests of Multinomial Models
## Response: ASSIGNMENT
##             Model Resid. df Resid. Dev   Test   Df LR stat. Pr(Chi)
## 1               1        598   659.1674
## 2 1 + MISTAKES        596   551.5162 1 vs 2    2 107.6512       0
pchisq(q=107.6512, df=2, lower.tail=FALSE)
## [1] 4.205706e-24
```

R^2 is next:

```
R2(m.01) ## [...]
## [1] 0.3392009
```

I don't know about you, but having to do all this stuff manually makes me wish
there was a way to get the results of a multinomial regression as easily as we got
them in the summary output of a linear model. So I used the logic from Section
3.5.4.2 above to write the crude but useful helper function that we already
sourced above, summarize.multinom, which only requires the model as input:

```
summarize.multinom(m.01)
## $Coefficients
##                          Estimate  Std.Error    zvalues      Pvalues
## (Intercept):oral_exam   3.7153819 0.82353035   4.511530 6.436168e-06
## (Intercept):thesis     -5.4355976 1.00187496  -5.425425 5.781677e-08
## MISTAKES:oral_exam     -0.2343503 0.05119224  -4.577849 4.697824e-06
## MISTAKES:thesis         0.2970226 0.05395567   5.504939 3.692971e-08
## $R2
## [1] 0.3392009
## $`Model significance test`
## LR statistic          Df      P-value
## 1.076512e+02 2.000000e+00 4.205796e-24
```

Ok, that's much better. Of course, you can also compute confidence intervals:

```
Confint(m.01) # return estimates w/ their 95%-CI
## , , oral_exam
##              Estimate     2.5 %     97.5 %
## (Intercept) 3.7153819  2.1012920  5.3294717
## MISTAKES   -0.2343503 -0.3346853 -0.1340154
## , , thesis
##              Estimate     2.5 %     97.5 %
## (Intercept) -5.4355976 -7.3992364 -3.4719587
## MISTAKES    0.2970226  0.1912715  0.4027738
```

Now we turn to the model's predictions. For multinom objects, the predict function actually offers two useful settings: one gives us a matrix of predicted probabilities for each case, namely how likely the model thinks each level of the response variable is in each case; the other gives us the level of the response variable with the highest predicted probability, i.e what above we did ourselves with PREDS.CAT <- ifelse(PREDS.NUM>=0.5, ...) etc. We compute both and add them to our data (and then use paste0 to make the names more informative):

```
x <- cbind(x, predict(m.01, type="prob"))
names(x)[5:7] <- paste0("PREDS.", names(x)[5:7])
x <- cbind(x, PREDS.CAT=predict(m.01, type="class"))
```

And with that, we can generate a confusion matrix and compute our accuracy:

```
table(x$ASSIGNMENT, x$PREDS.CAT)
##              lab_report oral_exam thesis
## lab_report          34        34     32
## oral_exam           24        59     17
## thesis              38         5     57
mean(x$ASSIGNMENT==x$PREDS.CAT)
## [1] 0.5
sum(dbinom(x=150:300, size=300, prob=baseline)) # > baseline
## [1] 1.918983e-09
```

We only get 50% right, but since the baseline is $1/3$, 50% is significantly better than that.

Finally, especially when it comes to interpretation, we visualize. There's the default multi-panel option but I show the same result in one panel:

```
plot(mist, type="probability", ylim=c(0, 1), grid=TRUE
plot(mist,type="probability", ylim=c(0, 1), grid=TRUE,
    multiline=TRUE, co fint=list(style="auto"),
    lattice=list(key.args=list(columns=3, cex.title=0)))
```

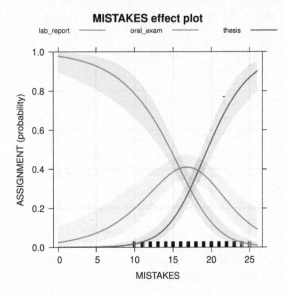

Figure 115: The effect of MISTAKES

You would summarize all the numerical stuff from above and conclude that low numbers of mistakes are associated with oral exam choices whereas high numbers of mistakes are associated with theses – lab reports are mostly chosen within a rather small window of intermediate numbers of mistakes.

Recommendation(s) for further study: You might want to check out the package mlogit, which offers a lot of multinomial regression functionality (but note that it requires a different kind of input format and formula notation, which is one reason I didn't use it here in the main text); also, it doesn't return the same kind of R^2 as my function R^2 (mine returns Nagelkerke's R^2).

5.4.1.2 A multinomial regression with a categorical predictor
Working with the same data frame, fitting the model now for REGION as a predictor is again straightforward.

```
summary(m.01 <- multinom(ASSIGNMENT ~ 1 + REGION, data=x,
    model=TRUE, na.action=na.exclude)) ## [...]
```

```
## Coefficients:
##             (Intercept) REGIONhispanic REGIONmid_east
## oral_exam    1.3581354      -1.106857     -3.0927262
## thesis      -0.4924459       2.072866     -0.6825258
## Std. Errors:
##             (Intercept) REGIONhispanic REGIONmid_east
## oral_exam    0.2642762      0.4436492      0.4097324
## thesis       0.3827056      0.4822823      0.4569334
```

But after that, everything is the same (nightmare) as before:
– exponentiating the intercept value for *oral_exam* (1.3581354) is 3.8889353, which is how much higher the predicted probability of *oral exam* is than that of *lab_report* (the first level of the response) when REGION is *centr_eur;*
– exponentiating the intercept value for *thesis* (-0.4924459) is 0.6111298, which is how much 'higher' the predicted probability of oral exam is than that of *lab_report* (the first level of the response) when REGION is *centr_eur.*

Thus, here are the predicted probabilities of the three levels of the response when REGION is *centr_eur*:

```
c(1,    exp(coef(m.01)[1,1]),  exp(coef(m.01)[2,1])) /
sum(c(1+exp(coef(m.01)[1,1]) + exp(coef(m.01)[2,1])))
## [1] 0.1818160 0.7070708 0.1111132
```

Since we agreed to not do this again, let's immediately move to ph:

```
ph <- data.frame(reg <- effect("REGION", m.01))
ph <- ph[,c(1, grep("prob", names(ph)))]
(ph <- ph[,c(grep("se.prob", names(ph), invert=TRUE))])[1:3,1:4]
##       REGION prob.lab_report prob.oral_exam prob.thesis
## 1 centr_eur       0.1818160      0.7070708   0.1111132
## 2  hispanic       0.1400038      0.1799983   0.6799979
## 3  mid_east       0.6732646      0.1188126   0.2079228
```

And let's abbreviate model significance and R^2 with our helper function:

```
summarize.multinom(m.01) ## [...]
## $R2
## [1] 0.466786
## $`Model significance test`
```

```
## LR statistic            Df        P-value
## 1.608025e+02 4.000000e+00 9.836040e-34
```

No change when it comes to the confidence intervals and the predictions, which his why I am only showing the code here, not also its output:

```
Confint(m.01) # return estimates w/ their 95%-CI
x <- cbind(x, predict(m.01, type="prob"))
names(x)[5:7] <- paste0("PREDS.", names(x)[5:7])
x <- cbind(x, PREDS.CAT=predict(m.01, type="class"))
```

And with that, we can generate a confusion matrix and compute our accuracy:

```
# we still have the baseline from above
table(x$ASSIGNMENT, x$PREDS.CAT)
##                  lab_report oral_exam thesis
##     lab_report          68        18     14
##     oral_exam           12        70     18
##     thesis              21        11     68
mean(x$ASSIGNMENT==x$PREDS.CAT)
## [1] 0.6866667
sum(dbinom(x=206:300, size=300, prob=baseline))
## [1] 9.396562e-36
```

We get nearly 70% right – not bad. And we conclude with the same kinds of plots: Either the default or the one-panel solution shown on the next page. A pretty clear separation, hence the good accuracy score: The Central European students seem to prefer the oral exam, the Hispanic students the thesis, and the Middle Eastern students the lab report.

5.4.1.3 Multinomial and binary logistic regression

In this section, I just want to prove the point that binary logistic regression is really just the limiting case of multinomial regression by comparing the output of the two. I will not discuss this here in the book to not waste space on just showing you two identical outputs, but run the code in the relevant section of the code file just to make you recognize the equivalence of the two approaches.

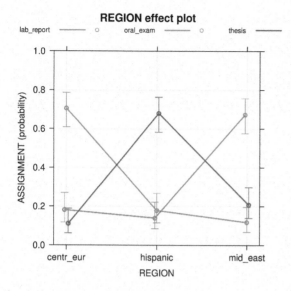

Figure 116: The effect of REGION

5.4.2 Ordinal logistic regression

For the final regression model type to be discussed in this chapter, we'll proceed very much like we did for multinomial regression. We'll look at just two models in a sequence of steps that'll be very similar to what we did above and we'll again just load one data set that contains all variables of interest to look at two hypotheses, namely (i) whether the choice of topic on which to write an essay or (ii) the average number of mistakes made per 20 words in the previous essay allow us to predict the CEFR levels of 600 learners at one university; i.e. we have

– an ordinal response CEFR: *A2* (the upper level of 'basic user') < *B1* < *B2* (both *B*-levels are for 'independent users') < *C1* (the lower level of 'proficient user'); these Common European Framework of Reference for Languages levels broadly label language learners' ability levels in reading, listening, speaking, and writing;

– a numeric predictor MISTKper20, the number of mistakes made per 20 words in the learners' short essays;

– a categorical predictor TOPIC: *deathpenalty* vs. *election* vs. *healthcare* vs. *immigration* vs. *incomeinequ* vs. *smoking*, describing essay topics learner chose to write on.

That means our two different hypotheses will be:

- that MISTKper20 predicts CEFR, i.e.,
    - H_0: There is no correlation between MISTKper20 and CEFR; $R^2=0$;
    - H_1: There is a correlation between MISTKper20 and CEFR; $R^2>0$;
- that TOPIC predicts CEFR, i.e.,
    - H_0: There is no correlation between TOPIC and CEFR; $R^2=0$;
    - H_1: There is a correlation between TOPIC and CEFR; $R^2>0$.

We load the data and make sure that is changed into an ordinal factor:

```
rm(list=ls(all.names=TRUE)); library(car); library(effects);
   library(MASS); source("helpers/R2.r"); source("helpers/ilogit.r")
summary(x <- read.delim(file="_inputfiles/05_CEFR.csv",
   stringsAsFactors=TRUE)) ## [...]
x$CEFR <- factor(x$CEFR, ordered=TRUE)
(baseline <- max(prop.table(table(x$CEFR))))
## [1] 0.2833333
```

We begin with the usual descriptive exploration. I will again not show the results but the tables and plots seem pretty ok in terms of not indicating many problems and there again seem to be some correlations with CEFR to be found.

```
# bivariate numerical exploration
table(x$CEFR, x$TOPIC)
table(cut(x$MISTKper20, 6), x$CEFR)
table(cut(x$MISTKper20, 6), x$TOPIC)
# bivariate graphical exploration
mosaicplot(table(x$CEFR, x$TOPIC), shade=TRUE)
plot(x$CEFR ~ x$MISTKper20)
   plot(x$MISTKper20 ~ x$CEFR)
plot(x$MISTKper20 ~ x$TOPIC)
   plot(x$TOPIC ~ x$MISTKper20)
```

5.4.2.1 An ordinal regression with a numeric predictor
The function we'll use is MASS::polr; with the exception of the additional argument Hess=TRUE, which we need not concern ourselves with, not much changes:

```
summary(m.01 <- polr(CEFR ~ 1 + MISTKper20, Hess=TRUE, data=x,
   na.action=na.exclude))
## [...] ## Coefficients:
```

```
##               Value Std. Error t value
## MISTKper20 -0.2287      0.0181  -12.64
## Intercepts:
##         Value    Std. Error t value
## A2|B1  -2.5819   0.1686     -15.3099
## B1|B2  -1.3136   0.1414     -9.2914
## B2|C1  -0.0608   0.1318     -0.4616
```

Looks similar to the output of `multinom`: Again, the summary table isn't quite structured as we might like it (from `lm`) and not quite as forthcoming in terms of the info that is provided. However, we can recycle pretty much everything from our work with multinomial models. For instance, we can compute the *p*-values of the coefficients in the same way as before:[14]

```
(m.01.tscores <- summary(m.01)$coefficients[,"t value"])
##  MISTKper20       A2|B1        B1|B2        B2|C1
## -12.6359478 -15.3099047  -9.2914133  -0.4615865
(m.01.pvalues <- 2*pnorm(abs(m.01.tscores), lower.tail=FALSE))
##    MISTKper20        A2|B1        B1|B2        B2|C1
## 1.337725e-36 6.566012e-53 1.522530e-20 6.443779e-01
Confint(m.01) # return estimates w/ their 95%-CI
##              Estimate      2.5 %      97.5 %
## MISTKper20 -0.22873438 -0.2648303 -0.1938215
## A2|B1      -2.58189120 -2.9124232 -2.2513592
## B1|B2      -1.31356624 -1.5906546 -1.0364779
## B2|C1      -0.06083141 -0.3191305  0.1974677
```

Same with the overall model significance test and the model's R^2:

```
anova(update(m.01, ~ 1), m.01, test="Chisq")
## Likelihood ratio tests of ordinal regression models ## [...]
##         Model Resid. df Resid. Dev   Test   Df LR stat. Pr(Chi)
## 1           1       597   1659.673
```

14 The really attentive reader might wonder why I'm using `pnorm` although the `polr` output says those are `t values` (meaning, shouldn't I be using `pt`?). I think that output involves a mistaken label, given what other packages return (`ordinal::clm`, `rms::lrm`, and `VGAM::vglm`) and how textbooks such as Agresti (2013, 2019:170f.) discuss the significance tests of these kinds of models; the package maintainer did not respond to multiple inquiries.

```
## 2 1+MISTKper20        596   1471.737 1 vs 2    1 187.9352        0
pchisq(q=187.9352, df=1, lower.tail=FALSE)
## [1] 8.975216e-43
R2(m.01)
## [1] 0.2869666
```

(All of this is of course a not-so-indirect speech act for you to, later, write a sister function to summarize.multinom, namely one called summarize.polr.) But now we're facing the same hell as before with regard to the coefficients – actually, it's even worse as you'll see in a moment: What do they mean? Let's start with the 'Intercepts' part: while MISTKper20 is 0,

– if you ilogit/plogis the negative version (!) of the intercept (!) for A2|B1,[15] you get the predicted probability that CEFR is greater than A2 (i.e. *B1* or *B2* or *C1*): faraway::ilogit(--2.5819) and plogis(--2.5819) return 0.9296876;

– if you ilogit/plogis the negative version of the intercept for B1|B2, you get the predicted probability that CEFR is greater than *B1* (i.e. *B2* and/or *C1*): 0.7881149;

– if you ilogit/plogis the negative version of the intercept for B2|C1, you get the predicted probability that CEFR is greater than *B2* (i.e. *C1*): 0.5151953.

If you look at the last two bullet points, you see how you can compute the predicted probability of CEFR: *B2*: 0.7881149-0.5151953=0.2729196 (with a bit of a difference to the value listed later, which is just due to rounding), how fun ... And the slope of MISTKper20?

– if you ilogit/plogis the sum of the negative version (!) of the intercept for A2| B1 and one time the slope of MISTKper20, you get the predicted probability that CEFR is greater than *A2* (i.e. *B1*, *B2*, or *C1*) when MISTKper20 is 1: plogis(--2.5819+-0.2287) returns 0.9131882;

– if you ilogit/plogis the sum of the negative version of the intercept for B1|B2 and one time the slope of MISTKper20, you get the predicted probability that CEFR is greater than *B1* (i.e. *B2* and/or *C1*) when MISTKper20 is 1: 0.7474201;

– if you ilogit/plogis the sum of the negative version of the intercept for A2|B1 and one time the slope of MISTKper20, you get the predicted probability that CEFR is greater than *B2* (i.e. *C1*) when MISTKper20 is 1: 0.4581233.

---

15 This is one unfortunate aspect of MASS::polr (and ordinal::clm): They reverse the sign of the intercepts so, to use the same logic as for the other models, one has to take the negative value of the intercepts rather than the positive one (as in all other regression models you're seeing in the book); see Harrell (2015:313) for a quick note on this and the corresponding equation, but we will mostly work with the effects plots anyway. Just FYI: the functions rms::lrm or VGAM::vglm work more in the way we might expect from everywhere else.

Can we agree that this is another one of these things we don't want to do again? Good, so we'll create our `effects`-based data frame – just make sure you check it and compare it with the above manual calculation (but don't forget that you usually need to add up multiple predicted probabilities for the proper results).

```
ph <- data.frame(mist <- effect("MISTKper20", m.01, xlevels=list(
   MISTKper20=0:20)))
ph <- ph[,c(1, grep("prob", names(ph)))]
(ph <- ph[,c(grep("se.prob", names(ph), invert=TRUE))])[1:3,1:5]
##   MISTKper20    prob.A2    prob.B1   prob.B2    prob.C1
## 1          0 0.07031300 0.1415777 0.2729061 0.5152032
## 2          1 0.08681518 0.1657775 0.2892847 0.4581226
## 3          2 0.10674565 0.1914097 0.2997241 0.4021205
```

From now on, everything else is just as with multinomial models: We generate predictions, add them to the original data frame, ... (showing only the code)

```
x <- cbind(x, predict(m.01, type="prob"))
names(x)[5:8] <- paste0("PREDS.", names(x)[5:8])
x <- cbind(x, PREDS.CAT=predict(m.01, type="class")) ## [...]
```

... compute our accuracy, ...

```
table(x$CEFR, x$PREDS.CAT)
##
##        A2  B1  B2  C1
##    A2 102  23  11  34
##    B1  61  17  18  47
##    B2  44  23  22  49
##    C1   0   0  49 100
mean(as.character(x$CEFR)==x$PREDS.CAT)
## [1] 0.4016667
```

... and check whether we did better than baseline (we did).

```
sum(dbinom(x=241:600, size=600, prob=baseline))
## [1] 3.216908e-10
```

Finally, we plot things using the default multi-panel plot or, as I show here, the one-panel variant:...

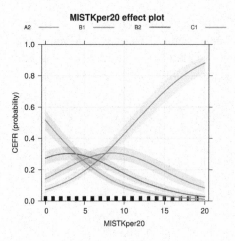

Figure 117: The effect of `MISTKper20`

We conclude that the highest numbers of mistakes are associated with the lowest CEFR level (in our sample) of *A2*, the lowest numbers of mistakes are associated with the highest CEFR level (in our sample) of *C1*, and mistake numbers in a small range in the middle are associated with the *B*-levels – unsurprising results.

5.4.2.2 An ordinal regression with a categorical predictor

The procedure now will be very similar (and again I am redefining the data frame because we added to x the predictions from the previous model):

```
x <- x[,1:4] # omitting predictions from previous model
summary(m.01 <- polr(CEFR ~ 1 + TOPIC, Hess=TRUE, data=x,
   na.action=na.exclude)) ## [...]
## Coefficients:
##                      Value Std. Error t value
## TOPICelection        0.3509     0.2797  1.2544
## TOPIChealthcare      1.2031     0.3064  3.9261
## TOPICimmigration     1.1015     0.2885  3.8179
## TOPICincomeinequ     2.8545     0.3516  8.1192
## TOPICsmoking        -0.1411     0.2911 -0.4846
## Intercepts:
##        Value   Std. Error t value
## A2|B1 -0.3008  0.2368     -1.2703
## B1|B2  0.8529  0.2414      3.5330
## B2|C1  2.0752  0.2543      8.1601
```

```
(m.01.tscores <- summary(m.01)$coefficients[,"t value"]) ## [...]
(m.01.pvalues  <-  2*pnorm(abs(m.01.tscores),  lower.tail=FALSE))  ##
[...]
Confint(m.01) # return estimates w/ their 95%-CI
anova(update(m.01, ~ 1), m.01, test="Chisq") ## [...]
## Response: CEFR
##         Model Resid. df Resid. Dev   Test    Df LR stat. Pr(Chi)
## 1           1       597   1659.673
## 2 1 + TOPIC       592   1529.598 1 vs 2     5 130.0745       0
pchisq(q=130.0745, df=5, lower.tail=FALSE)
## [1] 2.29491e-26
```

But there's the coefficients again, this time with the levels of TOPIC ... Let's start with the 'Intercepts' part because that's most like above: While TOPIC is the first level of *deathpenalty*,
- if you ilogit/plogis the negative version of the intercept for A2|B1, you get the predicted probability that CEFR is greater than *A2* (i.e. *B1* or *B2* or *C1*): plogis(--0.3008) returns 0.5746381;
- if you ilogit/plogis the negative version of the intercept for B1|B2, you get the predicted probability that CEFR is greater than *B1* (i.e. *B2* and/or *C1*): 0.2988249;
- if you ilogit/plogis the negative version of the intercept for B2|C1, you get the predicted probability that CEFR is greater than *B2* (i.e. *C1*): 0.1115307.

And the 'slopes' of TOPIC?
- if you ilogit/plogis the sum of the negative version of the intercept for A2|B1 and the slope of TOPIC: *election*, you get the predicted probability that CEFR is greater than *A2* (i.e. *B1*, *B2*, or *C1*) when TOPIC is *election*: plogis(--0.3008+0.3509) returns 0.6573935;
- if you ilogit/plogis the sum of the negative version of the intercept for B1|B2 and the slope of TOPIC: *election*, you get the predicted probability that CEFR is greater than *B1* (i.e. *B2* and/or *C1*) when TOPIC is *election*: 0.3770708;
- if you ilogit/plogis the sum of the negative version of the intercept for B2|C1 and the slope of TOPIC: *election*, you get the predicted probability that CEFR is greater than *B2* (i.e. *C1*) when TOPIC is *election*: 0.1513181.

We can easily – ahem – check this by looking at our effects-based data frame:

```
ph <- data.frame(topc <- effect("TOPIC", m.01))
ph <- ph[,c(1, grep("prob", names(ph)))]
```

```
(ph <- ph[,c(grep("se.prob", names(ph), invert=TRUE))])[1:6,1:5]
##           TOPIC     prob.A2     prob.B1    prob.B2    prob.C1
## 1 deathpenalty 0.42536203 0.27581422 0.1872936 0.11153017
## 2     election 0.34260509 0.28032377 0.2257528 0.15131830
## [...]
```

The rest is the same:

```
x <- cbind(x, predict( m.01, type="prob"))
names(x)[5:8] <- paste0("PREDS.", names(x)[5:8])
x <- cbind(x, PREDS.CAT=predict(m.01, type="class")) ## {…]
table(x$CEFR, x$PREDS.CAT)
##       A2  B1  B2  C1
##   A2 124   0  24  22
##   B1  93   0  19  31
##   B2  58   0  49  31
##   C1  40   0  25  84
mean(as.character(x$CEFR)==x$PREDS.CAT)
## [1] 0.4283333
sum(dbinom(x=257:600, size=600, prob=baseline))
## [1] 2.420691e-14
```

... and then we plot things, I am now only showing the one-panel plot:

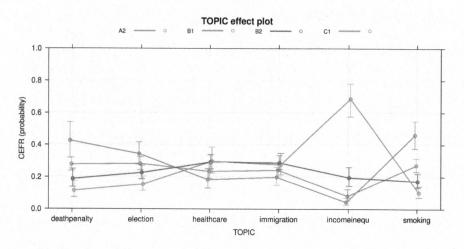

Figure 118: The effect of TOPIC

We conclude that
- the topics deathpenalty, election, and smoking are associated with A2 students;
- the topic incomeinequ is highly associated with C1 students;
- the remaining two topics – healthcare and immigration – do not have strong associations, but there's a slight preference for the two higher CEFR levels in the sample of B2 and C1.

This concludes the presentation of fixed-effects regression models.

Recommendation(s) for further study: Check out
- the package rms for its function lrm, which is useful for binary and ordinal logistic regression modeling, but rms also has many other useful regression-modeling functions;
- the packages ordinal and VGLM for additional functions to fit ordinal regression models (even mixed-effects models!);
- maybe quite a bit later, other regression model types such as Poisson regression, negative binomial regression, zero-inflated regression, and beta regression, all of which can be useful in different linguistic applications. Poisson regression is actually discussed in the second edition of this book and can, in certain circumstances, be equivalent to binary logistic regression modeling, so maybe start with that one; Faraway (2016) is a great place to start but Faraway (2015) is also very informative (for linear models).

The remainder of this chapter now discusses the more general aspects of model selection, diagnostics, evaluation, and validation, before Chapter 6 then turns to mixed-effects modeling.

5.5 Model formulation (and model selection)

With very few exceptions, all previous sections defined a regression model with a certain model equation, computed the model, and interpreted it on the basis of numeric and graphical output. In actual applications, you'll find a much wider range of approaches and procedures, plus the usual (sometimes heated) discussions about what is (the 'obviously' only) right way to do something and what isn't. In fact, probably for most questions you can think of in a regression-modeling context (and especially later in a mixed-effects modeling context), you'll find many different answers. Yes, those will come with different degrees of plausibility, evidence, and support – I'm not saying 'anything goes' – but it's really quite difficult to sort through oftentimes conflicting advice. (In Chapter 6, you'll see this kind of sentiment represented in several epigraphs throughout that chapter.) In what follows, I'll discuss a variety of notions or issues with regard to which you as the analyst will have to make and motivate or defend decisions. In addition to the initial kind of exploration/preparation discussed in Table 21 (Section 5.2), these notions/issues include the following (just about all of which need to be described in a methods section):

– **(initial) model formulation**: what is the structure of the predictor/response relations to be included in a/the model? What control variables may need to be included, what confounds, what moderators, what mediators? Does one need interactions for any of these? Does one need curvature for any of these? Does one need special kinds of contrasts? (Or even, what kind of modeling perspective does one adopt: frequentist vs. Bayesian, something I am not discussing in this book)?

– **model/variable selection**: does one want to check just one single model that tests one or a small set of *a priori* hypotheses? Or will there be model selection to arrive at one final model, or will there be model amalgamation? If any kind of model selection is involved, what is its direction (forward, backward, hybrid)? Is it conceptually restricted or completely data-driven? What is the model selection criterion – *p*-values or information criteria (e.g., *AIC*, *AICc*, *BIC*, *cAIC*, ...)?

– **model diagnostics**: is one's final model (which might be one's first model) 'well-formed' in the sense of meeting the assumptions of fixed- (and later mixed-)effects regression models such as residual distributions, multicollinearity, overdispersion, influence measures, autocorrelation, etc.?

– **model (cross-)validation**: is one's final model likely to generalize well to other data sets?

With regard to the formulation of the initial (and maybe only) model, the purest NHST scenario – read the beginning of Section 1.5 again if you need to refresh you memory about this! – would be to build a regression model equation that specifies exactly the relation(s) you expect to hold between the predictors and controls on the one hand and the response on the other, and to always imply this viewpoint, all sections in 5.2 to 5.4 started with such hypotheses determining our models. To give a more complex example now: If you have a numeric response Y, predictors A, B, and C, and controls M and N and you hypothesize

1. each predictor correlates with the response Y;
2. predictor B's correlation with the response will be curved;
3. predictor A's effect depends on what C does;
4. each control correlates with the response;
5. predictor B's effect might depend on what control M does.

then you could fit this (initial) model:

```
lm(Y ~ 1 +                    # Y ~ intercept
   A + poly(B, 2) + C + # point 1 & point 2
   A:C +                 # point 3
   M + N +               # point 4
   poly(B, 2):M,         # point 5
   data=...)
```

And if that regression model embodies exactly the hypothesis/hypotheses you want to test, you might already be nearly done (with model selection at least): The *p*-values for the predictors will tell you exactly what they were 'designed to do': they will tell you for each predictor the probability to get the observed result or one that deviates from H_0 even more and, thus, which of your predictors are significant, and the signs and values of the predictors will tell you about the effect direction and (to some degree) effect size, done.

But a lot of times the waters are a bit muddier and you'll find discussion of a process called **model selection**, which involves finding the best model for your data. You might think now, what could possibly be wrong with "finding the best model for your data"? Well, it depends (which is probably the most frequent answer I give in bootcamps), because model selection is more data-driven and exploratory than strict NHST, and when model selection is done using *p*-values/ significance testing, then the *p*-values are, so to speak, 'losing' their strict NHST meaning/function and are mutating into something more of a 'general importance indicator' (even if researchers superficially stick to the threshold of 0.05 and the 'significance' terminology'). But of course that's not what these *p*-values were supposed to mean and that makes some people very upset ...

For instance, remember what we did in Section 5.2.1 above? We fit lm(RT~FREQ) and found a significant correlation in the expected direction, but then we also explored the possibility that the effect of FREQ might be curved. In fact, we can be pretty certain it will be curved somewhere in the population because there's a physiological lower limit to our reaction times no matter how high the frequency will be – we just didn't know whether it was already going to be curved within the range of FREQ values of our sample. And so we fit a second model on the same data set (using poly(FREQ, 2)) and then did a model comparison with anova (returning another *p*-value!) to see whether the additional complexity was justifiable (and then it wasn't so we stuck with the simple linear FREQ effect). But the fact of the matter is that that procedure might already give some people a mild arrhythmia because we're now entering an area where many notions we've discussed before – especially NHST (Section 1.5 and passim), but also Occam's razor (Section 5.2.1.3), adjusting *p*-values for multiple *post-hoc* tests (Section 5.2.3.3), ... – come together and become intermingled with notions such as academic honesty and credit. Here're some scenarios and some thoughts on them that are worth considering to develop one's stance on this:

1. You hypothesize a *straight-line* relation between RT and FREQ, you fit lm(RT~FREQ), this is significant, great, and that's what you report, done. This is picture-perfect textbook null-hypothesis significance testing; from that perspective, one can really not find fault with it.

2. You hypothesize a *straight-line* relation between RT and FREQ, you fit lm(RT~FREQ), and this is significant. But then the results make you think 'but maybe there's curvature' and you check lm(RT~poly(FREQ, 2)); however, it turns out the curvature isn't needed. Thus, your initial hypothesis was still confirmed with your initial model, great – but you also fit a second model on the same data and what would you have done if the curvature had been significant? You would probably have reported that, but that second model with curvature you subjected to a hypothesis-testing approach when in fact you didn't have that curved-relation hypothesis at the very beginning. In other words, you used a hypothesis-testing tool but you used it for exploratory purposes by doing a second test on the same data (rather than seeing something in your first data set that makes you think 'maybe there's curvature', getting a new data set, and testing the curvature hypothesis there).

3. You hypothesize a *straight-line* relation between RT and FREQ, you fit lm(RT~FREQ), and it's significant. But then the results make you think 'but maybe there's curvature' and you check lm(RT~poly(FREQ, 2)) and this time there *is* significant curvature – how do you report that?

4. You hypothesize a *curved* relation between RT and FREQ, you fit lm(RT~poly(FREQ, 2)), but it turns out curvature isn't needed – lm(RT~FREQ) without any curvature is actually good enough, which means your prediction (of a curved relation) was strictly speaking wrong (even if there's of course still the significant straight-line effect of FREQ).

5. You hypothesize *some* relation between RT and FREQ, you fit lm(RT~FREQ), and it looks great, but you then still check lm(RT~poly(FREQ, 2)) but that one doesn't pan out so you can still retreat to 'well, but there's some relation, just like I said'.

So you see, much of this is about the questions (i) what did you hypothesize and when?, (ii) what did you test and when and in what order?, and (iii) how do you write that up? As discussed at the beginning of the book, picture perfect NHST has you formulate an alternative hypothesis and a null hypothesis before you see the data, and then do your test to get a yes/no answer from a p-value, and then you decide which hypothesis to adopt, as in the first of the above scenarios.

But now consider scenario 3 again – wouldn't 'everybody' be grateful if you didn't just report that you found the hypothesized linear relationships but also told everyone that you also found that, actually, the relationship between FREQ and RT is curved? Well, no, not if 'everybody' is super strict about hypothesis testing. But like I said, 'everybody' is of course not in agreement on everything (a.k.a. the understatement of the year ...). In fact, the notion of model selection is one of the most controversial issues, in particular, but not exclusively, model selection based on significance testing; that is because the more steps you do in your model selection process, the more p-values you compute on the same data, meaning the more pretend-hypotheses you are testing and the more you're 'perverting' a hypothesis-testing p-value into some kind of exploratory variable-importance measure (and the more the results could be biased).

Some authors make it very clear they are against model selection: Thompson (1995, 2001, and the references cited therein), Harrell (2015:67-69), Heinze, Wallisch, & Dunkler (2017:435), references cited in Heinze, Wallisch, & Dunkler (2017:432) are just a few and many of their reasons are compelling (in particular the risk of biased results and the fact that the order in which model selection happens can have a big impact on the final result).

Yet again, many research papers are using and, thus apparently more accepting of (different kinds of) model selection, there are textbooks that use/teach it (e.g., Zuur et al. 2009: Section 5.7, Crawley 2013:390ff., Faraway 2016:131), and there are packages/functions with associated reviewed publications for it in general and for mixed-effects modeling in particular such as FWDselect::selection by Sestelo et al. (2016), lmerTest::step by Kuznetsova et al. (2017), cAIC4::step by Säfken et al. (2018), orbuildmer::buildlmer by Voeten (2020). In addition, we find quotes in the relevant literature that indicate that in related areas that also deal with predictive modeling, e.g., "in machine learning, variable (or feature) selection seems to be the standard" (Heinze, Wallisch, & Dunkler 2017:432), or we find in a recent email on the R-sig-mixed-models Digest (Vol 161, Issue 20, 14 May 2020) contained the following advice to a poster:

> There are many approaches for [model selection/feature selection]. The easiest would be likelihood-ratio tests (LRTs, or AIC, or BIC, or some other criterion). Start with a full model (or as full as you can get while still achieving convergence) containing all combinations of predictors, remove one term, see if the model improves according to your criterion ... repeat until no terms are left to be eliminated.

Bolker et al. (2009a:133), probably referring to Pinheiro & Bates (2000:44f.) state what is probably the best way to look at it: "Whereas statisticians strongly discourage automatic stepwise regression with many potential predictors, disciplined hypothesis testing for small amounts of model reduction is still considered appropriate in some situations". So model selection does happen and can happen, but probably best with some limits. What kinds of approaches to model selection can one find? There are several hyperparameters to consider (where **hyperparameters** are parameters that determine the outcome of the modeling or, in machine learning contexts, the learning/training process):

– **direction of model selection:**
  – **forward** stepwise model selection: one starts with a relatively small model and tries to make it better by checking which one of several predictors, if added, would make the model better most and adding that one, and then you reiterate till the model cannot be made better by adding something;[16]
  – **backward** stepwise model selection: one starts with a relatively big (or even maximal) model and tries to make it better by checking which one of its predictors is least needed in the model and dropping that one, and then you reiterate till the model cannot be made better by dropping something;
  – **bidirectional** model selection: one starts with some model and tries to make it better by checking at each step what makes the model better most, adding something or dropping something, and you reiterate till the model cannot be made better;

– **criterion of model selection:**
  – **significance testing / p-values** using a certain significance threshold (typically, but not necessarily 0.05): a predictor is dropped if, of all the droppable predictors, it has the highest non-significant p-value (and, thus, makes no significant contribution to the model), or a predictor is added if, of all the addable predictors, it has the lowest significant p-value (and, thus, will make a significant contribution to the model);
  – **information criteria** such as *AIC* (or its corrected version *AICc*, corrected for small sample sizes) and others. *AIC* stands for **Akaike Information criterion**, which, like a p-value, is a value you can compute for any model, but, unlike a p-value, its absolute value isn't relevant – instead, you use it to compare competing models: All other things being equal, of two models applied to the same data, the one with the smaller *AIC*-score is preferred. That also means, you don't really say much if you report your (final) model's *AIC*-score on its own (i.e. when it is not compared/comparable to another model's *AIC*-score). Interestingly, while you can only do a p-value-based anova comparison of two models if one of them is a sub-model of the other (see above Section 5.2.1.3), *AIC* doesn't have that same restriction.

---

16 A special kind of forward model selection would be **hierarchical regression**, which we did in Section 5.1, when we checked (with anova) whether adding disp to a model prior.knowl (including everything else we already know to affect mpg) makes a significant difference.

As an interesting aside, I have met people (and/or had them as reviewers) who *hate* model selection with *p*-values with a vengeance but are much more open to model selection based on information criteria. Why is that interesting? Because (i) on an anecdotal level, anyone who has ever compared results of *p*-value-based model selection processes (e.g., using anova to compare models) and *AIC*-based model selection processes knows how similar the outcomes usually are (with the latter being more permissive/inclusive) and, more importantly, (ii) on a mathematical level, Heinze, Wallisch, & Dunkler (2017:435) show that this is so because the two are actually mathematically related in the first place:

> While at first sight selection based on information criteria seems different to significance-based selection, there is a connection between these two concepts. Consider two competing hierarchically nested models differing by one DF. Here, AIC optimization corresponds to significance-based selection at a significance level of 0.157. More generally, the significance level corresponding to AIC selection in hierarchical model comparisons is $\alpha_{AIC}(DF)=1-F_{\chi2,DF}(2\times DF)$ with $F_{\chi2,DF}(x)$ denoting the cumulative distribution function of the χ^2_{DF} distribution evaluated at x. Therefore, AIC-selected models will generally contain effects with *p*-values (in the final model) lower than approximately 0.157.

Now, my view on all of this is something like the following (and the next few paragraphs are the ones I rewrote most often while writing this book and they'll probably be the ones that will draw most ire):

To me, there are two main dimensions here to consider: one is **academic honesty and credit/merit**, the other the **exact methodological choice(s)**. By that I mean, as long as you truthfully state and motivate (i) the framing of your study – are you doing strict NHST of a small number of precise hypotheses? or are you more trying to answer questions such as 'do all my predictors correlate with my response?'? – and (ii) what you expected and what you did then, I might ultimately be ok with a more liberal view towards model selection than some others (unless of course what you did is unsuitable for finding out what you wanted to find out or you suddenly don't even discuss your own hypotheses anymore or ...). This is because if you test your hypotheses and report on those results, but then you also do more explicitly *post-hoc* and well-described testing than your hypotheses actually licensed, find some significant but initially unexpected interactions in there, and then do some explicitly *post-hoc* speculation why they might exist, then you are not asking for undeserved 'academic credit' for having had *a priori* hypotheses for these unexpected results – you're not pretending you were the genius who knew all along that these things would be there and why. Yes, you might be using a hypothesis-testing method in an exploratory way, I get that, but at the same time, let's be realistic:

First, so you used *p*-values in an exploratory variable-importance kind of way, ok, that is indeed not what they were designed for, I know that. But if you describe what you did, well, then I as the reader/reviewer can decide whether or not I want to consider these results or not (e.g., by computing my own *p*-values adjusted for multiple testing if you didn't do that or requesting you report those).

Second and even more practically-oriented, a lot of people are now using tree-based methods (see Chapter 7) as an alternative to regression modeling – either just because they think it's simpler (more on that below) or because they feel their data don't permit regression modeling; in other words, tree-based methods are often considered a perfectly valid alternative/plan B to regressions. Now, if someone else had used a tree-based predictive modeling method like random forests instead of a regression and identified the 'important predictors' to be discussed using variable importance scores, but the results were for all theoretical and practical implications identical to the results of a model selection process, then what? I'm supposed to reject your model selection paper just because of the philosophical hypothesis-testing discrepancy (that you were even open about and that statisticians give conflicting advice on) but accept the other paper whose only advantage over yours is then that it avoided the holy cow of significance testing and didn't (openly!) extend the use of *p*-values to some variable importance measure to identify the same important predictors? Frankly, while I realize what *p*-values are supposed to express, that's a little 'more Catholic than the Pope' for my taste especially given that this doesn't even acknowledge (i) the problems arising from treating tree-based approaches as a straightforward alternative to regressions in the first place, which they are *not* (see Breiman 2001b, Efron 2020 and Section 7.3 below) and that (ii) the fact that any alternative approach might involve decisions that are just as arbitrary as those we make in significance testing.

Third, within the limits of 'reasonable exploration', there might (!) be some value in reporting the unexpected findings because, even if you and I perhaps can't make sense of them, maybe another reader has a potential explanation for them and can now include them as *a priori* hypotheses in their own next study.

Thus, at least with regard to the philosophical controversies, I am fully aware of how model selection runs afoul of NHST proper, but I do think that, given how differently model/variable/feature selection is discussed even in statistical works, one should maybe not always exaggerate the philosophical purity tests – we have enough of those in other areas of life.

At the same time, model selection *does* have methodological problems (especially for the interpretation of results), like the above-mentioned fact that much of the final result hinges on the order of its steps, plus model selection can be overly optimistic and anticonservative. For such reasons, the above quote from Bolker et al. (2009a), is so useful/practical, in particular with regard to its rejection of completely automatic and exhaustive model selection. In other words, I think one should *not*, for instance, create the largest possible model given the number of predictors and controls one has and then leave it up to a completely automatic model selection function such as MASS::stepAIC to 'figure something out from there'. A more reasonable approach might be to fit a model that represents one's hypotheses as well as possible and maybe fine-tune it to get a better picture of what is happening in one's data. For instance, if I as a reviewer were to review a paper where someone said 'I hypothesized and fit lm(RT~FREQ) but then, to make sure I am not missing curvature, I also fit lm(RT~poly(FREQ, 2)), that one was significant, here are its results, too', I would be fine with that because (i) the author stated that they began with the linear effect (meaning, they're not pretending they were so smart to hypothesize the curved relation right away) and because (ii) I also get the useful information that the relation was curved, meaning the author of the next study can already legitimately consider that as well in their model. Similarly, if I as a reviewer were to review a paper where someone said 'I hypothesized an effect of FREQ and fit lm(RT~FREQ) but then, to make sure I am not reporting a main effect of FREQ and am missing an interaction, I also checked lm(RT~FREQ:IMA), that one was significant, here are its results', I would be fine with that as well for the same reasons as before.

On the other hand, I would definitely 'struggle' with an author saying 'I hypothesized an effect of FREQ and fit lm(RT~FREQ) but then I also let FREQ interact with all 13 other predictors in the model up to 3-way interactions, here are the eight most significant ones'. However, if that author made it very clear at the beginning of their study that their approach was *completely* exploratory, deep down inside I would probably not like this kind of 'completely exploratory significance testing' (because of the *contradictio in adjecto* it represents) and would prefer a different approach to this, but I might (!) not shoot it down right away just for that.

Given all this, the main recommendations I can make is (i) one that I made at the very beginning: be cautious and always consider how someone would try to criticize what you're doing and try to anticipate/preempt that criticism and (ii) write good methods sections in which you clearly explicate what you did and why so that reviewers/readers can see the principle(s) behind what you're doing and can acknowledge it's maybe, just maybe, not completely unreasonable even if – gasp! – it's not *their* favorite way of doing things (see Meteyard & Davies 2020 for a very sobering putting-things-into-perspective overview of the diversity of ways in which mixed-effects modeling is currently used in the field). Even that will not always work, but it's your best shot, and the applications below will hopefully give you some ideas on how one might proceed.

Recommendation(s) for further study: An alternative to model selection is what is called **model amalgamation** or **multi-model inferencing**. In a nutshell, the idea is to not try and find one best model (through model selection), but to identify a set of plausible models and amalgamate them into one 'composite model' in such a way that models from the set of plausible models shape the composite model to a degree that is proportional to their quality (operationalized by weights computed from *AIC*). For this approach in general, see Burnham & Anderson (2002) and for an excellent overview and application in linguistics, see Kuperman & Bresnan (2012).

5.6 Model assumptions/diagnostics

An important aspect of modeling that we have glossed over so far is concerned with the assumptions that models make about the data and with **model diagnostics**, i.e. the checks/tests one does after a having fit a model to determine whether the model can be fit on the data they way it was done. For the classical monofactorial tests in Chapter 4, we always checked assumptions of a test in advance – in regression modeling, many such diagnostics are done 'after the fact', so to speak, and if diagnostics flag our model as problematic, we have to take some action to address the problem(s) and then re-fit our model(s). What are those assumptions? I don't have space to discuss this in as much detail as I'd like – for that, see especially Fox & Weisberg's (2019) excellent chapter 8 and their car package – but I want to at least get you started; we will discuss a few assumptions of linear models using the following model as our starting point:

```
rm(list=ls(all.names=TRUE))
x <- read.delim(file="_inputfiles/05_rt_famfreq.csv",
    stringsAsFactors=TRUE, row.names=1)
x$FREQ <- log2(x$FREQ) # log FREQ to the base of 2
x$FAM <- factor(x$FAM, levels=levels(x$FAM)[c(2, 3, 1)])
summary(m.01 <- lm(RT ~ FREQ+FAM, data=x)) ## [...]
##              Estimate Std. Error t value Pr(>|t|)
## (Intercept)  675.291     14.202  47.548  < 2e-16 ***
## FREQ          -7.854      3.930  -1.998  0.05104 .
## FAMmed       -43.327     15.483  -2.798  0.00723 **
## FAMhi        -53.858     20.317  -2.651  0.01067 *
## [...]
## Multiple R-squared:  0.2904, Adjusted R-squared:  0.2487
## F-statistic: 6.959 on 3 and 51 DF,  p-value: 0.0005159
```

5.6.1 Amount of data

One seemingly trivial issue is concerned with how many data points we have. In order for a regression model to even be potentially reasonably reliable, one important notion is a value that Harrell (2015:72) calls the limiting sample size m: "in many situations a fitted regression model is likely to be reliable when the number of predictors (or candidate predictors if using variable selection) p is less than $m/10$ or $m/20$, [...] A good average requirement is $p<m/15$"; note that p here doesn't include the intercept. Harrell then states that,
- for models with numeric/continuous response variables, m is the overall sample size n;
- for models with binary response variables, m is min(table(RESPONSE));
- for models with ordinal response variables with k levels, $m=n{-}^1/_{(n\times n)}\times\Sigma n_i^3$.

With this kind of recommendation, you can clearly see why I always mentioned that this data set is more useful for explaining/teaching things than it would be for real research: Beyond the intercept, three parameters are estimated (the summary output has four rows in the coefficients table (minus the intercept) or the model matrix of m.01 has four columns (minus the intercept)), so we should have 45 data points, but better even 60, which we don't quite have (see nrow(x)). So, before embarking on some modeling, it's always useful to first check whether one is even close to the required number of data points. I recently reviewed a study involving a kind of regression model where the number of predictors p was in fact quite a bit greater than $^m/_{15}$, which did not instill confidence in the results (even with the understanding that recommendations of this kind never capture the whole truth, e.g. see van Smeden et al. 2016).

As an aside, a recent overview article stated that logistic regression assumes that all of the combinations of the various levels of all variables should be represented in the data set – not true at all, as far as I can tell! If anything, one might say logistic regression assumes that all combinations of levels of predictors *for which you're estimating a coefficient* must be attested, and each with both levels of the response (to avoid complete separation issues). But that means, if you're fitting a model glm(Y ~ A + B + C, family=binomial) with A, B, and C being ternary predictors, not all theoretically possible 27 levels of A:B:C must be attested in the data because you're not fitting a coefficient for them.

5.6.2 Residuals

Now, as for more typical regression diagnostics, a good way to start getting a first overview is to plot the model object, which generates a series of diagnostic plots that are helpful; we're focusing on the first two here:

```
par(mfrow=c(1, 2)); plot(m.01, which=1:2, col.smooth="black");
par(mfrow=c(1, 1))
```

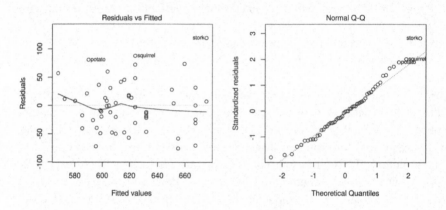

Figure 119: Model-diagnostic plots

The top left plot is essentially a slightly enriched version of plot(residuals(m.01) ~ predict(m.01)). What you want to see there is the smoother hugging the $y=0$ line pretty well and no particular pattern in the points (what's sometimes called a null plot), because that means the residuals are not correlated with the fitted/predicted values, as they shouldn't be. You also don't want to see signs of non-constant variance as in, e.g., a triangular shape, which would imply that the residuals grow as the predictions grow. Figure 120's left panel is a super obvious example of a data set through which no one who did their exploratory homework would ever fit a straight line, and the right panel then nicely illustrates how the diagnostic plot reacts to that:

Going from the left to the right (in either panel), the first residuals are all positive (the points are above the regression line), then they are all negative (the points are below the regression line), and then they are all positive again. Also, the regression line isn't *exactly* hugging the regression line [end of irony].

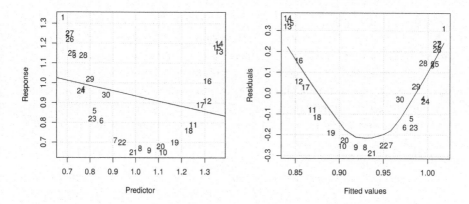

Figure 120: Data (left) and Residuals vs. fitted (right) for an inappropriate model

Thus, the diagnostic plot tells you something's wrong, and in this case it already also gives you a good idea of what that might be (although, again, that should have been obvious from prior exploration and the exact message from this kind of plot isn't always going to be this crystal-clear).

With regard to the residuals, it's also informative to plot them against the predictors because, given the definition of residuals, there should again not be much of a pattern left in those plots. There's a very nice function in the car package that generates the residuals-vs.-fitted plot but also the residuals-vs.-predictors plot in one go:

```
car::residualPlots(m.01, fitted=FALSE, col.quad="black")
```

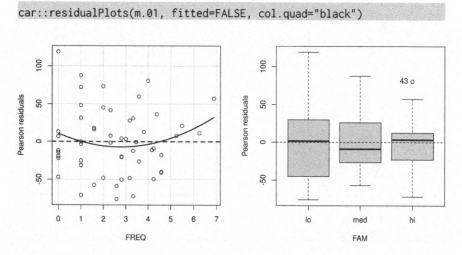

Figure 121: Residual plots

These two panels plot residuals against predictors. The right plot looks somewhat unremarkable (as it should): medians of the residuals for every level of FAM are very close to zero, for instance. The left plot is a bit more interesting because the black regression line suggests a bit of curvature in the residuals as a function of FREQ, which you will recall is something we considered in Section 5.2.3.1. But, the curvature isn't strong and the console output of residualPlots returns the *p*-value from testing whether FREQ should be a polynomial to the 2nd degree, and, as we see (again), it shouldn't; you can verify this by running round(summary(lm(RT ~ poly(FREQ,2)+FAM, data=x))$coefficients[3,3:4], 4).

The second model diagnostic plot in Figure 119 above is a quantile-quantile plot concerned with the assumption that the residuals of such a linear model should be normally distributed (around 0), meaning most residuals should be pretty symmetrically distributed around 0 and residuals further away from 0 should be rarer. This is actually important: it's the residuals that are supposed to be normally distributed – not so much the response or the predictors (as I sometimes see mentioned in papers I get to review)! And if that is the case, then the points should be on the line, which they pretty much are (with a few (labeled) data points as exceptions). More intuitively accessible, maybe, would be a histograms of the residuals. The three panels of Figure 122 show the histogram of the residuals for m.01 (left) as well as the Q-Q plot and the histogram of the terrible model of the *U*-shaped data (mid and right respectively): Especially the histogram of the model of the *U*-shaped data is quite different from a normal bell curve.

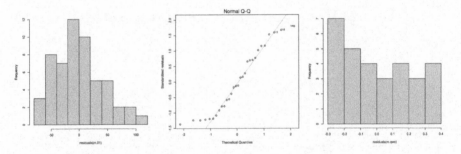

Figure 122: Normality of residuals for m.01 and an inappropriate model

---

Recommendation(s) for further study: Check out the functions car::ncvTest (to check for non-constant variance), car::qqPlot (as in car::qqPlot(residuals(m.01))), car::avPlots, and car::marginalModelPlots.

5.6.3 Influential data points

One other important characteristic of model diagnostics is a check whether the overall results are unduly influenced by maybe an only small number of data points. This notion evokes in many people the term *outlier* (e.g. as identified by boxplot), but regression modeling requires a more differentiated perspective. Consider Figure 123, in which the red line is the regression line of a model m1a for all points (50 black points and point #51 shown in red) whereas the black line is the regression line of a model m1b for all black points only.

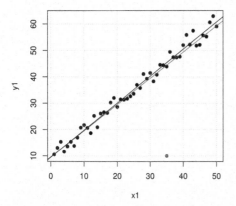

Figure 123: The effect of a non-influential data point w/ low leverage

Point 51 is not an outlier in terms of its *x*-value because its *x*-value isn't unusual at all, but it is an outlier in the bivariate correlation/regression scenario because its *y*-value is unusual given its *x*-value (remember my discussion of correlation in Section 3.3 above). At the same time, it has very little influence on the (interpretation of the) results: With the red point, the intercept and the slope are 9.63 and 0.99 respectively; without it, they are 9.52 and 1.03. Sure, they are not identical but you have to contextualize that a bit: First, there are actually 14 other data points whose removal would lead to a bigger change in the intercept, and the intercept change of 0.11 that removing #51 incurs happens on a scale of *y*-values with a range of 53. Similarly, while no other point's removal would lead to a bigger change in slope, the average absolute change in predictions that omitting #51 would bring about is a change of 0.69 on that same range of 53. Look at it this way: I bet that if I had mixed up the description, telling you that the red line is for all points but the red one, you wouldn't have blinked because that fit would also be pretty good! Thus, while you may be tempted to delete #51 – especially if you think this is due to a mistake during data entry, for instance – its presence doesn't do much damage but would of course cost you 1 *df* for the significance test (not that that makes much of a difference here nor that hunting a good *p*-value should be your ultimate goal).

Consider now Figure 124. #51 is a univariate outlier given how much its *x* value differs from all other *x*-values, same for the *y*-values. But, in the bivariate correlation/regression scenario it is *not* an outlier because its *y*-value is not unusual at all given its *x*-value.

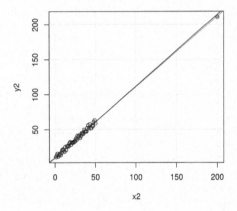

Figure 124: The effect of a non-influential data point w/ high leverage

And again it has actually very little influence because its removal results in very small changes to the models: For instance, the slope of m2a with #51 included is 1.01 whereas the slope of m2b without it 1.03; the average absolute change in predictions that omitting #51 would bring about is a change of 0.19 when the range of all *y*-values is 200.

Consider, finally, Figure 125. #51 is a univariate outlier on the *x*-dimension, but only perhaps, though not necessarily, one on the *y*-dimension. However, it also definitely is an outlier in the bivariate correlation/regression scenario seeing as how unusual its *y*-value is given its *x*-value. However, this time it also has huge influence on the regression models m3a and m3b. With the red point, the intercept and the slope of m3a are 25.82 and 0.35 respectively; without it, the intercept and the slope of m3b are 10.85 and 0.97. Those are pretty massive changes given that the *y*-values exhibit a range of 50. Also, the average absolute change in predictions that omitting #51 would bring about is a change of 7.72, which on a *y*-axis with the above-mentioned range of 50 is sizable.

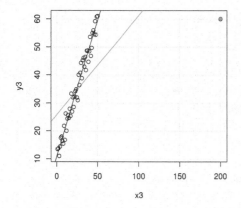

Figure 125: The effect of a non-influential data point w/ high leverage

Even visually, here you'd have noticed right away if I had mixed up the description and told you that the red line is for all points but the red one. Thus, this time, #51 is a candidate whose deletion should be considered even it comes with a loss of 1 *df*.

By the way, that recommendation to exclude #51 here is also supported by what we discussed in the previous section: check out the residuals-vs.-fitted plots of these last models m3a (with #51, left) and m3b (without it, right). Not sure any comment is needed here ...

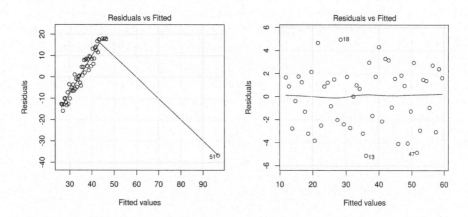

Figure 126: Comparing residuals vs. fitted plots with and without #51

Above, you saw me discuss how little or much the in- vs. exclusion of #51 changed the resulting intercepts and slopes. There are some useful statistics that can be computed very easily to get this kind of information from a model object. Three conceptually fairly straightforward statistics one might explore for this are the following:

- dfbeta, which answer the question "how much does deleting the i-th observation change the regression coefficient?"; this means, you get one *dfbeta*-value for each data point and each regression coefficient;
- dffits, which answer the question "how much does deleting the i-th observation change the prediction of the i-th data point?"; this means, you get one *dffits*-value for each data point;
- Cook's D with cooks.distance, which answer the question "how much does deleting the i-th observation change *all* predicted values? This means, you get one D-value for each data point,

In the code file, you find code for plots of these for m2 (top row) and m3 (bottom row); for both models, #51 is included so you see what it does. It is obvious that #51 is noticeable in all three upper plots for m2, but nowhere near like it is noticeable in the three lower plots for m3, clearly indicating the outsized impact it has on that model:

In sum, it is instructive to determine how much certain data points might affect a model's coefficients and other numeric results, no doubt about that, and that can lead to certain data points not being included in the main modeling process. It's often less instructive, however, to discard data points on the basis of univariate exploration (e.g., just because a box plot labels a certain point an outlier) before the modeling begins. Yes, univariate exploration has its merits – there's a reason it was discussed in Chapter 3 and done over and over again in Chapters 4 and 5 – but when it comes to modeling, it's often smarter to decide on deletion of data points after a first round of modeling when regression residuals or influence diagnostics can be looked at; in lexical decision studies, one might discard data points whose absolute standardized residuals are >2.5 (e.g., Dijkstra et al. 2010 or Carrasco Ortíz et al., to appear).

Recommendation(s) for further study: Check out
- functions such as influence.measures and rstandard;
- the above-mentioned chapter 8 of Fox & Weisberg (2019);
- maybe Field, Miles, & Field (2012: Sections 7.9, 8.6.7, and 8.8).

5.6.4 Excursus: autocorrelation/time & overdispersion

The above are probably among the most widely-used model diagnostics, but, of course there are others for linear models and of course also others for other kinds of regression models. (In fact, one was already discussed above in Section 5.2.5.3: multicollinearity). Another aspect that is often useful to consider in one's design and to statistically control for (and that might indeed be the focus of the study) is, maybe especially with observational/corpus data, captured in the notion of **autocorrelation**, which refers to the fact that a response variable is potentially correlated with (an earlier value of) itself. One realization of this is priming effects, where **priming** refers to the fairly well-established fact (although see Healey, Purver, & Howes 2014) that a certain linguistic choice at some point of time (e.g., the choice of a ditransitive construction over a prepositional dative) increases the probability that the same speaker or another speaker who heard the previous structural choice will use the same construction the next time he has to make a choice from the same set of alternants. In the language of spreadsheets and assuming the order of data points in the spreadsheet is chronological, that means the decision at a certain point in time may not only be affected by the values of cells in other columns of the same row (that's what we've been discussing), but also by cells in the same column but an earlier row; this is what I meant when I said the response variable is potentially correlated with (an earlier value of) itself. This is something quite important to control for. Imagine a corpus study of the dative alternation (ditransitives vs. prepositional datives) where you go over the cases in your spreadsheet and then you come across this weird example: a prepositional dative where
- the agent is a human;
- the patient is long, discourse-new, inanimate, and concrete;
- the recipient is short, discourse-given, and human;
- the verb used in the VP is *give*;
- the action denoted by the whole VP is literal transfer of the patient from the agent to the recipient.

In other words, all your annotation of this case (i.e. all columns in this case's row) screams the speaker should have been using a ditransitive, but he didn't. It's at least possible that the answer to this surprising choice is the case one row up (again, I'm assuming the rows are ordered chronologically). Maybe the speakers' interlocutor used a prepositional dative (maybe even in a situation in which that construction was a bit surprising), so that the current case's speaker was just so strongly primed from the *previous* case that he used a prepositional dative even though all *current*-case characteristics favor the opposite structural

choice. If you, minimally, added a column called LASTCHOICE to your data which always contained which alternant was chosen last time around, you could use that variable in your model predicting CURRENTCHOICE as a control variable to control for priming effects; similarly, as per Baayen, Davidson, & Bates (2008:399), you might consider to
- add a predictor RTPREVIOUSTRIAL to a model predicting reaction times to account for the fact that the preceding RT-value is usually a good predictor for the next one;
- add a predictor PREVIOUSTRIALCORRECT to a model to account for streaks, or **runs** of correct or false responses;
- add a predictor STIMULUSNUMBER to a model to statistically account for learning, habituation, fatigue over the time course of an experiment, i.e. changes in subjects' performance over experiment time; etc.

For example, in Gries & Wulff (2009), we found a within-subject accumulative priming effect (subjects priming themselves more over time); in Doğruöz & Gries (2012), we found that subjects became more accepting of novel expressions not attested in their dialects over less than a dozen stimuli, etc.; see the recommendations below for much more (!) advanced discussion). But note: it may be important to include such controls not just as main effects, but also have them interact with the main predictor(s) of interest. Why? Because interactions are when 'something doesn't do the same everywhere/always' ...

Imagine we want to do a very simple experimental study of the word frequency effect: our response is RT, our only predictor is FREQ (let's say logged already), but we want to control for subjects potentially fatiguing over time (or getting faster over time due to practice effects). In that case, it may be wise to add a predictor into our model that corresponds to experiment time (like a numeric stimulus counter called STIMULUSNUMBER). A significant positive effect of that predictor would then indicate that people slow down over the course of the experiment. So far so good, but if we want to know whether there's a fatigue effect with regard to or sensitive to FREQ, then it might be better to also check whether there's a significant interaction STIMULUSNUMBER:FREQ: If that interaction term is significant, then that means the effect of FREQ is not the same everywhere/always, i.e. at every point in time of the experiment – *that* is also something we might want to identify or statistically control for. Maybe subjects fatigue but especially with regard to lower-frequency words; for that you need the interaction!

More generally and as mentioned in Section 1.6, for the analysis of a factorial experimental design, we might add a variable to a multifactorial analysis that mentions for each presentation of an experimental condition how often it has been presented already and permit that variable to interact with other predictors, which might show that experimental time has different effects on different variable level combinations of your schematic token set.

As for priming effects in, say, a corpus study, it might be worthwhile to do some simple exploration beforehand. For example, here is some info on 300 instances of the dative alternation in a vector of constructional choices called CURRENTCHOICE. As you can see, the constructions are pretty evenly frequent, as is 'confirmed' by a (only heuristically-used!) chi-squared test:

```
(qwe <- table(CURRENTCHOICE))
## CURRENTCHOICE
## ditr prep
##  141  159
chisq.test(qwe, correct=FALSE)$p.value # show only p
## [1] 0.2986976
```

But one can easily show that this overall pretty even distribution doesn't at all entail that these two constructions alternate pretty much randomly back and forth all the time: In Figure 127, a line going down from the bold horizontal line in the middle means a prepositional dative was produced, a line going up means a ditransitive was produced, and horizontal lines at the bottom or the top indicate **runs** (a construction being used several times in succession), and we can clearly see that constructional choices 'cluster' (note esp. the long run or prepositional datives in the middle above the *a* of *prepositional* at the bottom).

ditransitive

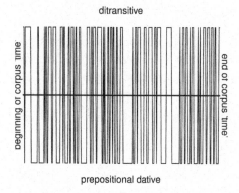

prepositional dative

Figure 127: Priming/runs of constructional choices

In fact, there's a nice function (rle) to show many runs there are and another function (tseries::runs.test or randtests::runs.test) to see if the distribution of two constructions is compatible with the H_0 of a random binary data series. In this case, there are too many and too long runs in order for this to look random (and that's because I biased the sequence that way so the test is right):

```
rle(as.character(CURRENTCHOICE)) # identify all runs in the data
## Run Length Encoding
##    lengths: int [1:89] 2 1 9 10 2 8 1 1 2 2 ...
##    values : chr [1:89] "ditr" "prep" "ditr" "prep" "ditr" ...
table(rle(as.character(CURRENTCHOICE))$lengths)
##  1  2  3  4  5  6  7  8  9 10 12 15
## 18 26 14 12  6  4  1  3  2  1  1  1
tseries::runs.test(CURRENTCHOICE)$p.value # p-value of runs test
## [1] 9.716989e-13
```

Which also means, if you wanted to build a regression modeling predicting CURRENTCHOICE, then including a predictor LASTCHOICE along the lines discussed above is probably useful, and we can see in this abbreviated summary output that, because of all the runs, LASTCHOICE has quite some impact on CURRENTCHOICE (R^2 isn't shown here but is a sizable 0.216).

```
summary(glm(CURRENTCHOICE ~ LASTCHOICE,
    family=binomial))$coefficients
##               Estimate Std. Error    z value     Pr(>|z|)
## (Intercept) -0.7801586  0.1820547  -4.285297 1.824950e-05
## LASTCHOICE2  1.7409011  0.2541000   6.851245 7.321024e-12
```

So, the notion of autocorrelation and its various incarnations is something you should be aware of when you formulate your models: It's often a good or even necessary control variable (and could be the main predictor in a priming study).

Recommendation(s) for further study: Check out
- the function acf as in acf(as.numeric(CURRENTCHOICE=="ditr")) and performance:: check_autocorrelation;
- Koplenig & Müller-Spitzer (2016) and Koplenig (2017) for studies exemplifying the importance of taking the temporal structure of data into account;
- while we haven't discussed mixed-effects modeling yet, the following sources are probably already still interesting, if only to give you ideas of how the above kinds of things can be statistically controlled for and, on a general/conceptual level, how: Baayen, Davidson, & Bates (2008, esp. p. 399), Baayen et al. (2017), and Baayen et al. (2018).

Another important concept for generalized linear models is **overdispersion**, which refers to something often observed in binary logistic regression (and Poisson regression), namely the undesirable situation that the variance of the response variable is greater than what the current model specifies or that the discrepancy between observed and predicted values is greater than the current model specifies. It can be tested for once you have a regression model object. For instance, if you have the model m.01, which we considered above, you can check for overdispersion by looking at the two 'deviance lines' at the bottom.

```
## Call:
## glm(formula=ORDER~1+CONJ*LENDIFF, family=binomial, data=x)
## Coefficients:
##                          Estimate Std. Error z value Pr(>|z|)
## (Intercept)             -2.504984   0.270435  -9.263  < 2e-16
## CONJbevor/before         2.148720   0.421964   5.092 3.54e-07
## CONJals/when             2.968349   0.352068   8.431  < 2e-16
## [...]
## (Dispersion parameter for binomial family taken to be 1)
##     Null deviance: 503.80  on 402  degrees of freedom
## Residual deviance: 368.59  on 395  degrees of freedom
```

Specifically, you look at the ratio of your model's residual deviance and its residual dfs, which shouldn't be much larger than 1 (and here it's fine because $^{368.59}/_{395} \approx 0.933$). Baayen (2008:199) uses as a diagnostic a chi-squared test of the residual deviance at the residual df and one hopes for a non-significant result:

```
pchisq(q=m.01$deviance, df=m.01$df.residual, lower.tail=FALSE)
## [1] 0.8257883
```

If this chi-squared test returns a significant result, you need to consider changes to your model. One would be to re-fit the model again with a different family argument: quasibinomial instead of the usual binomial, which will *in*crease the standard errors in the coefficients table, which will in turn *de*crease the *t*-values and *in*crease the *p*-values and can, therefore lead to different conclusions. If you re-fit the model, you get this result; the standard errors here are the ones from m.01 multiplied by the square root of the dispersion parameter R estimated (multiplied by $1.019053^{0.5}$). (Your G^2-value would also have to be adjusted for its significance test: you'd divide it by the dispersion parameter.)

```
summary(m.02 <- glm(ORDER ~ 1 + CONJ*LENDIFF, family=quasibinomial,
    data=x))
## Coefficients:
```

```
##                              Estimate Std. Error t value Pr(>|t|)
## (Intercept)                 -2.504984   0.272999  -9.176  < 2e-16
## CONJbevor/before             2.148720   0.425965   5.044 6.95e-07
## [...
## (Dispersion parameter for quasibinomial family taken to be
1.019053)
##     Null deviance: 503.80  on 402  degrees of freedom
## Residual deviance: 368.59  on 395  degrees of freedom
```

Another possibility of dealing with overdispersion would be to add additional predictors or controls (which might bring the unexplained variance down) or to switch to a different kind of regression model (e.g., in the case of a Poisson model with overdispersion, you could re-fit with family=quasipoisson or switch to a negative binomial model); see Faraway (2016: Sections 3.4-3.5) for input.

Multinomial and ordinal models also come with additional assumptions, but I won't discuss those here (and these are actually not discussed in many references I've seen) – instead, you can begin to read up on those here:

Recommendation(s) for further study: Check out
- for the Independence-of-Irrelevant-Alternatives assumption of multinomial models, mlogit::hmftest;
- for the ordinality and proportional-odds assumptions of ordinal models, see Harrell (2015:311-314), Agresti (2019: Section 8.2.5), or Fox & Weisberg (2019: Section 6.9.1).

5.7 Model validation (and classification vs. prediction)

The last major notion to be discussed here (all too briefly) is that of **model validation**, in particular determining how well the output of a model – notably, its predictions, which are of course a direct function of the model's coefficients – matches data that did not feature in the generation of the model. In the models above, we always evaluated the performance of the model using statistics resulting from applying the model to the exact same data set it was built on. For instance, in Section 5.3.4 above, we fit this model, ...

```
rm(list=ls(all.names=TRUE))
x <- read.delim(file="_inputfiles/05_scmc_conjmorethan2.csv",
   stringsAsFactors=TRUE) # change categorical variables into factors
data.frame(Estimate=coef(m.01 <- glm(ORDER ~ 1 +
   CONJ*MORETHAN2CL, data=x, family=binomial))) ## [...]
```

... and then we used predict to generate predictions from it, and then we computed the model's accuracy, which turned out to be 0.7667494.

However, while we used the predict function for this, one might say that these are not really *predictions* in a narrower sense. Even just colloquially, it seems weird to call this prediction given that, to anthropomorphize a bit, the model has already seen the ordering choices. You're not predicting the outcome of the Superbowl after having seen the game ... I often use the term *classification (accuracy)* to indicate that I'm aware that, even if the values I'm using in my accuracy computations are created by a function called predict, they're not really prototypical predictions – unless, of course, I'm providing predict with new data using its aptly named newdata argument (as we did in Sections 3.2.4 and 5.2.6.3 above). The problem with this kind of accuracy score is that it is usually too optimistic, meaning, with very few chance exceptions, a model will perform better on the data it was built on – or trained on, to use machine-learning language – if only because, I am still anthropomorphizing, it found things in the data set it was trained on that it could use for good predictions but that wouldn't exist in any other sample; this is often called **overfitting** A more formal definition of overfitting is "the fact that a classifier that adapts too closely to the learning sample not only discovers the systematic components of the structure that is present in the population, but also the random variation from this structure that is present in the learning data because of random sampling" (Strobl et al. 2009:327).

How does one obtain a more realistic assessment of one's model's true predictive accuracy? Simple: sample another data set from the same population that your first data set was representative for, annotate it for all the same predictors in exactly the same way, apply the model from the first data set to it, and see how well it's doing ... Yeah, that'd work, but of course it's not always possible or practical or affordable to do that, so researchers often go with another solution called **cross-validation**. In bootcamps, I usually discuss three approaches to this, but for lack of space, I will only discuss one particular type of it here, namely one that strikes a good balance between quality of results and computational costs: **10-fold cross-validation**. In this process, the data are randomly split into ten 10% parts/folds, and then each 10% fold is not used – often called held out – for computing/training the model. That means, the model is computed on 90% of your data, but its accuracy is tested by applying it to the 10% that were held out, i.e. not used for computing/training the model.

Let's go through this process: We begin by setting a random number seed so we get random but replicable results. Then, we add to the original data frame a column that assigns every row randomly to 1 of 10 folds:

```
set.seed(sum(utf8ToInt("Parmaschinken")))
x$FOLDS <- sample(rep(1:10, length.out=nrow(x)))
```

Then, because we will do this with a for-loop, we remember Section 3.5.2 and
create two collector structures. The more important one of the two is very simple: it's just a vector that has 10 slots (currently filled with NA), one for each accuracy score of each cross-validation iteration.

```
prediction.accuracies <- rep(NA, 10)
```

The other, less important one is a matrix in which we collect each of the 10 models coefficients (this is not usually done, but I sometimes find it informative):

```
# define a collector matrix for the 8 coefficients from each of the
10 models
model.coefficients <- matrix(rep(0, 80), ncol=10, dimnames=list(
   COEFS=names(coef(m.01)), MODELS=c(paste0("CV", 1:10))))
```

So how does the validation actually happen? (In what follows, I'm not showing
the shortest/most elegant way to do this, but one that's most in sync with how
things were discussed above.) We go through a for-loop 10 times letting i be a
number from 1 to 10 and, each time, we're subsetting the whole data frame x to
create a training set x.train (all the rows where FOLDS is not i) and a test set
x.test (all the rows where FOLDS is i); one could use split for this, too. Then, we
apply the model formula to the training set, and the model coefficients we get
from the training set are then applied to the test set to compute predictions.
Finally, we determine how well these predictions are doing on the test set and
store (i) the i-th prediction accuracy in prediction.accuracies[i] and (ii) all
model coefficients from this iteration in the i-th column of model.coeffi-
cients[,i]: (Check out the loop in the code, I only show the results here.)

```
## [...]
summary(prediction.accuracies)
##    Min. 1st Qu.  Median    Mean 3rd Qu.    Max.
##  0.6250  0.6872  0.7652  0.7418  0.8000  0.8293
```

In this case, the mean of the 10 prediction accuracies – 0.7418 – is really only a
bit smaller than the classification accuracy from all the data (which was 0.7667),
meaning that, in this case, our model on all the data wasn't really too overly optimistic. In fact, the classification accuracy is within the confidence interval of

the prediction accuracies (t.test(prediction.accuracies, mu=0.7667494)$ conf.int, remember this from Section 4.3.1.2? Don't forget the basics!) so this seems fine – if it could only always be like that ... We can also check out the volatility of the coefficients now, by looking at model.coefficients and, for instance, the ranges of values we get for them or, better, the middle 95% of the values. As you can see, even though the overall mean accuracy is close to our from the full data set, some coefficients change their sign in some models – i.e. the direction of their effect! – indicating a certain degree of volatility (as do some of the really low accuracies).

Cross-validation is something you should definitely be prepared to do (for fixed-effects models at least);[17] it's an important tool and asked for more and more often by reviewers and for good reason. Note, however, that model selection together with cross-validation is more tricky because you'd have to do model selection on each of the 10 training sets and then apply each final model to each corresponding test set, and of course it's quite possible that different training sets lead to different final models ... Since I personally would never do a fully automatic model selection process, this can increase demands on time and computational power considerably as well as require a complex amalgamation of different final models – if you consider only a single model, like we just did, cross-validation is much more unproblematic.

Recommendation(s) for further study: You should read up on cross-validation and bootstrapping in, e.g., Hamrick (2018) or Egbert & Plonsky (to appear); James et al. (2015: Ch. 5) is a more general intro chapter to resampling methods using R.

5.8 A thought experiment

Ok, now that we're nearly at the end of this chapter on fixed-effects-only regression, here's a little practice example for you: Look at the structure of this data

---

17 For mixed-effects models, cross-validation is much more complex because of the relatedness of the data points due to the random effects. One can theoretically do cross-validation on the basis of random sampling, but that can lead to overoptimistic model assessments, which is why Roberts et al. (2016), for instance, recommend cross-validation with blocking – however, even that approach isn't entirely straightforward (p. 915). I think it's fair to say that cross-validation for mixed-effects models is far from being an obvious standard (certainly not in linguistics), an assessment I feel is supported by the complete absence of the topic even in many of the standard references of the top people in the field that otherwise inform most mixed-effects modeling applications in linguistics.

set involving durations of words in 10-word turns (an altered version of one used in Rühlemann & Gries 2020):

```
str(x <- read.delim("_inputfiles/05_durations.csv",
  stringsAsFactors=TRUE))
'data.frame':        6383 obs. of  9 variables:
 $ CASE     : int  1 2 3 4 5 6 7 8 9 10 ...
 $ DURATION : int  105 89 78 100 368 251 167 418 238 419 ...
 $ POSINTURN: int  2 3 4 5 6 7 8 9 10 1 ...
 $ SEX      : Factor w/ 2 levels "female","male": 2 2 2 2 2 2 2 2 ...
 $ CLASS    : Factor w/ 5 levels "closed","number",..: 1 1 1 1 3 ...
 $ VOWELS   : Factor w/ 2 levels "one","two+": 1 1 1 1 2 2 2 2 ...
 $ LENGTH   : int  3 3 2 1 6 2 2 4 3 1 ...
 $ SURPRISAL: int  5 6 3 3 8 7 3 16 6 10 ...
 $ FREQ     : int  16 16 18 15 11 16 16 7 6 12 ...
```

Here is some information on all variables but CASE:
— DURATION: the response variable, the duration of a word in ms;
— POSINTURN: the main predictor of interest, the position of the word in the 10-word turn (from 1 to 10);
— SEX: the sex of the current turn's speaker;
— CLASS: the 'class' of the word in each position;
— VOWELS: whether the word in question contains one or more vowels;
— LENGTH: the length of the word in phonemes;
— SURPRISAL: an index quantifying how surprising the word is given the previous word;
— FREQ: how frequent the word is in a reference corpus (this isn't a raw frequency but an index derived from a raw frequency, the exact nature of that derivation isn't relevant now).

Imagine you're a statistical consultant and your task is to study the hypothesis that word durations increase at the end of 10-word turns (maybe speakers slow down to indicate to the hearer that they can take over the next turn) and that effect might not be the same for open- and closed-class words. Ideally, do *not* read on now but jot down some notes on what you'd be planning to do; make those detailed and only read on when you really think you're done. And by *detailed*, I mean, they are supposed to be so detailed that, if you got sick tomorrow and couldn't continue working on this project, your colleague in your data science company would take over this project and could hit the ground running from your notes (since the client was already billed for the exploration of the data and the deadline is very soon).

THINK BREAK (long!)

Now, with regard to
- data exploration and preparation, did you note down to consider
  - transforming (some of) the numeric variables?
  - doing something about the low-frequency levels of CLASS? If so, what: conflation? deletion?
- the formulation of the initial model, did you
  - remember that, ultimately, you will need to consider some form of the interaction of POSINTURN:CLASS (to see whether the effect of POSINTURN is the same across classes)?
  - think about what you want to do with the control variables CLASS, VOWELS, LENGTH, SURPRISAL, FREQ? Do you want to include them as main effects only so that POSINTURN cannot claim to explain variability that actually is already taken care of by the controls? Do you want the controls to interact with POSINTURN?
  - decide whether your first model will already contain all controls and POSINTURN*SEX or whether your first model will be a model with all controls but without POSINTURN*SEX (so you can see whether adding POSINTURN*SEX to the first model makes a significant difference like in the adding disp-to-everything-else example)?
- the initial model, but also model selection, did you
  - plan on doing model selection or sticking with whatever initial model you formulated? If you were planning on, say, backwards model selection, were you planning on allowing the controls to be deleted if they were non-significant (if you were planning on using p-values for model selection, that is) or would you have them stay in even if they were not significant (to not let POSINTURN explain variability that could be explained even by non-significant controls)?
  - think about whether you want POSINTURN to only have a straight-line effect or are you open to a curved effect? If so, when in the modeling process – as your first proper alternative hypothesis or as a follow-up?
  - plan on doing model amalgamation? If so, what was the 'set of reasonable models' you were considering for amalgamation? (This we have of course not talked about much; this is just a reminder that that option exists and is something you (c|sh)ould read up on.)

Don't get me wrong: this list, which isn't even complete, isn't supposed to be some 'gotcha, you didn't think of that!' moment – I'm just trying to give you an idea of the complexity of everything you need to consider before you even start writing your first line of code. I often get emails/questions from people who basically ask something like 'here's my question/hypothesis, I have these data, is this a good model?' or, worse, 'can we do a quick modeling thing in your office hours / during the lunch break?' And the answer is invariably some hopefully polite enough version of this:

'If you've answered all those kinds of questions above, I might (!) be willing to have a look at the model/data – otherwise, no, I can't really help you (yet). Plus, a proper modeling of some data will certainly take more than this lunch break because you need to make up your mind first about all sorts of things (many of which might require domain knowledge I often don't even have), Finally, any model's success or lack thereof requires familiarity with the data (to decide on proper conflations, transformations, etc.) that I most likely don't have either, so ...'

So, bottom line: when you have your spreadsheet prepared and you think you're ready to go, sit down for a while and think about how about you would answer the above kinds of questions and why (and note those things down in detail because these answers are likely to already make up a considerable part of your paper's methods section).

Finally, a few brief comments on how we write up results of some such regression modeling process. I already gave a few examples of how to summarize things in some regression sections above, but now that we've also talked about model selection, diagnostics, and validation, I want to add to this and recommend to provide at least

– all relevant details regarding the initial and the final model: what the first model was and why and, in terms of model selection, how you got from there to the final model;
– the overall final model's significance test and R^2(s);
– the droppable predictors' significance tests;
– a quick mention of what you did in terms of model diagnostics (e.g. checking residuals and collinearity); if you did model validation, describe that as well;
– effects plots of all relevant predictors (with confidence intervals/bands).

Some people insist on providing the summary model output. I agree that that can be useful because sometimes it can lead to questions about the model (diagnostic or otherwise) or certain effects – on the other hand, the more complex the model, the harder those tables become to interpret. So for the summary output, I'd say, if there's room for it, great, do include it, but maybe in an appendix so whoever wants to look at it can do so but, for other readers, the often huge table then wouldn't disrupt the flow. Now, if you provide a summary table, may I make a little plea for a certain way of reporting the coefficients table? A lot of times, people just copy and paste directly from R so the table may look like this:

```
##                Estimate Std. Error    t value      Pr(>|t|)
## (Intercept) 697.96237    22.65474 30.808667 9.871190e-34
## FREQ         -22.68790    12.19506 -1.860417 6.883343e-02
## FAMmed       -66.39724    26.81901 -2.475753 1.679960e-02
## FAMhi        -94.75672    37.78113 -2.508044 1.550114e-02
## FREQ:FAMmed   15.00512    13.22089  1.134955 2.619156e-01
## FREQ:FAMhi    19.59873    14.13690  1.386353 1.719154e-01
```

Fine, but I think it could be made more reader-friendly, especially when you have many more predictors with maybe many levels. In Table 31, I make explicit which contrast every coefficient/difference is representing and what the first/reference levels are for the intercept, which makes this so much easier to interpret than if one has to go back and look up for all your categorical predictors what the reference levels were etc. Also, I am reducing decimals to what is practical: if the response is milliseconds, I doubt we need more than one decimal for the estimates/CI of the response variable at least; for the other numbers, two or three is fine. These are small changes, I admit, but they can make a big difference in processability.

Table 31: What I think is a better summary/coefficients table

	Estimate	95%-CI	se	t	$p_{\text{2-tailed}}$
Intercept (FREQ=0, FAM=lo)	698	[652.4, 743.5]	22.65	30.81	<0.001
FREQ$_{0 \to 1}$	-22.7	[-47.2, 1.8]	12.2	-1.86	0.069
FAM$_{lo \to med}$	-66.4	[-120.3, -12.5]	26.82	-2.48	0.017
FAM$_{lo \to hi}$	-94.8	[-170.7, -18.8]	37.78	-2.51	0.016
FREQ$_{0 \to 1}$ FAM$_{lo \to med}$	15	[-11.6, 41.6]	13.22	1.13	0.262
FREQ$_{0 \to 1}$ FAM$_{lo \to hi}$	19.6	[-8.8, 48]	14014	1.39	0.172

Ok, time to complicate things some more and, finally, turn to mixed-effects modeling. I actually hope that, as you were thinking about the durations data, you were wondering "but wait, can we even do a regression of the Chapter 5-type there? The data points are not all independent of each other, minimally because all the words of one 10-word turn are related (by virtue of having been produced by the same speaker) and maybe every speaker contributed multiple turns, which are therefore related!" This kind of scenario, which is of course extremely frequent, is what we're turning to now – well, maybe not *now* but after you've done the exercises for Chapter 5!

Recommendation(s) for further study: Check out
- for more discussion on what to include when you write up your results, see Wilkinson & The Task Force on Statistical Inference (1999), Norris et al. (2015), and Gries & Paquot (to appear);
- for more information on all aspects of fixed-effects regression modeling, see Fox & Weisberg (2019: Chapters 4-6, 8), Faraway (2015), Faraway (2016: Ch. 1-9), Harrell (2015: Ch. 2, 4), Hilpert & Blasi (to appear), and especially the excellent Gelman, Hill, & Vehtari (2020), who discuss regression from a Bayesian perspective with `rstanarm::stan_glm`.

---

6 Mixed-effects regression modeling

Whereas GLMMs themselves are uncontroversial, describing how to use them to analyze data necessarily touches on controversial statistical issues such as the debate over null hypothesis testing], the validity of stepwise regression and the use of Bayesian statistics. Others have thoroughly discussed these topics; we acknowledge the difficulty while remaining agnostic. (Bolker et al. 2009a:128)

6.1 A very basic introduction

The whole previous chapter was, as per its title, about fixed-effects (henceforth *fixef*) regression modeling (not as the term is used in economics, though). But ever since 2008, which saw the publication of Baayen (2008)'s Chapter 7 and a special issue of the *Journal of Memory and Language* on "Emerging Data Analysis", whose contributors included again Baayen, but also Quené & van den Bergh, Jaeger, Barr, and others, mixed-effects modeling (henceforth MEM, which I will also use for *mixed-effects model(s)*) has taken linguistics by storm. The maybe most important advantage of MEM is how it 'modifies' or 'enriches' (generalized) linear models (GLMs) in the following way: As we saw above multiple times, nearly all monofactorial tests and regression models we discussed so far involve the assumption that the data points (or observations or – in the usual long format use by statistical software – the rows of the spreadsheet) are statistically independent of each other, an assumption that (i) ideally already informed the design of the data collection process and the data analysis and (ii) minimally is checked after the fact as part of model diagnostics (e.g. by checking (visually or otherwise) the structure of the residuals of especially linear models). In what way might data points or samples not be statistically independent of each other? I mentioned this briefly above, when we talked about test situations for which we require tests for dependent samples such as the *t*-test for dependent samples or the Wilcoxon test. The most common kinds of scenarios are probably these:
- data points might be temporally and/or autocorrelationally related as when subjects in experiments exhibit learning/habituation, practice, or fatigue effects and/or when speakers in observational data exhibit priming and/or resonance effects; diagnostically, this could show up in autocorrelation/autoregressive structures or runs as discussed above;

https://doi.org/10.1515/9783110718256-006

– more importantly, however, data points might be related because they share characteristics other than straightforward predictor variables, e.g. when subjects in experiments produce multiple measures of the response variable (so that all the subject's measurements might be affected by, say, the subject's idiosyncratic aptitude, motivation, etc.) or when stimuli are used for multiple measurements (so that certain characteristics of a stimulus might affect all measures performed on it). Diagnostically, that could show up in residual plots exhibiting structure (resulting from clumping of multiple measurements of one or more speakers) or from notable results in influence measures. Crucially, MEM allows to take both of these kinds of relations between different data points – subjects/speakers and items/words – into consideration at the same time, for instance, when in an experimental set-up, where each speaker and each stimulus 'contributes' multiple data points, this is dealt with by including what are called **crossed random effects**.

– in addition, data points might also be related because they share multiple taxonomically- or hierarchically-organized characteristics, giving rise to what are so-called **nested random effects**. A frequently-used example to explain this involves educational research where, when, say, high school students are tested in one state, then all students within the same classroom share the teacher (whose teaching style might have a certain impact on all of his students), but they also share the school (whose PTA might work in a way that is systematically different from that of other schools), but they also share the school district (whose funding situation might affect all its schools differently than those of other districts), etc. This, too, might diagnostically show up in residual structure and/or influence measures.

Just to clarify this distinction between crossed and nested one more time (even with considerable simplification), consider Table 32, which contains two schematic variables RESPONSE and PREDICTOR and then the corpus part the data in each row are from. Here, the corpus variables exhibit nesting: If I tell you the file name from which a data point was sampled, i.e. the level of FILE, then you also know the level of REGISTER and that of MODE that that data point is from (which in R can be written as MODE/REGISTER/FILE, see Gries 2015 for a simple 'exemplification' using corpus data). If I tell you the file name is a2, there's only file with that name in your data and so knowing the file's name makes you know the content of the other corpus variables/columns as well (although of course not necessarily the content of RESPONSE and PREDICTOR).

Table 32: A schematic example of nested variables (MODE/REGISTER/FILE)

CASE	RESPONSE	PREDICTOR	MODE	REGISTER	FILE
1	...	...	spk	dialog	a1
2	...	...	spk	dialog	a2
3	...	...	spk	dialog	a2
4	...	...	spk	dialog	a2
5	...	...	spk	monolog	b1
6	...	...	spk	monolog	b2
7	...	...	spk	monolog	b3
8	...	...	wrt	printed	c1
9	...	...	wrt	printed	c2
10	...	...	wrt	printed	c3
11	...	...	wrt	printed	c3
12	...	...	wrt	printed	c4
13	...	...	wrt	non-printed	d1
14	...	...	wrt	non-printed	d1
15	...	...	wrt	non-printed	d1

This is not the case with crossed variables, which should remind you of the fully factorial experimental design discussed in Section 1.6. Consider Table 33, for an example where SPEAKER and STIMULUS are crossed (because each of the three speakers saw each of the four stimuli used in the experiment): If I give you a stimulus number, say, 1, then you do not know what speaker etc. I am referring to because there are multiple speakers that saw that (or any other) stimulus.

By the way, very important piece of advice here: If you have multiple experiments each of which involves different speakers (such that the speakers are nested into the experiments), it's safest to *not* have your table – specifically the SPEAKER and EXPERIMENT columns – look like Table 34. Why? Because we said "experiments each of which involves *different speakers*". Unless we fix Table 34 in one of several ways or tell R in some other way, R wouldn't know that speaker 1 in experiment 1 is not the same speaker as speaker 1 in experiment 2 and would therefore do the stats all wrong. Yes, with the same kind of slash notation as above, you can tell R in the formula of a model that the levels of SPEAKER are supposed to be seen as nested into the level of EXPERIMENT (EXPERIMENT/SPEAKER), but it's probably safer to either change the content of the column SPEAKER or create a new column EXPSPK like in the code shown next (which also has the advantage that the new column cannot be misunderstood as a numeric variable).

Table 33: A schematic example of crossed variables (SPEAKER and STIMULUS)

CASE	RESPONSE	PREDICTOR	SPEAKER	STIMULUS
1	...	...	1	1
2	...	...	1	2
3	...	...	1	3
4	...	...	1	4
5	...	...	2	1
6	...	...	2	2
7	...	...	2	3
8	...	...	2	4
9	...	...	3	1
10	...	...	3	2
11	...	...	3	3
12	...	...	3	4

Table 34: How not to represent different speakers in different experiments

CASE	RESPONSE	PREDICTOR	EXPERIMENT	SPEAKER
1	...	...	1	1
2	...	...	1	2
3	...	...	1	3
4	...	...	1	4
5	...	...	2	1
6	...	...	2	2
7	...	...	2	3
8	...	...	2	4
9	...	...	3	1
10	...	...	3	2
11	...	...	3	3
12	...	...	3	4

```
EXPERIMENT <- rep(x=1:3, each=4)
SPEAKER <-    rep(x=1:4, times=3) # & the 'reverse Netflix notation':
(EXPSPK <- paste0("E", formatC(EXPERIMENT, width=2, flag="0"),
                 "S", formatC(SPEAKER,    width=2, flag="0")))
## [1] "E01S01" "E01S02" "E01S03" "E01S04" "E02S01" "E02S02"
## [7] "E02S03" "E02S04" "E03S01" "E03S02" "E03S03" "E03S04"
```

This way, every speaker across your complete data set has a unique ID and, because of the padding of the single digits with 0s, the names remain usefully sortable and/or easily processable with string manipulation functions. (Another useful option might be to take some variable like EXPSPK and combine it with a numbering of each speaker's data points and maybe even make the result of that the row names of the data frame; this can be useful because some diagnostic plotting functions plot the (row) names of notable data points, which then becomes more easily interpretable than just a case number.)

In the following four brief sub-sections, I will discuss how MEM accounts for non-independence-of-data points scenarios. In each section, we will look at a really small data set that was designed to have certain expositorily useful totally obvious characteristics and, in each section, we will first fit a 'normal' very simple linear model (regressing one response Y on one predictor X), then plot the data. I hope you're immediately thinking 'wait, what? I thought we were supposed to always do that the other way round?' Yes, you should, this is only for didactic reasons here. And then we'll see how certain kinds of MEM can handle what's going on in those data; all these examples involve just one source of random effect (henceforth *ranef*) variation, namely subjects/speakers, but the logic naturally extends to more complex scenarios.

6.1.1 Varying intercepts only

We load the data and immediately fit the linear model:

```
rm(list=ls(all.names=TRUE)); library(lme4); summary(x <- read.delim(
    file="_inputfiles/06_vi.csv", stringsAsFactors=TRUE))
##      CASE              X                Y              SPKR
## Min.   : 1.00    Min.   :0.03169   Min.   :0.5976   S1:10
## 1st Qu.: 8.25    1st Qu.:0.23185   1st Qu.:0.8335   S2:10
## Median :15.50    Median :0.39242   Median :1.0213   S3:10
## Mean   :15.50    Mean   :0.38963   Mean   :1.0277
## 3rd Qu.:22.75    3rd Qu.:0.54567   3rd Qu.:1.2201
## Max.   :30.00    Max.   :0.73020   Max.   :1.4142
summary(data1.model1 <- lm(Y ~ 1 + X, data=x)) ## [...]
##             Estimate Std. Error t value Pr(>|t|)
## (Intercept)  0.96212    0.09441  10.191 6.33e-11 ***
## X            0.16824    0.21415   0.786    0.439  ## [...]
## Multiple R-squared:  0.02157,    Adjusted R-squared:  -0.01338
## F-statistic: 0.6172 on 1 and 28 DF,  p-value: 0.4387
```

I want to focus on two things here in this output: (i) the one predictor and, thus, the whole model isn't significant and (ii) the predictor's slope is 0.1682, i.e. for every 1-unit increase of X, Y increases by that amount. But as you recognized in the summary output of the data frame x, however, the 30 data points were contributed by only three speakers. That actually means the data points can be argued to not be independent, which was one crucial assumption of linear models. If we now look at the residual diagnostic plot in the left panel of Figure 128 (the seemingly weird x/y-axis limits of the plot will become clear in a moment) and the data in the right panel (speakers are represented with numbers in both panels) and the regression line we just forced through those points in the right panel, it clearly seems there's a bit of structure remaining in the residuals ...

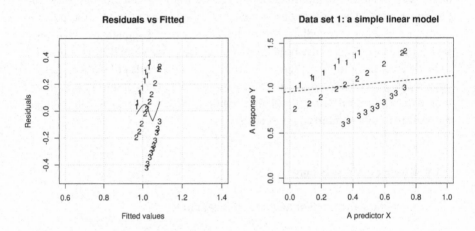

Figure 128: Residuals vs. fitted values and/of lm(Y~X) (data set 1)

In fact, the residual plot doesn't look 'unstructured' at all and the right plot makes it plain obvious that every speaker on their own exhibits what looks like a perfect correlation between Y and X and that the slopes of X for each speaker seem to be very similar and also much steeper than the estimate of 0.17 suggests. If all observations were independent of each other, using one intercept for all of the data points could theoretically (!) make sense, but here a MEM is needed to to take the relatedness of the data points per speaker into account. The simplest way it can do so statistically is by adjusting each speaker's intercept to accommodate their 'idiosyncracy' (meaning, each speaker will have their own intercept) while still letting them 'share' a common slope of X. This is how this can be done using lme4::lmer (I am showing only the coefficients part of the output, but now you will finally see why I always included the intercept as a 1 in all model formulae so far):

```
summary(data1.model2 <- lmer(Y ~ 1 + X + (1|SPKR),
    data=x))$coefficients
##               Estimate Std. Error   t value
## (Intercept) 0.6560563 0.20098223  3.26425
## X           0.9537659 0.01695631 56.24843
# what are the adjustments to the intercept for each speaker?
ranef(data1.model2)$SPKR
##    (Intercept)
## S1  0.31671378
## S2  0.05557053
## S3 -0.37228431
```

Now (as you can check with coef(data1.model2)),
– there is an overall 'shared' intercept of 0.656, but now every speaker gets their own personal adjustment to that 'shared' intercept:
  – speaker 1's personal intercept is the overall shared one of 0.656 plus his adjustment of 0.317 for a total of 0.973;
  – speaker 2's personal intercept is the overall shared one of 0.656 plus his adjustment of 0.056 for a total of 0.712;
  – speaker 3's personal intercept is the overall shared one of 0.656 plus his adjustment of -0.372 for a total of 0.284;
– all speakers are still 'sharing' the same slope of 0.954.

(Note: the speaker-specific adjustments add up to 0: all.equal(sum(ranef(data1.model2)$SPKR), 0).) The residual plot of this MEM in the left panel of Figure 129 now looks much better (i.e. much less structured): in that plot, the diagnostic results for the linear model are shown again but backgrounded in grey, and the diagnostic results for the MEM are shown in black. Not only were the residuals of the former far from an unstructured null plot, we can now in the comparison also see how narrow the range of the predictions was there: the fitted/predicted values of the lm are squeezed around 1 with huge residuals, whereas the fitted/predicted values of the lmer are much more varied and with much smaller residuals and a well-behaved smoother hugging the $y=0$ line.

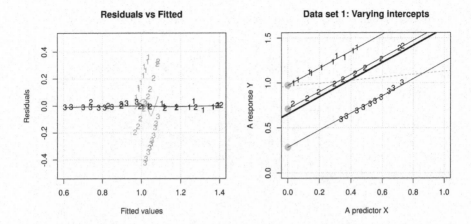

Figure 129: Residuals vs. fitted values and/of `lmer(Y~X+(1|SPKR))` (data set 1)

The right panel of Figure 129 shows why these results are so much better: There,
– the heavy solid line is the overall regression line of this model (resulting from the 'shared' intercept of 0.656 and the 'shared' slope of 0.954); note that this is the regression line you would use to predict a Y-value for a data point of X of the hitherto unseen speaker 4 that you found in the drier;
– the thin solid lines are the speaker-specific regression lines with different intercepts (as discussed above and as highlighted with the grey points at X=0) but the same slope (as can be seen from the lines being parallel); note that the line for speaker 1 is the regression line you would use to predict a Y-value for a new data point of X of speaker 1 that you found in your garbage disposal;
– the grey dashed line is the regression line from the inappropriate linear model above (just for comparison).

Recall also that the linear model had a terribly low R^2, the MEM's one is 0.9985 (this is a measure called $R^2_{conditional}$, which I will explain below). Also note that the slope of X in the linear model was small (0.1682) and not significantly different from 0, but the slope in the MEM is about six times as high (0.9538) and highly significantly different from 0 (for one, the absolute value of its t-value is greater than 2; I'll show later how to get a p-value for the slope, but let me already tell you the p-value would be $1.0795558 \times 10^{-28}$). In other words, taking into account how of data points produced by each speaker are related changed *everything*.

6.1.2 Varying slopes only

To look at a second kind of model, let's load a new data and immediately fit the linear model:

```
rm(list=ls(all.names=TRUE)); summary(x <- read.delim(file=
    "_inputfiles/06_vs.csv", stringsAsFactors=TRUE))
## [...]
summary(data2.model1 <- lm(Y ~ 1 + X, data=x)) ## [...]
##              Estimate Std. Error t value Pr(>|t|)
## (Intercept)  0.93510    0.04643  20.140  < 2e-16 ***
## X            0.40489    0.14504   2.792  0.00934 **  ## [...]
## Multiple R-squared:  0.2177, Adjusted R-squared:  0.1898
## F-statistic: 7.793 on 1 and 28 DF,  p-value: 0.009343
```

This time around, (i) the one predictor and, thus, the whole model is significant and (ii) the slope is 0.4049, i.e. for every 1-unit increase of X, Y increases by that amount. Again, however, the 30 data points were contributed by only three speakers so the data points are not independent. If we now look at the residual diagnostic plot in the left panel of Figure 130 on the next page and the data and its regression line in the right panel, there again is clearly 'some structure' remaining in the data.

The residual plot is 'not unstructured' again and in the right panel it is obvious that every speaker on their own exhibits what looks like a perfect correlation between Y and X but this time the speakers seem to share an overall intercept of around 0.8 while they have very different slopes. That we'll tell our MEM now to do (check the code for the explanation of the syntax):

```
summary(data2.model2 <- lmer(Y ~ 1 + X + (0+X|SPKR),
    data=x))$coefficients
##              Estimate  Std. Error     t value
## (Intercept) 0.7993878 0.006803557 117.495571
## X           1.5210556 0.874458880   1.739425
ranef(data2.model2)$SPKR
##          X
## S1  1.7195292
## S2 -0.5934691
## S3 -1.1260601
```

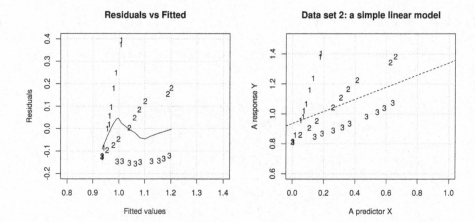

Figure 130: Residuals vs. fitted values and/of `lm(Y~X)` (data set 2)

Now (as you should verify with `coef(data2.model2)`),
– there is an overall 'shared' intercept of 0.799,
– there is an overall 'shared' slope of 1.521 but now every speaker gets their own specific adjustment to that 'shared' slope:
  – speaker 1's personal slope is the overall shared one of 1.521 plus his adjustment of 1.72 for an overall 3.241;
  – speaker 2's personal slope is the overall shared one of 1.521 plus his adjustment of -0.593 for an overall 0.928;
  – speaker 3's personal slope is the overall shared one of 1.521 plus his adjustment of -1.126 for an overall 0.395.

Again, this improves things quite a bit. The residuals plot is better – smaller residuals, more varied/realistic predictions – even if it's still not 'fully unstructured', but the improvement is especially obvious in the visual representation and the MEM's $R^2_{conditional}$ of 0.9988. However, note also that in the fixef model of this data set the slope of X was significantly different from 0 whereas in the MEM of this data set the slope of X is not (for one, the absolute values of its t-value is less than 2; again I'll show later how to compute this, but let me already tell you the p-value will be 0.2241). Thus, taking into account the fact that the set of data points produced by each speaker are related again changed pretty much everything.

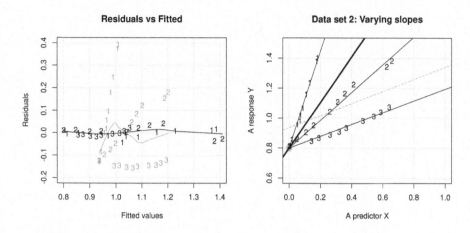

Figure 131: Residuals vs. fitted values and/of `lmer(Y~X+(0+X|SPKR))` (data set 2)

6.1.3 Varying intercepts and slopes

I am pretty sure you see where this is heading: Wouldn't it be something if there were models with varying intercepts and slopes ... Our final linear model:

```
rm(list=ls(all.names=TRUE)); library(lme4)
summary(x <- read.delim(file="_inputfiles/06_vis.csv",
   stringsAsFactors=TRUE))
##      CASE          X                Y              SPKR
## Min.   : 1.00  Min.   :0.006559  Min.   :-0.00692  S1:10
## 1st Qu.: 8.25  1st Qu.:0.312214  1st Qu.: 0.31551  S2:10
## Median :15.50  Median :0.564414  Median : 0.64572  S3:10
## Mean   :15.50  Mean   :0.625179  Mean   : 0.67326
## 3rd Qu.:22.75  3rd Qu.:0.897482  3rd Qu.: 1.00419
## Max.   :30.00  Max.   :1.511534  Max.   : 1.49708
summary(data3.model1 <- lm(Y ~ 1 + X, data=x)) ## [...]
##              Estimate Std. Error t value Pr(>|t|)
## (Intercept)   0.4524     0.1493   3.030  0.00521 **
## X             0.3533     0.2018   1.751  0.09095 .
## Multiple R-squared:  0.09866,   Adjusted R-squared:  0.06647
## F-statistic: 3.065 on 1 and 28 DF,  p-value: 0.09095
```

A weak effect of a single predictor that is not significant in a two-tailed test, but we encounter the by now familiar problems:

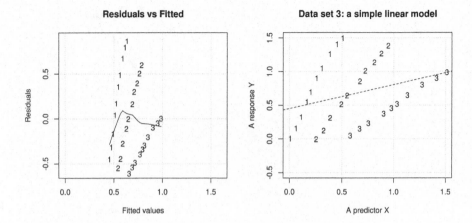

Figure 132: Residuals vs. fitted values and/of lm(Y~X) (data set 3)

6.1.3.1 Varying intercepts and slopes (correlated)

This time our MEM will allow both intercepts and slopes to vary for each subject. When we have both varying intercepts and varying slopes of a ranef for a predictor, there are two different ways to analyze the data. One of them involves modeling the intercept and slope adjustments of X for the speakers as correlated (which is what the syntax (1+X|SPKR) means; e.g. high adjustments to intercepts might be associated with high adjustments to intercepts):

```
summary(data3.model2 <- lmer(Y ~ 1 + X + (1+X|SPKR),
    data=x))$coefficients
##                  Estimate Std. Error    t value
## (Intercept) -0.3387724  0.1816883 -1.864580
## X            2.0491139  0.6024526  3.401286
ranef(data3.model2)$SPKR
##      (Intercept)           X
## S1    0.3555846  1.06981158
## S2   -0.1371513 -0.06275068
## S3   -0.2184333 -1.00706090
```

Now (as you should verify with coef(data3.model2)),
– there is an overall 'shared' intercept of -0.339, but now every speaker gets their own personal adjustment to that 'shared' intercept:
  – speaker 1's personal intercept is the overall shared one of -0.339 plus his adjustment of 0.356 for an overall 0.017;

- speaker 2's personal intercept is the overall shared one of -0.339 plus his adjustment of -0.137 for an overall -0.476;
- speaker 3's personal intercept is the overall shared one of -0.339 plus his adjustment of -0.218 for an overall -0.557;
- there is an overall 'shared' slope of 2.049 but now every speaker gets their own specific adjustment to that 'shared' slope:
  - speaker 1's personal slope is the overall shared one of 2.049 plus his adjustment of 1.07 for an overall 3.119;
  - speaker 2's personal slope is the overall shared one of 2.049 plus his adjustment of -0.063 for an overall 1.986;
  - speaker 3's personal slope is the overall shared one of 2.049 plus his adjustment of -1.007 for an overall 1.042.

As a result, the MEM's $R^2_{conditional}$ of 0.999 and the residuals plot has improved in all the usual ways. In the fixef model of this data set the slope of X was not significantly different from 0 – in the MEM of this data set, the slope of X isn't either (here, the t-value heuristic is failing; the (as usual two-tailed) p-value is 0.0767).

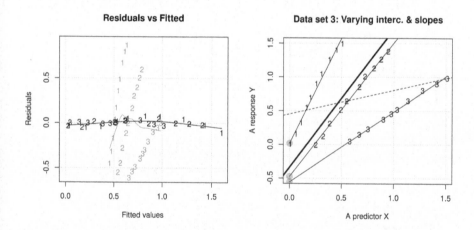

Figure 133: Residuals vs. fitted values and/of `lmer(Y~X+(1+X|SPKR))` (data set 3)

Thus, in this case, the MEM confirmed the lack of significance of the slope of X but the actual difference between the slopes is still massive: 0.3533 vs. 2.0491, not something one would want to just miss ...

6.1.3.2 Varying intercepts and slopes (uncorrelated)

The other way to model these data with both varying intercepts and varying slopes of a ranef for a predictor is to not assume a correlation between those intercept and slope adjustments (meaning, one sets that correlation to 0), which can be written in two ways:

– with a double vertical bar like this (1+X||SPKR);
– by separating out the intercept and slope like this: (1|SPKR) + (0+X|SPKR) (this is how a model with the double vertical bar notation will be shown in the non-abbreviated summary of such a model).

This next model is therefore a bit (one parameter) simpler than the previous one: we don't compute a correlation between intercept and slope adjustments:

```
summary(data3.model3 <- lmer(Y ~ 1 + X + (1+X||SPKR),
   data=x))$coefficients
##               Estimate Std. Error    t value
## (Intercept) -0.3371053  0.1812970  -1.859410
## X            2.0483584  0.6041711   3.390362
ranef(data3.model3)$SPKR
##      (Intercept)          X
## S1    0.3563624   1.06111566
## S2   -0.1545899  -0.03810088
## S3   -0.2017725  -1.02301478
```

Given the smallness of the data set and its artificially strong and homogeneous effects, the results can, for all practical intents and purposes at least, be considered virtually identical. The difference between the two models is just about not significant (p=0.056), meaning in a model selection or trimming-the-ranef-structure context, some might go with this latter model.

We see that, as per coef(data3.model3),
– there is an overall 'shared' intercept of -0.337, but now every speaker gets their own personal adjustment to that 'shared' intercept:
    – speaker 1's personal intercept is the overall shared one of -0.337 plus his adjustment of 0.356 for an overall 0.019;
    – speaker 2's personal intercept is the overall shared one of -0.337 plus his adjustment of -0.155 for an overall -0.492;
    – speaker 3's personal intercept is the overall shared one of -0.337 plus his adjustment of -0.202 for an overall -0.539;
– there is an overall 'shared' slope of 2.048 but now every speaker gets their own specific adjustment to that 'shared' slope:

- speaker 1's personal slope is the overall shared one of 2.048 plus his adjustment of 1.061 for an overall 3.109;
- speaker 2's personal slope is the overall shared one of 2.048 plus his adjustment of -0.038 for an overall 2.01;
- speaker 3's personal slope is the overall shared one of 2.048 plus his adjustment of -1.023 for an overall 1.025.

(I'm not showing the plots for this here in the book, given how similar they are to Figure 133.) Even in this small set of made-up examples, at least two of the advantages of MEM should be apparent: First, and trivially, one avoids violating the independence-of-data-points assumption of fixef modeling. Second, since the MEM addresses the dependence of the data points (and, thus, speaker- or stimulus-specific idiosyncrasies, for instance), the models are just doing so much better: their residuals are less structured, their predictions are much more varied and in line with the observed values, and, therefore, their fixef results (which are usually used to interpret the model and which one would use to predict unseen cases) will be more robust and likely generalize better. But there's more and I'm mentioning just a few: Third, MEM can in fact address multiple such sources of interdependence of data points at the same time, yet still avoids the information loss coming with, say, averaging across speakers or stimuli/items or the loss of power that comes with more traditional $F_1/F_2/minF$ approaches. Fourth, MEM handles missing data in much better ways than traditional repeated-measures ANOVA would, and fifth, allows for the inclusion of numeric predictors in the first place; a sixth advantage will be discussed below.

As always, there's no free lunch: These huge advantages come with huge costs in the sense of complexity that can quickly feel overwhelming; in fact, Bolker et al. (2009:127) explicitly state that "GLMMs are surprisingly challenging to use even for statisticians." Thus and without trying to be elitist or discouraging, successful MEM presupposes (in the strictest sense of the word) a thorough understanding of the central aspects of fixed-effects regression modeling: model formulation, selection, diagnostics, validation, and interpretation. I have taught dozens of workshops/bootcamps on regression modeling and MEM and participants that struggle most are always those who cannot take a results table of a fixed-effects regression with minimally two categorical and numeric predictors and at least one interaction term and explain what each coefficient/estimate means and/or compute a prediction for an unseen data point without using R's predict function. How is one supposed to understand adjustments to intercepts and slopes from, say, two separate crossed random effects, if one hasn't yet understood what the values mean that are being adjusted, which is exactly why I tortured you to no end with the meanings of intercepts and coefficients (for dif-

408 —— Mixed-effects regression modeling

ferences between means and slopes) in Chapter 5. You may have hated it then, but I hope it's slowly becoming clear why I did this ...

6.2 Some general MEM considerations

> Successful modeling of a complex data set is part science, part statistical methods, and part experience and common sense. (Hosmer, Lemeshow, & Sturdivant 2013:89)

Some of the above discussion of MEM – especially the third/fourth kinds of model with varying intercepts and slopes – might have reminded you of something we discussed on the basis of Figure 2 at the beginning of the book, namely the notions of Simpson's paradox and interactions.

The nature of that data set – FF being the site where the YY- and XX-values were collected, which is quite similar to SPKR being the person for whom YY and XX were collected – and even just the plot per se make this comparable to the MEM in which, if you look at the plot, each level of FF has a different intercept and a different slope. Thus, on a much simplified and coarse level at least, what the two models are really doing is comparable (even though there *are* also important differences!):

– the linear model of lm(YY~XX*FF) uses the fixef main effect of FF to let every level of FF have a different intercept and it uses the fixef interaction XX:FF to let XX's slope be different for every level of FF;
– the MEM of lmer(YY~XX+(1+XX|FF)) uses the fixef main effect of XX as an overall slope and then uses the ranef structure – the intercept adjustments in ranef(mixef.model)$FF[,1] and the slope adjustments in ranef(mixef.-model)$FF[,2] to let every level of FF have a different intercept and slope.

Both models' results for this data set (!) are indeed similar, but *not* identical. If the two are so similar (here at least– of course it won't always be like that), how do you decide when to use which – when do you use a fixef model with interactions and when an MEM with intercept and/or slope adjustments? One question this relates to is whether FF is, or should be treated as, a fixed effect or a random effect, and even that question isn't as straightforward as it seems.

As one of the probably most widely-cited sources, Gelman & Hill (2006:245-246) provide a good overview of different definitional approaches (and see Crawley 2013:523 for a different list). I don't always see people explain why they considered something a ranef rather than a fixef or vice versa, but what I do see most often in linguistic studies seems to be based on the following logic.

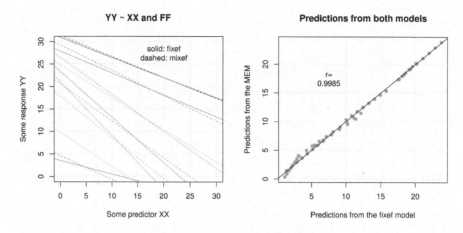

Figure 134: Comparing fixef and mixef results for XX, YY, and FF

Authors treat variables like SPEAKER and SENTENCE/STIMULUS as ranefs if
– the levels of that variable in the sample do not exhaust the levels that variable
  would have in the population: If you do a judgment experiment on contemporary American English with some stimulus sentences, then the 40 speakers
  you have participate are not the whole population, and the 20 stimulus sentences you have the speakers rate do not exhaust all possible sentences you
  could present to subjects.
– the real interest is not so much in what exactly these particular speakers and
  sentences/stimuli do but in generalizing from them to the population while
  'just' controlling for speakers' and stimuli's idiosyncrasies.

Of course, one point that gets in the way of maybe both criteria is that the levels
of the factors that are declared ranefs *should*, but usually *do not*, result from a
random/representative sample of the population but from the convenience sample that is the subject pool of our university (see Henrich, Heine, & Norenzayan
(2010) for an even more comprehensive critique). Gelman & Hill (2006:246)
claim that "[t]hese two recommendations (and others) can be unhelpful" – I am
not disputing that assessment but the two criteria certainly seem to underlie
most of the work I see in linguistics and other fields (such as ecology or psychology; for an example of the latter, see the excellent overview article by Brauer &
Curtin 2018:392).

However, the decision between different models – a fixef model with interactions and when an MEM with intercept and/or slope adjustments – also has
other important implications. While, like here, the results can be similar, they
are also conceptually different: The MEM does something that a 'fixed-effects-

only' model does not do, namely employs something called **shrinkage**, which amounts to reducing estimates for levels of random effects like, here, SPEAKER, in a way that reflects the number of observations available for them and their variance or, as Baayen (2008:277) puts it, "[considers] the behavior of any given subject in the light of what it knows about the behavior of all the other subjects". The computation of a linear model's coefficient for a speaker A would be (i) considered unconnected from those of the other speakers and (ii) not be 'filtered' or adjusted in any way even if there were only few observations for A. In an MEM, however, (i) a speaker's adjustments are connected to those of the other speakers (because they are assumed to come from, by default at least, a normal distribution) and (ii) potentially extreme adjustments from speakers with few data points get shrunk towards the overall intercept or slope, which makes the results more robust. Bell et al. (2019:1061 formulate this nicely concisely: "[i]n practice, the random intercepts in [MEMs] will correlate strongly with the fixed effects in a 'dummy variable' [fixef] models [which is what we saw above, STG], but [ranef] estimates will be drawn in or 'shrunk' towards their mean – with unreliably estimated and more extreme values shrunk the most."

Recommendation(s) for further study: Check out
- Bell et al. (2019:1061 for nice discussion, esp. in Section 3;
- Gelman & Hill (2006: Sections 12.1-12.5) for discussion of how MEM's way of 'partial pooling' differs from the complete-pooling of a single fixed-effects model on all data or the no pooling of separate fixed-effects models for each level of a random effect.

Other, related questions that come up a lot in this connection are (i) how many number of levels a ranef should minimally have and (ii) how many observations each level of a ranef should minimally have. As usual, you will find different recommendations in different sources. Gelman & Hill (2006:275) state there are essentially no such lower limits, pointing out that "[mixed-effects/multi-level modeling] should still work at least as well as classical regression" since mixed-effects modeling or "[m]ultilevel modeling includes classical regression as a limiting case".

On the other hand, Bolker (2013) shows in simulations that small numbers of ranef levels can lead to convergence problems and Bolker et al. (2009a:132) argue that the significance test I see most scholars using – the likelihood ratio test (*LR*-test) conducted by anova or drop1 – is "only adequate for testing fixed effects when both the ratio of the total sample size to the number of fixed-effect levels being tested and the number of random-effect levels (blocks) are large". Similarly, Meteyard & Davies (2020) state that "increasing numbers of sampling units is the best way to improve power (this held for the accuracy of estimating fixed effect coefficients, random effect variances and cross-level interactions). For psychological research, this means 30-50 participants, and 30-50 items or trials for each of those participants completing each condition". Meteyard & Davies (2020) also cite Brysbaert & Stevens (2018), who, assuming typical effect sizes of 0.3-0.4 *sd*s, recommend a minimum of 40 participants and 40 items; see Brauer & Curtin (2018:399) for more discussion and additional references. Given the fact that ranef selection is in part informed by the size of their variance, greater numbers of levels per ranef and greater numbers of data points per level are likely to lead to more robust results/stable (see the blog entry at https://www.muscardinus.be/2018/09/number-random-effect-levels/ for a nice exploration of this issue) and fewer convergence problems of the algorithms during model fitting (see also Maas & Hox 2005 or Austin & Leckie 2018 for discussion); some of those things we'll revisit in our applications below.

By the way, Gelman & Hill's statement that the "limiting case" of MEM is "classical regression" – Brauer & Curtin (2018:393) make a similar point: "A [generalized linear model] is a [linear MEM] without random effects" – is something we can actually easily verify by showing that the simplest repeated-measures/dependent-samples kind of test we discussed above – a *t*-test for dependent samples – essentially is a very simple linear MEM. If we reload the saccades data from Section 4.3.2.4 and compare the result of our *t*-test for dependent samples there (t.test(SACCADES~TASK, paired=TRUE)) with the corresponding MEM (lmer(SACCADES~TASK+(1|SUBJECT))), you can see how everything's the same (with the exception of two signs and you know those usually just differ because of differences in direction of subtraction):

Table 35: A *t*-test for dependent samples vs. a simple MEM

	Mean / Coef	*se*	*df*	*t*	*p*
t.test	-534.2188	480.7343	31	-1.1113	0.2750
lmer	534.2188	480.7343	31	1.1113	0.2750

By the way, can you imagine a way to do a *t*-test for dependent samples with lm – not lmer? It's admittedly not important per se, but it would indicate that you are really internalizing what the coefficients in the summary of an lm are …

THINK BREAK

```
sacc.diffs <- x$SACCADES[x$TASK=="direct"] -
              x$SACCADES[x$TASK=="inverse"]
summary(lm(sacc.diffs ~ 1))$coefficients
##             Estimate Std. Error   t value Pr(>|t|)
## (Intercept) -534.2187   480.7343 -1.111256 0.275003
```

Why does this work, you ask? It works because in the lm output the p-values of the coefficients table test whether the estimate could be 0. And if you fit a null model (remember, that's a model without any predictors but just with an overall intercept), then in a linear model that intercept becomes the overall mean (here of the differences) and so the p-value will test how likely that mean – the mean of the pairwise saccade differences – is to be 0, i.e. exactly what the t-test output told you explicitly what it would be testing: "alternative hypothesis: true difference in means is not equal to 0".

Back the MEMS: how will we proceed? We now have two kinds of effect structures to deal with, fixefs and ranefs, so we need to define each of them in some way and, maybe, grow each or trim each of them down or at least evaluate them in some way – but how, and in what order?

With regard to the fixefs, there's good news, sort of. Most of the above from Section 5.5 applies to MEM as well: Ideally, (the fixef part of) our model should come close to embodying our main hypotheses/questions of interest as possible just as before; at least that's my recommendation (and this is how I understand Bolker et al.'s (2009a:133, Box 4) and their supplementary material). However, another recommendation is that of Zuur et al. (2009:121), who attribute to Diggle et al. (2002) the suggestion to

> [s]tart with a model where the fixed component contains all explanatory variables and as many interactions as possible. This is called the *beyond optimal model*. If this is impractical, e.g. due to a large number of explanatory variables, interactions, or numerical problems, use a selection of explanatory variables that you think are most likely to contribute to the optimal model.

(See Crawley 2013:390-391 for similar advice on starting with a maximal model.) Given my discussion above, these days I would lean more towards less complex initial models, but, given all the conflicting recommendations regarding model selection we have seen by now, this is one decision we'll have to make for our fixefs (and note that Zuur et al.'s as well as Crawley's advice do leave room for researchers' domain knowledge or otherwise informed decisions).

With regard to ranefs, the story is more complicated and not only because of the above uncertainty with regard to what a ranef is to begin with – I'll assume we have answered that to our satisfaction. The question then becomes how complex a ranef structure to use. I think it's fair to say that for some time people just used varying intercepts, that was it. Then, in an influential paper, Barr et al. (2013) argued in favor of fitting maximal ranef structures, i.e. varying intercepts and slopes for all predictors of interest, which, once one thinks about it, makes a lot of sense: We want the fixef slope we're interested in to be 'clean' in the sense of 'not being tainted/skewed by speakers' or stimuli's idiosyncrasies', which would be taken care of by adjustments, leaving the overall slope nice and squeaky clean of such effects. Nevertheless, this 'policy' often leads to extremely complex ranef structures, which in turn often leads to model convergence issues and other problems. Follow-up discussion by Matuschek et al. (2017) and Bates et al. (2018) argued that it is acceptable or even better to be more parsimonious in one's ranef structures. The former show that "higher power is achieved without inflating Type I error rate if a model selection criterion is used to select a random effect structure that is supported by the data" (p. 305) and the latter discuss a series of steps of identifying the best ranef structure that informed the exposition below. We'll therefore begin our modeling with the maximal ranef structure that has varying intercepts and slopes for the predictors of interest, but we'll already be open to the necessity of simplifying it to make things work.

And in what order do we proceed? We'll follow Zuur et al. (2009: Section 5.7): After formulating our initial model's fixef and ranef structure as just discussed, we will, first, try to find the best ranef structure for the model – typically *best* means 'the most comprehensive one that doesn't cause numerical problems', and then we will try to find the best fixef structure for the model, where *best* means 'best explanatory power (relative to Occam's razor of course) without causing numerical problems'. There is one additional complication, but it's slight, we just need to remember it (and Zuur et al (2009: Section 5.6) discuss this in more detail than you ever wanted to know about): For linear MEM, i.e. MEMs with numeric response variables, you need to
– use something called **REML-estimation** as you work on the ranef structure;
– use something called **ML-estimation** as you work on the fixef structure;
– re-fit the final model again with REML-estimation.

The good news are that (i) REML-estimation is lmer's default so you really only need to worry about this one time when you switch to ML for the fixef exploration and another time at the end, and (ii) you do not need to worry about this for generalized linear MEMs (e.g. a binary logistic regression with ranefs).

Recommendation(s) for further study: I really strongly recommend that, once you're completely done with this chapter here, you read the references I've relied on so much for here, I recommend this order: Zuur et al (2009: Chapter 5) (maybe go easy on some technical sections first, depending on your experience), then Bolker et al. (2009a) (especially boxes 3 and 4 are super-useful), then Bates et al. (2018), then Matuschek et al. (2017). I know this sounds like a lot, but if you want to use a highly technical method, you need to invest a bit of time into that. There's a reason why, in many other disciplines, there's year-long stats sequences and separate follow-up courses for other statistical methods; these references are all very useful, you won't regret it.

Ok, let's get started ...

6.3 Linear MEM case study

> We emphasize that we do not claim that our illustrations are the only way to carry out these analyses, but the strategy outlined above has yielded satisfactory results. (Bates et al. 2018:5)

We're now going to work through one case study of a linear MEM. This case study will revisit the word duration data from the thought experiment in Section 5.8 above, but now with some additional information, namely for each data point which of altogether 20 speakers produced it and in which conversation. You've already thought about this data set above so I won't present the variables etc. again:

```
rm(list=ls(all.names=TRUE)); library(car); library(effects);
    library(lme4); library(MuMIn)
summary(x <- read.delim(file="_inputfiles/06_durations.csv",
    stringsAsFactors=TRUE))
```

(Note: in the interest of space, I will not show many of the plots in the book, but since you're running the code as you're reading this, you can see them in R.)

6.3.1 Preparation and exploration

As I've tried to make abundantly, tiringly, clear, we need to do some exploration first to get to know the data and prepare them for modeling. We begin with the response. As you can see, its distribution is fairly skewed with a long right tail, but a log transformation makes it look much better so we go with that; since that transformation is easy to reverse, we again just overwrite the DURATION column:

```
par(mfrow=c(1, 2))
hist(x$DURATION, main="")
hist(log2(x$DURATION), main="")
par(mfrow=c(1, 1)) ## [...]
x$DURATION <- log2(x$DURATION)
```

The main predictor of interest POSINTURN should be pretty evenly distributed: If we look at 10-word turns, then, with the exception of measurement problems, all word positions in turns should be about equally frequent, and they are (and thanks, but no thanks, I don't need a plot for this):

```
table(x$POSINTURN)
##   1   2   3   4   5   6   7   8   9  10
## 631 632 629 639 635 658 628 633 640 658
```

What about the source of ranef variation, speakers in conversations: Are there speakers for whom we have only very few data? No, this is looking pretty good.

```
table(x$SPEAKER)
## [...]
table(x$CONV)
## C01 C02 C03 C04 C05 C06 C07 C08 C09 C10
## 427 354 531 737 831 800 772 873 557 501
```

Just for the fun of it, let's realize my above suggestion to give every row a unique reverse-Netflix identifier stating the number of the observation for each conversation (C) and speaker (S); check out the code for how it's done, esp. for how we can determine these numbers from the data; here's part of the result:

```
x[1:3, 1:3] # part of the first 3 rows
##            CASE DURATION POSINTURN
## C01S01001     1 6.714246         2
## C01S01002     2 6.475733         3
## C01S01003     3 6.285402         4
x[6381:6383, 1:3] # part of the last 3 rows
##            CASE DURATION POSINTURN
## C10S19323 6381 7.169925         5
## C10S19324 6382 8.611025         6
## C10S19325 6383 8.071462         9
```

What about the other fairly central variable, whose interaction with POSINTURN we want to check?

```
table(x$CLASS)                          # table of frequencies
##   closed   number     open propname  unclear
##     4021      125     2086      110       41
round(prop.table(table(x$CLASS)), 4) # rounded table of proportions
##   closed   number     open propname  unclear
##   0.6300   0.0196   0.3268   0.0172   0.0064
```

This distribution is very uneven and 3 of the 5 levels are quite rare; it's unlikely we will get robust estimates for those. Given that these 3 rare levels only make up about 4.3% of the data, we will discard them. This will make modeling much easier at the cost of only a small proportion of the data, and we would probably not have wanted to generalize too much from those few data points anyway.[18]

```
x <- droplevels(x[x$CLASS %in% c("closed", "open"),])
table(x$CLASS)      # check the result
## closed    open
##   4021    2086
```

Now, what about the controls? Let's begin with LENGTH. Like DURATION, it has a long right tail, and, like DURATION, logging makes this look better. However, on top of the logging, we now also z-standardize the variable to make it have a mean of 0 and a value range around the mean of 0 (which, when other variables are transformed the same way, is often useful in how it reduces modeling problems later; see Brauer & Curtin 2018:404). The third plot just serves for us to see how the original variable (on the x-axis) and the new one we will use for modeling (on the y-axis) are related, i.e. how (much) the transformations have altered the distributional shape of this predictor.

```
par(mfrow=c(1, 3))
hist(x$LENGTH, main="")
hist(log2(x$LENGTH), main="")
x$LENGTH.log.sc <- as.numeric(scale(log2(x$LENGTH)))
plot(jitter(x$LENGTH), jitter(x$LENGTH.log.sc), pch=16,
   col="#00000030"); grid()
par(mfrow=c(1, 1)) ## [...]
```

SURPRISAL is next: The original distribution isn't even that bad, logging doesn't improve it much, but taking the square root makes it look really nice. (But remember, we're not requiring normality in the predictors, just the residuals.) Thus, we go with the square root, z-standardize, and plot to see how the new variable relates to the old one.

---

18 Alternative ways to proceed are sometimes possible: One could conflate the rarer levels into a new category (which might be called *other*); this might be useful if that conflation into a new level also makes at least some conceptual sense and if the frequency of that new level is then decent. Sometimes, it might also be possible (in the sense of 'making at least some conceptual sense') to conflate the rarer levels with one of the existing levels. These kinds of decisions obviously require domain knowledge, not just statistical considerations.

```
## [...]
x$SURPRISAL.sq.sc <- as.numeric(scale(sqrt(x$SURPRISAL))) ## [...]
```

Finally, let's check out FREQ: If we try logging, it doesn't help much, neither does taking the root, so maybe this is a good opportunity to try a power transformation (remember the recommendation for further study in Section 5.2.1?). As recommended above, we use car::powerTransform to get the parameters gamma and lambda that transform FREQ 'best' and use car::bcnPower to transform FREQ with these parameters; as usual, we z-standardize and plot. (If one doesn't z-standardize, the transformation results in values between 0 and 3000, which would later cause modeling problems in the form of the warning "Some predictor variables are on very different scales: consider rescaling" so this is how we avoid this early on, see Simoiu & Savage 2016 for discussion/exemplification).)

```
(bcn.parameters <- car::powerTransform(x$FREQ ~ 1,family="bcnPower"))
## Estimated transformation power, lambda
## [1] 2.999954
## Estimated location, gamma
## [1] 13.46412
hist(x$FREQ.bcn.sc <- as.numeric(scale(bcnPower(x$FREQ,
    lambda=bcn.parameters[[1]], gamma=bcn.parameters[[2]]))),
    main="", xlab="Power transform")
```

For lack of space, I will not do a comprehensive pairwise exploration of all variables, but it is something you would do; minimally (!), you'd run something like this (results not shown here). The pairs plot will show what you might already have expected, namely that there are quote noticeable intercorrelations here, maybe we will run into collinearity.

```
pairs(x[,c(2:3, 6:8, 12:14)], panel=panel.smooth, pch=16,
    col="#00000030")
sapply(x[,c(3, 6:8, 12:14)], function (af) {
    plot(x$DURATION ~ jitter(as.numeric(af)), pch=16, col="#00000020")
    lines(lowess(x$DURATION ~ as.numeric(af))) })
```

Ok, let's start with some modeling.

6.3.2 Model fitting/selection

Given the nature of the question, let's assume we make this our first model:
- for the fixef structure,
  - POSINTURN is our main predictor and, as per the above explanation, we have to include its interaction with CLASS;
  - all other controls are entered just as main effects;
- for the ranef structure,
  - we follow Matuschek et al.'s (2017) and Bates et al.'s (2018) follow-up of Barr et al. (2013) and include a maximal ranef structure involving varying intercepts and slopes for our main predictors of interest;
  - we include in our ranef structure the information that the speakers are nested into the conversations:

```
summary(m.01 <- lmer(DURATION ~ 1 + POSINTURN + POSINTURN:CLASS +
    CLASS + SEX + VOWELS + LENGTH.log.sc + SURPRISAL.sq.sc +
    FREQ.bcn.sc + (1 + POSINTURN*CLASS | CONV/SPEAKER),
    data=x, REML=TRUE), correlation=FALSE) ## [...]
## [I abbreviate SPEAKER as SPK in the ranef table to make it fit.]
## REML criterion at convergence: 11584.9
## Scaled residuals:
##     Min      1Q  Median      3Q     Max
## -4.3190 -0.6185  0.0164  0.6239  4.7416
## Random effects:
##  Groups      Name                   Variance  Std.Dev. Corr
##  SPK:CONV    (Intercept)            0.000e+00 0.000000
##              POSINTURN              8.414e-05 0.009173  NaN
##              CLASSopen              8.689e-04 0.029478  NaN   1.00
##              POSINTURN:CLASSopen    1.018e-04 0.010092  NaN  -1.00 -1.00
##  CONV        (Intercept)            1.551e-03 0.039383
##              POSINTURN              3.395e-05 0.005827 -1.00
##              CLASSopen              5.844e-05 0.007645  0.91 -0.87
##              POSINTURN:CLASSopen    6.842e-06 0.002616  1.00 -0.99  0.92
##  Residual                          3.851e-01 0.620604
## Number of obs: 6107, groups:  SPEAKER:CONV, 20; CONV, 10
##
## Fixed effects:
##              Estimate Std. Error t value
## (Intercept)  7.204175   0.027986 257.423
## POSINTURN    0.014855   0.004475   3.319
```

```
## CLASSopen              0.082138   0.042917   1.914
## SEXmale               -0.039599   0.021755  -1.820
## VOWELStwo+            -0.127659   0.018975  -6.728
## LENGTH.log.sc          0.288819   0.011142  25.922
## SURPRISAL.sq.sc        0.143540   0.010434  13.757
## FREQ.bcn.sc           -0.147523   0.013567 -10.874
## POSINTURN:CLASSopen    0.033546   0.006508   5.155
## optimizer (nloptwrap) convergence code: 0 (OK)
## boundary (singular) fit: see ?isSingular
```

A lot to unpack – this is different from all outputs we've seen so far. As with linear models, we start at the bottom, where we can see what may well become one of the most frequent MEM output lines you will see: convergence: 0 and a short cryptic added note. Non-convergence means that the algorithm didn't arrive a final, numerically satisfactory result ("the numerical optimization algorithm cannot reliably determine the maximum of the log-likelihood function", Brauer & Curtin 2018:403), which means the results might not be trustworthy. Common reasons for non-convergence are lack of data (in general or in certain 'pockets' of the data and models that are too complex on the fixef and/or ranef side of things; I'll return to this in Section 6.5. Above that, we find a fixef table that looks similar to what we've seen from lm or glm, but no *p*-values again; however, as per our current heuristic, most *t*-values have an absolute value >2 so there seem to be significant predictors including our interaction of interest.

Above that, there's a ranef table that shows for all our ranefs – SPEAKER:CONV being the speakers nested into the conversations, CONV being just the conversations – a variance and a standard deviation and a correlation score indicating how highly the ranefs are intercorrelated; high correlations often mean that ranef structures can be simplified, as we will explore in a moment. We also get to see the number of data points and the number of "groups", which is the number of levels of each of our ranefs: 20 levels of SPEAKER, 10 levels of CONV.

Finally, above that we get a brief overview of the scaled residuals and it's good to see that those look good: a median close to 0 and fairly symmetric 1st/3rd quartiles and minimum/maximum values; the REML criterion, we'll ignore.

So, we have a convergence warning and some pretty high correlations between the ranefs, a relatively good indication that the ranef structure is more complex than it should or needs to be. This assessment is supported by running a principal components analysis on the ranefs like this (to see how much we will likely be able to reduce the ranef structure).

```
rePCA(m.01) ## [...]
```

The console contains results for each ranef part, and the first line of each of those two outputs, the standard deviations, suggest that we might get away with having only one ranef component (because the first standard deviation and, hence, the first variance, makes up so much of the variability in the ranefs). We could therefore simplify the ranef structure in pretty much the same way we'd do this in any other model, namely by removing what seems to do least while at the same time respecting the principle of marginality (see above Section 5.2.5.1); in this case that might mean removing the interaction term in the ranef structure, simplifying POSINTURN*CLASS to POSINTURN+CLASS. Another possibility would be to consider the question of whether, if we already include SPEAKER as a ranef, also including CONV is worth the considerable amount of complexity it adds to the model, especially since we only have two speakers per conversation in the first place. Since addressing the latter question would reduce the complexity of the ranef structure so much, we begin with that option (using update) and then immediately do a model comparison (using anova) to see whether simplifying the ranef structure led to a significantly worse model:

```
summary(m.02 <- update(m.01, .~. - (1 + POSINTURN*CLASS | CONV/
   SPEAKER) + (1 + POSINTURN*CLASS | SPEAKER)), correlation=FALSE)
## [...]
## optimizer (nloptwrap) convergence code: 0 (OK)
## boundary (singular) fit: see ?isSingular
anova(m.01, m.02, test="Chisq", refit=FALSE)
## Models:
## m.02: DURATION ~ POSINTURN + CLASS + SEX + VOWELS +
## m.02: LENGTH.log.sc + SURPRISAL.sq.sc + FREQ.bcn.sc +
## m.02: (1 + POSINTURN * CLASS | SPEAKER) + POSINTURN:CLASS
## m.01: DURATION ~ 1 + POSINTURN + POSINTURN:CLASS + CLASS + SEX +
## m.01: VOWELS + LENGTH.log.sc + SURPRISAL.sq.sc + FREQ.bcn.sc +
## m.01: (1 + POSINTURN * CLASS | CONV/SPEAKER)
##        npar   AIC   BIC  logLik deviance Chisq Df Pr(>Chisq)
## m.02    20 11622 11756 -5790.9    11582
## m.01    30 11645 11846 -5792.5    11585     0 10          1
```

This is looking better: while we still have the same convergence warning, removing CONV had hardly any effect: the *LR*-test leads to such a high *p*-value that R rounds up to 1. That means, we can now try the other option already entertained above, removing the interaction term in the ranef structure:

```
summary(m.03 <- update(m.02, .~. - (1 + POSINTURN*CLASS | SPEAKER)
  + (1 + POSINTURN+CLASS | SPEAKER)), correlation=FALSE) ## [...]
## optimizer (nloptwrap) convergence code: 0 (OK)
## Model failed to converge with max|grad| = 0.0323719 (tol = 0.002,
## component 1)
anova(m.02, m.03, test="Chisq", refit=FALSE) ## [...]
##       npar   AIC   BIC  logLik deviance Chisq Df Pr(>Chisq)
## m.03    16 11614 11722 -5791.1    11582
## m.02    20 11622 11756 -5790.9    11582 0.412  4     0.9815
```

Removing that interaction term did certainly not make a significant difference, but also didn't help with convergence: now a new warning showed up. That convergence warning value of 0.0323719 is ideally below the threshold value of 0.002 mentioned there. What part of the ranef structure do we remove next? The one with the smallest variance/standard deviation:

```
summary(m.04 <- update(m.03, .~. - (1 + POSINTURN+CLASS | SPEAKER)
  + (1 +             CLASS | SPEAKER)), correlation=FALSE) ## [...]
## optimizer (nloptwrap) convergence code: 0 (OK)
## boundary (singular) fit: see ?isSingular
anova(m.03, m.04, test="Chisq", refit=FALSE) ## [...]
##       npar   AIC   BIC  logLik deviance  Chisq Df Pr(>Chisq)
## m.04    13 11609 11696 -5791.4    11583
## m.03    16 11614 11722 -5791.1    11582 0.6848  3     0.8768
```

Same as before: the deletion was fine, but we still have convergence problems. We continue, the next smallest variance is the one for CLASS|SPEAKER:

```
summary(m.05 <- update(m.04, .~. - (1 + CLASS | SPEAKER)
  + (1         | SPEAKER)), correlation=FALSE) ## [...]
anova(m.04, m.05, test="Chisq", refit=FALSE)  ## [...]
##       npar   AIC   BIC  logLik deviance  Chisq Df Pr(>Chisq)
## m.05    11 11607 11681 -5792.4    11585
## m.04    13 11609 11696 -5791.4    11583 1.9448  2     0.3782
```

Now we're talking: again no significant difference and now, with only one ranef component left (the intercepts for SPEAKER), we have no convergence problems anymore – just like rePCA made us hope for. That means we can now turn to the fixef structure, for which we first re-fit the model with ML.

```
summary(m.05 <- update(m.05, .~., REML=FALSE), correlation=FALSE)
## [...]
```

We also look at collinearity – now that we turn to the fixefs – and the *VIF*s are
better than we might have feared, all are <10 at least:

```
sort(round(vif(m.05), 2))
##                SEX           VOWELS        POSINTURN
##               1.00             1.40             1.57
## SURPRISAL.sq.sc    LENGTH.log.sc     FREQ.bcn.sc
##               1.72             1.96             2.91
## POSINTURN:CLASS          CLASS
##               6.27             6.36
```

Finally, we use drop1: can we drop any variables from the model?

```
drop1.m.05 <- drop1(m.05, test="Chisq")
drop1.m.05[order(drop1.m.05[,"Pr(Chi)"]),] ## [...]
##                   npar    AIC     LRT    Pr(Chi)
## LENGTH.log.sc        1  12177  636.83  < 2.2e-16 ***
## SURPRISAL.sq.sc      1  11726  186.26  < 2.2e-16 ***
## FREQ.bcn.sc          1  11658  118.04  < 2.2e-16 ***
## VOWELS               1  11586   45.52  1.511e-11 ***
## POSINTURN:CLASS      1  11571   30.73  2.960e-08 ***
## SEX                  1  11541    1.00     0.3161
## <none>                  11542
```

The predictor SEX can go, meaning the word durations don't differ between
female and male speakers. So, next round:

```
summary(m.06 <- update(m.05, .~. - SEX), correlation=FALSE) ## […]
anova(m.05, m.06, test="Chisq") ## […]
sort(round(vif(m.06), 2)) ## […]
drop1.m.06 <- drop1(m.06, test="Chisq")
drop1.m.06[order(drop1.m.06[,"Pr(Chi)"]),] ## [...]
##                   npar    AIC     LRT    Pr(Chi)
## LENGTH.log.sc        1  12176  637.19  < 2.2e-16 ***
## SURPRISAL.sq.sc      1  11725  186.01  < 2.2e-16 ***
## FREQ.bcn.sc          1  11657  117.83  < 2.2e-16 ***
## VOWELS               1  11585   45.68  1.391e-11 ***
```

```
## POSINTURN:CLASS      1 11570   30.71 3.004e-08 ***
## <none>                 11541
```

And it seems we're done: no convergence problems, no collinearity, all remaining predictors significant. So, following Zuur et al. (2009), we re-fit what seems to be the final model with REML again and move on to some model diagnostics.

```
summary(m.06 <- update(m.06, .~., REML=TRUE), correlation=FALSE)
```

6.3.3 Quick excursus on update

In this section, you saw the first more comprehensive uses of update, which I want to briefly comment on. I think this function is really important in how it helps make code interpretable esp. when you return to code file after a longer period of time – like when you send off your paper/revision somewhere and have the pleasure of waiting 7? 11? months for the reviews ...). This is because update automatically focuses your attention on what the difference is between two models and makes recovering these differences very much easier for your future self. I once saw a discussion (the following is 'altered for anonymization') of model comparisons using two models model1 and model2 that were defined exactly like this:

```
model1 <- glmer(primedconstruction ~ predictor1 + predictor2 + pre-
dictor3 + (1 + predictor1 + predictor2||item) + (1 + predictor1 +
predictor2 + predictor3||subj), data=somestuff, family=binomial,
control=glmerControl(optimizer="Nelder_Mead"))
model2 <- glmer(primedconstruction ~ predictor1 + predictor2 + (1 +
predictor1 + predictor2|| item) + (1 + predictor2 + predictor1 ||
subj), data=somestuff, family=binomial, control=glmerControl(
optimizer="Nelder_Mead"))
```

With all due respect, but this is just torture. No one who hasn't looked at this script for 7 months (but worked on 12 other analysis scripts in the meantime) will look at this and immediately recover how model2 differs from model1. I know it's not cool but anal, OCD, and whatever else to want to pay as much attention to this kind of stuff and formatting issues as I'm doing here, but is there really anybody out there who doesn't think that the following way of defining model2 is more easily interpretable than the above (esp. with the comments/spacing)?

```
model2 <- update(model1, .~., # make model2 the update of model1:
  - predictor3,                # remove predictor3 from fixefs
  - (1+predictor1+predictor2+predictor3|subj)  # remove ranef str
  + (1+predictor1+predictor2          |subj)) # reinsert w/out p3
```

I rest my case.

6.3.4 Model diagnostics

Let's first look at the residuals of the model (I'm only showing the first plot):

```
hist(residuals(m.06), main="") ## [...]
plot(m.06, col="#00000020", type=c("p", "smooth"), pch=16, id=0.001)
```

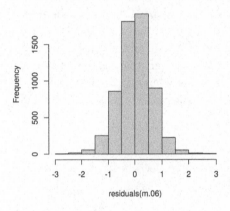

Figure 135: Residuals of m.06

(If we had added idLabels=rownames(x) to the above plotting call, we would have gotten the more specific row names we created as point labels, see ?plot.merMod for more details) The histogram looks great, the residuals-vs.-fitted plot is perhaps a bit tricky: There seems to be a slight non-constant variance problem: The vertical spread of the points is wider on the left than on the right.

Let's look in more detail by plotting the residuals against the predictors: We start with CLASS and VOWELS and those are pretty good: The vast majority of the points seem to be rather symmetric around 0 in the interval [-1, 1] and the grey lines are right on top of y=0.

What about the numeric predictors? As you see in the code/plots, now the pain begins ... There's a strong suggestion of curvature for LENGTH.log.sc, weak to no evidence of curvature for SURPRISAL.sq.sc, some evidence of curvature for FREQ.bcn.sc. What about our main predictor of interest? There's again some suggestion of curvature, now even for our main predictor of interest, and that's certainly not something we want to ignore; you better get ready for some interesting result(s) ... Ok, "back to model fitting/selection" it is!

6.3.5 Model fitting/selection, part 2

Since we're going to check fixefs for curvature, we go back to ML-estimation:

```
summary(m.06 <- update(m.06, .~., REML=FALSE), correlation=FALSE)
## [...]
```

The 'visual evidence' for curvature of LENGTH.log.sc seemed strongest so we start with this one by changing it into an orthogonal polynomial to the second degree:

```
summary(m.07 <- update(m.06, .~. - LENGTH.log.sc
    + poly(LENGTH.log.sc, 2)), correlation=FALSE) ## [...]
anova(m.06, m.07, test="Chisq") ## [...]
##       npar   AIC   BIC  logLik deviance  Chisq Df Pr(>Chisq)
## m.06    10 11541 11608 -5760.6    11521
## m.07    11 11498 11572 -5737.9    11476 45.456  1  1.561e-11 ***
```

Wow, no convergence issues, excellent. Did 'polynomializing' LENGTH.log.sc the model significantly better? Definitely, and there's also a big *AIC* decrease.

```
sort(round(vif(m.07)[,1], 2)) ## [...] still no problems
```

And still no collinearity issues. (Note that the syntax to get the *VIFs* has changed a bit because, now that the polynomial term is in the model, car::vif returns a data frame as a result, of which I am extracting the first column with a generalized *VIF* for MEMs).

```
drop1.m.07 <- drop1(m.07, test="Chisq")
drop1.m.07[order(drop1.m.07[,"Pr(Chi)"]),] ## [...]
##                      npar   AIC   LRT  Pr(Chi)
```

```
## poly(LENGTH.log.sc, 2)   2 12176 682.65 < 2.2e-16 ***
## SURPRISAL.sq.sc          1 11672 175.85 < 2.2e-16 ***
## FREQ.bcn.sc              1 11589  93.54 < 2.2e-16 ***
## VOWELS                   1 11528  32.29 1.327e-08 ***
## POSINTURN:CLASS          1 11520  24.43 7.712e-07 ***
## <none>                     11498
```

And, nothing else became insignificant because of how we changed this control – it doesn't get much better than that (don't get used to it tho ...). What about the next weaker predictor maybe needing/benefitting from curvature?

```
summary(m.08 <- update(m.07, .~. - FREQ.bcn.sc + poly(FREQ.bcn.sc,
   2)), correlation=FALSE) ## [...]
anova(m.07, m.08, test="Chisq") ## [...]
##      npar   AIC   BIC  logLik deviance  Chisq Df Pr(>Chisq)
## m.07  11 11498 11572 -5737.9   11476
## m.08  12 11482 11563 -5729.2   11458 17.379  1  3.062e-05 ***
```

Stlll no collinearity problems and still nothing turning non-significant:

```
sort(round(vif(m.08)[,1], 2)) ## [...]
drop1.m.08 <- drop1(m.08, test="Chisq")
drop1.m.08[order(drop1.m.08[,"Pr(Chi)"]),] ## [...]
##                          npar   AIC    LRT   Pr(Chi)
## poly(LENGTH.log.sc, 2)      2 12137 658.80 < 2.2e-16 ***
## SURPRISAL.sq.sc             1 11642 161.29 < 2.2e-16 ***
## poly(FREQ.bcn.sc, 2)        2 11589 110.92 < 2.2e-16 ***
## VOWELS                      1 11515  34.80 3.662e-09 ***
## POSINTURN:CLASS             1 11500  19.91 8.128e-06 ***
## <none>                        11482
```

Same thing: the model is significantly better, but raises no red flags. What about SURPRISAL.sq.sc then? [I am skipping some code regarding m.09 here, but you should of course run it in R as you follow along.] Same thing, so now all the numeric controls' effects are curved. Now, are we lucky and the way the model has changed takes care of the curvature in the residuals-vs.-POSINTURN plot? (Hint before you check Figure 136: you believe in Santa?)

I am gonna take this as a 'no(t really)' ... because then life would be too easy. Ok, so now the maybe most important one: POSINTURN. It's in an interaction so we need to be careful to replace this properly:

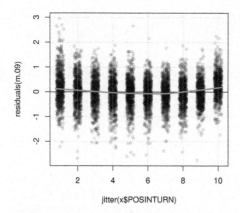

Figure 136: Residuals of m.09 against POSINTURN

```
summary(m.10 <- update(m.09, .~. - POSINTURN - POSINTURN:CLASS
    + poly(POSINTURN, 2) + poly(POSINTURN, 2):CLASS),
    correlation=FALSE) ## {...]
anova(m.09, m.10, test="Chisq")
##      npar   AIC   BIC  logLik deviance  Chisq Df Pr(>Chisq)
## m.09   13 11471 11558 -5722.5    11445
## m.10   15 11216 11317 -5593.1    11186 258.83  2   < 2.2e-16 ***
sort(round(vif(m.10)[,1], 2)) ## [...] fine!
drop1.m.10 <- drop1( # drop each droppable predictor at a time
    m.10,            # from the model m.10 &
    test="Chisq")    # test its significance w/ a LR-test
drop1.m.10[order(drop1.m.10[,"Pr(Chi)"]),] ## [...]
##                           npar   AIC    LRT   Pr(Chi)
## poly(LENGTH.log.sc, 2)       2 11909 696.85 < 2.2e-16 ***
## poly(FREQ.bcn.sc, 2)         2 11369 156.87 < 2.2e-16 ***
## poly(SURPRISAL.sq.sc, 2)     2 11336 123.73 < 2.2e-16 ***
## VOWELS                       1 11247  32.81 1.017e-08 ***
## CLASS:poly(POSINTURN, 2)     2 11219   7.00   0.03018 *
## <none>                         11216
```

No collinearity, the model is getting highly significantly better, and the *AIC* decrease is massive, much bigger than any other improvement we have seen so far! As a small brain teaser, why don't you try and figure out by looking up sapply, grep, and get how these two lines (i) identify all *AIC*-scores of all models we've fit and (ii) their differences as the models got better and the *AIC* got smaller?

```
(qwe <- sapply(sapply(grep("^m.", ls(), value=TRUE), get), AIC))
round(diff(qwe), 3)
```

Given how the *p*-value of `poly(POSINTURN, 2):CLASS` is still significant, this seems to be our new final model ...

6.3.6 A brief interlude

What did I just say? "[T]his **seems** to be our new final model ..." Our next step depends on our stance towards model selection (and a couple of other considerations), but before we go there, let's face the fact that even this model might raise some people's eyebrows. We found that curvature was needed to deal with structure in the residuals, so we added it for some controls, which should be uncontroversial (because we're not claiming academic-genius credit for those being significant). But then we also added curvature for the main predictor, which might be less uncontroversial. Did we really hypothesize a curved relationship? No, not really, the description of the data/scenario in Section 5.8 said "study the hypothesis that word durations increase at the end of 10-word turns" – that doesn't specify the nature of the regression line of POSINTURN, which means, according to Occam's razor and Grice's maxims, this could be understood as stipulating a linear trend only. Thus, we cannot take full credit for the significant result of the *curved* relationship because it's not like we suspected it in advance. However, I personally still would not consider the reporting of the significant result for the curved relationship of POSINTURN a problem here because I am assuming (in this hypothetical scenario) that
- the hypothesis formulated in the paper will be the one quoted above, meaning we're not going to pretend we knew it was curved *a priori* and of course our hypothesis, that durations are higher at turn ends (rather than lower, for example), will still be evaluated only once we see the exact nature of the effects plot for POSINTURN's polynomial effect (because right now, from the summary output for the polynomial effects, we actually have no real good idea what the nature of POSINTURN's effect is);
- we will describe in our paper that the introduction of the curvature happened to deal with the residual problems, not because of our brilliance of suspecting it in the first place.

Thus, one way to proceed would be the above: consider m.10 the final model and write it up as just described. But here's the thing, and this may make some colleagues' ears perk up in terror ... Once we've determined that the polynomial to the 2nd degree is needed, we might even decide to see whether that's all that's needed and/or the best we can do. Glossing over one technicality now just for the sake of the argument,[19] it turns out that each of the models m.11, m.12, and m.13 with 3rd, 4th, and 5th degree polynomials respectively is significantly better than the previous one, and none of them has collinearity issues and all of them do in fact show the hypothesized increase of DURATION late in the turns (which I will show you later in a plot).

```
m.11 <- update(m.09, .~. - POSINTURN - POSINTURN:CLASS
   + poly(POSINTURN, 3) + poly(POSINTURN, 3):CLASS)
m.12 <- update(m.09, .~. - POSINTURN - POSINTURN:CLASS
   + poly(POSINTURN, 4) + poly(POSINTURN, 4):CLASS)
m.13 <- update(m.09, .~. - POSINTURN - POSINTURN:CLASS
   + poly(POSINTURN, 5) + poly(POSINTURN, 5):CLASS)
anova(m.10, m.11, test="Chisq")[2,"Pr(>Chisq)"]
## [1] 5.667598e-06
anova(m.11, m.12, test="Chisq")[2,"Pr(>Chisq)"]
## [1] 7.66633e-11
anova(m.12, m.13, test="Chisq")[2,"Pr(>Chisq)"]
## [1] 0.01181964
```

But of course we only included a polynomial to the 2nd degree to address the residual problem and we certainly didn't hypothesize a polynomial to the 5th degree so can we in fact use this? Personally, I still tend to say yes, *iff* we remain honest in (i) our characterization of the hypothesis, (ii) the use of the polynomial to the 2nd degree as a tool to address residuals and (iii) the fact that the higher-order polynomials were done exploratorily to get the best fit possible while, hopefully, still seeing the hypothesized increase at the ends of turns. I know some colleagues may frown on this, but to my mind some of the work done with generalized (mixed) additive models is, in spirit at least, not *that* dissimilar: In such studies, researchers might use a function like mgcv::bam/gam to zoom in on the right amount of curvature / number of knots 'automatically' from the data (using *edf*-values or automatic shrinkage methods), or they might use model-diagnostic functions such as mgcv::gam.check to identify the best smoothing parameter/λ; for predictors (which can sometimes lead to very squiggly regression lines) It's not obvious to me how doing that to find the best smoothing parame-

---

19 We haven't adjusted the ranef structure for the fact that we now have a polynomial effect of POSINTURN in the fixef structure (see Barr 2013, Barr et al. 2013).

ters/k-values (with residuals diagnostics or *AIC*) is oh-so-obviously fine but looking for the best degree of polynomial curvature (with residual diagnostics or model comparisons maybe also with *AIC*) is oh-so-obviously bad ...

For now, we will remain conservative and stick with m.10, but I did want to discuss this briefly and I'll briefly show the effect of POSINTURN:CLASS for the 5th-degree polynomial in Section 6.3.7 below (because it is awesome). Thus, for now we re-fit m.10 with REML and do diagnostics again:

```
summary(m.final <- update(m.10, .~., REML=TRUE), correlation=FALSE)
## [...]
## Random effects:
##  Groups   Name        Variance Std.Dev.
##  SPEAKER  (Intercept) 0.00248  0.0498
##  Residual             0.36508  0.6042
## Number of obs: 6107, groups:  SPEAKER, 20
## Fixed effects:
##                               Estimate Std. Error t value
## (Intercept)                    7.26999    0.01662 437.531
## CLASSopen                      0.24187    0.02505   9.654
## VOWELStwo+                    -0.10726    0.01872  -5.730
## poly(LENGTH.log.sc, 2)1       23.36200    0.86081  27.140
## poly(LENGTH.log.sc, 2)2        3.49860    0.69035   5.068
## poly(FREQ.bcn.sc, 2)1        -14.44268    1.15748 -12.478
## poly(FREQ.bcn.sc, 2)2          4.06666    0.71764   5.667
## poly(SURPRISAL.sq.sc, 2)1      7.52995    0.85609   8.796
## poly(SURPRISAL.sq.sc, 2)2     -2.60469    0.71671  -3.634
## poly(POSINTURN, 2)1            5.05720    0.76749   6.589
## poly(POSINTURN, 2)2           11.12943    0.77445  14.371
## CLASSopen:poly(POSINTURN, 2)1  1.94507    1.37325   1.416
## CLASSopen:poly(POSINTURN, 2)2 -3.13874    1.29801  -2.418
```

6.3.7 Model diagnostics, part 2

Here we are again but we'll speed this up now: If we look at the residuals, there's still a bit of non-constant variance, but otherwise this looks fine. The residual plots for CLASS and VOWELS were pretty unproblematic before, but now there are even more homogeneous (in terms of their range), so this is good. The residual plots for LENGTH.log.sc, SURPRISAL.sq.sc, and FREQ.bcn.sc are not picture-perfect, but I hope you agree they're better than before. What about POSINTURN?

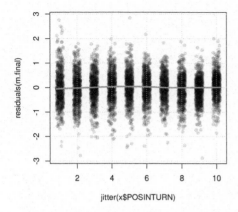

Figure 137: Residuals of m.final against POSINTURN

Ok, that one's fine now so we'll stick with this model. I hope you now recognize why I gave this 'don't trust anything, least of all an analysis you just did yourself' speech at the beginning of the book ... modeling is 'detective work'!

Let's also quickly check the varying intercepts for the speakers, which in the MEM are supposed to be normally-distributed around 0.[20]

```
lattice::dotplot(ranef(m.final, condVar=TRUE))
```

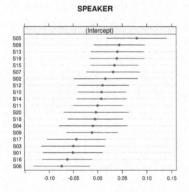

Figure 138: A dotchart of the ranef adjustments for SPEAKER

---

20 Bell et al. (2019:1051) state that "assuming random intercepts are normally distributed, when they are not, introduces only modest biases", thus, deviations from normality are less of a concern than one might fear.

Figure 138 looks fine, I'd say: Nearly all speakers have adjustments whose 95%-CI overlaps with 0, which leaves only 3 speakers with 'notably stronger' adjustments, i.e. speakers whose word durations are notably shorter or longer in general (an alternative plot could be generated with plot(m.final, SPEAKER ~ resid(.))). It seems like we're there: we can finally interpret this thing.

6.3.8 Model interpretation

Let's begin by computing the significance test for the overall model, for which we use the same logic as a few times before: We compute a null model, which in the context of MEM is a model with no fixefs, but the same ranef structure as the model we're trying to test, and then we compare our final model to that model with anova.

```
m.nofixef <- lmer(DURATION ~ 1 + (1|SPEAKER), data=x)
anova(m.final, m.nofixef, test="Chisq")
##             npar   AIC   BIC  logLik deviance  Chisq Df Pr(>Chisq)
## m.nofixef      3 15451 15471 -7722.5    15445
## m.final       15 11216 11317 -5593.1    11186 4258.8 12  < 2.2e-16
```

We would report that the model is highly significant (*LR*-test=4258.8, *df*=12, *p*<0.0001). We might also compute the so-called **relative likelihood** of the final model compared to the null model, which quantifies, so to speak, how much more plausibly the final model is 'the right model' for the data compared to the null model, which here gives a fairly convincing value of Inf:

```
(exp((AIC(m.nofixef)-AIC(m.final))/2))
## [1] Inf
```

(If we were to compare m.final and m.13, we'd find a relative likelihood of ≈ 7×1015 ((exp((AIC(m.final)-AIC(m.13))/2)) in favor of the latter!; I'm jus' sayin' ...) We can also compute R^2-values, but for MEM there are two: $R^2_{marginal}$ quantifies the explanatory power of the fixefs whereas $R^2_{conditional}$ quantifies the explanatory power of both fixefs and ranefs (see Nakagawa et al. 2017). For a lot of studies, the ideal outcome is that both values are high and $R^2_{marginal}$ is only a bit smaller than $R^2_{conditional}$. That'd be nice because then the model accounts for a lot of variability and that explanatory power doesn't simply come from (often less relevant) idiosyncrasies captured in the ranefs. Thus, if $R^2_{marginal}$ and $R^2_{conditional}$ are 0.05 and 0.07 respectively, you just don't have a very explanatory model – that's not great. If $R^2_{marginal}$ and $R^2_{conditional}$ are 0.05 and 0.7 respectively, your fixefs don't do much but there's a lot of, say, speaker-specific variation – also not great. But if $R^2_{marginal}$ and $R^2_{conditional}$ are 0.6 and 0.7 respectively, you have a nicely explanatory fixef structure, which is 'helped' a bit by some ranef structure. Most studies are (more) interested in the fixefs than the ranefs, but I would nevertheless always report both values. In our case, we can be happy to see that nearly all variability that is accounted for is so by the fixefs; however, what counts as 'a good R^2' is dependent on the discipline and previous work on the topic/phenomenon.

```
r.squaredGLMM(m.final)
##              R2m        R2c
## [1,] 0.5002701 0.5036425
```

Ok, what about the coefficients etc.? We saw them already above, but we also saw that we're not getting any p-values; this is because deciding how to compute them isn't straightforward. One way we can get p-values is by using a different package such as lmerTest. Here's how I would do this: I plug the formula of the final model into the lmer function from the package lmerTest: [output doesn't fit here so check it out in R]

```
summary(lmerTest::lmer(formula(m.final), data=x)) ## [...]
```

Now you might ask, 'if lmerTest has an lmer function that provides p-values, why didn't I use lmerTest::lmer throughout the whole process?' That's because I once wasted an afternoon loading lmerTest, whose lmer function returned a model object that is slightly different from lmer's, which led to follow-up functions from other packages that I wanted to apply to my model object not working: these follow-up functions required an lmer-object created by lme4::lmer, not one from lmerTest::lmer – hence this approach.

The functions fixef and ranef give you the fixef estimates and all ranef adjustments – i.e., here just the intercept adjustments per speaker – respectively:

```
fixef(m.final) ## [...]
ranef(m.final) ## [...]
```

(The conditional variances, which you would use to compute CIs of these adjustments, like in the above dot chart, you would retrieve here with something slightly convoluted: as.numeric(attr(ranef(m.final)$SPEAKER, "postVar")).) Note that I said there that fixef on a merMod object (i.e. a model fitted, in this book, with lme4::lmer or lme4::glmer) is the same as coef is for lm/glm. Does that mean `coef` wouldn't work on `m.final`? No, it works (and you saw it referred to in Section 6.1), it just gives you something different:

```
coef(m.final)$SPEAKER[1:3,1:4]
    (Intercept) CLASSopen VOWELStwo+ poly(LENGTH.log.sc, 2)1
S01    7.218628 0.2418731 -0.1072573                  23.362
S02    7.286268 0.2418731 -0.1072573                  23.362
S03    7.219541 0.2418731 -0.1072573                  23.362
```

What is this? `coef.merMod`, which means the function `coef` applied to an merMod object (which is what lmer creates) is a list with a component for each source of ranef variation, i.e. here just one for SPEAKER. That component in turn is a data frame with the coefficients of the model adjusted for each level of the ranef, i.e. here for each speaker. Since we only have varying intercepts, you can see that all slopes are constant, but each speaker has a different intercept; in other words, the first column of `coef(m.final)$SPEAKER` is the same as if you did this:

```
fixef(m.final)["(Intercept)"] +
ranef(m.final)$SPEAKER["(Intercept)"]
```

You can also compute confidence intervals for your fixef coefficients and display them together with the estimates from the summary output like we always did in Chapter 5. The best way to do this is using the simulation-based method of bootstrapping you read about in Section 5.2.1.5, which is what the following code chunk exemplifies. Since bootstrapping for MEMs can sometimes take a really long time – I have waited hours in the past – I'm showing a version here that uses multiple threads of my laptop. If you have fewer than 24 threads available, you should adjust the argument `ncpus` accordingly and if this doesn't work at all, omit the arguments `parallel` and `ncpus` and this will just take longer. (Learning about how to parallelize things in R is worth it, though, for many statistical and corpus-linguistic applications.)

```
set.seed(utf8ToInt("Brokkoliauflauf"))
m.final.cis <-confint(m.final, parm="beta_", method="boot",
    nsim=1000, parallel="snow", ncpus=22)
round(data.frame(COEF=fixef(m.final),
    LOWER=m.final.cis[,1], UPPER=m.final.cis[,2]), 3)
##                COEF  LOWER  UPPER
## (Intercept)   7.270  7.238  7.301
## CLASSopen     0.242  0.195  0.293
```

```
## VOWELStwo+                              -0.107  -0.145  -0.071
## poly(LENGTH.log.sc, 2)1                 23.362   21.716  24.961
## [...]
```

There are two faster alternatives to the above:
– use method="profile" (and then you can omit the arguments nsim, parallel and ncpus), which takes only 3.5 seconds on my laptop;
– use car::Confint(m.final), which returns results instantaneously.

While the results of these three approaches may not always differ markedly, bootstrapping with a decent number of simulations (like above) is probably the safest option especially for mixed-effects modeling.

Let's now see what the effect of our main predictor is (in its interaction with CLASS of course). This part can essentially be dealt with like all the fixef models above. You can generate an effects object and data frame (which, note!, is based only on the fixefs) and plot that object:

```
(ph <- data.frame(ia <- effect("CLASS:poly(POSINTURN, 2)",
    m.final, xlevels=list(POSINTURN=1:10))))
##       CLASS POSINTURN       fit          se      lower      upper
## 1    closed         1  7.299134  0.02738855  7.245443  7.352825
## 2      open         1  7.435451  0.04316252  7.350837  7.520065
## 3    closed         2  7.164662  0.02165910  7.122203  7.207122
## [...]
## 18     open         9  7.571739  0.02923803  7.514423  7.629056
## 19   closed        10  7.500764  0.02981207  7.442322  7.559206
## 20     open        10  7.715488  0.03578503  7.645336  7.785639
plot(ia, ylim=range(x$DURATION), grid=TRUE
```

Given our super honest plotting – I am referring to how we defined ylim – this doesn't look like much, but it is significant and in the expected direction; check how much more 'impressive' you can make this appear if you leave out the ylim argument in the call to plot or, more defensibly, set ylim like this: ylim=quantile(x$DURATION, probs=c(0.025, 0.975)) ... Anyway, we see that the hypothesis is confirmed: Durations are predicted to be longer/longest at the end of the 10-word turns, but especially so if the word there is an open-class word.

But now what about m.13 with its 5th-degree polynomial? I will show the effect of that by generating my own plot, but based on the same logic as above

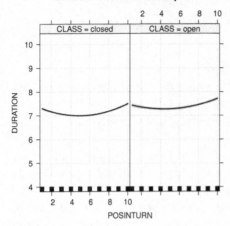

Figure 139: The effect of CLASS:POSINTURN

I begin by redefining ph to use m.13, then I am setting the y-axis limits to be identical to the plots we will generate for all control variables in a moment, and I define a right y-axis that contains the 'back-transformed' DURATION values (just as a heuristic, of course those are not the values we modeled):

```
ph <- data.frame(effect("CLASS:poly(POSINTURN, 5)", m.13,
    xlevels=list(POSINTURN=1:10)))
ph.split <- split(ph, ph$CLASS, drop=TRUE)
par(mfrow=c(1, 2)); for (i in seq(ph.split)) {
    plot(main=paste0("POSINTURN when CLASS is '",
        names(ph.split)[i], "'"), xlab="Position in turn",
        xlim=c(1, 10), x=ph.split[[i]]$POSINTURN,
        ylab="Predicted duration", ylim=c(5.5, 9), y=ph.split[[i]]$fit,
        type="b", pch=16); grid(); abline(h=0.5, lty=2)
    axis(4, at=seq(6.5, 9, 0.5), labels=round(2^seq(6.5, 9, 0.5)))
    polygon(c(ph.split[[i]]$POSINTURN, rev(ph.split[[i]]$POSINTURN)),
        c(ph.split[[i]]$lower, rev(ph.split[[i]]$upper)),
        col="#00000020", border=NA)
    }; par(mfrow=c(1, 1))
```

The effect of POSINTURN looks really fairly similar for both classes (at least with regard to our hypothesis). In general and when everything else is controlled for (in the way effects does it), open-class words have higher durations (not surprising) and turn-medial words are shortest.

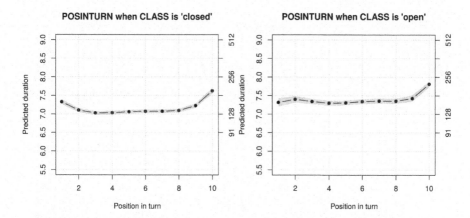

Figure 140: The effect of CLASS:POSINTURN

At the very beginning of turns – slot 1 – there's no difference, but right after that we find a bit of a difference depending on whether the next words are closed-class words (shorter durations) or open-class words (longer durations). However, in both panels, there's a very clear effect especially at position 10 on the right. Like I said, as long as authors clearly outline how they got to their results, I would really prefer seeing this plot over the previous plot even if the authors didn't hypothesize a 5th-degree polynomial *a priori*.

Let's quickly look at whether the controls work as one might suspect with just one quick effects plot. On the whole, the results makes sense: longer and more surprising words have longer durations, more frequent words and words with more vowels have shorter durations.

```
plot(allEffects(m.final)[1:4], ylim=c(5.5, 9), grid=TRUE) ## [...]
```

6.3.9 A bit on MEM predictions

I want to briefly discuss how you can get predictions from this model, both with and without ranefs. If you just apply predict to the final model created with lmer, you get the model's predictions for all your data points and those predictions will be based on both fixefs and ranefs, which we might add to the original data frame. But with the argument re.form, whose default setting NULL means 'include all random effects'), we can also specify that we do not want any ranefs included (re.form=NA), and theoretically you can also specify a (certain part of a) ranef structure you want to use (check ?predict.merMod).

```
x$PREDS.alleff <- predict(m.final)            # this uses all ranefs
x$PREDS.fixeff <- predict(m.final, re.form=NA) # this uses no ranefs
```

We can also compute confidence intervals for the predictions using the function bootMer. We won't do anything with those here but I did want to show how this can be done:

```
set.seed(utf8ToInt("Schokonüsse"))
PREDS.boot.obj <- bootMer(x=m.final, FUN=function (af) {
   predict(af) }, nsim=1000, parallel="snow", ncpus=22)
x <- cbind(x, t(apply(X=PREDS.boot.obj$t, MARGIN=2, quantile,
   probs=c(0.025, 0.975))))
x[1:3,c(1:3, 15:18)]
## CASE DURATION POSINTURN PREDS.alleff PREDS.fixeff    2.5%   97.5%
##    1 6.714246        2     7.214322     7.265685 7.179433 7.35273
##    2 6.475733        3     7.145279     7.196643 7.112163 7.28328
##    3 6.285402        4     6.663836     6.715200 6.620824 6.80936
```

If we want to apply predictions to unseen cases, you use newdata, just like before. Here, I first define a data frame with the combination of predictor values we're interested in (and, if we want to use speaker information, what the speaker level is), and then we pass this on to predict. This is what we could do if we wanted to know the fixef prediction (hence re.form=NA) for the first case in the data but when VOWELS was *two+*:

```
nd <- data.frame(CLASS="closed", VOWELS="two+",
   LENGTH.log.sc=0.4449693, SURPRISAL.sq.sc=-0.1424065,
   FREQ.bcn.sc=0.5137626, POSINTURN=2)
predict(m.final, newdata=nd, re.form=NA)
##        1
## 7.158428
```

This is of course x$PREDS.fixeff[1]+fixef(m.final)["VOWELStwo+"]. As a little brain teaser and to end this part, try to see how/why the following line is the fixef prediction for the first case:

```
sum(model.matrix(m.final)[1,] * coef(m.final)[[1]][x$SPEAKER[1],])
## [1] 7.214322
```

6.4 Generalized linear MEM case study

> [...] how should one actually use GLMMs to analyze data? Unfortunately, we cannot recom-
> mend a single, universal procedure because different methods are appropriate for different
> problems and, as made clear by recent debates, how one analyzes data depends strongly
> on one'sphilosophical approach (e.g. hypothesis testing versus model selection, frequen-
> tist versus Bayesian). (Bolker et al. 2009a:133)

The second MEM case study will involve a binary logistic regression with ranefs.
We will look at subject realization in spoken conversational Japanese involving
native and non-native speakers to test the hypothesis that the intermediately
proficient non-native speakers in the sample data will react differently to two of
the main predictors governing subject realization, namely the givenness of the
subject referent and whether it is used contrastively (this study is based on an altered version of the data in Gries & Adelman 2014). We load the data set, which
contains the following variables:

- SPEAKERTYPE: *nns* (non-native speaker) vs. *ns* (native speaker);
- SPEAKER: a unique code for each speaker;
- SUBJREAL: *no* vs. *yes*, the dependent variable representing whether a subject
  was realized or not;
- CONTRAST: *no* vs. yes, a predictor representing whether the referent of the subject would be contrastive or not;
- GIVENNESS: 0 to 10, a discrete scale indicating how 'given' from the preceding
  discourse the referent of the subject is (essentially, 10 - distance to last mention in clauses):

```
rm(list=ls(all.names=TRUE)); library(car); library(effects);
   library(lme4); source("helpers/C.score.r"); source("helpers/
   overdisp.mer.r")
summary(x <- read.delim(file="_inputfiles/06_subjreal.csv",
   stringsAsFactors=TRUE)) ## [I'm omitting the CASE column here]
##        SPEAKER      SPEAKERTYPE SUBJREAL    CONTRAST      GIVENNESS
## S14    : 372    nns:1895    no :3136    no :4121    Min.   : 0.000
## S12    : 359    ns :2436    yes:1195    yes: 210    1st Qu.: 8.000
## S08    : 318                                        Median :10.000
## S02    : 299                                        Mean   : 7.814
## S15    : 290                                        3rd Qu.:10.000
## S03    : 278                                        Max.   :10.000
## (Other):2415
```

6.4.1 Preparation and exploration

Given the smallness of the data set (in terms of number of variables), there's not that much to explore, but if the summary output above didn't make you want to look at the distribution of GIVENNESS, then either you're not paying attention or this book has failed its mission ... I really hope you saw that (i) the first quartile is already 8 and (ii) in a slight variation on "a rose is a rose is a rose", the median is the third quartile is the maximum.

```
plot(main="", xlab="Observed frequency values", x=ecdf(x$GIVENNESS),
    ylab="Cumulative percentage", verticals=TRUE); grid()
```

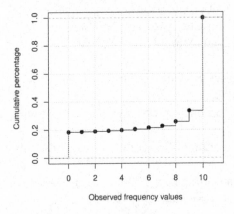

Figure 141: The ecdf of GIVENNESS

Ugh – not something that we can easily make look better with a transformation. While factorizing numeric variables is definitely always only a *last*-resort option – because of the information loss it invariably incurs – this *might* be a case where this is defensible. In your spare time, you should of course also explore the option of making GIVENNESS an ordinal ternary variable, but for now, we make every case where GIVENNESS is 0 *new* and everything else *given*:

```
x$GIVENNESS.fac <- factor(ifelse(x$GIVENNESS==0, "new", "given"))
tapply(x$GIVENNESS, x$GIVENNESS.fac, function (af) sort(unique(af)))
## $given
##  [1] 1  2  3  4  5  6  7  8  9  10
## $new
## [1] 0
```

Since the number of variables involved is so small, let's do some quick cross-tabulating: We can see that CONTRAST: *yes* might become a problem simply because it's so rare comparatively speaking that we don't have many observations for the regression 'to work with', especially in interaction terms, which we'll need.

```
table(x$CONTRAST, x$GIVENNESS.fac) ## [...]
table(x$CONTRAST, x$SPEAKERTYPE) ## [...]
table(x$GIVENNESS.fac, x$SPEAKERTYPE) ## [...]
```

Let's cross-tabulate the response with the predictors:

```
table(x$SUBJREAL, x$CONTRAST) ## [...]
table(x$SUBJREAL, x$GIVENNESS.fac) ## [...]
table(x$SUBJREAL, x$SPEAKERTYPE) ## [...]
```

Again, CONTRAST: yes might be challenging: With the ratio of 3104:32 in the first table (i.e., nearly 99% to 1%), we're getting close to complete separation (recall Section 5.3.4). We'll see how it goes ...

Do all speakers use all levels of both predictors? Yes, but with CONTRAST: *yes* we see the familiar low-frequency issue.

```
table(x$GIVENNESS.fac, x$SPEAKER) ## [...]
table(x$CONTRAST, x$SPEAKER) ## [...]
```

Note that SPEAKERTYPE is nested into SPEAKER: if you know SPEAKER, you know SPEAKERTYPE:

```
table(x$SPEAKERTYPE, x$SPEAKER) ## [...]
```

For a 3-way interaction of our central predictors, we *might* have too imbalanced a distribution, though:

```
ftable(x$SPEAKERTYPE, x$CONTRAST, x$GIVENNESS.fac, x$SUBJREAL)
## [...]
```

Several combinations are really rare (and running that same table with SPEAKER instead of SPEAKERTYPE leads to a table with more than a third of cells with 3 or fewer observations).

Finally, since we'll be predicting categorical outcomes, let's already compute the baselines we want to exceed:

```
(baseline.1 <- max(prop.table(table(x$SUBJREAL))))
## [1] 0.7240822
(baseline.2 <- sum(prop.table(table(x$SUBJREAL))^2))
## [1] 0.6004257
```

Note that this data set is involves a bit of the so-called **class imbalance** problem, which refers to the fact that the levels of the response variable to be predicted are not at all evenly distributed. The more massive the imbalance between the levels of the response variable, the more this can cause problems because it essentially means that whatever model/algorithm you use on the data will have (much) fewer instances of the rarer level(s) to extract predictive patterns from, plus it of course becomes harder and harder to beat the baseline(s). Imagine a study that models a response variable VOICE with the levels *active* and *passive* with a distribution of 0.9 vs. 0.1: here even baseline.1 would already be 0.9! In this particular case, it's not nearly as bad, but this is something to bear in mind in general (see Kuhn & Johnson 2013: Ch. 16).

6.4.2 Model fitting/selection

Given our above interest – do non-native speakers' decisions to realize subjects (based on givenness and contrast) differ from those of native speakers? – our first model should probably look like this:

```
summary(m.01 <- glmer(SUBJREAL ~ 1 +
    CONTRAST*GIVENNESS.fac*SPEAKERTYPE +
    (1+CONTRAST*GIVENNESS.fac|SPEAKER),
    family=binomial, data=x), correlation=FALSE)
## [...]
## optimizer (Nelder_Mead) convergence code: 0 (OK)
## Model failed to converge with max|grad| = 0.00834076 (tol = 0.002,
## component 1)
```

Note the ranef structure: We have (i) varying intercepts and (ii) varying slopes for everything that can vary within speakers, but (iii) we're not including varying slopes for SPEAKERTYPE as well (not even in the interaction): For every speaker, there's only one level of SPEAKERTYPE (plus we also saw above how sparse the distribution per speaker is anyway). And it's of course gratifying to see our good ol' friend, the convergence warning, again ... how would we survive without it? However, the value that we're being warned about (0.0083408) is actually quite close to the threshold value to which it is compared (0.002), which is quite reassuring. Let's see how much less complex our ranef structure can likely be, given the very high correlations we see up there (half of them ≥0.9)?

```
rePCA(m.01) ## [...]
```

Seems like we will end up with two sources of ranef variation. Let's do a quick check for collinearity and overdispersion:

```
unname(sort(round(vif(m.01), 2))) # unname only to save space in book
[1] 1.59 2.30 2.65 4.00 4.10 4.19 4.38
overdisp.mer(m.01)
##         chisq        ratio           rdf             p
## 4238.5066724    0.9827282 4313.0000000    0.7880134
```

Let's proceed as before and remove the interaction from the ranef structure:

```
summary(m.02 <- update(m.01, .~.
    - (1+CONTRAST*GIVENNESS.fac|SPEAKER)
+ (1+CONTRAST+GIVENNESS.fac|SPEAKER)), correlation=FALSE) ## [...]
## optimizer (Nelder_Mead) convergence code: 0 (OK)
## Model failed to converge with max|grad| = 0.00420693 (tol = 0.002,
## component 1)
anova(m.01, m.02, test="Chisq") ## [...]
##       npar    AIC    BIC  logLik deviance  Chisq Df Pr(>Chisq)
## m.02    14 3690.9 3780.1 -1831.4   3662.9
## m.01    18 3698.8 3813.5 -1831.4   3662.8 0.0757  4     0.9993
unname(sort(round(vif(m.02), 2))) # still fine
overdisp.mer(m.02)                # still fine
```

Ok, no significant difference between the models, that's good. The convergence warning is down to an even smaller value (of 0.0042069). We will continue to try and simplify things, but this is already not bad. In the next step, we delete CONTRAST from the ranef structure, because of the two slopes, it has the smaller variance and the higher correlation value:

```
summary(m.03 <- update(m.02, .~.
    - (1+CONTRAST+GIVENNESS.fac|SPEAKER)
    + (1        +GIVENNESS.fac|SPEAKER)), correlation=FALSE)
anova(m.02, m.03, test="Chisq")
```

```
##       npar   AIC    BIC  logLik deviance Chisq Df Pr(>Chisq)
## m.03    11 3689.2 3759.3 -1833.6  3667.2
## m.02    14 3690.9 3780.1 -1831.4  3662.9 4.361  3     0.225
unname(sort(round(vif(m.03), 2))) # still fine
overdisp.mer(m.03)                # still fine
```

Excellent: deleting the slope adjustments for CONTRAST did no significant damage, but it got rid of the (already minor) convergence problem we still had. We
will therefore stick with the ranef structure we have now and work on the fixef
structure;[21] from the summary table, it doesn't seem that the 3-way interaction
will remain in the model.

```
drop1(m.03, test="Chisq") ## [...]
##                                   npar   AIC    LRT Pr(Chi)
## <none>                                  3689.2
## CONTRAST:GIVENNESS.fac:SPEAKERTYPE    1 3687.5 0.22319  0.6366
```

Yup, that interaction had 1 *df* so drop1 just returns the *p*-value from the summary table, which means the three-way interaction should go, which means,
whatever a potential interaction between CONTRAST and GIVENNESS.fac might involve, non-native and native speakers do it the same way.

```
summary(m.04 <- update(m.03, .~.
   - CONTRAST:GIVENNESS.fac:SPEAKERTYPE), correlation=FALSE)
anova(m.03, m.04, test="Chisq")
##       npar   AIC    BIC  logLik deviance  Chisq Df Pr(>Chisq)
## m.04    10 3687.5 3751.2 -1833.7  3667.5
## m.03    11 3689.2 3759.3 -1833.6  3667.2 0.2232  1     0.6366
unname(sort(round(vif(m.04), 2))) # still fine
overdisp.mer(m.04)                # still fine
```

We can already pretty much guess where this is most likely headed:
GIVENNESS.fac:SPEAKERTYPE will go first, then CONTRAST:SPEAKERTYPE. To save
space here in the book, I will therefore skip ahead to m.06:

```
drop1(m.06, test="Chisq")
## Model:
## SUBJREAL ~ CONTRAST + GIVENNESS.fac + SPEAKERTYPE +
```

---

21 If you're in the mood, you can check that at least deleting GIVENNESS.fac|SPEAKER wouldn't
be permitted anyway, because it would make that new model significantly worse.

```
## (1 + GIVENNESS.fac | SPEAKER) + CONTRAST:GIVENNESS.fac
##                       npar    AIC    LRT   Pr(Chi)
## <none>                       3684.4
## SPEAKERTYPE              1 3687.1  4.648   0.03109 *
## CONTRAST:GIVENNESS.fac   1 3736.2 53.840 2.176e-13 ***
m.final <- m.06; rm(m.06)
```

... and we are: all remaining predictors are significant. Our hypothesis that native and non-native speakers would differ in how CONTRAST and GIVENNESS would make them realize subjects is not confirmed: CONTRAST and GIVENNESS do interact but only with each other. Thus, given my definition of interaction, whatever it is that these variables do (in combination), 'they do it everywhere/always', i.e. with both speaker types. If you've really internalized regression outputs, you can already see in the fixef table what's happening here ... On the other hand, SPEAKERTYPE is a significant main effect, and again its effect is quite clear from the table when you think back to what these coefficients mean.

6.4.3 Model diagnostics

We have been keeping track of collinearity and overdispersion as we were modeling and they were fine but let's quickly check the ranef structure. The histograms (see the code file) look pretty ok, and this also shows the confidence intervals; nearly all adjustments are 'within reach' of 0 (see Figure 142).

All in all, this is looking fairly unproblematic and, to be honest, I see very little discussion of glmer-model diagnostics. Not that that's a good thing, but it suggests that firm standards/expectations are not yet available.

Recommendation(s) for further study: Check out the DHARMa package for more advanced checks of residuals, like so:
```
m.final.simres <- simulateResiduals( # simulate residuals for
    m.final, refit=FALSE, n=1000, plot=TRUE, set.seed(utf8ToInt("simres")))
testResiduals(m.final.simres) # check for residual uniformity & dispersion
```

6.4.4 Model interpretation

Now that we have a final model, much of what follows is actually very similar to what we did in the sections on fixef regressions and in Section 6.3. We first compute an overall significance test for our final model by, first, fitting a null model with no fixef predictors but the same ranef structure as the final model and, second, doing a model comparison with anova between those two:

SPEAKER

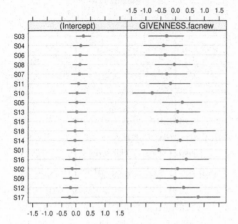

Figure 142: A dotchart of the ranef adjustments for SPEAKER

```
m.nofixef <- glmer(SUBJREAL ~ 1 +  (1+GIVENNESS.fac|SPEAKER),
   family=binomial, data=x)
anova(m.final, m.nofixef, test="Chisq")
##              npar    AIC    BIC  logLik deviance  Chisq Df Pr(>Chisq)
## m.nofixef      4 4033.5 4058.9 -2012.7   4025.5
## m.final        8 3684.4 3735.4 -1834.2   3668.4 357.05  4  < 2.2e-16
(exp((AIC(m.nofixef)-AIC(m.final))/2))  # relative likelihood
## [1] 6.227179e+75
```

We would report that the model is highly significant (*LR*-test=357.05, *df*=4, *p*<0.0001) and that its relative likelihood (of >1074) makes it vastly more plausible than the null model.

We can also compute confidence intervals of the coefficients, which I am doing as above for the lmer object – but consider yourself reminded that computing CIs of glmer models with bootstrapping like this can take a really long time because the model needs to be re-fitted as many times as you specify (that's why I'm only using nsim=200 here); thus, don't forget about the alternatives described above.

```
set.seed(utf8ToInt("PolkHigh"))
m.final.cis <-confint(m.final, parm="beta_", method="boot", nsim=200,
   parallel="snow", ncpus=22)
round(data.frame(COEF=fixef(m.final),
```

```
   LOWER=m.final.cis[,1], UPPER=m.final.cis[,2]), 3)
##                              COEF   LOWER   UPPER
## (Intercept)                -1.696 -1.872  -1.528
## CONTRASTyes                 3.649  3.201   4.192
## GIVENNESS.facnew            3.068  2.752   3.389
## SPEAKERTYPEns              -0.267 -0.478  -0.015
## CONTRASTyes:GIVENNESS.facnew -3.320 -4.148 -2.580
```

Then, we compute R^2; note that I haven't seen any discussion whether to use the theoretical or the delta score in any papers reporting these values but, as far as I can remember, an older version of the function returned only one of those, which corresponded to the theoretical one. We also compute the C-score, the accuracy of our final model, and precision as well as recall; thankfully, C exceeds the desired threshold value of 0.8:

```
MuMIn::r.squaredGLMM(m.final)
##                   R2m        R2c
## theoretical 0.3405870 0.3538001
## delta       0.2696623 0.2801239
C.score(m.final)
## [1] 0.8081525
x$PREDS.NUM <- predict(m.final, type="response")
x$PREDS.CAT <- factor(ifelse(x$PREDS.NUM>=0.5,
   levels(x$SUBJREAL)[2], levels(x$SUBJREAL)[1]))
(qwe <- table(x$SUBJREAL, x$PREDS.CAT)) ## [...]
##          no  yes
##   no   2938  198
##   yes   471  724
##   Class. acc. Prec. for yes  Rec. for yes  Prec. for no
##      0.8455322     0.7852495     0.6058577     0.8618363
##   Rec. for no
##      0.9368622
sum(dbinom(x=3662:4331, size=4331, prob=baseline.1))
## [1] 2.811504e-80
```

As before, we can compute confidence intervals for these predictions and, as before with the CI for the `glmer` coefficients, this can take a long time especially if you use a higher number of simulations and even if you parallelize the workload onto as many processor cores/threads as you can spare:

```
set.seed(utf8ToInt("Gorp.Fnark.Schmegle."))
PREDS.boot.obj <- bootMer(x=m.final, FUN=function (af) { predict(af,
   type="response") }, nsim=50, parallel="snow", ncpus=22)
x <- cbind(x, t(apply(X=PREDS.boot.obj$t, MARGIN=2, quantile,
   probs=c(0.025, 0.975))))
```

Lastly, we can interpret the model based on the predictions. We begin with the main effect of SPEAKERTYPE; here's the effects data frame and the plot [not shown here in book]:

```
(ph.spkt <- data.frame(spkt <- effect(m.final)))
##     SPEAKERTYPE       fit         se      lower      upper
## 1           nns 0.2723818 0.01676393 0.2407896 0.3064459
## 2            ns 0.2228302 0.01399089 0.1966140 0.2514481
plot(spkt, type="response", main="The effect of speaker type",
   xlab="Speaker type", ylab="Predicted probability of SUBJREAL:
   'yes'", ylim=c(0, 1), grid=TRUE, lines=list(col=c("black")))
## [...]
```

Native speakers are more likely to not realize the subject than non-native speakers (to which, in a write-up, we might add the drop1 statistics for this predictor (*LR*-statistic=4.648, *df*=1, *p*=0.03109).

What about the interaction effect of CONTRAST and GIVENNESS.fac? We first generate the usual effects data frame and then a plot summarizing the results:

```
(ph.ia <- data.frame(ia <- effect("CONTRAST:GIVENNESS.fac",
   m.final)))
##    CONTRAST GIVENNESS.fac       fit         se      lower      upper
## 1        no         given 0.1363612 0.008070936 0.1213007 0.1529660
## 2       yes         given 0.8585632 0.032444939 0.7824045 0.9110951
## 3        no           new 0.7724753 0.025192511 0.7193836 0.8180627
## 4       yes           new 0.8252114 0.044772180 0.7198420 0.8966409
```

Rather straightforward: There's in general a strong tendency to realize the subject, but not when the referent of the subject is highly given but not contrastive (which of course makes sense, *LR*-statistic=53.84, *df*=1, $p<10^{-12}$); see the simple effects plot in the code.

Most studies do not explore or utilize the ranef results in any way other than them providing 'cleaner' fixef results, which is a bit of a shame and a waste. Not only can they be relevant for assessing model quality, the ranef structure can also be instructive in its own right: In Miglio (et al. 2013), for instance, we found in *post-hoc* exploration that sizes and directions of varying intercepts were correlated with the dialects of the speakers for which the intercepts were computed. It can therefore be useful to pay attention to ranef structures – either to explore them in a *post-hoc*/bottom-up way or to correlate them with other variables or just to visualize them to understand the spread that comes with the fixef results.

I won't really be able to discuss this in as much detail as would be nice (esp. the plotting parts), but let me give you at least one example: I first create a data frame ph that contains all theoretically possible combinations of all predictors and speaker names – that's what expand.grid does (remember that recommendation for further study from Section 2.5.2?).

```
dim(ph <- expand.grid(CONTRAST=levels(x$CONTRAST),
   GIVENNESS.fac=levels(x$GIVENNESS.fac),
   SPEAKERTYPE=levels(x$SPEAKERTYPE),
   SPEAKER=levels(x$SPEAKER)))
## [1] 144    4
```

However, since all theoretically possible combinations are created, ph now also crosses non-native speaker IDs with native-speaker speaker types:

```
head(ph, 6)
##    CONTRAST GIVENNESS.fac SPEAKERTYPE SPEAKER
## 1        no         given         nns     S01
## 2       yes         given         nns     S01
## 3        no           new         nns     S01
## 4       yes           new         nns     S01
## 5        no         given          ns     S01
## 6       yes         given          ns     S01
```

So we get rid of those by retaining only those rows of ph where the speaker type for a speaker is the same as the speaker type for that same speaker in x:

```
dim(ph <- ph[ph$SPEAKERTYPE == (x$SPEAKERTYPE[
   match(ph$SPEAKER, x$SPEAKER)]),])
## [1] 72    4
```

Then we can generate predictions for all actually possible situations using predict, split the data frame up speaker-by-speaker, and then plot all speakers' lines just like in the overall effects plot of the interaction above.

The result of what you see in the code file is the front cover of this book:

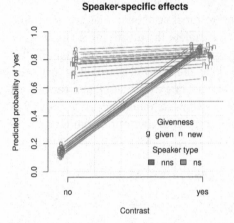

Figure 143: Speaker specificity of CONTRAST:GIVENNESS.fac

Of course one can do more (detailed) things, but it's already clear, for instance, that the spread of the regression lines is wider when CONTRAST is new and that one native speaker in particular (*S10*) has somewhat astonishingly low predicted probabilities of realizing new subject referents. I hope this gives you at least some ideas about how actually exploring ranefs rather than just 'leaving them aside' can be useful.

6.5 On convergence and final recommendations

> However, GLMMs are surprisingly challenging to use even for statisticians.
> (Bolker et al. 2009a:127)

One of the probably most important things to discuss at least briefly, given its frequency in real-life applications, is that of convergence warnings, one of the most frequent problems of MEM. There are many options with regard to how to proceed from here: Impressionistically, what we did above seems to me to be one of the most frequently-adopted solutions, namely simplifying the ranef structure (especially when 'advised' to do so by the results of rePCA, typically by dropping the ranef component with the smallest *sd* while respecting the principle of marginality). There are other options but not only do those become increasingly technical, but, to my knowledge at least, there are also no uniformly accepted rules how to decide which option(s) to take and in which order etc., and of course different orders can change results quite a bit. Here are some options for dealing with convergence issues with a given model m, some easy to do, some requiring more knowledge and experience than I can convey here:

- re-fit m
  - after removing some or more of the rarer levels of one or more of the ranefs. For instance, I sometimes use a function I wrote called random.effects. distribution to help me see things like 'if I delete all levels of this ranef that are attested only *n* or fewer times, I only lose *p*% of the data' (I'm aware that seems to go against the discussion of Gelman & Hill (2006) in Section 6.2 above, but I have seen it make huge differences in 'convergability'). Based on the results from that function, in Gries (to appear a), I removed all levels of a lemma-based ranef that are attested fewer than 10 times (which, given the Zipfian distribution of the lemmas actually only cost me 2.1% of the data points), and I removed all levels of a file-/speaker-based ranef that were attested fewer than 4 times (at the cost of an additional 13.8% of the data points);
  - after removing data points that, early on in the modeling process, have very high residuals; recall from Section 5.6.2 above that, for instance, Dijkstra et al. 2010 or Carrasco Ortíz et al. to appear deleted data points whose absolute standardized residuals in a first maximal model exceeded 2.5;
  - after checking whether there are (more) variables that can be usefully transformed to address problems arising from skewness and/or vastly different value ranges of predictors (for example);
  - with more iterations to give (g)lmer more 'time' to find a converging solution like so: control=glmerControl(optCtrl=list(maxfun=50000));
  - with the start values you get from the just fitted version of m (using getME on m like so: m <- update(m, start=getME(m, c("theta", "fixef"))));
- experiment with different optimizer settings, for instance,
  - re-fit m which was fit with, say, glmer's default settings with a different optimizer (see ?glmerControl);
  - try all sorts of optimizers by, e.g., using something like summary(tryopts.m <- allFit(m)) and then check the variability of the effects with, say, t(summary(tryopts.m)$fixef) or t(summary(tryopts.m)$sdcor);
  - switch to Bayesian modeling, which is of course a huge step, given that that entails learning a whole new approach to modeling (but an extremely useful one), see the recommendations below;
- consult the packages merTools and performance for many functions designed to evaluate a model's performance, convergence, and potential problems.

In a book like this one, that's about all I have space for – once you become a bit more experienced, you will need to read up on things, e.g. read the page on lme4 convergence warnings, Bolker (2015), the reference manual of lme4, and/or the section on convergence warnings in the GLMM FAQ for even more background/ options; Brauer & Curtin's (2018: Table 17) list of suggestions for how to deal with convergence issues is the most comprehensive one I've seen so far.

Here are some final recommendations, before we leave regressions behind and move on to the last chapter.

Recommendation(s) for further study: Check out
- for more discussion on what to include when you write up your MEM results, see Meteyard & Davies (2020), which is also a good general overview;
- for more information on all sorts of aspects of mixed-effects modeling, see Brauer & Curtin (2018), Fox & Weisberg (2019: Ch. 7), Faraway (2016: Ch. 10-11, 13), Schäfer (to appear);
- for a recent discussion on (un)standardized effect sizes for MEM, check out the thread on R-sig-ME beginning with the posting at https://stat.ethz.ch/pipermail/r-sig-mixed-models/ 2020q3/028942.html;
- the package ordinal (especially for its function clmm, which allows you to fit MEMs to ordinal response variables);
- the packages rstanarm (Goodrich et al. 2020) and brms (Bürkner 2017, 2018) for Bayesian fixed- and mixed-effects modeling; for a not too technical intro, see Muth, Oravecz, & Gabry (2018), for a more demanding one, see Vasishth et al. 2018, and see Gelman, Hill, & Vehtari (2020) or McElreath (2020) on Bayesian modeling in general.

Also, running mixed-effects models (esp. with glmer, but also Bayesian ones with brms) and some of the follow-up computations (confidence intervals with bootstrapping) can take a very long time, which means you don't want to do it more often than necessary. It is therefore a good idea to occasionally save objects whose creation took a lot of time or steps so that you can just re-load them rather than having to run the whole script again. I recommend that you either save relevant objects (e.g., your m.final, m.final.cis, or PREDS.boot.obj) with save/saveRDS or periodically the whole workspace with save.image to avoid having to waste time by re-running the code that created those objects; this is why I recommended those functions up in Section 2.5.

7 Tree-based approaches

While regression modeling is probably still the most frequent kind of multifactorial data analysis approach in linguistics, there's another family of methods that's becoming increasingly popular as well, namely approaches based on trees and, by extension, (random) forests. Tree-based methods, a term I'll use to cover both 'simple trees' and random forests, try to identify structure in the relation(s) between a response and multiple predictors by determining how the data set can be split up repeatedly into successively smaller groups (based on the values of the predictors) in such a way that each split leads to the currently best possible improvement in terms of classification accuracy or some other criterion (such as deviance, entropy, the Gini coefficient, or others) for the response variable. As Strobl et al. (2009:326) – a fantastic overview paper on tree-based methods that I cannot help but borrow from quite a bit – put it, "each split in the tree-building process results in daughter nodes that are more pure than the parent node in the sense that groups of [cases] with a majority for either response class are isolated." That also means, with the move from regression modeling to tree-base methods, we're crossing from the domain of **statistical modeling** (Ch. 5-6) into that of **machine learning** (Ch. 7), which comes with a whole new world of goals, emphases, terminology, and challenges, which is something that is often not appreciated enough and which I cannot discuss much here, but I will recommend two papers that will give you a good overview of this below.

In this chapter, I will first discuss two kinds of trees (Section 7.1) and then turn to the corresponding two kinds of random forests (Section 7.2). After that, I will offer a bit of a discussion of their advantages and disadvantages/risks and how they can be used better than they often have in linguistics so far (Section 7.3); I will mostly focus on classification trees/forests (trees/forests with a categorical response) but most of the general logic also applies to regression trees/forests (trees/forests with a numeric response).

https://doi.org/10.1515/9783110718256-007

7.1 Trees

7.1.1 Classification and regression trees

We'll start our discussion of trees with an example we know all too well by know and which will therefore make for an easy comparison, the clause-ordering data discussed in Section 5.3:

```
rm(list=ls(all.names=TRUE)); library(tree)
x <- read.delim(file="_inputfiles/07_scmc.csv",
   stringsAsFactors=TRUE) # change categorical variables into factors
levels(x$CONJ) <- gsub("^.*?/", "", levels(x$CONJ), perl=TRUE)
baseline.1 <- max(prop.table(table(x$ORDER)))
baseline.2 <- sum(prop.table(table(x$ORDER))^2)
```

Let's begin with an extremely simple, monofactorial scenario, in which we'll re-visit a question from Section 5.3.1: do the subordinate clause types correlate with the clause-ordering choices? We first do a simple descriptive cross-tabulation and then use the function tree::tree (Ripley 2019) to create a first classification tree, which we also immediately summarize:

```
addmargins(table(x$SCTYPE, x$ORDER))
##          mc-sc sc-mc Sum
##    caus    184    15 199
##    temp     91   113 204
##    Sum     275   128 403
summary(cart.0 <- tree(  ORDER ~ SCTYPE, data=x)) ## [...]
## Number of terminal nodes:  2
## Residual mean deviance:  0.9646 = 386.8 / 401
## Misclassification error rate: 0.263 = 106 / 403
```

Let's start at the bottom, where the results indicate that

- the tree makes 106 incorrect classifications and, thus, 403-106=297 correct ones, i.e. it has an accuracy of 0.737 (the same as in Section 5.3.1 from the glm);
- after the tree was fit, there's a residual mean deviance of $^{386.8}/_{401}$=0.9646, which is also what you would get from the corresponding glm.

These correspondences of the results of this current, simplest `tree` with those of a `glm` are exemplified here:

```
m <- glm(ORDER~SCTYPE, data=x, family=binomial); c(
   "Residual mean deviance"=m$deviance / m$df.residual,
   "Misclassification error rate"=
      1-sum(diag(table(predict(m)>=0, x$ORDER))/length(x$ORDER)))
##       Residual mean deviance Misclassification error rate
##                    0.9646492                    0.2630273
```

The tree that the algorithm came up with has two terminal nodes – what does it look like?

```
plot(cart.0); text(cart.0, pretty=0, all=TRUE)
```

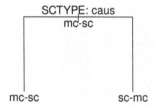

Figure 144: The classification tree of `cart.0`

The way to read this is quite simple: we start at the top, the so-called root (node) and see a first (and, here, only) split and then right below it you see *mc-sc*. That *mc-sc* means 'if you don't do this split, you should predict *mc-sc* (because it's the more frequent level of ORDER)'. The expression above the split is read as a question or a conditional expression: Is SCTYPE caus? If 'yes', you go to the left and down that branch to the first terminal node, which 'predicts' *mc-sc*; if 'no', you go to the right and down that branch to the second terminal node, which 'predicts' *sc-mc*. In other words, the tree says, if SCTYPE is *caus*, I predict *mc-sc*, otherwise (i.e. for all temporal ones), I predict *sc-mc* – seems refreshingly simple, doesn't it? No intercept, no coefficients to add, ... But let's extend this now to something more realistic:

```
summary(cart.1 <- tree(ORDER ~ SCTYPE + CONJ + MORETHAN2CL +
   LENMC + LENSC + LENDIFF, data=x)) ## [...]
## Variables actually used in tree construction:
```

```
## [1] "SCTYPE"       "LENMC"        "LENDIFF"       "MORETHAN2CL" "CONJ"
## Number of terminal nodes:  7
## Residual mean deviance:  0.883 = 349.7 / 396
## Misclassification error rate: 0.2134 = 86 / 403
```

We get the same info as before, but now also a first (coarse) indication of variable importance, namely a list of the variables that actually feature in the tree.
From the absence of LENSC in that list, we can infer that LENSC was not relevant
to the tree. At the same time, the tree with its five predictors doesn't do much
better (in terms of accuracy) than the previous tree using only SCTYPE. But let's
look at this in more detail:

```
cart.1
## node), split, n, deviance, yval, (yprob)
##       * denotes terminal node
##  1) root 403 503.80 mc-sc ( 0.68238 0.31762 )
##    2) SCTYPE: caus 199 106.40 mc-sc ( 0.92462 0.07538 )
##      4) LENMC < 12.5 159  99.36 mc-sc ( 0.90566 0.09434 )
##        8) LENDIFF < 0.5 105  40.20 mc-sc ( 0.95238 0.04762 ) *
##        9) LENDIFF > 0.5 54  51.75 mc-sc ( 0.81481 0.18519 ) *
##      5) LENMC > 12.5 40   0.00 mc-sc ( 1.00000 0.00000 ) *
##    3) SCTYPE: temp 204 280.40 sc-mc ( 0.44608 0.55392 )
##      6) LENDIFF < -2.5 61  81.77 mc-sc ( 0.60656 0.39344 )
##       12) MORETHAN2CL: no 26  28.09 mc-sc ( 0.76923 0.23077 ) *
##       13) MORETHAN2CL: yes 35  48.49 sc-mc ( 0.48571 0.51429 ) *
##      7) LENDIFF > -2.5 143 189.60 sc-mc ( 0.37762 0.62238 )
##       14) CONJ: before 36  48.90 mc-sc ( 0.58333 0.41667 ) *
##       15) CONJ: when,after 107 132.20 sc-mc ( 0.30841 0.69159 ) *
```

How do we read this? I think often this isn't read at all (because the tree is of
course easier to interpret), but just to give you an idea (and the beginning of the
output at the top is like a legend): Node 1 is the (topmost) root node of the tree,
which comprises (all) 403 observations and an overall deviance (amount of variability in the data, same as the null deviance in a glm) of 503.8; the prediction
from that node alone is *mc-sc*, which occurs in 0.68238 of all cases. The first split
then leads to nodes 2 and 3. Node 2 describes all cases where SCTYPE is *caus*,
which are 199 cases with a remaining deviance of 106.4 and for which the tree
predicts *mc-sc*, because that level accounts for 0.92462 of those 199 cases. Node 3
describes all cases where SCTYPE is *temp*, which are 204 cases with a remaining
deviance of 280.4 and for which the tree predicts *sc-mc*, because that level ac-

counts for 0.55392 of those 204 cases, and so on. The 7 terminal nodes are the ones marked with asterisks; in the output of cart.1$frame, these terminal nodes are the ones called <leaf>. You can then also easily get the classifications from this tree and the confusion matrix in a way that is fairly similar to how we proceeded with a glm:

```
x$PREDS.NUM.t <- predict(cart.1)[,"sc-mc"]
x$PREDS.CAT.t <- predict(cart.1, type="class")
(qwe <- table(x$ORDER, x$PREDS.CAT.t)) ## [...]
##          mc-sc sc-mc
##   mc-sc   225    50
##   sc-mc    36    92
##       Class. acc. Prec. for sc-mc  Rec. for sc-mc
##        0.7866005        0.6478873       0.7187500
## Prec. for mc-sc  Rec. for mc-sc
##        0.8620690       0.8181818
```

Now, what does the tree look like? Let's make it a bit nicer (ignore the (code for the) shading for now):

```
plot(cart.1); grid(); axis(2); mtext("Deviance", 2, 3)
text(cart.1, pretty=0, all=TRUE) ## [...]
```

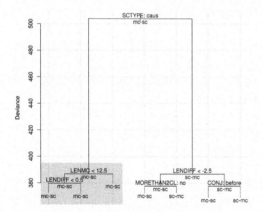

Figure 145: The classification tree of cart.1

Note that the length of the vertical lines reflect the importance of the split, because they indicate how much a split reduces the deviance; that's why the topmost (root) node is at y=503.8 (the deviance of the whole data set) whereas the next two splits are at y=386.82 (the summed deviances of node 2 and 3: sum(cart.1$frame$dev[c(2,7)])) etc. One interesting aspect to note: For the numeric predictors, tree finds the best possible cut-off point, i.e. the value where to split the numeric predictor into 2 groups to predict the response variable best (not unlike we did in Section 5.3.3.3); some approach like this can be useful when numeric predictors in a regression have such a skewed distribution that factorization/binning – cutting it up into an ordinal factor with a few levels – seems the only solution; see Gries (to appear a) for multiple applications of this to recalcitrant data.

Given this tree, you should ask yourself two related questions: (i) why are there so many splits on the left side when they all make the same prediction (*mc-sc*, this is what the grey polygon is supposed to draw your attention to) and, thus and more generally, (ii) when do trees stop splitting (because this one apparently went on splitting even when that didn't change predictions anymore)? In general, a tree stops splitting when
– the improvement, however that is measured (deviance, Gini, ...), resulting from any possible next split doesn't reach a certain threshold anymore; this is also the answer to question (i): the tree doesn't optimize classification/prediction accuracy per se, it optimizes something else and that something else licensed more splits even when accuracy did not increase anymore;
– the number of cases in the nodes resulting from a split being considered doesn't reach a certain threshold;
– when the tree depth exceeds another threshold value.

Those criteria are all tweakable (see ?tree::tree.control) and differ across packages and functions.

Before we interpret the plot, two other things merit brief discussion. One is concerned with validation again, which we discussed above in Section 5.7 for regression modeling. Let's do a quick attempt at validation that follows the above logic/code as closely as possible. We prepare a column called FOLDS for the 10-fold cross-validation, plus we create a vector to collect 10 prediction accuracies:

```
set.seed(sum(utf8ToInt("Himbeertörtchen")))
x$FOLDS <- sample(rep(1:10, length.out=nrow(x)))
prediction.accuracies <- rep(NA, 10)
```

Then we do the exact same kind of for-loop as above:

```
for (i in 1:10) {
    x.train <- x[x$FOLDS!=i,] # all data points where x$FOLDS isn't i
    x.test <-  x[x$FOLDS==i,] # all data points where x$FOLDS is i
    tree.curr <- tree(ORDER ~ SCTYPE+LENMC+LENDIFF+MORETHAN2CL+CONJ,
        data=x.train)
    x.test$PREDS.CAT <- predict(tree.curr, type="class",
        newdata=x.test)
    prediction.accuracies[i] <- mean(x.test$ORDER==x.test$PREDS.CAT)
}
summary(prediction.accuracies)
##    Min. 1st Qu.  Median   Mean 3rd Qu.    Max.
## 0.6000  0.7500  0.7561 0.7492  0.7937  0.8500
```

We find that the cross-validated prediction accuracies are a bit lower an average (a mean of 0.7492) compared to the classification accuracy of cart.1 fitted on all the data, which was 0.7866, but a one-sample *t*-test says that the classification accuracy is within the confidence interval of the prediction accuracies (t.test(prediction.accuracies, mu=0.7866005)$conf.int) so this isn't too bad.

The other topic is related to validation, but also concerned with question (ii) from above: Classification trees like this one are often likely to split more than would be necessary for best accuracy; we saw this in the left part of the tree featuring splits that didn't change the prediction. To deal with this, we can **prune** the tree. We first tell the tree we want to run some cross-validation that does not use deviance or Gini, but the number of misclassifications, i.e. accuracy:

```
set.seed(sum(utf8ToInt("Mozzarella")))
pruning <- cv.tree(cart.1, FUN=prune.misclass)
```

Then we plot the result (not shown here): the *x*-axis has the tree sizes that resulted from the cross-validation (in numbers of terminal nodes) and the *y*-axis portrays how much worse the trees are with those sizes. The tree in cart.1 had 7, i.e. is on the very right, but, with an Occam's razor perspective, we can see that a tree with only 4 or 5 terminal nodes is just as good but with fewer distinctions – what in regression modeling would be 'fewer parameters' – so we pick 4 as the 'best' tree size (*best* in the sense of 'a good compromise between fit and parsimony').

```
plot(pruning$size, pruning$dev, type="b"); grid() ## [...]
```

With that info, we prune our original tree and plot it right away:

```
cart.1.pruned <- prune.tree(cart.1, best=4)
plot(cart.1.pruned); axis(2); mtext("Deviance", 2, 3); grid()
text(cart.1.pruned, pretty=0, all=TRUE)
```

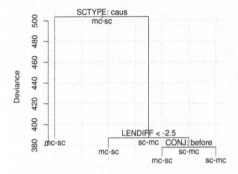

Figure 146: The classification tree of cart.1.pruned

This looks much easier to interpret and you can see how all the branching on the left was eliminated, given how it didn't contribute to a better accuracy in the first place. But before we interpret this, let's see how much worse accuracy became due to the pruning. As you can see from running the code in the code file, there's hardly any difference: the pruned tree gets 0.7841 right when the non-pruned tree got 0.7866 right, meaning we got a much more concise/parsimonious and easier-to-explain tree with practically no loss in explanatory power.

How do we interpret the tree? Now that it's been pruned, it's actually very easy to interpret: Rather than formulate many long and complex *if-then* sentences, as one often has to when summarizing a tree, here we can just paraphrase it by saying: 'predict *mc-sc* unless (i) the subordinate clause is headed by *als/when* or *nachdem/after* and (ii) LENDIFF is ≥-2, i.e. when the subordinate clause length is shorter than, or equal to, the main clause length or up to maximally two words longer than the main clause'. As you hopefully recognize, those findings are very similar to the effects plots of shown in Section 5.3.5, thereby providing what seems like converging machine-learning evidence for the statistical-modeling regression results there.

7.1.2 Conditional inference trees

An alternative tree-based approach that has gained some popularity in linguistic applications is that of conditional inference trees, in particular as implemented in the packages party (Hothorn et al. 2006) and partykit (Hothorn et al. 2015), which address concerns regarding the degree to which classification trees of the above kind can (i) overfit (which can be countered by pruning as shown above) and (ii) overestimate the importance of predictors with many different values (i.e. numeric predictors or categorical ones with many levels, see Strobl et al. 2009:342). This approach is conceptually similar to the kind of trees discussed above, but uses a p-value (adjusted for multiple tests) as a splitting criterion. Creating a conditional inference tree in R is (deceptively) simple, given everything we've discussed so far:

```
library(partykit) # the newer reimplementation of the package party
plot(ctree.1 <- ctree(ORDER ~ SCTYPE + CONJ + MORETHAN2CL +
    LENMC + LENSC + LENDIFF, data=x))
```

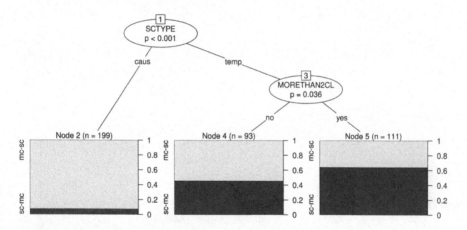

Figure 147: The conditional inference tree of ctree.1

The resulting plot essentially says
- if SCTYPE is *caus* (node 2 with 199 cases), *mc-sc* is extremely likely (>90%) whereas *sc-mc* is rather unlikely (<10%);
- if SCTYPE is *temp* and MORETHAN2CL is *no* (node 4 with 93 cases), *mc-sc* is considerably less likely (but, with ≈55%) still more likely than *sc-mc* and thus predicted);
- if SCTYPE is *temp* and MORETHAN2CL is *yes* (node 5 with 111 cases), *mc-sc* is even less likely and now also not predicted (because *sc-mc* occurs in ≈64% of all those cases).

Some people use the fancier-looking plot resulting from the following line (output not shown), which shows bar plots for every single node, even the non-terminal ones, which, to my mind, can quickly lead to visual overkill.

```
plot(ctree.1, inner_panel=node_barplot) ## [...]
```

I sometimes just resort to the following tree; here, to use node 2 as an example, we see that in the 199 cases where SCTYPE is *caus*, ORDER is predicted to be *mc-sc* and 7.5% (0.075) of those predictions are then false, meaning of course that 92.5% (0.925) are correct, and analogously for the other nodes, plus I show how to extract the predicted probabilities of each ordering for each node:

```
plot(ctree.1, type="simple") ## [...]
```

BTW, this is how can retrieve the bar plot's proportions for each node:

```
qwe <- predict(ctree.1, type="prob")
qwe[sort(unique(rownames(qwe))),]
##        mc-sc       sc-mc
## 2 0.9246231 0.07537688
## 4 0.5483871 0.45161290
## 5 0.3603604 0.63963964
```

What's the accuracy of this tree?

```
x$PREDS.NUM.ct <- qwe[,"sc-mc"]
x$PREDS.CAT.ct <- predict(ctree.1)
(qwe <- table(x$ORDER, x$PREDS.CAT.ct)) ## [...]
##          mc-sc sc-mc
##   mc-sc    235    40
##   sc-mc     57    71
##      Class. acc. Prec. for sc-mc  Rec. for sc-mc
##        0.7593052       0.6396396       0.5546875
## Prec. for mc-sc  Rec. for mc-sc
##        0.8047945       0.8545455
```

We get a similar accuracy to all the other accuracy scores for this data set we've seen so far (the accuracy of the conditional inference tree isn't significantly worse than that of the pruned classification tree. Fortunately and because conditional inference trees use *p*-values (corrected for multiple testing) as their main splitting criterion (see ?ctree_control for other options), they do not require pruning (Strobl et al. 2009:328) or cross-validation; in the code file, I show how you get the *p*-values that ctree used for deciding on what to split where.:

However, one major problem of both kinds of trees is

> their instability to small changes in the learning data [...] the entire tree structure could be altered if the first splitting variable [something to which we will return in detail below], or only the first cutpoint, was chosen differently because of a small change in the learning data. Because of this instability, the predictions of single trees show a high variability (Strobl et al. 2009:330).

Another problem of trees is that "the prediction of single trees is piecewise constant and thus may jump from one value to the next even for small changes of the predictor values" (Strobl et al. 2009:331, see Section 7.3 below for an example). Both of these problems can be dealt with to some degree using so-called ensemble methods such as random forests, to which we turn now.

7.2 Ensembles of trees: forests

Random forests (Breiman 2001a, Hastie, Tibshirani, & Friedman 2014: Ch. 15, James et al. 2014: Section 8.2) are an instance of what are called **ensemble methods** because "an ensemble or committee of classification trees is aggregated for prediction" (Strobl et al. 2009:325). In other words, a random forest consists of ntree different trees, but with two additional layers of randomness, namely randomness
- **on the level of the data points**: random forests involve running (and then amalgamating) ntree trees on ntree different data sets that were bootstrapped – sampled with replacement – from the original data (recall Section 5.2.1.5);
- **on the level of predictors**: at every split in every tree, only a randomly-selected subset of the predictors is eligible to be chosen, namely mtry predictors.

Random forests usually overfit much less than individual trees or even training/ test validation approaches and can be straightforwardly evaluated given that random forest accuracies are prediction, not classification, accuracies: While classification trees, strictly speaking, only return classification accuracies (i.e. accuracies in classifying cases on which the tree was trained, unless you cross-validate yourself later like we did above), random forests return actual prediction accuracies. Why/how is that? If you bootstrap with replacement from your data, then, like I mentioned above, each of the ntree trees will

– be based only on the cases that were sampled (with replacement) this time around, i.e. their training set, which, on average, will be 63.2% of all your different cases);
– not 'have seen' the, on average, remaining 36.8% of the cases that were not sampled for the current tree, i.e. cases that the current tree was not trained on, which are referred to as the **held-out** cases or the **OOB (out of bag)** cases.

The predictive accuracy of a forest can then be tested by aggregating (by some statistical voting procedure), for each case separately, the predictions of only those trees for which the case in question was OOB; that way, cross-validation is inbuilt into the random forest algorithm. Now you might ask, 'where are those numbers coming from, that the training sample and the test sample will on average be 63.2% and 36.8% of the data? (Especially if you read James et al. (2014:317), who, to keep things simpler, state that the ratio of the training to the test sample is $\approx^2/_3$ to $\approx^1/_3$.) To answer that question, we can quickly simulate the boostrapping approach (no pun intended):

```
set.seed(sum(utf8ToInt("Currywurst")))
some.data <- 1:500
collector <- rep(NA, 10000)
for (i in 1:10000) {
   collector[i] <- length(unique(sample(some.data, 500,
      replace=TRUE)))
}; median(collector/500) # tadaah!
## [1] 0.632
```

The above also begins to point to one disadvantage of random forests: While they excel at prediction (often outperforming regression models in that sense), interpreting them can be hard: There is no single model, no single tree from a single data set that can be straightforwardly plotted – there's a forest of, say, ntree=500 different trees fit on 500 differently-sampled data sets, with thousands of different splits in different locations in trees with differently-sampled mtry predictors available for splits. (And below I hope to convince you that the practice of trying to appealingly interpret/summarize such a forest of ntree trees with a single tree fitted to the same data is in fact misguided.)

With regard to the size or importance of an effect/predictor, the random forest implementations that seem to be most widely used in linguistics – randomForest::randomForest and party::cforest/partykit::cforest – offer the functionality of computing so-called variable importance scores, some version of which (permutation-based scores, conditional importance scores, scaled or unscaled ones) is regularly reported. **Variable importance scores** basically answer the question "how much (if at all) does a certain predictor contribute to predicting the response?". (Note the *exact* formulation I'm using here: There's an important reason why I did not simply say "how much is a predictor correlated with the response?" This is me setting the stage for Section 7.3.)

These importance scores can be computed in different ways, but one common strategy involves taking a predictor in the forest, randomizing it in some way (thereby 'destroying' its association with the response), and determining how much worse the forest's prediction accuracy becomes as a result, which should remind you of some of the simulation examples above, e.g. in Sections 4.2.2.1 or 4.3.2.2, where we did just that; more complex versions of this kind of permutation accuracy and stratified randomization are also available and used.

With regard to the nature/direction of an effect, on the other hand, one can report **partial dependence scores**, which answer the question "how do values/levels of a certain predictor help predict the response?", but for no good reason I see those much less often. Let's now discuss how this all works; thankfully, in terms of R code, it's all pretty (but again deceptively) straightforward.

7.2.1 Forests of classification and regression trees

Let's revisit the clause-ordering data from the perspective of random forests, for now using the maybe best-known implementation in `randomForest::randomForest` (Liaw & Wiener 2002). The following shows that we use the familiar formula notation, but we also tweak a few hyperparameters and arguments:
– the main hyperparameters:
  – `ntree`: how many trees we want the forest to have; the default is 500 but since the data set is small, we can straightforwardly increase that number because "[i]n general, the higher the number of trees, the more reliable the prediction and the interpretability of the variable importance" (Strobl et al. 2009:343);
  – `replace`: whether we want sampling with replacement or not (the default is TRUE);
  – `mtry`: how many predictors we want to be available at each split; the default for a forest of classification trees is the square root of the number of predictors in the formula (for a forest of regression trees, the default is $1/3$ of the number of predictors); note that "[w]hen predictor variables are highly correlated, [...] a higher number of randomly preselected predictor variables is better suited to reflect conditional importance" (Strobl et al. 2009:343); check out `?randomForest::tuneRF` to determine the best `mtry` for a data set;

- additional arguments:
  - keep.forest: whether the forest is kept in the output object (the default is FALSE);
  - keep.inbag: whether we want to retain the info which data points were sampled into the training data for each tree (but, strangely enough, not how often ...) (the default is FALSE);
  - importance: whether we want predictor importance to be computed (the default is FALSE).

```
library(randomForest); set.seed(sum(utf8ToInt("Bacon bits")))
(rf.1 <- randomForest(ORDER ~ LENMC + LENSC + LENDIFF + CONJ +
    SCTYPE + MORETHAN2CL, data=x, ntree=1500, replace=TRUE, mtry=3,
    keep.forest=TRUE, keep.inbag=TRUE, importance=TRUE))
## [...]
## Confusion matrix:
##        mc-sc sc-mc class.error
## mc-sc    226    49   0.1781818
## sc-mc     60    68   0.4687500
```

The output shows that our forest obtained a prediction accuracy of 1-0.2705=0.7295 and that the accuracy was much lower for *sc-mc* (0.46875) than for *mc-sc* (0.17818). We can also compute precision and recall by retrieving the actual predictions:

```
x$PREDS.NUM.rf <- predict(rf.1, type="prob")[,"sc-mc"]
x$PREDS.CAT.rf <- predict(rf.1)
qwe <- table(x$ORDER, x$PREDS.CAT.rf)
## [...]
##      Class. acc. Prec. for sc-mc  Rec. for sc-mc
##        0.7295285       0.5811966       0.5312500
## Prec. for mc-sc  Rec. for mc-sc
##        0.7902098       0.8218182
```

But which variables are driving this prediction accuracy? We can get those from rf.1 with importance (and plot them, if we think that's really necessary):

```
varimps <- importance(rf.1, type=1)
dotchart(sort(varimps[,1]), xlim=c(0, 40), pch=4) ## [...]
```

Apparently, SCTYPE and CONJ are most important and nearly equally so – in part because CONJ is a more fine-grained version of SCTYPE of course and because the biggest difference between the conjunctions is between those that constitute the two levels of SCTYPE). Of the numeric predictors LENMC and LENDIFF are most important (with hardly any difference). Note, by the way, that predictors can be considered 'important' or 'worth retaining in a forest', if their variable importance score is greater than the absolute value of the smallest negative importance score (Strobl et al. 2009:339, 343) (of which we have none here).

I've seen many papers/talks that leave it at this or do something really (sorry ...) self-contradictory, namely compute the nature/direction of the effects in a monofactorial way (!), but just like it doesn't make sense to summarize a multifactorial regression with monofactorial tests/plots (see Section 5.2.6.3), it also makes no sense to summarize a multifactorial forest with monofactorial tables –[22] this is what we use partial dependence plots for.

There is a function partialPlot available in the package randomForest but we will not use it for two reasons. First and to be frank, it annoys me to no end that that function forces you to accept blue bar plots (the color is hard-coded into the function – why?!) and, second, because we need to use another package to compute partial dependence scores of conditional inference forests anyway (the package pdp) so we'll simply use pdp::partial for both; when we do so, I always set the which.class argument to the second level of the response because I'm so used to that from regression modeling (just like I did above for computing x$PREDS.NUM.rf, force of habit ...). Let's look at scores for one categorical and one numeric predictor to then discuss a visualization option for each:

```
library(pdp)
(pd.c <- partial(object=rf.1, pred.var="CONJ", which.class=2,
   train=x))
##        CONJ       yhat
## 1     when -0.02583917
## 2   before -0.40144125
## 3    after -0.05646455
## 4  because -1.90299511
```

---

22 I once reviewed a submission for a journal where the authors applied a random forest to some data but (i) only used about a third of the predictors they had (for no good reason at all: random forests can even be used when you have more predictors than cases!) and (ii) then proceeded to discuss the results of the forest on the basis of a series of separate monofactorial chi-squared tests – you do not want to do that ...

```
pd.lm <- partial(object=rf.1, pred.var="LENMC", which.class=2,
   train=x); pd.lm[sort(sample(nrow(pd.lm), 5)),]
##    LENMC       yhat
## 2      3 -0.9378265
## 12    14 -1.1623414
## 17    19 -0.6488276
## 18    20 -0.6574969
## 27    31 -0.4999908
```

And then we could plot those in a way that also shows the distribution of the predictors – with bar widths reflecting the frequencies of the levels of CONJ and point sizes reflecting the frequencies of main clause lengths:

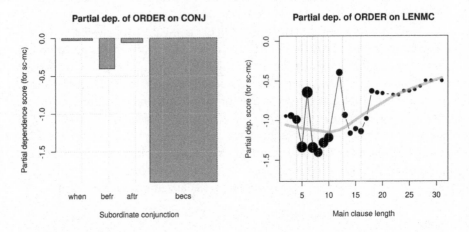

Figure 148: Partial dependence plots for rf.1

The left panel shows, as we already know from above, that *because* strongly suppresses (negative *y*-values!) *sc-mc*, etc. The right panel shows a fairly erratic patterning, but we can see, if we try real hard, an overall pattern of the line going more up then down, namely
– overall with the really low values on the left and the continually high values on the right;
– where most of the data are according to the decile grid, e.g. in the interval [5, 12.6];
– from the smoother I added in grey.

7.2.2 Forests of conditional inference trees

Building a forests of conditional inference trees is only a bit different from the use of randomForest above:[23]

```
library(partykit); set.seed(sum(utf8ToInt("Gummibären")))
cf.1 <- cforest(ORDER ~ LENMC + LENSC + LENDIFF + CONJ + SCTYPE +
   MORETHAN2CL, data=x, ntree=1500, perturb=list(replace=TRUE),
   mtry=3)
```

As before, we can compute predictions and all the usual statistics:

```
x$PREDS.NUM.cf <- predict(cf.1, type="prob")[,"sc-mc"]
x$PREDS.CAT.cf <- predict(cf.1)
(qwe <- table(x$ORDER, x$PREDS.CAT.cf)) ## [...]
##          mc-sc sc-mc
##   mc-sc   243    32
##   sc-mc    31    97
##      Class. acc. Prec. for sc-mc  Rec. for sc-mc
##       0.8436725       0.7519380       0.7578125
## Prec. for mc-sc  Rec. for mc-sc
##       0.8868613       0.8836364
```

Similarly, we can compute variable importance scores with varimp, which computes importance measures whose logic is comparable to the permutation-accuracy one used in randomForest::importance above, where predictors' associations with the response gets destroyed to measure the impact this has on

---

23 Note that partykit::cforest can take an argument cores=..., where you can provide a number >1 specifying how many cores/threads you want to use; while this can speed up the execution greatly, at least in partykit version 1.2-10 this also leads to the results being random but not replicable anymore, which is why I'm not using this here. (I'm suspecting that the random number seed is not being passed on to the different cores/threads correctly, but I'm not sure; contacting the package maintainer about this led to no response other than "This is beyond my control". Thus, if replicability is relevant, maybe don't use partykit (but party) and/ or check whether this ever gets fixed.) Also and completely by the way, here's an interesting little nugget that I've never seen or heard acknowledged in linguistics: This is what the documentation of cforest for both party (at least till version 1.3-5) and partykit (at least till version 1.2-10) says about itself (my emphasis): "Ensembles of conditional inference trees haven't yet been extensively tested, so this routine is meant for the expert user only and **its current state is rather experimental**"; I genuinely wonder how many users of cforest are aware of that.

prediction accuracy. However, with an argument called `conditional` you can choose how the permutation is done: `conditional=FALSE` refers to the default of randomly permuting the column of interest, `conditional=TRUE` means that the variable of interest is permuted in a way that takes its correlation with other predictors into consideration and can avoid exaggerating the importance of predictors that are correlated with other predictors (which is also why computing conditional scores takes *considerably* longer than computing unconditional ones):

```
sort(varimp(cf.1))    # sort the variable importance scores of cf.1
##        LENSC         LENMC MORETHAN2CL      LENDIFF
##   0.02764128  0.09007466  0.09759636   0.10013999
##         CONJ        SCTYPE
##   0.74460031  1.33480127
sort(varimp(cf.1, conditional=TRUE, cores=20))
##        LENSC       LENDIFF        LENMC        SCTYPE
## 0.003453228 0.018572660 0.020469838 0.042069597
## MORETHAN2CL          CONJ
## 0.071758366 0.426737230
```

As you can see, the kind of permutation makes a difference. All forests agree that CONJ is quite important and that LENSC is not, but in the middle they disagree a bit, especially with regard to MORETHAN2CL. With a caveat to be discussed in Section 7.3, I would tend to trust the conditional `varimp` scores of `partykit` most.

Let's use the `pdp` package already introduced above to again compute partial dependence scores for just two predictors:

```
(pd.c <- partial(object=cf.1, pred.var="CONJ", which.class=2,
   train=x))
##       CONJ        yhat
## 1     when -0.05567753
## 2   before -0.40479045
## 3    after -0.10700286
## 4  because -0.87776710
pd.lm <- partial(object=cf.1, pred.var="LENMC", which.class=2,
   train=x); pd.lm[sort(sample(nrow(pd.lm), 5)),]
##    LENMC       yhat
## 2      3 -0.6379518
## 8      9 -0.5212465
## 9     10 -0.5560669
```

```
## 11      13 -0.6600751
## 12      14 -0.6634140
## [...]
```

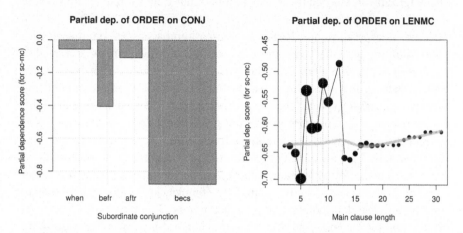

Figure 149: Partial dependence plots for `cf.1`

Here, too, the overall picture is similar to what we found before – just make sure you write it up well: we need variable importance scores (to know what's doing something in our data) and partial dependence scores (to know what is doing what in our data).

Recommendation(s) for further study: If you used the `party` package for your forest, check out `party::varimpAUC` for an alternative variable importance measure, whose logic is similar to that of the *C*-score and which are supposed to be better for imbalanced response variables (see Janitza et al. 2013).

7.3 Discussion

Trees and especially forests have become increasingly frequent in linguistic applications in part because this family of approaches is said to have several attractive/advantageous features. At the same time, I'm also sometimes concerned with how a variety of potential problems of tree-based approaches are under-appreciated or -estimated in linguistic studies. In this section, I will discuss tree-based approaches to highlight some of the issues that not everyone might be aware of – I certainly wasn't for too long: introductory/textbook discussion of forests in particular that I consulted didn't cover all the subtleties I later found discussed in methodological research papers on forests. Hopefully, this discussion will make users abandon certain misconceptions and alert them to pitfalls in data analysis and interpretation; as always, the situation will not be always characterizable in easy black-vs.-white strokes, but it helps to at least be aware of some of the relevant issues.

One widespread notion is that tree-based approaches are often seen as a **good 'plan B'**, i.e. a methodological fall-back position when regression modeling is seen as too difficult or (near) impossible for a certain data set; some might even go so far as to say that tree-based methods outperform regression modeling in many – most? – respects (and I'm assuming/hoping they mean that like I did above, namely as 'outperform in terms of prediction'). For example, tree-based approaches don't rely on estimations as parametric regression models do but can essentially be seen as a non-parametric alternative that is, potentially at least, much less affected by many kinds of problems that can plague regression modeling such as data sparsity, collinearity, complete separation, small-n-large-p situations (few data points, many predictors), etc. In addition, there's a perception that the visualization of at least trees is **more intuitively interpretable** than the summary/coefficients table usually reported for regression models (see, e.g., Baayen et al. 2013:265 for such an assessment). Similarly, there's also a perception that trees are particularly good, or even better than regression modeling, at **exploring/revealing interactions**; a somewhat related notion, which I hardly ever see mentioned in linguistics, however, is that tree-based approaches are good at detecting **non-linear and non-monotonic patterns** in the associations between predictors and a response.

Then, let's not forget that fitting trees/forests seems 'so easy': Even for data that would be very hard to model with statistical-modeling tools such as regression methods and would, therefore, require much preparation, exploration, diagnostics, and (cross-)validation, machine-learning tools like trees seem to take one or two lines of code and then you have a random forest with a good prediction accuracy (without diagnostics, validation, etc.), and easy-to-obtain variable importance scores. And we find statements that variable importance scores from tree-based methods are less volatile than the results from stepwise model selection in regression, which also means that "the overall importance ranking of a variable is much more reliable than its position in stepwise selection" (Strobl et al. 2009:341, also p. 324). For all these reasons, tree-based approaches are also sometimes used as a way of validating regression analyses – if a tree-based method, with its completely different underpinnings, returns results that are compatible with the regression results, that provides converging-evidence kind of support for the regression model; recent applications of tree-based methods in linguistics include Tagliamonte & Baayen (2012), Dilts (2013), Hansen &

Schneider (2013), Bernaisch et al. (2014), Klavan, Pilvik, & Uiboaed (2015), Matsuki et al. (2016), Szmrecsanyi et al. (2016), Heller et al. (2017), Rezaee & Golparvar (2017), Hundt (2018), Tomaschek, Hendrix, & Baayen (2018), and many more.

Now, not to rain on the parade – after all, I have used tree-based methods myself – but the situation is not quite as simple and clear-cut. First, the ease of interpretation of trees is often overstated. For instance, in order to represent what in a regression is a simple slope, a tree might have to represent multiple binary splits that a user/reader needs to then 'piece back together' to recognize the slope. Let's just look at one very simple example: The left panel of Figure 150 shows the result of a monofactorial tree (using tree::tree) modeling mpg ~ wt (weight) in the mtcars data discussed above a few times. If you try to interpret this, your eyes have to dart back and forth quite a bit in order for you to piece together from (i) the observed/predicted values decreasing from left to right (30.07>21.18>17.80>14.70) and (ii) the predictor ranges increasing from left to right (<2.26, [2.26,3.325), [3.325, 3.49), and ≥3.49) that the left panel amounts to nothing more than a simple slope – the right panel, by contrast, makes that much easier; in fact, at this point in the book, I really hope you cannot look at it and not get that fact right away. (A regression tree from partykit::ctree would also be easier to interpret than the result of tree::tree.)[24]

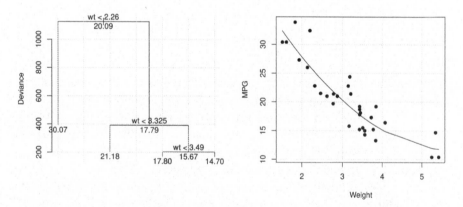

Figure 150: A slope in a regression tree vs. in a regression

---

24 For another example like this, run plot(partykit::ctree(SUBJREAL ~ GIVENNESS, data=x)) on the data from Section 6.4: You will see how much cognitive and visual work you'll have to do to find out whether GIVENNESS has a monotonic effect on SUBJREAL, and then compare that to the ease of plot(allEffects(glm(SUBJREAL ~ GIVENNESS, data=x, family=binomial)), type="response").

Also, note that the regression model makes more fine-grained predictions (and heterogeneity of predictions is in part a reflection of discriminatory/predictive power): The following plot repeats the right panel from above but adds the predictions of the tree (horizontal grey lines) within the predictor ranges of the tree (dashed vertical lines). While the predictions of the regression are not necessarily better here, they do discriminate more within each bin, which can make a difference: For example, the tree predicts the same mpg-value (14.7) for a car weighing 3520 lbs and one weighting 5424 lbs, the regression does not (it predicts 17.3 for the former and 11.8 for the latter).

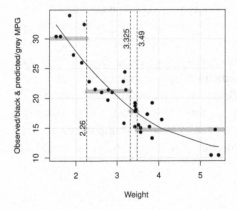

Figure 151: Predictions from a regression and the tree

Finally, with regard to ease of interpretability, I once saw authors argue that a regression result involving three-way interactions was 'hard to grasp intuitively', which the authors then used as a reason to show a classification tree, half of whose terminal nodes *also* involved three binary splits; while admittedly the rest of their tree was indeed simpler than a regression result, such assessments, I think, muddy the waters more than they clear things up. Plus, trees can also be really complex. While I will not waste a page here to show you a really terribly opaque plot, if you have time, check out Figure 1 of Bernaisch et al. (2014:17): Characterizing that monstrosity took us more than one page of densely-packed super-ugly conditional sentences and a big table, followed by some more paraphrases – ease of interpretation? Not necessarily ...

Another, much more important issue is concerned with the notion of interactions, in particular their identifiability and their relation to variable importance scores. Let's first consider how an interaction would be represented in a tree.

If you go back to Figure 97 in Section 5.2.4.2, you will recall that the variables CLAUSE and GRAMREL were interacting – how does that surface in a tree? Like in Figure 152 (if you use the easier-to-interpret partykit::ctree, not tree::tree): When CLAUSE is *main*, then the length for GRAMREL being *subj* is lower (by ≈3) than that for GRAMREL being *obj* , but when CLAUSE is *subord*, then the length for GRAMREL being *subj* is higher (by ≈2) than that for GRAMREL being *obj*.

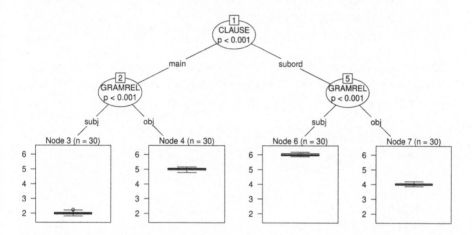

Figure 152: A 2-by-2 interaction in a regression tree

But there are cases where trees are not as great at interactions as one might think. First, while Figure 152 isn't too bad at all in how it requires only a bit of visual scanning to recover the interaction, it is also a simple tree involving just two predictors – in a tree with much more variables, such effects will definitely be much harder to recognize. Second, as the depth/complexity of a tree grows, the interactions it can reveal become more and more intricate or specialized; it's not uncommon to look at a more complex tree and see the equivalent of 4- or 5-way interactions, which are (i) extremely hard to describe and interpret and (ii) probably often not really explainable (let alone motivatable *a priori*). If one uses these methods for prediction only, that of course doesn't matter – all that matters is the often exceptional prediction accuracy – but in linguistics, we usually do not 'just' want to predict, we also want to explain, and then these kinds of results are often much more challenging than trees-are-so-easy proponents admit.

But it gets worse because the situation is even trickier: Sometimes, tree-based approaches don't even see what they are supposedly so good at and/or provide quite importance results that are ambiguous and regularly misinter-preted; the following discussion is based on Gries (2020).

Consider the following tiny data set of three binary predictors and one bi-nary response (the *s* in the variable names stands for 'small'):

```
P1s <- factor(rep(c("b","a","b","a"), c(1,7,9,3)) )
P2s <- factor(rep(c("e","f","e"), c(6,10,4)))
P3s <- factor(rep(c("m","n","m","n"), c(6,4,6,4)))
Rs <- factor(rep(c("x","y"), c(10, 10)))
Ds <- data.frame(P1s, P2s, P3s, Rs)
```

The relation between the predictors and the response is such that P1s is most as-sociated with the response Rs, P2s is less associated with Rs, and P3s is not asso-ciated with Rs at all:

```
table(P1s, Rs) # accuracy=0.7
##    Rs
## P1s x y
##   a 7 3
##   b 3 7
table(P2s, Rs) # accuracy=0.6
##    Rs
## P2s x y
##   e 6 4
##   f 4 6
table(P3s, Rs) # accuracy=0.5
##    Rs
## P3s x y
##   m 6 6
##   n 4 4
```

However, there's an interaction effect here: P2s:P3s predicts Rs perfectly:

```
ftable(P2s, P3s, Rs)
##          Rs x y
## P2s P3s
## e   m       6 0
##     n       0 4
## f   m       0 6
##     n       4 0
```

Thus, this data set exemplifies something that is at least relatable to the so-called **XOR problem,**

> a situation where two variables show no main effect [not true of P2s here, though, which has a 'main effect'] but a perfect interaction. In this case, because of the lack of a marginally detectable main effect, none of the variables may be selected in the first split of a classification tree, and the interaction may never be discovered" (Strobl et al. 2009:341).

And indeed, `tree::tree` doesn't see the perfectly predictive interaction – instead, it returns a tree with an accuracy of 0.75 that uses the interaction `P1s:P3s` (I am referring to that as an interaction because it's possible to say 'the effect of P3s is not the same everywhere: it does something when `P1s` is *a*, but not when `P1s` is *b*'). (Note that `rpart::rpart` doesn't fare better, neither does `party(kit)::ctree`, which makes no split at all.)

```
plot(tree.tree <- tree(Rs ~ P1s+P2s+P3s)); grid()
axis(2); mtext("Deviance", 2, 3)
text(tree.tree, pretty=0, all=TRUE)
text(x=2.5, y=21, paste0("accuracy=", mean(predict(
    tree.tree, type="class")==Rs)))
```

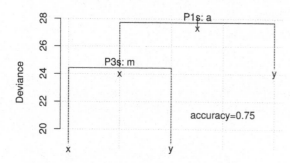

Figure 153: A tree on the (small) example data

But then, maybe this is because the data set is so small (esp. for the *p*-value-based trees of `party/partykit`) so let's increase it by one order of magnitude (the *l* in the variable names stands for 'larger') and try again:

```
P1l <- rep(P1s, 10); P2l <- rep(P2s, 10); P3l <- rep(P3s, 10);
    Rl <- rep(Rs, 10); Dl <- data.frame(P1l, P2l, P3l, Rl)
```

```
plot(tree.tree <- tree(R1 ~ P11+P21+P31)); grid()
axis(2); mtext("Deviance", 2, 3)
text(tree.tree, pretty=0, all=TRUE)
text(x=5.5, y=125, paste0("accuracy=", mean(predict(
   tree.tree, type="class")==R1)))
```

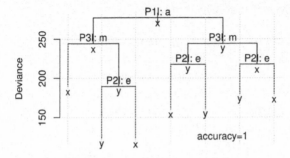

Figure 154: A tree on the (large) example data

Now we get perfect accuracy (also from `rpart::rpart` or `party(kit)::ctree`), but the result is still not great in terms of parsimony: We're not easily shown that P11 is not needed at all – we're essentially presented with a 3-way interaction when a 2-way interaction is all that's needed (and no, pruning the tree does not take care of that, try it out). The reason is that

> the split selection process in regular classification trees is only locally optimal in each node: A variable and cutpoint are chosen with respect to the impurity reduction they can achieve in a given node defined by all *previous splits*, but *regardless of all splits yet to come*" (Strobl et al. 2009:333, my emphasis).

In other words, in all cases so far, the algorithm sees that P1 has the highest monofactorial association and runs with it, but it never 'backtracks' to see whether starting with a split on the 'monofactorially inferior' P2 or P3 would ultimately lead to an overall superior outcome.[25] But this is of course where random forests should be able to help, because, in some of the trees of the forest,
– the random sampling of the data might have (i) weakened the association of
   P11 to R1 and (ii) strengthened the association of P21 or P31 to R1, maybe giv-

---

25 And this is why a recent overview article's statement that recursive partitioning as in trees 'can literally be understood as an optimal algorithm for predicting an outcome given the predictor values' is problematic: As per Strobl et al., the algorithm is *locally* optimal, which is not the same – a truly optimal algorithm would backtrack.

ing these monofactorially weaker predictors 'a leg up' to be chosen on the first split;

– P11 will not be available for the first split, so that P21 will be chosen instead, and if then P31 is available for the second split, the tree will get perfect accuracy (and such results will augment these variables' importance scores).

Indeed, this is what happens:

```
set.seed(sum(utf8ToInt("Knoblauchwürste")))
rf1 <- randomForest(R1 ~ P11+P21+P31, mtry=2)
mean(predict(rf1)==R1) # prediction accuracy
## [1] 1
```

Prediction accuracy goes up to 1, which is great, but ...

```
importance(rf1)
##       MeanDecreaseGini
## P11          13.13008
## P21          19.57731
## P31          50.19747
(pd.1 <- partial(object=rf1, pred.var="P11", which.class=2,
   train=D1))
##   P11      yhat
## 1   a -5.58267
## 2   b  5.14978
(pd.2 <- partial(object=rf1, pred.var="P21", which.class=2,
   train=D1))
##   P21       yhat
## 1   e -4.395955
## 2   f  5.775961
(pd.3 <- partial(object=rf1, pred.var="P31", which.class=2,
   train=D1))
##   P31         yhat
## 1   m -0.12614422
## 2   n -0.03812862
```

... the variable importance scores and partial dependence scores are still not great: The fact that P21:P31 is what really matters is still nowhere to be seen and even though the variable importance scores for P31 are high, its partial dependence scores are low. And all that counterintuitive mess in a data set as small and actually simple as this! Does a conditional inference forest perform better?

If you run the code you will see, that it does a bit better when the conditional variable importance scores are used because those are (nicely) small for P11 – but we *still* don't get the one piece of information everyone would want, that P21:P31 'does it all'. And we again have the seemingly counterintuitive result that the variable we know does nothing monofactorially – P31 – has low partial dependence scores (ok) but the by far highest variable importance score. So you need to understand the following (which is something I figure many users of forests do actually not know, judging from how they discuss their forests): What we're getting shown from the variable importance score looks like a main effect, like 'P31 (on its own) does a lot!', but what the variable importance score *really* means is 'P31 is (somehow!) important for making good predictions', where "somehow" means P31 might

- theoretically be a strong main effect (which, here, we know it is not from the simple cross-tabulation at the beginning);
- be involved in one or more strong two-way interactions with P11 and/or P21;
  - be involved in a strong three-way interactions with P11 and P21, i.e. P11:P21.

To make this really obvious with regression formula syntax: A high variable importance score for P31 can mean that any one or more of the following things are important: P31, P11:P31, P21:P31, or P11:P21:P31, and *this* is why in Section 5.2.8, I alerted you to anova(rms::ols(...)) and then, later, anova(rms::lrm(...)): Like I said there, anova applied to ols/lrm objects returns significance tests that do something like that in a regression context. But this fact about variable importance scores is something that most papers using random forests that I've seen seem to have not fully understood. Most papers I've seen arrive at a high variable importance score of some predictor like P31 and then interpret the effect of that 'important' variable in a monofactorial main-effect kind of way. But, as we see very clearly here and as Strobl et al. (2009:337) put it, "the random forest permutation accuracy importance [...] covers the impact of each predictor variable *individually as well as in multivariate interactions with other predictor variables*" (my emphasis); similarly, "the random forest variable importance may reveal higher importance scores for variables working in complex interactions" (Strobl et al. 2009:336), and that's what's happening here. That also means that many studies that used random forests might have made a big monofactorial deal out of the predictors for which they obtained a high variable importance score without ever realizing that the real reason for them was the predictors' participation in (an) interaction(s), and you shouldn't trust the discussion if the authors don't make it clear how they followed up on the variable importance score(s).

The way this issue is discussed in the fundamental literature on forests is concerned with how good forests and their variable importance measures are at capturing interactions and/or detecting interactions, where **capturing interactions** refers to a random forest identifying a variable that "contributes to the classification with an interaction effect" and where **detecting interactions** refers to a random forest identifying "the interaction effect per se and the predictor variables interacting with each other" (Wright, Ziegler, & König 2016:1). Unfortunately for the corpus linguists among us, it is especially corpus data that might be a perfect-storm kind of data for forests:

– Wright, Ziegler, & König (2016:7) demonstrate that "random forests are capable of capturing [...] interactions" but that both single and pairwise importance measures "are unable to detect interactions in the presence of marginal effects" (!) and of course in corpus-linguistic data, we often have both strong marginal effects and interactions, i.e. exactly the combination that makes variable importance measures bad at detecting interactions;

– Boulesteix et al. (2015:341) argue that "strong association between predictor variables may in some cases hinder the detection of interaction effects, especially in datasets of moderate size", and of course in corpus data we often have highly associated/correlated predictors and only moderate data sizes (compared to the kind of data that much work on random forests is done on, i.e. genetics data with hundreds of thousands of data points).

Thus and exactly as demonstrated by our above data, "RF methodologies are commonly claimed, often in rather vague terms, to be able to handle interactions [...], although, by construction, the predictor defining the first split of a tree is selected as the one with the strongest main effect on the response variable" (Boulesteix et al. 2015:344).

So how can we address this? As I discuss in Gries (2020), we can address this by following

– Forina et al. (2009), who "augment [...] the prediction data with addition of complex combinations of the data" (Kuhn & Johnson 2013:48, also see p. 57f.);

– Strobl et al. (2009:341), who state that "an interaction effect of two variables can also be explicitly added as a potential predictor variable";

– Baayen (2011:305f.), whose application of Naïve Discriminative Learning includes "pairs of features" as "the functional equivalent of interactions in a regression model".

That means, we force the tree-based approach to consider the combined effect of P21 and P31 by explicitly including in the formula the combination/interaction of these two predictors or, more generally, all predictors in whose interactions one might be interested in. For here, it means we create three new predictors:

```
P11xP21 <- P11:P21; P11xP31 <- P11:P31; P21xP31 <- P21:P31
D1 <- cbind(D1, P11xP21, P11xP31, P21xP31)
```

And this solves everything for the trees (perfect accuracy and they only use P21xP31) ...

```
(tt1 <- tree(R1 ~ P11+P21+P31+P11xP21+P11xP31+P21xP31)) ## [...]
## 1) root 200 277.3 x ( 0.5 0.5 )
##    2) P21xP31: e:m,f:n 100    0.0 x ( 1.0 0.0 ) *
##    3) P21xP31: e:n,f:m 100    0.0 y ( 0.0 1.0 ) *
(ct1 <- ctree(R1 ~ P11+P21+P31+P11xP21+P11xP31+P21xP31))
## [...]
## Fitted party:
## [1] root
## |   [2] P21xP31 in e:m, f:n: x (n = 100, err = 0.0%)
## |   [3] P21xP31 in e:n, f:m: y (n = 100, err = 0.0%)
```

... and for the random forest ...

```
set.seed(sum(utf8ToInt("Hanuta")))
rf1 <- randomForest(R1 ~ P11+P21+P31+P11xP21+P11xP31+P21xP31, mtry=2)
mean(predict(rf1)==R1)
## [1] 1
   importance(rf1)
##           MeanDecreaseGini
## P11              2.942730
## P21              4.237394
## P31              5.871964
## P11xP21         11.071039
## P11xP31         17.340106
## P21xP31         54.049938
partial(object=rf1, pred.var="P21xP31", which.class=2, train=D1)
##   P21xP31       yhat
## 1     e:m -5.0590514
## 2     e:n  0.8263312
```

```
## 3      f:m   5.5113559
## 4      f:n  -0.8561893
```

... and for the conditional inference forest (which I don't show here in the book). Every tree/forest returns perfect accuracy, the forests return the by far highest variable importance scores for P21xP31, and the partial dependence scores of that predictor reveal the interaction pattern we knew is in the data ... finally! And if you also add the three way interaction P11xP21xP31 to the formula, then tree, ctree, and cforest all still recover that P21xP31 is most important – only randomForest assigns a variable importance score to P11xP21xP31 that's slightly higher than that of P21xP31).

Thus, bottom line, trees and especially more robust/powerful forests can be good at detecting interactions, but things are more complex than they seem. One should always (i) compute a forest, its accuracy, precision, and recall, but also (ii) variable importance scores and (iii) partial dependence scores. High variable importance scores for a predictor can mean many things: don't take them at face value and let them fool you into automatically assuming they reflect an important 'main effect' and then you plot/interpret that, and you're done – a high variable importance score only means 'that predictor does something, somehow' and you need to do follow-up analyses to find out what exactly that is. And studying that can be done with interaction predictors (or in other ways, see Gries (2020) for, e.g., an application of **global surrogate models**) and the beauty here is, if you're doing 'random foresting' already, you're avoiding convergence and model selection/significance testing philosophy issues ... In fact, Strobl et al. (2009:339) go so far as to advise as follows:

> In general, however, the complex random forest model, involving high-order interactions and nonlinearity, should be compared to a simpler model (e.g., a linear or logistic regression model including only low-order interactions) whenever possible to decide whether the simpler, interpretable model would be equally adequate.

Did you catch that?? Random forests are the *more* complex models, because each tree of a forest can easily involve 3-, 4-, 5-, ... way interactions that people would never dream of fitting in a regression model but that they rely on unquestioningly in a forest, no questions asked. Don't let the apparent simplicity of the R code for a forest trick you into believing that forests are the simpler method; part of why they are doing so much better in predictions than regressions is that they can involve very complex partitioning of the data.

Given this underappreciated complexity of random forests, Strobl et al. (2009:341) conclude that random forests can at least serve as a benchmark predictor: If a linear or other parametric model with a limited number and degree of interaction terms can reach the (cross-validated or test sample) prediction accuracy of the more complex model, the extra complexity may be uncalled for and the simpler, interpretable model should be given preference. If, however, the prediction accuracy cannot be reached with the simpler model, and, for example, the high importance of a variable in a random forest is not reflected by its respective parameters in the simpler model, relevant nonlinear or interaction effects may be missing in the simpler model, and it may not be suited to grasping the complexity of the underlying process.

In other words, 'consider doing both!' – a regression and a tree-based method.

Recommendation(s) for further study: Check out
- the package randomForestSRC, in general, but also esp. for its function find.interactions;
- the package ranger for what seems to be the fastest random forest implementation;
- the package RLT for reinforcement learning trees;
- the package stablelearner, to follow up on random/conditional inference forests;
- the package glmertree, to be able to combine trees with random effects as in MEM; see also Hajjem et al. (2014);
- Faraway (2016: Ch. 16) or Levshina (to appear) for discussion of trees and forests and Matloff (2017) as a book on regression and classification covering modeling and classifiers well;
- Gries (to appear b) for more discussion on how to explore random forests (using representative trees and especially global surrogate models).

A final few recommendations here at the end of the book: The very next two things you should *definitely* read are Breiman (2001b) and Efron (2020). Those two discussion papers were so eye-opening to me in how they put many things into perspective, in particular the relationship between more statistical (in the sense of 'mathematical') methods such as regression modeling and the apparent alternative/plan B machine-learning/prediction methods such as random forests; I wish I had known everything those papers discussed many years ago so hopefully you'll benefit from them at an earlier time in your career.

Then, the next thing to read are these websites: https://stackoverflow.com/help/minimal-reproducible-example and https://stackoverflow.com/questions/5963269/how-to-make-a-great-r-reproducible-example, which you will need for whenever you want to ask someone a question! Also, look up the function system.time, which in the long run will help you with writing better/faster code.

Finally, if you ever saw the 2nd edition of this book, you will have noticed that this 3rd edition has no chapter on exploratory methods anymore – this is mostly for space constraints, but also for the realization that it would be hard to do a better job on cluster analysis than Moisl (2015, the book) or Moisl (to appear, an overview article) or on exploratory methods more generally than Desagulier (to appear); these are all good references I'm happy to recommend for these kinds of important methods.

References

Agresti, Alan. 2013. Categorical data analysis. 3rd ed. Hoboken, NJ: John Wiley & Sons.
Agresti, Alan. 2019. An introduction to categorical data analysis. 3rd ed. Hoboken, NJ: John Wiley & Sons.
Anscombe, Francis J. 1973. Graphs in statistical analysis. American Statistician 27. 17-21.
Austin, Peter C. & George Leckie. 2018. The effect of number of clusters and cluster size on statistical power and Type I error rates when testing random effects variance components in multilevel linear and logistic regression models. Journal of Statistical Computation and Simulation 88(16). 3151-3163.
Baayen, R. Harald. 2008. Analyzing linguistic data: a practical introduction to statistics using R. Cambridge: Cambridge University Press.
Baayen, R. Harald. 2010. A real experiment is a factorial experiment? The Mental Lexicon 5(1). 149-157.
Baayen, R. Harald. 2011. Corpus linguistics and naïve discriminative learning. Brazilian Journal of Applied Linguistics 11(2). 295-328.
Baayen, R. Harald, D.J. Davidson, & Douglas M. Bates. 2008. Mixed-effects modeling with crossed random effects for subjects and items. Journal of Memory and Language 59(4). 390-412.
Baayen, R. Harald, Jacolien van Rij, Cecile de Cat, & Simon Wood. 2018. Autocorrelated errors in experimental data in the language sciences: some solutions offered by generalized additive mixed models. In Dirk Speelman, Kris Heylen, & Dirk Geeraerts (eds.), Mixed-effects regression models in linguistics, 48-69. Berlin & New York: Springer.
Baayen, R. Harald & Maja Linke. 2020. An introduction to the generalized additive model. In Magali Paquot & Stefan Th. Gries (eds.), A practical handbook of corpus linguistics. Berlin & New York: Springer.
Baayen, R. Harald, Shravan Vasishth, Reinhold Kliegl, & Douglas Bates. 2017. The cave of shadows: Addressing the human factor with generalized additive mixed models. Journal of Memory and Language 94. 206-234.
Baguley, Thom. 2012. Serious Stats: A Guide to Advanced Statistics for the Behavioral Sciences. Houndmills, Basingstoke, Hampshire: Palgrave MacMillan.
Barr, Dale J. 2013. Random effects structure for testing interactions in linear-mixed-effects models. Frontiers in Psychology 4(328).
Barr, Dale J., Roger Levy, Christoph Scheepers, & Harry J. Tily. 2013. Random effects structure for confirmatory hypothesis testing: Keep it maximal. Journal of Memory and Language 68(3). 255-278.
Bates, Douglas, Martin Maechler, Ben Bolker, & Steve Walker. 2015. Fitting Linear Mixed-Effects Models Using lme4. Journal of Statistical Software 67(1). 1-48.
Bates, Douglas, Reinhold Kliegl, Shravan Vasishth, & R. Harald Baayen. 2018. Parsimonious mixed models. Pre-publication version 2 at https://arxiv.org/abs/1506.04967, last accessed 20 May 2020.
Bell, Andrew, Malcolm Fairbrother, & Kelvyn Jones. 2019. Fixed and random effects models: making an informed choice. Quality and Quantity 53. 1051-1074.
Bencini, Giulia & Adele E. Goldberg. 2000. The contribution of argument structure constructions to sentence meaning. Journal of Memory and Language 43(3). 640-651.
Benjamin, Daniel J. et al. 2017. Redefine statistical significance. Nature Human Behavior 2. 6-10.

https://doi.org/10.1515/9783110718256-008

Berez, Andrea L., & Stefan Th. Gries. 2010. Correlates to middle marking in Dena'ina iterative verbs. International Journal of American Linguistics 76(1). 145-165.

Bernaisch, Tobias, Stefan Th. Gries, & Joybrato Mukherjee. 2014. The dative alternation in South Asian English(es): Modelling predictors and predicting prototypes. English World-Wide 35(1). 7-31.

Bolker, Benjamin M. 2015. Exploring convergence issues. Online ms.

Bolker, Benjamin M., Mollie E. Brooks, Connie J. Clark, Shane W. Grange, John R. Poulsen, M. Henry H. Stevens, & Jada-Simone S. White. 2009a. Generalized linear mixed models: a practical guide for ecology and evolution. Trends in Ecology & Evolution 24(3). 127-135.

Bolker, Benjamin M., Mollie E. Brooks, Connie J. Clark, Shane W. Grange, John R. Poulsen, M. Henry H. Stevens, & Jada-Simone S. White. 2009b. GLMMs in action: gene-by-environment interaction in total fruit production wild populations of Arabidopsis thaliana. online supplement to Bolker et al. (2009a).

Bortz, Jürgen. 2005. Statistik for Human- und Sozialwissenschaftler. 6th ed. Heidelberg: Springer Medizin Verlag.

Bortz, Jürgen, Gustav A. Lienert & Klaus Boehnke. 2008. Verteilungsfreie Methoden in der Biostatistik. 3rd ed. Berlin & New York: Springer.

Boulesteix, Anne-Laure, Silke Janitza, Alexander Hapfelmeier, Kristel Van Steen, & Carolin Strobl. 2015. Letter to the editor: On the term 'interaction' and related phrases in the literature on Random Forests. Briefings in Bioinformatics 16(2). 338-345.

Brauer, Markus & John J. Curtin. 2018. Linear mixed-effects models and the analysis of nonindependent data: A unified framework to analyze categorical and continuous independent variables that vary within-subjects and/or within-items. Psychological Methods 23(3). 389-411.

Breiman, Leo. 2001a. Random forests. Machine Learning 45. 5-32.

Breiman, Leo. 2001b. Statistical modeling: The two cultures. Statistical Science 16. 199-231.

Brew, Chris, & David McKelvie. 1996. Word-pair extraction for lexicography. In Kemal O. Oflazer & Harold Somers (eds.), Proceedings of the 2nd International Conference on New Methods in Language Processing, 45-55. Ankara: Bilkent University.

Brysbaert, Marc & Michaël Stevens. 2018. Power Analysis and Effect Size in Mixed Effects Models: A Tutorial. Journal of Cognition 1(1). 9.

Bürkner, Paul-Christian. 2017. brms: An R package for Bayesian multilevel models using Stan. Journal of Statistical Software 80(1). 1-28.

Bürkner, Paul-Christian. 2018. Advanced Bayesian multilevel modeling with the R package brms. The R Journal 10(1). 395-411.

Burnham, Kenneth P. & David R. Anderson. 2002. Model selection and multimodel inference. Berlin & New York: Springer.

Carrasco Ortíz, Elia Haydee, Mark Amengual, & Stefan Th. Gries. Cross-language effects of phonological and orthographic similarity in cognate word recognition: the role of language dominance. Linguistic Approaches to Bilingualism.

Chen, Ping. 1986. Discourse and Particle Movement in English. Studies in Language 10(1). 79-95.

Cleveland, W. & R. McGill. 1985. Graphical perception and graphical methods for analyzing scientific data. Science 229(4716). 828-833.

Cowart, Wayne. 1997. Experimental Syntax: Applying Objective Methods to Sentence Judgments. Thousand Oaks, CA: Sage.

Crawley, Michael J. 2007. The R book. 1st ed. Chichester: John Wiley.

Crawley, Michael J. 2013. The R book. 2nd ed. Chichester: John Wiley.

Desagulier, Guillaume. to appear. Multivariate exploratory approaches. In Magali Paquot & Stefan Th. Gries (eds.), A practical handbook of corpus linguistics. Berlin & New York: Springer.

Dijkstra, Ton, Koji Miwa, Bianca Brummelhuis, Maya Sappelli, & R. Harald Baayen. 2010. How cross-language similarity and task demands affect cognate recognition. Journal of Memory and Language 62(3). 284-301.

Dilts, Philip. 2013. Modelling phonetic reduction in a corpus of spoken English using random forests and mixed-effects regression. Unpublished Ph.D. dissertation, University of Alberta, Edmonton.

Doğruöz, A. Seza & Stefan Th. Gries. 2012. Spread of on-going changes in an immigrant language: Turkish in the Netherlands. Review of Cognitive Linguistics 10(2). 401-426.

Dolgalev, Igor & G Brazovskaia, N & S Karpov, R. (2013). Spousal Concordance of Blood Pressure Levels (Results of 17-year Follow-up). Kardiologiia. 53. 43-7.

Efron, Bradley. 2020. Prediction, estimation, and attribution. Journal of the American Statistical Association 115(530). 636-655.

Egbert, Jesse & Luke Plonsky. to appear. Bootstrapping techniques. In Magali Paquot & Stefan Th. Gries (eds.), A practical handbook of corpus linguistics. Berlin & New York: Springer.

Ellis, Nick C. 2007. Language acquisition as rational contingency learning. Applied Linguistics 27(1). 1-27.

Faraway, Julian J. 2015. Linear models with R. 2nd ed. Boca Raton, FL: Chapman & Hall/CRC.

Faraway, Julian J. 2016. Extending the linear model with R: Generalized linear, mixed effects and nonparametric regression models. 2nd ed. Boca Raton, FL: Chapman & Hall/CRC.

Field, Andy, Jeremy Miles, & Zoë Field. 2012. Discovering Statistics Using 8 Los Angeles & London: Sage Publications.

Fokkema, Marjolein, Niels Smits, Achim Zeileis, Torsten Hothorn, & Henk Kelderman. 2018. Detecting treatment-subgroup interactions in clustered data with generalized linear mixed-effects model trees. Behavior Research Methods 50(5). 2016-2034.

Forina, Michele, Monica Casale, Paolo Oliveru, & Silvia Lanteri. 2009. CAIMAN brothers: A family of powerful classification and class modeling techniques. Chemometrics and Intelligent Laboratory Systems 96(2). 239-245.

Fox, John. 2003. Effect displays in R for generalised linear models. Journal of Statistical Software 8(15). 1-27.

Fox, John. 2016. Applied regression analysis and generalized linear models. Los Angeles: Sage.

Fox, John & Jangman Hong. 2009. Effect displays in R for multinomial and proportional-odds logit models: Extensions to the effects package. Journal of Statistical Software 32(1). 1-24.

Fox, John & Sanford Weisberg. 2019. An R companion to applied regression. 3rd ed. Thousand Oaks, CA: Sage.

Fraser, Bruce. 1966. Some remarks on the VPC in English. In Francis P. Dinneen (ed.), Problems in Semantics, History of Linguistics, Linguistics and English, 45-61. Washington, DC: Georgetown University Press.

Gaudio, Rudolf P. 1994. Sounding gay: pitch properties in the speech of gay and straight men. American Speech 69(1). 30-57.

Gelman, Andrew & Jennifer Hill. 2007. Data Analysis Using Regression and Multilevel/Hierarchical Models. Cambridge: Cambridge University Press.

Gelman, Andrew, Jennifer Hill, & Aki Vehtari. 2020. Regression and other stories. Cambridge: Cambridge University Press.

Gilquin, Gaëtanelle, Sylvie De Cock, & Sylviane Granger. 2010. Louvain International Database of Spoken English Interlanguage. Louvain-la-Neuve: Presses universitaires de Louvain.

Granger, Sylviane, Estelle Dagneaux, Fanny Meunier, & Magali Paquot. 2009. International Corpus of Learner English v2. Louvain-la-Neuve: Presses universitaires de Louvain.

Greenland, Sander, Stephen J. Senn, Kenneth J. Rothman, John B. Carlin, Charles Poole, Steven N. Goodman & Douglas G. Altman. 2-16. Statistical tests, P values, confidence intervals, and power: a guide to misinterpretations. European Journal of Epidemiology 31. 337-350.

Greenwell, Brandon M. 2017. pdp: An R package for constructing partial dependence plots. The R Journal 9(1). 421-436.

Gries, Stefan Th. 2003. Multifactorial analysis in corpus linguistics: a study of particle placement. London, New York: Continuum.

Gries, Stefan Th. 2006. Cognitive determinants of subtractive word-formation processes: a corpus-based perspective. Cognitive Linguistics 17 (4). 535-558.

Gries, Stefan Th. 2013a. Statistics for linguistics with R: a practical introduction. 2nd rev. & ext. ed. Berlin, New York: Mouton de Gruyter.

Gries, Stefan Th. 2013b. 50-something years of work on collocations: what is or should be next … International Journal of Corpus Linguistics 18(1). 137-165.

Gries, Stefan Th. 2015. The most underused statistical method in corpus linguistics: Multi-level (and mixed-effects) models. Corpora 10(1). 95-125.

Gries, Stefan Th. 2016. Quantitative corpus linguistics with R: a practical introduction. 2nd rev. & ext. ed. London, New York: Taylor & Francis.

Gries, Stefan Th. 2020. On classification trees and random forests in corpus linguistics: some words of caution and suggestions for improvement. Corpus Linguistics and Linguistic Theory.

Gries, Stefan Th. to appear. (Generalized linear) Mixed-effects modeling: a learner corpus example. Language Learning.

Gries, Stefan Th. & Allison S. Adelman. 2014. Subject realization in Japanese conversation by native and non-native speakers: exemplifying a new paradigm for learner corpus research. In Jesús Romero-Trillo (ed.), Yearbook of Corpus Linguistics and Pragmatics 2014: New empirical and theoretical paradigms, 35-54. Berlin & New York: Springer.

Gries, Stefan Th. & Magali Paquot. to appear. Writing up a corpus-linguistic paper. In Magali Paquot & Stefan Th. Gries (eds.), A practical handbook of corpus linguistics. Berlin & New York: Springer.

Gries, Stefan Th., & Stefanie Wulff. 2005. Do foreign language learners also have constructions? Evidence from priming, sorting, and corpora. Annual Review of Cognitive Linguistics 3. 182-200.

Gries, Stefan Th. & Stefanie Wulff. 2009. Psycholinguistic and corpus linguistic evidence for L2 constructions. Annual Review of Cognitive Linguistics 7. 163-186.

Gries, Stefan Th. & Stefanie Wulff. to appear. Adverbial clause ordering in learner production data. Applied Psycholinguistics.

Groyecka, Agata, Agnieszka Sorokowska, Anna Oleszkiewicz, Thomas Hummel, Krystyna Łysenko, & Piotr Sorokowski. 2018. Similarities in smell and taste preferences in couples increase with relationship duration. Appetite 120. 158-162.

Hajjem, Ahlem, François Bellavance, & Denis Larocque. 2014. Mixed-effects random forest for clustered data. Journal of Statistical Computation and Simulation 84(6). 1313-1328.

Hamrick, Phillip. 2018. Adjusting regression models for overfitting in second language research. Journal of Research Design and Statistics in Linguistics and Communication 5(1-2). 107-122.

Hansen, Sandra & Roman Schneider. 2013. Decision tree-based evaluation of genitive classification: an empirical study on CMC and text corpora. In Iryna Gurevych, Chris Biemann, & Torsten Zesch (eds.), Language processing and knowledge in the web, 83-88. Berlin & New York: Springer.

Harrell, Frank E. Jr. 2015. Regression Modeling Strategies. With Applications to Linear Models, Logistic Regression, and Survival Analysis. Berlin & New York: Springer.

Hastie, Trevor, Robert Tibshirani, & Jerome Friedman. 2014. The elements of statistical learning: Data mining, inference, and prediction. 2nd ed. Berlin & New York: Springer.

Hawkins, John A. 1994. A Performance Theory of Order and Constituency. Cambridge: Cambridge University Press.

Healey, Patrick G.T., Matthew Purver, & Christine Howes. 2014. Divergence in dialogue. PLOS ONE 9(6). e98598.

Heinze, Georg, Christine Wallisch, & Daniela Dunkler. 2018. Variable selection – A review and recommendations for the practicing statistician. Biometrical Journal 60(3). 431-449.

Heller, Benedikt, Tobias Bernaisch, & Stefan Th. Gries. Empirical perspectives on two potential epicenters: The genitive alternation in Asian Englishes. ICAME Journal 41. 111-144.

Henrich, Joseph, Steven J. Heine, & Ara Norenzayan. 2010. The weirdest people in the world? Behavioral and Brain Sciences 33(2-3). 61-83.

Hilpert, Martin & Damián E. Blasi. to appear. Fixed-effects regression modeling. In Magali Paquot & Stefan Th. Gries (eds.), A practical handbook of corpus linguistics. Berlin & New York: Springer.

Hosmer, David W. Stanley Lemeshow, Rodney X. Sturdivant. 2013. Applied Logistic Regression 3rd ed. Chichester: John Wiley.

Hothorn, Torsten, Peter Buehlmann, Sandrine Dudoit, Annette Molinaro, & Mark Van Der Laan. 2006. Survival Ensembles. Biostatistics 7(3). 355-373.

Hothorn, Torsten, Kurt Hornik, & Achim Zeileis. 2006. Unbiased Recursive Partitioning: A conditional inference framework. Journal of Computational and Graphical Statistics 15(3). 651-674.

Hothorn, Torsten & Achim Zeileis. 2015. partykit: A Modular Toolkit for Recursive Partytioning in R. Journal of Machine Learning Research 16. 3905-3909.

Hundt, Marianne. 2018. It is time that this (should) be studied across a broader range of Englishes: A global trip around mandative subjunctives. In Sandra C. Deshors (ed.), Modeling World Englishes: Assessing the interplay of emancipation and globalization of ESL varieties, 217-244. Amsterdam & Philadelphia: John Benjamins.

James, Gareth, Daniela Witten, Trevor Hastie, & Robert Tibshirani. 2014. An introduction to statistical learning with applications in R. 4th printing. Berlin & New York: Springer.

Janitza, Silke, Carolin Strobl, & Anne-Laure Boulesteix. 2013. An AUC-based permutation variable importance measure for random forests. BMC Bioinformatics 14(119).

Jenset, Gard B. & Barbara McGillvray. 2017. Quantitative historical linguistics. Oxford: Oxford University Press.

Johnson, Keith. 2008. Quantitative methods in linguistics. Malden, MA: Wiley-Blackwell.

Joseph, Brian D. 2008. Last scene of all ... Language 84(4). 686-690.

Keen, Kevin J. 2010. Graphics for Statistics and Data Analysis with R. Boca Raton, FL: Chapman & Hall/CRC.

Klavan, Jane, Maarja-Liisa Pilvik, & Kristel Uiboaed. 2015. The use of multivariate statistical classification models for predicting constructional choice in spoken, non-standard varieties of Estonian. SKY Journal of Linguistics 28. 187-224.

Krishnamoorthy, Kalimuthu & Meesook Lee. 2014. Improved tests for the equality of normal coefficients of variation. Computational Statistics 29. 215-232.

Kuhn, Max & Kjell Johnson. 2013. Applied predictive modeling. Berlin & New York: Springer.

Kuperman, Victor & Joan Bresnan. 2012. The effects of construction probability on word durations during spontaneous incremental sentence production. Journal of Memory and Language 66. 588-611.

Kuznetsova Alexandra, Per Bruun Brockhoff, & Rune Haubo Bojesen Christensen. 2017. lmerTest Package: Tests in linear mixed effects models. Journal of Statistical Software 82(13). 1-26.

Lester, Nicholas A. 2018. The syntactic bits of nouns: How prior syntactic distributions affect comprehension. Ph.D. dissertation UC Santa Barbara, URL https://escholarship.org/uc/item/25r9w1t1, last accessed 15 May 2020.

Levshina, Natalia. to appear. Conditional inference trees and random forests. In Magali Paquot & Stefan Th. Gries (eds.), A practical handbook of corpus linguistics. Berlin & New York: Springer.

Liaw, Andy & Matthew Wiener. 2002. Classification and Regression by randomForest. R News 2(3). 18-22.

Maas, Cora J.M. & Joop J. Hox. 2005. Sufficient sample sizes for multilevel modeling. Methodology 1(3). 86-92.

Mair Patrick & Rand Wilcox. 2020. Robust Statistical Methods in R Using the WRS2 Package. Behavior Research Methods 52 464-488.

Makin, Tamar R. & Jean Jacques Orban de Xivry. 2019. Ten common statistical mistakes to watch out for when writing or reviewing a manuscript. eLife 2019;8:e48175.

Matloff, Norman. 2017. Statistical regression and classification. Boca Raton, FL: Chapman & Hall/CRC.

Matsuki, Kazunaga, Victor Kuperman, & Julie A. Van Dyke. 2016. The Random Forests statistical technique: An examination of its value for the study of reading Scientific Studies of Reading 20(1). 20-33.

McElreath, Richard. 2020. Statistical rethinking: a Bayesian course with examples in R and Stan. 2nd ed. Boca Raton, FL: CRC Press.

Meteyard, Lotte & Robert A.I. Davies. 2020. Best practice guidance for linear mixed-effects models in psychological science. Journal of Memory and Language 112(104092).

Miglio, Viola G., Stefan Th. Gries, Michael J. Harris, Eva M. Wheeler, & Raquel Santana-Paixão. 2013. Spanish lo(s)-le(s) clitic alternations in psych verbs: a multifactorial corpus-based analysis. In: Jennifer Cabrelli Amaro, Gillian Lord, Ana de Prada Pérez, & Jessi E. Aaron (eds.), Selected Proceedings of the 15th Hispanic Linguistics Symposium, 268-278. Somerville, MA. Cascadilla Press.

Moisl, Hermann. 2015. Cluster analysis for corpus linguistics. Amsterdam & Philadelphia: John Benjamins.

Moisl, Hermann. to appear. Cluster analysis. In Magali Paquot & Stefan Th. Gries (eds.), A practical handbook of corpus linguistics. Berlin & New York: Springer.

Muth, Chelsea, Zita Oravecz, & Jonah Gabry. 2018. User-friendly Bayesian regression modeling: A tutorial with rstanarm and shinystan. *The Quantitative Methods for Psychology* 14(2). 99-119.

Nagata, Hiroshi. 1987. Long-term effect of repetition on judgments of grammaticality. Perceptual and Motor Skills 65(5): 295-299.

Nagata, Hiroshi. 1989. Effect of repetition on grammaticality judgments under objective and subjective self-awareness conditions. Journal of Psycholinguistic Research 18(3). 255-269.

Nakagawa, Shinichi, Paul C.D. Johnson, & Holger Schielzeth. 2017. The coefficient of determination R2 and intra-class correlation coefficient from generalized linear mixed-effects models revisited and expanded. Journal of the Royal Society Interface 14: 20170213.

Norris, John M., Luke Plonsky, Steven J. Ross, & Rob Schoonend. 2015. Guidelines for reporting quantitative methods and results in primary research. Language Learning 65(2). 470-476.

Pedersen, Eric J., David L. Miller, Gavin L. Simpson, & Noam Ross. 2019. Hierarchical generalized additive models in ecology: an introduction with mgcv. PeerJ 7:e6876.

Pek, Jolynn & David B. Flora. 2018. Reporting effect sizes in original psychological research: A discussion and tutorial. Psychological Methods 23(2). 208-225.

Peters, Julia. 2001. Given vs. new information influencing constituent ordering in the VPC. In Ruth Brend, Alan K. Melby, & Arle Lommel (eds.), LACUS Forum XXVII: Speaking and Comprehending, 133-140. Fullerton, CA: LACUS.

Philipp, Michel, Achim Zeileis, & Carolin Strobl. 2016. A toolkit for stability assessment of tree-based learners." In Ana Colubi, Angela Blanco, & Cristian Gatu (eds.), Proceedings of COMPSTAT 2016 - 22nd International Conference on Computational Statistics, 315-325.

Rezaee, Abbas Ali & Seyyed Ehsan Golparvar. 2017. Conditional inference tree modelling of competing motivators of the positioning of concessive clauses: the case of a non-native corpus. Journal of Quantitative Linguistics 24(2-3). 89-106.

Roberts, David R. et al. 2016. Cross-validation strategies for data with temporal, spatial, hierarchical, or phylogenetic structure. Ecography 40. 913-929.

Rühlemann, Christoph & Stefan Th. Gries. 2020. Speakers advance-project turn completion by slowing down: a multifactorial corpus analysis. Journal of Phonetics 80(3).

Säfken, Benjamin David Rügamer, Thomas Kneib, & Sonja Greven. 2018. Conditional model selection in mixed-effects Models with cAIC4. Pre-publication version 2 at https://arxiv.org/abs/1803.05664, last accessed 15 May 2020.

Sandra, Dominiek & Sally Rice. 1995. Network analyses of prepositional meaning: Mirroring whose mind – the linguist's or the language user's? Cognitive Linguistics 6(1). 89-130.

Schad, Daniel J., Shravan Vasishth, Sven Hohenstein, & Reinhold Kliegl. 2019. How to capitalize on a priori contrasts in linear (mixed) models: A tutorial. Journal of Memory and Language 110.104038.

Schäfer, Roland. to appear. Mixed-effects regression modeling. In Magali Paquot & Stefan Th. Gries (eds.), A practical handbook of corpus linguistics. Berlin & New York: Springer.

Scheepers, Christoph. 2003. Syntactic priming of relative clause attachments: persistence of structural configuration in sentence production. Cognition 89(3). 179-205.

Schielzeth, Holger. 2010. Simple means to improve the interpretability of regression coefficients. Methods in Ecology and Evolution 1. 103-113.

Sestelo, Marta, Nora M. Villanueva, Luis Meira-Machado, & Javier Roca-Pardiñas. 2016. FWDselect: An R package for variable selection in regression models. The R Journal 8(1). 132-148.

Sheskin, David J. 2011. Handbook of Parametric and Nonparametric Statistical Procedures. 5th ed. Boca Raton, FL: Chapman & Hall/CRC.

Shirai, Yasuhiro & Roger W. Andersen. 1995. The acquisition of tense-aspect morphology: A prototype account. Language 71(4). 743-762.

Simoiu, Camelia & Jim Savage. 2016. A bag of tips and tricks for dealing with scale issues. Online ms at https://rpubs.com/jimsavage/scale_issues, last accessed 08 Oct 2020.

Singmann, Henrik & David Kellen. 2019. An introduction to mixed models for experimental psychology. In Daniel H. Spieler & Eric Schumacher (eds.), New Methods in Cognitive Psychology, 4-31. Psychology Press.

Smith, Michael L. 2014. Honey bee sting pain index by body location. PeerJ 2. e338.

Speelman, Dirk, Kris Heylen, & Dirk Geeraerts (eds.). 2018. Mixed-effects regression models in linguistics. Berlin & New York: Springer.

Steinberg, Danny D. 1993. An introduction to psycholinguistics. London: Longman.

Strobl, Carolin, Anne-Laure Boulesteix, Achim Zeileis, & Torsten Hothorn. 2007. Bias in Random Forest Variable Importance Measures: Illustrations, Sources and a Solution. BMC Bioinformatics 8(25).

Strobl, Carolin, Anne-Laure Boulesteix, Thomas Kneib, Thomas Augustin, & Achim Zeileis. 2008. Conditional Variable Importance for Random Forests. BMC Bioinformatics 9(307).

Strobl, Carolin, James Malley, & Gerhard Tutz. 2009. An introduction to recursive partitioning: rationale, application and characteristics of classification and regression trees, bagging and random forests. Psychological Methods 14(4). 323-348.

Szmrecsanyi, Benedikt, Jason Grafmiller, Benedikt Heller, & Melanie Röthlisberger. 2016. Around the world in three alternations: Modeling syntactic variation in varieties of English. English World-Wide 37(2). 109-137.

Tagliamonte, Sali A. & R. Harald Baayen. 2012. Models, forests, and trees of York English: Was/were variation as a case study for statistical practice. Language Variation and Change 24(2). 135-178.

Tjur, Tue. 2009. Coefficients of determination in logistic regression models—a new proposal: The coefficient of discrimination. The American Statistician 63(4). 366-372.

Tomaschek, Fabian, Peter Hendrix, & R. Harald Baayen. 2018. Strategies for addressing collinearity in multivariate linguistic data. Journal of Phonetics 71. 249-267.

Tufte, E. 2001. The visual display of quantitative information. 2nd ed. Graphics Press: Cheshire, CT.

Van Dongen. W. A. Sr. 1919. He Puts on His Hat & He Puts His Hat on. Neophilologus 4. 322-353.

van Smeden, Maarten, Joris A.H. de Groot , Karel G.M. Moons, Gary S. Collins, Douglas G. Altman, Marinus J.C. Eijkemans, & Johannes B. Reitsma. 2016. No rationale for 1 variable per 10 events criterion for binary logistic regression analysis. BMC Medical Research Methodology 16. 163.

Vasishth, Shravan, Bruno Nicenboim, Mary E. Beckman, Fangfang Li, & Eun Jong Kong. 2018. Bayesian data analysis in the phonetic sciences: A tutorial introduction. Journal of Phonetics 71. 147-161.

Venables, William N. & Brian D. Ripley. 2002. Modern applied statistics with S. 4th ed. Berlin & New York: Springer.

Verbeke, Geert, Geert Molenberghs, Steffen Fieuws, & Samuel Iddi. 2018. Mixed models with emphasis on large data sets. In Dirk Speelman, Kris Heylen, & Dirk Geeraerts (eds.), Mixed-effects regression models in linguistics, 11-28. Berlin & New York: Springer.

Wieling, Martijn. 2018. Analyzing dynamic phonetic data using generalized additive mixed modeling: A tutorial focusing on articulatory differences between L1 and L2 speakers of English. Journal of Phonetics 70(1). 86-116.

Wieling, Martijn, Simonetta Montemagni, John Nerbonne, & R. Harald Baayen. 2014. Lexical differences between Tuscan dialects and standard Italian: accounting for geographic and sociodemographic variation using generalized additive mixed modeling. Language 90(3). 669-692.

Wilcox, Rand. 2012. Introduction to robust estimation and hypothesis testing. 3rd ed. Amsterdam: Elsevier.

Wilcox, Rand. 2017. Modern statistics for the social and behavioral sciences. 2nd ed. Amsterdam: Elsevier.

Wilkinson, Leland & The Task Force on Statistical Inference. 1999. Statistical methods in psychology journals: guidelines and explanations. American Psychologist 54(8). 594-604.

Wright, Marvin N. & Andreas Ziegler. 2017. ranger: a fast implementation of random forests for high dimensional data in C++ and R. Journal of Statistical Software 77(1). 1-17.

Wright, Marvin N., Andreas Ziegler, & Inke R. König. 2016. Do little interactions get lost in dark random forests? BMC Bioinformatics 17(145).

Wulff, Stefanie, Stefan Th. Gries, & Nicholas A. Lester. 2018. Optional that in complementation by German and Spanish learners. In Andrea Tyler, Lihong Huan, & Hana Jan (eds.), What is Applied Cognitive Linguistics? Answers from current SLA research, 99-120. Berlin & Boston: De Gruyter Mouton.

Zar, Jerrold H. 2010. Biostatistical Analysis. 5th ed. Upper Saddle River, NJ: Prentice Hall.

Zhu, Ruoqing, Donglin Zeng, & Michael R. Kosorok. 2015. Reinforcement learning trees. Journal of the American Statistical Association 110(512). 1770-1784.

Zuur, Alain F., Elena N. Ieno, & Chris S. Elphick. 2010. A protocol for data exploration to avoid common statistical problems. Methods in Ecology & Evolution 1. 3-14.

Zuur, Alain F., Elena N. Ieno, & Graham. M. Smith. 2007. Analysing Ecological Data. Berlin & New York: Springer.

Zuur, Alain F., Elena N. Ieno, Neil Walker, Anatoly A. Saveliev, & Graham M. Smith. 2009. Mixed effects models and extensions in ecology with R. Berlin & New York: Springer.

Packages

Packages are listed by name with a link; if the package doesn't come with an associated publication, I cite it as "(Name YEAR)", if the package is part of a publication, I cite it as "see Name (YEAR)" and you will find the reference in the reference section for books, papers, … You can also always enter citation("PACKAGENAME") for more info on a package.

buildmer: Stepwise Elimination and Term Reordering for Mixed-Effects Regression (Voeten 2020)

car: Companion to Applied Regression, see Fox & Weisberg 2019

cvequality: Tests for the Equality of Coefficients of Variation from Multiple Groups, see Krishnamoorthy & Lee 2014

DHARMa: Residual Diagnostics for Hierarchical (Multi-Level / Mixed) Regression Models (Hartig 2020)

doParallel: Foreach Parallel Adaptor for the 'parallel' Package (Microsoft Corporation & Steve Weston 2019)

effects: Effect Displays for Linear, Generalized Linear, and Other Models, see Fox (2003), Fox & Weisberg (2019)

faraway: Functions and Datasets for Books by Julian Faraway, see Farawy (2015, 2016)

FWDselect: Selecting Variables in Regression Models (Sestelo, Villanueva, & Roca-Pardinas 2015)

glmertree: Generalized Linear Mixed Model Trees, see Fokkema et al. (2018)

lme4: Linear Mixed-Effects Models using 'Eigen' and S4, see Bates et al. (2015)

lmerTest: Tests in Linear Mixed Effects Models, see Kuznetsova et al. (2017)

magrittr: A Forward-Pipe Operator for R (Bache & Wickham 2014)

merTools: Tools for Analyzing Mixed Effect Regression Models (Knowles & Frederick 2020)

mlogit: Multinomial Logit Models (Croissant 2020)

MuMIn: Multi-Model Inference (Bartoń 2020)

nortest: Tests for Normality (Gross & Ligges 2015)

nnet: Feed-Forward Neural Networks and Multinomial Log-Linear Models, see Venables & Ripley (2002)

party: A Laboratory for Recursive Partitioning, see Hothorn et al. (2006)

partykit: A Toolkit for Recursive Partitioning, see Hothorn & Zeileis (2015)

pdp: Partial Dependence Plots, see Greenwell (2017)

randomForest: Breiman and Cutler's Random Forests for Classification and Regression, see Liaw & Wiener (2002)

ranger: A Fast Implementation of Random Forests, see Wright & Ziegler (2017)

randomForestSRC: Fast Unified Random Forests for Survival, Regression, and Classification (RF-SRC), see Ishwaran & Kogalur (2019)

rgl: 3D Visualization Using OpenGL (Adler, Murdoch, et al. 2020)

RLT: Reinforcement Learning Trees, see Zhu, Zeng, & Kosorok (2015)

rstanarm: Bayesian Applied Regression Modeling via Stan (Goodrich et al. 2020)

snow: Simple Network of Workstations (Tierney et al. 2018)

stablelearner: Stability Assessment of Statistical Learning Methods, see Philipp et al. (2016)

vioplot: Violin Plot (Adler & Kelly 2020)

tree: Classification and Regression Trees (Ripley 2019)

WRS2: A Collection of Robust Statistical Methods, see Mair & Wilcox (2020)

About the Author

Stefan Th. Gries is Professor of Linguistics at the University of California, Santa Barbara and Chair of English Linguistics (Corpus Linguistics with a focus on quantitative methods, 25%) at the Justus Liebig University Giessen. He was a Visiting Chair (Linguistics and English Language) at the ESRC Centre for Corpus Approaches to Social Science (at Lancaster University, 2013-2017), Visiting Leibniz Professor at the Research Academy Leipzig of the University of Leipzig (2017), and a Visiting Professor at five recent LSA Linguistic Institutes. He is a quantitative corpus linguist with additional interests in usage-based/cognitive linguistics, computational linguistics, psycholinguistics, and applications of corpus linguistics to the law. Research-active since 1999, he has (co)-authored more than 80 journals articles, more than 45 articles in edited volumes, 40 survey articles, and 10(co-)edited volumes, handbooks, or special issues in these research areas; he is on the editorial board of more than a dozen journals in corpus and cognitive linguistics. He has published two editions of a textbook on R in corpus linguistics and the previous 2nd edition of this statistics textbook was translated into Brazilian Portuguese, Chinese, and Korean.

https://doi.org/10.1515/9783110718256-009